Frommer's

W9-BJS-333

Maine Coast

1st Edition

by Paul Karr

20th Wed Rockport MA
21 Thurs Boothbay Harbor
22 Fri
23 Sat } Acadia / Bar Harbor
24 Sun
25 Mon
26 Tues Boston (airport)

Here's what critics say about Frommer's:

"Amazingly easy to use. Very portable, very complete."

—*Booklist*

"Detailed, accurate, and easy-to-read information for all price ranges."
—*Glamour Magazine*

"Hotel information is close to encyclopedic."

—*Des Moines Sunday Register*

"Frommer's Guides have a way of giving you a real feel for a place."
—*Knight Ridder Newspapers*

WILEY

Wiley Publishing, Inc.

About the Author

Paul Karr has written, co-authored, or edited more than 25 guidebooks, including Wiley's *Vancouver and Victoria For Dummies* and *Frommer's Vermont, New Hampshire & Maine*. He has also contributed to Discovery Channel/Insight Guides to Montréal, Atlanta, Vienna, Austria, and Switzerland; Wiley Publishing's Irreverent Guides to Rome and Vancouver; and *Scandinavia: The Rough Guide* while writing articles for *Sierra* and *Sports Illustrated,* among other publications. He divides his time between New England, both coasts of Canada, and Europe.

Published by:

Wiley Publishing, Inc.

111 River St.
Hoboken, NJ 07030-5774

ISBN 0-7645-7789-1

Editor: Cate Latting
Production Editor: Bethany André
Cartographer: Roberta Stockwell
Photo Editor: Richard Fox
Production by Wiley Indianapolis Composition Services
Chapter 8 illustrations by Kelly Emkow, Joni Burns, and Mary Virgin

Front cover photo: Cape Elizabeth, Portland Head Light
Back cover photo: Lobster cookout in Maine

For information on our other products and services or to obtain technical support, please contact our Customer Care Department within the U.S. at 800/762-2974, outside the U.S. at 317/572-3993 or fax 317/572-4002.

Wiley also publishes its books in a variety of electronic formats. Some content that appears in print may not be available in electronic formats.

Manufactured in the United States of America

5   4   3   2   1

Contents

List of Maps   vi

What's New Along the Coast of Maine   1

1   The Best of the Maine Coast   3

1 The Seven Natural Wonders
of Coastal Maine 3

2 The Best Small Towns 6

3 The Best Places to See
Fall Foliage 6

4 The Best Coastal Views 6

5 The Best Active Vacations 7

6 The Best Destinations
for Families 8

7 The Most Intriguing
Historic Homes 8

8 The Best Places to Rediscover
America's Past 8

9 The Best Resorts 9

10 The Best Bed & Breakfasts 9

11 The Best Moderately Priced
Accommodations 10

12 The Best Alternative
Accommodations 10

13 The Best Restaurants 10

14 The Best Local Dining
Experiences 11

15 The Best Destinations
for Serious Shoppers 11

2   Planning Your Trip to the Maine Coast   12

1 The Regions in Brief 12

*Destination: Coastal Maine—
Red Alert Checklist* 13

2 Visitor Information 13

3 Money 13

4 When to Go 16

*The Maine Coast
Calendar of Events* 18

5 Travel Insurance 20

6 Health & Safety 21

7 Specialized Travel Resources 23

8 Planning Your Trip Online 27

*Frommers.com: The Complete
Travel Resource* 28

9 The 21st-Century Traveler 29

Online Traveler's Toolbox 31

10 Getting There 31

Flying with Film & Video 35

11 The Active Vacation Planner 36

12 Getting Around
Coastal Maine 41

*Your Car: Leave Home
Without It!* 42

Moose X-ing 44

13 Tips on Accommodations 44

14 Suggested Itinerary 48

15 Recommended Reading 50

Fast Facts: The Maine Coast . . .50

3 For International Visitors 53

1 Preparing for Your Trip 53

2 Getting to & Around Coastal Maine 59

Fast Facts: For the International Traveler 61

4 The Southern Coast: Kittery to the Kennebunks 67

1 Kittery & the Yorks 68

Sayward-Wheeler House 71

A Detour to South Berwick 72

Packing a Picnic 76

2 Ogunquit 77

The Diner Denizen: Eating Like a Local . . . At 1940s Prices ...84

3 The Kennebunks 86

Parsons Beach 89

Packing a Picnic 90

4 A Side Trip to Biddeford-Saco 97

5 Portland 99

1 Orientation 100

2 Where to Stay 102

3 Where to Dine 106

Packing a Picnic 110

4 Exploring the City 112

Lucky 77: Hitting the Beaches 117

5 Portland After Dark 119

A Hundred Beers Old 120

6 Side Trips 121

6 Freeport to Monhegan Island 123

1 Freeport 123

Tale of the Tags: Freeport vs. Kittery 126

Packing a Picnic 130

2 Brunswick & Bath 131

Packing a Picnic 133

3 Harpswell Peninsula 136

4 Wiscasset & the Boothbays ...138

5 Pemaquid Peninsula 145

6 Monhegan Island 148

7 Midcoast 152

1 Enjoying the Great Outdoors 152

2 Rockland & Environs 153

Boat & Breakfast 159

3 Camden 161

Packing a Picnic 164

Crafting a Vacation 165

4 Belfast to Bucksport 172

Packing a Picnic 175

5 Castine & Environs 178

6 Deer Isle 181

7 Blue Hill 187

8 Bangor, Orono & Old Town ...190

8   Mount Desert Island & Acadia National Park   193

1 Enjoying the Great
Outdoors 193

2 Acadia National Park 196

*Avoiding Crowds
in the Park* 198

*Driving Tour: Driving
the Park Loop Road* 200

Packing a Picnic 204

3 A Nature Guide to Acadia
National Park 206

4 Bar Harbor 219

Packing a Picnic 223

Eating Lobster by the Pound . . .228

5 Elsewhere on Mount
Desert Island 232

9   The Downeast Coast   238

1 Essentials 238

2 Enjoying the Great
Outdoors 240

3 Exploring Downeast Maine . . .241

You Light Up My Life 243

Radar Love 244

4 What to See & Do 245

*Touring Eastport Via
the "Woody"* 246

5 Passamaquoddy Bay 248

6 Where to Stay & Dine 251

10   Side Trips from the Maine Coast   258

1 Portsmouth, New
Hampshire 258

Packing a Picnic 263

2 Baxter State Park &
Mount Katahdin 268

*The Debate over Maine's
North Woods* 270

3 St. Andrews & Grand Manan
Island, New Brunswick 274

Appendix: The Maine Coast in Depth   285

1 The Maine Coast Today 286

2 History 101 287

Dateline 287

A Literary Legacy 290

3 Maine Architecture 292

4 A Taste of Maine 293

5 Lighthouses: A Tour
Up the Coast 294

Index   299

General Index 299

Accommodations Index 306

Restaurant Index 307

List of Maps

The Maine Coast   4
The Southern Maine Coast   69
Ogunquit   81
Kennebunk & Kennebunkport   91
Greater Portland   101
Downtown Portland   103
Freeport   125
Penobscot Bay   154

Camden   163
Isle au Haut   186
Mount Desert Island/Acadia
   National Park   195
Bar Harbor   221
Downeast Coast   239
Portsmouth, New Hampshire   259
Baxter State Park   269

An Invitation to the Reader

In researching this book, we discovered many wonderful places—hotels, restaurants, shops, and more. We're sure you'll find others. Please tell us about them, so we can share the information with your fellow travelers in upcoming editions. If you were disappointed with a recommendation, we'd love to know that, too. Please write to:

Frommer's Maine Coast, 1st Edition
Wiley Publishing, Inc. • 111 River St. • Hoboken, NJ 07030-5774

An Additional Note

Please be advised that travel information is subject to change at any time—and this is especially true of prices. We therefore suggest that you write or call ahead for confirmation when making your travel plans. The authors, editors, and publisher cannot be held responsible for the experiences of readers while traveling. Your safety is important to us, however, so we encourage you to stay alert and be aware of your surroundings. Keep a close eye on cameras, purses, and wallets, all favorite targets of thieves and pickpockets.

Other Great Guides for Your Trip:

Frommer's Vermont, New Hampshire & Maine
Frommer's New England
Frommer's Portable Maine Coast
Frommer's Best Loved Driving Tours: New England
Frommer's Family Vacations in the National Parks
Unofficial Guide to Campgrounds in the Northeast

Frommer's Star Ratings, Icons & Abbreviations

Every hotel, restaurant, and attraction listing in this guide has been ranked for quality, value, service, amenities, and special features using a **star-rating system.** In country, state, and regional guides, we also rate towns and regions to help you narrow down your choices and budget your time accordingly. Hotels and restaurants are rated on a scale of zero (recommended) to three stars (exceptional). Attractions, shopping, nightlife, towns, and regions are rated according to the following scale: zero stars (recommended), one star (highly recommended), two stars (very highly recommended), and three stars (must-see).

In addition to the star-rating system, we also use **seven feature icons** that point you to the great deals, in-the-know advice, and unique experiences that separate travelers from tourists. Throughout the book, look for:

Finds	Special finds—those places only insiders know about
Fun Fact	Fun facts—details that make travelers more informed and their trips more fun
Kids	Best bets for kids and advice for the whole family
Moments	Special moments—those experiences that memories are made of
Overrated	Places or experiences not worth your time or money
Tips	Insider tips—great ways to save time and money
Value	Great values—where to get the best deals

The following abbreviations are used for credit cards:

AE	American Express	DISC	Discover	V	Visa
DC	Diners Club	MC	MasterCard		

Frommers.com

Now that you have the guidebook to a great trip, visit our website at **www.frommers.com** for travel information on nearly 3,000 destinations. With features updated regularly, we give you instant access to the most current trip-planning information available. At Frommers.com you'll find the best prices on airfares, accommodations, and car rentals—and you can even book travel online through our travel booking partners. At Frommers.com, you'll also find the following:

- Online updates to our most popular guidebooks
- Vacation sweepstakes and contest giveaways
- Newsletter highlighting the hottest travel trends
- Online travel message boards with featured travel discussions

What's New Along the Coast of Maine

THE SOUTHERN MAINE COAST

In Kittery, the **Portsmouth Harbor Inn and Spa** (© 207/439-4040) has a new name and two new owners (one a former state tourism official), but the same good rooms and increasingly popular day spa.

Peter and Kate Morency have renovated and updated the former Seascapes fine-dining restaurant in Cape Porpoise; it's now known as the **Pier 77 Restaurant** (© 207/967-8500), but still serves a Continental menu.

Just north of York, the Cape Neddick Inn's fine restaurant has closed its doors.

Kennebunk's esteemed **White Barn Inn** (© 207/967-2321) has acquired a handful of cottages on the tidal Kennebunk River, a bit down the road from the main inn, and will shortly be developing a wharf on that site to encourage boating interests. The cottages are cozy, nicely equipped with modern kitchens and bathrooms, and will continue to see future upgrades. The inn's restaurant was also recently selected one of America's top inn restaurants by readers of *Travel + Leisure* magazine. See chapter 4.

GREATER PORTLAND

Two major hotels have both cut their ribbons in Portland's Old Port section. The luxury **Portland Harbor Hotel** (© 888/798-9090), based around a central garden and right in the heart of the neighborhood's dining and nightlife, offers top-of-the-line accommodations and services. And the Hilton brand unveiled a new waterfront **Hilton Garden Inn** (© 207/780-0780) right across the street from the city's ferry dock.

Off the lobby of the Eastland Park Hotel in the heart of Portland's Arts District, the fine **Aucocisco Gallery** has opened, with a focus on Maine artists. Watch for openings and ongoing shows of work.

And, in the "Meet the New Boss . . ." department, the popular Exchange Street gift shop formerly known as Fibula changed its name to **Folia** (© 207/761-4432), yet it still offers the same intriguing assortment of jewelry, and retains the same owners. Go figure. See chapter 5.

FREEPORT TO MIDCOAST MAINE

Sadly, the early-August **Maine Festival** has apparently ceased to exist; one can only hope it might be resurrected someday in the future.

In Boothbay Harbor, Christopher's Boathouse restaurant has closed.

However, the **Sea Dog Brewing Co.** brewpub has moved from its original home in Camden to a restored mill in **Topsham**. See chapter 6.

MIDCOAST MAINE

Camden lost a notable fine-dining experience when **Cork** closed. Happily, however, the new **Francine Bistro** (© 207/230-0083) has moved into town at 55 Chestnut St., and is already garnering rave reviews as the next great Camden dining experience. See p. 171.

The Kelmscott Rare Breeds Foundation just inland from Lincolnville Beach, which formerly conserved rare breeds of livestock such as Gloucestershire old spots pigs and Cotswolds sheep, has transferred some of its stock to other organizations and is no longer open to the public.

ACADIA NATIONAL PARK & MOUNT DESERT ISLAND

There's hotel news afoot in Bar Harbor. Converted from a family-style motel into wonderfully luxury waterside accommodations, the **Harborside Hotel & Marina** (© 800/328-5033) features whale-watching, a lobster restaurant, and stunning ocean views from the dining room and many of the nicer rooms.

The large and new **Bar Harbor Grand Hotel** (© 888/766-2529 or 207/288-5226) in the heart of downtown echoes the design of the town's original grand hotel—the one that helped put the town on the tourist map in the first place.

However, the popular Bar Harbor B&B Sunset on West has been sold and is now a private residence.

In non-hotel Bar Harbor news, the **Abbe Museum**—Maine's largest Native American museum—has created a new year-round annex (© 207/288-3519) located in the heart of downtown, greatly adding to its exhibit space and accessibility. The original museum location, inside Acadia National Park, also remains open from May to October.

Win one, lose one: Elaine's Stardust Oasis in Bar Harbor has closed, but the **Eden Vegetarian Café** (© 207/288-4422) has capably replaced it at 78 West St.

Finally, a number of new (and surprisingly modern) seafood and fusion restaurants have recently sprouted up in, of all places, the sparsely settled Southwest Harbor area. The best three are **Red Sky** (© 207/244-0476), **Fiddlers' Green** (© 207/244-9416), and the **Seaweed Café** (© 207/244-0572). See chapter 8.

SIDE TRIPS

On New Castle Island just outside Portsmouth, New Hampshire, the **Wentworth by the Sea** (© 866/240-6313) resort has reopened to the public after being boarded up for years, and it's now the classiest lodging on the New Hampshire coast. There are more than 160 rooms, with 17 luxury units added in 2004; there's also a full-service spa, two pools, and a wonderful dining room.

In Portsmouth itself, **Pesce Blue** (© 603/430-7766) is a hot new Italian seafood restaurant right on the main drag at 106 Congress St. Reservations are recommended.

Also in Portsmouth, the popular French bakery Café La Brioche closed down, but the great coffeehouse **Breaking New Grounds** (© 603/436-9555) has move into its former location—and retained the outdoor tables on Market Square. See chapter 10.

The Best of the Maine Coast

Humorist Dave Barry once wryly suggested that Maine's state motto should be "Cold, but damp."

Cute, but true. There's spring, which tends to last a few blustery, rain-soaked days. There's November, in which Arctic winds alternate with gray sheets of rain. And then winter brings a character-building mix of blizzards and ice storms to the fabled coast.

Ah, but then there's summer. Summer in Maine brings ospreys diving for fish off wooded points, gleaming cumulus clouds building over the rounded peaks of Acadia, and the haunting whoop of loons echoing off the dense forest walls bordering the lakes. It brings languorous days when the sun rises before most visitors and it seems like noontime at 8am. Maine summers bring a measure of gracious tranquillity, and a placid stay in the right spot can rejuvenate even the most jangled nerves.

The trick is finding that right spot. Those who arrive here without a clear plan might find themselves cursing their travel decision. Maine's Route 1 along the coast has its moments, but it's mostly charmless—an amalgam of convenience stores, tourist boutiques, and restaurants catering to bus tours. Acadia National Park, for all its vaunted ocean vistas, also has world-class congestion along some of the byways in and around the park. In this it's no different from other national parks of its stature—whether Yosemite or Yellowstone. You need strategy to avoid the worst moments.

Fortunately, Maine's size works to the traveler's advantage. Maine is nearly as large as the other five New England states combined. Straighten out the state's convoluted coast and you'll discover you've got more than a continent's worth of exploring—some 5,500 miles of mainland shoreline. Add to that the possibility of exploring even a few of Maine's thousands of coastal islands and numberless coves, peninsulas, and bays, and you'll soon realize that with a little planning, you should easily be able to find your place far from the crowds.

One of the greatest challenges of planning a vacation in coastal Maine is narrowing down the options: Where to start? Here's an entirely biased list of destinations, the places I enjoy returning to time and again. Over years of traveling through the region, I've discovered that these places merit more than just a quick stop when I'm in the area; they're worth a major detour.

1 The Seven Natural Wonders of Coastal Maine

- **The beaches of southern Maine** (southern Maine): The flat, white-sand beaches of southernmost Maine are gorgeous and perfect for Frisbee, walking, tanning, kite-flying, or photography. Just watch your tootsies: that water's cold. See chapter 4.

- **The Calendar Islands** (southern Maine): Locals call 'em the Calendar Islands for a very simple reason: There must be *at least* 365 of

The Maine Coast

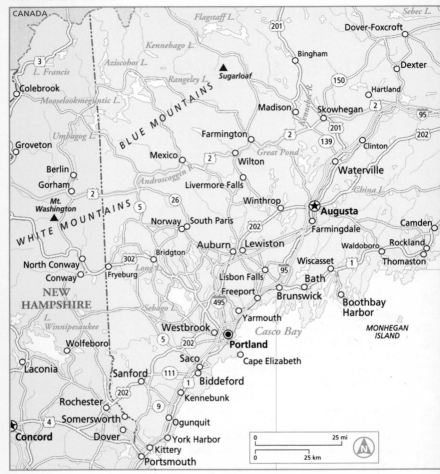

these rocky islands dotting Casco Bay, in every shape and size. Take a mailboat from Portland harbor and see how many you can count. See chapter 5.

- **Rocky peninsulas** (southern, midcoast, and Downeast Maine): Everywhere you go—from the Cape Neddick area to just south of Portland area, from Harpswell to Georgetown to Blue Hill to Boothbay and Schoodic Point—

you'll find long fingerlings and headlands carved of sheer bedrock. Once these were mountaintops high above an ancient sea; now they comprise some of the East Coast's most beautiful scenery. Try some backroads wandering to find the best ones.

- **The Camden Hills** (midcoast Maine): They're not huge, but this run of hills comes with a bonus you'll only understand when you

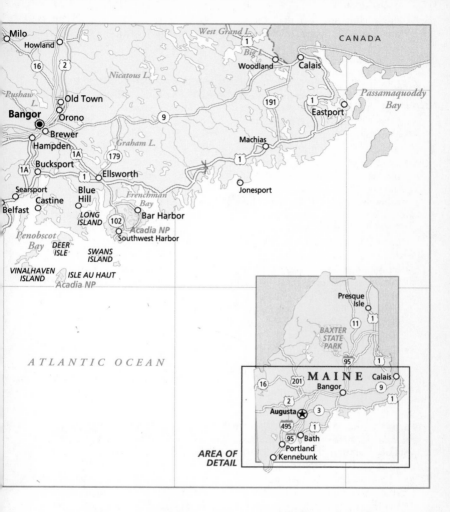

get to the top: eye-popping coastal vistas of boats, villages, and more hills like these. See chapter 7.

- **Acadia National Park** (Downeast Maine): New England's only national park is also one of the most popular in the U.S. The fractured, rocky, surf-pounded coastline is the main attraction, but don't overlook the quiet, boreal forests and open summits of low mountains that afford spectacular coastal views. See chapter 8.

- **The Appalachian Trail and Mount Katahdin** (side trip from Downeast Maine): All right, they're not directly on the coast. But Maine's highest peak is well worth a detour. Rising abruptly from a thick blanket of North Woods forest, the nearly mile-high Mount Katahdin has an ineffable spiritual quality to it. It's the centerpiece of equally inspiring Baxter State Park, one of the last, best wildernesses of the eastern states. While here, don't forget to check out the trail, which stretches 2,100 rugged miles from Georgia before winding uphill to the finish line here on Katahdin.

The stretches in Maine include some of the most magnificent scenery in northern New England. See chapter 10.

2 The Best Small Towns

- **York Village** (southern Maine): What else can you say? It's Maine's oldest settlement, so it's got history and fine architecture. It's also got a set of beaches and a coastal trail nearby. And people just seem friendlier here. See Chapter 4.
- **Camden** (midcoast Maine): This seaside town has everything—a beautiful harbor, great Federal, Queen Anne, and Greek Revival architecture, even its own tiny mountain range affording great hikes with sweeping ocean views. With lots of elegant bed-and-breakfasts, it's a perfect base for explorations further afield. See chapter 7.
- **Castine** (midcoast Maine): Soaring elm trees, a peaceful harborside setting, grand historic homes, and a selection of good inns make this a great spot to soak up some

of Maine's coastal ambience off the beaten path. See chapter 7.
- **Blue Hill** (midcoast Maine): A tiny town with fine harbor views, a general store, a green, a lazy, summery feeling, and absolutely no pretense or T-shirt shops (yet). See chapter 7.
- **Northeast Harbor** (Downeast Maine): A waterside setting, a gentle mixture of seafaring locals and art-loving summer folks, and a century-ago aura pervade the single, sleepy main street of one of Mount Desert Island's best little towns. See chapter 8.
- **Eastport** (Downeast Maine): Sure, it's the saltiest town on my list, but Eastport is making a slow transition from working-class sea town to tourist (and life) destination. See chapter 9.

3 The Best Places to See Fall Foliage

- **The Camden Hills** (midcoast Maine): The surrounding countryside is full of blazing color, with whitewashed homes and sailboats to offset it. Perfect. See chapter 7.
- **Acadia National Park** (Downeast Maine): This national park possesses some of the finest foliage views I've ever seen, all the more so when placed beside the dramatic, rocky coastline. See chapter 8.
- **Blueberry barrens** (Downeast Maine): Maine's wild blueberry barrens turn a brilliant cranberry-red in fall, setting the fields ablaze with color. Wander the dirt roads northeast of Cherryfield through the upland barrens, or drive Route 1 between Harrington and Machias past the experimental farm atop, of course, Blueberry Hill. See chapter 9.

4 The Best Coastal Views

- **Hike Monhegan Island:** The village of Monhegan is clustered around the harbor of this island far off the Maine coast. The rest of this

700-acre island is comprised of picturesque wildlands, with miles of trails crossing open meadows and tracing rocky bluffs. See chapter 6.

- **Cruising Maine on a windjammer:** See Maine as many saw it for centuries—from the ocean, looking inland. Sailing ships depart from various harbors along the coast, particularly Rockland and Camden. Spend between a night and a week exploring the dramatic shoreline. See chapter 7.

- **Merchant's Row by sea kayak:** The islands between Stonington and Isle au Haut, rimmed with pink granite and capped with the stark spires of spruce trees, are among the most spectacular anywhere. Inaccessible by motorboat, a wonderful way to explore them is by sea kayak. Outfitters offer overnight camping trips on the islands. See chapter 7.

- **Drive the Park Loop Road at Acadia National Park:** This is the region's premier ocean drive. Start along a ridge with views of Frenchman Bay and the Porcupine Islands, then dip down along the rocky shores to watch the surf crash against the dark rocks. Plan to do this 20-mile loop at least twice to get the most out of it. See chapter 8.

- **Sit in a rocking chair:** Views are never better than when you're caught unaware—such as looking up from an engrossing book on the front porch of an ocean-side inn. This book includes many hotels and inns on the water. Some of the better ones for so-called rusticating: Beachmere Inn (Ogunquit), Black Point Inn (Scarborough), Grey Havens (Georgetown Island), East Wind Inn (Tenant's Harbor), Samoset Resort (Rockport), Inn on the Harbor (Stonington), The Tides Inn (Bar Harbor), and the Claremont (Southwest Harbor).

- **Bicycle Route 1A, Hampton Beach to Portsmouth** (New Hampshire): With a sampling of all sorts of coastal scenery on New Hampshire's minuscule coastline, you begin with sandy beaches, then pass rocky headlands and handsome mansions before coasting into Portsmouth, New Hampshire's scenic seaside city. See chapter 10.

5 The Best Active Vacations

- **Mountain biking at Acadia:** John D. Rockefeller, Jr., built the carriage roads of Mount Desert Island so that the gentry could enjoy rambles in the woods with their horses—away from pesky cars. Today, this extensive network offers some of the most enjoyable, aesthetically pleasing mountain biking anywhere. See chapter 8.

- **Kayaking the coast:** With its massive and serpentine coastline and thousands of islands, most uninhabited, Maine is a world-class destination for those who like to snoop around by kayak. The Stonington area is considered the best spot for kayaking in Maine, but it's hard to go wrong anywhere north and east of Portland. Beware of dangers in the form of tides and weather—kayak with a guide if you're a novice.

- **Canoeing the North Woods:** Maine has thousands of miles of flowing rivers and streams, and hundreds of miles of shoreline along remote ponds and lakes. Bring your tent, sleeping bag, and cooking gear, and come prepared to spend a night under the stars listening to the sounds of the loons. See chapter 10.

6 The Best Destinations for Families

- **York Beach** (southern Maine): This beach town is actually a set of three towns; head for Short Sands with the kids, where they can watch a taffy-pulling machine, play video games in an arcade, ogle seashells in a trinket shop, or scarf cotton candy at a small amusement park. The Long Sands section is ideal for Frisbee and kite-flying, and nearby Nubble Light is close to a kid-friendly ice cream shop, Brown's (to get there, keep going uphill past the lighthouse). See chapter 4.
- **Old Orchard Beach** (southern Maine): This place has a carny atmosphere—there are French fries and hotdogs and fried-dough galore. Though it might be a bit much for you, the kids will probably love it. See chapter 5.
- **Monhegan Island** (southern Maine): Kids from 8 to 12 years old especially enjoy overnight excursions to Monhegan Island. The mail boat from Port Clyde is rustic and intriguing, the hotels are an adventure, and the 700-acre island's scale is perfect for kids to explore. See chapter 6.

7 The Most Intriguing Historic Homes

- **Victoria Mansion** (Portland): Donald Trump has nothing on the Victorians when it comes to material excess. You'll see Victorian decorative arts at their zenith in this elaborate Italianate mansion, built during the Civil War. It's open to the public for tours throughout the summer. See chapter 5
- **Parson Fisher House** (Blue Hill): Parson Jonathan Fisher, who served as minister to the quiet town of Blue Hill in the late 18th century, was a man of extraordinary talents, from designing his own house to building his own clocks to preaching sermons in five languages (including Aramaic). As if that wasn't enough, his primitive landscapes of the region are widely regarded as among the best to come from the area. See chapter 7.

8 The Best Places to Rediscover America's Past

- **Sabbathday Lake Shaker Community** (New Gloucester): This is the last of the active Shaker communities in the nation and the only one that voted to accept new converts rather than die out. The 1,900-acre farm about 45 minutes outside of Portland has a number of exceptional buildings, including some dating from the 18th century. Visitors can view examples of Shaker craftsmanship and buy locally grown Shaker herbs to bring home. See chapter 5.
- **Mount Desert Island & Bar Harbor:** In the mid-1800s, America launched a love affair with nature and never looked back. See where it started, amid surf-wracked rocks, and where some of the nation's most affluent families ventured to erect vacation "cottages," with bedrooms by the dozen. The area still offers lessons on how to design with nature as accomplice, rather than adversary. See chapter 8.
- **Portsmouth** (New Hampshire): Portsmouth is a salty coastal city that just happens to have some of the most impressive historic homes in New England. Start at Strawbery Banke, a 10-acre compound of 42 historic buildings. Then visit the many other grand homes in nearby neighborhoods,

including the house John Paul Jones lived in while building his warship during the Revolution. See chapter 10.

9 The Best Resorts

- **The Colony Hotel** (Kennebunkport; ✆ **800/552-2363** or 207/967-3331): This rambling and gleaming white resort dates from 1914 and has been upgraded over the years without losing any of its charm. You can play shuffleboard, putt on the green, or lounge in the ocean-view pool. More vigorous souls cross the street to brave the cold Atlantic waters. See p. 93.

- **Black Point Inn** (Scarborough; ✆ **800/258-0003** or 207/883-2500): This compound of shingled buildings near two beaches dates from 1878 but has been impeccably maintained ever since. New owners have brought back the luster without obscuring the old-fashioned charm. See p. 102.

- **White Barn Inn** (Kennebunkport; ✆ **207/967-2321**): Much of the White Barn staff hails from Europe, and they treat guests graciously. The rooms are a delight, and the meals (served in a gloriously restored barn) may be the best in Maine. See p. 92.

10 The Best Bed & Breakfasts

- **The Captain Lord Mansion** (Kennebunkport; ✆ **800/522-3141** or 207/967-3141): You'll transcend the "wannaB&Bs" at this genuine article, with grandfather clocks, Chippendale highboys, and other wonderful antiques. This uncommonly handsome mansion is right in the village of Kennebunkport, perfectly situated for relaxing strolls. See p. 92.

- **Pomegranate Inn** (Portland; ✆ **800/356-0408** or 207/772-1006): Whimsy and history combine with good effect at this fine B&B in one of Portland's most stately neighborhoods. The Italianate mansion is stern on the outside yet alive on the inside with creative paintings and an eclectic collection of unique antiques. See p. 104.

- **Grey Havens** (Georgetown Island; ✆ **800/431-2316** or 207/371-2616): This graceful, 1904-shingled home with prominent turrets sits on a high, rocky bluff overlooking the sea. Inside, it's all richly mellowed pine paneling, with a spacious common room where you can relax in cozy chairs in front of the cobblestone fireplace while listening to classical music. See p. 134.

- **Lindenwood Inn** (Southwest Harbor; ✆ **800/307-5335** or 207/244-5335): It's hard to argue with a jovial owner, outstanding rooms, a refreshingly laid-back feel, and proximity to one of Mount Desert Island's key lobster piers. This place delivers in every sense of the word. See p. 235.

- **The Claremont** (Southwest Harbor; ✆ **800/244-5036** or 207/244-5036): The 1884 Claremont is a Maine classic. This waterside lodge has everything a Victorian resort should, including sparely decorated rooms, creaky floorboards in the halls, great views of water and mountains, and a croquet pitch. The dining room is only so-so, but Southwest Harbor has other dining options. See p. 234.

11 The Best Moderately Priced Accommodations

- **Franciscan Guest House** (Kennebunkport; ℂ **207/967-4865**): No daily maid service, cheap paneling on the walls, and industrial carpeting. What's to like? Plenty, including the location (on the lush riverside grounds of a monastery), price, and a great Lithuanian-style breakfast spread in the morning. You can walk to Dock Square at Kennebunkport or bike to the beach. See p. 90.

- **Driftwood Inn & Cottages** (Bailey Island; ℂ **207/833-5461**): Where else can you find rooms at the edge of the rocky Maine coast for around $70 and up? This classic shingled compound dates from 1910 and offers mostly rooms with a shared bathroom, but the views alone are worth that inconvenience. See p. 137.

- **Maine Idyll Motor Court** (Freeport; ℂ **207/865-4201**): The 1932 Maine Idyll Motor Court is a classic—a cluster of 20 cottages scattered about a grove of beech and oak trees. Each cottage has a tiny porch, wood-burning fireplace (birch logs provided), TV, modest kitchen facilities (no ovens), and timeworn furniture. The downside? Highway noise. Cottages are $44 to $70 for two. See p. 129.

12 The Best Alternative Accommodations

- **Maine Island Trail:** About 70 remote islands along the Maine coast are open to camping, and from these remote, salty wildernesses, you'll see some of the best sunsets imaginable. See "Outdoor Activity," in chapter 2, for an introduction.

- **Windjammers** (Maine): Maine has the East Coast's largest fleet of windjammers, offering adventures on the high seas throughout the summer. You can explore offshore islands and inland estuaries, and learn how sailors once made the best of the wind. Accommodations in private cabins are typically spartan, but you'll spend most of your time on the deck luxuriating in the stunning views. See chapter 7.

13 The Best Restaurants

- **Arrows** (Ogunquit; ℂ **207/361-1100**): The emphasis at this elegant spot is local products—often very local, including many ingredients from nearby organic vegetable gardens. Prices are not for the fainthearted (it's expensive by New York City standards), but the experience is top-rate, from the cordial service to the silver and linens. Expect New American fare informed by an Asian sensibility. See p. 83.

- **Hurricane** (Ogunquit); ℂ **800/649-6348** (Maine and New Hampshire only) or 207/646-6348: Brooks MacDonald's longtime favorite emphasizes local seafood and lobster with a creative flair. There's now a second branch of the popular eatery in Kennebunkport's Dock Square (ℂ **207/967-1111**), too. See p. 84 and p. 96.

- **White Barn Inn** (Kennebunkport; ℂ **207/967-2321**): The setting, in an ancient, rustic barn, is magical. The tables are draped with floor-length tablecloths, and the chairs feature Italian upholstery. The food is to die for. Enjoy entrees such as grilled duckling breast with ginger and sundried cherry sauce, or rack of lamb with pecans and homemade barbecue sauce. See p. 97.

- **Fore Street** (Portland; © 207/775-2717): Fore Street is one of New England's most celebrated restaurants—listed as one of *Gourmet* magazine's 100 best restaurants in 2001, and the chef has been getting lots of press elsewhere. His secret? Simplicity, and lots of it. Some of the most memorable meals are prepared over an applewood grill. See p. 107.

- **Primo** (Rockland; © 207/596-0770): Melissa Kelly and Price Kushner create culinary magic on two floors of a century-old home at this winning Rockland bistro. Expect fancy treatments of foie gras, scallops, duck, steak, and the like, plus outstanding desserts and an impressively long wine list. See p. 161.

14 The Best Local Dining Experiences

- **Becky's** (Portland; © 207/773-7070): Five different kinds of home fries on the menu? It's breakfast nirvana at this local institution on the working waterfront. It's a favored hangout of fishermen, high school kids, businessmen, and just about everyone else. See p. 111.

- **Silly's** (Portland; © 207/772-0360): Hectic and fun, this tiny, informal, kitschy restaurant serves up delicious finger food, such as pita wraps, hamburgers, and pizza. The milkshakes alone are worth the detour. See p. 112.

- **Dolphin Marina** (South Harpswell; © 207/833-6000): The fish chowder and lobster stew are reasonably priced and delicious at this hidden spot, part of a marina at the end of a dead-end road. Blueberry muffins come with most meals. See chapter 6.

- **Thurston's Lobster Pound** (Bernard; © 207/244-7600). It doesn't get much more local than this place, perched above the water with atmospheric views on the so-called "quiet side" of Mount Desert Island. Order lobsters, of course (choose your size from the tank at the counter), plus sides of corn on the cob, steamed clams, blueberry cake, and beer. Then join the happy crowds upstairs or down. See chapter 8.

15 The Best Destinations for Serious Shoppers

- **Kittery:** There are tons of outlets on Route 1 of this otherwise sleepy hamlet; you're bound to find something good at a low price, whether it's at Crate & Barrel, or Coach, or Seiko, or GAP, or . . . well, wherever. See chapter 4.

- **Portland:** A city this size really ought to have more than it does— the Old Port, the chief shopping district, is in serious danger of becoming Tweesville—but you can still find great little boutiques and shops if you look hard enough. See chapter 5.

- **Freeport:** L.L.Bean is the anchor store for this thriving town of outlets, but you'll also find Patagonia, J. Crew, Dansk, Brooks Brothers, Levi's, and about 100 others. This is the most aesthetically pleasing of the several outlet centers in northern New England. See chapter 6.

- **Portsmouth, New Hampshire:** Downtown Portsmouth offers a grab bag of small, manageable, eclectic shops, ranging from funky shoe stores to classy art galleries. The downtown district is small enough to browse leisurely on foot, but you'll find a broad assortment of stuff for sale that will appeal to almost any taste. See chapter 10.

2

Planning Your Trip to the Maine Coast

This chapter provides the nuts-and-bolts travel information you'll need before setting off for coastal Maine. Browse through this section before hitting the road to ensure you've touched all the bases.

1 The Regions in Brief

Southern Maine Stretching from the state line at Kittery to roughly the Freeport-Bath-Brunswick area, Maine's southern coast features most of the state's best beaches and beach resorts. It's also home to the region's largest and most vibrant city, Portland. It's also worth dipping a few miles south of the Piscataqua River to experience the adjacent New Hampshire coast and its anchor city, Portsmouth. For the purposes of this guidebook, I have divided southern Maine into three chapters: Kittery to the Kennebunks, Portland, and Freeport to Monhegan Island.

Midcoast Maine Midcoast Maine begins, depending on whom who ask, somewhere across the Bath bridge and ends somewhere up in the Bucksport or Ellsworth area. In between, you'll discover more rocky headlands, bays, and coves than you ever dreamed existed, as well as quaint villages with names like Blue Hill, Camden, and Rockport. In this book, I have shoe-horned all of this wonderfully scenic region into one (action-packed, wind-jamming) chapter.

Downeast Maine Maine's rocky coast is the stuff of legend, art, and poetry, and in "Downeast" Maine—

which goes from perhaps Ellsworth all the way up the coast to the Canadian border— you'll find plenty of empty back roads and room to roam, not to mention rocky islands, foggy mornings, lobster boats aplenty, and breathtakingly beautiful Acadia National Park. In this book, I have dedicated one entire chapter to MDI, as Mount Desert Island is known by locals—and that chapter is dominated by the park. Another chapter details the quieter pleasures of cruising north and east from the Mount Desert area to the Canadian border.

Side Trips from the Maine Coast Finally, once here, it's worth exploring nearby areas and attractions. In a final chapter, I describe three such side trips: swinging a few miles south of the Piscataqua River to experience the adjacent Portsmouth, New Hampshire, coast; pushing inland from Belfast or Bangor to sample the Great North Woods region of Maine, the northeast's last bit of untrammeled wilderness; and heading a few miles north of the Canadian border by car or boat to experience coastal New Brunswick.

Destination: Coastal Maine—Red Alert Checklist

- Did you make sure to book advance reservations for popular tours and restaurants you don't want to miss?
- Did you make sure your favorite attractions are open? Especially if you're traveling early or late in the season, you should call ahead for opening and closing hours if you have your heart set on seeing certain places.
- Do you have a safe, accessible place to store money?
- Did you bring identification that could entitle you to discounts, such as AAA and AARP cards, student IDs, and so on?
- Did you bring emergency drug prescriptions and extra glasses and/ or contact lenses?
- Do you have your credit card PINs?
- If you have an e-ticket, do you have documentation?
- Did you leave a copy of your itinerary with someone at home?
- If renting a car, have you checked your insurance and credit card policies to see what's covered? You may be able to save money by declining the extra insurance (collision damage waiver) offered by the rental agency.

2 Visitor Information

For a comprehensive overview of what's what in the state, contact Maine's state office of tourism (© **888/624-6345;** www.visitmaine.com). The **Maine Tourism Association** (© **207/623-0363;** www.mainetourism.com), which publishes a stout "official" travel guide entitled "Maine Invites You" (also available free at official information centers; you often have to ask for it), is also very helpful.

For local and regional information, chambers of commerce addresses and phone numbers are provided for each region in the chapters that follow. If you're a highly organized traveler, you'll call in advance and ask for information to be mailed to you long before you depart. (If you're like the rest of us, you'll swing by when you reach town and hope the office is still open.)

3 Money

Here's a scene I've seen repeated more than once. A young couple stands at a tourist information center looking despondent. "Isn't there *anything* cheaper?" one asks. "No, and that's a good price," responds the staff person behind the desk. "You won't find anything better."

Budget travelers accustomed to finding basic motels for $30 or $35 in other parts of the country are in for a bit of sticker shock on the Maine coast, at least during peak travel seasons. In midsummer, there's simply no such thing as a cheap motel along the Maine coast. Places where you might reasonably expect to pay $40 per night will command upward of $90 on a Saturday in August. (To be fair, many of the innkeepers in these northern latitudes must make all their profits in what amounts to a 2- or 3-month season.)

To save money on accommodations, consider these alternatives:

- **Travel in the off-season.** Inexpensive rooms are often available in April, May, November, and early December. Granted, it's a bit bleak then (winter may be out the door in April, but it still hasn't left the driveway), but you can find good deals if you're just looking for a quiet retreat. Or consider the period between Memorial Day and Fourth of July, when you can still often find discounts or budget-priced packages as innkeepers ready themselves for the crowds of high summer. The best off-season period, to my mind, is September. The weather is great, and many inns and hotels cut their prices for 2 or 3 weeks between the summer and foliage periods. Early fall is growing more popular with travelers each year, however, and you may find it harder to find discounts than in the past.

- **Commute from lower-priced areas.** If you're willing to drive a half-hour to an hour to reach prime destinations, you can often find cheaper lodging in less glamorous settings. Bangor is within striking distance of Acadia National Park; Biddeford and Saco are no more than 20 minutes apiece from Portland and Kennebunkport. Study a map and be creative.

- **Camp.** Maine's coast isn't so congested that campgrounds have been driven out to make room for condominiums. You should be able to find great camping at both public and private campgrounds, with prices usually ranging from $10 to $30 per night; camping out for a few nights can then free up some cash for a much-earned splurge at a nicer spot. Be aware, however, that coastal campgrounds south of Portland tend to be fewer in number, a bit more crowded, and more expensive than those to the north; northward, the opportunities expand and the prices tend to fall (except on Mount Desert Island in high summer season).

Prices here fall somewhere in the middle of the price range for the United States. Meals, rooms, and day-to-day expenses are certainly less than you'd pay in major non–New England cities—for example, you can find excellent entrees at upscale, creative restaurants for under $20, compared with similar dishes at some larger-city restaurants topping $30.

On the other hand, this region is more expensive than many other parts of the United States (see above about the scarcity of cheap motels), particularly in the short summer season. Summer and fall travel here can definitely prove a challenge for budget-minded travelers.

ATMs

ATMs (automated teller machines) are easy to find in coastal Maine's more populated areas and regions that cater to tourists. The machines are even making their way to the smaller villages, but don't count on finding them in the more remote parts of the region. Stock up on cash when you can. As in many locales these days, most ATMs assess a fee of about $1 or $1.50 for each transaction.

ATMs are linked to a network that most likely includes your bank at home. **Cirrus** (© **800/424-7787;** www.mastercard.com) and **PLUS** (© **800/843-7587;** www.visa.com) are the two most popular networks in the U.S.; use a phone or the Web to case for ATM locations at your next destination. Be sure you know your four-digit PIN (personal identification number) before you leave home, and be sure to find out your daily withdrawal limit before you depart. You can also get cash advances on your credit card at an ATM. Keep in mind that credit card companies try to protect themselves from theft by limiting the funds someone can withdraw away from home. It's therefore best to call your credit card company before you leave and let them know where you're going and how much you plan to spend. For foreign travelers, you'll get the best exchange rate if you withdraw money from an ATM, but keep in mind that many banks impose a fee every time a card is used at an ATM in a different city or bank. On top of this, the bank from which you withdraw cash may charge its own fee.

TRAVELER'S CHECKS

Traveler's checks are something of an anachronism from the days before the ATM made cash accessible at any time. Traveler's checks used to be the only sound alternative to traveling with dangerously large amounts of cash. They are as reliable as currency, but, unlike cash, can be replaced if lost or stolen.

These days, traveler's checks are less necessary because most cities have 24-hour ATMs that enable you to withdraw small amounts of cash as needed. However, keep in mind that you will likely be charged an ATM withdrawal fee if the bank is not your own, so if you're withdrawing money every day, you might be better off with traveler's checks—provided that you don't mind showing identification every time you want to cash one.

You can get traveler's checks at almost any bank. **American Express** offers denominations of $20, $50, $100, $500, and (for cardholders only) $1,000. You'll pay a service charge ranging from 1% to 4%. You can also get American Express traveler's checks over the phone by calling ℂ **800/221-7282;** Amex gold and platinum cardholders who use this number are exempt from the 1% fee.

Visa offers traveler's checks at Citibank locations nationwide, as well

as at several other banks. The service charge ranges between 1.5% and 2%; checks come in denominations of $20, $50, $100, $500, and $1,000. Call ℂ **800/732-1322** for information. AAA members can obtain Visa checks without a fee at most AAA offices or by calling ℂ **866/339-3378. MasterCard** also offers traveler's checks. Call ℂ **800/ 223-9920** for a location near you.

If you choose to carry traveler's checks, be sure to keep a record of their serial numbers separate from your checks in the event that they are stolen or lost. You'll get a refund faster if you know the numbers.

CREDIT CARDS

Credit cards are invaluable when traveling. They are a safe way to carry money and provide a convenient record of all your expenses. You can also withdraw cash advances from your credit cards at any bank (though you'll start paying hefty interest on the advance the moment you receive the cash). At most banks, you don't even need to see a teller; you can get a cash advance at the ATM if you know your PIN. If you've forgotten your PIN, or didn't even know you had one, call the number on the back of your credit card and ask the bank to send it to you. It usually takes 5 to 7 business days, though some banks will provide the number over the phone if you tell them your mother's maiden name or pass some other security clearance.

For tips and telephone numbers to call if your wallet is stolen or lost, see the "Lost & Found" entry in the "Fast Facts" section at the end of this chapter.

Cards widely accepted in Maine include American Express, MasterCard, and Visa. I've found Diner's Club and Discover to be less commonly accepted, but check ahead if you carry these cards; they may well be accepted. (Also check the listings of hotels and restaurants in this guidebook.)

4 When to Go

THE SEASONS

The well-worn joke about the climate in coastal Maine is that it has just two seasons: winter and August. There's a kernel of truth in that, but it's mostly a canard to keep outsiders from moving here, the same way the Pacific Northwest "celebrates" its 11-month "rain festival." In fact, the ever-shifting seasons are one of those elements that make this part of the world so distinctive, and with one exception, the seasons are long and well defined.

SUMMER   The peak summer season runs from July 4th to Labor Day. Vast crowds surge up the Maine coast during and between the two holiday weekends, swelling traffic on the turnpike and Route 1, and causing countless motels and inns to hang NO VACANCY signs. Expect to pay premium prices at hotels and restaurants along the coast in midseason. This should be no surprise: Summers are exquisite here, in spite of the occasional stretch of fog or rain for a few days. (In Portland, it tops 90°F/32°C only 4 or 5 days a year, on average.)

Forests are verdant and lush; the sky can be an almost lurid blue, the cumulus clouds painfully white. In the mountains, warm (rarely hot) days are the rule, followed by cool nights. On the coast, ocean breezes keep temperatures down and often produce vichyssoise fogs that linger for days.

Maine's coastal weather is largely determined by the prevailing winds. Southwest winds bring haze, heat, humidity, and often thunderstorms. The northwest winds bring cool weather and knife-sharp vistas. These systems tend to alternate during the summer, with the heat arriving stealthily and slowly, then getting exiled by stiff, cool winds rising from the north a few days later. (The change from hot to cool will sometimes occur in a matter of minutes.) Along the immediate coast it's often warmest in the late morning, since sea breezes typically kick up around lunchtime, pushing temperatures back down in the afternoons. Rain is rarely far away—some days it's an afternoon thunderstorm, and sometimes it's a steady drizzle that brings a 4-day soaking. On average, about 1 day in 3 will bring some rain. Travelers should come prepared for it.

Also be aware that early summer brings out the black flies and the mosquitoes in great multitude, a state of affairs that has spoiled many camping and hiking trips. While this is especially true in the inland areas, it applies along the coast and offshore islands as well. Outdoors enthusiasts are best off waiting until after July 4 for longer adventures if they want to avoid a fate as human pincushions.

AUTUMN   Don't be surprised to smell the tang of fall approaching as early as mid-August, a time when you'll also notice a few leaves turning blaze-orange on the lush maples at the edges of wetlands. Fall comes early to Maine, puts its feet up on the couch, and stays for some time. The foliage season begins in earnest in the northern part of the region by the third week in September; in the south, it reaches its peak by mid-October.

Fall is to Maine what the Grand Canyon is to the Southwest. It's one of the great natural spectacles of the United States, and with its rolling hills saturated in brilliant reds and stunning oranges, fall is garish in a way that seems determined to embarrass understated Yankees in these parts. But even many locals get dewy-eyed at the sight of the annual colors.

Happily, thanks to the low elevation and moderating influences of the ocean temperatures along the coast, the foliage season tends to run even longer along the coast. Inland mountains can be brown and brittle by mid-October, but coastal foliage is just hitting its stride by then, and the tart colors can linger into the first few days of November.

Keep in mind that this is also the most popular time of year to travel—bus tours flock like migrating geese to New England in early October. As a result, hotels are invariably booked solid, and reservations are strongly encouraged. Some years, local radio stations put out calls for residents to open their doors to stranded travelers who otherwise would have to sleep in their cars. Reservations are essential. Don't be surprised if you're assessed a foliage surcharge of $10 or $20 per room at some inns.

Maine maintains a recorded **foliage hot line** to let you know when the leaves are at their peak: call ✆ **800/777-0317** for the latest info.

WINTER Maine winters are like wine—some years are good, some are lousy. During a good season, mounds of light, fluffy snow blanket the deep woods and fill the ski slopes. A good winter offers a profound peace and tranquillity. The muffling qualities of fresh snow bring a thunderous silence to the region, and the hiss and pop of a wood fire at a country inn can sound like an overwrought symphony. During these winters, exploring the forest on snowshoes or cross-country skis is an experience bordering on the magical.

During the *other* winters, the lousy ones, the weather brings a nasty mélange of rain, freezing rain, and sleet. The woods are filled with dirty crusty snow, the cold is damp and numbing, and it's bleak, bleak, bleak. In 1998, a destructive ice storm wreaked havoc on trees (you'll see broken trunks and branches almost everywhere) and citizens, stranding over half of Maine's homes without power for up to 2 weeks. Look into the eyes of residents on the street during this time. They're all longing for the Caribbean.

Ergo, visiting Maine in winter is something of a high-risk venture.

The higher you go in the mountains, and the further north you head, the better your odds of finding snow and avoiding rain. Winter coastal vacations can be spectacular (not much beats cross-country skiing at the edge of the pounding surf), but it's a high-risk venture that could well yield rain rather than snow.

Where to go? Beach towns like York Beach and Ogunquit and tourist destinations like Boothbay Harbor tend to be shuttered and melancholy in the winter. Intrepid winter travelers are better off heading to places with more substantial year-round communities and a good selection of year-round lodging, like Kennebunkport, Portland, and Camden.

SPRING Maine's spring seemingly lasts only a weekend or so, often appearing around mid-May but sometimes as late as June. One day the ground is muddy, the trees barren, and gritty snow is still collected in shady hollows. The next day, it's in the 70s or 80s, trees are blooming, and kids are jumping off the docks into the ocean. Travelers need to be very crafty and alert if they want to experience spring in Maine; spring is also known as "mud season" in these parts, and many innkeepers and restaurateurs close up for a few weeks for repairs or to venture someplace warm.

That said, April and May can offer superb days when a blue sky arches overhead and it's warm in the sun. And this might be the most peaceful time of year—a good season for taking solitary walks on the beach or sitting on rocky promontories with only seagulls for company. Just be aware that as soon as the sun slips behind a cloud or over the horizon, it'll quickly feel like winter again. Don't leave your parka or gloves behind if you venture here in spring.

Portland, Maine's Average Temperatures

	Jan	Feb	Mar	Apr	May	June	July	Aug	Sept	Oct	Nov	Dec
Avg. High (°F)	31	32	40	50	61	72	76	74	68	58	45	34
(°C)	–1	0	4	10	16	22	24	23	20	14	7	1
Avg. Low (°F)	16	16	27	36	47	54	61	59	52	43	32	22
(°C)	–9	–9	–3	2	8	12	16	15	11	6	0	–6

THE MAINE COAST CALENDAR OF EVENTS

January

New Year's Portland. Ring in the New Year with a smorgasbord of events and entertainment throughout downtown Portland. Events for families are scheduled in the afternoon; adult entertainment, including loads of live music, kicks off later in the evening at numerous auditoriums, shops, and churches. One admission price buys entrance to all events. December 31/January 1.

February

U.S. National Toboggan Championships, Camden, Maine. Raucous and lively athletic event where being overweight is an advantage. Held at the Camden Snow Bowl's toboggan chute. Call ✆ **207/236-3438.** Early February.

March

Maine Boatbuilders' Show, Portland. More than 200 exhibitors and 9,000 boat aficionados gather as winter fades to make plans for the coming summer. A great place to meet boatbuilders and get ideas for your dream craft. Call ✆ **207/774-1067.** Late March.

Maine Maple Sunday. Maple sugarhouses throughout the state open their doors to visitors. Call ✆ **207/287-3491.** Third Sunday in March.

April

Boothbay Harbor Fisherman's Festival. Local fishermen display their talents in fish filleting, clam shucking, and even lobster eating. Enjoy seafood feasts, exhibits, games, and a Blessing of the Fleet on Sunday afternoon. Call ✆ **207/633-2353.** End of April.

May

Annual Fiddlers Contest, Ogunquit. Rosin up your bow and whip out your best version of Sally Goodin. Or just come and listen to others. Call ✆ **207/646-2939** or 207/646-6170. Late May.

Fiddlehead, Antique Car, & Antique Aeroplane Festival, Owls Head. A combination fiddlehead-cooking show and gathering of hundreds of antique planes (no trains) and automobiles. Held at the Owls Head Transportation Museum on Rte. 73. Call ✆ **207/594-4418.** Late May.

June

Old Port Festival, Portland, Maine. A daylong block party in the heart of Portland's historic district with live music, food vendors, and activities for kids. Call ✆ **207/772-6828.** Early June.

Market Square Day, Portsmouth, New Hampshire. This lively street fair attracts hordes from all over southern New Hampshire and Maine to dance, listen to music, sample food, and enjoy summer's arrival. Call ✆ **603/436-3988.** Early June.

Annual Windjammer Days, Boothbay Harbor, Maine. For nearly 4 decades, windjammers have gathered in Boothbay Harbor to kick off the summer sailing season. Expect music, food, and a parade of magnificent sailboats. Call ✆ **207/633-2353.** Late June.

July

Independence Day, region wide. Communities all along the coast celebrate with parades, greased-pole climbs, cakewalks, cookouts, road races, and fireworks. The bigger the town, the bigger the fireworks. But many small coastal towns feature seafood and/or lobster-boat racing, an unusual and fun way to celebrate the occasion; Eastport's celebration is particularly impressive (it's 4 days long); see chapter 9. Check local newspapers or contact chambers of commerce for details. July 4.

Summer Performance Series, Portland. Relax and enjoy 50 free noontime performances in Portland's downtown parks. Music includes classical, folk, jazz, rock, country, and children's shows. Call ✆ **207/874-8793** for a complete listing. July and August.

August

Maine Lobster Festival, Rockland. Fill up on the local harvest at this event marking the importance and delectability of Maine's favorite crustacean. Enjoy a boiled lobster or two, and take in the ample entertainment during this informal waterfront gala. Call ✆ **800/LOB-CLAW** or 207/596-0376. Usually held the first weekend of August.

York Days, York Village. Enjoy a quintessential coastal Maine celebration complete with crafts, road races, parades, dances, concerts, fireworks, and much more. Call ✆ **207/363-1040.** Early August.

Wild Blueberry Festival, Machias. Marks the harvest of the region's wild blueberries. Eat to your heart's content. Call ✆ **207/794-3543** or 207/255-6665. Mid-August.

Blue Hill Fair, Blue Hill. A classic country fair outside one of Maine's most elegant villages. Call ✆ **207/374-3701.** Late August.

September

Windjammer Weekend, Camden. Visit Maine's impressive fleet of old-time sailing ships; open houses throughout the weekend at this scenic harbor. Call ✆ **207/236-4404.** Early September.

Thomas Point Bluegrass Festival, Brunswick. New England's best roots-music festival, held at attractive Thomas Point Beach State Park. Bring your instrument and join a fireside song circle; guests and musicians jam and improvise late into the night. Call ✆ **207/725-6009.** Early September.

Common Ground Country Fair, Unity. An old-time state fair with a twist: emphasis is on organic foods, recycling, and wholesome living. Call ✆ **207/568-4142.** Late September.

October

Fall Festival Arts & Crafts Show, Camden. More than 80 artists purvey their wares near peak foliage time in this cute coastal town. Call ✆ **207/236-4404** for details. Early October.

Fall Foliage Fair, Boothbay. More than 100 exhibitors display their arts and crafts at the Railroad Village; plenty of festive foodstuffs and live music too. Call ✆ **207/633-4743.** Mid-October.

Mount Desert Island Marathon, Bar Harbor. Scenic 26.2-mile race through gorgeous island scenery. Call **207/288-4725** for more information. Mid-October.

Festival of Scarecrows and Harvest Day, Rockland. A local scarecrow-making contest, plus a farmers' market and other activities, spread over a 2-week period. Call ✆ **207/596-6256** for details. Late October.

Ogunquit Fest, Ogunquit. A 3-day pre-Halloween bash, featuring arts, crafts, costumes, and a parade. Call © **207/646-2939.** Late October.

November

Festival of Lights, Rockland. Horse-drawn carriages, singing, shopping, and open houses of local inns. Call © **207/596-0376** for details. Late November.

Victorian Holiday, Portland. From late November until Christmas, Portland decorates its Old Port in a Victorian Christmas theme. Enjoy the window displays, take a free hayride, and listen to costumed carolers sing. Call © **207/772-6828** or 207/780-5555. Late November to Christmas.

December

Christmas Prelude, Kennebunkport. This scenic coastal village greets Santa's arrival in a lobster boat, and marks the coming of Christmas with street shows, pancake breakfasts, and tours of the town's inns. Call © **207/967-0857.** Early December.

Candlelight Stroll, Portsmouth, New Hampshire. Historic Strawbery Banke gets in a Christmas way with old-time decorations and more than 1,000 candles lighting the 10-acre grounds. Call © **603/433-1100.** First 2 weekends of December.

York Village Festival of Lights. This beautiful festival displays an entire York Village and York Beach lit with Christmas lights, carolers, a parade, and much more. Call © **207/363-4974.** Early December.

5 Travel Insurance

Check your existing insurance policies and credit card coverage before you buy travel insurance. You may already be covered for lost luggage, canceled tickets, or medical expenses. The cost of travel insurance varies widely, depending on the cost and length of your trip, your age, your health, and the type of trip you're taking.

TRIP-CANCELLATION INSURANCE

Trip-cancellation insurance helps you get your money back if you have to back out of a trip, if you have to go home early, or if your travel supplier goes bankrupt. Allowed reasons for cancellation can range from sickness to natural disasters to the State Department declaring your destination unsafe for travel. In this unstable world, trip-cancellation insurance is a good buy if you're getting tickets well in advance—who knows what the state of the world, or of your airline, will be in 9 months? Insurance policy details vary, so read the fine print—and especially make sure that your airline or cruise line is on the list of carriers covered in case of bankruptcy.

For information, contact one of the following insurers: **Access America** (© **866/807-3982;** www.accessamerica.com); **Travel Guard International** (© **800/826-4919;** www.travelguard.com); **Travel Insured International** (© **800/243-3174;** www.travelinsured.com); and **Travelex Insurance Services** (© **888/457-4602;** www.travelex-insurance.com).

MEDICAL INSURANCE

Most health insurance policies cover you if you get sick away from home—but check, particularly if you're insured by an HMO.

If you require additional medical insurance, try **MEDEX International** (© **800/527-0218** or 410/453-6300; www.medexassist.com) or **Travel Assistance International** (© **800/821-2828;** www.travelassistance.com; for general information on services, call the company's Worldwide Assistance Services, Inc., at © **800/777-8710**).

LOST-LUGGAGE INSURANCE

On domestic flights, checked baggage is covered up to $2,500 per ticketed passenger. On international flights (including U.S. portions of international trips), baggage is limited to approximately $9 per pound, up to approximately $635 per checked bag. If you plan to check items more valuable than the standard liability, see if your valuables are covered by your homeowner's policy, get baggage insurance as part of your comprehensive travel-insurance package, or buy Travel Guard's "BagTrak" product. Don't buy insurance at the airport, as it's usually overpriced. Be sure to take any valuables or irreplaceable items with you in your carry-on luggage, as many valuables (including books, money, and electronics) aren't covered by airline policies.

If your luggage is lost, immediately file a lost-luggage claim at the airport, detailing the luggage contents. For most airlines, you must report delayed, damaged, or lost baggage within 4 hours of arrival. The airlines are required to deliver luggage, once found, directly to your house or destination free of charge.

6 Health & Safety

STAYING HEALTHY

Mainers by and large consider themselves a healthy bunch, which they ascribe to clean living, brisk northern air, vigorous exercise (leaf raking, snow shoveling, and so on), and a sensible diet. Other than picking up a germ that may lead to a cold or flu, you shouldn't face any serious health risks when traveling the region.

Exceptions? Well, yes—you may find yourself at higher risk when exploring the outdoors, particularly in the backcountry. A few things to watch for when venturing off the beaten track:

- **Poison ivy:** The shiny, three-leafed plant is common throughout the region. If touched, you may develop a nasty, itchy rash that will seriously erode the enjoyment of your vacation. The reaction tends to be worse in some people than others. It's safest to simply avoid it. If you're unfamiliar with what poison ivy looks like, ask at a ranger station or visitor information booth for more information. Many have posters or books to help with identification.

- **Giardia:** That crystal-clear stream coursing down a backcountry peak may seem as pure as pure gets, but consider the possibility that it may be contaminated with animal feces. Disgusting, yes, and also dangerous. Giardia cysts may be present in some streams and rivers. When ingested by humans, the cysts can result in copious diarrhea and weight loss. Symptoms may not surface until well after you've left the backcountry and returned home. Carry your own water for day trips, or bring a small filter (available at most camping and sporting goods shops) to treat backcountry water. Failing that, at least boil water or treat it with iodine before using it for cooking, drinking, or washing. If you detect symptoms, see a doctor immediately.

- **Lyme disease:** Lyme disease has been a growing problem in New England since 1975 when the disease was identified in the town of Lyme, Connecticut, with some 14,000 cases now reported nationwide annually. The disease is transmitted by tiny deer ticks—smaller than the more common, relatively harmless wood ticks. Look for a bull's-eye-shaped rash (3–8 in. in diameter); it may feel warm but usually doesn't itch.

Symptoms include muscle and joint pain, fever, and fatigue. If left untreated, heart damage may occur. It's more easily treated in early phases than later, so it's best to seek medical attention as soon as any symptoms are noted.

• **Rabies:** Since 1989, rabies has been spreading northward from New Jersey into New England. The disease is spread by animal saliva and is especially prevalent in skunks, raccoons, bats, and foxes. It is always fatal if left untreated in humans. Infected animals tend to display erratic and aggressive behavior. The best advice is to keep a safe distance between yourself and any wild animal you may encounter. If bitten, wash the wound as soon as you can and immediately seek medical attention. Treatment is no longer as painful as it once was, but still involves a series of shots.

Those planning longer excursions into the outdoors may find a compact first aid kit with basic salves and medicines very handy to have along. Those traveling mostly in the towns and villages should have little trouble finding a local pharmacy, Rite Aid, or Wal-Mart to stock up on common medicines (such as calamine lotion or aspirin) to aid with any minor ailments picked up along the way.

WHAT TO DO IF YOU GET SICK AWAY FROM HOME

If you get sick, consider asking your hotel concierge, motel desk clerk, or B&B innkeeper to recommend a local doctor—even his or her own. You can also try the emergency room at a local hospital. Many hospitals also have walk-in clinics for emergency cases that are not life-threatening; you may not get immediate attention, but you won't pay the high price of an emergency room visit. See "Fast Facts," p. 51, for hospitals and emergency numbers.

If you worry about getting sick away from home, consider purchasing **medical travel insurance** and carry your ID card in your purse or wallet. In most cases, your existing health plan will provide the coverage you need. See the preceding section, "Travel Insurance," for more information.

If you suffer from a chronic illness, consult your doctor before leaving. For conditions such as epilepsy, diabetes, or heart problems, wear a **MedicAlert identification tag** (© **800/825-3785; www.medicalert.org**), which will immediately alert doctors to your condition and give them access to your records through MedicAlert's 24-hour hot line.

Pack **prescription medications** (make sure they're in their original containers) in your carry-on luggage. Also, bring along copies of your prescriptions in case you lose your pills or run out. And don't forget sunglasses and an extra pair of contact lenses or prescription glasses.

STAYING SAFE

Maine boasts some of the lowest crime rates in the country. The odds of anything bad happening during your visit here are very slight. But all travelers are advised to take the usual precautions against theft, robbery, and assault.

Travelers should avoid any unnecessary public displays of wealth. Don't bring out fat wads of cash from your pocket, and save your best jewelry for private occasions. If you are approached by someone who demands money, jewelry, or anything else from you, hand it over. Don't argue. Don't negotiate. Just comply. Afterward, immediately contact the police; dialing © **911** from almost any phone will connect you to an emergency dispatcher, who will record the details of the crime and send a police officer, if necessary. (If 911 doesn't work, dial 0 [zero] and inform the operator that you have an emergency to report.)

The crime you're statistically most likely to encounter is theft of items from your car. Break-ins can occur anytime. Don't leave anything of value in plain view. At the least, lock valuables in your trunk. Better still, keep them with you at all times.

Late at night, you should look for a well-lighted area if you need gas or you need to step out of your car for any reason. Also, it's not advisable to sleep in your car late at night at highway rest areas, which can leave you vulnerable to robbers.

Take the usual precautions against leaving cash or valuables in your hotel room when you're not present. Many hotels have safe-deposit boxes. Smaller inns and hotels often do not, although it can't hurt to ask to leave small items in the house safe. Some small inns don't even have locks on guest-room doors. Don't be alarmed; if anything, this is a good sign, indicating that the inn has had no problems there in the past. If you're feeling at all nervous about this, lock your valuables in your car's trunk.

7 Specialized Travel Resources

TRAVELERS WITH DISABILITIES

Most disabilities shouldn't stop anyone from traveling, with more options and resources out there than ever before.

Prodded by the Americans with Disabilities Act, a growing number of New England inns and hotels are retrofitting some of their rooms for people with special needs. Most innkeepers are quite proud of their improvements—when Frommer's arrives for a site visit, they're invariably quick to show their new rooms with barrier-free entrances, wheelchair-accessible showers, and fire alarms equipped with strobe lights. Outdoor-recreation areas, especially on state and federal lands, are also providing more trails and facilities for those who've been effectively barred in the past. Accessibility is improving region wide, but improvements are far from universal. When in doubt, call ahead to ensure that you'll be accommodated.

The U.S. National Park Service offers a Golden Access Passport that gives free lifetime entrance to all properties administered by the National Park Service—national parks, monuments, historic sites, recreation areas, and national wildlife refuges—for persons who are visually impaired or permanently disabled, regardless of your age. You may pick up a Golden Access Passport at any NPS entrance fee area by showing proof of medically determined disability and eligibility for receiving benefits under federal law. Besides free entry, the Golden Access Passport also offers a 50% discount on federal-use fees charged for such facilities as camping, swimming, parking, boat launching, and tours. For more information, go to www.nps.gov/fees_passes.htm or call © **888/467-2757.**

Many travel agencies offer customized tours and itineraries for travelers with disabilities. **Flying Wheels Travel** (© **507/451-5005;** www.flyingwheelstravel.com) offers escorted tours and cruises that emphasize sports and private tours in minivans with lifts. **Accessible Journeys** (© **800/846-4537** or 610/521-0339; www.disabilitytravel.com) caters specifically to slow walkers and wheelchair travelers and their families and friends.

Organizations that offer assistance to travelers with disabilities include **Moss-Rehab** (www.mossresourcenet.org), which provides a library of accessible-travel resources online; the **Society for Accessible Travel and Hospitality** (© **212/447-7284;** www.sath.org; annual membership fees: $45 adults, $30 seniors and students), which offers a wealth of travel resources for all types of disabilities and informed recommendations on destinations, access guides, travel agents, tour operators, vehicle rentals, and companion services; and the **American Foundation for the Blind** (© 800/232-5463; www.afb.org), which provides information on traveling with Seeing Eye dogs.

For more information specifically targeted to travelers with disabilities, the community website **iCan** (www.icanonline.net) has destination guides and several regular columns on accessible travel. Also check out the quarterly magazine **Emerging Horizons** ($14.95 per year, $19.95 outside the U.S.; www.emerginghorizons.com); **Twin Peaks Press** (© 360/694-2462), offering travel-related books for travelers with special needs; and *Open World Magazine,* published by the Society for Accessible Travel and Hospitality (see above; subscription: $18 per year, $35 outside the U.S.).

GAY & LESBIAN TRAVELERS

Though coastal Maine isn't exactly a hotbed of gay culture, it has been rapidly growing as a gay travel destination, and many gays and lesbians now live and travel here. Larger cities tend to be more accommodating to gay travelers than smaller towns, but many small coastal towns now also show gay and lesbian presence. In general, gay and lesbian travelers should feel very comfortable in all vacation areas of coastal Maine.

Portland is now home to a substantial gay population, attracting many refugees who've fled the crime and congestion of Boston and New York. The city hosts a sizable Pride festival early each summer that includes a riotous parade and a dance on the city pier, among other events. In early 1998, Maine narrowly repealed a statewide gay-rights law that had been passed earlier by the state legislature. In Portland, however, the vote was nearly four to one against the repeal and in support of equal rights. Portland also has a municipal ordinance that prohibits discrimination in jobs and housing based on sexual orientation.

Blackstones (© 207/775-2885), at 6 Pine St., is a low-key neighborhood bar, while **Sisters** (© 207/774-1505), 45 Danforth, is the city's most popular lesbian hangout.

Ogunquit, on the southern Maine coast, is hugely popular among gay travelers, a longtime (even historic) gay resort area which features a lively beach and bar scene in the summer. In the winter, it's still active but decidedly more mellow. Several Ogunquit B&Bs are owned by gay entrepreneurs A well-designed website, **www.gayogunquit.com**, is a great place to start to find information on gay-owned inns, restaurants, and nightclubs in the town.

For a more detailed directory of gay-oriented enterprises in New England, track down a copy of **The Pink Pages,** published by KP Media (66 Charles St., #283, Boston, MA 02114; kpmedia@aol.com). The price is $8.95, plus $2 shipping and handling. Call © 617/423-1515 or visit the firm's website at **www.pinkweb.com**, which also contains much of the information in the published version.

More adventurous souls should consider linking up with the **Chiltern Mountain Club,** P.O. Box 407, Boston, MA 02117 (© 888/831-3100 or 617/556-7774; www.chiltern.org), an outdoor-adventure club for gays and lesbians; about two-thirds of its 1,200 members are men. The club organizes trips to northern New England throughout the year.

The International Gay & Lesbian Travel Association (IGLTA) (© 800/448-8550 or 954/776-2626; www.iglta.org) is the trade association for the gay and lesbian travel industry, and offers an online directory of gay- and lesbian-friendly travel businesses; go to their website and click on "Members."

Many agencies offer tours and travel itineraries specifically for gay and lesbian travelers. **Now, Voyager**

(© **800/255-6951;** www.nowvoyager.com) is a well-known San Francisco–based gay-owned and -operated travel service.

SENIOR TRAVEL

Mention the fact that you're a senior when you first make your travel reservations. All major airlines and many hotels offer discounts for seniors. Major airlines also offer coupons for domestic travel for seniors over 60. Typically, a book of four coupons costs less than $700, and each coupon is good for a single one-way flight. In other words, a round-trip in the continental United States ends up costing under $350. In most cities, people over the age of 60 qualify for reduced admission to theaters, museums, and other attractions, as well as discounted fares on public transportation.

Coastal Maine is generally well suited to older travelers, with a wide array of activities for seniors and discounts commonly available (not to mention the low crime rate, quiet nights, and scenic roads). It's wise to request a discount at hotels or motels when booking the room, not when you arrive. An identification card from **AARP** (formerly known as the American Association of Retired Persons), 601 E St. NW, Washington, DC 20049 (© **800/424-3410** or 202/434-2277; www.aarp.org), can aid in getting discounts on hotels, airfares, and car rentals. AARP offers members a wide range of benefits, including *AARP: The Magazine* and a monthly newsletter. Anyone over 50 can join.

The **U.S. National Park Service** offers a **Golden Age Passport** that gives seniors 62 years or older lifetime entrance to all properties administered by the National Park Service—national parks, monuments, historic sites, recreation areas, and national wildlife refuges—for a one-time processing fee of $10, which must be purchased in person at any NPS facility that charges

an entrance fee. Besides free entry, a Golden Age Passport also provides a 50% discount on federal-use fees charged for such facilities as camping, swimming, parking, boat launching, and tours. For more information, go to www.nps.gov/fees_passes.htm or call © **888/467-2757.**

Many reliable agencies and organizations target the 50-plus market. **Elderhostel** (© **877/426-8056;** www.elderhostel.org) arranges study programs for those aged 55 and over (and a spouse or companion of any age) in the U.S. and in more than 80 countries around the world. Most courses last 5 to 7 days in the U.S. (2–4 weeks abroad), and many include airfare, accommodations in university dormitories or modest inns, meals, and tuition. **ElderTreks** (© **800/741-7956;** www.eldertreks.com) offers small-group tours to off-the-beaten-path or adventure-travel locations, restricted to travelers 50 and older.

Recommended publications offering travel resources and discounts for seniors include: the quarterly magazine *Travel 50 & Beyond* (www.travel50andbeyond.com); *Travel Unlimited: Uncommon Adventures for the Mature Traveler* (Avalon); *101 Tips for Mature Travelers,* available from Grand Circle Travel (© **800/221-2610** or 617/350-7500; www.gct.com); *The 50+ Traveler's Guidebook* (St. Martin's Press); and *Unbelievably Good Deals and Great Adventures That You Absolutely Can't Get Unless You're Over 50* (McGraw-Hill).

FAMILY TRAVEL

The family vacation is a rite of passage for many households, one that in a split second can evolve into a *National Lampoon* farce. But as any veteran family vacationer will assure you, a family trip can be among the most pleasurable and rewarding times of your life.

Families rarely have trouble finding things to do with kids along the

Maine coast. The natural world seems to hold tremendous wonder for the younger set—an afternoon exploring a tide pool can be a huge adventure. Older kids may like the challenge of learning to paddle a sea kayak in choppy seas or playing video games at an arcade. And there's always the beach, which is usually good for hours of sunny diversion.

Recommended destinations for families include **York Beach**—with long strips of sand, an arcade, and an amusement park—and **Old Orchard Beach,** as well as Acadia National Park's home base town of **Bar Harbor.** Teens may enjoy shopping the outlets of **Freeport** and **Kittery** or the more substantial boutiques and shops in the Old Port section of **Portland**. **Sebasco Harbor Resort** south of Bath, the **Samoset Resort** in Rockport, and the rocky headland and nearby beach of **Pemaquid Point** are also notably family-friendly.

Be aware that many inns in Maine cater to couples looking for a romantic getaway, and kids aren't exactly welcomed with open arms. In fact, some inns don't allow kids at all, or strongly prefer only children over a certain age. Innkeepers will let you know when you make your reservation (I have also noted policies about children in the listings in this book), but you should mention that you're traveling with kids when booking anyway.

Several specialized guides offer more detailed information for families on the go. Try *Best Hikes with Children in Vermont, New Hampshire & Maine,* by Cynthia and Thomas Lewis (Mountaineers, 2000); *Fun Places to Go with Children in New England,* by Pamela Wright and Diane Bair (Chronicle Books, 1998); Howard Stone's *25 Bicycle Tours in Maine* (W.W. Norton, 1998), reissued by Countryman Press; and *Great Family Vacations North East,* by Candyce Stapen (Globe Pequot, 1999). The

Maine Department of Transportation also publishes an excellent biking map, available online at www.explore maine.org/bike.

In addition, *The Unofficial Guide to New England & New York with Kids* (Wiley Publishing) is a good overview of the region's offerings for families. *How to Take Great Trips with Your Kids* (The Harvard Common Press) is full of good general advice that can apply to travel anywhere.

Finally, be sure to ask about family discounts when visiting attractions. Many places offer a flat family rate that is less than paying for each ticket individually. Some parks and beaches charge by the car rather than the head.

STUDENT TRAVEL

Although discounts aren't as widespread as in Europe, students can sometimes save a few dollars on tours or museum admissions along the coast of Maine by presenting a current ID card from a college or university or by presenting the **International Student Identity Card (ISIC),** which offers substantial savings on rail passes, plane tickets, and entrance fees. It also provides basic health and life insurance and a 24-hour help line. The card is available for $22 from **STA Travel** (© **800/781-4040;** www.statravel. com), the biggest student travel agency in the world. If you're no longer a student but are still under 26, you can get an **International Youth Travel Card (IYTC)** for the same price from the same people, which entitles you to some discounts (but not on museum admissions). (**Note:** In 2002, STA Travel bought competitors **Council Travel** and **USIT Campus** after they went bankrupt. It's still operating some offices under the Council name, but it's owned by STA.)

Travel CUTS (© **800/667-2887** or 416/614-2887; www.travelcuts.com) offers similar services for both Canadians and U.S. residents. Irish students

---

> **Tips The Peripatetic Pet**
>
> Never leave your pet inside a parked car in hot climates with the windows rolled up. It's a good idea never to leave a pet inside a hot car even with the windows rolled down for any length of time.
>
> Make sure your pet is wearing a name tag with the name and phone number of either a contact person who can take the call if your pet is lost while you're away from home or a voice mail system that enables you to easily check remotely for any calls related to a lost pet.

---

should turn to **USIT** (© **01/602-1600;** www.usitnow.ie).

TRAVELING WITH PETS

No surprise: Some places allow pets, some don't. I've noted here inns that allow pets, but even here I don't recommend showing up with a pet in tow unless you've cleared it over the phone with the innkeeper. Note that many establishments have only one or two rooms (often a cottage or room with exterior entrance) set aside for guests traveling with pets, and they won't be happy to meet Fido if the pet rooms are already occupied. Also, it's increasingly common for a surcharge of $10 or $20 to be charged to pet owners to pay for the extra cleaning.

Some innkeepers will accept pets but don't want the fact mentioned in this guide. Their policy is to have travelers ask them first so that they can explain the ground rules and ascertain that the pet in question isn't a hyperactive terrier with unresolved barking issues. It doesn't hurt to inquire, even if a pet policy isn't mentioned in these pages.

An excellent resource is **www.pets welcome.com,** which dispenses medical tips, names of animal-friendly lodgings and campgrounds, and lists of kennels and veterinarians. Also check out **www.pettravel.com** and **www. travelpets.com** for more information.

Keep in mind that dogs are prohibited on hiking trails and must be leashed at all times on federal lands administered by the National Park Service, which include Acadia National Park in Maine. No pets of any sort are allowed at any time (leashed or unleashed) at Baxter State Park in Maine. Other Maine state parks do allow pets on a leash.

8 Planning Your Trip Online

SURFING FOR AIRFARES

The "big three" online travel agencies—**Travelocity, Expedia.com,** and **Orbitz**—sell most of the air tickets bought on the Internet. (Canadian travelers should try expedia.ca and Travelocity.ca; U.K. residents can go to expedia.co.uk and opodo.co.uk.) Each has different business deals with the airlines and may offer different fares on the same flights, so it's wise to shop around. Expedia and Travelocity will also send you **e-mail notification**

when a cheap fare becomes available to your favorite destination.

Also remember to check **airline websites,** especially those for low-fare carriers such as JetBlue and Southwest, whose fares are often misreported or simply missing from travel agency websites. Even with major airlines, you can often shave a few bucks from a fare by booking directly through the airline and avoiding a travel agency's transaction fee. But you'll get these discounts only by

booking online: Most airlines now offer online-only fares that even their phone agents know nothing about. For the websites of airlines that fly to and from your destination, go to "Getting There," later in this chapter.

Great **last-minute deals** are available through free weekly e-mail services provided directly by the airlines. Most of these are announced on Tuesday or Wednesday and must be purchased online. Most are only valid for travel that weekend, but some (such as Southwest's) can be booked weeks or months in advance. Sign up for weekly e-mail alerts at airline websites or check megasites that compile comprehensive lists of last-minute specials, such as **Smarter Living** (smarterliving.com). For last-minute trips, **site59.com** often has better deals than the major-label sites.

If you're willing to give up some control over your flight details, use an **opaque fare service** such as **Priceline** (www.priceline.com; www.priceline.co.uk for Europeans) or **Hotwire** (www.hotwire.com). Both offer rock-bottom prices in exchange for travel on a "mystery airline" at a mysterious time of day, often with a mysterious change of planes en route. The mystery airlines are all major, well-known carriers—and the possibility of being sent from Philadelphia to Chicago via Tampa is remote; the airlines' routing computers have gotten a lot better than they used to be. But your chances of getting a 6am or 11pm flight are pretty high. Hotwire tells you flight prices before you buy; Priceline usually has better deals than Hotwire, but you have to play their "name our price" game. If you're new at this, the helpful folks at **BiddingForTravel** (www.biddingfortravel.com) do a good job of demystifying Priceline's prices. Priceline and Hotwire are great for flights within North America.

For much more about airfares and savvy air-travel tips and advice, pick up a copy of *Frommer's Fly Safe, Fly Smart* (Wiley Publishing, Inc.).

SURFING FOR HOTELS

Shopping online for hotels is much easier in the U.S., Canada, and certain parts of Europe than it is in the rest of the world. If you try to book a Chinese hotel online, for instance, you'll probably overpay. Also, many smaller hotels and B&Bs don't show up on websites at all. Of the "big three" sites, **Expedia.com** may be the best choice,

---

Frommers.com: The Complete Travel Resource

For an excellent travel-planning resource, I highly recommend **Frommers.com** (www.frommers.com). We're a little biased, of course, but we guarantee that you'll find the travel tips, reviews, monthly vacation giveaways, and online-booking capabilities thoroughly indispensable. Among the special features are our popular **Message Boards,** where Frommer's readers post queries and share advice (sometimes even our authors show up to answer questions); the **Frommers.com Newsletter,** for the latest travel bargains and insider travel secrets; and **Frommer's Destinations Section,** where you'll get expert travel tips, hotel and dining recommendations, and advice on the sights to see for more than 3,000 destinations around the globe. When your research is done, the **Online Reservations System** (www.frommers.com) takes you to Frommer's preferred online partners for booking your vacation at affordable prices.

thanks to its long list of specials. **Travelocity** runs a close second. Hotel specialist sites **hotels.com** and **hotel discounts.com** are also reliable. An excellent free program, **TravelAxe** (www.travelaxe.net), can help you search multiple sites at once, even ones you may never have heard of.

Priceline and Hotwire are even better for hotels than for airfares; with both, you're allowed to pick the neighborhood and quality level of your hotel before offering up your money. Priceline's hotel product even covers Europe and Asia, though it's much better at getting five-star lodging for

three-star prices than at finding anything at the bottom of the scale. *Note:* Hotwire overrates its hotels by one star—what Hotwire calls a four-star is a three-star anywhere else.

SURFING FOR RENTAL CARS

For booking rental cars online, the best deals are usually found at rental-car company websites, although all the major online travel agencies offer rental-car reservations. Priceline and Hotwire work well for rental cars, too; the only "mystery" is which major rental company you get.

9 The 21st-Century Traveler

INTERNET ACCESS AWAY FROM HOME

Travelers have any number of ways to check their e-mail and access the Internet on the road. Of course, using your own laptop—or even a PDA (personal digital assistant) or electronic organizer with a modem—gives you the most flexibility. But even if you don't have a computer, you can still access your e-mail and even your office computer from cybercafes.

WITHOUT YOUR OWN COMPUTER

It's hard nowadays to find a city that *doesn't* have a few cybercafes. Although there's no definitive directory for cybercafes—these are independent businesses, after all—three places to start looking are at **www.cybercaptive.com**, **www.netcafeguide.com**, and **www. cybercafe.com**. Portland has a couple of cybercafes; in small towns, though, it's hit or miss (usually miss).

Fortunately, coastal Maine's **public libraries** are superb at offering Internet access, nearly always for free (you may need to submit a driver's license or library card or other piece of identification as a deposit). The local library in a large coastal town such as

York, Kennebunk, or Belfast could prove vital in a pinch—but be courteous, and do not overstay your welcome. Avoid **hotel business centers,** which often charge exorbitant rates.

To retrieve your e-mail, ask your **Internet service provider (ISP)** if it has a Web-based interface tied to your existing e-mail account. If your ISP doesn't have such an interface, you can use the free **mail2web** service (www.mail2web. com) to view and reply to your home e-mail. For more flexibility, you may want to open a free, Web-based e-mail account with **Yahoo! Mail** (http://mail. yahoo.com). (Microsoft's Hotmail is another popular option, but Hotmail has severe spam problems.) Your home ISP may be able to forward your e-mail to the Web-based account automatically.

If you need to access files on your office computer, look into a service called **GoToMyPC** (www.gotomypc. com). The service provides a Web-based interface through which you can access and manipulate a distant PC from anywhere—even a cybercafe—provided your "target" PC is on and has an always-on connection to the Internet (such as with Road Runner cable). The service offers top-quality security, but if you're worried about hackers, use your own laptop rather than a cyber café to access the GoToMyPC system.

WITH YOUR OWN COMPUTER

Major Internet service providers (ISPs) have **local access numbers** around the world, enabling you to go online by simply placing a local call. Check your ISP's website or call its toll-free number and ask how you can use your current account away from home, and how much it will cost.

If you're traveling outside the reach of your ISP, the **iPass** network has dial-up numbers in most of the world's countries. You'll have to sign up with an iPass provider, who will then tell you how to set up your computer for your destination(s). For a list of iPass providers, go to www.ipass.com and click on "Reseller Locator." Under "Select a Country" pick the country that you're coming from, and under "Who is this service for?" pick "Individual." One solid provider is **i2roam** (www.i2roam.com; © **866/811-6209** or 920/235-0475).

Wherever you go, bring a **connection kit** of the right power and phone adapters, a spare phone cord, and a spare Ethernet network cable.

Most business-class hotels offer dataports for laptop modems, and some even offer high-speed Internet access using an Ethernet network cable. You'll have to bring your own cables either way, so **call your hotel in advance** to find out what the options are. Many business-class hotels in the U.S. also offer a form of computer-free Web browsing through the room TV set. Yahoo! Mail, Hotmail, and sometimes AOL mail can be checked on these systems.

If you have an 802.11b/**Wi-Fi** card for your computer, several commercial companies have made wireless service available in airports, hotel lobbies, and coffee shops, primarily in the U.S. I have recently been surprised and pleased to discover a number of inns and hotels along the coast of Maine adding Wi-Fi access points, usually at no extra charge (except a deposit in case you break the connection "bridge" you may need to borrow at reception).

T-Mobile Hotspot (www.t-mobile.com/hotspot) serves up wireless connections at more than 1,000 Starbucks coffee shops nationwide. **Boingo** (www.boingo.com) and **Wayport** (www.wayport.com) have set up networks in airports and upscale hotel lobbies. IPass providers (see above) also give you access to a few hundred wireless hotel lobby setups. Best of all, you don't need to be staying at the Four Seasons to use that hotel's network; just set yourself up on a nice couch in the lobby. Unfortunately, the companies' pricing policies are byzantine, with a variety of monthly, per-connection, and per-minute plans.

Community-minded individuals have also set up **free wireless networks** in major cities around the world. These networks are spotty, but you get what you (don't) pay for. Each network has a home page explaining how to set up your computer for their particular system; start your explorations at www.personaltelco.net/index.cgi/WirelessCommunities.

USING A CELLPHONE

Just because your cellphone works at home doesn't mean it'll work in coastal Maine (thanks to our nation's fragmented cellphone system). It's a good bet that your phone will work in major cities, a bad bet it will bail you out of trouble on an offshore island. Maine is far off the beaten track, so you may pay through the nose even if it does work; be sure to take a look at your wireless company's coverage map on its website before heading out—T-Mobile, Sprint, and Nextel are particularly weak in rural areas, and you

Online Traveler's Toolbox

Veteran travelers usually carry some essential items to make their trips easier. Following is a selection of online tools to bookmark and use:

- **Visa ATM Locator** (www.visa.com), for locations of PLUS ATMs worldwide, or **MasterCard ATM Locator** (www.mastercard.com), for locations of Cirrus ATMs worldwide.
- **Intellicast** (www.intellicast.com) and **Weather.com** (www.weather.com). These sites provide weather forecasts for all 50 states and for cities around the world.
- **MapQuest** (www.mapquest.com) and **Yahoo! Maps** (maps.yahoo.com). These are the best of the mapping sites; in seconds, from an input address, they return a map and detailed driving directions.

may pay exorbitant premiums to both make and receive calls while in Maine if your plan only includes a local calling area. If you need to stay in touch at a destination where you know your phone won't work, **rent** a phone that does from **InTouch USA** (✆ 800/872-7626; www.intouchglobal.com) or a rental-car location, but beware that you'll pay $1 a minute or more for airtime.

If you're venturing deep into the backcountry or offshore, places where cell towers might never be built, you may want to consider renting a **satellite phone (satphone),** which differs from a cellphone in that it connects to satellites, rather than ground-based towers. A satphone is more costly than a cellphone but works where there's no cellular signal and no towers. Unfortunately, you'll pay at least $2 per minute to use the phone, and it only works where you can see the horizon (i.e., usually not indoors). In North America, you can rent Iridium satellite phones from **RoadPost** (www.roadpost.com; ✆ **888/290-1606** or 905/272-5665).

InTouch USA (see above) offers a wider range of satphones but at higher rates. As of this writing, satphones were amazingly expensive to buy, so don't even think about it.

If you're not from the U.S., you'll be appalled at the poor reach of our **GSM (Global System for Mobiles) wireless network,** which is used by much of the rest of the world (see below). Your phone will probably work in most major U.S. cities; it definitely won't work in many rural areas. (To see where GSM phones work in the U.S., check out www.t-mobile.com/coverage/national_popup.asp) And you may or may not be able to send SMS (text messaging) home—something Americans tend not to do anyway, for various cultural and technological reasons. (International budget travelers like to send text messages home because it's much cheaper than making international calls.) Assume nothing—call your wireless provider and get the full scoop. In a worst-case scenario, you can always rent a phone; InTouch USA delivers to hotels.

10 Getting There

BY PLANE

Several commercial carriers serve Portland and Bangor. Airlines most commonly fly to these airports from New York or Boston, although direct connections from other cities, such as Chicago and Philadelphia, are also available. Many of the scheduled flights to Maine from Boston are aboard smaller prop planes; ask the airline or your travel agent if this is an issue for you.

Portland International Jetport (abbreviation PWM) is the coast's largest airport. It's served by regularly scheduled flights on **American Airlines** (© 800/433-7300; www.aa.com), **Delta** (© 800/221-1212; www.delta.com), **Continental** (© 800/525-0280; www.continental.com), **US Airways** (© 800/428-4322; www.usairways.com), **United Express** (© 800/241-6522; www.ual.com), and **Northwest Airlines** (800/225-2525; www.nwa.com). For general airport information, see www.portlandjetport.org or call © (**207/774-7301**).

Several smaller coastal airports in the region are served by feeder airlines and charter companies, including Rockport and Bar Harbor (actually, it's Trenton, which is just across the causeway from Mount Desert Island). Contact **Colgan Air** (© **800/428-4322;** www.usairways.com). Airlines most commonly fly to these airports from New York or Boston, although direct connections from other cities, such as Chicago, Cincinnati, and Philadelphia, are available. Many of these scheduled flights to northern New England from Boston are also aboard smaller prop planes.

Visitors to northern New England often find cheaper fares and a wider choice of flight times by flying into Boston's Logan Airport and then renting a car or connecting by bus to their final destination. (Boston is about 1 hr. by car from Kittery and Portsmouth, New Hampshire, 2 hr. by car from Portland, perhaps 5–6 hr. by car from Mount Desert Island.)

But travelers should note that Boston can be very congested, and delayed flights are endemic. Following the September 11, 2001, terrorist attacks, increased security has led to periodic but massive delays during check-in and screening. With far fewer flights, the smaller airports (such as Bangor and Burlington) have not been subject to such huge disruptions, and travelers may find that the increased expense and less flexible flight times using these airports are more than offset by the much less stressful experience of checking in and boarding.

In the last few years, the airport in Manchester, New Hampshire, has also grown in prominence thanks to the arrival of budget-friendly **Southwest Airlines,** which has brought competitive, low-cost airfares and improved service. Manchester has gone from a sleepy backwater airport to a bustling destination, recently eclipsing Portland in numbers of passengers served. (Like Boston, it's about 2 hr. away by car.) Travelers looking for good deals to the region are advised to first check with Southwest (© **800/435-9792;** www.iflyswa.com) before pricing other gateways.

Travel in the Age of Bankruptcy

At press time, two major U.S. airlines were struggling in bankruptcy court and most of the rest weren't doing very well either. To protect yourself, **buy your tickets with a credit card,** as the Fair Credit Billing Act guarantees that you can get your money back from the credit card company if a travel supplier goes under (and if you request the refund within 60 days of the bankruptcy). **Travel insurance** can also help, but make sure it covers "carrier default" for your specific travel provider. And be aware that if a U.S. airline goes bust midtrip, a 2001 federal law requires other carriers to take you to your destination (albeit on a space-available basis) for a fee of no more than $25, provided you rebook within 60 days of the cancellation.

Another relatively new discount carrier is **Pan Am,** once a dominant (then bankrupt) air carrier. Now back to life under the auspices of entrepreneurs who purchased the name, Pan Am serves Portsmouth, New Hampshire—but only from Bedford, Massachusetts, Trenton, New Jersey, and Sanford, Florida. Call ℂ **800/359-7262** or book flights at **www.flypanam.com**.

GETTING THROUGH THE AIRPORT

With the federalization of airport security, security procedures at U.S. airports are more stable and consistent than ever. Generally, you'll be fine if you arrive at the airport **1 hour** before a domestic flight; if you show up late, tell an airline employee and she'll probably whisk you to the front of the line.

Bring a **current, government-issued photo ID** such as a driver's license or passport. Keep your ID at the ready to show at check-in, the security checkpoint, and sometimes even the gate. (Children under 18 do not need photo IDs for domestic flights, but the adults checking in with them should have them.)

In 2003, the TSA phased out **gate check-in** at all U.S. airports. Passengers with e-tickets can still beat the ticket-counter lines by using **electronic kiosks** or even **online check-in.** Ask your airline which alternatives are available, and if you're using a kiosk, bring the credit card you used to book the ticket or your frequent-flier card. If you're checking bags or looking to snag an exit-row seat, you will be able to do so using most airlines' kiosks; again, call your airline for up-to-date information. **Curbside check-in** is also a good way to avoid lines, although a few airlines still ban curbside check-in; call before you go.

Security checkpoint lines are getting shorter than they were during 2001 and 2002, but some doozies remain. If you have trouble standing for long periods of time, tell an airline employee; the airline will provide a wheelchair. Speed up security by **not wearing metal objects** such as big belt buckles. If you've got metallic body parts, a note from your doctor can prevent a long chat with the security screeners. Keep in mind that only **ticketed passengers** are allowed past security, except for folks escorting passengers with disabilities or children.

Federalization has stabilized **what you can carry on** and **what you can't.** The general rule is that sharp things are out, although nail clippers are okay, and food and beverages must be passed through the X-ray machine—but security screeners can't make you drink from your coffee cup. Bring food in your carry-on rather than checking it, as explosive-detection machines used on checked luggage have been known to mistake food (especially chocolate, for some reason) for bombs. Travelers in the U.S. are allowed one carry-on bag, plus a "personal item" such as a purse, briefcase, or laptop bag. Carry-on hoarders can stuff all sorts of things into a laptop bag; as long as it has a laptop in it, it's still considered a personal item. The Transportation Security Administration (TSA) has issued a list of restricted items; check its website (www.tsa.gov/public/index.jsp) for details.

At press time, the TSA is also recommending that you **not lock your checked luggage** so screeners can search it by hand if necessary. The agency says to use plastic "zip ties" instead, which can be bought at hardware stores and are easily cut off.

FLYING FOR LESS: TIPS FOR GETTING THE BEST AIRFARE

Passengers sharing the same airplane cabin have rarely paid the same fare. Travelers who need to purchase tickets at the last minute, change their itinerary at a moment's notice, or fly one-way

> **Tips** **Don't Stow It—Ship It**
>
> If ease of travel is your main concern and money is no object, you can ship your luggage with one of the growing numbers of luggage-service companies that pick up, track, and deliver your luggage (often through couriers such as Federal Express) with minimum hassle for you. Traveling luggage-free may be ultraconvenient, but it's not cheap: One-way overnight shipping can cost from $100 to $200, depending on what you're sending. Still, for some people, especially the elderly or the infirm, it's a sensible solution to lugging heavy baggage. Specialists in door-to-door luggage delivery are **Virtual Bellhop** (www.virtualbellhop.com), **SkyCap International** (www.skycap international.com), and **Luggage Express** (www.usxpluggageexpress.com).

often get stuck paying the premium rate. Here are some ways to keep your airfare costs down:

- Passengers who can book their ticket **long in advance,** who can **stay over Saturday night,** or who are able to **fly midweek** or **during low-traffic hours** will pay a fraction of the full fare. If your schedule is flexible, say so, and ask if you can secure a cheaper fare by changing your flight plans.
- You can also save on airfares by checking local newspapers for **promotional specials** or **fare wars,** when airlines lower prices on their most popular routes. You rarely see fare wars offered for peak travel times, but if you can travel in the off months, you may snag a bargain.
- Search **the Internet** for cheap fares (see "Planning Your Trip Online," earlier in this chapter).
- **Consolidators,** also known as bucket shops, are great sources for international tickets, although they usually can't beat the Internet on fares within North America. Start by looking in Sunday newspaper travel sections; U.S. travelers should focus on the *New York Times, Los Angeles Times,* and *Miami Herald.* For less-developed destinations, small travel agents who cater to immigrant communities in large cities often have the

best deals. *Beware:* Bucket shop tickets are usually nonrefundable or rigged with stiff cancellation penalties, often as high as 50% to 75% of the ticket price, and some put you on charter airlines with questionable safety records.

- **STA Travel** is now the world's leader in student travel, thanks to their purchase of Council Travel. It also offers good fares for travelers of all ages. **ELTExpress (Flights. com) (© 800/TRAV-800;** www. eltexpress.com) started in Europe and has excellent fares worldwide, but particularly to that continent. It also has "local" websites in 12 countries. **FlyCheap (© 800/FLY-CHEAP;** www.1800flycheap.com) is owned by package-holiday megalith MyTravel and thus has especially good access to fares for sunny destinations.
- Join **frequent-flier clubs.** Accrue enough miles, and you'll be rewarded with free flights and elite status. It's free, and you'll get the best choice of seats, faster response to phone inquiries, and prompter service if your luggage is stolen, your flight is canceled or delayed, or if you want to change your seat. You don't need to fly to build frequent-flier miles—using **frequent-flier credit cards** can provide thousands of miles just for doing your everyday shopping.

- For many more tips about air travel, including a rundown of the major frequent-flier credit cards, pick up a copy of *Frommer's Fly Safe, Fly Smart* (Wiley Publishing, Inc.).

BY CAR

Coming from Boston or the New York City area, you can take several routes to reach coastal Maine. **Interstate 95** parallels the Atlantic coast to Boston, after which it skirts the New Hampshire coast briefly and then proceeds along the southern Maine coast for a stretch before heading north toward the Canadian border.

Tip: I-95 from Boston to Maine is often sluggish on Friday afternoons and evenings as weekend traffic backs up the toll gates for miles; Route 1 along the coast can also bottleneck where two-lane bridges span tidal rivers. To avoid the worst of the tourist traffic, try to stay put on weekends and during big summer holidays; if your schedule allows it, take an extra day off work and head back after the holiday crush. It'll pay handsome dividends in lowered blood pressure.

You'll need to break off at **Route 1** or **Route 3** at some point if you're heading to midcoast or Downeast Maine.

Another tip: If you're driving to Camden or Belfast on western Penobscot Bay, you can avoid coastal traffic by taking the turnpike to Augusta, then connecting via Route 17 (to

Flying with Film & Video

Never pack unprotected, undeveloped film in checked bags, which may be scanned. The film you carry with you can be damaged by scanners, too. X-ray damage is cumulative; the faster the film, and the more times you put it through a scanner, the more likely the damage. Film under 800 ASA is usually safe for up to five scans. If you're taking your film through additional scans, request a hand inspection. In domestic airports, the Federal Aviation Administration guarantees hand inspections. In international airports, you're at the mercy of airport officials. On international flights, store your film in transparent baggies so that you can remove it easily before you go through scanners. Keep in mind that airports are not the only places where your camera may be scanned: Highly trafficked attractions are X-raying visitors' bags with increasing frequency.

Most photo supply stores sell protective pouches designed to block damaging X-rays. The pouches fit both film and loaded cameras. They should protect your film in checked baggage, but they also may raise alarms and result in a hand inspection.

An organization called **Film Safety for Traveling on Planes,** or **FSTOP** (© 888/301-2665; www.f-stop.org), can provide additional tips for traveling with film and related equipment.

Carry-on scanners will not damage **videotape** in video cameras, but the magnetic fields emitted by the walk-through security gateways and handheld inspection wands will. Always place your loaded camcorder on the screening conveyor belt or have it hand-inspected. Be sure your batteries are charged, as you will probably be required to turn the device on to ensure that it's what it appears to be.

Camden) or Route 3 (to Belfast). Those heading directly to Acadia National Park may find it most expedient to follow interstates to Bangor, then Route 1A to Ellsworth, where you can connect to Route 3 onward to Mount Desert Island.

From New York City, I-95 can sometimes can be congested for much of its length, particularly on summer weekends. It's often quicker to take **I-91** north from New Haven, Connecticut, then cutting north on **I-84** toward Boston but circumventing Beantown via **I-495** north which then joins **I-95** again near Portsmouth, New Hampshire and the Maine state line.

Either way, note that some stretches of I-95 are toll roads.

BY TRAIN

Train service to coastal Maine is very limited but it does exist. After more than a decade of delays, Amtrak finally relaunched rail service to Maine in December 2001, restoring a line that had been discontinued in the 1960s. The **Down Easter** now operates between North Station in Boston and Portland, with intermediate stops in Wells, Saco, and Old Orchard Beach en route. Travel time is about 2 hours and 45 minutes between Boston and Portland, with that duration expected to decrease as track upgrades are completed. And the fare is surprisingly affordable, at just $25 one-way from Boston to Portland. Bikes may be loaded and off-loaded at Boston, Wells, and Portland. Four trips daily are offered.

For more information on train service, contact **Amtrak** (✆ **800/ 872-7245**; www.amtrak.com). The Portland-to-Boston line also has its own website, at www.thedowneaster. com, with fares, schedules, and other useful information.

BY BUS

Express bus service is well run (if a bit spotty) in coastal Maine. You'll be able to reach the major cities and tourist destinations by bus, but few of the smaller towns or villages. Tickets from Boston to Portland cost between $15 and $30 per person, one-way, depending on such factors as day of week, time of day, and how far in advance you purchase the tickets. Taking the bus requires no advance planning or reservations, but in summer it's still a good idea to buy as early as possible; often you can also save money this way.

Two major bus lines serve coastal Maine from Boston and New York City. **Vermont Transit Lines** (✆ **800/ 552-8737**; www.vermonttransit.com) is affiliated with **Greyhound** and serves Portsmouth, New Hampshire; Portland; Bangor; and points in-between with frequent departures from Boston's South Station, connecting (in summer only) onward to Ellsworth and Bar Harbor.

Concord Trailways (✆ **800/639- 3317**; www.concordtrailways.com) also serves Portsmouth, New Hampshire; Portland; and Bangor from Boston, but does not continue onward to the smaller towns; you'll need to transfer at Bangor. However, Concord Trailways buses are a bit more luxurious (and thus a few dollars more expensive) than Vermont Transit's rides, and often entertain travelers with movies and music (piped through headphones) en route.

11 The Active Vacation Planner

Coastal Maine is a superb destination for those who don't consider it a vacation unless they spend some time far away from their cars. Hiking, canoeing, and skiing are among the most popular outdoor activities, but you can also try rock climbing, sea kayaking, mountain biking, road biking, sailing, winter mountaineering, and snowmobiling. In general, the farther north you go in the region, the more remote and wild the terrain becomes. For pointers on where to head, see "Outdoor Activity," below. More detailed information on local services is included in each regional section.

OUTDOOR ACTIVITY

BEACHGOING Swimming at Maine's ocean beaches is for the hardy. The Gulf Stream, which prods warm waters south toward the Cape Cod shores, veers toward Iceland south of Maine and leaves the state's 5,500-mile coastline washed by a brisk Nova Scotia current, an offshoot of the arctic Labrador current. During summer, water temperatures along the south coast may top 60°F (16°C) during an especially warm spell where water is shallow, but it's usually cooler than that.

Maine's best beaches are found mostly between the New Hampshire border and Portland. Northeast of Portland, a handful of fine beaches await—including popular **Reid State Park** (p. 137) and **Popham Beach State Park** (p. 137)—but rocky coast defines this territory for the most part. The southern beaches are beautiful but rarely isolated. Summer homes occupy the low dunes in most areas; midrise condos give **Old Orchard Beach** a "mini-Miami" air.

Some of the best swimming beaches in the region can be found at **Ogunquit,** which boasts a 3-mile-long sandy strand (some of which has a mildly remote character), and **Long Sands Beach** (p. 72) and **Short Sands Beach** (p. 72) at York: Long Sands possesses great views of the sea and a nearby lighthouse plus great walking at low tide (at high tide, the sand disappears completely), while Short Sands has a festive, carnival atmosphere. Both lie right on Route 1A. There are also a number of fine beaches in the greater **Portland** area; for a primer on the very best, see chapter 5.

If you love swimming but aren't especially keen on shivering, head inland to the sandy beaches at Maine's wonderful lakes, where the water is tepid by comparison. A number of state and municipal parks offer access. Among the most accessible to the coast are **Sebago Lake State Park** (© **207/693-6613**), about 20 miles northwest of Portland; there's a small admission fee charged.

BIKING In southern Maine, **Route 103** and **Route 1A** offer pleasant scenery for bikers as well. Offshore, bring your bike to the bigger islands for car-free cruising. In Casco Bay, **Chebeague Island** offers a pleasant wooded excursion, **Peaks Island** (p. 116) an easy ride and convenient ferry connection.

Serious mountain biking is also available, in parts of coastal Maine, for those who like to get technical on two wheels. Your best bet is to consult area bike shops for the best trails, which are typically a matter of local knowledge.

The Maine Department of Transportation publishes a booklet, *Explore Maine by Bike,* describing 25 popular bike trips around the state; log onto **www.exploremaine.org/bike** to get it. The Maine DOT also publishes a map marked up with state biking information, including traffic volumes and road shoulder conditions along popular routes. Order it by e-mailing bikeinfo@maine.gov or by calling the DOT at © **207/624-3252.**

BIRDING Birders from southern and inland states should lengthen their life lists along the Maine coast, which attracts migrating birds cruising the Atlantic flyway (there are warblers galore in spring) and boasts populations of numerous native shorebirds, such as plovers (including the threatened piping plover), terns, whimbrels, sandpipers, and dunlins. Gulls and terns are frequently seen; you'll see a surfeit of herring and great black-backed gull, along with the common tern. Less frequently seen are Bonaparte's gull, the laughing gull, the jaeger, and the arctic tern.

For a recording of recent sightings of rare birds, call © **207/781-2332.**

CAMPING   For information about state parks, many of which offer camping, contact the **Department of Conservation,** State House Station #22, Augusta, ME 04333 (© **207/287-3821**). To make camping reservations at most state park campgrounds, call on a weekday between February and mid-September (© **800/332-1501** in Maine, or 207/287-3824).

Maine also has more than 200 private campgrounds spread throughout the state, many offering full hookups for RVs. For a guide to the private campgrounds, contact the **Maine Campground Owners Association,** 10 Falcon Rd., Suite #1, Lewiston, ME 04240. Campsites get booked quickly for summer weekends, so call ahead for reservations.

FISHING   Anglers from all over the Northeast indulge their grand obsession on Maine's 6,000 lakes and ponds and its countless miles of rivers and streams. And deep-sea fishing charters are available at many of the harbors along the Maine coast, with options ranging from inshore fishing expeditions for stripers and bluefish, to offshore voyages in search of shark, cod, and pollack. Prices range from $25 per person for day trips to $395 to charter an offshore boat for the day. Visitor information centers and chambers of commerce listed in this guide will be able to match you up with the right boat to meet your needs.

Saltwater fishing in Maine requires no license. For freshwater fishing, nonresident **licenses** are $53 for the season or $24 for 3 days. Seven- and 15-day licenses are also available. Fees are reduced for juniors (age 12–15); no license is required for those under 12. Licenses are available at many outdoor

shops and general stores throughout the state, or by mail from the address below. For a booklet of fishing regulations, contact the **Department of Inland Fisheries and Wildlife,** State House Station #41, Augusta, ME 04333 (© **207/287-8000;** www.state.me.us/ifw).

GOLFING   Most of southern Maine's best courses are private, but a few are open to the public. Try Kennebunkport's **Cape Arundel Golf Club** (© **207/967-2222**), which is favored by a certain ex-president when he's in town.

HIKING   Southern Maine's walks are not hikes, but rather less-demanding strolls; many of these are a matter of local knowledge. Two fine pathways skirt the water in **York** (see chapter 4), and even in **Portland** (see chapter 5) you can saunter on well-maintained (and heavily used) recreational pathways along about 5 miles of tidal waters.

SEA KAYAKING   Sea kayakers nationwide migrate to Maine for world-class sea kayaking. Thousands of miles of deeply indented coastline and thousands of offshore islands have created a wondrous kayaker's playground. Paddlers can explore protected estuaries far from the surf or test their skills and determination with excursions across choppy, open seas to islands far offshore. It's a sport that can be extremely dangerous (when weather shifts, the seas can turn on you in a matter of minutes), but can yield plenty of returns with the proper equipment and skills.

The nation's first long-distance water trail, the **Maine Island Trail,** was created here in 1987. This 325-mile waterway winds along the coast from Portland to Machias, incorporating some 70 state and privately owned islands on its route. Members of the Maine Island Trail Association, a private nonprofit group, help maintain and monitor the islands and in turn are granted permission to visit and camp on them as long as they follow certain restrictions (for example, no visiting designated islands during seabird nesting season). The association seeks to encourage low-impact, responsible use of these natural treasures, and joining is a good idea if you'll be doing some kayaking. The MITA guidebook, published annually, provides descriptions of all the islands in the network and is free with association membership (note that the guide is available only to members).

Membership is $45 per year for individuals, $65 per family; contact the **Maine Island Trail Association,** 328 Main St., Rockland, ME 04841 (© **207/596-6456** or 207/761-8225).

The islands and protected bays around **Portland** make for great kayaking, as do the cliffs, parks, and beaches just south of the city—though surf can be rough at times. Make sure you're experienced enough to handle it.

For novices, Maine has a number of kayak outfitters offering guided excursions ranging from an afternoon to a week. Recommended outfitters that offer a wide array of trips in Maine include the **Maine Island Kayak Co.,** 70 Luther St., Peaks Island, ME 04108 (© **800/796-2373** or 207/766-2373; www.maineislandkayak.com) and **Maine Sport Outfitters,** P.O. Box 956, Rockport, ME 04856 (© **800/722-0826** or 207/236-8797; www.maine sport.com).

GENERAL ADVICE

The best way to enjoy the outdoors is to head to public lands where the natural landscape is preserved. For my money, Acadia National Park is one of the nation's finest parks, and inland you could also day-trip to majestic Baxter State Park. You can often find adventure-travel outfitters and suppliers in towns around the perimeter of these areas.

A bit of added advice: To find real adventure, plan to stay put. I've run across too many gung-ho travelers who try to bite off too much—some biking, some hiking, and then maybe a little kayaking off Acadian coast. All in a week. That's only a good formula for developing a close, personal relationship with the paved road. I'd advise prospective adventurers to pick just one area, then settle in for a few days or a week, spending the long summer days exploring locally by foot, canoe, or kayak. This will give you the time to enjoy an extra hour lounging at a remote back-country lake, or to spend an extra day camped in the backcountry. You'll also learn a lot more about the area. Few travelers ever regret planning to do too little on their vacations. A lot of travelers regret attempting to do too much.

FINDING YOUR WAY

Travelers used to hire guides to ensure they could find their way out of the woods. With development encroaching on many once-pristine areas, it's now helpful to have guides to find your way *into* the woods and away from civilization and its long reach. Clear-cuts, second-home developments, and trails teeming with weekend hikers are all obstacles to be avoided. Local knowledge is the best way to find the most alluring, least congested spots.

Travelers have three options: Hire a guide, sign up for a guided trip, or dig up the essential information yourself.

HIRING A GUIDE   Guides of all kinds may be hired throughout the region, from grizzled fishing hands who know local rivers like their own homes to young canoe guides attracted to the field because of their interest in the environment. Alexandra and Garrett Conover of **North Woods Ways,** RR#2, Box 159A, Guilford, ME 04443 (© **207/997-3723**), are among the most experienced in the region. The couple offers canoe trips on northern Maine rivers (and as far north as Labrador), and they are well versed in North Woods lore.

Maine has a centuries-old tradition of guides leading "sports" into the backwoods for hunting and fishing, although many now have branched out to include recreational canoeing and more specialized interests, such as bird-watching. Professional guides are certified by the state; you can learn more about hiring Maine guides by contacting the **Maine Professional Guides Association,** P.O. Box 336, Augusta, ME 04332 (© 207/751-3797). The association's website (www.maine guides.com) features links to many of its members.

Elsewhere, contact the appropriate chambers of commerce for suggestions on local guides.

GUIDED TOURS   Guided tours have boomed in recent years, both in number and variety. These range from 2-night guided inn-to-inn hiking trips to weeklong canoe and kayak expeditions, camping each night along the way. A few reputable outfitters to start with include the following:

- **Country Walkers,** P.O. Box 180, Waterbury, VT 05676 (© **800/ 464-9255** or 802/244-1387; www. countrywalkers.com), has a glorious color catalog (more like a wishbook) outlining supported walking trips around the world. Among the offerings: walking tours in coastal Maine. Trips run 4 or 5 nights and include all meals and lodging at appealing inns.

- **Maine Island Kayak Co.,** 70 Luther St., Peaks Island, ME 04108 (© **800/796-2373** or 207/766-2373; www.sea-kayak.com), has a fleet of seaworthy kayaks for camping trips up and down the Maine coast. The firm has a number of 2- and 3-night expeditions each summer and has plenty of experience training novices.

- **New England Hiking Holidays,** P.O. Box 1648, North Conway, NH 03860 (© **800/869-0949** or 603/356-9696; www.nehiking holidays.com), has an extensive inventory of trips, including week-end trips in the White Mountains as well as more extended excursions to the Maine coast. Trips typically involve moderate day hiking coupled with nights at comfortable lodges.

- **Vermont Bicycle Touring,** P.O. Box 711, Bristol, VT 05442 (© **800/245-3868;** www.vbt. com), is one of the more established and well-organized touring operations, with an extensive bike tour schedule in North America, Europe, and New Zealand. VBT offers three trips in Maine, including a 6-day Acadia trip with some overnights at the grand Claremont Hotel.

GETTING MORE INFORMATION   Guidebooks to the region's backcountry are plentiful and diverse. L.L. Bean in Freeport, Maine has an excellent selection of guidebooks for sale, as do many local bookshops throughout the region. An exhaustive collection of New England outdoor guidebooks for sale may be found on the Web at **www.mountainwanderer. com**. The **Appalachian Mountain Club,** 5 Joy St., Boston, MA 02108 (© **617/523-0636;** www.outdoors. org), publishes a number of definitive guides to hiking and boating in the region.

Map Adventures, P.O. Box 15214 Portland, ME 04112 (© **207/879-4777**), is a small firm that publishes a growing line of recreational maps covering popular northern New England areas, including the Stowe and Mad River Valley areas and the White Mountains. See what they offer on the Web at **www.mapadventures.com**.

Local outdoor clubs are also a good source of information, and most offer trips to nonmembers. The largest of the bunch is the Appalachian Mountain

Club (see address above), whose chapters run group trips almost every weekend throughout the region, with northern New Hampshire especially well represented.

SPECIAL-INTEREST VACATIONS

A richly rewarding way to spend a vacation is to learn a new outdoor skill or add to your knowledge while on holiday. You can find plenty of options in northern New England, ranging from formal weeklong classes to 1-day workshops.

Among the options are these:

- **Learn to fly-fish on New England's fabled rivers.** Among the region's most respected schools are those offered by **L.L. Bean** (© **800/341-4341**) in Freeport,

Maine. (L.L. Bean also offers a number of shorter workshops on various outdoor skills through its **Outdoor Discovery Program;** call © **888/552-3261.**)

- **Learn about birds and coastal ecosystems in Maine.** Budding and experienced naturalists can expand their understanding of marine wildlife while residing on 333-acre Hog Island in Maine's wild and scenic Muscongus Bay. Famed birder Roger Tory Peterson taught birding classes here in the past, and the program has a stellar reputation. Contact the **Maine Audubon Society,** 20 Gilsland Farm Rd., Falmouth ME 04105 (© **207/781-2330;** www.maine audubon.org).

12 Getting Around Coastal Maine

One of my most fervent wishes is that someday I'll be able to travel around coastal Maine without a car, as my ancestors did. I'd love to see a reversion to historical times, when travelers could venture to Mount Desert Island via luxurious rail car or steamship. Early in this century, visitors could even link one trolley line with the next to travel great distances between seaboard cities and inland towns.

BY CAR

The major airports in Maine (see the "Getting There" section, earlier in this chapter) all host national car-rental chains. Some handy phone numbers and websites are **Avis** (© 800/230-4898; www.avis.com), **Budget** (© 800/527-0700; www.budget.com), **Enterprise** (© 800/736-8222; www.enterprise.com), **Hertz** (© 800/654-3131; www.hertz.com), **National** (© 800/227-7368; www.nationalcar.com), and **Thrifty** (© 800/847-4389; www.thrifty.com). You may also find independent car-rental firms in the bigger towns, sometimes at better rates than those offered by the chains. Look in the Yellow Pages under "Automobile–Renting."

A famous local joke ends with the punch line, "You can't get there from here," but you may conclude it's no joke as you try to navigate through the region. Travel can be convoluted and often confusing, and it's handy to have someone adept at map reading in the car with you if you veer off the main routes for country-road exploring.

North-south travel is fairly straightforward, thanks to I-95 and Route 1. Day-trips by car up and down the coast can be done quite comfortably if you consult a map and understand the distances involved. Don't underestimate the size of the Maine coast—Kittery to Eastport (the easternmost city in the United States) is 293 miles. Driving times can be longer than you'd expect due to narrow roads and zigzagging peninsulas, not to mention high-season traffic. Also beware of two-sided maps that alter the scale

Your Car: Leave Home Without It!

Options exist for a vacation without a car. Here are a few suggestions:

- Bus, fly, or train to Portland, where you can sign up for a guided sea-kayak excursion. **Maine Island Kayak Co.** (© 207/766-2373) is just 20 minutes outside of the city by ferry (the terminal is at the corner of Commercial and Franklin sts.) on Peaks Island, and offers trips throughout the state all summer long. You can camp within the city limits on remote Jewell Island at the edge of Casco Bay, or head out for a few days along more remote parts of the coast. Spend an extra day or two in Portland to visit museums and sample the excellent restaurants.

- Bus or fly to Bar Harbor, and then settle into one of the numerous inns or B&Bs downtown. (There's a free shuttle bus from the airport to downtown.) Rent a mountain bike and explore the elaborate network of carriage roads at Acadia National Park, and then cruise along picturesque Park Loop Road. Another day, sign up for a sea-kayak tour or whale-watching excursion. By night, enjoy lobster or other fine meals at Bar Harbor's fine restaurants. Mountain bikes may be easily rented along Cottage Street in Bar Harbor. A free bus connects downtown Bar Harbor with more than a half-dozen bus routes into and around the park, making travel hassle-free. Try **Bar Harbor Bicycle Shop** (© 207/288-3886) at 141 Cottage St.; **Acadia Outfitters** (© 207/288-8118) at 106 Cottage St.; or **Acadia Bike & Canoe** (© 207/288-9605) at 48 Cottage St. For sea kayaking, the following outfitters offer half- and full-day tours: **Acadia Outfitters** (© 207/288-8118) at 106 Cottage St.; **Coastal Kayaking Tours** (© 207/288-9605) at 48 Cottage St.; and **National Park Sea Kayak Tours** (© 800/347-0940 or 207/288-0342) at 39 Cottage St.

- Fly to Bangor on a commercial flight. **KT Aviation** (© 207/945-5087) can meet you at the airport and take you by van to a nearby lake for a seaplane flight to a remote sporting camp. Here you can spend a week or so hiking, dubbing around in canoes, or reading and relaxing. Among the better sporting camps is **Bradford Camps** (© 207/746-7777; www.bradfordcamps.com), a compound of rustic log cabins on an unpopulated lake right out of an L.L. Bean catalog. Meals are served in a 1940s-style dining room. Also of interest is the tiny fishing community of Grand Lake Stream, which has several sporting camps (try **Weatherby's, The Fisherman's Resort,** © 207/796-5558; www.weatherbys.com). Link up with **Grand Lake Outfitters** (© 207/796-5561) for kayak or rafting tours of lakes and rivers. Charter rates to Grand Lake Stream, which is about a 30-minute flight from Bangor, start at $120 (one-way) for one person, up to $180 for three people.

from one side to the other, and remember when budgeting your time that Portland is closer to New York City than it is to Madawaska at the state's extreme northern tip.

If you're a connoisseur of back roads and off-the-beaten-track exploring, the **Maine Atlas and Gazetteer,** produced by DeLorme Mapping (© 888/227-1656) in Yarmouth, is an invaluable tool. It offers an extraordinary level of detail, right down to logging roads and canoe launch sites. DeLorme's atlases are available at many local book and convenience stores, or at the company's headquarters and map store in Yarmouth, a few minutes north of Portland and just off I-95.

Traffic is generally light compared to most urban and suburban areas along the East Coast.

If you're still in doubt about a route, use a Web service such as **MapQuest** (www.mapquest.com) or **Yahoo! Maps** (maps.yahoo.com). These handy websites calculate distances and driving directions from any point in the country to any other point. Type in where you want to start and where you want to go, and the online software calculates the total distance and provides detailed driving instructions, along with maps if you want them. Before departing, you can plot your route and print out a daily driving itinerary.

Here are some representative distances between points:

New York City to:		
	Bar Harbor, Maine	493 miles
	Portland, Maine	319 miles
Boston, Massachusetts, to:		
	Bar Harbor, Maine	281 miles
	Portland, Maine	107 miles
	Portsmouth, New Hampshire	56 miles
Portland, Maine, to:		
	Bar Harbor, Maine	174 miles
	Manchester, New Hampshire	95 miles
Burlington, Vermont, to:		
	Portland, Maine	232 miles
North Conway, New Hampshire, to:		
	Bar Harbor, Maine	216 miles
	Portland, Maine	65 miles

BY BUS

As mentioned in the "Getting There" section earlier in this chapter, express bus service *into* the region is quite good, but beware of trying to travel *within* the region by bus. Quirky schedules and routes may send you well out of your way, and what may seem a simple trip could take hours. One example: A clerk at Vermont Transit once explained that a 65-mile trip from Portland to North Conway, New Hampshire was necessarily via Boston and, with layovers, would require approximately 9 hours—somewhat longer than it would require a moderately fit person to travel between these points by bicycle.

Traveling north-south between towns along a single bus route (for example, Portland to Bangor) is feasible, but east-west travel across Maine is, by and large, impractical. For information on travel within northern New England, call **Vermont Transit Lines** (© **800/451-3292** or 800/642-3133; www.vermonttransit.com) or **Concord Trailways** (© **800/639-3317**; www.concordtrailways.com) for service in New Hampshire and Maine.

Tips   Moose X-ing

Driving across the northern tier of Maine, you'll often see MOOSE CROSSING signs, complete with silhouettes of the gangly herbivores. These are not placed here to amuse the tourists. In Maine, the state with the most moose (an estimated 30,000, at last count), crashes between moose and cars are increasingly common.

These encounters are usually more dramatic than deer-car collisions. For starters, the large eyes of moose don't reflect in headlights like those of deer, so you often come upon them with less warning when driving late at night. Moose can weigh up to 1,000 pounds, with almost all of that weight placed high atop spindly legs. When a car strikes a moose broadside in the road, it usually knocks the legs out and sends a half-ton of hapless beast right through the windshield. Need we dwell on the results of such an encounter? I thought not. In 1998 alone, the state of Maine recorded 859 crashes involving moose, with 247 injuries and five fatalities. When in moose country, drive slowly and carefully.

BY PLANE

Service between airports within the region is sketchy at best. You can find limited direct flights between some cities (such as Portland to Bangor), but for the most part, you'll have to backtrack to Boston and fly out again to your final destination. Convenient it's not. See the "Getting There" section, earlier in this chapter.

Contact **Colgan Air** (© **800/428-4322** or 207/596-7604), owned by U.S. Airways, for information on scheduled flights to Rockland and Bar Harbor. **Quoddy Air** (© **207/853-0997**), based in Eastport, offers charter service to airports in and around Downeast Maine.

BY TRAIN

Amtrak provides limited rail travel within the region, and is mostly confined to a few stops in Vermont, New Hampshire, and southern Maine. See the "Getting There" section, earlier in this chapter. For more information, call **Amtrak** at © **800/872-7245;** www.amtrak.com.

13 Tips on Accommodations

"The more we travel," said an unhappy couple next to me one morning at a New Hampshire inn, "the more we realize why we go back to our old favorites time and again." The reason for their disgruntlement? They were up and switching rooms at 2am when rain began dripping on them through the ceiling.

Coastal Maine is famous for its plethora of country inns and bed-and-breakfasts (B&Bs). These offer a wonderful alternative to the cookie-cutter chain-hotel rooms that line U.S. highways coast-to-coast, but as that unhappy couple learned, there are good reasons why some people prefer cookie-cutter sameness. Predictability isn't always a bad thing. In a chain hotel, you can be reasonably certain water won't drip through your ceiling at night. Likewise, you can bet that beds will be firm, that the sink will be relatively new and lacking in interesting sepia-toned stains, and that you'll have a TV, telephone, and a lot of counter space next to the bathroom sink.

If you're heading for an inn or B&B, just keep in mind that every place is different, and you still need to match the personality of a place with your own personality. Some are more polished and fussier than others. Many lack the amenities travelers have grown accustomed to in chain hotels. (In-room phones and air-conditioning lead the list.)

The difference between an inn and a B&B may be confusing for some travelers, since the gap between the two narrows by the day. A couple of decades ago, inns were full-service affairs, whereas B&Bs consisted of private homes with an extra bedroom or two and a homeowner looking for a little extra income. These old-style B&Bs still exist around the region. I've occupied a few evenings sitting in a well-used living room watching Tom Brokaw with the owner, as if visiting with a forgotten aunt.

Today, B&Bs are more commonly professionally run affairs, where guests have private bathrooms, a separate common area, and attentive service. The owners have apartments tucked away in the back, prepare sumptuous breakfasts in the morning (some B&Bs offer "candlelight breakfasts"), and offer a high level of service. All of the B&Bs in this guide are of the more professionally run variety (although several or more still have shared bathrooms). Other guidebooks are available for those searching for home-stay lodging.

The sole difference between inns and B&Bs—at least as defined by this guide—is that inns serve dinner (and sometimes lunch). B&Bs provide breakfast only. Readers shouldn't infer that B&Bs are necessarily more informal or in any way inferior to a full-service inn. Indeed, the places listed in "The Best Bed & Breakfasts" section in chapter 1 all have the air of gracious inns that just happened to have overlooked serving dinner. That's true for many of the other B&Bs listed in this guide; and with a little luck, you'll stumble into Ralph Waldo Emerson's idea of simple contentment: "Hospitality consists in a little fire, a little food, and an immense quiet," he wrote in his journal.

As innkeeping evolves into the more complex and demanding "hospitality industry," you're bound to bump up against more restrictions, rules, and regulations at places you're staying. It's always best to ask in advance to avoid unpleasant surprises.

A few notes on recent trends:

SMOKING   Smokers looking to light up are being edged out the door to smoke on front lawns and porches. It's no different in the region's inns and B&Bs than in other public spaces. A decade or two ago, only a handful of places prohibited smoking. Today, I'd wager that the great majority of inns and B&Bs have banned smoking within their buildings entirely, and some have even exiled smokers from their property—front lawn included.

Frommer's has stopped mentioning whether smoking is allowed or not in inns because it has rapidly become a nonissue—almost everyone has banned it. Assume that no smoking is allowed at any of the accommodations listed in this guide. (As in other regions, the larger, more modern hotels—say a Radisson or Holiday Inn—will have guest rooms set aside for smokers.) If being able to smoke in your room or the lobby is paramount to your vacation happiness, be sure to inquire first. Likewise, if you're a nonsmoker who finds the smell of cigarette smoke obnoxious in the extreme, it also wouldn't hurt to confirm that you're at a fully nonsmoking establishment.

ADDITIONAL   GUESTS   The room rates published in this guide are for two people sharing a room. Many places charge $10 and up for each extra guest sharing the room. Don't assume that children traveling with you are free—ask first about extra charges—and don't assume that all places are able to accommodate children or extra guests. The guest rooms at some inns are quite cozy and lack space for a cot. Ask first if you don't want to end up four to a bed.

MINIMUM STAY It's become increasingly common for inns to require guests to book a minimum of 2 nights or more during busy times. These times typically include weekends in the summer (or in the winter, near ski areas), holiday periods, and the fall foliage season. These policies are mentioned in the following pages when known, but they're in constant flux, so don't be surprised if you're told you need to reserve an extra day when you make reservations.

Note that minimum-stay policies typically apply only to those making advance reservations. If you stop by an inn on a Saturday night and find a room available, innkeepers won't charge you for a second night. Also, thanks to erratic travel planning, the occasional stray night sometimes becomes available during minimum-stay periods. Don't hesitate to call and ask if a single night is available when planning your itinerary.

DEPOSITS Many establishments now require guests to provide a credit card number to hold a room. What happens if you cancel? The policies are Byzantine at best. Some places have a graduated refund—cancel 1 week in advance, and you'll be charged for 1 night's stay; cancel 1 day in advance, and you're charged for your whole reserved stay—unless they can fill the room. Then you'll be charged for half. Other places are quite generous about refunding your deposit. It's more than a bit tedious to figure it all out if you're booking a half-dozen places

over the course of your trip, and the policies can often seem irrational. One Frommer's reader wrote to say that she made a reservation at a New England motel 3 days before her arrival, but called to cancel the next day because a hurricane had veered to hit her home state and she wanted to head back. Sorry, she was told, cancellations must be made 1 week in advance; she was billed for the room. Go figure.

Most hotels and inns are fair and will scrupulously spell out their cancellation policy when you make reservations, but always ask about it before you give your credit card number, and if possible, ask to have it e-mailed, faxed, or mailed to you before you agree to anything. Most travelers experience no unpleasant surprises on their credit card bills, but it's better to err on the side of caution.

PETS Sometimes yes, sometimes no. Always ask. See the "Traveling with Pets" section, earlier in this chapter.

SERVICE CHARGES Rather than increase room rates in the face of rising competition, hotels, inns, and B&Bs are increasingly tacking on unpublicized fees to guests' bills. Most innkeepers will tell you about these when you reserve or check in; the less scrupulous will surprise you at checkout. In my opinion, this is not a welcome trend.

The most common surcharge is an involuntary "service charge" of 10% to 15%. Coupled with state lodging taxes (even "sales-tax-free" New Hampshire hits tourists with an 8% levy), that bumps the cost of a bed up by nearly 25%. (The rates listed in this guide don't include service charges or sales tax.)

Other charges may include a pet fee (as much as $10 per day extra), a foliage-season surcharge ($10 or more per room), or a "resort fee." Other fees are more irksome than financially burdensome.

TIPS FOR SAVING ON YOUR HOTEL ROOM

Smaller inns and B&Bs have pretty straightforward rate structures—usually an in-season rate and an off-season rate, and according to the room's attributes, including size, view, and opulence. Larger hotels employ more complicated pricing systems that are constantly refined by computer, based on current bookings and demand.

The **rack rate** is the maximum rate that a hotel charges for a room. It's the rate you'd get if you walked in off the street and asked for a room for the night. Hardly anybody pays these prices, however, and there are many ways around them:

- **Don't be afraid to bargain.** Most rack rates include commissions of 10% to 25% for travel agents, which some hotels may be willing to reduce if you make your own reservations and haggle a bit. Always ask whether a room less expensive than the first one quoted is available, or whether any special rates apply to you. You may qualify for corporate, student, military, senior citizen, or other discounts. Be sure to mention membership in AAA, AARP, frequent-flier programs, or trade unions, which may entitle you to special deals as well.

- **Rely on a qualified professional.** Certain hotels give travel agents discounts in exchange for steering business their way, so if you're shy about bargaining, an agent may be better equipped to negotiate discounts for you.

- **Dial direct.** When booking a room in a chain hotel, compare the rates offered by the hotel's local line with that of the toll-free number. Also, check with an agent and online. A hotel makes nothing on a room that stays empty, so the local hotel reservation desk may be willing to offer a special rate unavailable elsewhere.

- **Remember the law of supply and demand.** Resort hotels are most crowded and, therefore, most expensive on weekends, so discounts are usually available for midweek stays. Business hotels in downtown locations are busiest during the week, so you can expect big discounts over the weekend. Avoid high-season stays whenever you can: planning your vacation just a week before or after official peak season can mean big savings.

- **Look into group or long-stay discounts.** If you come as part of a large group, you should be able to negotiate a bargain rate, as the hotel can then guarantee occupancy in a number of rooms. Likewise, if you're planning a long stay (at least 5 days), you may qualify for a discount. As a general rule, expect 1 night free after a 7-night stay.

- **Avoid excess charges.** When you book a room, ask whether the hotel charges for parking. Many hotels charge a fee just for dialing out on the phone in your room. Find out whether your hotel imposes a surcharge on local and long-distance calls. A pay phone, however inconvenient, may save you money, although many calling cards charge a fee when you use them on pay phones. Finally, ask about local taxes and service charges, which could increase the cost of a room by 25% or more.

- **Carefully consider your hotel's meal plan.** If you enjoy eating out and sampling the local cuisine, it makes sense to choose a **Continental Plan (CP),** which includes breakfast only, or a **European Plan (EP),** which doesn't include any meals and allows you maximum flexibility. If you're more interested in saving money, opt for a **Modified American Plan (MAP),** which includes breakfast and one meal, or the **American Plan (AP),** which includes three meals. If you must choose a MAP, see if you can get a free lunch at your hotel if you decide to do dinner out.

- **Watch for coupons and advertised discounts.** Scan ads in your local Sunday newspaper travel section, an excellent source for up-to-the-minute hotel deals.
- **Consider a suite.** If you are traveling with your family or another couple, you can pack more people into a suite (which usually comes with a sofa bed) and thereby reduce your per-person rate. Remember that some places charge for extra guests.
- **Book an efficiency.** A kitchenette allows you to shop for groceries and cook your own meals. This is a money saver, especially for families on long stays.
- **Many hotels offer frequent-flier points.** Don't forget to ask for yours when you check in.
- **Investigate reservations services.** These outfits usually work as consolidators, buying up or reserving rooms in bulk, and then dealing them out to customers at a profit. You can get 10% to 50% off; but remember, these discounts apply to inflated rack rates that savvy travelers rarely end up paying. You may get a decent rate, but always call the hotel as well to see if you can do better.

LANDING THE BEST ROOM

Somebody has to get the best room in the house. It may as well be you.

You can start by joining the hotel's frequent-guest program, which may make you eligible for upgrades. A hotel-branded credit card usually gives it owner "silver" or "gold" status in frequent-guest programs for free.

Always ask about a corner room. They're often larger and quieter, with more windows and light, and they often cost the same as standard rooms.

When you make your reservation, ask if the hotel is renovating; if it is, request a room away from the construction. Ask about nonsmoking rooms, rooms with views, and rooms with twin, queen- or king-size beds. If you're a light sleeper, request a quiet room away from vending machines, elevators, restaurants, bars, and discos. Ask for one of the rooms that have been most recently renovated or redecorated.

If you aren't happy with your room when you arrive, say so. If another room is available, most lodgings will be willing to accommodate you.

14 Suggested Itinerary

I can't emphasize enough not overreaching when planning your trip. Many travelers coming from a distance look at this trip as their only chance to see coastal Maine, and make the rash decision to race madly across the region in a valiant effort to see everything from Kittery to Portland to Acadia, and (of course) a moose up in those Maine Woods too along the way. All in a week.

A formula for disappointment, you end up seeing little except the inside of your windshield. New England has few attractions that lend themselves to pit-stop tourism—you remember these kinds of trips: you pay your fee, look around for a few minutes, take some photos, grab a snack, and get back on the road to the next "attraction." New England is best seen by not moving, or at least moving rather slowly, by foot or canoe or bike. The happiest visitors to the region tend to be those who stay put the most, getting to know their selected patch more intimately through well-crafted day trips.

With that in mind, here's a suggested itinerary that you can use as a starting point, mixing and matching depending on how much time you have. (See also the suggested trips without a car, in "Your Car: Leave Home Without It!" earlier in this chapter.)

NINE DAYS ON MAINE'S COAST

Maine's coast tends to confound hurry-up tourism—there are too many dead-end peninsulas to backtrack along, too many inlets that cleave the coast far inland, forcing tourists to drive great distances to get from one rocky, wave-beaten point to the next. Finding a couple of welcoming bases and using these to explore farther afield is a good strategy.

Day 1 Drive in to Maine from the south on I-95, and head immediately to York Village. Spend some time snooping around the historic homes of the Old York Historical Society, and stretch your legs on a walk through town or the woods. Drive northward through York Beach (stocking up on saltwater taffy), and arrive in Kennebunkport in time to stroll the leafy town, gawk at George Bush the Elder's summerhouse, settle into your room for the evening, and have a relaxed dinner out.

Day 2 Pick and choose your diversions en route to Portland: maybe a birding hike at Laudholm Farms, a visit to the beach or an excellent small art museum at Ogunquit, or antiquing up Route 1. In Portland by afternoon, stroll the Old Port, take a ferry to one of the islands, or prowl the Portland Public Market in search of picnic supplies. Pick from the abundance of restaurants to suit your mood.

Day 3 Head north early to beat the shopping crowds at the outlet haven of Freeport. (You can't leave too early for L.L. Bean—it never closes.) Continue onward with possible side trips in Brunswick (for the Bowdoin College Museum of Art or the intriguing Arctic Museum) and Bath (to the Maine Maritime Museum and Shipyard). Detour down to Pemaquid Point for a late picnic and to watch the surf roll in,

and then head back to Route 1 and make it to Camden in time for dinner. Plan on 2 nights in this area.

Day 4 Wander around Camden's downtown, poking into shops and galleries, hike up one of the impressive hills at Camden Hills State Park, hop a ferry to an island (North Haven and Isleboro are both great for biking), sign up for a daylong sail on a windjammer, or just spend a long afternoon unwinding on the deck at The Waterfront Restaurant. Turn in early.

Day 5 Drive up and around the head of Penobscot Bay and then down the bay's eastern shore. The roads here are great for aimless drives, but aim for Stonington, far down at the end of the peninsula. If distant Isle au Haut, visible from town docks, makes you pine for an offshore adventure, plan on a boat trip out early the next morning, securing lodging for the night and adjusting your schedule accordingly. Otherwise, explore around the area, or sign up for a kayak tour with Old Quarry Charters. Then head to scenic Blue Hill for dinner and lodging.

Day 6 Off to Bar Harbor and Mount Desert Island. Book a room for three nights at the place of your choosing—Bar Harbor is a handy and central location, with access to movies, bike and kayak rentals, free shuttle buses all over the island, and numerous restaurants. Spend the day getting oriented—perhaps with a shuttle bus trip around the scenic Park Loop Road, which offers a great introduction to what's in store.

Day 7 Hike, bike, boat, whatever. Explore the island at your own pace. A beginner's kayak trip down the eastern shore, a hike out to Bar Island, or a mountain bike trip along the carriage roads are all good options.

Day 8 Those things that you wanted to do yesterday but didn't have time? Do them today. Cap it off with a cold-water swim at Sand Beach and tea and popovers at Jordan Pond House.

Day 9 With luck, you'll still have some time to do a few things before it's time to zip up to Bangor and begin your long southward trek home on I-95. Maybe watch a sunrise from the top of Cadillac Mountain? Or paddle a canoe on Long Pond? Or enjoy a last lobster atop a pier before setting off?

15 Recommended Reading

If you're looking for reading to broaden your understanding of the region, you need not look much further than the many excellent bookstores (both new and used) you'll find scattered throughout the region. Among my favorite books are these:

- *Inventing New England,* by Dona Brown (1995). A University of Vermont professor tells the epic tale of the rise of 19th-century tourism in New England in this uncommonly well-written study.
- *The Lobster Chronicles,* by Linda Greenlaw (2002). Written by a real, live lobsterwoman with street cred—her flirtations with maritime disaster made it into the book and film *The Perfect Storm*—talks of lobsters and life on tiny Isle au Haut.
- *Lobster Gangs of Maine,* by James M. Acheson (1988). This exhaustively researched book answers every question you'll have about the lobsterman's life, and then some.
- *One Man's Meat,* by E. B. White. White was a sometime resident of a saltwater farm on the Maine coast and frequent contributor to *The New Yorker.* His essays, from the late 1930s and early 1940s, are only incidentally about Maine, but you get a superb sense of place by observing the shadows. Still in print in paperback.
- *Serious Pig,* by John Thorne, with Matt Lewis Thorne (1996). The way to a region's character is through its stomach. The Thornes' finely crafted essays on Maine regional cooking are exhaustive in their coverage of chowder, beans, pie, and more.

FAST FACTS: The Maine Coast

AAA The automobile club's Maine headquarters (© 207/780-6900) is on Marginal Way in Portland, just off I-295, and can help members with trip planning and discount tickets to events and attractions. Call © 800/222-4357 for general membership information.

American Express American Express offers travel services, including check cashing and trip planning, through several affiliated agencies in the region. The office in Portland is at 480 Congress St. (© 207/772-8450).

Area Codes Maine's area code is 207.

ATM Networks Cirrus (© 800/424-7787; www.mastercard.com/cardholder services/atm) and PLUS (© 800/843-7587; www.visa.com/atms) are the two most popular networks; check the back of your ATM card to see which network your bank belongs to. Use the 800 numbers to locate ATMs in your destination.

Car Rentals See "Getting Around Coastal Maine," earlier in this chapter.

Climate See "When to Go," earlier in this chapter.

Embassies & Consulates See chapter 3, "For International Visitors."

Emergencies In the event of an emergency, find any phone and dial ℂ **911.** If this fails, dial 0 (zero) and tell the operator you need to report an emergency.

Hospitals The largest hospital in Maine is the **Maine Medical Center** (ℂ **207/662-0111**), a busy professional facility located improbably on a hilltop in a residential neighborhood of Portland at 22 Bramhall St. **Mercy Hospital** (ℂ **207/879-3000**) is a second, Catholic-owned hospital very close to Maine Medical at 144 State St. Smaller admitting hospitals are easily located in larger towns and small cities such as York, Biddeford, Brunswick, Damariscotta, Ellsworth, and Bar Harbor; once you're north of Camden, however, things thin out considerably. Consult your hotel, inn, or the phone book when you arrive to get details on the nearest outpatient clinic if you're concerned you may need access to a hospital facility.

Internet Access Many of Maine's public libraries have free terminals with Internet access, enabling travelers to check their e-mail through a Web-based e-mail service such as Yahoo!, Hotmail, or AOL. Internet cafes have come and gone in the last few years; it's best to ask around locally, or try visiting **www.netcafeguide.com** or **www.cybercafe.com**.

Liquor Laws The legal age to consume alcohol in Maine is 21. Hard liquor is sold through state-run stores as well as "agency stores," which are often found as sections in larger supermarkets. Beer and wine are available in grocery and convenience stores. Purchasing is strictly regulated; even those clearly above age 21 might be asked to show ID. Restaurants that don't have liquor licenses sometimes allow patrons to bring in their own. Ask first.

Lost & Found Be sure to notify all of your credit card companies the minute you discover your wallet has been lost or stolen, and file a report at the nearest police precinct. Your credit card company or insurer may require a police report number or record of the loss. Most credit card companies have an emergency toll-free number to call if your card is lost or stolen; they may be able to wire you a cash advance immediately or deliver an emergency credit card in a day or two. Visa's U.S. emergency numbers are ℂ **800/847-2911** or 410/581-9994. American Express cardholders and traveler's check holders should call ℂ **800/221-7282.** MasterCard holders should call ℂ **800/307-7309** or 636/722-7111. For other credit cards, call the toll-free number directory at ℂ **800/555-1212.**

If you need emergency cash over the weekend when all banks and American Express offices are closed, you can have money wired to you via **Western Union** (ℂ **800/325-6000**; www.westernunion.com).

Identity theft or fraud are potential complications of losing your wallet, especially if you've lost your driver's license along with your cash and credit cards. Notify the major credit-reporting bureaus immediately; placing a fraud alert on your record may protect you against liability for criminal activity. The three major U.S. credit-reporting agencies are **Equifax** (ℂ **800/766-0008**; www.equifax.com), **Experian** (ℂ **888/397-3742**; www.experian.com), and **TransUnion** (ℂ **800/680-7289**; www.transunion.com). Finally, if you've lost all forms of photo ID, call your airline and explain the situation; they might allow you to board the plane if you have a copy of your passport or birth certificate and a copy of the police report you've filed.

Maps Maine offers plenty of free maps at well-stocked visitor information centers; ask at the counter if you don't see them. For incredibly detailed maps, consider purchasing one or more of the DeLorme atlases, which depict every road, bay, and cove, along with many hiking trails, local beaches, and access points for canoes. DeLorme's headquarters and map store (© **800/561-5105** or 800/642-0970) are in Yarmouth, but their products are available at bookstores and convenience stores throughout the region.

Newspapers & Magazines Almost every small town seems to have a daily or weekly newspaper covering the events and happenings of the area. These are good sources of information for small-town events and specials at local restaurants—the day-to-day things that slip through the cracks at the tourist bureaus. The three largest papers in the region are the *Portland Press Herald* (Portland), the *Portsmouth Herald* (Portsmouth, New Hampshire) and the *Bangor Daily News* (Bangor), with good smaller local papers in such towns as Brunswick, Bar Harbor, and Camden.

Portland and Portsmouth also share a free alternative weekly paper, the *Phoenix*, that is a very handy source of information on concerts and shows at local clubs, and the *Press Herald* maintains an active website (**http://pressherald.mainetoday.com**) which is good for getting a sense of the state before you arrive. The *New York Times* and *The Wall Street Journal* are also now often available daily in many shops around the region, except in the smallest towns and at the farthest fringes of the region.

Pets See "Traveling with Pets," earlier in this chapter.

Smoking Maine has banned smoking in restaurants, although taverns still permit it. Most inns and B&Bs have banned smoking from guest rooms (see "Tips on Accommodations," earlier in this chapter).

Taxes Maine levies a 5% sales tax on goods, a 7% tax on meals and lodging, and a 10% tax on auto rentals.

Time Zone Maine is in the eastern time zone (the same one as New York and Boston). Daylight saving time is in effect (move clocks forward 1 hr. from Eastern Standard Time) between early April and late October.

3

For International Visitors

Whether it's your 1st visit or your 10th, a trip to the United States may require an additional degree of planning. This chapter will provide you with essential information, tips, and advice.

1 Preparing for Your Trip

ENTRY REQUIREMENTS

Check at any U.S. embassy or consulate for current information and requirements. You can also obtain a visa application and other information online from the **U.S. State Department** at **www.travel.state.gov**.

VISAS The U.S. State Department has a **Visa Waiver Program** allowing citizens of certain countries to enter the United States without a visa for stays of up to 90 days. At press time, these included Andorra, Australia, Austria, Belgium, Brunei, Denmark, Finland, France, Germany, Iceland, Ireland, Italy, Japan, Liechtenstein, Luxembourg, Monaco, the Netherlands, New Zealand, Norway, Portugal, San Marino, Singapore, Slovenia, Spain, Sweden, Switzerland, and the United Kingdom. Citizens of these countries need only a valid passport and a round-trip air or cruise ticket in their possession upon arrival. If they first enter the United States, they may also visit Mexico, Canada, Bermuda, and/or the Caribbean islands and return to the United States without a visa. Further information is available from any U.S. embassy or consulate. Canadian citizens may enter the United States without visas; they need only proof of residence.

Citizens of all other countries must have (1) a valid passport that expires at least 6 months later than the scheduled end of their visit to the United States, and (2) a tourist visa, which may be obtained without charge from any U.S. consulate.

To obtain a visa, the traveler must submit a completed application form (either in person or by mail) with a 1½-inch-square photo, and must demonstrate binding ties to a residence abroad. Usually you can obtain a visa at once or within 24 hours, but it may take longer during the summer rush from June through August. If you cannot go in person, contact the nearest U.S. embassy or consulate for directions on applying by mail. Your travel agent or airline office may also be able to provide you with visa applications and instructions. The U.S. consulate or embassy that issues your visa will determine whether you will be issued a multiple- or single-entry visa and any restrictions regarding the length of your stay.

British subjects can obtain up-to-date visa information by calling the **U.S. Embassy Visa Information Line** (✆ **0891/200-290**) or by visiting the "Consular Services" section of the American Embassy's London website at www.usembassy.org.uk.

Irish citizens can obtain up-to-date visa information through the **Embassy of the USA Dublin,** 42 Elgin Rd., Dublin 4, Ireland (✆ **353/1-668-8777;** or by checking the "Consular

> **Tips Prepare to Be Fingerprinted**
>
> Starting in January 2004, many international visitors traveling on visas to the United States are now photographed and fingerprinted at Customs in a new program created by the Department of Homeland Security called **US-VISIT.** Non-U.S. citizens arriving at airports and on cruise ships must undergo an instant background check as part of the government's ongoing efforts to deter terrorism by verifying the identity of incoming and outgoing visitors. Exempt from the extra scrutiny are visitors entering by land or those from 28 countries (mostly in Europe) that don't require a visa for short-term visits. For more information, go to the Homeland Security website at **www.dhs.gov/dhspublic.**

Services" section of the website at www.usembassy.ie.

Australian citizens can obtain up-to-date visa information by contacting the **U.S. Embassy Canberra,** Moonah Place, Yarralumla, ACT 2600 (© **02/6214-5600**), or by checking the U.S. Diplomatic Mission's website at http://usembassy-australia.state.gov/consular.

Citizens of **New Zealand** can obtain up-to-date visa information by contacting the **U.S. Embassy New Zealand,** 29 Fitzherbert Terrace, Thorndon, Wellington (© **644/472-2068**), or get the information directly from the "Services to New Zealanders" section of the website at http://usembassy.org.nz.

MEDICAL REQUIREMENTS

Unless you're arriving from an area known to be suffering from an epidemic (particularly cholera or yellow fever), inoculations or vaccinations are not required for entry into the United States. If you have a medical condition that requires **syringe-administered medications,** carry a valid signed prescription from your physician—the Federal Aviation Administration (FAA) no longer allows airline passengers to pack syringes in their carry-on baggage without documented proof of medical need. If you have a disease that requires treatment with **narcotics,** you should also carry documented proof with you—smuggling narcotics aboard a plane is a serious offense that carries severe penalties in the U.S.

For **HIV-positive visitors,** requirements for entering the United States are somewhat vague and change frequently. According to the latest publication of *HIV and Immigrants: A Manual for AIDS Service Providers,* the Immigration and Naturalization Service (INS) doesn't require a medical exam for entry into the United States, but INS officials may stop individuals because they look sick or because they are carrying AIDS/HIV medicine.

If an HIV-positive noncitizen applies for a nonimmigrant visa, the question on the application regarding communicable diseases is tricky no matter which way it's answered. If the applicant checks "no," INS may deny the visa on the grounds that the applicant committed fraud. If the applicant checks "yes" or the INS suspects the person is HIV-positive, it will deny the visa unless the applicant asks for a special waiver for visitors. This waiver is for people visiting the United States for a short time, to attend a conference, for instance, to visit close relatives, or to receive medical treatment. It can be a confusing situation. For up-to-the-minute information, contact **AIDSinfo** (© **800/448-0440** or 301/519-6616 outside the U.S.; www.aidsinfo.nih.gov) or the **Gay Men's Health Crisis** (© **212/367-1000;** www.gmhc.org).

DRIVER'S LICENSES Foreign driver's licenses are mostly recognized in the U.S., although you may want to get an international driver's license if your license is not written in English.

PASSPORT INFORMATION

Safeguard your passport in an inconspicuous, inaccessible place like a money belt. Make a copy of the critical pages, including the passport number, and store it in a safe place, separate from the passport. If you lose your passport, visit the nearest consulate of your country as soon as possible for a replacement. Passport applications are downloadable from the websites listed below.

Note that the International Civil Aviation Organization (ICAO) has recommended a policy requiring that *every* individual who travels by air have his or her own passport. In response, many countries are now requiring that children must be issued their own passport, whereas previously those under 16 or so may have been able to travel on a parent or guardian's passport.

FOR RESIDENTS OF CANADA

You can pick up a passport application at one of 28 regional passport offices or most travel agencies. Canadian children who travel must have their own passport. However, if you hold a valid Canadian passport issued before December 11, 2001, that bears the name of your child, the passport remains valid for you and your child until it expires. Passports cost C$85 for those 16 years and older (valid 5 years), C$35 for children 3 to 15 (valid 5 years), and C$20 for children under 3 (valid for 3 years). Applications, which must be accompanied by two identical passport-sized photographs and proof of Canadian citizenship, are available at travel agencies throughout Canada or from the central **Passport Office,** Department of Foreign Affairs and International Trade, Ottawa, ON K1A 0G3 (© **800/567-6868;** www.ppt.gc.

ca). Processing takes 5 to 10 days if you apply in person, or about 3 weeks by mail.

FOR RESIDENTS OF THE UNITED KINGDOM

As a member of the European Union, you need only an identity card, not a passport, to travel to other EU countries. However, if you already possess a passport, it's always useful to carry it. To pick up an application for a standard 10-year passport (5-year passport for children under 16), visit the nearest Passport Office, major post office, or travel agency. You can also contact the **United Kingdom Passport Service** at © **0870/571-0410** or visit its website at www.passport.gov.uk. Passports are £33 for adults and £19 for children under 16, with an additional £30 fee if you apply in person at a Passport Office. Processing takes about 2 weeks (1 week if you apply at the Passport Office).

FOR RESIDENTS OF IRELAND

You can apply for a 10-year passport, costing €57, at the **Passport Office,** Setanta Centre, Molesworth Street, Dublin 2 (© **01/671-1633;** www.irlgov.ie/iveagh). Those under age 18 and over 65 must apply for a €12 3-year passport. You can also apply at 1A South Mall, Cork (© **021/272-525**) or over the counter at most main post offices.

FOR RESIDENTS OF AUSTRALIA

You can pick up an application from your local post office or any branch of Passports Australia, but you must schedule an interview to present your application materials. Call the **Australian Passport Information Service** at © **131-232 o**r visit the government website at www.passports.gov.au. Passports for adults are A$144; for those under 18, they are A$72.

FOR RESIDENTS OF NEW ZEALAND

You can pick up a passport application at any New Zealand Passports Office or download it from their website. Contact the **Passports Office** at ✆ **0800/ 225-050** (in New Zealand) or 04/474-8100, or log on to www.passports.govt. nz. Passports for adults are NZ$80; and for children under 16, they are NZ$40.

CUSTOMS
WHAT YOU CAN BRING IN

Every visitor over 21 years of age may bring in, free of duty, the following: (1) 1 liter of wine or hard liquor; (2) 200 cigarettes, 100 cigars (but not from Cuba), or 3 pounds of smoking tobacco; and (3) $100 worth of gifts. These exemptions are offered to travelers who spend at least 72 hours in the United States and who have not claimed them within the preceding 6 months. It is altogether forbidden to bring into the country foodstuffs (particularly fruit, cooked meats, and canned goods) and plants (vegetables, seeds, tropical plants, and the like). Foreign tourists may bring in or take out up to $10,000 in U.S. or foreign currency with no formalities; larger sums must be declared to U.S. Customs on entering or leaving, which includes filing form CM 4790. For more specific information regarding U.S. Customs, contact your nearest U.S. embassy or consulate, or the **U.S. Customs** office (✆ **202/927-1770**; www.customs.ustreas.gov).

WHAT YOU CAN TAKE HOME

U.K. citizens returning from a non-EU country have a customs allowance of 200 cigarettes; 50 cigars; 250 grams of smoking tobacco; 2 liters of still table wine; 1 liter of spirits or strong liqueurs (over 22% volume); 2 liters of fortified wine, sparkling wine, or other liqueurs; 60cc (ml) of perfume; 250cc (ml) of toilet water; and £145 worth of all other goods, including gifts and souvenirs. People under 17

cannot have the tobacco or alcohol allowance. For more information, contact HM Customs & Excise at ✆ **0845/010-9000** (from outside the U.K., 020/8929-0152), or consult their website at www.hmce.gov.uk.

For a clear summary of **Canadian** rules, request the booklet *I Declare,* issued by the **Canada Customs and Revenue Agency** (✆ **800/461-9999** in Canada, or 204/983-3500; www. ccra-adrc.gc.ca). Canada allows its citizens a C$750 exemption, and you're allowed to bring back one carton of duty-free cigarettes, one can of tobacco, 40 imperial ounces of liquor, and 50 cigars. In addition, you're allowed to mail gifts to Canada valued at less than C$60 a day, provided they're unsolicited and don't contain alcohol or tobacco (write on the package "Unsolicited gift, under $60 value"). All valuables should be declared on the Y-38 form before departure from Canada, including serial numbers of valuables you own, such as expensive foreign cameras. *Note:* The C$750 exemption can only be used once a year and only after an absence of 7 days.

The duty-free allowance in **Australia** is A$400 or, for those under 18, A$200. Citizens age 18 and over can bring in 250 cigarettes or 250 grams of loose tobacco, and 1,125 milliliters of alcohol. If you're returning with valuables you already own, such as foreign-made cameras, you should file form B263. A helpful brochure available from Australian consulates or Customs offices is *Know Before You Go.* For more information, call the **Australian Customs Service** at ✆ **1300/363-263,** or log on to www.customs.gov.au.

The duty-free allowance for **New Zealand** is NZ$700. Citizens over 17 can bring in 200 cigarettes, 50 cigars, or 250 grams of tobacco (or a mixture of all three if their combined weight doesn't exceed 250g); plus 4.5 liters of wine and beer, or 1.125 liters of liquor. New Zealand currency does not carry import or export restrictions. Fill out a certificate of export, listing the valuables you are taking out of the country; that way, you can bring them back without paying duty. Most questions are answered in a free pamphlet available at New Zealand consulates and Customs offices: *New Zealand Customs Guide for Travellers, Notice no. 4.* For more information, contact **New Zealand Customs,** The Customhouse, 17–21 Whitmore St., Box 2218, Wellington (© **0800/428-786** or 04/473-6099; www.customs. govt.nz).

HEALTH INSURANCE

Although it's not required of travelers, health insurance is highly recommended. Unlike many European countries, the United States does not usually offer free or low-cost medical care to its citizens or visitors. Doctors and hospitals are expensive, and in most cases will require advance payment or proof of coverage before they render their services. Policies can cover everything from the loss or theft of your baggage and trip cancellation to the guarantee of bail in case you're arrested. Good policies will also cover the costs of an accident, repatriation, or death. See "Health & Insurance" in chapter 2 for more information. Packages such as **Europ Assistance's "Worldwide Healthcare Plan"** are sold by European automobile clubs and travel agencies at attractive rates. **Worldwide Assistance Services, Inc.** (© **800/821-2828;** www.worldwide assistance.com), is the agent for Europ Assistance in the United States.

Though lack of health insurance may prevent you from being admitted to a hospital in nonemergencies, don't worry about being left on a street corner to die: The American way is to fix you now and bill the living daylights out of you later.

INSURANCE FOR BRITISH TRAVELERS   Most big travel agents offer their own insurance and will probably try to sell you their package when you book a holiday. Think before you sign. **Britain's Consumers' Association** recommends that you insist on seeing the policy and reading the fine print before buying travel insurance. **The Association of British Insurers** (© **020/ 7600-3333;** www.abi.org.uk) gives advice by phone and publishes *Holiday Insurance,* a free guide to policy provisions and prices. You might also shop around for better deals: Try **Columbus Direct** (© **020/7375-0011;** www. columbusdirect.net).

INSURANCE FOR CANADIAN TRAVELERS   Canadians should check with their provincial health plan offices or call **Health Canada** (© **613/ 957-2991;** www.hc-sc.gc.ca) to find out the extent of their coverage and what documentation and receipts they must take home in case they are treated in the United States.

MONEY

CURRENCY   The U.S. monetary system is very simple: The most common **bills** are the $1 (colloquially, a "buck"), $5, $10, and $20 denominations. There are also $2 bills (seldom encountered), $50 bills, and $100 bills (the last two are usually not welcome as payment for small purchases). All the paper money was recently redesigned, making the famous faces adorning them disproportionately large. The old-style bills are still legal tender.

There are seven denominations of coins: 1¢ (1 cent, or a penny); 5¢ (5 cents, or a nickel); 10¢ (10 cents, or a dime); 25¢ (25 cents, or a quarter); 50¢ (50 cents, or a half dollar); the new gold-colored "Sacagawea" coin worth $1; and, prized by collectors, the rare, older silver dollar.

Note: The "foreign-exchange bureaus" so common in Europe are rare even at airports in the United States, and nonexistent outside major cities. It's best not to change foreign money (or traveler's checks denominated in a currency other than U.S. dollars) at a small-town bank, or even a branch in a big city; in fact, leave any currency other than U.S. dollars at home—it may prove a greater nuisance to you than it's worth.

Note: Canadian dollars are often accepted in Maine, New Hampshire, and Vermont (all of which border Canada), although it's generally easier to use Canadian currency closer to the border. Most hotels and many restaurants will accept Canadian currency at a discount close to its current trading value. Increasingly common in border towns on the Canadian side are ATMs (automated teller machines) that dispense U.S. dollars from your Canadian account.

TRAVELER'S CHECKS   Though traveler's checks are widely accepted, make sure that they're denominated in U.S. dollars, as foreign-currency checks are often difficult to exchange. The three traveler's checks that are most widely recognized—and least likely to be denied—are **Visa, American Express,** and **Thomas Cook.** Be sure to record the numbers of the checks, and keep that information in a separate place in case the checks are lost or stolen. Most businesses are pretty good about taking traveler's checks, but you're better off cashing them in at a bank (in small amounts, of course) and paying in cash. Remember: You'll need ID, such as a driver's license or passport, to change a traveler's check.

CREDIT CARDS & ATMs   The following credit cards are the most widely used form of payment in the United States: **Visa** (Barclaycard in Britain), **MasterCard** (EuroCard in Europe, Access in Britain, Chargex in Canada), **American Express, Diners Club,** and **Discover.** However, a handful of stores and restaurants do not take credit cards, so ask in advance. Most businesses display a sticker near their entrance to let you know which cards they accept. (*Note:* Businesses may require a minimum purchase, usually around $10, to use a credit card.)

It is strongly recommended that you bring at least one major credit card. You must have one to rent a car. Hotels and airlines usually require a credit card imprint as a deposit, and in an emergency a credit card can be priceless.

You'll find **automated teller machines (ATMs)** at almost any bank in coastal Maine, and others at shopping malls or inside gas stations or convenience stores (these may levy a high fee). Some ATMs will allow you to draw U.S. currency against your bank and credit cards. Check with your bank before leaving home, and remember that you will need your personal identification number (PIN) to do so. Most accept Visa, MasterCard, and American Express, as well as ATM cards from other U.S. banks. Expect to be charged up to $3 per transaction if you're not using your own bank's ATM.

One way around these fees is to ask for cash back at grocery stores that accept ATM cards and don't charge usage fees. Of course, you'll have to purchase something first.

Travel Tip

Be sure to keep a copy of all your travel papers separate from your wallet or purse, and leave a copy with someone at home should you need it faxed in an emergency.

ATM cards with major credit card backing, known as *debit cards,* are now a commonly acceptable form of payment in most stores and restaurants. Debit cards draw money directly from your checking account. Some stores enable you to receive "cash back" on your debit-card purchases as well.

SAFETY

Maine has some of the lowest crime rates in the country, and the odds of being a victim of a crime during your visit here are slight, but all travelers are advised to take the usual precautions against theft, robbery, and assault.

Avoid carrying valuables with you on the street, and keep expensive cameras or electronic equipment bagged up or covered when not in use. If you're using a map, try to consult it inconspicuously—or better yet, study it before you leave your room. Hold onto your pocketbook, and place your billfold in an inside pocket. In theaters, restaurants, and other public places, keep your possessions in sight.

Always lock your room door—don't assume that once you're inside the hotel you are safe and no longer need to be aware of your surroundings. Hotels are open to the public, and in a large hotel, security may not be able to screen everyone who enters.

Park in well-lit and well-traveled areas whenever possible. Always keep your car doors locked, whether the vehicle is attended or unattended. Never leave any packages or valuables in sight. If someone attempts to rob you or steal your car, don't try to resist the thief/carjacker. Report the incident to the police department immediately by calling ℂ **911.**

For additional information, see the "Staying Safe" section in chapter 2.

2 Getting To & Around Coastal Maine

GETTING THERE   There are few international flights into Maine, so the odds are good you'll arrive by way of Boston or New York. Bus and train services reach parts of Maine, New Hampshire, and Vermont, but both tend to be spotty and relatively expensive, especially if two or more are traveling together (it's often much cheaper to rent a car than to pay for two tickets). Note also that these states are best seen by exploring the countryside, which is virtually inaccessible by mass transportation. If you're dead set against renting a car, see the section "Your Car: Leave Home Without It" in chapter 2. For information on renting a car, see "Getting Around Coastal Maine" in chapter 2.

BY PLANE   Most international travelers come to the coast of Maine via Boston's Logan Airport or one of the three New York City–area airports. Boston offers the easiest access to northern New England: Maine's southernmost beaches are an hour away by car, Portland is 2 hours away by car, and Acadia National Park 5 to 6 hours away by car. Figure on 6 to 8 hours of driving time to most attractions if you're coming by car from New York–area airports. For info on getting to the coast of Maine from within the U.S., see "Getting There," in chapter 2.

Dozens of airlines serve New York and Boston airports from overseas, although New York and Newark see far more overseas traffic. Airlines serving Boston, New York, and Newark transcontinentally include **American Airlines** (ℂ 0845-778-9789; www.aa. com), **British Airways** (ℂ 0870/ 850-9850; www.british-airways.com), **Continental** (ℂ 0800/776-464; www. continental.com), **Delta** (ℂ 0800/ 414-767; www.delta.com), **United** (ℂ 0845/8444-777; www.united airlines.co.uk), and **Virgin Atlantic**

(☎ 0870/380-2007; www.virgin-atlantic.com).

Those coming from Latin America, Asia, Australia, or New Zealand will probably arrive in New England through gateway cities such as Miami, Los Angeles, or San Francisco, clearing Customs there before connecting onward to Boston. Bus service is available from Boston's Logan Airport to several cities in northern New England. Limited train service is also offered. See "Getting Around Coastal Maine" in chapter 2.

Airports with regularly scheduled flights within New England include Portland, Rockland, Trenton, and Bangor; all connect directly to Boston.

AIRLINE DISCOUNTS The smart traveler can find many ways to reduce the price of a plane ticket simply by taking time to shop around. For example, overseas visitors can take advantage of the APEX (Advance Purchase Excursion) reductions offered by all major U.S. and European carriers. For more money-saving airline advice, see "Getting There," in chapter 2. For the best rates, compare fares and be flexible with your dates and times of travel.

Some large airlines (for example, Northwest and Delta) offer travelers on their transatlantic or transpacific flights special discount tickets under the name **Visit USA,** allowing mostly one-way travel from one U.S. destination to another at very low prices. These discount tickets are not for sale in the United States and must be purchased abroad in conjunction with your international ticket. This system is the best, easiest, and fastest way to see the United States at low cost. You should obtain information well in advance from your travel agent or the office of the airline concerned, as the conditions attached to these discount tickets can be changed without advance notice.

IMMIGRATION & CUSTOMS CLEARANCE Visitors arriving by air, no matter what the port of entry, should cultivate patience before setting foot on U.S. soil. Getting through immigration control can take as long as 2 hours on some days, especially on summer weekends, so be sure to carry this guidebook or something else to read.

People traveling by air from Canada, Bermuda, and certain countries in the Caribbean can sometimes clear Customs and Immigration at the point of departure, which is much quicker.

BY TRAIN Several **Amtrak** (☎ 800/USA-RAIL;** www.amtrak.com) trains per day also run from Boston up the southern coast of Maine as far north as Portland. International visitors (excluding Canada) can also buy a **USA Rail Pass,** good for 15 or 30 days of unlimited travel on the Amtrak network. The pass is available through many overseas travel agents. As of press time prices for a 15-day pass are $295 off-peak, $440 peak; a 30-day pass cost $385 off-peak, $550 peak. With a foreign passport, you can also buy passes at some Amtrak offices in the United States, including locations in San Francisco, Los Angeles, Chicago, New York, Miami, Boston, and Washington, D.C. Reservations are generally required and should be made as early as possible. Regional rail passes are also available.

BY BUS Although bus travel is often the most economical form of public transit for short hops between U.S. cities, it can also be slow and uncomfortable—certainly not an option for everyone (particularly when Amtrak, which is far more luxurious, offers similar rates). **Greyhound/Trailways** (☎ 800/231-2222; www.greyhound.com) offers an **International Ameripass** that must be purchased before coming to the United States, or by phone through the Greyhound International Office at the Port Authority Bus Terminal in New York City (☎ 212/971-0492). The pass can be obtained from foreign travel agents or through Greyhound's website (order at least 21 days before your departure to the U.S.), and costs less than the domestic version. At press time passes are priced as follows: 4 days ($140), 7 days ($199), 10 days ($249), 15 days ($289), 21 days ($339), 30 days ($379), 45 days ($429), or 60 days ($519). You can get more info on the pass at the website, or by calling ℂ **402/330-8552.** Special rates are available for seniors and students.

The regional bus lines **Vermont Transit** (ℂ **800/451-3292;** www.vermonttransit.com) and **Concord Trailways** (ℂ **800/639-3317;** www.concordtrailways.com) link Boston to Bangor, Portland, Portsmouth, New Hampshire, and some of the smaller cities and towns in coastal Maine. See the individual town and city sections for more information on local bus depots and contact information.

BY CAR The most cost-effective, convenient, and comfortable way to get around the coast of Maine is by car. Some of the national car-rental companies include **Alamo** (ℂ 800/462-5266; www.alamo.com), **Avis** (ℂ 800/230-4898; www.avis.com), **Budget** (ℂ 800/527-0700; www.budget.com), **Dollar** (ℂ 800/800-3665; www.dollar.com), **Hertz** (ℂ 800/654-3131; www.hertz.com), **National** (ℂ 800/227-7368; www.nationalcar.com), and **Thrifty** (ℂ 800/847-4389; www.thrifty.com).

If you plan to rent a car in the United States, you probably won't need the services of an additional automobile organization. If you're planning to buy or borrow a car, automobile association membership is recommended. **AAA, the American Automobile Association** (ℂ **800/222-4357**), is the country's largest auto club and supplies its members with maps, insurance, and, most important, emergency road service. The cost of joining runs from $63 for singles to $87 for two members, but if you're a member of a foreign auto club with reciprocal arrangements, you can enjoy free AAA service in America.

FAST FACTS: **For the International Traveler**

Abbreviations On highway signs and publications, you'll see Maine abbreviated as "Me." All capital letters (ME) are used when addressing mail for the U.S. Postal Service.

Automobile Organizations Becoming a member of an automobile club is handy for obtaining maps and route suggestions, and it can be helpful should an emergency arise with your automobile. The nation's largest automobile club is the American Automobile Association (AAA), which has nearly 1,000 offices nationwide. AAA offers reciprocal arrangements with many overseas automobile clubs; if you're a member of an automobile club at home, find out whether your privileges extend to the United States. For more information on AAA, call ℂ **800/222-4357;** www.aaa.com. There's a handy AAA office located in Portland right off I-295 at 68 Marginal Way (ℂ **207/780-6800**), open Monday through Friday from 8:30am to 5pm and Saturdays from 9am to 1pm. Other local branches can be found in Bangor, Brunswick, Kennebunk, South Portland, and Portsmouth, New Hampshire.

Business Hours Most offices are open from 8 or 9am to 5 or 6pm. Shops usually open around 9:30 or 10am. Banks typically close at 3 or 4pm, but many have automated teller machines (ATMs) available 24 hours. Post offices in larger cities may be open past 5pm, but it's best to call ahead before going out of your way. A few supermarkets are open 24 hours a day, but they're not terribly common in this part of the world. If you need quick provisions, look for one of the brightly lit convenience stores, which are usually open until at least 10 or 11pm.

Drinking Laws You must be 21 years old to legally drink alcohol in the U.S. No matter what your age, state laws in Maine are notoriously harsh on those who drive under the influence of alcohol. Know your tolerance and don't even think about driving drunk.

Driving A current overseas license is valid on U.S. roads. If your license is in a language other than English, it's recommended that you obtain an International Drivers Permit from an American Automobile Association affiliate or other automobile organization in your own country prior to departure (see "Automobile Organizations," above).

Drivers may make a right turn at a red light, provided that they first stop fully and confirm that no other driver is approaching from the left. At some intersections, signs prohibit such a turn.

Electricity Electrical incompatibility makes it tricky to use appliances manufactured for Europe in the United States. The current here is 110 to 120 volts, 60 cycles, compared to the 220 to 240 volts, 50 cycles used in much of Europe. If you're bringing an electric camera flash, portable computer, or other gadget that requires electricity, be sure to bring the appropriate converter and plug adapter.

Embassies & Consulates Embassies are located in the nation's capital, Washington, D.C. Some consulates are located in major U.S. cities, and most nations have a mission to the United Nations in New York City. If your country isn't listed below, call for directory information in Washington, D.C. (© **202/555-1212**), or log on to **www.embassy.org/embassies**.

The embassy of **Australia** is at 1601 Massachusetts Ave. NW, Washington, DC 20036 (© **202/797-3000**; www.austemb.org).

The embassy of **Canada** is at 501 Pennsylvania Ave. NW, Washington, DC 20001 (© **202/682-1740**; www.canadianembassy.org). Other Canadian consulates are in Buffalo (NY), Detroit, Los Angeles, New York, and Seattle.

The embassy of **Ireland** is at 2234 Massachusetts Ave. NW, Washington, DC 20008 (© **202/462-3939**; www.irelandemb.org).

The embassy of **Japan** is at 2520 Massachusetts Ave. NW, Washington, DC 20008 (© **202/238-6700**; www.embjapan.org).

The embassy of **New Zealand** is at 37 Observatory Circle NW, Washington, DC 20008 (© **202/328-4800**; www.nzemb.org).

The embassy of the **United Kingdom** is at 3100 Massachusetts Ave. NW, Washington, DC 20008 (© **202/462-1340**; www.britainusa.com).

A handful of countries also maintain consulates in Boston, including **Canada,** 3 Copley Place, Suite 400, Boston, MA 02116 (© **617/262-3760**); **Great Britain,** Federal Reserve Plaza, 600 Atlantic Ave. (25th floor), Boston, MA 02210 (© **617/248-9555**); **Ireland,** 535 Boylston St., Boston, MA 02116 (© **617/267-9330**); and **Israel,** 1020 Statler Office Building, 20 Park Plaza, Boston, MA 02116 (© **617/535-0200**). For other countries, contact directory assistance (© **617/555-1212**).

Emergencies In the event of any type of emergency—whether medical, fire, or if you've been the victim of a crime—simply dial ✆ **911** from any phone. You do not need a coin to make this call. A dispatcher will immediately send medics, the police, or the fire department to assist you, though you may need to provide your location to the dispatcher. If 911 doesn't work (some of the more remote areas haven't yet been connected to the network), dial 0 (zero) and report your situation to the operator. If a hospital is nearby when a medical emergency arises, look for the "Emergency" entrance, where you will be quickly attended to.

Gasoline Gasoline is widely available throughout the region, with the exception of the North Woods, where you can travel many miles without seeing a filling station. Gas tends to be cheaper farther to the south and in larger towns and cities, where the competition is a bit stiffer; you're better off filling up before setting off into remote or rural areas. Gas is available in several different grades at each station; the higher the octane, the more expensive it is.

Many of the filling stations in Maine have both **self-serve** and **full-service** pumps; look for signs as you pull up. Full service pumps are slightly more expensive per gallon, but an attendant will pump your gas and check your oil (you may have to ask for this). The self-serve pumps often have simple directions posted on them. If you're at all confused, ask the station attendant for instructions.

Holidays With some important exceptions, national holidays usually fall on Mondays to allow workers to enjoy a 3-day holiday. The exceptions are New Year's Day (Jan 1), Independence Day (July 4), Veterans Day (Nov 11), Thanksgiving (last Thurs in Nov), and Christmas (Dec 25). Other holidays include Martin Luther King, Jr., Day (third Mon in Jan), President's Day (third Mon in Feb), Easter (first Sun following a full moon occurring Mar 21 or later), Memorial Day (last Mon in May), Labor Day (first Mon in Sept), and Columbus Day (second Mon in Oct). In Maine, Patriot's Day is also celebrated on the third Monday in April.

On these holidays, banks, government offices, and post offices are closed. Shops are sometimes open on holidays, but assume almost all will be closed on Thanksgiving and Christmas Day.

Languages Some of the larger hotels may have multilingual employees, but don't count on it. Outside of the cities, English is the only language spoken. The exception is along the Canadian border and in some coastal Maine locales (including Old Orchard Beach and Biddeford), where French is commonly spoken or at least understood.

Legal Aid If a foreign tourist accidentally breaks a law, it's most likely to be for exceeding the posted speed limit on a road (it's the law U.S. residents frequently run afoul of). If you are pulled over by a policeman, don't attempt to pay the fine directly—that may be interpreted as a bribe, and you may find yourself in graver trouble. If pulled over, your best bet is to put on a display of confusion or ignorance of local laws (this may be feigned or legitimate), combined with a respect for authority. You may be let off with a warning. Failing that, you'll be issued a summons with a court date and a fine listed on it; if you pay the fine by mail, you don't have to appear in court. If you are arrested for a more serious infraction, you'll be allowed one phone call from jail. It's advisable to contact your embassy or consulate for further instruction.

Mail If you aren't sure what your address will be in the United States, mail can be sent to you, in your name, c/o General Delivery at the main post office of the city or region where you expect to be. (Call ℂ **800/275-8777** for information on the nearest post office.) The addressee must pick up mail in person and must produce proof of identity (driver's license, passport, etc.). Most post offices will hold your mail for up to one month, and are open Monday to Friday from 8am to 6pm, and Saturday from 9am to 3pm.

Generally found at intersections, mailboxes are blue with a red-and-white stripe and carry the inscription U.S. MAIL. If your mail is addressed to a U.S. destination, don't forget to add the five-digit postal code (or zip code), after the two-letter abbreviation of the state to which the mail is addressed. This is essential to prompt delivery.

At press time, domestic postage rates are 23¢ for a postcard and 37¢ for a letter. For international mail, a first-class letter of up to one-half ounce costs 80¢ (60¢ to Canada and Mexico); a first-class postcard costs 70¢ (50¢ to Canada and Mexico); and a preprinted postal aerogramme costs 70¢.

Newspapers & Magazines Foreign newspapers and magazines are commonly found in Boston, but are harder to track down in northern New England. Your best bet is to head for Borders (in Portland and Bangor, Maine), or Barnes & Noble (in Augusta, Maine). Both bookstore chains have large stores and offer a limited selection of overseas newspapers and magazines.

Taxes Visitors to the United States are assessed a $10 customs tax upon entering the country and a $6 tax on departure. The United States does not have a value-added tax (VAT). Maine's sales tax is 5% for most goods and services, 7% for hotel rooms and prepared meals. There is no refund of these taxes available for foreign travelers.

Telephone, Telegraph, Telex & Fax The telephone system in the United States is run by private corporations, so rates, especially for long-distance service and operator-assisted calls, can vary widely. Generally, hotel surcharges on long-distance and local calls are astronomical, so you're usually better off using a **public pay telephone,** which you'll find clearly marked in most public buildings and private establishments as well as on the street. Convenience grocery stores and gas stations always have them. Many convenience groceries and packaging services sell **prepaid calling cards** in denominations up to $50; these can be the least expensive way to call home. Many public phones at airports now accept American Express, MasterCard, and Visa credit cards. **Local calls** made from public pay phones in most locales cost either 25¢ or 35¢ (or sometimes 50¢). Pay phones do not accept pennies, and few will take anything larger than a quarter.

You may want to look into leasing a cellphone for the duration of your trip.

Most long-distance and international calls can be dialed directly from any phone. **For calls within the United States and to Canada,** dial 1 followed by the area code and the seven-digit number. **For other international calls,** dial

011 followed by the country code, the city code, and the telephone number of the person you are calling.

Calls to area codes **800, 888, 877,** and **866** are toll-free. However, calls to numbers in area codes **700** and **900** (chat lines, bulletin boards, "dating" services, and so on) can be very expensive—usually involving a charge of 95¢ to $3 or more per minute, and they sometimes have minimum charges that can run as high as $15 or more.

For **reversed-charge or collect calls,** and for person-to-person calls, dial 0 (zero, not the letter O) followed by the area code and number you want; an operator will then come on the line, and you should specify that you are calling collect, or person-to-person, or both. If your operator-assisted call is international, ask for the overseas operator.

For **local directory assistance** ("information"), dial 411; for long-distance information, dial 1, followed by the appropriate area code and 555-1212.

Telegraph and telex services are provided primarily by Western Union. You can bring your telegram into the nearest Western Union office (there are hundreds across the country) or dictate it over the phone (© **800/ 325-6000**). You can also telegraph money, or have it telegraphed to you, very quickly over the Western Union system, but this service can cost as much as 15% to 20% of the amount sent.

Most hotels have **fax machines** available for guest use (be sure to ask about the charge to use it). Many hotel rooms are even wired for guests' fax machines. A less expensive way to send and receive faxes may be at stores such as **The UPS Store** (formerly Mail Boxes Etc.), a national chain of retail packing service shops; somewhat surprisingly (to me, anyhow), there are at present five UPS stores strung out along the coast of Maine. They are located in Bangor, Belfast, Boothbay Harbor, Ellsworth, and Rockland.

There are two kinds of telephone directories in the United States. The so-called **White Pages** list private households and business subscribers in alphabetical order. The inside front cover lists emergency numbers for police, fire, ambulance, the Coast Guard, the poison-control center, the crime-victims hot line, and so on. The first few pages tell you how to make long-distance and international calls, complete with country codes and area codes. Government numbers are usually printed on blue paper within the White Pages. Printed on yellow paper, the so-called **Yellow Pages** list all local services, businesses, industries, and houses of worship according to subject, with an index at the front or back. (Drugstores/pharmacies and restaurants are also listed by geographic location.) The Yellow Pages also include city plans or detailed area maps, postal zip codes, and public transportation routes.

Time All of Maine is in the eastern time zone—the same zone as Boston, New York, and the rest of the eastern seaboard. All three states shift to daylight saving time in summer, setting clocks ahead 1 hour in the spring (the first Sun in Apr) and back again in the fall (the last Sun in Oct).

Tipping Tips are a very important part of certain workers' income, and gratuities are the standard way of showing appreciation for services provided. (Tipping is certainly not compulsory if the service is poor!) In hotels, tip **bellhops** at least $1 per bag ($2–$3 if you have a lot of luggage) and tip the **chamber staff** $1 to $2 per day (more if you've left a disaster area to clean up). Tip the **doorman** or **concierge** only if he or she has provided you with some specific service (for example, calling a cab for you or obtaining difficult-to-get theater tickets). Tip the **valet-parking attendant** $1 every time you get your car.

In restaurants, bars, and nightclubs, tip **service staff** 15% to 20% of the check, tip **bartenders** 10% to 15%, tip **checkroom attendants** $1 per garment, and tip **valet-parking attendants** $1 per vehicle.

As for other service personnel, tip **cab drivers** 15% of the fare; tip **skycaps** at airports at least $1 per bag ($2–$3 if you have a lot of luggage); and tip **hairdressers** and **barbers** 15% to 20%.

Toilets You won't find public toilets or "restrooms" on the streets in most U.S. cities, but they can be found in libraries, bars, restaurants, museums, department stores, railway and bus stations, some hotel lobbies, and most service stations. Failing all else, try a fast-food restaurant. If possible, avoid the toilets at parks and beaches, which tend to be dirty; some may be unsafe. Restaurants and bars in resorts or heavily visited areas may reserve their restrooms for patrons. Some establishments display a notice indicating this. You can ignore this sign or, better yet, avoid arguments by paying for a cup of coffee or a soft drink, which will qualify you as a patron.

The Southern Coast: Kittery to the Kennebunks

Maine's southern coast runs roughly from the state line at Kittery to Portland, and this is the destination of the majority of travelers into the state (the numbers are swelled by day-trippers from the Boston area). While it will take some doing to find privacy and remoteness here, you'll turn up at least two excellent reasons for a detour: the long, sandy beaches that are the region's hallmark, and the almost tactile sense of history in the coastal villages.

Thanks to quirks of geography, nearly all of Maine's sandy beaches are located in this 60-mile stretch of coastline. It's not hard to find a relaxing sandy spot, whether you prefer dunes and the lulling sound of the surf or the carnival atmosphere of a festive beach town. The waves are dependent on the weather—during a good northeast blow they pound the shores and threaten decades-old beach houses. During the balmy days of midsummer the ocean can be as gentle as a farm pond, with barely audible waves lapping timidly at the shore.

One characteristic all of the beaches have in common: the chilly waters of the Gulf of Maine. Except for those of the very young, who seem immune to blood-chilling temperatures, swimming sessions in these waters tend to be very brief and often accompanied by shrieks, whoops, and agitated hand-waving. The beach season itself is brief yet intense, running from July 4th to Labor Day. Of late it seems to be stretching out into fall at an increasing number of beach towns (Columbus

Day usually brings the remaining businesses to a close), but after Labor Day shorefront communities adopt a slower, more somnolent pace.

On foggy or rainy days, plan to search out the southern coast's rich history, which one can still glimpse in places like York. More than 3 centuries ago the early European newcomers first settled here, only to be driven out by hostile Native Americans who had been pushed to the brink by treaty-breaking British settlers and prodded by the mischievous French. Settlers later reestablished themselves, and by the early 19th century, the southern Maine coast was one of the most prosperous regions in the nation. Shipbuilders constructed brigantines and sloops, and merchants and traders constructed warehouses along the rivers to store their goods. Even today, many handsome and historic homes here can attest to the region's former prosperity.

A second wave of settlers, wealthy city dwellers from Boston and New York, came to Maine's coast in the mid– to late 19th century seeking respite from the summer heat and city congestion. They built shingled estates (which they coyly called "cottages") with views of the Atlantic. Soon these wealthy rusticators were followed by the emerging middle class, who built or rented bungalows near the shore and congregated at ocean-side boarding houses to splash in the waves.

That tradition continues unabated today—and you can be part of it.

1 Kittery & the Yorks ✦✦

Driving into Maine from the south, as most travelers do, **Kittery** ✦ is the first town to appear. Once famous for its (still operating) naval yard, it's now better known for dozens of factory outlets. Maine has the second-highest number of outlet malls in the nation (after California), and Kittery is home to a good many of them—though the reasons they chose to spring up here, and not a few miles away in sales tax-free New Hampshire, remain an enduring mystery.

"The Yorks," just to the north, are three towns that share a name but little else. In fact, it's rare to find three such well-defined and diverse New England archetypes within such a compact area. **York Village** ✦ is full of early (17th-century) American history and architecture, and has a good library. **York Harbor** ✦✦ reached its zenith during America's late Victorian era, when wealthy urbanites constructed cottages at the ocean's edge; it's the most relaxing and scenic of the three. But it's **York Beach** ✦✦ I like the best: a beach town with amusements, taffy shops, a small zoo, gabled summer homes set in crowded enclaves, a great lighthouse, and two good beaches—a long one perfect for walking or tanning, plus a shorter one within a minute's walk of restaurants, souvenir shops, candy shops, an arcade, and even a palm reader.

Just outside York Village, the protrusion of land known as **Cape Neddick** ✦✦ is an excellent back-road route to Ogunquit, *if* you can find it (go past the police station in Short Sands, then bear right at the sign for the Cape Neddick Lobster Pound).

ESSENTIALS

GETTING THERE

Kittery is accessible from **I-95** or **Route 1,** with exits well marked. The Yorks are reached most easily from Exit 1 of the Maine Turnpike. Look for Route 1A, just south of the turnpike exit. Turn left onto Route 1A for the Yorks. This route connects all three York towns.

Amtrak (© 800/872-7245; www.amtrak.com) operates four trains daily from Boston's North Station to southern Maine, stopping outside Wells, about 10 miles away from the Yorks; a one-way ticket costs $17, and the trip takes 2 hours. You'll need to phone for a taxi or arrange for a pickup to get to your destination if you arrive by train.

Greyhound (© 800/229-9424), **C&J Trailways** (© 800/258-7111), and **Vermont Transit** (© 800/552-8737) all run a few buses daily from Boston's South Station to southern Maine, but they only stop in Wells, and not even in the beach or commercial area. Bus fare is comparable to train fare; the trip can be up to a half-hour shorter. Buses also run a bit more frequently from South Station to downtown Portsmouth, New Hampshire, which is close to Kittery and a more convenient place to get off. Taking a Greyhound from New York City's Port Authority to Portsmouth is about $44 one-way and takes about 6½ hours.

VISITOR INFORMATION

Travelers entering the state on I-95 can stock up on travel information for the region and beyond at the **Kittery Information Center** (© 207/439-1319), located at a well-marked rest area. Open 8am to 6pm in summer, 9am to 5:30pm the rest of the year, it's amply stocked with brochures, and the helpful staff can answer most questions.

The **York Chamber of Commerce,** 1 Stonewall Lane, York, ME 03909 (© 207/363-4422; www.yorkme.org), operates a helpful information center at

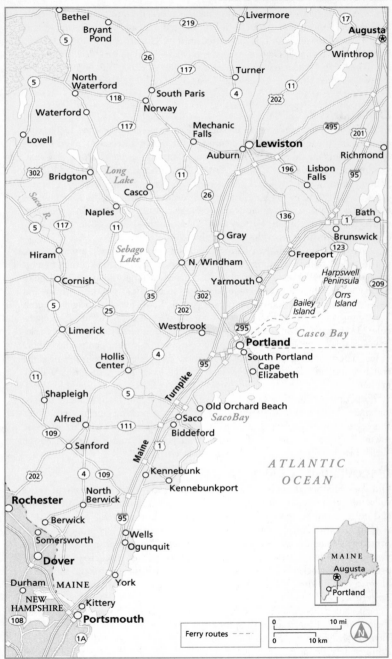

Bethel
Livermore
219
17
Augusta ⊛
Bryant
Pond
5
Winthrop
26
North
Waterford
117
Turner
5
118
South Paris
4
11
202
Norway
Waterford
Mechanic
Falls
495
201
302
117
Lovell
Auburn
Lewiston
Richmond
Long
Lake
11
Lisbon
Falls
196
95
Bridgton
302
Casco
26
136
Bath
Naples
Saco R.
Sebago
Lake
1
5
117
11
Brunswick
Hiram
Gray
Freeport
123
Cornish
N. Windham
Harpswell
Peninsula
209
Yarmouth
35
302
Orrs
Island
Bailey
Island
Westbrook
202
Casco Bay
Limerick
25
295
Portland
5
Hollis
Center
4
South Portland
Cape
Elizabeth
95
11
Shapleigh
5
Turnpike
Old Orchard Beach
Alfred
111
Saco
Saco Bay
109
Biddeford
Sanford
Maine
1
202
4
109
Kennebunk
ATLANTIC
OCEAN
Rochester
North
Berwick
Kennebunkport
95
Berwick
Wells
Somersworth
Ogunquit
Dover
Durham
MAINE
York
NEW
HAMPSHIRE
Kittery
108
Portsmouth
1A

MAINE
Augusta ⊛
Portland

Ferry routes - - - -

0   10 mi
0   10 km

571 Rte. 1, a short distance from the turnpike exit. It's open year-round, daily in summers 9am to 5pm (until 6pm Fri), limited days and hours in the off-season. A trackless trolley (a bus retrofitted to look like an old-fashioned trolley) links all three York towns and provides a convenient way to explore without having to be hassled with parking. Hop on the trolley (© **207/748-3030**) at one of the well-marked stops; an all-day pass costs $7 per adult, $4 for kids (children 3 and under ride free).

EXPLORING KITTERY

Kittery's consumer mecca is 4 miles south of York on Route 1. Some 120 factory outlets flank the highway, scattered among more than a dozen strip malls. Name-brand retailers include Dansk, Eddie Bauer, Corning Revere, Coldwater Creek, Le Creuset, Calvin Klein, Crate & Barrel, Donna Karan, Converse, Polo/Ralph Lauren, Tommy Hilfiger, Levi's, Old Navy, Bose, Nautica, and Noritake. The area can be aggravating to navigate during the summer, owing to the four lanes of often heavy traffic and capricious restrictions on turns. Information on current outlets is available from the **Kittery Outlet Association.** Call © **888/KITTERY,** or visit the website at www.thekitteryoutlets.com.

Departing from downtown Kittery (south of the outlet zone), a scenic route north to York follows winding Route 103. (It's perfect for a drive, although a bit busy and narrow for a bike ride.) The road passes through the historic village of Kittery Point, where homes seem to be located just inches from the roadway, and past two historic forts (both in public parks). Look for the **Lady Pepperell House** on your right at the first left elbow in the road. The handsome cream-colored Georgian home was built in 1760 and is considered one of the most elegant Georgian-style homes in the nation. However, it is not open to the public.

Just before coming into the village of York, keep an eye on your left near the marshes and tidal inlets for the Wiggly Bridge (see "Two Wonderful Walks," below).

Tip: Portsmouth, New Hampshire, makes a very worthwhile side trip once ensconced in Kittery or the Yorks—in fact, if you're seeking culture, arts, coffee shops, and top-flight restaurants, it's a much better base than either of those towns. Best of all, it's just a half-mile from Kittery, a few minutes' drive from the Yorks. I've described this city as a side trip in chapter 10.

DISCOVERING LOCAL HISTORY

Old York Historical Society   This historical society oversees the bulk of York's collection of historic buildings, some of which date to the early 18th century and most of which are astonishingly well preserved or restored.

John Hancock is famous for his oversize signature on the Declaration of Independence, his tenure as governor of Massachusetts, and the insurance company named after him. What's not so well known is his earlier checkered past as proprietor of Hancock Wharf, a failed enterprise that is but one of the intriguing historic sites in **York Village** ★★★, a fine destination for those curious about early American history.

First settled in 1624, York Village opens several early homes to the public. Tickets are available at all of the properties, but a good place to start is **Jefferds Tavern** ★, across from the handsome **old burying ground** ★. Changing exhibits here document various facets of early life. Next door is the **School House,** furnished as it might have been in the last century. A 10-minute walk along lightly traveled Lindsay Road will bring you to **Hancock Wharf,** next

Finds **Sayward-Wheeler House**

For those who'd like a taste of local history but lack the stamina for the full-court Old York visit, stop by the Sayward-Wheeler House ✶ at 9 Barrett Lane Extension in York Harbor, a rambling 18th-century merchant's home retaining the original furniture and family portraits now run by the Society for the Preservation of New England Antiquities. You'll see china captured during the 1745 Siege of Louisbourg, which routed the French out of Nova Scotia. It's open weekends only, June through October. Tours are given hourly from 11am to 4pm. Admission is $5 for adults, $4 for seniors, and $2.50 for children. For information, call the house (✆ 207/384-2454) or SPNEA's office in New Hampshire at ✆ 603/436-3205.

door to the **George Marshall Store.** Nearby is the **Elizabeth Perkins House,** with its well-preserved Colonial Revival interiors.

The two don't-miss buildings in the society's collection are the intriguing **Old Gaol** and the **Emerson-Wilcox House.** The **Old Gaol** ✶✶, a former jail with now-musty dungeons, was built in 1719 as a jail for criminals and debtors. It is the oldest surviving public building in the United States. Just down the knoll from the jail is the **Emerson-Wilcox House** ✶, built in the mid-1700s and added to periodically over the years. It's a virtual catalog of architectural styles and early decorative arts.

207 York St., York. ✆ 207/363-4974. Admission per building $5 adult, $4 senior, $3 children 3–15; pass to all buildings $10 adult, $7 senior, $5 children 4–15. Children under 4 free. Mon–Sat 10am–5pm; Sun 1–5pm. (Last tour leaves at 4pm.) Closed mid-Oct to mid-June.

TWO WONDERFUL WALKS
Two local strolls will allow visitors to stretch their legs and get the cobwebs out of their heads.

York Harbor and York Village are connected by a quiet pathway that follows a river and passes through gently rustling woodlands. **Fisherman's Walk** ✶ departs from below Edward's Harborside Inn, near the Stage Neck Inn. (There's limited parking at tiny York Harbor Beach.) Follow the pathway along the river, past lobster shacks and along lawns leading up to grand shingled homes. Cross Route 103 and walk over the **Wiggly Bridge** (said to be, not implausibly, the smallest suspension bridge in the world), then head into the woods. You'll soon connect with a dirt lane; follow this and you'll emerge at Lindsay Road near Hancock Wharf (see above). The entire walk is about a mile and, depending on your pace, will take a half-hour to 45 minutes.

Also departing from near York Harbor Beach is the **Cliff Walk** ✶✶, a scenic little trail that follows rugged terrain along rocky bluffs and offers sweeping views of the open ocean as well as glimpses of life in some of the town's grandest cottages. The far end of this trail has been destroyed by ocean waves and has not been rebuilt; you'll have to retrace your steps back to the beach. The pathway remains the subject of recent disputes between the town and landowners seeking to limit access. Check signs for any new restrictions on trespassing before you set off.

Finally, there's the small peninsula ending at an island capped by the scenic **Nubble Light** ★★★ lighthouse. This lighthouse, probably one of the most photographed in the world, is undeniably attractive—and absolutely free to view from the safety of a parking lot set across the swift little inlet that separates it from the mainland. There's little walking to be done, but this is a terrific spot for a picnic; walk a minute uphill to **Brown's Ice Cream** ★★ for some of Maine's best homemade ice cream for dessert. (The lighthouse is lit up for the holiday season around Thanksgiving each year, by the way; if you happen to be here in late November—who knows? it's possible—inquire about the shuttle from Short Sands Beach out to the vantage point.) For information on additional lighthouses see "Lighthouses: A Tour Up the Coast," in the appendix of this guide.

BEACHES

York Beach actually consists of two beaches—**Long Sands Beach** ★★ and **Short Sands Beach**—separated by a rocky headland. Both offer plenty of room for sunning and Frisbees when the tide is out. When the tide is in, they're both narrow and cramped. Short Sands fronts the town of York Beach with its candlepin bowling and video arcades. It's the better bet for families traveling with

---

⟮Tips A Detour to South Berwick

It's not on the tourist map and it's not on or near the coast, but little South Berwick provides a worthwhile detour back into Maine's colonial—and literary—history. Think about taking a few hours to explore it on a day when the raindrops are pelting York Beach.

The two structures of highest note are the late-18th-century **Hamilton House** (② 207/384-2454) at 40 Vaughan's Lane—a solid riverside home with fine gardens and lawns—and its contemporary, the **Sarah Orne Jewett House** at 5 Portland St. (② 207/384-2454), a 1774 Georgian where the noted author lived; her desk overlooks the village's main crossroads. Both homes open to the public June through mid-October, Wednesday to Sunday from 11am to 5pm with hourly tours offered. Admission costs $8 per person for Hamilton House, $5 per person for the Sarah Orne Jewett House.

If you're looking for some nature, drop by one of the area farms or orchards, or take the kids to **Vaughn Woods State Park** (② 207/384-5160), down Old Fields Road just off Route 236 (a bit south of the town center). Set along the quiet Salmon Falls River, the park features picnic areas and a hiking trail through groves of old-growth pine and hemlock. It's open Memorial Day to Labor Day; the admissions fee is $2 per adult, $1 per child age 5 to 11, free for children under 5.

For golfers, the outstanding **The Links at Outlook** golf course (② 207/384-GOLF; www.outlookgolf.com) on Route 4 is a fine, links-style track of bent grass fairways and greens. The greens fees for 18 holes will run you $41 to $48 per person in high summer season, cheaper weekdays, afternoons and in spring and fall.

From York, South Berwick is quickly reached via Route 91 (which shoots west off Rte. 1 just south of the Maine Turnpike interchange for York). It's a ride of about 20 minutes.

kids who have short attention spans. Long Sands runs along Route 1A, across from a profusion of motels, summer homes, and convenience stores. Parking at both beaches is metered in summer (50¢ per hour, quarters only); pay heed, as enforcement is strict and you must pay from 9am until 9pm, 7 days a week.

Public restrooms are available at both beaches; other services, including snacks, are provided by local restaurants and vendors.

WHERE TO STAY

York Beach has a number of motels facing Long Sands Beach. Reserve ahead during high season. Among those with simple accommodations on or near the beach are the **Anchorage Inn** (℃ 207/363-5112) and **Sea Latch** (℃ 800/441-2993 or 207/363-4400).

In Kittery

Portsmouth Harbor Inn and Spa ★★   Now operated by a former Maine tourism official and his wife, this handsome 1899 home is located just across the river from downtown Portsmouth, New Hampshire—about a pleasant, half-mile walk across a drawbridge and the state line from the action. Guests here get a taste of small coastal town life, yet with access to the restaurants and shopping of a small city. The rooms here are tastefully restored and furnished with eclectic antiques, although most are on the small side. But all are boldly furnished and fun—the Valora room has ruby red walls, attractive antiques, and an above average–size bathroom with historic accents; the Royal Gorge is on the third floor and has limited skylight views of the harbor and a cast-iron tub with hand-held shower. The whimsically decorated sitting room downstairs has two couches, where you can sprawl and browse through intriguing and readable books. Breakfasts are flat-out great: They're large and tasty, with fresh-squeezed juice and such selections as corn pancakes with smoked salmon. The spa services are a recent addition, but already quite popular with guests and locals alike; try to book your treatment ahead if you're coming.

6 Water St., Kittery, ME 03904. ℃ 207/439-4040. Fax 207/438-9286. www.innatportsmouth.com. 5 units. May–Oct $139–$209 double; Nov–Apr $99–$139 weekdays, $129–$189 weekends. Rates include full breakfast. 2-night minimum in summer, holidays. MC, V. Children over 16 welcome. **Amenities:** Jacuzzi, spa. *In room:* A/C, dataport, hair dryer.

In The Yorks

Dockside Guest Quarters ★   David and Harriet Lusty established this quiet retreat in 1954, and recent additions (mostly new cottages) haven't changed the friendly, maritime flavor of the place. Situated on an island connected to the mainland by a small bridge, the inn occupies nicely landscaped grounds shady with maples and white pines. Five of the rooms are in the main house, built in 1885, but the bulk of the accommodations are in small, modern town house–style cottages constructed between 1968 and 1998. These are simply furnished, bright, and airy, and most have private decks that overlook the entrance to York Harbor. (Several rooms also feature wood stoves and/or kitchenettes.) The inn also operates a locally popular restaurant on the property, serving traditional New England meals such as broiled halibut, baked stuffed lobster, and braised lamb.

Harris Island (P.O. Box 205), York, ME 03909. ℃ 888/860-7428 or 207/363-2868. Fax 207/363-1977. www.docksidegq.com. 25 units (2 with shared bathroom). Mid-June to early Sept $169–$182 double (from $114 with shared bathroom), $239–$249 suite; early summer and late fall $150–$175 double, $215—$225 suite; winter–spring (open weekends only) $85–$150. 2-night minimum July–Sept. DISC, MC, V. Drive south on Rte. 103 from Rte. 1A in York Harbor; after bridge over York River, turn left and follow signs. **Amenities:** Restaurant; ocean swimming; rowboats; bike rentals; badminton; croquet; laundry service; sundeck; *In room:* AC, kitchenette (some).

Edwards' Harborside Inn ⭐ *Finds* Work your way downhill off Route 1A toward the sprawling Stage Neck Inn, and before you get there you'll stumble across a beautifully kept home right on the water, with a private dock and a lawn whose Adirondack chairs possess wonderfully quaint views of fishing boats. That's Jay Edwards's place. Edwards, who runs the place as his father and grandfather did, is just as likely to be in the kitchen cooking breakfast as he is to be out in the parlor tickling the ivories on the house piano. Ten units vary from simple to elegant (the York Suite is otherwise known as the "Spoil Me Suite," with a tiled Jacuzzi and water views on all sides), but all are lovely and homey with touches such as welcoming chocolates. Add in the fireplace in winter, the hearty hospitality, board games for relaxing, and the splendiferous views from the front rooms, and you've discovered a cozy little place you might never want to leave.

Stage Neck Rd., York Harbor, ME 03911. ✆ **800/273-2686** or 207/363-3037. www.edwardsharborside.com. 10 units (8 with shared bathroom). July–Aug from $180 double (from $120 with shared bathroom), from $270 suite; May–June and Sept–Oct from $130 double (from $70 with shared bathroom), from $210 suite; Nov–Apr from $90 double (from $50 with shared bathroom), from $180 suite. MC, V. Breakfast included with rates. Extra 8% service charge in addition to tax. Holidays and weekends higher. Minimum stay some times of year. *In room:* A/C, Jacuzzi (1 room).

Stage Neck Inn ⭐⭐ Since about 1870, a hotel in one form or another has been housing guests on this windswept bluff located between the harbor and the open ocean. The most recent incarnation was constructed in 1972, and furnished with an understated, country club–like elegance. The hotel, while indisputably up-to-date, successfully creates a sense of old-fashioned intimacy and avoids the overbearing grandeur to which many modern resorts aspire. Almost every room has a view of the water, and guests enjoy low-key recreational pursuits. York Harbor Beach is only steps away. The inn has two dining rooms: the Sandpiper Bar and Grille and Harbor Porches. Both offer three meals daily, as well as terrific views of the sea. Dinner entrees at the more elegant Harbor Porches range from blackened Maine crab cakes to grilled lamb chops. Less formal fare is served at Sandpiper's.

Stage Neck (P.O. Box 70), York Harbor, ME 03911. ✆ **800/340-1130** or 207/363-3850. www.stageneck.com. 58 units. Mid-May to Labor Day $235–$275 double; spring $165—$200 double; fall $185–$255 double; winter $135–$185 double. Ask about off-season packages. AE, DISC, MC, V. Head north on 1A from Rte. 1; make 2nd right after York Harbor post office. **Amenities:** 2 restaurants; indoor and outdoor pools; ocean swimming; tennis courts; fitness room; Jacuzzi, sauna. *In room:* A/C, VCR, CD player.

Union Bluff Hotel ⭐ With its stumpy turrets, dormers, and prominent porches, the Union Bluff has the look of an old-fashioned beach hotel. So it's a bit of a surprise to learn that it was built in 1989 (the fifth hotel to rise on this site since the late 1800s). Inside is a generic-modern building; rooms have oak furniture, wall-to-wall carpeting, and small refrigerators. There's a comfortable and quiet deck on the top floor for getting away from it all (alas, no ocean view). Step outside and you're virtually at the beach and the Fun-O-Rama arcade with its candlepin bowling and banks of video games. (It can be noisy in the evening if your room faces this direction.) Twenty-one rooms are located in a motel annex next door, and the rooms here are also simply furnished. Stick to the main inn for better views; the best rooms are the suites on the top floor, which offer beach vistas from sitting areas within the turrets. There's also a lounge and a restaurant, both of which are open daily during the warmer months (weekends only in the off-season). The restaurant features mostly traditional New England fare, like clam chowder and steamers, along with baked haddock, prime rib, and a number of pasta selections.

Fun Fact **One of a kind**

Maine is the only state in the U.S. that borders only one other state (New Hampshire).

Beach St. (at the N end of Short Sands Beach), York Beach, ME 03910. ©️ **800/833-0721** or 207/363-1333. www.unionbluff.com. 61 units. Summer $129–$209 double, $189–$279 suite; late spring and early fall $59–$159, $129–$209 suite; spring, late fall, and winter $49–$129 double, $99–$189 suite. AE, DISC, MC, V. **Amenities:** Restaurant; lounge. *In room:* A/C, some refrigerators.

WHERE TO DINE
In Kittery

Bob's Clam Hut *Value* FRIED FISH   Operating since 1956, Bob's manages to retain an old-fashioned flavor—despite now being surrounded by slick new factory outlet malls—while serving up heaps of fried clams and other diet-busting enticements with great efficiency. (From Bob's brochure: "Our suppliers marvel at the amount of Fryolator oil we order.") Order at the front window, get a soda from a vending machine, then stake out a table inside or on the deck (with a Rte. 1 view) while waiting for your number to be called. The food is surprisingly light, cooked in cholesterol-free vegetable oil; the onion rings are especially good. To ensure that your diet plans have been irrevocably violated, Bob's also offers Ben & Jerry's ice cream.

Kittery. ©️ **207/439-4233.** Reservations not accepted. Sandwiches $1.50–$3.95; dinners $3.95–$18. AE, MC, V. Daily Memorial Day to Labor Day 11am–9pm; closing times vary in off-season, call ahead. Located just N of the Kittery Trading Post.

Chauncey Creek Lobster Pier ★★ *Finds* LOBSTER   It's not on the wild, open ocean, but Chauncey's remains one of the most scenic lobster pounds in the state, not the least because the Spinney family, which has been selling lobsters here since the 1950s, takes such pride in their place. You reach the pound by walking down a wooden ramp to a broad deck on a tidal inlet, where some 42 festively painted picnic tables await. Lobster, served hot and fresh, is the specialty, of course, but they also serve steamed mussels (in wine and garlic) and clams. This place is a la carte—buy a crock of baked beans and sodas and a bag of ice while waiting for your lobsters to cook. Want a drink? BYOB. In fact, feel free to bring along your own cooler full of beer, wine, soda, chips, watermelon, and what-have-you. Everyone else does.

Kittery Point. ©️ **207/439-1030.** No reservations. Lobsters priced to market; other items $1.50–$8.95. MC, V. Daily 11am–8pm (until 7pm during shoulder seasons). Closed Mon after Labor Day and Columbus Day to Mother's Day. Located between Kittery Point and York on Rte. 103; watch for signs.

IN THE YORKS

Goldenrod Restaurant *Kids* TRADITIONAL AMERICAN   This beach-town classic is *the* place for local color—it has been a summer institution in York Beach since it first opened in 1896. It's easy to find: Look for visitors gawking through plate-glass windows at the ancient taffy machines hypnotically churning out taffy in volumes enough (9 million candies a year) to make busloads of dentists very wealthy. The restaurant is behind the taffy and fudge operation and is low on frills and long on atmosphere. Diners sit on stout oak furniture around a stone fireplace, or at the antique soda fountain. There are dark beams overhead and the sort of linoleum floor you don't see much anymore. Breakfast offerings are the standards (omelets, waffles, griddle cakes, and bakery items). Lunch features

Packing a Picnic

In York, the best place for a picnic is on the beach—any of them. **Long Sands** (p. 72) and **Short Sands** (p. 72) are best; the former has views of a lighthouse and boats far out to sea, the latter is more compact, and surrounded by quaintly appealing arcades, hotels, and grand summer homes. Parking can be tight at both—and tickets are written with regularity. Bring lots of quarters.

Speaking of that lighthouse, **Nubble Light** (p. 72) is hard to beat for the quintessential Maine postcard-view picnic. Reach it from Long Sands. If you need sweets, stock up at **The Goldenrod** (p. 75), a real live working candy shop just a block off Short Sands beach. For a bite, I like the Long **Sands General Store** (© **206/363-5383** near the northern end of Long Sands beach, with pizzas, sandwiches, and other essential picnicking supplies.

traditional American fare: soups, club sandwiches, milkshakes, burgers, hot dogs, and somewhat overpriced sandwiches. But what saves the place is that outstanding candy counter, where you watch the taffy being stretched and then buy boxfuls of it as souvenirs for envious neighbors back home. The almond-studded "birch barks" are mighty good, too; I've been eating the dark-chocolate version (you can also get milk-chocolate and white-chocolate incarnations) for approximately 3 decades running now. As for dinner, you'd be better served heading somewhere more creative—just don't forget to first grab a sampler bag of taffy or some raspberry-chocolate malted milk balls for dessert.

Railroad Rd. and Ocean Ave., York Beach. © **207/363-2621**. www.thegoldenrod.com. Breakfast $2.65–$5.25; lunch and dinner entrees $2.75–$7.50. MC, V. Memorial Day to Labor Day daily 8am–10pm (until 9pm in June); Labor Day to Columbus Day Wed–Sun 8am–3pm. Closed Columbus Day to Memorial Day.

Lobster Cove *(Value* SEAFOOD/FAMILY-STYLE   Set right across the street from the pounding Atlantic, dependable Lobster Cove is a good choice when you don't wish to stray from the beach for lunch or dinner. Breakfast consists of standard, though surprisingly inexpensive, choices like omelets, pancakes, and eggs Benedict. Lunch runs to burgers and sandwiches, but I prefer dinner, when a standard shore dinner of lobster, corn on the cob, clam chowder, and steamed clams is hefty and good. The lobster pie is an old-fashioned New England favorite (if a little heavy on the bread crumbs). The Captain's Platter is a selection of fried seafood. They also do lobster rolls, clam rolls, and traditional Maine desserts like wild blueberry pie, tollhouse cookie pie, and warm bread pudding with whiskey sauce. The bar whips up fun drinks and pours good local drafts, albeit in plastic cups if you order from the dining room. Both the regular dining room and an outdoor terrace provide outstanding beach and lighthouse views; service, though, is young and a bit erratic.

756 York St., York (south end of Long Sands Beach). © **207/351-1100**. Breakfast items $2–$6, main courses $6–$8. AE, MC, V. Daily 7:30am–9pm.

Stonewall Kitchen Café CAFE   Stonewall Kitchen's York-based gourmet foods operation has taken a step to the front with this cafe, smartly located in its York headquarters/store and just beside the local tourist information office. The café features simple, hearty meals of fish chowder, French onion soup, crispy duck confit with Damson plum and a balsamic glaze, pan-seared salmon with a sun-dried tomato and olive relish or a grapefruit beurre blanc sauce, chicken pot pie, steak fries, burgers, panini (including one of meatloaf), and sandwiches. Finish with a dessert such as toasted coconut crème brûlée, flourless chocolate torte, lemon sorbet, or house-made chai ice cream topped with bittersweet chocolate sauce. The kitchen also prepares gourmet meals to go, serves a variety of delicious brunch items on Sunday, and stocks a surprisingly deep wine list. Still hungry? Stock up on jams, jellies, and sauces at the adjacent retail store.

Stonewall Lane, York. © 207/351-2719. www.stonewallkitchen.com. Entrees $8–$14. AE, DC, DISC, MC, V. Mon–Sat takeout 8am–6pm, lunch 11am–3pm; Sun takeout 9am–6pm, brunch 10am–3pm.

2 Ogunquit

Ogunquit is 15 miles NE of Kittery.

Ogunquit is a bustling beachside town that has attracted vacationers and artists for well over a century. While notable for its elegant summer resort architecture, Ogunquit is most famous for its 3½-mile white-sand beach, which is backed by grassy dunes. The beach serves as the town's front porch, and everyone drifts over there at least once a day when the sun is shining.

Ogunquit's fame as an art colony dates from around 1890, when Charles H. Woodbury arrived and declared the place an "artist's paradise." He was followed by artists such as Walt Kuhn, Elihu Vedder, Yasuo Kuniyoshi, and Rudolph Dirks.

In the latter decades of the 19th century, the town also found quiet fame as a destination for gay travelers, at a time when one's sexual orientation was not publicly acknowledged. Ogunquit has retained its appeal for gays through the years. The scene here is very low-key compared to Provincetown, Massachusetts—it's more like an understated family resort, where a good many family members just happen to be gay.

Despite the architectural gentility and the overall civility of the place, the town is overrun with tourists during the peak summer season, especially on weekends. The teeming crowds are part of the allure for some Ogunquit regulars. If you're not a crowd person, you would do well to visit here in the off-season.

Those hoping to avoid the close company of others might consider other destinations along the coast, or at the least come early or late in the season. If you arrive early in the morning, you can hike a bit and stake out one of the more remote sections of the town's famous beach, which is long enough to allow most of the teeming masses to disperse. There's even something to do here in autumn. A new pre-Halloween festival in late October, the Ogunquit Fest, offers 3 days of arts, crafts, costumes, and a parade; it's best for families with kids. Call © 207/646-2939 for more information.

ESSENTIALS
GETTING THERE
Ogunquit is located on Route 1 between York and Wells. It's accessible from either Exit 1 or Exit 2 of the Maine Turnpike.

VISITOR INFORMATION
The **Ogunquit Welcome Center,** P.O. Box 2289, Ogunquit, ME 03907 (© 207/646-2939; www.ogunquit.org), is on Route 1 south of the village center. It's open daily 9am to 5pm Memorial Day to Columbus Day (until 8pm weekends during

> **Tips   Trolley Ho!**
>
> A number of trackless "trolleys" (© **207/646-1411**)—actually buses—with names like Dolly and Ollie (you get the idea) run all day from mid-May to Columbus Day between Perkins Cove and the Wells town line to the north, with detours to the sea down Beach and Ocean streets. A day pass costs $5 per adult, $3 per child under 10, though it might be worth the expense to avoid driving and parking hassles.

the peak summer season), and Monday to Saturday during the off-season—and it has restrooms.

GETTING AROUND

The village of Ogunquit is centered around an awkward three-way intersection that seems fiendishly designed to cause massive traffic foul-ups during the summer. Parking in and around the village is also tight and relatively expensive (expect to pay $6 or more per day). As a result, Ogunquit is best explored on foot or by bike.

EXPLORING OGUNQUIT

The village center is good for an hour or two of browsing among the boutiques or sipping a cappuccino at one of the several coffee emporia.

From the village, you can walk a mile to scenic Perkins Cove along **Marginal Way** ★★, a mile-long ocean-side pathway once used for herding cattle to pasture. Earlier in this century, the land was bought by a local developer who deeded the right-of-way to the town. The pathway, which is wide and well-maintained, departs across from the Seacastles Resort on Shore Road. It passes tide pools, pocket beaches, and rocky, fissured bluffs, all of which are worth exploring. The seascape can be spectacular (especially after a storm), but Marginal Way can also be spectacularly crowded during fair-weather weekends. To elude the crowds, we recommend heading out in the very early morning.

Perkins Cove ★★, accessible either from Marginal Way or by driving south on Shore Road and veering left at the Y intersection, is a small, well-protected harbor that seems custom-designed for photos. As such, it attracts visitors by the busload, carload, and boatload, and is often heavily congested. A handful of galleries, restaurants, and T-shirt shops catering to the tourist trade occupy a cluster of quaint buildings between the harbor and the sea. An intriguing pedestrian drawbridge is operated by whoever happens to be handy, allowing sailboats to come and go. (*Warning:* If crowds of tourists make you unpleasantly edgy, steer well clear of Perkins Cove.)

Excursions Coastal Maine Outfitting Co., Route 1, Cape Neddick (© **207/ 363-0181;** www.excursionsinmaine.com), offers half-day ($55–$60) and multiday sea-kayaking tours along area rivers near the coast. For more dramatic paddling, ask about sunrise, sunset, and full-moon kayaking trips. Excursions is located on Route 1 approximately 4 miles north of Exit 1 on I-95.

Perkins Cove is also home to a handful of deep-sea fishing and tour-boat operators who offer trips of various durations. The *Deborah Ann* (© **207/361-9501**) chugs some 25 miles offshore twice daily in summer (once daily in the shoulder seasons) in search of whales, usually of the humpback, minke, and finback variety. There are two 4½-hour tours daily from mid-June to mid-October ($40 for adults,

$25 for children, and $35 for seniors) For deep-sea fishing, the *Ugly Anne* ((C) 207/ 646-7202) runs half- and full-day trips for up to 35 passengers between April and November. The fare is $45 for a half-day trip, $60 for a full-day trip; reservations are encouraged.

Not far from the cove is The **Ogunquit Museum of American Art** ★★★, 543 Shore Rd. ((C) **207/646-4909;** www.ogunquitmuseum.org), one of the best small art museums in the nation. Set back from the road in a grassy glen overlooking the rocky shore, the museum's spectacular view initially overwhelms the artwork as visitors walk through the door. But stick around a few minutes—the changing exhibits in this architecturally engaging modern building of cement block, slate, and glass will get your attention soon enough, since the curators have a track record of staging superb shows and attracting national attention. (Be sure to note the bold, underappreciated work of Henry Strater, the Ogunquit artist who founded the museum in 1953.) A 1,400-square-foot wing opened in 1996, adding welcome new exhibition space. The museum is open July 1 to October 15 from 10:30am to 5pm Monday to Saturday, and 2 to 5pm on Sunday. Admission is $5 for adults, $4 for seniors, and $3 for students; children under 12 are free.

For evening entertainment, head to the **Ogunquit Playhouse** ★, Route 1 ((C) **207/646-5511**), a 750-seat summer stock theater that has garnered a solid reputation for its careful, serious attention to stagecraft. The theater has entertained Ogunquit since 1933, attracting noted actors such as Bette Davis, Tallulah Bankhead, and Gary Merrill. Tickets generally cost $29 to $45 per person.

Another evening alternative is the **Booth Theatre,** at the Betty Doon Motor Hotel, Village Square ((C) **207/646-8142**), which bills itself, somewhat peckishly, as "Ogunquit's true repertory summer theater." Summer season runs for 11 weeks; each Sunday night features a magic show. Recent shows have included favorites such as *Snoopy* and *Kiss Me Kate*. Tickets are generally $10 to $15.

BEACHES

Ogunquit's **main beach** is more than 3 miles long, and its width varies with the tides. There are three paid parking lots (around $2 per hr.) along its length. The most popular access point is at the foot of Beach Street, which connects to

---

Moments **Doing Doughnuts in Wells**

While cruising the Wells-Ogunquit axis, you *must* experience **Congdon's Doughnuts Family Restaurant & Bakery** ★★, 1090 Post Rd. (Rte. 1), (C) **207/ 646-4219.** Clint and Dot "Nana" Congdon of New Hampshire moved to the Maine coast and opened a family-style restaurant in 1945. Nana's sinkers proved so popular she relocated the operation to Wells ten years later and went into the doughnut business full-time. These are some of New England's best. Chocolate-chocolate is ever-popular, but you can't go wrong with almost anything else among three dozen choices—a pillowy raised doughnut, a filled blueberry, a butter crunch, a honey-dip, a sugar twist, a chocolate honey, or one of the seasonal specials, such as maple, apple, or pumpkin. You can also get diner-style meals here, mostly fried food and breakfast fare. The shop recently added a drive-through window, but retains its original character (and that includes the characters dining inside). Yes, they use lard. You have been warned. Open daily except Tuesday, from 6am to 2pm.

Ogunquit Village. The beach ends at a sandy spit, where the Ogunquit River flows into the sea; facilities here include changing rooms, bathrooms, and a handful of informal restaurants. It's also the most crowded part of the beach. Less congested options are at **Footbridge Beach** (turn on Ocean Ave. off Rte. 1 north of the village center) and **Moody Beach** (turn on Eldridge Ave. in Wells). Restrooms are maintained at all three beaches.

A ROAD TRIP TO LAUDHOLM FARM

A short drive north of Ogunquit, just above the beach town of Wells, is **Laudholm Farm** ★★ (© 207/646-4521), a historic saltwater farm owned by the nonprofit Laudholm Trust since 1986. The 1,600-acre property was originally the summer home of 19th-century railroad baron George Lord, but is now used for estuarine research. The farm has 7 miles of trails through diverse ecosystems, which range from salt marsh to forest to dunes. A visitor center in the regal Victorian farmhouse will get you oriented. Tours are available, or you can explore the grounds on your own. Parking costs $2 per adult ($10 per car maximum) daily in summer and on spring weekends; it's by donation the rest of the year. There's no admission charge to the grounds or visitor center. The trails are open daily from 7am to dusk; the visitor center is open 10am to 4pm Monday to Saturday, and noon to 4pm on Sunday (closed weekends in the off-season, also closed mid-Dec to mid-Jan).

The farm is reached by turning east from Route 1 on Laudholm Farm Road at the blinking light just north of Harding Books. Bear left at the fork, then turn right into the farm's entrance.

WHERE TO STAY

Just a few steps from Ogunquit's main downtown intersection is the meticulously maintained **Studio East Motel,** 267 Main St. (© 207/646-7297). It's open April to mid-November, with peak-season rates running $119 to $149 double. The rooms are basic, but all have refrigerators, telephones, and televisions, and there are a few two-bedroom suites for $20 to $30 more per night. Microwaves are available for free to those staying 3 nights or more.

Above Tide Inn ★   This nicely-sited inn rises from where a lobster shack once stood . . . until a 1978 blizzard took it to sea. That fact (and the inn's name) should suggest its great location—on a lazy tidal river between town and the main beach, which is an easy stroll away. It's right by the start of Marginal Way, the town's popular walking path. The location's a good thing, as the rooms are a bit smaller and darker than one might hope for during a beach vacation. If the weather's good, you're in luck—each room has its own outdoor sitting area, most located off the room (though two tables are reserved on the front deck for guests in the two back rooms that don't face the water). Room 1 is my favorite, thanks to its view of the river. The building could be more solidly constructed, but children aren't permitted here, so noise shouldn't be much of an issue.

66 Beach St. Ogunquit, ME 03907. © 207/646-7454. www.abovetideinn.com. 9 units. Peak season $145–$210 double; off-season from $110. Rates include continental breakfast. MC, V. 3-night minimum stay in summer. No children. Closed Columbus Day to mid-May. *In room:* A/C, TV, fridge, no phone.

Beachmere Inn ★   Run by the same family since 1937, the Beachmere Inn sprawls across a grassy hillside (the inn occupies about 4 acres) and nearly every room has a view northward up Ogunquit's famous beach. Guests choose from two buildings on the main grounds. The Beachmere Victorian dates from the 1890s and is all turrets and porches; two rooms have fireplaces. Next door is the

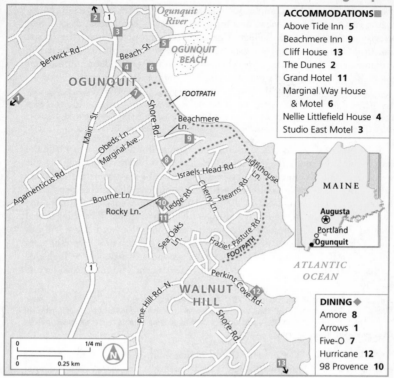

ACCOMMODATIONS ■
Above Tide Inn **5**
Beachmere Inn **9**
Cliff House **13**
The Dunes **2**
Grand Hotel **11**
Marginal Way House
  & Motel **6**
Nellie Littlefield House **4**
Studio East Motel **3**

DINING ◆
Amore **8**
Arrows **1**
Five-O **7**
Hurricane **12**
98 Provence **10**

midcentury modern Beachmere South, a two-story motel-like structure designed in 1960s style, featuring concrete slathered with a stucco finish. The rooms at Beachmere South are spacious (some are minisuites, and these rooms cost more), interestingly angled, and all have private balconies or patios and great views. The inn is located on Marginal Way, which is great for walks and offers foot access to the beach. When rooms in the two main buildings are filled, guests are offered rooms in the cottages nearby; rates in these vary. The five units are darker, lack views, and are less impressively furnished, but they are spacious and appropriate for families. Larger families or groups of friends traveling together should ask about Hearthstone, an elegant cottage with fireplace and barbecue shelter a short walk from the inn.

Beachmere Rd., Ogunquit, ME 03907. ℂ **800/336-3983** or 207/646-2021. Fax 207/646-2231. www.beachmere inn.com. 53 units. Peak season $100–$250 double; midseason $75–$185 double; off-season $65–$130 double. Cottage $175–$360. Rates include continental breakfast. 3-night minimum in summer. AE, DC, DISC, MC, V. Closed mid-Dec to Apr 1. **Amenities:** Beach access. *In room:* A/C, kitchenette (some), fireplace (some), balcony/ patio (some).

Cliff House Resort and Spa ⭐   The Cliff House was for many years a favored old-money seaside resort in these parts, with classic architecture topping a scenic rise and a turn-back-the-clock feel. Progress has apparently caught up with the old place, however, because the attractive Victorian building was recently demolished and replaced with a rather characterless (okay, ugly) set of modern structures. The complex includes a number of different styles of rooms, many with stunning sea views and most with modern comforts such as digital televisions, recliners, and the like. A new and highly touted state-of-the-art spa and fitness facility dispenses a wide range of soothing treatments and exercise programs (ask about package deals); there are also several indoor and outdoor pools. If you're coming in summer, there's a 3-night minimum stay.

Shore Rd. (P.O. Box 2274), Ogunquit, ME 03907. ✆ **207/361-1000.** Fax 207/361-2122. www.cliffhousemaine. com. 200 units. Mid-Mar to June and Sept–Dec $155–$255 double; July–Aug $230–$310 double. Meal plans also available. 3-night minimum during holidays and July–Aug, 2-night minimum most weekends. AE, DISC, MC, V. Closed early Jan to late Mar. **Amenities:** Fitness center, spa. *In room:* A/C, TV, hair dryer.

The Dunes ⭐⭐   This classic motor court (built around 1936) has made the transition to the modern age more gracefully than any other vintage motel I've seen. With one six-unit motel-like building, most of the rooms are found in gabled cottages, all white clapboard with green shutters. The kitchens and bathrooms have all been updated in the past 10 years, but plenty of old-fashioned charm remains in many of the units, with vintage maple furnishings, oval braided rugs, maple floors, knotty pine paneling, and louvered doors. All but one of the cottages has a wood-burning fireplace. It's set on 12 peaceful acres (away from Rte. 1) with Adirondack chairs overlooking a lagoon; at high tide guests can borrow a rowboat to get across to the beach. The cottages all feature full kitchens.

518 U.S. Rte. 1, Ogunquit, ME 03907. ✆ **207/646-2612.** www.dunesmotel.com. 36 units. Peak season $160–$285; off-season $120–$225. MC, V. July–Aug 1-week minimum stay in cottages; 3-night minimum stay in motel. Closed late Oct to late Apr. **Amenities:** Outdoor pool; watersports equipment rental. *In room:* A/C, TV, dataport, fridge, coffeemaker.

Grand Hotel ⭐   The modern Grand Hotel, built in 1990, seems a bit ill at ease in Victorian Ogunquit; frankly, it's a bit jarring at first glance. But the hotel centers on a three-story atrium and consists of 28 two-room suites. All rooms have refrigerators and VCRs (tapes available for rent). The modern, tidy guest rooms have a generic, chain-hotel character, and each has a private deck from which to enjoy the Maine air (no ocean views). The five top-floor penthouses are airy and bright, with cathedral ceilings and Duraflame-log fireplaces. The hotel is located on busy Shore Road and is about a 10-minute walk to the beach. Other nice touches: Parking (one car per party) is underground and connected to the rooms by elevator, and there's a small indoor pool.

276 Shore Rd. (P.O. Box 1526), Ogunquit, ME 03907. ✆ **800/806-1231** or 207/646-1231. www.thegrandhotel. com. 28 suites. Late June to early Sept $145–$230 double; Apr–June and Sept–Nov $70–$210. Rates include continental breakfast. 2- or 3-night minimum on weekends and peak season. AE, DISC, MC, V. Underground parking. Closed early Nov to early Apr. **Amenities:** Indoor pool; video rental. *In room:* A/C, VCR, refrigerators, some fireplaces.

Marginal Way House and Motel ⭐   This old-fashioned, nothing-fancy compound centers on a four-story, mid-19th-century guest house with summery, basic rooms that feature white-painted furniture. Room 7 is among the best, with a private porch and canopy and an ocean view. The guest house is surrounded by four contemporary buildings, which lack charm and feature motel-style rooms yet are generally comfortable and bright. The whole affair is situated on a large, grassy lot on a quiet cul-de-sac. It's hard to believe that you're smack in the middle of Ogunquit, with both the beach and the village just a few minutes' walk away. All rooms have refrigerators; one- and two-bedroom efficiencies are available for longer stays.

Wharf Lane (P.O. Box 697), Ogunquit, ME 03907. ℭ 207/646-8801. www.marginalwayhouse.com. 30 units (1 with private bathroom down hall). Mid-June to early Sept $114–$187 double; shoulder seasons $49–$139 double. Minimum stay requirements on some weekends. MC, V. Closed mid-Oct to mid-Apr. Pets allowed off-season; advance notice required. *In room:* A/C, refrigerator, some balconies.

Nellie Littlefield House ★★   This 1889 home stands impressively at the edge of Ogunquit's compact commercial district. This prime location and the handsome Queen Anne architecture are the main draws here. All of the rooms are carpeted and feature a mix of modern and antique reproduction furnishings; several have refrigerators. Four rooms to the rear have private decks, but views are limited—mostly to the unlovely motel next door. The most spacious room is the third-floor J. H. Littlefield suite, with two TVs and a Jacuzzi. The most unique? The circular Grace Littlefield room, located in the upper turret and overlooking the street. The basement features a compact fitness room with modern equipment.

27 Shore Rd., Ogunquit, ME 03907. ℭ 207/646-1692. www.visit-maine.com/nellielittlefieldhouse. 8 units. July to Labor Day $165–$220 double; Memorial Day to June, Labor Day to Columbus Day $95–$170 double; Late Apr, May, and late Oct $85–$140 double. Rates include full breakfast. 2-night minimum weekends, 3 nights on holidays. DISC, MC, V. Closed late Oct to late Apr. Children over 12 are welcome. **Amenities:** Fitness center. *In room:* A/C, TV.

WHERE TO DINE

For breakfasts in Ogunquit, it's hard to beat **Amore** (178 Shore Rd. ℭ **207/ 646-6661**). This isn't the place for dainty pickers and waist-watchers, but hey . . . you're on vacation. Look for numerous variations on the eggs Benedict theme, along with Belgian waffles, bananas Foster, and more than a dozen types of omelets. Breakfast is served daily until 1pm.

Arrows ★★★ NEW AMERICAN   When owner/chefs Mark Gaier and Clark Frasier opened Arrows in 1988, they quickly put Ogunquit on the national culinary map. They've done so not only by creating an elegant and intimate atmosphere, but by serving up some of the freshest, most innovative cooking in New England. The emphasis is on local products—often very local. The salad greens are grown in gardens on the grounds, and much of the rest is produced or raised locally. The food transcends traditional New England fare and is deftly prepared with exotic twists and turns. The menu changes nightly, but among the more popular recurring appetizers is the homemade prosciutto—hams are hung in the restaurant to cure in the off-season. Entrees might include wild salmon in four preparations (including a portion steamed with pine needles); a pair of roasted quail with preserved lemon; a plate of six pastas, six cheeses and six herbs; grilled Maine lobster tail with crispy shallots, lime leaf-cilantro vinaigrette and coconut "jello." The wine list is top-rate. The prices are not for the faint-hearted, but committed foodies will find an evening here memorable. Note that there is a moderate dress code: jacket preferred for men, no shorts allowed.

Berwick Rd. ℭ 207/361-1100. www.arrowsrestaurant.com. Reservations strongly recommended. Main courses $40–$43; tasting menu $95. MC, V. Generally open Apr to mid-Dec 6–9:30pm. Days of the week that Arrows is open vary widely. We strongly recommend you call ahead for specifics. Closed mid-Dec to Mar. Turn uphill at the Key Bank in the village; the restaurant is 2 miles on your right.

Five-O ★ NEW AMERICAN   A fine choice if you're looking for a more casual alternative to the two more formal restaurants listed here, Five-O is one of those spots where just reading the menu offers a decent evening's entertainment. Much of the fare is tropical inspired, such as scallops with vanilla and dark rum sauce and halibut with plantains and Caribbean spices.

The Diner Denizen: Eating Like a Local . . . At 1940s Prices

One thing you'll notice as you traverse the Maine coast is a preponderance of diners.

What gives? This isn't New Jersey, after all, yet the humble diner remains as much a culinary staple of coastal Maine as the lobster shack—probably more so, in fact. Locals congregate daily in their coffee klatches on the diner stools; expect a steady stream of hunting caps, thick accents, doughnuts and eggs, and Red Sox or Patriots talk (depending on the season). You'd do well to sample one or two of them while on the road; here are a few that are easily reached if you're taking Route 1.

From the New Hampshire state line, heading north, your first opportunity on Route 1 comes rather quickly, near the town line that separates York and Kittery (a few miles north of the Kittery outlets). The **Line House** (© 207/439-3401) has been serving heralded fried clams and other local favorites in this location since 1945, and remains a steady favorite among locals.

Heading north from York to Ogunquit along Route 1, you could easily blow right by the reddish-hut icon that is **Flo's Steamed Hot Dogs** (no phone) in Cape Neddick—it's a couple of miles north of York, in the middle of nowhere, at a bend in the road—without noticing. But if you crave a winner of a wiener, screech to a halt in the dirt parking lot and give it a whirl. You'll probably wait in the line, which resembles an assembly line: The steamed dogs here are cheap and good, but they can only do them 50 at a time. If your dog is number 51, bring a paperback. There are only six seats inside, so you'll probably have to eat in the car. Go anyway. And get your dogs with Flo's special sauce.

A little farther north, also on Route 1 but in Wells, the **Maine Diner** (© 207/646-4441) is a classic, though perhaps getting a little too famous for its own good. (They'll page you when a table is ready. How retro is that? Not retro enough.) But worry not. The lobster pie and hot lobster roll are still famous and delicious, as is a plate of baked scallops. Red flannel hash? Pot roast? They've got it—as well as the "clam-o-rama," a sampler of clam items. Very unusually, they serve wine and beer here, too.

Set on a pedestal and surrounded by a small screen of trees, the red little **Palace Diner** (© 207/283-8462) is smack in the middle of downtown Biddeford but a bit hard to find. This 1920s-model dining car was hauled up here in 1927 by none other than Louis Pollard, he of the famous Pollard family diner-manufacturing company in Lowell, Massachusetts.

---

50 Shore Rd. © 207/646-5001. Reservations recommended in summer. Main courses $17–$29. AE, DISC, MC, V. Daily 5–10pm.

Hurricane ★★★ NEW AMERICAN   Tucked away amid the T-shirt kitsch of Perkins Cove is one of southern Maine's classiest and most enjoyable dining experiences. The plain-shingled exterior of the building, set along a curving, narrow lane, doesn't hint at what you'll find inside. The narrow dining room is divided

Today it is Maine's oldest surviving diner, serving reliable eggs, burgers, and daily specials heavy on the gravy. Find it at 18 Franklin St., between Washington and Main streets.

On Route 1 in Scarborough, a new **Bintliff's Diner** (© 207/885-1523) is the new offshoot from a slightly fancy diner/burger joint in Portland. It's geared more to younger folks who want to eat updated comfort food, rather than to old-time Mainers who'd be happy to eat liver and onions and black coffee for breakfast. As a result, some of the food here is a bit too prettied up—lobster ravioli? wine? Caesar salad?—but the times are a'changing, and these nouveau diners are beginning to find a niche. And you can get very good pancakes here.

In a low-slung, red-and-neon, Worcester-style car on outer Pleasant Street (Rte. 1) as you approach downtown Brunswick, the **Miss Brunswick Diner** (© 207/729-5948) doesn't deserve the highest marks for its food. But it does retain the atmosphere and pricing of a bygone era.

On Route 1 as you roll downhill into the tiny center of pretty Wiscasset, the **Miss Wiscasset Diner** (© 207/882-9272) is a beat-up shack of a place—and the handwritten sign has seen better days, too. But it's a winner, serving the usual breakfasts, chowders, burgers, and fried seafood.

An entire book could be written about little **Moody's Diner** (© 207/832-7785) in Waldoboro—in fact, it has. This is *the* place to stop on Route 1 when traversing north toward Acadia and points beyond. From the sublime cream pies to the only-in-Maine specials (boiled dinner on Thurs; haddock with egg sauce on Fri; and, of course, baked beans on Sat), the place simply serves food you can find almost nowhere else in the state. The old food ways are disappearing that fast. Finish with Indian pudding or one of those mile-high pies—walnut cream and rhubarb are two good choices, though any of them will satisfy. The prices, too, seem nearly locked in 1948, when Moody's opened.

Finally, way farther Down East, I'd be remiss if I didn't mention the two **Helen's** restaurants, one on Route 1 in Ellsworth just north of the Route 3 split (© 207/667-2433) and one on Main Street in downtown Machias (© 207/255-8423). Though neither eatery is strictly speaking a diner, these Helen's serves up some of the very best home-cooked meals and pies in all of the great state o'Maine, in fine old diner tradition. Look for seasonal specials like turkey with the fixins, pork with fiddleheads, or just order a piece of the marvelous seasonal blueberry, strawberry, chocolate cream, and other pies.

into two smallish halves, but soaring windows overlooking the Gulf of Maine create a sense that this place is larger than it actually is. At lunch, look for a variety of grilled fish and burgers. The dinner menu changes daily, and owner Brooks MacDonald is known for his consistently creative concoctions, beginning with a raft of small-plate appetizers and continuing on to entrees such as a wonderful lobster cioppino (his signature dish), roasted chicken with cheddar biscuits,

---

Tips **Borealis Bread**

A good spot for bread and snacks in southern Maine is **Borealis Breads** (© **207/641-8800**) on Route 1 in a strip mall just north of the turnoff to Wells Beach, between Ogunquit and Kennebunkport. You'll find a good selection of hearty, warm-from-the-oven breads, along with sandwiches, Maine specialties such as dilly beans, and regular and almond macaroons. It's a great pit stop before an afternoon on the beach.

---

cumin-encrusted pork chops with molé sauce, herb-encrusted venison, or fire-roasted Alaskan king salmon with sautéed beets in lemon butter. Nightly desserts could include a milk chocolate crème brûlée, a strawberry-lavender Napoleon, or a raspberry-lemon-verbena panna cotta. Added bonus: Hurricane makes the best martini in town.

111 Perkins Cove Rd. © 800/649-6348 (Maine and New Hampshire only) or 207/646-6348. www.perkins cove.com. Reservations recommended for either lunch or dinner. Lunch items $8–$16; main dinner courses $18–$32; lobster dishes priced daily (to $39). AE, DC, DISC, MC, V. May–Oct daily 11:30am–3:30pm, 5:30–10:30pm; Nov–Apr daily 5:30–9:30pm. Closed briefly in Jan (call ahead).

98 Provence *★★* BISTRO Candlelight reflects off the warm wood interior and infuses the surroundings with a romantic glow; tables are covered with two layers of Provençal-style linens, lace curtains drape the windows, and diners eat off colorful china. 98 Provence is charming, if a bit on the precious side. The decor almost, but not quite, distracts one from the delicious food. Chef Pierre Gignac relies on fresh, local ingredients to create such dishes as terrine of lobster delicately flavored with mandarin orange. The menu changes thrice yearly to reflect the seasons. You might start with the seared duck foie gras with cheese buccatini, green peas, and morel mushrooms, scallops seared in Basque pepper, lobster poached in cream with morels and asparagus, a fisherman's soup—or just simple, fresh Nova Scotia mussels. Entrees wander the barnyard, from rabbit to cassoulet to lamb in puff pastry; potential offerings could include veal mignon wrapped in smoked bacon; slow-braised lamb shank *tagine* with plums, arti-chokes and couscous; stewed rabbit daube with porcini, country olives, and papardelle; and a beef filet roasted in a pine crust with prosciutto and sage demiglace. The roasted venison is quite popular; in fall, it's prepared with stuffed pumpkin and dried fruits.

262 Shore Rd. © 207/646-9898. www.98provence.com. Reservations recommended. Main courses $24–$31, *table d'hôte* (appetizer, main course, and dessert) $32. AE, MC, V. Summer Wed–Mon 5:30–9:30pm; off-season Thurs–Mon 5:30–9pm.

3 The Kennebunks *★★*

The Kennebunks are 10 miles NE of Ogunquit.

"The Kennebunks" consist of the villages of Kennebunk and Kennebunkport, both situated along the shores of small rivers. The region was first settled in the mid-1600s and flourished after the American Revolution, when ship captains, shipbuilders, and prosperous merchants constructed the imposing, solid homes. The Kennebunks are famed for their striking historic architecture and expansive beaches; leave time to explore both.

A quick primer: Kennebunk proper begins just south of the Kennebunk River bridge, stretching south and inland to the junction of Route 9 and U.S.

Highway 1. This is where you'll find the White Barn Inn, Tom's of Maine, and a few fast-food joints. The town also includes, a few miles to the east, the beachside community of Kennebunk Beach.

Kennebunkport's compact, trim downtown begins across the Kennebunk River, on the north side, and extends eastward to take in both million-dollar oceanfront homes (including the Bush family estate at Walker's Point) and the fishing village of Cape Porpoise.

While summer is the busy season along the coast, winter has its charms: The grand architecture is better seen through leafless trees. When the snow flies, guests find solace in front of a fire at one of the inviting inns.

ESSENTIALS
GETTING THERE
Kennebunk is located off Exit 3 of the Maine Turnpike. Kennebunkport is 3½ miles southeast of Kennebunk on Port Road (Rte. 35).

VISITOR INFORMATION
The Kennebunk-Kennebunkport Chamber of Commerce, 17 Western Ave. (P.O. Box 740), Kennebunk, ME 04043 (© **800/982-4421** or 207/967-0857), can answer your questions year-round by phone or at their offices on Route 9 next to Meserve's Market. The **Kennebunkport Information Center** (© **207/ 967-8600**), operated by an association of local businesses, is off Dock Square (next to Ben & Jerry's) and is open daily throughout the summer and fall.

The local trolley (actually a bus) makes several stops in and around Kennebunkport and also serves the beaches. The fare, a day pass costing $10 per adult or $5 per child age 3 to 14, includes unlimited trips. Call © **207/967-3686** or check www.intowntrolley.com for details.

EXPLORING KENNEBUNK
Kennebunk's downtown, located inland, is just off the turnpike and is a dignified, small commercial center of white clapboard and brick. The **Brick Store Museum** ✸, 117 Main St. (© **207/985-4802**), hosts shows of historical art and artifacts throughout the summer, switching to contemporary art in the off-season. The museum is housed in a historic former brick store—yes, a store that once sold bricks!—and three adjacent buildings. The buildings have been renovated and all have the polished gloss of a well-cared-for gallery. Admission is free, but tours cost $5 per person. The museum is open Tuesdays to Fridays 10am to 4:30pm and Saturdays from 10am to 1pm from March to December. Call for winter hours.

Tom's of Maine (© **800/FOR-TOMS** or 207/985-2944), a natural toothpaste maker, is headquartered here. Tom and Kate Chappell sell their all-natural toothpaste and other personal-care products worldwide, but they are almost as well known for their green, socially conscious business philosophy. (Tom wrote a 1993 book on the subject.) Tom's factory outlet sells firsts and seconds of its own products (some at a tremendous markdown), as well as a selection of other natural products. The shop is at Lafayette Center (corner of Main and Water sts.), a historic industrial building converted to shops and offices. It's open Monday to Saturday 10am to 5pm. There's another store located nearby at 1 Storer St.

When en route to or from the coast, be sure to note the extraordinary homes that line Port Road (Rte. 35). This includes the famously elaborate **Wedding Cake House** ✸, which you should be able to identify all on your own. (It looks like . . . well, you know.) Local lore claims that the house was built by a guilt-ridden ship captain who left for sea before his bride could enjoy a proper wedding cake. It's made of brick, with a surfeit of ornamental trim. It's sometimes mistakenly regarded as a fine example of Gothic architecture, but it's nothing of the sort. Underneath all the trimmings is a plain house with a classic Federal form. The house is privately owned but can be enjoyed from the outside.

EXPLORING KENNEBUNKPORT

Kennebunkport is the summer home of former President George Bush, whose family has summered here for decades. Given that, it has the tweedy, upper-crust feel that one might expect of the place. This historic village, whose streets were laid out during days of travel by boat and horse, is subject to monumental traffic jams around the town center. If the municipal lot off the square is full, head north on North Street a few minutes to the free long-term lot and catch the trolley back into town. Or walk—it's a pleasant walk of about 10 or 15 minutes from the satellite lot to Dock Square.

Dock Square has a pleasantly wharflike feel to it, with low buildings of mixed vintages and styles, but the flavor is mostly clapboard and shingles. The boutiques in the area are attractive, and many feature creative artworks and crafts. But Kennebunkport's real attraction is found in the surrounding blocks, where the side streets are lined with one of the nation's richest assortments of early-American homes. The neighborhoods are especially ripe with examples of Federal-style homes; many have been converted to B&B's (see "Where to Stay," below).

Aimless wandering is a good tactic for exploring Kennebunkport, but at the least make an effort to stop by the **Richard A. Nott House,** 8 Maine St. (© 207/ 967-2751), during your travels. Situated on Maine Street at the head of Spring Street, this imposing Greek Revival house was built in 1853 and is a Victorian-era aficionado's dream. It remained untouched by the Nott family through the years and was donated to the local historical society with the stipulation that it remain forever unchanged. It still has the original wallpaper, carpeting, and furnishings. Tours run about 40 minutes; it's open mid-June to mid-October 1 to 4pm Tuesday to Friday, and Saturday 10am to 1pm. Admission is $5 for adults.

For a clear view of the coast, sign up for a 2-hour sail aboard the ***Schooner Eleanor*** ★★ (at the Arundel Wharf Restaurant, Kennebunkport; © 207/967-8809), a 55-foot gaff-rigged schooner, built in Kennebunkport in 1999 after a classic Herreshoff design. If the weather's willing, you'll have a perfect view of the Bush compound and Cape Porpoise. Fare is $38 per person.

A bit farther afield, in an affluent neighborhood near the Colony Hotel (about 1 mile east on Ocean Ave.), is a superb collection of homes of the uniquely American shingle style. It's worth a detour on foot or bike to ogle these icons of the 19th- and early-20th-century leisure class.

Ocean Drive from Dock Square to **Walkers Point** ★ and beyond is lined with opulent summer homes overlooking surf and rocky shore. You'll likely recognize the Bush family compound when you arrive. If it's not familiar from the time it has spent in the national spotlight, look for crowds with telephoto lenses. If they're not out, look for a shingle-style secret service booth at the head of a driveway. That's the place.

The Seashore Trolley Museum ★ A short drive north of Kennebunkport is a local marvel: a scrap yard masquerading as a museum ("world's oldest and largest museum of its type"). Quirky and engaging, this museum was founded in 1939 to preserve a disappearing way of life, and today the collection boasts more than 200 trolleys, including specimens from Glasgow, Moscow, San Francisco, and Rome. (Naturally, there's also a streetcar named Desire from New Orleans.)

About 40 of the cars still operate, and the admission charge includes rides on a 2-mile track. Other cars, some of which still contain early-20th-century advertising, are on display outdoors and in vast storage sheds. A good museum inspires awe and educates its visitors on the sly. This one does so deftly. It's not until you drive away that you're likely to realize how much you've learned about transportation before there were cars in every garage.

195 Log Cabin Rd., Kennebunkport. © 207/967-2800. www.trolleymuseum.org. Admission $7.50 adults, $5 children 6–16, $5.50 seniors. Daily June to mid-Oct (10am–5pm), weekends only May and late Oct. Closed Nov–May (except May weekends). Head north from Kennebunkport on North St. for 1¾ miles; look for signs.

BEACHES

A word about beach parking: Finding a spot is often difficult, and all beaches require a parking permit, which can be obtained at the town offices or from your hotel. You can avoid parking hassles by renting a bike and leaving your car behind at your inn or hotel. A good spot for rentals is **Cape Able Bike Shop** (© **800/ 220-0907** or 207/967-4382), which rents a variety of bikes for $20 and up per day or $80 and up per week. There are also mountain bikes, along with kid trailers and baby seats. (Helmets and locks are free with rental.) The bike shop is on North Street north of Kennebunkport at Arundel Road. Some inns (such as The Colony) also rent bikes to guests; others offer free bikes for guests, no strings attached (except that you have to return the bike). Ask about these services when you first call an inn to reserve a room.

The local trolley also offers beach access (see above); the fare is $10 per adult, $5 per child per day for unlimited trips. The coastal area around Kennebunkport is home to several of the state's finest beaches.

Southward across the river (technically, this is Kennebunk, although it's much closer to Kennebunkport) are **Gooch's Beach** and **Kennebunk Beach** ✦. Head eastward on Beach Street (from the intersection of Rtes. 9 and 35) and you'll soon wind into a handsome colony of eclectic shingled summer homes (some improbably grand, some modest). The narrow road twists past sandy beaches

Finds Parsons Beach

It's certainly the most attractive *approach* to a beach in Maine, and the beach itself is lovely and often much less populated than others in the area. Find the beach by heading south on Route 9 from the Kennebunks; after you cross a marsh and the Mousam River, take your first left on Parson's Beach Road.

You'll drive down a country lane lined with maples, and at the end there's limited parking for the beach, though you can also park on the north side of the road if that's full. It may not be the best beach for swimming—it's rocky at the mouth of the river—but it's without parallel for lounging and reading. Be on your best behavior here (don't trample the dunes, don't take stuff from the tide pool). You cross private land to reach the beach, and signs ominously proclaim that access can be denied if the landowner so chooses.

Packing a Picnic

Kennebunk Beach is a fine spot for a picnic, with long sands and good waves. Watch your parking meter here, however. This is away from the downtown, and there are no shops on the beach; so, to pick up supplies, you'll need to backtrack (or plan ahead). For those, go to **H.B. Provisions** (℃ **207/967-5762**), in a grand old country store building formerly known as Meserve's Market, back near the bridge.

Farther up the coast, the unlikely city of Biddeford has a few good spots, including **Rotary Park,** with river views, and **Fortunes Rock Beach.** See "A Side Trip to Biddeford-Saco" later in this chapter for more details.

and rocky headlands. The area can be frightfully congested when traveling by car in the summer; avoid the local version of gridlock by exploring on foot or bike.

Goose Rocks Beach, north of Kennebunkport off Route 9 (watch for signs, or just turn east at the barn topped by a giant clock), is a good choice for those who like their crowds light and prefer beaches to beach scenes. You'll find an enclave of beach homes set amid rustling oaks just off a fine sand beach. Just offshore is a narrow barrier reef that has historically attracted flocks of geese—the geese, in turn, lent their name to the beach.

WHERE TO STAY

A unique choice for local accommodations is the **Franciscan Guest House,** 28 Beach Ave. (℃ 207/967-4865), a former dormitory on the 200-acre grounds of the St. Anthony's Monastery. The 60 or so rooms are institutional, basic, and clean, with private bathrooms; guests can stroll the very attractive riverside grounds or walk over to Dock Square, about 10 minutes away. Only drawback? It's not nearly as inexpensive as it used to be—the brothers have wised up to modern times, and rates have slowly escalated as a result. Nevertheless, the place is still an outstanding bargain, especially given the fine walking trails. Rooms range from $55 to $269 double per night. No credit cards are accepted; the guest house is open mid-May to October.

VERY EXPENSIVE

Beach House Inn ★★   This is a good choice if you'd like to be amid the action of Kennebunk Beach. The inn was built in 1891 but has been extensively modernized and expanded—in 1999, it was purchased by the same folks who own the legendary White Barn Inn and was upgraded with down comforters and pillows. The rooms aren't necessarily historic, but they are carpeted and most have Victorian furnishings and accenting. The main draw is the lovely porch, where you can stare out at the pebble beach across the road and idly watch the bikers and in-line skaters. The inn has bikes and canoes for guests to use and provides beach chairs and towels.

211 Beach Ave., Kennebunk Beach, ME 04043. ℃ 207/967-3850. Fax 207/967-4719. www.beachhseinn.com. 35 units. Late June to mid-Sept $255–$390; June, mid-Sept to Oct $185–$390; Nov–Dec $155–$300. Closed Jan–May. Rates include continental breakfast. 2-night minimum on weekends. AE, MC, V. **Amenities:** Bikes; canoes; beach chairs. *In room:* VCR, CD player.

Kennebunk & Kennebunkport

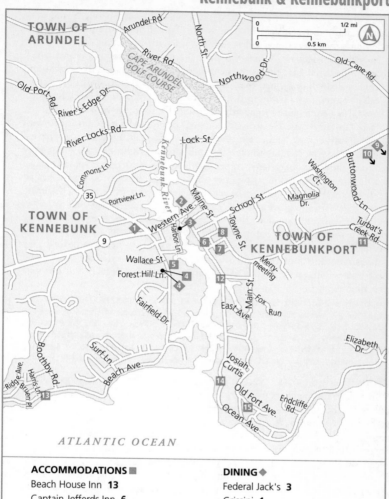

ACCOMMODATIONS ■

Beach House Inn **13**

Captain Jefferds Inn **6**

The Captain Lord Mansion **7**

The Colony Hotel **14**

Franciscan Guest House **5**

Lodge at Turbat's Creek **11**

Maine Stay Inn & Cottages **8**

Old Fort Inn **15**

The Tides Inn **10**

White Barn Inn **4**

The Yachtsman Lodge & Marina **12**

DINING ◆

Federal Jack's **3**

Grissini **1**

Hurricane **2**

Pier 77 Restaurant **9**

White Barn Inn **4**

The Captain Lord Mansion ★★★ The Captain Lord is one of the most architecturally distinguished inns anywhere, housed in a pale-yellow Federal-style home that peers down a shady lawn toward the river. The adjective *stately* is laughably inadequate. When you enter the downstairs reception area, you'll know immediately that this is the genuine article, with grandfather clocks and Chippendale highboys—and that's just the front hallway. Off the hall is a comfortable common area with piped-in classical music and a broad brick fireplace. There's also a conference room with a sofa and TV for those who need their fix.

Head up the elliptical staircase to the guest rooms, which are furnished with splendid antiques; all feature gas fireplaces. The Captain Lord does not have a single unappealing room (although the Union room is a little dark). Among my favorites: the Excelsior, a large corner room with a massive four-poster, a love seat in front of the gas fire, a two-person Jacuzzi in the bathroom with heated tile floor; the Hesper, which is the nicest of the less expensive rooms, featuring a burnished historic gloss and a bathroom with a large stained-glass window; and the Merchant, a spacious first-floor suite that pampers you with two large rooms, a marble-floored bathroom with large Jacuzzi, and a minispa with a NordicRider bike and foot massager. Four rooms are at Phebe's, a historic gray clapboard home behind the main inn, where guests are served breakfast at a long table in a colonial-style kitchen. The rooms here are less opulent but still very well appointed.

Pleasant St. and Green St. (P.O. Box 800), Kennebunkport, ME 04046. (© **800/522-3141** or 207/967-3141. Fax 207/967-3172. www.captainlord.com. 16 units. June–Oct $234–$399 double, $475 suite; Jan to late May $125–$329 double, $225–$375 suite;. Nov–Dec $125–$329 double midweek; $234–$399 double weekends; $375 suite midweek; $475 weekends. Rates include full breakfast. 2-night minimum weekends and holidays year-round (some holidays 3-night minimum). DISC, MC, V. Children 12 and older welcome. **Amenities:** Lounge; conference room. *In room:* A/C, Jacuzzi (some), fireplace (some).

White Barn Inn ★★★ Part of the exclusive Relais & Châteaux group, the White Barn Inn pampers its guests like no other in Maine. Upon checking in, guests are shown to one of the parlors and offered port or brandy while valets gather luggage and park cars. The atmosphere is distinctly European, with an emphasis on service. The rooms are individually decorated in an upscale country style, and I know of no other inn of this size that offers as many unexpected niceties such as robes, fresh flowers in the rooms, and turndown service at night. Nearly half the rooms have wood-burning fireplaces, while the suites (in a separate facility across from the main inn) are truly spectacular; each is themed with a separate color, and most have LCD televisions, whirlpools, or similar perks. Guests can avail themselves of the inn's free bikes (including a small fleet of tandems) to head to the beach, take a cruise on its Hinckley charter yacht, or stroll across the street to explore the shady grounds and pathways of St. Anthony's Franciscan Monastery. You might also lounge around the beautiful outdoor pool. In 2003, the inn acquired a handful of cottages on the tidal Kennebunk River, a bit down the road from the main inn, and will develop a wharf on that site to encourage boating interests. The cottages are cozy, nicely equipped with modern kitchens and bathrooms, and will continue to see future upgrades; an adjacent "friendship cottage" is stocked at all times with snacks, wine, and the like. They are a wonderful addition to a property that previously lacked nothing except water views.

Ocean Ave. (¼ mile east of junction of Rtes. 9 and 35; P.O. Box 560-C), Kennebunk, ME 04043. (© **207/ 967-2321.** Fax 207/967-1100. www.whitebarninn.com. 25 units, 4 cottages. $275–$390 double; $530–$750 suite; $460–$1,230 cottage. Rates include continental breakfast and afternoon tea. 2-night minimum weekends; 3 nights holiday weekends. AE, MC, V. Valet parking. **Amenities:** Outdoor heated pool; nearby ocean beach; bikes; concierge; conference rooms; room service (breakfast only); in-room massage; free newspaper; twice-daily maid service. *In room:* A/C, safe, robes, fireplace (some).

EXPENSIVE

Captain Jefferds Inn ★★   This 1804 Federal home was fully redone in 1997, and the innkeepers have done a superb job in coaxing out the historic feel of the place while giving each room its own personality. Fine antiques abound throughout, and guests will need some persuading to come out of their wonderful rooms once they've settled in. Among the best are the Manhattan, with a four-poster bed, fireplace, and beautiful afternoon light; and the Assisi, with a restful indoor fountain and rock garden (sounds weird, but it works). The Winterthur is the only room with a television (though there is a TV in the common room), and the Winterthur and the Santa Fe both have whirlpools. The price range reflects the varying room sizes, but even the smallest rooms—like the Katahdin—are comfortable and far exceed the merely adequate. Bright common rooms on the first floor offer alluring lounging space; an elaborate breakfast is served before a fire on cool days and on the terrace when summer weather permits.

5 Pearl St. (P.O. Box 691), Kennebunkport, ME 04046. © **800/839-6844** or 207/967-2311. Fax 207/967-0721. www.captainjefferdsinn.com. 15 units. June–Oct $165–$340 double; Nov–May $110–$285 double. Rates include full breakfast. AE, MC, V. 2-night minimum weekends. Dogs $20 additional by advance reservation. *In room:* A/C, hair dryer, Jacuzzi (some), fireplace (some), CD player.

The Colony Hotel ★★   The Colony is one of the handful of ocean-side resorts that has preserved, intact, the classic New England vacation experience. This mammoth white Georgian Revival (built in 1914) lords over the ocean and the mouth of the Kennebunk River. The three-story main inn has 91 rooms, all of which have been renovated over the last 3 years. The rooms are bright and cheery, simply furnished with summer cottage antiques. Rooms in two of the three outbuildings carry over the rustic elegance of the main hotel; the exception is the East House, a 1950s-era motor hotel at the back edge of the property with 20 uninteresting motel-style rooms.

Guest rooms lack TVs in the main inn, and that's by design. The Boughton family, which has owned the hotel since 1948, encourages guests to socialize in the evening downstairs in the lobby, on the porch, or at the shuffleboard court, which is lighted for nighttime play.

The Porch Dining Room seats 100 (open to the public). Dinners begin with a classic relish tray and then progress to creative regional entrees. On Fridays there's a lobster buffet, and lunch is served daily (poolside in July–Aug).

140 Ocean Ave. (P.O. Box 511), Kennebunkport, ME 04046. © **800/552-2363** or 207/967-3331. Fax 207/967-8738. www.thecolonyhotel.com/maine. 123 units. July to early Sept $190–$435 double; mid-May to June and Sept–Oct $135–$270 double. Rates include breakfast. 3-night minimum on summer weekends and holidays in main hotel. Closed late Oct to mid-May. AE, MC, V. Pets allowed. **Amenities:** Restaurant; cocktail lounge; afternoon tea in lobby; heated saltwater pool; small beach; putting green; health club nearby; bike rental; social director; library; room service; free newspaper. *In room:* A/C (some), TV (some), safe.

Maine Stay Inn and Cottages ★   Innkeepers Janice and George Yankowski have maintained a strong sense of history in this 1860 home. Guest room decor might best be described as traditional without going overboard to be authentic. The common room is comfortably furnished; be sure to note the exceptional staircase in the main hall. The cottages, arrayed along the property's perimeter, are equally appealing. Constructed in the 1950s, they've been updated with small kitchens, and many have gas or wood fireplaces. The inn is happy to accommodate children in cottage rooms (minimum age is 6 in the main building), and there's a small playground on the edge of the lawn. The full breakfast is exceptional—it includes such treats as spinach frittata or very fresh fruit—and can be delivered to your room or your cottage if you wish. Feeling stressed? Six rooms have Jacuzzis. There's also a new studio apartment with a king bed, fireplace, sitting room with loveseat, home theater system, wet bar, double whirlpool tub, and high-speed Internet access.

34 Maine St. (P.O. Box 500-A), Kennebunkport, ME 04046. ℂ **800/950-2117** or 207/967-2117. Fax 207/967-8757. www.mainestayinn.com. 3 rooms, 14 cottages. $109–$219 double, $109–$269 suite. Apt $299–$359. Rates include full breakfast. 2-night minimum stay on weekends; 3 nights on major holiday weekends. AE, MC, V. **Amenities:** Playground. *In room:* A/C, VCR, some kitchens, Jacuzzi (some), fireplace (some).

Old Fort Inn 🦆🌟🌟   The sophisticated Old Fort Inn is located on 15 acres in a quiet and picturesque neighborhood of magnificent late-19th-century summer homes about 2 blocks from the ocean and not far from The Colony Hotel. Guests check in at a tidy antiques shop, and most park around back at the large carriage house, an interesting amalgam of stone, brick, shingle, and stucco. Rooms here all have creature comforts yet retain the charm of yesteryear: They are solidly wrought and delightfully decorated with antiques and reproductions. About half of the rooms have in-floor heated tiles in the bathrooms; all have welcome amenities like robes, refrigerators, irons, coffeemakers, hair dryers, Aveda products, and a discreet self-serve snack bar with microwave and sink. Two large suites are located in the main house; light-filled no. 216 faces east and looks out over the pool. A full buffet breakfast is served in the main house; in nice weather, guests often take waffles, pancakes, croissants, or fresh fruit on wicker trays outside to enjoy the morning sun.

Old Fort Rd. (P.O. Box M), Kennebunkport, ME 04046. ℂ **800/828-3678** or 207/967-5353. Fax 207/967-4547. www.oldfortinn.com. 16 units. High season $160–$375 double; low season $99–$295 double. Rates include full breakfast. AE, DC, DISC, MC,V. 2-night minimum weekends and July to Labor Day. **Amenities:** Heated outdoor pool; beach within walking distance; tennis court (1 hr. free daily); laundry service and self-serve laundry; dry cleaning. *In room:* A/C, minibar, fridge, coffeemaker, hair dryer, iron, robe.

The Tides Inn 🌟 *Kids*   This is the best bet in the region for a peaceful getaway—and maybe the best lodgings in the area for families as well. Located just across the street from Goose Rocks Beach, the Tides Inn is a yellow clapboard-and-shingle affair from 1899 that retains a seaside boarding house feel while providing up-to-date comfort. (Past guests have included Teddy Roosevelt and Sir Arthur Conan Doyle.) The rooms tend toward the small side but are comfortable, and you can hear the lapping of surf from all of them. Among the brightest and most popular rooms are nos. 11, 15, 24, and 29, some of which have bay windows and all of which have ocean views. The parlor has old wicker, TV, and chess for those rainy days. The pub is cozy and features a woodstove and dartboard.

The Belvidere Club offers upscale traditional dining in a Victorian setting with options such as rack of lamb, shellfish ragout, filet mignon, and boiled lobster. Less elaborate meals, including salads, burritos, and burgers, are served in the pub. Breakfast is also offered but is not included in room rates.

252 King's Hwy., Goose Rocks Beach, Kennebunkport, ME 04046. ℂ **207/967-3757.** www.tidesinnbythesea. com. 22 units (4 share 2 bathrooms). Early June to Labor Day $195–$325 double; off-season $145–$225 double. Closed mid-Oct to mid-May. 3-night minimum stay in peak season (mid-June to Labor Day and all weekends). AE, MC, V. **Amenities:** Restaurant; pub; lounge. *In room:* No phone.

MODERATE

Lodge at Turbat's Creek *Value*   This classy, unusually clean motel sits in a quiet residential neighborhood about a 5-minute drive from Dock Square. The grounds are attractive and amply endowed with Adirondack chairs. The inn has eight mountain bikes for guests to borrow (no charge), and there's also a heated pool. The rooms, located on two floors, are standard motel size, decorated with rustic pine furniture, and painted a cheerful lemony-yellow color. The complimentary continental breakfast can be enjoyed on the lawn in pleasant weather.

7 Turbat's Creek Rd. (P.O. Box 2722), Kennebunkport, ME 04046. © 877/594-5634 or 207/967-8700. 26 units. June–Aug $119–$169 double, off-season $89–$139 double. Rates include continental breakfast. AE, MC, V. Closed Dec–Mar (but open briefly in early Dec). From Dock Sq., drive to top of hill, turn right on Maine St., turn left at first fork, and turn right at 2nd fork. Pets allowed; inquire before arriving. **Amenities:** Heated pool; free use of mountain bikes. *In room:* A/C.

The Yachtsman Lodge & Marina ★★   The White Barn Inn took over this riverfront motel in 1997 and made it an appealing base for exploring the southern Maine coast. Within walking distance of Dock Square, nice touches abound, such as down comforters, granite-topped vanities, high ceilings, CD players, and French doors that open onto patios just above the river. Every room is a first-floor room and basically the same, but while standard motel sized, their simple, classical styling is far superior to anything you'll find at a chain motel.

Ocean Ave. (P.O. Box 2609), Kennebunkport, ME 04046. © 207/967-2511. Fax 207/967-5056. www.yachtsman lodge.com. 30 units. Peak season $195–$255; off-season $129–$253. Rates include continental breakfast. AE, MC, V. 2-night minimum stay on weekends and holidays. *In room:* A/C, TV/VCR, dataport, fridge, coffeemaker, hair dryer, iron.

WHERE TO DINE

Those looking for a quick lobster have a couple of options in the Kennebunkport area, although the prices tend to be a bit more expensive than at other casual lobster spots farther north along the coast. **Nunan's Lobster Hut** (© **207/967-4362**), Route 9 north of Kennebunkport at Cape Porpoise, is a classic lobster shack, often crowded with diners and full of atmosphere, which helps make up for disappointments such as potato chips (rather than a baked potato) served with the lobster dinner. No reservations are taken, nor are credit cards accepted; it's open daily for dinner, starting at 5pm in summer. There's also **Cape Porpoise Lobster Co.,** 15 Pier Rd. (© **800/967-4268** or 207/967-4268), a compact spot overlooking the sparkling water. There's limited outdoor dining, but most everything is served on Styrofoam plates, so beware of rogue winds that strive to dump your meal on your lap. No reservations are taken; credit cards are accepted. It's usually open daily from 9am to 7pm for breakfast, lunch, and dinner in season; it's closed from late fall to around Memorial Day.

Federal Jack's Restaurant and Brew Pub ★ PUB FARE   This light, airy, and modern restaurant, named after a schooner built at Cape Porpoise a century

---

Moments   **A Picnic on Cape Porpoise**

Cape Porpoise ★★ is a lovely little village, nearly forgotten by time, between Kennebunk and Biddeford. (And you've got to love the name.) It makes for a superb day-trip or bike ride. While in the village, think about packing a picnic and taking it to the rocks where the lobster boats are tied up; watch the fishermen, or train your binoculars on Goat Island and its lighthouse. Drop by **Bradbury Brothers Market** (© **207/967-3939**) for basic staples, or the **Cape Porpoise Kitchen** (© **800/488-1150** or 207/ 967-1150) for gourmet-style prepared meals, cheeses, and baked goods. There are two good lobster shacks (see above), a handful of shops, and even a postage-stamp-size library.

ago, is in a retail complex of recent vintage that sits a bit uneasily amid the boat-yards lining the south bank of the Kennebunk River. From the second-floor perch (look for a seat on the spacious three-season deck in warmer weather), you can gaze across the river toward the shops of Dock Square. The upscale pub menu features regional fare with a creative twist and also offers standards like hamburgers, steamed mussels, and pizza. This is good bet for a basic meal without any pretensions; locals keep a sharp eye on the specials board, which features treats like a grilled crab and havarti sandwich. The restaurant is best known for its Shipyard ales, lagers, and porters, which they've been brewing since 1992 and are among the best in New England. Nontipplers can enjoy a zesty homemade root beer or fresh-roasted coffees at the coffee bar.

8 Western Ave., Lower Village (S bank of Kennebunk River), Kennebunk, ME 04043. ℂ 207/967-4322. www.federaljacks.com. Main courses (lunch or dinner) $2.95–$16; lobster dinners priced to market. AE, DISC, MC, V. Daily 11:30am–9pm (bar to 1am), also Sun brunch served 10:30am–2pm.

Grissini ★★ TUSCAN Opened by the same folks who run the White Barn Inn, Grissini is a handsome trattoria that offers great value for the money. The mood is a sort of elegant but writ large rustic Italian: Oversize Italian advertising posters line the walls of the soaring, barnlike space, and burning logs in the handsome stone fireplace take the chill out of a cool evening. In fact, everything seems larger than life, including the plates, flatware, and water goblets. The menu changes weekly; meals are likewise luxuriously sized and nicely presented, and include a wide range of pastas and pizza served with considerable flair: Think fresh fettuccine with chicken breast and garlic tomato sauce, linguini tossed with mahogany clams, leeks and fennel in a pinot grigio sauce, rotini green beans and sun-dried tomatoes tossed with pesto and goat cheese. Simple meals can be had of a grilled half-chicken over garlic mashed potatoes or a Portobello mushroom layered with a zucchini pancake, while more far-ranging entrees include osso buco with vegetables, lemon zest and rosemary served over garlic mashed potatoes, and wood-grilled salmon served with a roasted pepper ragout. Desserts include crème caramel and tiramisu.

27 Western Ave., Kennebunk, ME 04043. ℂ 207/967-2211. www.restaurantgrissini.com. Reservations encouraged. Entrees $2.95–$14. AE, MC, V. Sun–Fri 5:30–9:30pm; Sat 5–9:30pm. Closed Wed Jan–Mar.

Hurricane ★★★ AMERICAN/ECLECTIC An offshoot of Brooks MacDonald's award-winning Hurricane in Ogunquit (reviewed earlier in this chapter), this kitchen prepares food in a similar vein. Lunch might start with a cup of lobster chowder, the "Ice Cube" (a block of iceberg lettuce with blue cheese dressing, toasted pecans, roasted pears, and croutons), a lobster Cobb salad, a bento box of shrimp, scallop and salmon lumpia, lobster rangoon, vegetable nori rolls and marinated beef, a pepper-seared tenderloin carpaccio, or some Penobscot Bay mussels steamed in fresh tomato, garlic, and basil; the main course could be a gourmet sandwich, some pan-roasted halibut over coconut purple rice, or seared diver-caught scallops. Dinner entrees run to such items as lobster cioppino, grilled veal chops, "stuffed" risotto, roasted chicken on a cheddar biscuit, rack of lamb, a modern take on pork and beans, garlic shrimp over linguine, or baked or boiled lobster. Finish with a vanilla bean crème brûlée, Key lime tart with coconut rum sauce, a raspberry/lemon panna cotta, or a course of cheeses.

29 Dock Sq., Kennebunkport. ℂ 207/967-1111. www.hurricanerestaurant.com. Reservations recommended. Main courses $18–$32, small plates $6–$22. AE, DC, DISC, MC, V. Daily 11:30am–10:30pm (winter to 9:30pm).

Pier 77 Restaurant ★★ CONTEMPORARY NEW ENGLAND Long a tony restaurant with a wonderful ocean view, Pier 77 was recently renovated and renamed by husband-and-wife team Peter and Kate Morency. The food, drawing on Peter's training at the Culinary Institute of America and 20 years in top kitchens in Boston and San Francisco, is more contemporary and skillful than most anything else in Maine. The menu offers traditional favorites along with more adventurous dishes such as cashew-crusted Chilean sea bass served with citrus-tamari sauce and pan roasted haddock with spinach gnocchi. The restaurant has earned *Wine Spectator*'s award of excellence annually since 1993.

77 Pier Rd., Cape Porpoise, Kennebunkport. ℭ **207/967-8500.** www.pier77restaurant.com. Reservations recommended. Main courses $14–$25. AE, MC, V. Tues–Sat 11:30am–2:30pm and 5–10pm; Sun 10am–2pm.

White Barn Inn ✦✦✦ REGIONAL/NEW AMERICAN   The White Barn Inn's (see earlier in this chapter) classy dining room attracts gourmands from New York and Boston, who make repeat trips up the Maine Turnpike to dine here. The restaurant is housed in a rustic barn attached to the inn, with a soaring interior and eclectic collection of country antiques displayed in a hayloft; this setting is magical. One window throws in coastal light, and staff gussies it up with changing window dressings (bright pumpkins, corn stalks, and other reminders of the harvest in fall, for example). Chef Jonathan Cartwright's menu also changes frequently, nearly always incorporating local ingredients: You might start with a lobster spring roll of daikon, carrots, snow peas, and Thai sauce or pan-seared diver scallops; glide through an *intermezzo* course of fruit soup or sorbet; then graduate to a roasted New England duck with a juniper sauce, roasted halibut filet with Matsutake mushrooms with sautéed shrimp and a champagne foam, or a simply steamed Maine lobster over fettuccine with cognac coral butter sauce. The tasting menu runs to seasonal items such as three variations of Maine oyster, sautéed veal over butternut squash ragout, and smoked haddock rarebit. The White Barn's service is astonishingly attentive and knowledgeable, capping the experience; anticipate a meal to remember. It's no surprise this was recently selected one of America's finest inn restaurants by the readers of *Travel + Leisure* magazine.

Beach Ave., Kennebunkport. ℭ **207/967-2321.** Reservations recommended. Fixed-price dinner $85, tasting menu $105 per person. AE, MC, V. Mon–Thurs 6:30–9:30pm; Fri 5:30–9:30pm. Closed 2 weeks in Jan.

4 A Side Trip to Biddeford-Saco

Biddeford and Saco won't show up on any tourist itineraries of the Maine coast, but they might be worth a detour since you must physically pass through the two workaday cities en route from southern Maine (Kittery, the Yorks, Ogunquit) to Portland and points north. And, since they're technically located on the coast, they belong in this book.

Of the two, **Biddeford** (*Bid*-duh-ford), originally known as Pepperrellborough—and how's that for a Scrabble score?—is a bit more strongly associated with Maine's Franco-American heritage. The city was a market town from the outset, owing to its position at the falls of the Saco River; cotton and shoe mills were among the many manufacturers who set up shop. As did Saco, Biddeford grew by leaps and bounds during the late 19th century due to waves of immigrants pouring down from Quebec in search of factory jobs here and in its sister city. To this day, diner fare influenced by Franco cooking (baked beans, fried foods, french fries with cheese and gravy) abound in both. Biddeford's also home to a sizable Greek population and a small university.

Saco's (*Sah*-ko's) main street also contains a private academy and some fine city hall and residential architecture which harkens back to the day when this was a center of commerce. Among the prime attractions here are the **Saco Museum** at 371 Main St. in Saco (℗ **207/282-3031**), open Tuesday to Friday and also Sunday from noon to 4pm; it costs $4 for adults, $2 for seniors and children under 16. Thurs afternoons the museum stays open until 8pm and is free during those afternoon hours. Golfers may wish to inspect the Biddeford-Saco Country Club (℗ **207/282-5883**) on Old Orchard Rd. in Saco; it's a 6,200-yard, par 71 course. For more information on the city, consult www.saco maine.org.

Two of the beguiling features of the twin-city area have nothing whatsoever to do with its denizens; they're natural features. One is the Saco River, which pushes east from a trickle in the White Mountains to become a slow, pretty waterway popular with local canoeing types before emptying into the ocean at the predictable mill wheels and factories (now mostly converted to offices and condominiums). You can view (and canoe or kayak in) the river at **Rotary Park** on Outer Main Street.

Also often missed by coastal tourists is **Biddeford Pool,** the ocean-side resort section of Biddeford; it's nothing like the rather pedestrian downtown. Here you'll find a huge tidal inlet and 30-acre **East Point Sanctuary** ✸, full of rocks, tidal pools, marine mammals—and scads of migrating waterfowl. The Pool is said to be one of the top migration spots on the East Coast; look for loons, gannets, ducks, terns, eiders, mergansers, and other birds. There are also two quite nice city-operated beaches on the ocean side of Biddeford—**Boucher Memorial Park** and **Fortunes Rocks Beach.** Parking is quite limited, however. For a bite after, head for the family restaurant Buffleheads (℗ **207/284-6000**), at Hills Beach, open daily for lunch and dinner; it's all about straightforward seafood and pasta.

The most cultural feature in these parts is La Kermesse, an annual festival of Franco cooking, sports contests, dances, and the like held at Biddeford's Alumni Field. It's poorly promoted, but worth a look if you're truly a connoisseur of things Franco; check the local newspaper the *Journal Tribune* (www.journal tribune.com) around mid- to late June if you want to experience it.

Portland

Portland is Maine's largest city and easily one of the most attractive and livable small cities on the East Coast. Actually, it feels more like a large town than a small city. Strike up a conversation with a resident, and you're likely to get an earful about how easy it is to live here. You can buy gourmet coffee, see art-house movies, and get good Vietnamese or Thai food to go. There's even some terrific residential architecture.

Yet Portland is still compact enough that you can walk from one end to the other; despite its outward appearance of being an actual metropolis, the city has a population of just 65,000. Traffic isn't bad at all. And there's a salty tang to local culture that you'll occasionally still glimpse in the waterfront bars and chowder houses.

Like most New England cities, Portland has been forced to reinvent itself every couple of generations as economic and cultural trends overturn old paradigms. The city was a center for maritime trade in the 19th century, when a forest of ship masts obscured the view of the harbor. It's been a manufacturing hub, with locomotive factories, steel foundries, and fish-packing plants. It's been a mercantile center, with impressive downtown department stores and a slew of wholesale dealers.

Today, as a sprawling, could-be-anywhere mall in South Portland siphons off much of the commercial business, this city is bent on reshaping its downtown core as a tourist destination, regional center for the arts, and incubator for high-tech startups. The latest effort in this redesigning and upscaling of a rather pedestrian place has been the city's public market, featuring Maine-grown foods and flowers. It opened in the summer of 1998 to a mixture of fanfare and outcry; like so much else here, however, it has struggled mightily to find an audience.

The verdict is still out on whether Portland's current reincarnation as a mini-Boston (right down to the fish market, train station, and beloved local baseball team) will succeed.

But unlike so many other deteriorating downtowns, Portland's has few vacant storefronts. Office space is in short supply, and there's a sort of brisk urban vitality that has eluded cities many times its size. A recent wave of immigration from Africa and Asia has given this formerly white-bread town a shot in the cultural arm. The city's art museum is outstanding for a community this size. An arts college brings a youthful spirit to the streets. Best of all, there's always an offshore island to escape to when the cruise ships on the waterfront unload a few too many fellow tourists for your taste.

1 Orientation

Portland is 107 miles N of Boston and 319 miles NE of New York City

GETTING THERE

BY CAR

Portland is off the Maine Turnpike (I-95). Coming from the south, downtown is most easily reached by taking Exit 6A and then following I-295 to downtown. Exit at Franklin Street and follow this eastward until you arrive at the waterfront at the Casco Bay Lines terminal. Turn right on Commercial Street, and you'll be at the lower edge of the Old Port. Continue on a few blocks to the visitors center (see below).

BY BUS

Concord Trailways (© 800/639-3317 or 207/828-1151) and **Vermont Transit** (© 800/552-8737 or 207/772-6587) offer bus service to Portland from Boston and Bangor. The Vermont Transit bus terminal is located at 950 Congress St., about a mile downhill from and south of the downtown core. Concord Trailways, which is a few dollars more expensive, offers movies and headsets on its trips; its terminal is inconveniently located on Thompson Point Rd. (a 35-min. walk from downtown), but it is served by local buses from nearby Congress Street.

BY PLANE

Portland International Jetport (© 207/774-7301; www.portlandjetport.org) is served by **Air Nova** (© 902/873-5000; www.airnova.ca), **American Airlines** (© 800/433-7300; www.aa.com), **Delta/Business Express** (© 800/638-7333; www.delta-air.com), **Continental** (© 800/525-0280; www.flycontinental.com), **Northwest** (© 800/225-2525; www.nwa.com), **US Airways** (© 800/428-4322; www.usairways.com), and **United** (© 800/241-6522; www.ual.com). The airport is across the Fore River from downtown. Local METRO buses ($1) connect the airport to downtown; cab fare runs about $15. The airport has grown in fits and starts in recent years (ongoing construction and tight parking can be frustrating at times) but is still quite easily navigated. It's located just across the Fore River from downtown. Metro buses connect the airport to downtown; cab fare runs about $12.

VISITOR INFORMATION

The **Convention and Visitor's Bureau of Greater Portland,** 245 Commercial St., Portland, ME 04101 (© **207/772-5800** or 207/772-4994; www.visitportland. com), stocks a large supply of brochures and is happy to dispense information about local attractions, lodging, and dining. The center is open in summer weekdays 8am to 6pm and Saturdays 10am to 5pm; hours are shorter during the off-season. Ask for the free "Greater Portland Visitor Guide" with map. There's also a tourist information kiosk at the **Portland International Jetport** (© **207/775-5809**), open mid-May through mid-October from around 10am to around 10:30pm daily.

Portland has a free weekly alternative newspaper, the *Portland Phoenix,* offering close-to-comprehensive listings of local events, films, nightclub performances and the like. Copies are widely available at restaurants, bars, and convenience stores.

CITY LAYOUT

The city of Portland is divided into two areas: on-peninsula and off-peninsula. (There are also the islands, but more on that below.) Most travelers are destined

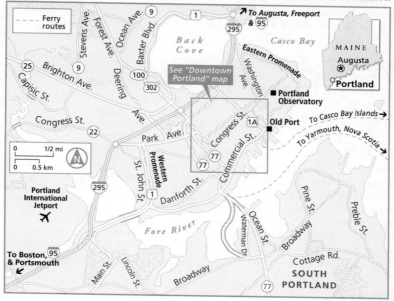

for the compact peninsula, which is home to the downtown and where most of the city's cultural life and retail activity takes place.

Viewed from the water, Portland's peninsula is shaped a bit like a sway-backed horse, with the Old Port lying in the belly near the waterfront and the peninsula's two main residential neighborhoods (Munjoy Hill and the West End) topping gentle rises overlooking downtown. Congress Street, Portland's main artery of commerce, connects these two neighborhoods. The western stretch of Congress Street (roughly between Monument Sq. and State St.) is home to Portland's emerging Arts District, where you can find the handsome art museum, several theaters, the campus of the Maine College of Art (located in an old department store), an L.L. Bean outlet, and a growing number of restaurants and boutiques.

PARKING

Parking is notoriously tight in the Old Port, and the city's parking enforcement is notoriously efficient. Several parking garages are convenient to the Old Port, with parking fees less than $1 per hour; you can also park in some residential neighborhoods, often for a maximum of 2 hours. Read signs carefully for news of nighttime street-sweeping hours; you *will* be towed (don't ask how I know) if you run afoul of them.

SPECIAL EVENTS

New Year's Portland rings in January with a smorgasbord of events and entertainment throughout downtown Portland. Events for families are scheduled in the afternoon; entertainment more oriented for adults—including loads of live music—kicks off later in the evening at numerous locales, including auditoriums, shops, and churches. The emphasis is on enjoying New Year's without alcohol. One admission button buys entrance to all events.

The **Old Port Festival** (© 207/772-6828) takes place in early June when tens of thousands of revelers descend upon the historic Old Port section to herald the arrival of summer. Several blocks of the Old Port are blocked to traffic, and the throngs order food and buy goods from street vendors. Several stages provide entertainment, ranging from kids' singalongs to raucous blues. Admission is free.

2 Where to Stay

If you're simply looking for something central, Hilton has unveiled a brand-new waterfront hotel across the street from the city's island ferry dock. The **Hilton Garden Inn** (65 Commercial St.; © 207/780-0780), though made from a cookie-cutter plan, is convenient to the Old Port's restaurants, bakeries, and pubs—not to mention the islands of Casco Bay. Double rooms run $89 to $289 per night.

The **Holiday Inn by the Bay,** 88 Spring St. (© 207/775-2311), offers great views of the harbor from about half the rooms, along with the usual chain-hotel creature comforts. Peak-season rates are approximately $140 for a double. Budget travelers seeking chain hotels typically head toward the area around the Maine Mall in South Portland, about 8 miles south of the attractions of downtown. Try **Days Inn** (© 207/772-3450) or **Coastline Inn** (© 207/772-3838).

The new **Extended Stay America** (2 Ashley Dr., Scarborough; © 207/883-0554; fax 207/883-1705; www.exstay.com) is a few minute's drive south of the Maine Mall and 6 miles from downtown Portland. At this branch, doubles start at about $50 nightly.

VERY EXPENSIVE

Black Point Inn ⭐⭐   Located 10 miles south of Portland (about 15 min. from downtown), the Black Point Inn is a Maine classic. Situated on 9 acres with views along the coast both north and south, the Black Point was built as a summer resort in 1873 in an area enshrined in some of the work of noted American painter Winslow Homer. It's been under new ownership since 1998 (by the same people who own the Portland Regency), and the new owners have retained its famous old-world graciousness and charm. Sixty guest rooms are located in the main shingled lodge. Even the smaller rooms are generously sized, with enough room for two wing chairs and a writing desk. All are carpeted and have a quaint, summery feel, with Martha Washington bedspreads, original glass doorknobs, and reproduction furnishings. There are also four tidy cottages on the property, and the guest rooms here have more of a rustic L.L. Bean look to them; my pick would be the Sprague Cottage, with its flagstone floors in the common area and five rooms with private balconies, some with ocean views. Note that it's popular for weddings on summer weekends, when you'll encounter accompanying bustle and noise.

The main dining rooms have heavy beams, Windsor chairs, toile wallpaper, views of the garden or ocean, and a menu that favors creative resort fare, such as seafood fettuccine, cedar-planked salmon, crusted rack of lamb, and, of course, boiled lobster with butter and lemon. On staff are a social director and, in summer, a children's program director.

510 Black Point Rd., Prouts Neck, ME 04074. © 800/258-0003 or 207/883-2500. Fax 207/883-9976. www. blackpointinn.com. 80 units (includes 12 two-room suites). July to Labor Day $450–$630 double; spring and fall $300–$430 double; winter $129–$199 double. Rates include breakfast and dinner in spring, summer, and fall; breakfast only in winter. AE, DC, DISC, MC, V. Free valet parking. Closed Dec. **Amenities:** Outdoor pool; indoor pool; shuttle to golf courses; fitness room; Jacuzzi; sauna; children's program (summers); limited room service; massage; babysitting; laundry; dry cleaning. *In room:* A/C, hair dryer, iron, safe.

Portland Harbor Hotel ⭐⭐⭐   Situated right on the corner of Fore and Union streets, only steps from a long row of bars and restaurants, the semicircular town-house-like structure—designed to fit in with the brick facades you'll see

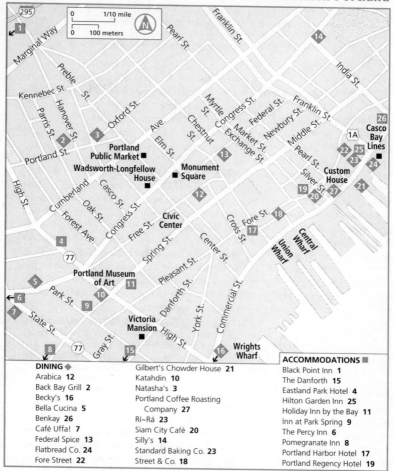

DINING ◆

Arabica **12**
Back Bay Grill **2**
Becky's **16**
Bella Cucina **5**
Benkay **26**
Café Uffa! **7**
Federal Spice **13**
Flatbread Co. **24**
Fore Street **22**

Gilbert's Chowder House **21**
Katahdin **10**
Natasha's **3**
Portland Coffee Roasting
    Company **27**
Rí~Rá **23**
Siam City Café **20**
Silly's **14**
Standard Baking Co. **23**
Street & Co. **18**

ACCOMMODATIONS ■

Black Point Inn **1**
The Danforth **15**
Eastland Park Hotel **4**
Hilton Garden Inn **25**
Holiday Inn by the Bay **11**
Inn at Park Spring **9**
The Percy Inn **6**
Pomegranate Inn **8**
Portland Harbor Hotel **17**
Portland Regency Hotel **19**

prevailing throughout the Old Port—goes for the boutique crowd with lots of amenities. The interior courtyard and garden throw off European ambiance; large, exquisite rooms are furnished with comfy queen and king beds (each with 250-count thread sheets) and spacious work desks. Even the standard rooms are outfitted with big, deep baths in granite-faced bathrooms; armoires; comfy duvets and down coverlets; two-line phones; and big TVs offering 70 channels of digital television with Internet access. Deluxe rooms and suites add Jacuzzis and sitting areas, and many units look out onto an attractive central garden area where guests dine or sip drinks in good weather; turndown service with chocolates is always available. Choose from garden, ocean, or city views, and give the chic bar a look.

The dining room, located just off the pleasant second-floor lobby, serves an upscale menu of meat, fish, and fowl. This hotel already seems to exemplify the best of what a luxury hotel should be—its one possible disadvantage is the same location that makes it so desirable. The proximity to so many bars means proximity to late-night noise, drunks, and sirens on weekends.

468 Fore St., Portland, ME 04101. © **888/798-9090** or 207/775-9090. Fax 207/775-9990. www.theportland harborhotel.com. 100 units. Mid-May to mid-Oct $229–$249 double, $329 suite; off-season $159–$179 double, $259 suite. AE, DC, DISC, MC, V. Parking $10 per day. **Amenities:** Dining room; bar; fitness center; concierge; limited room service; dry cleaning. In room: A/C, digital TV, Internet access, hair dryer, safe, Jacuzzi (some).

Portland Regency Hotel ★★★ Centrally located on a cobblestone court-yard in the middle of the trendy Old Port, the Regency boasts one of the city's premier hotel locations. But it's got more than location going for it—it's also one of the most architecturally striking and better-managed hotels in the state. Housed in an 1895 brick armory, the hotel inside is thoroughly modern and offers attractive guest rooms nicely appointed and furnished with all the expected amenities. The architects have had to work within the quirky layout of the building; as a result, the top-floor rooms lack windows but have skylights, and the windows are knee-high in some other rooms. The hotel has several different types of rooms and suites; for a splurge, ask for one of the luxurious corner rooms featuring handsome (nonworking) gas log fireplaces, sitting areas, CD players, lovely city views out the big windows, and Jacuzzis. Staff is extremely professional, the health club is a good one, and the hotel is also home to both a good downstairs restaurant (**The Armory;** fine dining) and a **bar** ★ that's the best quiet place in Portland to sip a drink and talk business, hold hands, or watch a ballgame on the TV. The only complaint I've heard is that some walls are a bit thin; on weekends, Old Port revelry may penetrate even the dense brick outer walls. But that's a small price to pay for such luxury, location, and professionalism.

20 Milk St., Portland, ME 04101. © **800/727-3436** or 207/774-4200. Fax 207/775-2150. www.theregency. com. 95 units. Early July to late Oct $249–$269 double; $289–$389 suite; off-season $159–$219 double, $209–$329 suite. AE, DISC, MC, V. Valet parking $8 per day. **Amenities:** Restaurant; bar; fitness club; aerobics classes; Jacuzzi; sauna; courtesy car to airport; business center; conference rooms; limited room service; babysitting (with prior notice); dry cleaning (Mon–Fri). In room: A/C, CD player, minibar, safe, Jacuzzi (some).

EXPENSIVE

The Danforth ★★ Located in an exceptionally handsome brick home constructed in 1821, The Danforth opened in 1994 and is now one of Portland's most desirable small inns. The guest rooms are handsomely decorated, many in rich and vibrant tones. The inn's extra touches are exceptional throughout, from working fireplaces in all guest rooms (but one) to the richly paneled basement billiards room, to the direct-line phones. Especially appealing is room no. 1, with a sitting room and private second-floor deck, and room no. 2, with high ceilings and superb morning light; room nos. 5 and 6, housed in the old servant's wing, are smaller. The inn is located at the edge of the Spring Street Historic District and is within a 10-minute walk from downtown attractions. It's very popular for weddings and other events, so if you're in search of a quiet weekend retreat, ask first if anything is planned.

163 Danforth St., Portland, ME 04102. © **800/991-6557** or 207/879-8755. Fax 207/879-8754. www.danforth maine.com. 10 units. Late May to Oct $139–$329 double; off-season $119–$249. Rates include continental breakfast. AE, MC, V. Pets sometimes allowed ($10 fee), call ahead. **Amenities:** Bike rental; billiards room; massage; laundry service. In room: A/C, hair dryer, iron.

Pomegranate Inn ★★ This could be Portland's most appealing B&B and one of the best choices in all of northern New England. Housed in an imposing, dove-gray 1884 Italianate home in the architecturally distinctive Western Prom neighborhood, the interiors are wondrously decorated with whimsy and elegance—a fatally cloying combination when attempted by someone without impeccably good taste. Look for the bold and exuberant wall paintings by a local artist, and the eclectic antique furniture collected and tastefully arranged by owner Isabel Smiles. If you have the chance, peek in some of the unoccupied rooms—they're all different with painted floors and boisterous faux-marble woodwork. Most rooms have gas fireplaces; the best of the lot is in the carriage house, which has its own private terrace, kitchenette, and fireplace. Tea and wine are served upon arrival, and the sit-down breakfasts in the cheery dining room are invariably creative and tasty. The inn is well situated for exploring the West End, and downtown is about a 20-minute walk away.

49 Neal St., Portland, ME 04102. (C) 800/356-0408 or 207/772-1006. Fax 207/773-4426. www.pomegranate inn.com. 8 units. Memorial Day to Oct $175–$265 double; off-season $95–$165. Rates include full breakfast. 2-night minimum summer weekends and holidays. AE, DISC, MC, V. On-street parking. From the Old Port, take Middle St. (which turns into Spring St.) to Neal St. in the West End (about 1 mile); turn right and proceed to inn. Children 16 and older are welcome. **Amenities:** Tea; wine. *In room:* A/C, kitchenette (1 room), fireplace (some).

MODERATE

The Eastland Park Hotel ★ Open since 1927, this longtime Portland doyenne had been fading into oblivion for years until new ownership purchased the former Sonesta and spruced it up to the tune of $4 million; as one of Portland's most central lodgings, it's once again a viable choice. The spacious lobby has been restored to its former glory, with crystal chandeliers, luxe furnishings, and a small bar and good restaurant (see below); there's also an attached art gallery. Rooms on lower floors are standard-grade, while the top two floors make up the concierge level. Rooms here have been recently upgraded and are much more impressive, with comfortable beds, gold-toned duvets, Australian toiletries, and two-line phones. Double rooms are rather tiny but have better views; king rooms feature spacious work areas and bathrooms. Guests also have access to the Bay Club (one of Portland's top gyms) and an airport shuttle service, and the respected Aucocisco fine art gallery is housed on the ground floor. The hotel restaurant, Adeline's Grill, serves an upscale version of pub food.

157 High St., Portland, ME 04101. (C) 888/671-8008 or 207/775-5411. Fax 207/775-2872. www.eastlandpark hotel.com. 202 units. June–Oct $129–$229 double; Nov–May $89–$129 double. AE, DISC, MC, V. Pets allowed ($25 fee). **Amenities:** Restaurant; bar; fitness center; meeting rooms; room service; valet laundry service; art gallery; newspaper delivery. *In room:* A/C, coffeemaker.

Inn at Park Spring ★★ This small, tasteful B&B is located on a busy downtown street in a historic brick home that dates back to 1835. It's well located for exploring the city on foot. The Portland Museum of Art is just 2 blocks away, the Old Port is about 10 minutes away, and great restaurants are all within easy walking distance. Guests can linger or watch TV in the front parlor, or chat at the table in the adjacent room. The rooms are all corner rooms, and most are bright and sunny. Especially nice is "Spring," with its great morning light and wonderful views of the historic row houses on Park Street, and "Gables," on the third floor, which gets abundant afternoon light and has a nice bathroom. The friendly new owners promise to gradually upgrade the inn.

135 Spring St., Portland, ME 04101. (C) 800/437-8511 or 207/774-1059. www.innatparkspring.com. 6 units. Mid-June to Oct and holidays $149–$175 double; mid-Apr to mid-June $129–$165 double; Nov to mid-Apr $109–$135 double. Rates include full breakfast and off-street parking. 2-night minimum weekends. AE, MC, V. Children over 10 are welcome. *In room:* A/C, hair dryer.

The Percy Inn ★★ The Percy Inn, based at the edge of Portland's West End, is housed in a pair of handsome early-19th-century brick town houses in an up-and-coming but not-quite-there-yet area. Close to good restaurants and the Center for Cultural Exchange (see below), it's about a 15-minute walk to the

Old Port. Guest rooms in the main building are reached via a narrow, twisting staircase. The Henry W. Longfellow Room has wonderful random-width floorboards, a small snack room with fridge, and a corner sitting area with marble cafe table. In 2001, the inn expanded into the adjacent town house and other buildings around town; at 1,000 square feet, Pine Suite 1 is the largest unit, a two-bedroom suite in a former art gallery. For families, another two-bedroom suite is in the carriage house. Other rooms possess good views of city architectures, and touches abound in these rooms as well: All have weather radios, CD players, VCRs, complimentary soft drinks, and coolers with beach blankets for day trips.

15 Pine St., Portland ME 04104. ⓒ 207/871-7638. Fax 207/775-2599. www.percyinn.com. 12 units. Mid-May to Oct $129–$229 double; Nov to mid-May $89–$209. Rates include continental breakfast. MC, V. Children over 8 welcome. **Amenities:** Free soft drinks. *In room:* A/C, TV/VCR, fax (some), kitchenette (some), fireplace (some).

3 Where to Dine

More than anything else, Portland is a city of creative cheap eats. In addition to the places listed under the "Inexpensive" category below, you'll find filling (if not exactly gourmet) fare at Italian trattorias scattered around town. Also don't neglect local bakeries and coffee shops while trolling for budget eats. My favorite bakery in New England, hands-down, is **Standard Baking Company** ★★★ at 75 Commercial St. (ⓒ **207/773-2112**), across from the ferry terminal and behind the new Hilton hotel. Allison Bray and Matt James bake the best sticky buns (with or without nuts) and focaccia I've tasted in America, plus top-rate breads, brioche, cookies, and more. There's good coffee, too. The bakery is open 7am to 6pm weekdays, to 5pm weekends.

Among the many coffee shops around the city, I frequent both **Arabica** at 16 Free St. (ⓒ **207/879-0792**), with house-roasted beans, a good choice of teas, plus pie, bagels, scones, and even toast with peanut butter, and **Portland Coffee Roasting Co.** (ⓒ **207/761-9525**) at 111 Commercial St., with inventive coffee drinks, a daily trivia quiz, and a display case of fun snacks such as sushi and energy bars.

For a pizza, head for **Flatbread** Company (see below); **Angelone's** (ⓒ **207/775-3114;** 788 Washington Ave.), which makes outstandingly authentic local pie; or **Ricetta's** (ⓒ **207/775-7400;** 29 Western Ave., South Portland). When Ricetta's opened in the early '90s, it was at the forefront of Portland's gradual transformation from a diner town into a kind of bistro town; already, though, it almost seems like an anachronism. Still, the wood-fired pizzas are pretty good, if a bit ostentatiously topped. The location, tucked into a small nondescript shopping mall en route to the much bigger Maine Mall, does leave something to be desired.

For takeout or a picnic, I'm crazy about **Supper at Six** ★ (ⓒ **207/761-6600**) at 16 Veranda St. near Back Cove and Washington Ave. Their sandwiches, made with Standard Baking Company breads (see above), are the best in the city; they also do a variety of to-go gourmet meals.

Portland claims to be the original home of the Italian sandwich—which may have been the original sub sandwich in American, as well—and locals maintain the best example can still be found at the (purported) inventor of this creation, **Amato's** (ⓒ **207/773-1682**) at 71 India St. in what's left of Portland's Italian neighborhood.

Finally, don't ignore the **Portland Public Market** (ⓒ **207/228-2000**), off the beaten tourist track at 25 Preble St., with a collection of stalls dispensing eat-in or take-out soup, salad, sushi, coffee, baked goods, and seafood meals. The mix of vendors seems to change fairly regularly as fortunes rise and fall, but you can always find something to go; get the merchant to stamp your parking ticket while you're there—the first 2 hours are free at the adjacent garage if you buy anything inside the market.

EXPENSIVE

Back Bay Grill ★★★ NEW AMERICAN Back Bay Grill is one of Portland's consistently best restaurants, offering an upscale, contemporary ambiance amid a rather downscale neighborhood near the main post office. There's light jazz on the stereo in the background and bold artwork on the walls that goes several notches above mere atmosphere. The menu is revamped seasonally, although dishes change more frequently to emphasize the local produce and meats that are available. Diners begin an evening with Maine crab cakes with lemon-pepper crème fraîche, or perhaps potato soup with a salmon mousse or some local mussels steamed in white wine, garlic, and shallots. Among main courses, look for heavenly dishes such as rack of lamb in Burgundy sauce, with butter-braised potatoes and fava beans; a grilled filet mignon with mashed potatoes, Maytag blue cheese, and pancetta; a plate of soft-shell crab and seared jumbo scallops served with basmati rice and a truffle sauce; or Scottish salmon with roasted peppers, grilled zucchini, and local fingerling potatoes. The fresh pastas are memorable, as well—previous creations have included hand-rolled fettuccini with smoked tomatoes and oyster mushrooms; the same fettuccini with Maine chèvre, spring peas, and pine nuts; and ravioli filled with maple-butternut squash and served with a tangy cranberry, orange, and ginger sauce. The restaurant also offers a good selection of moderately priced wines by the glass. Top off your meal with crème brûlée.

65 Portland St. ⓒ 207/772-8833. www.backbaygrill.com. Reservations recommended. Main courses $19–$33. AE, DC, DISC, MC, V. Mon–Thurs 5–9pm; Fri–Sat 5–9:30pm.

Fore Street ★★★ CONTEMPORARY GRILL During the long summer evenings, light floods in through the huge windows in this loft-like space; later at night, it takes on a more intimate glow with soft lighting against the brick walls, buttery narrow-plank maple floors, and copper-topped tables. But the place always feels bustling—the sprawling open kitchen is located in the middle of it all and filled with a team of chefs busy stoking the wood-fired brick oven and grilling fish and meats. Indeed, Fore Street has emerged to take its place as one of New England's most celebrated restaurants—chef Sam Hayward has been profiled in *Saveur* and *House Beautiful,* and the restaurant has been listed in *Gourmet's* 100 Best list. Its secret is simplicity: Local ingredients are used when possible (note the rustic vegetable cooler overflowing with what's fresh), and the kitchen shuns fussy presentations. The menu changes nightly; some of the most memorable meals are prepared over an applewood grill, such as Maine pheasant, or two-texture duckling with grilled pears. Lobster and rabbit courses never disappoint. Though it can be mighty hard to snag a reservation here, particularly on a summer weekend, Fore Street actually sets aside a few tables each night for walk-ins. Smart move. Now, you make one: Get there.

288 Fore St. ⓒ 207/775-2717. Reservations recommended. Main courses $13–$29. AE, MC, V. Mon–Thurs 5:30–10pm; Fri–Sat 5:30–10:30pm; Sun 5:30–9:30pm.

Street & Co. ★★★ MEDITERRANEAN/SEAFOOD A pioneering establishment on now-bustling Wharf Street, Dana Street's intimate, brick-walled bistro specializes in seafood cooked just right. There's no smoke and mirrors—

you pass the open kitchen as you're seated, and you can watch the talented chefs perform their magic in their tiny space. The kitchen specializes in seafood that's fresh as can be (the docks are close by) and cooked just right. Diners sit at cop-per-topped tables, designed so that the waiters can deliver steaming skillets directly from the stove. Looking for lobster? Try it grilled and served over lin-guini in a butter-garlic sauce. If you're partial to calamari, they know how to cook it here so that it's perfectly tender, a knack that's been lost elsewhere. Oth-erwise, go for seared tuna, fresh mussels, or a grilled piece of whatever's come in (swordfish, perhaps). This place often fills up early, so reservations are strongly recommended. But, like Fore Street (see above), one-third of the tables are reserved for walk-ins; it can't hurt to check if you're in the neighborhood. In summer, outdoor seating is available at a few tables on the alley.

33 Wharf St. © 207/775-0887. Reservations recommended. Main courses $14–$24. AE, MC, V. Sun–Thurs 5:30–9:30pm; Fri–Sat 5:30–10pm.

MODERATE

Beale Street BBQ ✮ *Finds* BARBECUE   Beale Street BBQ owner Mark Quigg once operated a takeout grill on Route 1 outside Freeport, but he chucked that life when notables such as author Stephen King got wind of his cooking; soon he was catering movie shoots, joining forces with his two brothers, and the Quiggs have never looked back. Of all the barbecue joints in Maine, this is my favorite, with its appealing roadhouse atmosphere, friendly staff, and great smoked meats. Though I like everything here—check the board for intriguing daily specials, which usually include a fish preparation as well as Creole or Cajun offerings—I usually order the barbeque sampler (subtitled "All You Really Need to Know About BBQ"). This entitles you to a choice of pulled pork, chicken, or beef brisket (go with the brisket); ample sweet and crunchy cornbread; a half slab of ribs; a quarter chicken; and delicious spicy smoked links that remind me of East Texas, plus a mound of barbeque beans and coleslaw. Two people could comfortably split it. This location, in South Portland's commercial Mill Creek and Knightville neighborhoods, is a bit hard to find (it's almost beneath the Casco Bay Bridge). There's another fancier location (© **207/442-9514**) at 215 Water St. in the gritty maritime town of Bath, a half-hour north up Route 1.

90 Waterman Dr., South Portland. © 207/767-0130. Reservations not accepted. Main courses $9–$18. MC, V. Mon–Sat 11:30am–10pm; Sun 11:30am–9pm.

Bella Cucina ✮ RUSTIC ITALIAN   Situated in one of Portland's less elegant commercial neighborhoods, Bella Cucina sets an inviting mood with rich col-ors, stylized fish sculptures, soft lighting, and pinpoint spotlights over the tables that carve out alluring islands of light. The eclectic menu changes every night, dancing deftly between rustic Italian and regional, with options like a robust cioppino and a mélange of veal, pork, and chicken served with a prosciutto and mushroom ragout. Three or four vegan selections are always offered. About half the seats are kept open for walk-ins, so take a chance and stop by even if you don't have a reservation. There's a fitting selection of wines and free parking at night behind Joe's Smoke Shop.

653 Congress St. © 207/828-4033. Reservations recommended. Main courses $12–$19. AE, DISC, MC, V. Sun and Tues–Thurs 5–9pm; Fri–Sat 5–10pm.

Benkay ✮ *Value* JAPANESE/SUSHI   Of Portland's sushi restaurants, Benkay is the hippest, usually teeming with a lively crowd lured by good value. Ask about $1 sushi nights (usually weeknights). The regular sushi platter is inexpensive and delivers a lot for the money, though nothing very exotic. Teriyaki and tempura round out the menu. Expect harried service on busy nights. It stays open until 1am Thursdays through Saturdays—a boon in early-closing Portland.

2 India St. (at Commercial). (C) 207/773-5555. Reservations not accepted. Main courses $7.95–$17. AE, MC, V. Mon–Fri 11:30am–2pm; Mon–Sat 5–10pm; Sun noon–9pm.

Café Uffa! CONTEMPORARY AMERICAN   Café Uffa! offers a little bit of everything, from vegetarian entrees to grilled steak, but try the fish, which is grilled to a wonderful tenderness over a wood-stoked fire (the salmon is especially good). Dishes might include grilled mahimahi on a shiitake mushroom risotto cake, pan-seared scallops with a pesto broth, seared catfish over parsley-jasmine rice, beef Wellington, grilled steelhead trout with potato gratin, or a bouillabaisse incorporating mussels, fish, shrimp, and half a lobster. Lunches are simpler, with salmon salad and chicken salad among the offerings. With its mismatched chairs, last week's flea market style of decor, aggressively informal styling, and high ceilings, Uffa appeals to a young (and young-minded) crowd. Sunday brunches are superb, but be prepared to wait. There's often a line to get in, but you can check out outstanding art on the walls while waiting—the restaurant also functions as a working art gallery.

190 State St. (C) 207/775-3380. www.uffarestaurant.com. Breakfast $3–$7, dinner $10–$18. MC, V. Wed 11am–2:30pm and 5:30–10pm, Thurs–Fri 7am– 2:30pm and 5:30–10pm, Sat 8am–noon and 5:30–10pm, Sun 9am–2pm.

Flatbread Company ✦ PIZZA   This upscale, hippie-chic pizzeria—an offshoot of the original Flatbread Company in Waitsfield, Vermont—may have the best waterfront location in town. It sits on a slip overlooking the Casco Bay Lines terminal, so you can watch fishermen at work while you eat. (Picnic tables are on the deck in fair weather.) The inside brings to mind a Phish concert, with Tibetan prayer flags and longhaired staffers stoking wood-fired ovens and slicing nitrate-free pepperoni and organic vegetables. The laid-back atmosphere makes the place; the pizza is quite good, though toppings tend to be skimpy.

72 Commercial St. (C) 207/772-8777. Reservations accepted for parties of 10 or more. Pizzas $12–$15. AE, MC, V. Mon–Tues 5–9pm; Wed–Sun 11:30am–9pm.

Katahdin ✦ CREATIVE NEW ENGLAND   Katahdin is a lively, often noisy spot that prides itself on its eclectic cuisine. Artists on slim budgets dine on the nightly blue-plate special, which typically features something basic like meatloaf or pan-fried catfish. Wealthy business folks dine on more delicate fare, like the restaurant's crab cakes. Nightly specialties could include a plate of grilled sea scallops with an apricot-lobster reduction, or a London broil marinated in a ginger, scallion, and garlic mix. Sometimes the kitchen nods, but for the most part, food is good, made more palatable by the reasonable prices. There's a small but decent selection of wines. No reservations are accepted, but you can enjoy one of the restaurant's fine martinis while waiting at the bar for a table.

106 High St. (C) 207/774-1740. www.katahdinrestaurant.com. Reservations not accepted. Main courses $12–$18. DISC, MC, V. Tues–Thurs 5–9:30pm; Fri–Sat 5–10:30pm.

Natasha's ✦ NEW AMERICAN   Natasha's menu is delightfully creative in its simplicity—a lobster stew with leek and potatoes or a Maine crab and goat cheese Rangoon serve as typical starters. Dinner entrees (served Tues–Sat) include lobster and crab ravioli served with leeks and lemon, pork loin grilled and served with a spicy pepper jam, and a crispy peanut tofu with *pad Thai* seasoning. Lunch is inviting, with options including creative sandwiches (like a

Packing a Picnic

Portland and its surrounding area is so stuffed with picnic spots you might need a week to sample them all.

For starters, don't miss the **Eastern Promenade** (p. 113), a hilltop park with expansive views of Casco Bay and its myriad (more than one for each day of the year) islands. Some have favorably compared this view with San Francisco's; even if that's stretching it a bit, you can't go wrong here watching the weather and light come and go.

The **Western Promenade** (p. 113), reached across town via Congress Street, has distant westerly views of the White Mountains (you can just make out the massive outline of Mount Washington on a clear day). The mall, airport, and paper mill in the foreground make for uninspiring scenery—but it's still a great spot for sunsets. There are a few benches. In summer, there are free musical performances here of a pretty high caliber.

If you enjoy scenes of a gritty working waterfront, the **Casco Bay Lines** ferry terminal on Commercial Street (at the foot of Franklin Arterial) has plenty of free benches.

If you seek a more tranquil water view, **Back Cove** loops around from Forest Avenue to Washington Avenue. Stopping places are scattered about the circular path around the cove, which is full of joggers, baby-strollers, and walkers in good weather. A full loop takes about an hour.

---

vegetarian napoleon with artichoke hearts, mozzarella cheese, portobello mushrooms, and roasted red peppers) and salads, along with wraps and noodles. Owner Natasha Carleton believes in giving back to the community: On Mondays lunch is free—you pay what you can afford, with the more affluent covering the cost for the less so.

82 Exchange St. ✆ 207/774-4004. Reservations recommended. Main courses: lunch $4.50–$9.95 (mostly $5–$6); dinner $13–$20. AE, DISC, MC, V. Mon–Fri 11am–2:30pm and 5–9:30pm; Sat 5–9:30pm.

Rí~Rá ✪ IRISH   This fun restaurant and bar (next to Flatbread Company) is styled after a friendly Irish pub. The doors were imported from a shop pub in Kilkenny, and the back bar and counter are from County Louth. Old and new blend seamlessly; it sometimes seems more Irish than the real thing—save for a lack of smoke and a large-screen TV with football and baseball, not soccer. Upstairs beyond the pub is a nice dining room with a great view of the ferry slip; look for basic pub fare such as smoked turkey wrap, cheeseburgers, shepherd's pie, and Guinness bread pudding, along with some more upscale dishes acceptably done. This is part of a small chain with other Rí~Rás in North Carolina, Rhode Island, and Vermont.

72 Commercial St. ✆ 207/761-4446. www.rira.com. Main courses: pub fare $6.95–$9.95; entrees $18–$22. AE, MC, V. Mon–Sat 11:30am–10pm; Sun 11am–10pm.

Siam City Cafe ✪ THAI   This pleasant little cafe resides on a revived stretch of Fore Street around the corner from the Portland Regency Hotel. The Thai food here is creatively presented. Start off with a traditional spring roll filled with shrimp, rice vermicelli, and vegetables or the deep-fried lobster egg rolls.

Just a few miles north of Portland along Route 1 in Falmouth, the Maine Audubon Society's **Gilsland Farm Sanctuary** is one of the best picnic spots I've found. Gaze out on grassy fields, wildflowers, and tidewater. Afterward, explore the society's intriguing displays, demonstration projects, and gift shops; this is clearly an organization that cares deeply about the state's natural resources. What the heck? Become a member while you're there.

And, of course, the beaches and parks in Cape Elizabeth (south of Portland, reached via Rte. 77) are all superlative picnic spots. **Two Lights State Park** and **Fort Williams Park** (which includes oft-photographed Portland Head Light) both offer sweeping vistas of lighthouses and craggy waves crashing onto dramatic rocks; **Crescent Beach State Park** is a very pleasing, sandy crescent, reached by a walk through beach roses. There's a concessions stand, too. A bit farther south, **Scarborough Beach Park** is another good choice. It's a long, sandy beach.

For picnicking supplies in metro Portland, I like **Supper at Six** for sandwiches and **Standard Baking Co.** for sweets and coffee; see "Where to Dine" for more details. Cape Elizabeth has a few general stores good for stocking up pre-beach; they're heavy on sodas, beer, and candy, but you can also score an Italian sandwich or an ice-cream treat at most.

For the main course, you might go with the jazzy *pad Thai*—here, a mélange of rice stick noodles, shrimp, scallops, and lobster, crunchy roasted peanuts, scrambled egg, crisp bean sprouts, and scallions—or choose one of the curries (red, green, or massaman) with chicken, scallops, shrimp, or tofu. Somewhat surprisingly, there's an extensive wine list, featuring a healthy selection of reds and whites for dousing the fiery food.

339 Fore St., Portland ME 04102. (?) 207/773-8389. Entrees $12–$22. AE, MC, V. Tues–Sun 11:30am–2pm and 5–9:30pm.

INEXPENSIVE

Becky's BREAKFAST/LUNCH   Becky's got a glowing write-up by noted food writers Jane and Michael Stern in *Gourmet* magazine in 1999, but it obviously hasn't gone to the proprietor's head (she's a mother of six and doesn't have time for a swelled head). This waterfront institution is located in a squat maroon building of concrete block on the not-so-quaint end of the waterfront; it has drop ceilings, fluorescent lights, and scruffy counters, booths, and tables. It's populated early (it opens at 4am) and often by local fishermen grabbing a cup of joe and a plate o' eggs before setting out; later in the day, it attracts high school kids, businessmen and just about everyone else. The menu is extensive, offering about what you'd expect, including lots of inexpensive sandwiches (fried haddock and cheese, corn dogs, tuna melt). But it's most noted for its breakfasts, including 13 different omelets, eggs anyway you'd like them, fruit bowls (made with fresh fruit in season), pancakes, and French toast. And where else can you choose among five different types of home fries? The place is open daily from

4am until 9pm and is a good spot to grab a booth, tuck into the daily special, and people-watch real Portlanders chatting, chewing, flirting, sassing, and then hurrying off to work.

390 Commercial St. ℂ 207/773-7070. www.beckysdiner.com. Main courses: breakfast $2.25–$7.50; sandwiches $1.95–$5.25; dinners $2.25–$7.95. AE, DISC, MC, V. Sun–Mon 4am–3pm; Tues–Sat 4am–9pm.

Federal Spice WRAPS/GLOBAL   Tucked in a drab location across from a post office, this is one of Portland's best bets for a quick, cheap nosh. Located beneath a parking garage (just off Temple St.), Federal Spice is a breezy, informal spot with limited dining inside and a few tables outside. There are quesadillas, salads, and soft tacos, along with wraps full of a choice of interesting fillings. The yam fries are an unusual side dish choice.

225 Federal St. ℂ 207/774-6404. Main courses $3–$7. No credit cards. Mon–Sat 11am–9pm.

Gilbert's Chowder House CHOWDER/SEAFOOD   Gilbert's is an unprepossessing waterfront spot that's nautical without being too cute. Angle for the outdoor tables overlooking a parking lot and the working waterfront; sometimes it smells pleasantly marine, sometimes unpleasantly so. The chowders are flavorful, if pasty. If you're looking to bulk up, consider getting your chowder in a bread bowl. Other meals include fried clams and haddock sandwiches, and a mess of other seafood available broiled or fried. There's also a basic lobster dinner, which includes corn on the cob and a cup of clam chowder. Limited microbrews are on tap; the homemade cheesecake makes a fitting dessert.

92 Commercial St. ℂ 207/871-5636. Reservations not accepted. Chowders $2.50–$9.75; sandwiches $2.25–$9.95; main courses $6.95–$23. Mon–Thurs 11am–10pm; Fri–Sat 11am–11pm; Sun 11am–9pm (closed earlier in winter).

Silly's ⚡ Finds Kids ECLECTIC/TAKEOUT   Silly's is the favored cheap-eats joint among even jaded Portlanders, and despite moving to a new location in the '90s, it has never lost favor. Situated on a ragged commercial street, the interior is informal, bright, and funky, with mismatched 1950s dinettes and an equally hodgepodge back patio beneath improbable trees. (There's also a weird fascination with Einstein here.) Like Einstein, the menu is creative, everything made fresh and from scratch. The place is noted for its roll-ups ("fast Abdullahs"), a series of tasty fillings piled into fresh tortillas. Among the best: the shish kebab with feta and the sloppy "Diesel," made with pulled pork barbecue and coleslaw. The fries here are hand-cut, the burgers big and delicious, and there's beer on tap with musicians sometimes performing as a bonus. Don't overlook the playful, changing dessert menu of pies, ice creams, and cakes—and absolutely do not leave without sampling one of the huge milkshakes. Silly's whip's 'em up with peanut butter, tahini, bananas, malt, or just about anything else you like. The rotating selection of homemade ice creams varies, but tend to be, shall we say, unique (such as cinnamon-basil or avocado and lime).

40 Washington Ave. ℂ 207/772-0360. www.sillys.com. Lunch and dinner $3.25–$7.50; pizza $8.50–$11. MC, V. Tues–Thurs 11:30am–9pm; Fri–Sat 11:30am–10pm; Sun 11:30am–8pm.

4 Exploring the City

Any visit to Portland should start with a stroll around the historic **Old Port** ⚡. Bounded by Commercial, Congress, Union, and Pearl streets, this several-square-block area near the waterfront contains the city's best commercial architecture, a plethora of fine restaurants, a mess of boutiques, and one of the thickest concentrations of bars you'll find anywhere. (The Old Port tends to transform as night lengthens, with the crowds growing younger and rowdier.) The narrow streets and intricate brick facades reflect the mid-Victorian era during which most of the area was rebuilt following a devastating fire in 1866. Leafy, quaint **Exchange Street** ⚓ is the heart of the Old Port, with other attractive streets running off and around it.

Just outside the Old Port, don't miss the **First Parish Church** ⚓, at 425 Congress St., an uncommonly beautiful granite meeting house with an impressively austere interior that has changed little since it first opened its doors in 1826. The church also boasts a small garden, one of the few green spaces in downtown Portland. A few doors down the block is **City Hall,** at the head of Exchange Street. Modeled after New York's City Hall, Portland's seat of government was built of granite in 1909. It houses the Merrill Auditorium, the city's classiest venue for concerts and Broadway-type road shows. In a similarly regal vein is the **U.S. Custom House,** at 312 Fore St. During business hours, feel free to wander inside to view the elegant woodwork and marble floors dating from 1868.

Flanking the Old Port on the two low hills are downtown's main residential areas. Drive eastward on Congress Street up and over Munjoy Hill, and you'll come to the **Eastern Promenade** ⚓⚓, a 68-acre hillside park with broad, grassy slopes extending down to the water and superb views of Casco Bay and its islands. Along the base of the park you'll find the Eastern Prom Pathway, which wraps along the waterfront between the Casco Bay Lines ferry terminal near the Old Port and the East End Beach. The pathway is suitable for walking or biking, and offers wonderful views of the harbor and its constant boat traffic. The easiest place to park is at the bottom of the hill near the beach and boat ramp.

Atop Munjoy Hill, above the Eastern Promenade, is the distinctive **Portland Observatory,** a quirky shingled tower dating from 1807, used to signal the arrival of ships into port. After 4 years of extensive structural repairs, the tower reopened in the summer of 2000. Exhibits inside provide a quick glimpse of Portland's past, but the real draw is the expansive view ⚓ from the top of the city and the harbor. It is open daily (when flags are flying from the cupola); admission is $5 for adults and $4 for children 6 to 16. For more information, call ℭ **207/774-5561.**

On the other end of the peninsula is the **Western Promenade** ⚓. (Follow Spring St. westward to Vaughan; turn right and then take your first left on Bowdoin St. to the prom.) This narrow strip of lawn atop a forested bluff has views across the Fore River, which is lined with less-than-scenic light industry, to the White Mountains in the distance. It's a great spot to watch the sunset. Around the Western Prom are some of the grandest and most imposing houses in the city that include a wide array of architectural styles, from Italianate to shingle to stick.

THE TOP ATTRACTIONS: FROM LIGHTHOUSES TO LONGFELLOW

Children's Museum of Maine ⚓ *(Kids*   The centerpiece exhibit here is the camera obscura, a room-size "camera" located on the top floor of this stout, columned downtown building next to the art museum. Children gather around a white table in a dark room, where they see magically projected images that include cars driving on city streets, boats plying the harbor, and seagulls flapping by. The camera obscura never fails to enthrall, and it provides a memorable lesson in the workings of a lens—whether in a camera or an eye.

That's just one attraction. There's plenty more to do here, from running a supermarket checkout counter to sliding down the firehouse pole, to piloting a mock space shuttle from a high cockpit. The Explore Floor offers a series of interactive science exhibits focusing on Maine's natural resources. Make a deal with your kids: They behave during a trip to the art museum (just next door), and they'll be rewarded with a couple of hours in their own museum.

142 Free St. (next to the Portland Museum of Art). (C) 207/828-1234. Admission $6. Free 5–8pm first Fri of each month. AE, MC, V. Mon–Sat 10am–5pm; Sun noon–5pm. Closed Mon fall–spring. Discounted parking at Spring St. parking garage.

Maine Narrow Gauge Railroad Co. & Museum ★ *Kids*   In the late 19th century, Maine was home to several narrow-gauge railways, operating on rails 2 feet apart. Most of these versatile trains have disappeared, but this nonprofit organization is dedicated to preserving the examples that remain. Admission is free, with a charge for a short ride on a train that chugs on a rail line along Casco Bay at the foot of the Eastern Prom. Views of the islands are outstanding; the ride itself is slow-paced and somewhat yawn-inducing unless you're very young.

58 Fore St. (C) 207/828-0814. www.mngrr.org. Museum admission free; train fare $6 adults, $5 seniors, $4 children. Daily 10am–4pm; trains run on the hour from 11am. Closed Jan to mid-Feb. From I-295, take Franklin St. exit and follow to Fore St.; turn left, continue to museum, on the right.

Portland Head Light & Museum ★★   A short drive (15–20 min. depending on traffic) from downtown Portland, this 1794 lighthouse is one of the most picturesque in the nation. (You'll probably recognize it from its cameo role in numerous advertisements and posters.) The light marks the entrance to Portland Harbor and was occupied continuously from its construction until 1989, when it was automated and the graceful keeper's house (1891) was converted to a small town-owned museum focusing on the history of navigation. The lighthouse itself is still active and thus closed to the public, but visitors can stop by the museum, browse for lighthouse-themed gifts at the gift shop, wander the park grounds, and watch the sailboats and cargo ships come and go. The park has a pebble beach, grassy lawns with ocean vistas, and picnic areas well suited for informal barbecues.

Fort Williams Park, 1000 Shore Rd., Cape Elizabeth. (C) 207/799-2661. www.portlandheadlight.com. Free admission for grounds; museum admission $2 adults, $1 children 6–18. Park grounds open daily year-round sunrise–sunset (until 8:30pm in summer); museum open daily June–Oct 10am–4pm; open weekends only in spring and late fall. From Portland, follow State St. across bridge to South Portland; bear left on Broadway. At 3rd light, turn right on Cottage Rd. (Rte. 77), which becomes Shore Rd.; follow until you arrive at the park, on your left.

Portland Museum of Art ★★   This bold, modern museum was designed by I.M. Pei & Partners in 1983, and it features selections from its own fine collections along with a parade of touring exhibits. (Summer exhibits are usually targeted at a broad audience.) The museum is particularly strong in American artists with Maine connections, including Winslow Homer, Andrew Wyeth, and Edward Hopper, and it has fine displays of early American furniture and crafts. The museum shares the Joan Whitney Payson Collection with Colby College (the college gets it one semester every other year), which includes wonderful European works by Renoir, Degas, and Picasso. Guided tours are daily at 2pm.

7 Congress Sq. (corner of Congress and High sts.). (C) 207/775-6148. www.portlandmuseum.org. Admission $8 adults, $6 students and seniors, $2 children 6–17. (Free admission Fri 5–9pm.) Tues–Thurs and Sat–Sun 10am–5pm (Memorial Day to mid-Oct also open Mon 10am–5pm); Fri 10am–9pm.

Portland Public Market *Kids*   The Portland Public Market features some of the best food that Maine is producing, and it's the perfect place to lay in supplies for a picnic or snacks. There are more than two dozen vendors selling fresh foods and flowers, much of which is Maine-grown. The architecturally distinctive building is at once classic and modern, and it houses fishmongers, butchers, fresh fruit dealers, a seafood cafe, and a wine shop. There's free parking (with validated ticket) at the connected garage on the west side of Cumberland Avenue; ask any merchant to stamp your ticket.

25 Preble St. (½ block west of Monument Sq.). ℭ **207/228-2000**. www.portlandmarket.com. Open year-round. Mon–Sat 9am–7pm; Sun 10am–5pm.

Victoria Mansion ★★ *Finds*   Widely regarded as one of the most elaborate Victorian brownstone homes ever built in the United States, this mansion (also known as the Morse-Libby House) is a remarkable display of high Victorian style. Built between 1858 and 1863 for a Maine businessman who made a fortune in the New Orleans hotel trade, the towering, slightly foreboding home is a prime example of the Italianate style once in vogue. Inside, it appears that not a square inch of wall space was left unmolested by craftsmen or artisans (11 painters were hired to create the murals). The decor is ponderous and somber, but it offers an engaging look at a bygone era. This home is a must for architecture buffs and is often mentioned in books on the history of American architecture. A gift shop sells Victorian-themed gifts and books. December is a particularly special time here, with a month of holiday events, decorations, and festivities.

109 Danforth St. ℭ **207/772-4841**. Admission $10 adults, $9 seniors, $3 children 6–17, free for children under 6. May–Oct Tues–Sat 10am–4pm, Sun 1–5pm; tours offered at quarter past and quarter of each hour. Closed Nov–Apr, except for holiday tours from end of Nov to mid-Dec. From the Old Port, head west on Fore St., and veer right on Danforth St. at light near Giobbi's restaurant; proceed 3 blocks to the mansion, at the corner of Park St.

Wadsworth-Longfellow House & Center for Maine History   Maine Historical Society's "history campus" includes three widely varied buildings on busy Congress Street in downtown Portland. The austere brick Wadsworth-Longfellow House dates from 1785 and was built by Gen. Peleg Wadsworth, father of noted poet Henry Wadsworth Longfellow. It's furnished in an early 19th century style, with many samples of Longfellow family furniture on display. Adjacent to the home is the Maine History Gallery, located in a garish post-modern building, formerly a bank. Changing exhibits here explore the rich texture of Maine history. Just behind the Longfellow house is the library of the Maine Historical Society, a popular destination among genealogists.

489 Congress St. ℭ **207/774-1822** or 207/879-0427. www.mainehistory.org. $7 adults, $6 seniors and students, $3 children (6–18). Longfellow House open May–Oct daily Mon–Sat 10am–4pm, Sun noon–5pm.

ON THE WATER

The 3½-mile **Back Cove Pathway** ★ loops around Portland's Back Cove, offering attractive views of the city skyline across the water, glimpses of Casco Bay, and a bit of exercise. The pathway is the city's most popular recreational facility; after work in summer, Portlanders flock here to walk, bike, jog, and windsurf (there's enough water 2½ hours before and after high tide). Part of the pathway shares a noisy bridge with I-295, and it can be fulsome at a dead low tide; when the tides and the weather cooperate, however, it's a pleasant spot for a walk. The main parking lot is located across from Hannaford Plaza at the water's edge. Take Exit 6 (Forest Ave. north) off I-295; turn right at the first light on Baxter Boulevard. At the next light, turn right again and park in the lot ahead on the left.

Another fine place to take in a water view is the **Eastern Prom Pathway** ★, which wraps for about a mile along the waterfront between the Casco Bay Lines ferry terminal and the East End Beach (the path continues onward to connect with the Back Cove Pathway). The paved pathway is suitable for walking or biking and offers wonderful views out toward the islands and the boat traffic on the harbor. The easiest place to park is near the beach and boat ramp. From downtown, head east on Congress Street until you can't go any farther; turn right and then take your first left on the road down the hill to the water's edge.

Casco Bay Lines   Six of the Casco Bay islands have year-round populations and are served by scheduled ferries from downtown Portland. Except for Long Island, the islands are part of the city of Portland. The ferries offer an inexpensive way to view the bustling harbor and get a taste of island life. Trips range from a 20-minute (one-way) excursion to Peaks Island (the closest thing to an island suburb, with 1,200 year-round residents), to the 5½-hour cruise to Bailey Island (connected by bridge to the mainland south of Brunswick) and back. All of the islands are well suited for walking; Peaks Island has a rocky back shore that's easily accessible via the island's paved perimeter road (bring a picnic lunch). Cliff Island is the most remote of the bunch and has a sedate turn-of-the-20th-century island retreat character. Peaks is easily biked, and there's a rental outfit right on the island, a few blocks from the ferry: Brad's Bike Shop, at 115 Island Ave. (© **207/766-5631**). Food options are few and far between, so stock up at the island's lone general store, just off the ferry. The islands are too spaced out to visit on a hop-skip-and-jump itinerary, so pick one and stick with it; Peaks is easiest.

Commercial and Franklin sts. © 207/774-7871. www.cascobaylines.com. Fares vary depending on the run and the season, but summer rates typically are $6–$18 round-trip. Frequent departures 6am–10pm.

Eagle Island Tours ☆   Eagle Island was the summer home of famed Arctic explorer and Portland native Robert E. Peary, who claimed in 1909 to be the first person to reach the North Pole. (His accomplishments have been the subject of exhaustive debates among Arctic scholars, some of whom insist he inflated his claims.) In 1904, Peary built a simple home on a remote, 17-acre island at the edge of Casco Bay; in 1912, he added flourishes in the form of two low stone towers. After his death in 1920, his family kept up the home; they later donated it to the state, which has since managed it as a state park. The home is open to the public, maintained much the way it was when Peary lived here. Island footpaths through the scant forest allow exploration to the open, seagull-clotted cliffs at the southern tip. Eagle Tours offers one trip daily from Portland. The 4-hour excursion includes a 1½-hour stopover on the island.

Long Wharf (Commercial St.) © 207/774-6498. www.eagleislandtours.com. $24 adults, $22 seniors, $13 children under 12 (includes state park fee of $2.50). 1 departure daily at 10am, daily late June–Labor Day, weekends June and Sept.

Olde Port Mariner Fleet   This fleet of three boats tied up off Commercial Street offers a number of ways to enjoy the bay. The *Indian II* runs deep-sea fishing trips far beyond Portland Harbor in search of cod, cusk, hake, pollack, and more. Most are daylong trips (8am–5pm), but several times each summer they offer marathons (5am–5pm) for real die-hards. On the *Odyssey* you search for whales by day and on Friday evenings you can enjoy music and food, including a 4-hour Downeast lobster bake. You're advised to book these cruises in advance if you're set on going.

Commercial St. (Long Wharf and Custom House Wharf). © 800/437-3270 or 207/774-2022. www.mariner fleet.com. Excursions $30–$60, short cruises $10. Several departures daily.

FERRIES TO NOVA SCOTIA

A trip to northern New England can serve as a springboard for an excursion to Atlantic Canada. The most hassle-free way to link the two is by ferry. Two ferries

Moments   Lucky 77: Hitting the Beaches

One of the supreme pleasures of visiting the Portland area is the opportunity to sample some of its many great beaches and lighthouse and ocean views. Even within Portland city limits, you can laze on the Eastern Promenade's tiny **East End Beach** (see above) for free; though I wouldn't swim there—a wastewater treatment plant looms nearby—you can take in great views. Across the bridge in South Portland, **Willard Beach** is a good neighborhood beach: small, with friendly locals, dogs, and tidal rocks to scramble over. There's plenty of parking here.

For the best of the out-of-town beaches and views, though, strike out for **Cape Elizabeth,** a moneyed suburb just south. (From Portland's State Street, cross the Rte. 77 bridge going south, then follow signs.) You can choose from a trio of good beaches as you meander along Route 77, a lovely lane that occasionally recalls England with its sweeping views of marsh, ocean, or cultivated field.

Two Lights State Park (© 207/799-5871) is impressively scenic, and has the advantage of a decent lobster-and-seafood hut beside it: **Two Lights Lobster Shack**, open late spring through October. The lobsters are smallish, lobster rolls meaty, clam chowder pretty good; the views are sublime. Farther south on 77, **Crescent Beach State Park** (© 207/799-5871) is a lovely mile-long curve of sand with ample parking, barbecue pits, picnic tables, and a snack bar. Both charge a fee from Memorial Day to Columbus Day. The town-operated **Fort Williams State Park**, located on Shore Road in Cape Elizabeth just off Route 77; is a bit harder to find, but offers free access and supreme views of both the ocean and the much-photographed **Portland Head Light** (see "Exploring the City," earlier in this chapter). There is also a small museum and a gift shop inside the lighthouse.

Two to 3 miles farther south, turn left onto Route 207 for two more options: **Scarborough Beach Park**, on the left, another long strip of clean sand and dunes with changing facilities ($3.50 for access in summer) or—a bit farther along, on the right at the end of Ferry Road—quieter **Ferry Beach,** which is free and has good views of Old Orchard to the south.

connect Yarmouth, Nova Scotia, with Maine, saving hours of driving time and providing a relaxing minicruise along the way.

The *Scotia Prince* departs each evening from Portland for an 11-hour crossing to Nova Scotia. The ship is bustling with activity, from its cafe and restaurant to casino and glitzy floor show in the lounge. When the party winds down, you can retire to a cabin for a good night's sleep and awake for breakfast before disembarking in Nova Scotia. Day cabins are available on the return trip, but you'll save some money sitting in the lounge or relaxing on a deck chair (or in the new hot tubs!) and watching for whales.

The Portland to Yarmouth crossing aboard the *Scotia Prince* is approximately 11 hours and in peak season costs $75 to $85 for adult passengers, $38 to $45 for children ages 5 to 12, and $95 to $105 for each vehicle under 75 feet long.

Cabins are available for an additional fare, ranging from $32 for a day cabin to $190 for an overnight suite with a king bed. Advance reservations are essential. Prices are lower in the off-season. Call **Scotia Prince Cruises** at ℂ **800/845-4073** or 207/775-5616; visit online at www.scotiaprince.com.

Bay Ferries (ℂ **888/249-7245** or 207/288-3395) operates the Bar Harbor–Yarmouth ferry aboard *The Cat* (short for catamaran), which claims to be the fastest ferry in North America. Since going into service in 1998, the new ship has cut the crossing time from 6 hours to less than 3 hours, zipping along at up to 50 miles per hour. There's an open deck on the rear, but passengers trying to enjoy the fresh air sometimes find it mingled with exhaust fumes. Summer season rates, one way, are $55 for adults, $50 for seniors, $35 for children ages 11 to 17, $25 for children ages 5 to 11, and $95 for most automobiles. Off-season rates are lower. The ferry leaves Bar Harbor twice daily in summer at 8am and 4pm (except Wed, when there's only a morning departure); as with the Scotia Prince line, advance reservations are vital during the peak summer season.

MINOR LEAGUE BASEBALL

Portland Sea Dogs ★★   A Double-A team affiliated with the Boston Red Sox (a perfect marriage in baseball-crazy northern New England), the Sea Dogs play through summer at Hadlock Field, a small stadium near downtown that still retains an old-time feel despite aluminum benches and other updating. Activities are geared toward families, with lots of entertainment between innings and a selection of food that's a couple of notches above basic hot dogs and hamburgers. (Try the tasty french fries and grilled sausages.) You might even catch future pro stars—Josh Beckett, Brad Penny, Alex Gonzalez, Charles Johnson, and Kevin Millar all did time here as farmhands before they made "the show."

Hadlock Field, 217 Park Ave. (P.O. Box 636), Portland, ME 04104. ℂ **800/936-3647** or 207/879-9500. www.seadogs.com. Tickets $3–$10. Season runs Apr to Labor Day.

SHOPPING

Aficionados of antique and secondhand furniture stores love Portland. Good browsing can be had on Congress Street. Check out the stretches between State and High streets in the arts district, and from India Street to Washington Avenue on Munjoy Hill. About a dozen shops of varying quality (mostly low end) can be found in these two areas.

More serious antique hounds may choose to visit an **auction** or two. Two or three times per week you'll be able to find an auction within an hour's drive of Portland. A good source of information is the *Maine Sunday Telegram*. Look in the classifieds for listings of auctions scheduled for the following week.

For new items, the Old Port, with its dozens of boutiques and storefronts, is well worth browsing. It's especially strong in contemporary one-of-a-kind clothing that's a world apart from generic stuff you'll find at a mall. Artisan and crafts shops are also well represented.

Business hours are generally 10am to 6pm for most retail stores, but individual store hours may vary. Many stores stay open later in summer. Always call ahead before heading out.

Abacus American Crafts   A wide range of bold, inventive crafts of all varieties—from furniture to jewelry—is displayed on two floors of this centrally located shop. Even if you're not in a buying frame of mind, this is a great place for browsing. 44 Exchange St. ℂ 207/772-4880.

Amaryllis Clothing Co.   Portland's original creative clothing store, Amaryllis offers unique clothing for women that's as comfortable as it is casually elegant.

The colors are rich, the patterns are unique, and some items are designed by local artisans. It's open until 6pm weekdays, to 8pm weekends. 41 Exchange St. © 207/772-4439.

D. Cole Jewelers   I love this place for little gifts of jewelry. Longtime Old Port denizens Dean and Denise Cole produce wonderfully handcrafted gold and silver jewelry that's always attractive and often surprisingly affordable. Browse from elegant traditional designs as well as more eccentric work at the bright, low-pressure shop; staff are extremely helpful. 10 Exchange St. © 207/772-5119.

Folia   Original, handcrafted jewelry by Maine's top designers is nicely displayed at this tasteful shop in the heart of the Old Port. There's also a collection of loose gemstones on display. 50 Exchange St. © 207/761-4432.

Green Design Furniture   This inventive shop sells a line of beautiful mission-inspired furniture that disassembles for easy storage and travel. These beautiful works are creatively crafted of cherry. 267 Commercial St. © 800/853-4234 or 207/775-4234.

Harbor Fish Market   This classic waterfront fish market is worth a trip just to see the mounds of fresh fish. It's a great spot for lobsters to go (they're packed for travel and will easily last 24 hr.) or to buy smoked fish for a local picnic. 9 Custom House Wharf (across from end of Pearl St.). © 800/370-1790 or 207/775-0251.

LeRoux Kitchen   Look for great kitchen gadgets, Maine-made food products, and a good selection of wine at this Old Port shop that replaced a similar shop of different ownership. 161 Commercial St. © 207/553-7665.

L.L. Bean Factory Store   Sporting goods retailer L.L. Bean opened its first downtown factory outlet here in 1996. Look for last year's fashions, returns, and slightly damaged goods, along with a small selection of first-run, full-price items. 542 Congress St. © 207/772-5100.

Maine Potters Market   Maine's largest pottery collective has been in operation for nearly 2 decades. You can select from a variety of styles; shipping is easily arranged. 376 Fore St. © 207/774-1633.

Resourceful Home   Environmentally sound products for the home and garden, linens, and cleaning products are the specialties here. 111 Commercial St. © 207/780-1314.

Stonewall Kitchen   Stonewall is a frequent winner in food trade shows for its innovative and delicious mustards, jams, and sauces. Among them: ginger peach tea jam, sun-dried tomato and olive relish, and maple chipotle grill sauce. You can browse and sample at their Old Port store (also stores in Camden and in York). 182 Middle St. © 207/879-2409.

5 Portland After Dark

BARS & MUSIC

Portland is usually lively in the evenings, especially on summer weekends when the testosterone level in the Old Port seems to rocket into the stratosphere, with young men and women prowling the dozens of bars and spilling out onto Fore Street and the surrounding alleys and streets.

Among the Old Port bars favored by locals are **Three-Dollar Dewey's,** at the corner of Commercial and Union streets (the popcorn is free); atmospheric **Gritty McDuff's Brew Pub** ⚓ on Fore Street at the foot of Exchange Street, where you'll find live music and a cast of regulars quaffing great beers brewed on-site; and the slightly rowdy Irish pub **Brian Ború,** on Center Street, with a rooftop patio. All three bars are casual and pubby, with guests sharing long tables with new companions.

Portland's newest gay club has replaced its longest-running one. **Styxx** (© 207/ **828-0822;** www.styxxportland.com) is located at 3 Spring St., just uphill from the Old Port. Half of the place is a tidy, friendly bar and hangout; the other half is a dance club with pulsing lights and music. It features movie nights, karaoke, and other special promotions.

Beyond the active Old Port bar scene, a number of clubs offer a mix of live and recorded entertainment throughout the year. As is common in other small cities where there are more venues than attendees, the clubs have come and gone, sometimes quite rapidly. Check the city's free weekly *Portland Phoenix* for current venues, performers, and show times.

FILM

Downtown Portland is still blessed with two downtown movie houses, enabling travelers in the mood for a flick to avoid the disheartening slog out to the boxy, could-be-anywhere mall octoplexes. **Nickelodeon Cinemas,** 1 Temple St. (© 207/ **772-9751**), has six screens showing first- and second-run films at reasonable prices. **The Movies** ☆, 10 Exchange St. (© 207/772-9600 or 207/772-8041), is a compact art-film showcase in the heart of the Old Port featuring a lineup of foreign and independent films of recent and historic vintage.

Moments **A Hundred Beers Old**

Once upon a time back in the day—alright, during the Clinton years—my girlfriend's father used to meet us at the legendary **Great Lost Bear** (540 Forest Ave.; © 207/772-0300) for a beer and a few burgers. Turns out he never liked me much, and she ran off with a married man soon enough—but that's another story.

My point is, if you're going to get your heart broken and cry in your beer afterward, might as well do it here: They've got the best brew selection in all of northern New England, 50 to 60 on offer at any given moment, including what seems like every last one of the numerous local brews crafted here in Maine. Some of the choicest ales are even dispensed from one of three cask-conditioned hand pumps, just like they do it in Jolly Olde England. As if that weren't enough, every Thursday the bartender showcases a particular brewer or style—a good way to get educated about the nuances of good beer.

This is definitely off the beaten track, though, in a locals'-only neighborhood separated from the other Portland attractions and eateries listed in this book. To find the Bear, head about two miles out Forest Avenue (*away* from the Old Port), or ask a local for directions. Only quibble? The food offerings here are spectacularly unspectacular; there's a great bakery close at hand tucked behind on a side street, though I don't suppose that would do you much good at two in the morning. Instead, come for the brews and the convivial atmosphere.

Travel Tip: He who finds the best hotel deal has more to spend on facials involving knobbly vegetables.

Hello, the Roaming Gnome here. I've been nabbed from the garden and taken round the world. The people who took me are so terribly clever. They find the best offerings on Travelocity. For very little cha-ching. And that means I get to be pampered and exfoliated till I'm pink as a bunny's doodah.

travelocity®

1-888-TRAVELOCITY / travelocity.com / America Online Keyword: Travel

PERFORMING ARTS

Portland has a growing creative corps of performing artists. Theater companies typically take the summer off, but it doesn't hurt to call or check the local papers for special performances.

Center for Cultural Exchange ✩   The center is devoted to bringing acts from around the globe to Portland. Venues range from area theaters and churches to the center's small but handsome performance space located in a former dry-cleaning establishment facing a statue of the pensive poet Henry Wadsworth Longfellow. Acts range from pan-Caribbean dance music to klezmer bands, to Quebecois step-dancing. It's worth stopping by the center (it hosts a tiny cafe) to see what's coming up. You just never know. Longfellow Sq. (corner of Congress and State sts.) ⓒ **207/761-1545.** www.centerforculturalexchange.org. Tickets $8–$32.

Portland Stage Company   The most polished and consistent of the Portland theater companies, Portland Stage offers crisply produced shows staring local and imported equity actors in a handsome, second-story theater just off Congress Street. About a half-dozen shows are staged throughout the season, which runs from October to May. Recent productions have included *Proof, Arcadia,* and *Fences.* Performing Arts Center, 25A Forest Ave. ⓒ **207/774-0465.** www.portland stage.com. Tickets $20–$32.

Portland Symphony Orchestra ✩✩   The well-regarded Portland Symphony, headed by Toshiyuki Shimada, offers a variety of performances throughout the season (typically Sept–May), ranging from pops to Mozart. Summer travelers should consider a Portland detour on the week of July Fourth, when the "Independence Pops" is held (weather permitting) at various sites around southern Maine, including the grounds of the Portland Head Lighthouse in Cape Elizabeth. The latter is a memorable outdoor picnic concert that features the "1812 Overture" and concludes with fireworks. 477 Congress St. ⓒ **207/842-0800** for tickets, or 207/773-6128 for more information. www.portlandsymphony.com. Tickets $15–$50.

6 Side Trips

OLD ORCHARD BEACH

About 12 miles south of Portland is the unrepentantly honky-tonkish beach town of Old Orchard Beach, which offers considerable stimulus for the senses (not to mention bikers, fried dough, and French-Canadians aplenty). This venerable Victorian-era resort is famed for its amusement park, pier, and long, sandy beach, which attracts sun worshippers from all over. Be sure to spend time and money on the stomach-churning rides at the beachside amusement park of **Palace Playland** (ⓒ **207/934-2001**), and then walk on the 7-mile-long beach past the midrise condos that sprouted in the 1980s like a scale-model Miami Beach.

The beach is broad and open at low tide; at high tide, space to plunk your towel down is at a premium. In the evenings, teens and young adults dominate the town's culture, spilling out of the video arcades and cruising the main strip. For dinner, do as the locals do and buy hot dogs and pizza and cotton candy; save your change for the arcades.

Old Orchard is just off Route 1 south of Portland. The quickest route is to leave the turnpike at Exit 5 and then follow I-195 and the signs to the beach. Don't expect to be alone here: Parking is tight, and the traffic can be horrendous during the peak summer months.

SEBAGO LAKE & DOUGLAS HILL

Maine's second-largest lake is also its most popular. Ringed with summer homes of varying vintages, many dating from the early part of this century, Sebago Lake attracts thousands of vacationers to its cool, deep waters.

You can take a tour of the outlying lakes and the ancient canal system between Sebago and Long lakes on the *Songo River Queen,* a faux-steamship berthed in the town of Naples (© 207/693-6861). For 2½-hour trips tickets cost $10 for adults and $8 for children 12 and under. For 1 hour trips, $6 for adults, $5 children 12 and under. Group rates are also available. Or just lie in the sun along the sandy beach at bustling **Sebago Lake State Park** (© 207/693-6613), on the lake's north shore (the park is off Rte. 302; look for signs between Raymond and South Casco). The park has shady picnic areas, a campground, a snack bar, and lifeguards on the beach (entrance fee charged). It can be uncomfortably crowded on sunny summer weekends; it's best on weekdays. Bring food and charcoal for barbecuing at the shady picnic areas off the beach. The park's campground has a separate beach (you need not camp to enjoy it, though), is at a distance from the day-use area, and is less congested during good weather. It books up early in the season, but you might luck into a cancellation if you need a spot to pitch your tent.

To the west of the lake, the rolling wooded uplands are very attractive. The closest prominent rise to Portland with public access is **Douglas Mountain,** whose summit is capped with a medieval-looking 16-foot stone tower. The property is open to the public; the summit is reached via an easy quarter-mile trail from the parking area. Look for wild blueberries at the end of July and the beginning of August.

SABBATHDAY LAKE SHAKER COMMUNITY ✮

Route 26, from Portland to Norway, is a speedy highway that runs past new housing developments and through hilly farmland. At one point the road pinches through a cluster of stately historic buildings that stand proudly beneath towering shade trees. That's the **Sabbathday Lake Shaker Community** (© 207/926-4597), the last active Shaker community in the nation. The half-dozen or so Shakers living here today still embrace their traditional beliefs and maintain a communal, pastoral way of life. The bulk of the community's income comes from the sale of herbs, which have been grown here since 1799.

Tours are offered daily in summer and early fall except on Sundays (when visitors are invited to attend services). Docents provide tours of the grounds and several buildings, including the graceful 1794 meeting house. Exhibits in the buildings showcase the famed furniture handcrafted by the Shakers and include antiques made by Shakers at other U.S. communes. You'll learn plenty about the Shaker ideology, with its emphasis on simplicity, industry, and celibacy. After your tour, browse the gift shop for Shaker herbs and teas. The introductory tour lasts 1 hour and 15 minutes ($6 for adults, $2 for children 6–12, and free for children under 6). In July and August, the community also offers an extended tour, which lasts 2 hours ($7.50 for adults, $2.75 for children). Tours run Monday through Saturday 10am to 4:30pm Memorial Day to Columbus Day. The last tour is at 3:15pm.

The Shaker village is about 45 minutes from Portland. Head north on Route 26 (Washington Ave. in Portland). The village is 8 miles from Exit 63 (Gray) of the Maine Turnpike; after exiting, follow signs into the center of downtown Gray, then follow Route 26 north right to the village.

6

Freeport to Monhegan Island

Veteran Maine travelers contend that this part of the coast is fast losing its native charm—it's too commercial, too developed, too much like the rest of the United States. The grousers do have a point, especially regarding Route 1's roadside, but get off the main roads and you'll find pockets where you can catch glimpses of another Maine. Among the sights back-road travelers will stumble upon are quiet inland villages, dramatic coastal scenery, and a rich sense of history, especially maritime history.

The best source of information for the region in general is found at the **Maine State Information Center** (© **207/846-0833**), just off Exit 17 of I-95 in Yarmouth. This state-run center is stocked with hundreds of brochures and free newspapers, and is staffed with a helpful crew that can provide information on the entire state but that is particularly well informed about the midcoast region. It's open daily from 8am to 6pm (8:30am–5pm in winter), and the attached restroom facilities are always open.

1 Freeport

Freeport is 123 miles NE of Boston, 333miles NE of New York City, and17 miles NE of Portland.

If Freeport were a mall (and that's not a far-fetched analogy), L.L. Bean would be the anchor store. It's the business that launched Freeport, elevating its status from just another town off the interstate to one of the two outlet capitals of Maine (the other is Kittery). Freeport still has the form of a classic coastal village, but it's a village that's been largely taken over by the national fashion industry. Most of the old homes and stores have been converted to upscale shops and now sell name-brand clothing and housewares. Banana Republic occupies an exceedingly handsome brick Federal-style home; even the McDonald's is in a tasteful, understated Victorian farmhouse—you really have to look for the golden arches.

While a number of more modern structures have been built to accommodate the outlet boom, strict planning guidelines have managed to preserve much of the local charm, at least in the village section. Huge parking lots off Main Street are hidden from view, making this one of the more aesthetically pleasing places to shop. But even with these large lots, parking can be scarce during the peak season, especially on rainy summer days when every cottage-bound tourist between York and Camden decides that a trip to Freeport is a winning idea. Bring a lot of patience, and expect teeming crowds if you come at a busy time.

ESSENTIALS
GETTING THERE
Freeport is on Route 1 but is most commonly reached via I-95 from either Exit 19 or Exit 20.

Finds **Mapping Your Next Stop**

Just across the road from the state information center in Yarmouth is the **DeLorme Map Store** (© 800/642-0970), open daily 9:30am to 6pm. You'll find a wide selection of maps here, including the firm's trademark state atlases and a line of CD-ROM map products. The store's fun to browse even if you're not a map buff, but what makes the place really worth a detour off the interstate is Eartha, "the world's largest rotating and revolving globe." The 42-foot-diameter globe occupies the entire atrium lobby and is constructed on a scale of 1:1,000,000, the largest satellite image of the earth ever produced. Far out.

VISITOR INFORMATION

The **Freeport Merchants Marketing Association,** P.O. Box 452, Freeport, ME 04032 (© **800/865-1994** or 207/865-1212; www.freeportusa.com), publishes a map and directory of businesses, restaurants, and overnight accommodations. The free map is widely available around town, or you can contact the association to send you one.

EXPLORING FREEPORT

While Freeport is nationally known for its outlet shopping, that's not all it offers. Just outside of town you'll find a lovely pastoral landscape, picturesque picnicking spots, and scenic drives that make for a handy retreat from all that spending.

By car head east on Bow Street (down the hill from L.L. Bean's main entrance), and wind around for 1 mile to the sign for **Mast Landing Sanctuary** ✪ (© 207/781-2330). Turn left and then right in ⅒ mile into the sanctuary parking lot. A network of trails totaling about 3 miles crisscrosses through a landscape of long-ago eroded hills and mixed woodlands; streams trickle down to the marshland estuary. The 140-acre property is owned by the Maine Audubon Society and is open to the public until dusk.

Back at the main road, turn left and continue eastward for 1½ miles; then turn right on Wolf Neck Road. Continue 1¾ miles and then turn left for a half-mile on a dirt farm road. **Wolfe's Neck Farm** ✪, owned and operated by a nonprofit trust, has been experimenting with ways to produce beef without chemicals, and it sells its own line of chemical-free meat. All this happens to take place at one of the most scenic coastal farms in Maine (it's especially beautiful near sunset). Stop at the gray farmhouse and pick up some tasty frozen steaks or flavorful hamburger. (Open Mon–Fri 1–6pm, Sat 9am–3pm; © **207/865-4469**).

Continue south on Wolf Neck Road, and you'll soon come to the 233-acre **Wolfe Neck Woods State Park** (© **207/865-4465**). This compact, attractive park has quiet woodland trails that run through forests of white pine and hemlock, past estuaries, and along the rocky shoreline of the bay. Googins Island, just offshore and reached by following the park's Casco Bay Trail, has an osprey nest on it. This is a good destination for enjoying a picnic brought from town or for bringing the kids—there are guided nature walks at 2pm daily during the summer. The day-use fee for the park is $3 per adult, $1 for children ages 5 to 11.

SHOPPING

Freeport has more than 100 retail shops between Exit 19 of I-95 at the far lower end of Main Street and Mallett Road, which connects to Exit 20. Shops have recently begun to spread south of Exit 19 toward Yarmouth. If you don't want

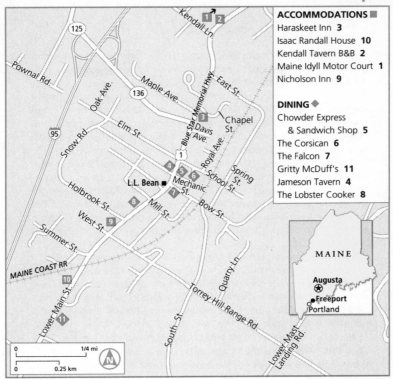

to miss a single shopping opportunity, get off at Exit 17 and head north on Route 1. The bargains can vary from extraordinary to "huh?," so plan on racking up some mileage if you're intent on finding outrageous deals. The national chains in Freeport include Abercrombie & Fitch (in a former Carnegie library!), Banana Republic, Gap, Levi's, Calvin Klein, Patagonia, North Face, Nike, Chaudier Cookware ("the cookware of choice aboard Air Force One"), Mikasa, Nine West, Timberland, and Maidenform, among others. Many others.

Stores in Freeport are typically open daily 9am to 9pm during the busy summer season and close much earlier (at 5 or 6pm) outside the summer; between Thanksgiving and Christmas, they remain open late once more. To avoid hauling your booty around for the rest of your vacation, stop by the **Freeport Trading & Shipping Co.,** 18 Independence Dr. (✆ **207/865-0421**), which can pack and ship everything home.

Cuddledown of Maine Cuddledown started producing down comforters in 1973 and now makes a whole line of products much appreciated in northern climes and beyond. Down pillows are made right in the outlet shop, which carries a variety of European goose-down comforters in all sizes and weights. Look also for linens and home furnishings. There's another outlet in Kittery. 475 U.S. Rte. 1 (between exits 17 and 19). ✆ **888/235-3696.** www.cuddledown.com.

Freeport Knife Co. This might be the sharpest company in the state of Maine, so to speak. In any case, it sports a wide selection of knives for kitchen and camp

Tale of the Tags: Freeport vs. Kittery

When visiting the Maine coast, many travelers only find time to shop once. Trouble is, there are *two* significant outlet centers on the southern coast; how to choose? Here's my quick take.

In **Kittery,** located at the southern edge of Maine, the malls are clumped along Route 1 just a couple of miles north of the New Hampshire border. Though the area appears at first glance to be a conglomerated, single huge mall, in fact there are five or six distinct areas with separate entrances. Choose carefully before you make your turn!

Generally speaking, Kittery is best for the name-brand shopper who wants to hit a large volume of places in a short time. It's easier to do Kittery quickly than Freeport, because of the side-by-side arrangement of the various stores and the malls. The tradeoff is the blandness of the experience; each of these side malls offers vast parking lots and boring architecture, and you cannot safely walk from one mall to another; you need wheels.

Among the best places to try are **GAP** outlet, a **Reebok** outlet (I picked up swim trunks here for a fraction of the retail cost), a **Stride-Rite** outlet (excellent changing collections of cut-rate shoes), a **J. Crew** outlet (good prices on sweaters), a **Seiko** watch outlet, and the brand-new **Crate & Barrel** outlet. The Indian-themed **Kittery Trading Post** is not all it's hyped up to be, but prices are low at least.

As well, there are a couple good places right here for a snack: **Bob's Clam Hut,** with a long line of hungry patrons awaiting superlative fried clams, and **Ben & Jerry's** for ice cream. For a sit-down meal, I like the **Weathervane,** a small New England fish-house chain that delivers value at moderate prices and is an excellent choice for families.

Freeport is a different animal. The outlets here are crunched together and interspersed throughout Freeport's Main Street. That makes driving around town a headache, as pedestrians and cars cruising for parking brings things to a constant halt. My advice? Strap on your walking shoes, park anywhere you can find it—even in a distant satellite lot—and just resign yourself to a lot of hoofing it. Bring a portable dolly or luggage rack to carry packages if you're expecting to buy a lot.

Freeport's outlets generally offer a higher grade of product than Kittery, and the stores have a great deal more architectural (and corporate) personality, too. You will actually find local, small manufacturers here, not just the big guys, and inventive big brands that go beyond the usual.

You can troll **L.L. Bean's** factory store, of course, tucked down a side street, for top-grade outdoors equipment and clothing, but even just

alike. Look for the custom knives, and bring your dull camp blade for sharpening. They also sell replacement parts and do repairs on any knives, not just their own brand. 148 Main St. ✆ 800/645-8430 or 207/865-0779. www.freeportknife.com.

J.L. Coombs Footwear and Fine Casuals A Maine shoemaker since 1830, J.L. Coombs today carries a wide assortment of imported and domestic footwear at its two Freeport shops, including Finn Comfort, Dr. Martens, Ecco, and sticking to Main Street you'll also find **Chaudier's** Canadian-made cookware; **Cuddledown of Maine's** comfy pillows and comforters; **Mikasa's** striking, simple kitchenware; **Freeport Knife Co.'s** knife shop; **Abercrombie & Fitch's** ever-young fashions (the girls will love this place), housed in a former Carnegie library; excellent bi-level **GAP** and **Banana Republic** outlets; and **Brooks Brothers, Burberry, Coach,** and **Patagonia** stores, among many other distinctive factory shops.

If you love shopping and you love quality, it's a genuinely enjoyable experience to stroll around here for a day, taking a snack of chowder or lobster (see "Where to Dine" in the Freeport section, p. 130); pausing to assess your finds; grabbing a soda, grilled hot dog, or ice cream from a vendor; then planning dinner somewhere. Parking and traffic are negatives to consider, however—you may cruise a half-hour before finding an open spot (if you ever do). You'll also probably spend more on a trip to Freeport, as price tags are generally higher.

The winner? It's close, but I'll take Freeport for its walkability.

There's also a third option to consider, by the way. That's the big **Maine Mall,** which takes up a huge chunk of real estate near the Portland Jetport in South Portland (easily reached off the Maine Turnpike via its own exit). The options here are uniformly bland—this could be Anywheresville, America—and there are no outlet or factory stores; you'll pay full price, plus Maine state tax.

Still, if there's something reassuring about being able to bop among a **Filene's** discount clothing shop, **Macy's, The Body Shop, Victoria's Secret, Pottery Barn, The Disney Store,** and **babyGAP,** then grabbing some chocolates from **Godiva** before settling down to coffee and a book or CD at **Borders Books & Music,** you might enjoy it. There's not much distinctive here, though the bookstore is very well stocked with books and CDs and staff are helpful. Also check out **The Sports Authority** for low-priced sporting goods; watch for specials on exercise equipment, golf balls, camping gear, and the like, and hit **Williams-Sonoma** for a look at upscale cooking gear.

Needless to say, there's a food court here, though it isn't very good. Consider dining at a nearby restaurant instead; a number of them surround the moatlike ring road that surrounds the mall and its acres of parking lots. Good choices include **The Weathervane,** for seafood, or even the Canadian chain **Tim Horton's** (rarely seen in the U.S. outside Michigan and upstate New York) for doughnuts.

Mephisto. There's also outerwear by Pendleton and Jackaroos. 15 Bow St. and 262 Rte. 1 (between exits 17 and 19). ℂ **800/683-5739** or 207/865-4333. www.jlcoombs.com.

L.L. Bean ★★ Monster outdoor retailer L.L. Bean traces its roots from the day Leon Leonwood Bean decided that what the world really needed was a good weatherproof hunting shoe. He joined a watertight gum shoe with a laced leather upper. Hunters liked it. The store grew. An empire was born.

Today L.L. Bean sells millions of dollars' worth of clothing and outdoor goods to customers nationwide through its well-respected catalogs, and it continues to draw hundreds of thousands through its door. This modern, multilevel store is the size of a regional mall, but it's tastefully done with its own indoor trout pond and lots of natural wood. L.L. Bean is open 365 days a year, 24 hours a day (note the lack of locks or latches on the front doors), and it's a popular spot even in the dead of night, especially in summer and around holidays. Selections include Bean's own trademark clothing, along with home furnishings, books, shoes, and plenty of outdoor gear for camping, fishing, and hunting. A 2-minute walk away is the L.L. Kids store, with goods for the younger set.

In addition to the main store, L.L. Bean stocks an **outlet shop** with a relatively small but rapidly changing inventory at discount prices. It's in a back lot between Main Street and Depot Street—ask at the front desk of the main store for walking directions. L.L. Bean also has outlets in Portland and Ellsworth. Main and Bow sts. © **800/341-4341** or 800/441-5713. www.llbean.com.

Mangy Moose A souvenir shop with a twist: Virtually everything in the place is moose-related. There are moose wine glasses, moose trivets, moose cookie cutters, and, of course, moose T-shirts. And much more. The merchandise is a notch above what you'll find in other tourist-oriented shops. 112 Main St. © **800/606-6517** or 207/865-6414. www.themangymoose.com.

Thos. Moser Cabinetmakers Classic furniture reinterpreted in lustrous wood and leather is the focus at this shop, which, thanks to a steady parade of ads in *The New Yorker* and elsewhere, has become almost as much an icon of Maine as L.L. Bean. Shaker, mission, and modern styles have been wonderfully reinvented by the shop's designers and woodworkers, who produce heirloom-quality signed pieces. Nationwide delivery is easily arranged. 149 Main St. © **207/865-4519**. www.thomasmoser.com.

WHERE TO STAY

Freeport has more than 700 guest rooms, ranging from quiet B&Bs with just three rooms to chain motels with several dozen. Reservations are strongly recommended during the peak summer season; the recent opening of several new midrange chain hotels and motels south of town on Route 1 has helped accommodate the summer crush, and in a pinch you might try the adjacent **Comfort Suites** (© **877/424-6423** or 207/865-9300) at 500 Rte. 1 or **Super 8** (© **800/ 800-8000** or 207/865-1408), adjacent to it on Route 1. Both are relatively new and good enough for a night's rest.

Harraseeket Inn The Harraseeket Inn is a large, thoroughly modern hotel 2 blocks north of L.L. Bean. It's to the inn's credit that, despite its size, a traveler could drive down Main Street and not immediately notice it. A late-19th-century home is the soul of the hotel, but most of the rooms are in later additions built in 1989 and 1997. Guests can relax in the well-regarded dining room, read the paper in the common room with the baby grand player piano, or sip a cocktail in the homey Broad Arrow Tavern, with its wood-fired oven and grill. The guest rooms are on the large side and tastefully done, with quarter-canopy beds and a nice mix of contemporary and antique furniture. About a quarter have gas or wood-burning fireplaces, and more than half feature whirlpools.

There are two restaurants on the premises. The Maine Dining Room offers New American dining with an emphasis on local ingredients. The Broad Arrow Tavern has a more informal setting with a less ambitious menu, which includes an array of burgers, steaks, pizzas, and pastas.

162 Main St., Freeport, ME 04032. © **800/342-6423** or 207/865-9377. www.harraseeketinn.com. 84 units. July–Oct $199–$279 double, $279 suite; mid-May to June $145–$239 double, $260 suite; winter $115–$219 double, $245 suite. All rates include breakfast buffet and afternoon tea. MAP plans also available. AE, DC, DISC, MC, V. Take Exit 20 off I-95 to Main St. **Amenities:** Dining room; indoor pool; concierge; business center; conference rooms; room service; laundry service; dry cleaning. *In room:* A/C, coffeemaker, some hair dryers, safe, fireplace (some), whirlpool (some).

Isaac Randall House   Freeport's first bed-and-breakfast, the Isaac Randall House is located in an 1823 farmhouse that's been refurbished with a dozen handsome guest rooms, all with private bathrooms, phones, and air-conditioning; about half the rooms also sport televisions. The most charming of the bunch is the Pine room, built in an adjoining shed with rustic barnboards and decorated in a Southwestern motif. (It also features a unique antique copper tub.) The least charming are two smaller modern rooms in an addition in back, and a dark loft upstairs. Breakfast is served in a homey country kitchen, while a Mexican-style library is also a good place to pass a bad-weather day. Kids may enjoy the playground outside. The inn is well situated for exploring Freeport; its main disadvantage is the location, sandwiched between Route 1 and I-95. The sound of traffic is never far away.

5 Independence Dr., Freeport, ME 04032. © **207/865-9295**. Fax 207/865-9003. 12 units (1 private hall bathroom). $75–$135 double. 2-night minimum on holiday and midsummer weekends. AE, DISC, MC, V. Rates include full breakfast. "Well-behaved" pets and children welcome. Located ½ mile S of the L.L. Bean store on Rte. 1. *In room:* A/C, TV (some), VCR (some), fridge (some), fireplace (some).

Kendall Tavern Bed & Breakfast   If you want to be out of the bustle of town but not too far from the shopping, this is a good choice. This handsome B&B is in a cheerful yellow farmhouse on 3½ acres at a bend in the road a half-mile north of the center of Freeport. The rooms are all plushly carpeted and appointed with comfort in mind. Everything is decorated in a bright and airy style, with framed prints of New England scenes and Victorian ladies on the walls and a mix of antique and new furniture. The rooms facing Route 1 (Main St.) might be a bit noisier than the others, but the traffic is still not likely to be too disruptive. There's a piano in one of the two downstairs parlors and a sizable hot tub in a spacious private room in the back (no extra charge). An all-you-can-eat breakfast is served in the pine-floored dining room.

213 Main St., Freeport, ME 04032. © **800/341-9572** or 207/865-1338. Fax 207/865-3544. 7 units. Peak season $95–$155 double; off-season and midweek discounts. Rates include full breakfast. AE, DISC, MC, V. **Amenities:** Hot tub.

Maine Idyll Motor Court   The 1932 Maine Idyll Motor Court is a Maine classic—a cluster of 20 cottages scattered about a grove of beech and oak trees. Each has a tiny porch, a wood-burning fireplace (birch logs provided), a TV, modest kitchen facilities (no ovens), and time-worn furniture. The cabins are not lavishly sized but are comfortable and spotlessly clean. If you need a phone, you're out of luck—the cabins lack them, and there's no pay phone on the premises (the owners are good about letting guests use the office phone if they're in a pinch). The only interruption to an idyll here is the omnipresent sound of traffic: I-95 is just through the trees on one side, and Route 1 is on the other side. Get past the drone, and you'll find very good value for your money here.

1411 U.S. Rte. 1, Freeport, ME 04032. © **207/865-4201**. www.freeportusa.com/maineidyll. 20 cottages. $49–$90 double. Rates include continental breakfast. No credit cards (checks okay). Closed early Nov to late Apr. Pets on leash allowed. *In room:* Kitchenette, fireplace (some), no phone.

Nicholson Inn   If your goal in Freeport is to visit as many outlets as humanly possible, then as far as proximity to the shopping goes, there's no better place.

Located right on Main Street just a minute's walk from the heart of the shopping district, this comfortable home built in the mid-1920s has just three guest rooms, all with private bathrooms. The common rooms and guest rooms have a pleasant floral motif. Furnishings are country contemporary and oak Victorian; a huge three-course breakfast is served daily. A front porch with wicker furniture is a good spot to rest up between forays, and there's plenty of parking for guests, who are allowed to leave their cars in the inn lot even after they check out.

25 Main St., Freeport, ME 04032. (C) **800/344-6404** or 207/865-6404. 3 units (showers only). Peak season $120 double; off-season $75 double. Rates include full breakfast. No credit cards. *In room:* A/C.

WHERE TO DINE

Despite all the outlet glitz of Freeport, a couple of small-town restaurants have persisted. For a quick and simple meal, you might head down Mechanic Street (near the Mangy Moose, at 112 Main St.) to the **Corsican Restaurant** ✦, 9 Mechanic St. ((C) **207/865-9421**), for a surprisingly healthful 10-inch pizza, calzone, or king-size sandwich. A favored spot for a quick, reasonably priced lunch close to L.L. Bean is the **Falcon Restaurant,** 8 Bow St. ((C) **207/865-4031**). The **Lobster Cooker,** 39 Main St. ((C) **207/865-4349**), serves daily seafood, sandwich, and chowder specials on an outdoor patio with views of the shopping hordes; go for salmon, lobster, or crab. Also nearby is the **Chowder Express & Sandwich Shop,** 2 Mechanic St. ((C) **207/865-3404**), with counter seating for about a dozen. They serve somewhat pricey fish, lobster, and clam chowder in paper bowls with plastic spoons. This is by no means a destination restaurant—there's no atmosphere, and the food is middling—but it is good for a quick bite because it's tucked right among the shops.

For another option, see also the Harraseeket Inn, above.

Gritty McDuff's BREWPUB Spacious, informal, and air-conditioned in summer, Gritty's is an offshoot of Portland's first and most successful brewpub. It's located a short drive south of the village center and is best known for its fine and varied selection of craft (*locally created and brewed*) beers. The pub offers a wide-ranging bar menu for both lunch and dinner, with few standout offerings but decent, consistent fare. The burgers and stone-oven pizzas are reliable; pub classics like shepherd's pie and barley-coated fish also tend to be popular. During the busy summer season, the kitchen and wait staff can get a bit overwhelmed; bring your patience and a newspaper.

187 Rte. 1., Freeport. (C) **207/865-4321**. Reservations not accepted. Main courses $6.50–$14. AE, DISC, MC, V. Daily 11:30am–11pm.

Harraseeket Lunch & Lobster ✦ *Finds* LOBSTER Located at a boatyard on the Harraseeket River about a 10-minute drive from Freeport's main shopping district, this lobster pound is an especially popular destination on sunny

Packing a Picnic

South Freeport's **Winslow Park** offers camping but also day use; it's very scenic for this part of the coast, a great spot for picnics with a family. (There's a playground, too.) However, you've got to be sure to pick up food beforehand—perhaps a cup of chowder at nearby **Harraseeket Lunch and Lobster** (see above for more details).

days—although, with its heated dining room, it's a worthy destination any time. Order a crustacean according to how hungry you are (1 lb. on up), and then take in the river view from the dock while waiting for your number to be called. Be prepared for big crowds; a good alternative is to come in late afternoon between the crushing lunch and dinner hordes. If you don't happen to like lobster, you can also order fried fish, burgers, chowder, and the like.

Main St., South Freeport. 🕿 207/865-4888. Lobsters market price (typically $8–$12). No credit cards. Daily 11:30am–8:30pm. Closed mid-Oct to May 1. From I-95, take Exit 17 and head north on Rte. 1; turn right on S. Freeport Rd. at the huge Indian statue; continue to stop sign in South Freeport; turn right to waterfront. From Freeport, take South St. (off Bow St.) to Main St. in South Freeport; turn left to waterfront.

Jameson Tavern 🏵 AMERICAN   Located in a handsome historic farmhouse literally in the shadow of L.L. Bean (it's just north of the store), the Jameson Tavern touts itself as the birthplace of Maine. In 1820, the papers were signed here legally separating Maine from Massachusetts. Today it's dual restaurants under the same ownership. As you enter the door, you can head left to the historic Tap Room, a compact, often crowded spot filled with the smell of fresh-popped popcorn. (Ask to sit outside on the brick patio if the weather's good.) Meals here include fare like crab-cake burgers, lobster croissants, and a variety of build-your-own burgers. The other part of the house is the Dining Room, which is rather more formal in a country-colonial sort of way. Meals here are more sedate and gussied up, with an emphasis on steak and hearty fare. Entrees include filet mignon Oscar (with asparagus, crabmeat, and hollandaise), seafood fettuccini, and pan-blackened haddock. (Look also for heart-healthy selections.) While not overly creative, the meals in both the dining room and the tap room will hit the spot.

115 Main St. 🕿 207/865-4196. Reservations encouraged. Main courses: tap room and lunch $6.95–$18; dining room dinner $13–$25. AE, DC, DISC, MC, V. Tap room daily 11am–11pm; dining room daily in summer 11am–10pm, winter 11:30am–9pm.

2 Brunswick & Bath 🏵

Brunswick is 10 miles NE of Freeport. Bath is 8 miles E of Brunswick.

Brunswick and Bath are two handsome, historic towns that share a strong commercial past. Many travelers heading up Route 1 pass through both towns eager to reach areas with higher billing on the marquee. That's a shame, for both are well worth the detour to sample the sort of slower pace that's being lost elsewhere.

Brunswick was once home to several mills along the Androscoggin River; these have since been converted to offices and the like, but Brunswick's broad Maine Street still bustles with activity. (Idiosyncratic traffic patterns can lead to snarls of traffic in the late afternoon.) Brunswick is also home to **Bowdoin College** 🏵, one of the nation's most respected small colleges. The school was founded in 1794, offered its first classes 8 years later, and has since amassed an illustrious roster of prominent alumni, including Nathaniel Hawthorne, Henry Wadsworth Longfellow, President Franklin Pierce, and Arctic explorer Robert E. Peary. Civil War hero Joshua Chamberlain served as president of the college after the war. The campus green is full of interesting buildings and museums (see below), and is well worth a short stroll.

Eight miles to the east of Brunswick, **Bath** is pleasantly situated on the broad Kennebec River and is a noted center of shipbuilding. The first U.S.-built ship was constructed downstream at the Popham Bay colony in the early 17th century; in the years since, shipbuilders have constructed more than 5,000 ships hereabouts. Bath shipbuilding reached its heyday in the late 19th century, but the business of shipbuilding continues to this day. Bath Iron Works is one of the nation's preeminent boatyards, constructing and repairing ships for the U.S. Navy. The scaled-down military has left Bath shipbuilders in a somewhat tenuous state, but it's still common to see the steely gray ships in the dry dock (the best view is from the bridge over the Kennebec) and the towering red-and-white crane moving supplies and parts around the yard.

Bath is gaining attention from young professional émigrés attracted by its fine old houses, but it's still at heart a blue-collar town, with massive traffic tie-ups weekdays at 3pm when the shipyard changes shifts. Architecture buffs will find a detour here worthwhile. (Look for the free brochure "Architectural Tours: Walking and Driving in the Bath Area," available at information centers listed below.) The Victorian era in particular is well represented. Washington Street, lined with maples and impressive homes, is one of the best-preserved displays in New England of late-19th-century residences. The compact downtown, on a rise overlooking the river, is also home to some pretty remarkable Victorian commercial architecture that even many Mainers don't realize is there.

Note that Christmas is a big time in Bath; for a full month, from Thanksgiving to the holiday, downtown features fun window displays, a parade, and other events. Contact the local tourist office for more details.

ESSENTIALS
GETTING THERE
Brunswick and Bath are both on Route 1. Brunswick is accessible via Exits 22 and 23 off I-95. If you're bypassing Brunswick and heading north up Route 1 to Bath or beyond, continue up I-95 and exit at the "coastal connector" exit in Topsham, which avoids some of the slower traffic going through Brunswick.

For bus service from Portland or Boston, contact **Vermont Transit** (© **800/ 451-3292;** www.vermonttransit.com) or **Concord Trailways** (© **800/639-3317;** www.concordtrailways.com).

VISITOR INFORMATION
The **Bath-Brunswick Region Chamber of Commerce,** 59 Pleasant St., Brunswick, ME 04011 (© **207/725-8797** or 207/443-9751; www.midcoast maine.com), offers information and lodging assistance Monday to Friday 8:30am to 5pm from its offices near downtown Brunswick. The chamber also staffs an information center 10am to 7pm daily in summer on Route 1 between Brunswick and Bath.

FESTIVALS
In mid-August, look for posters for the ever-popular **Thomas Point Beach Bluegrass Festival** (© **877/TPB-4321** or 207/725-6009), now more than a quarter-century old. It takes place over Labor Day Weekend at Thomas Point Beach between Brunswick and Bath. What started as a sort of counterculture celebration of folksy instruments has grown somewhat, but at its heart it's still just a bunch of like-minded folks collecting in song circles for some old-fashioned pickin' and grinnin'. Performers from throughout Maine gather at this pretty cove-side park (it's a private campground the rest of the summer) and put on shows from noon past dark. Admission varies, but generally it costs $3.50 per adult and $2 per child under 12; weekend "carload" and two-for-one specials can significantly reduce the cost of a group outing, however.

Packing a Picnic

The campus of **Bowdoin College** (p. 131) in Brunswick is an attractive (though technically not public) place for a stroll and a bite on a bench. Better to eat in Brunswick's grassy public park (look for the gazebo), then walk it off afterward around campus. There's a big Hannaford's supermarket right downtown with a deli, but you may prefer the more natural fare of **Wild Oats Bakery and Café** (© **207/725-2855**) in the tiny Tontine Mall right on Maine Street.

WHAT TO SEE & DO

Collectibles buffs and aficionados of antiques malls should schedule in an hour or so at **Cabot Mill Antiques,** 14 Maine St., Brunswick (© **207/725-2855;** www.cabotiques.com), located on the ground floor of a restored textile mill in downtown Brunswick. In the 15,000-square-foot showroom, more than 140 dealers purvey a wide variety of books, bottles, dolls, art, china, and porcelains. Quality is highly variable. The facility is open daily 10am to 5pm.

IN BRUNSWICK

Bowdoin College Museum of Art ★★   This stern neoclassical building on the Bowdoin campus was designed by the prominent architectural firm of McKim, Mead, and White. While the collections are small, they include a number of exceptionally fine paintings from Europe and America, along with early furniture and artifacts from classical antiquity. The artists include Andrew and N.C. Wyeth, Marsden Hartley, Winslow Homer, and John Singer Sargent. The older upstairs galleries have soft, diffused lighting from skylights high above; it feels a bit as if you're underwater. The basement galleries, which feature rotating exhibits, are modern and spacious.

Walker Art Building, Bowdoin College. © 207/725-3275. Free admission. Tues–Sat 10am–5pm, Sun 2–5pm.

Peary-MacMillan Arctic Museum ★ *Finds*   While Admiral Robert E. Peary (class of 1887) is better known for his accomplishments (he "discovered" the North Pole at age 53 in 1909), Donald MacMillan (class of 1898) also racked up an impressive string of achievements in Arctic research and exploration. You can learn about both men and the wherefores of Arctic exploration in this altogether manageable museum on the Bowdoin campus. The front room features mounted animals from the Arctic, including some impressive polar bears. A second room outlines Peary's historic 1909 expedition, complete with excerpts from Peary's journal. The last room includes varied displays of Inuit arts and crafts, some historic and some modern. You can visit this compact museum in about 20 minutes or so; the art museum (see above) is just next door.

Hubbard Hall, Bowdoin College. © 207/725-3416. Free admission. Tues–Sat 10am–5pm; Sun 2–5pm.

IN BATH

Maine Maritime Museum & Shipyard ★   On the shores of the Kennebec River, this museum (just south of the very obvious Bath Iron Works shipyard) features a wide array of displays and exhibits related to the boatbuilder's art. The museum is housed at the former shipyard of Percy and Small, which built some 42 schooners in the late 19th and early 20th centuries. (The largest wooden ship built in the U.S.—the 329-foot *Wyoming*—was constructed on this lot in 1909.) The centerpiece of the museum is the handsomely modern Maritime History Building, which houses exhibits of maritime art and artifacts. There's also a gift shop with a nice selection of books about ships. The 10-acre property houses a fleet of additional displays, including an intriguing exhibit on lobstering and a complete boat-building shop. Kids enjoy the play area (they can search for pirates from the crow's nest of the play boat). Be sure to wander down to the docks on the river to see what's tied up, or to inquire about the occasional river cruises ($30 per person), which include lighthouse tours and adventures up the Kennebec River to Merrymeeting Bay.

243 Washington St. © 207/443-1316. www.bathmaine.com. Admission $9.75 adults, $8.75 seniors, $6.75 children 6–17, $28 families. Daily 9:30am–5pm.

WHERE TO STAY

Brunswick Bed & Breakfast ⭐   This handsome B&B is located in a rambling Federal-style house with a wraparound porch smack dab in downtown Brunswick, facing the soothing town green; even better, it's run by exceptionally enthusiastic and friendly owners. The place is positioned perfectly, within walking distance of Bowdoin College, a summer music theater, and the restaurants lining Maine Street. Rooms are quite spacious, furnished in a sort of country-modern style—some with wingback or wicker chairs, and all with attractive quilts; ask about the bright, cheery corner rooms or the two suites. There's a TV downstairs in the common room for those staying in rooms without televisions. A new cottage with six rooms and a carriage house have also been added. Note that room phones can only make outgoing calls.

165 Park Row, Brunswick, ME 04011. © **800/299-4914** or 207/729-4914. www.brunswickbnb.com. 14 units, 1 cottage. $110–$170 double, $225 cottage. All prices include full breakfast. MC, V. Closed Jan. Children 6 and over accepted. **Amenities:** Lounge. *In room:* A/C, TV (some).

Galen C. Moses House ⭐   This 1874 inn is an extravagant, three-story Italianate home done up in exuberant colors by innkeepers Jim Haught and Larry Keift. The whole of the spacious first floor is open to guests and includes a TV room, lots of loudly ticking clocks, and an appropriately cluttered Victorian double parlor. Note the old friezes and stained glass original to the house. Guest rooms vary in decor and size, but all are quite welcoming. The Victorian Room occupies a corner and gets a lot of afternoon light, though the bathroom is dark; the Suite is ideal for families, with two sleeping rooms and a small kitchen.

1009 Washington St., Bath, ME 04530. © **888/442-8771** or 207/442-8771. www.galenmoses.com. 6 units, 1 with shared bathroom. Mid-May to Oct $99–$199 double; Nov to mid-May $99–$129 double. Rates include breakfast. 2-night minimum stay on summer weekends. AE, DISC, MC, V. *In room:* A/C, hair dryer, iron.

Grey Havens ⭐   This is the inn first-time visitors to Maine fantasize about when planning their vacation. Located on Georgetown Island off the beaten track southeast of Bath, this graceful, 1904 shingled home with prominent turrets sits on a high, rocky bluff overlooking the sea. Inside and out, it feels like the setting of a novel involving several generations. In the spacious common room, you can relax in cozy chairs in front of the cobblestone fireplace while listening to classical music. The guest rooms are simple but comfortably furnished. The oceanfront rooms command a premium but are worth it. (If you're looking to save a few dollars, ask for an oceanfront room where the bathroom is located just across the hall from the room.) Guests can use the inn's canoe or bikes to explore the outlying area. One caveat: The inn itself has been only lightly modernized, which is good but means rather thin walls. If you have loud neighbors, you'll learn more about their lives than you might care to know.

Seguinland Rd. (P.O. Box 308), Georgetown Island, ME 04548. (**©** 800/431-2316 or 207/371-2616. Fax 207/371-2274. www.greyhavens.com. 13 units (2 with private hall bathrooms). $100–$230 double including full breakfast. Closed Nov–May. From Rte. 1, head S on Rte. 127 and then follow signs for Reid State Park; watch for inn on left. MC, V. No children under 12. **Amenities:** Canoes; bikes.

Sebasco Harbor Resort ★   Sebasco Harbor is a grand old seaside resort that's fighting a generally successful battle against time and irrelevance. It's a self-contained resort of the sort that flourished 50 years ago and today is being rediscovered by families. Some guests have been coming here for 60 years and love the timelessness of it; newcomers are starting to visit now that much of it has benefited from a face-lift. The 664-acre grounds remain the real attraction here—guests enjoy sweeping ocean views, a lovely seaside pool, and great walks around well-cared-for property. The guest rooms, it should be noted, are adequate rather than elegant and might seem a bit short of the mark, given the high prices charged. Most lack a certain style—especially the 40 rooms in the old inn, which are dated, and I don't mean that in a good way. (The small wooden decks on many rooms are a plus, though.) Better are the quirky rooms in the octagonal Lighthouse Building—room nos. 12 and 20 have among the best views in the state. Most (not all) rooms have TVs; ask first if it's important to you. If you're coming for more than 2 days, it's probably best to book one of the cottages, which come in all sorts and sizes.

The Pilot House Dining Room is airy, contemporary, and the best place to enjoy the sunsets. You'll find white linens, and jackets are recommended for men; the menu is contemporary resort style, with dishes like grilled swordfish with a pesto butter, and prime rib with a Parmesan Yorkshire pudding. Another restaurant, Ledges, is a more informal spot downstairs that serves a lighter menu.

Rte. 217 (P.O. Box 75), Sebasco Estates, ME 04565. (**©** 800/225-3819 or 207/389-1161. Fax 207/389-2004. www.sebasco.com. 115 units (23 cottages). Mid-June to Labor Day $209–$315 double, $375–$1,890 cottage; spring and fall $139–$269 double, $249–$1,490 cottage. Service charge of 10% not included in rates; ask about modified American plan rates. AE, DISC, MC, V. 2-night minimum on weekends. Closed late Oct to early May. South from Bath 11 miles on Rte. 209; look for Rte. 217 and signs for Sebasco. **Amenities:** Dining room; saltwater pool; 9-hole golf course; tennis courts; health club; sauna; hot tub; canoe and kayak rentals; sailing lessons; bike rentals; children's center and programs; video games; shuffleboard; candlepin bowling; movies; nature trails; bay cruises. In room: TV (some), Jacuzzi (1).

WHERE TO DINE

Both downtown Brunswick and downtown Bath offer plenty of casual places to dine, ranging from burgers to barbecue and better. For informal fare, it's hard to go wrong at these cafes and restaurants.

Five Islands Lobster Co. Finds LOBSTER POUND   The drive alone makes this lobster pound a worthy destination. It's located about 12 miles south of Route 1 down winding Route 127, past bogs and spruce forests with glimpses of azure ocean inlets. (Head south from Woolwich, which is just across the bridge from Bath.) Drive until you pass a cluster of clapboard homes, and then keep going until you can't go any farther.

Wander out to the wharf, with its unbeatable island views, and place your order. This is a down-home affair, owned jointly by local lobstermen and the proprietors of Grey Havens, a local inn (see above). While you're awaiting your lobster, you can wander next door to the Love Nest Snack Bar for extras like soda or the sinful onion rings. Gather up your grub and settle in at one of the wharf picnic tables, or head over to the grassy spots at the edge of the dirt parking lot. And bring some patience: Despite its edge-of-the-world feel, the lobster pound draws steady traffic, and it can be crowded on weekends.

1447 Five Islands Rd. (Rte. 127), Georgetown. ✆ 207/371-2990. Typically $6–$9 per lobster; 75¢ for corn on the cob. MC, V. Daily 11am–8pm July–Aug; shorter hours during the off-season. Closed Columbus Day to Mother's Day.

Robinhood Free Meetinghouse ★★ FUSION   Chef Michael Gagne seems to follow architect Daniel Burnham's dictum: "Make no little plans." His menu features a raft of entrees, and they're wildly eclectic—from saltimbocca to scallops Niçoise in a puff pastry, from Szechuan Delmonico to Wiener schnitzel with German potato pancakes and lingonberries. Starters are equally wild: Thai crab, or grilled shrimp *adobo* on homemade tortillas (served with banana salsa), anyone? Ordering from the menu is like playing stump the chef: Let's see you make *this!* And, you know what? Gagne almost always hits a high note; consequently, you can't go wrong—the careening menu is backed up by substance in the kitchen. The Meetinghouse has attracted legions of dedicated local followers, who appreciate the extraordinary attention paid to detail, like foam baffles glued discreetly to the underside of the seats to dampen the echoes in the sparsely decorated, immaculately restored 1855 Greek Revival meetinghouse. Even sorbet served between courses is homemade. Though by no means a budget restaurant, this restaurant offers good value for its prices.

Robinhood Rd., Robinhood. ✆ 207/371-2188. www.robinhood-meetinghouse.com. Reservations encouraged. Main courses $18–$25. AE, DISC, MC, V. Daily May–Oct 5:30–9pm. Limited days late fall to spring; call first.

Sea Dog Brewing Co. PUB FARE   Relocated to a historic old mill astride the Androscoggin River dividing Brunswick and Topsham, this is one of a handful of brewpubs that have found quick acceptance in Maine, and it makes a reasonable destination for quick pub food such as nachos or hamburgers, as well as a few more adventurous offerings such as a lobster bisque and a char-grilled tuna sandwich. These eats won't necessarily set your taste buds dancing, but they will satisfy basic cravings. In any case, the beers are consistently excellent, especially the Hazelnut Porter and the India Pale Ale—and that's why you're here, right?

1 Main St., Topsham. ✆ 207/725-0162. Main courses $6.95–$15. AE, DISC, MC, V. Daily 11:30am–1am.

Star Fish Grill ★★ *Finds* SEAFOOD   Rising above a lackluster location (in a strip mall across from the Miss Brunswick Diner), the Star Fish Grill serves up great seafood, excellent service, and an atmosphere that's fun, upbeat, whimsical, and (naturally) maritime. This intimate restaurant has just 50 seats, but provides big-restaurant food and service. The emphasis is on seafood, and you can find whatever's fresh (scallops, pompano, grouper, trout, mahimahi) cooked professionally and well. I'd recommend the lobster paella if it's available. Don't let the unlovely setting throw you off. This is a favorite restaurant in southern Maine, especially if you're a fan of seafood.

100 Pleasant St., Bath. ✆ 207/725-7828. Reservations recommended. Main courses $14–$26. MC, V. Tues–Sun 5–9pm.

3 Harpswell Peninsula ★★

Extending southwest from Brunswick and Bath is the picturesque Harpswell region. It's actually three peninsulas, like the tines of a pitchfork, if you include the islands of Orrs and Bailey, which are linked to the mainland by bridges. While close to some of Maine's larger towns (Portland is only 45 min. away), the Harpswell Peninsula has a remote, historic feel with sudden vistas across meadows to the blue waters of northern Casco Bay. No hiking trails, no garish attractions—just winding roads good for country drives. (Narrow shoulders and fast cars make for poor biking, however.)

The region is an amalgam—old houses with picturesque peeling paint next to manufactured homes, and summer houses next to the homes of Brunswick commuters. Toward the southern tips of the peninsulas, the character changes as clusters of colorful Victorian-era summer cottages displace the farmhouses found farther inland. Some of these cottages rent by the week, but savvy families book up many of them years in advance. If you're interested, ask local real estate agents,.

There's no set itinerary for exploring the area. Just drive south from Brunswick on Route 24 or Route 123 until you can't go any farther, and then backtrack for a bit and strike south again. Among the "attractions" worth looking for are the wonderful ocean and island views from **South Harpswell** at the tip of the westernmost peninsula (park and wander around for a bit), and the clever **Cobwork Bridge** ★★ connecting Bailey and Orrs islands. The humpbacked bridge was built in 1928 of granite blocks stacked in such a way that the strong tides could come and go and not drag the bridge out with it. No cement was used in its construction.

BEACHES

This part of Maine is better known for rocky cliffs and lobster pots than swimming beaches, with two notable exceptions.

Popham Beach State Park (© 207/389-1335) is located at the tip of Route 209 (head south from Bath). This handsome park has a long and sandy strand, plus great views of knobby offshore islands such as Seguin Island, capped with a lonesome lighthouse. Parking and basic services, including changing rooms, are available. Admission is $2 for adults, 50¢ for children 5 to 11.

At the tip of the next peninsula to the east is **Reid State Park** (© 207/371-2303), an idyllic place to picnic on a summer day. Arrive early enough and you can stake out a picnic table among the wind-blasted pines. The mile-long beach is great for strolling and splashing around. Services include changing rooms and a small snack bar. Admission is $3 for adults, 50¢ for children 5 to 11. To reach Reid State Park, follow Route 127 south from Bath and Route 1.

WHERE TO STAY

Driftwood Inn & Cottages   The ocean-side Driftwood Inn dates from 1910. This family-run rustic summer retreat on 3 acres at the end of a dead-end road is a compound of four weathered, shingled buildings and a handful of housekeeping cottages on a rocky, ocean-side property. The rooms of time-aged pine have a simple turn-of-the-last-century flavor that hasn't been gentrified in the least. Most rooms share bathrooms down the hall, but some have private sinks and toilets. (The inn has seven rooms for solo travelers, which are a rare find these days; single prices start at $65.) Cottages are set along a small and private cove, and they are furnished in a budget modern style. It's nothing fancy: Expect industrial carpeting and plastic shower stalls. Some beds could stand replacing, yet where else can you sleep at the water's edge for under $100 per night? The inn has an old saltwater pool and porches with wicker furniture to while away the afternoons; bring plenty of books and board games.

The dining room serves basic fare (roasts, fish, etc.) in a wonderfully austere setting overlooking the sea; meals are extra, although a weekly American plan is available. Dining is open to outside guests if you make reservations by 4:30pm.

Washington Ave. (P.O. Box 16), Bailey Island, ME 04003. ℂ 207/833-5461. 21 double units, 7 single units, 6 cottages (most units share hallway bathrooms). $70–$110 double; weekly $410 per person, including breakfast and dinner (July–Aug only); cottages $600–$635 per week. Open mid-May to mid-Oct; dining room open late June to Labor Day. No credit cards. **Amenities:** Saltwater pool; games.

WHERE TO DINE

If a steamed lobster is on your mind, several sprawling establishments specialize in delivering crustaceans fresh from the sea. On the Bailey Island side, there's **Cook's Lobster House** (ℂ 207/833-2818), which has been serving up a choice of shore dinners since 1955. The restaurant has two decks for outdoor dining. Near Harpswell is the **Estes Lobster House** (ℂ 207/833-6340), which serves lobster (including an artery-clogging triple lobster plate) amid relaxed, festive surroundings.

Dolphin Marina ⭐ *Finds* TRADITIONAL NEW ENGLAND   One of the premier places for chowder in the state is the down-home Dolphin Marina (now also known as the Dolphin Chowder House) at Basin Point. Drive 12 miles south of Brunswick on Rte. 123, turn right at Ash Point Road near the West Harpswell School, then take the next right on Basin Point Road and continue to the end. At road's end you'll find a boatyard; wander inside the adjacent shingled building with small-paned windows and you'll discover a tiny counter seating six and a handful of pine tables and booths with stunning views of Casco Bay. If it's crowded, you can get a meal to go—except the chowder. It's against Dolphin tradition to walk out with chowder; you have to sit down and enjoy it here. The chowders and lobster stew are reasonably priced ($4.95–$12) and absolutely delicious, and the blueberry muffins are often warm and capped with a crispy crown. Note that the servers can sometimes seem flummoxed at busy times, so bring your patience.

Basin Point, South Harpswell. ℂ 207/833-6000. Breakfast items $1.25–$3; sandwiches $3.50–$7.95; complete dinners $14–$17. Open for breakfast Fri–Sun only 8–10:30am; daily 11am–8pm. MC, V. Closed Nov–Apr. Drive 12 miles south of Brunswick on Rte. 123, turn right at Ash Point Rd. near the West Harpswell School, and then take the next right on Basin Point Rd. and continue to the end.

4 Wiscasset & the Boothbays ⭐⭐

Wiscasset is 11 miles NE of Bath. The Boothbays are 11 miles S of Wiscasset.

Wiscasset ⭐⭐ is a lovely riverside town, and it's not shy about letting you know: THE PRETTIEST VILLAGE IN MAINE is the boast on the sign at the edge of town and on many brochures. Whether or not you agree with this self-assessment, the town is attractive (although the sluggish and persistent line of traffic snaking through on Rte. 1 diminishes the charm) and makes a good stop for stretching legs, taking in an attraction or two, or grabbing a bite to eat en route to coastal destinations farther along. Take the time to walk through the elegant neighborhoods both north and south of Route 1, which have kept much of their historic integrity in tact.

The **Boothbays** ⭐, 11 miles south of Route 1 on Route 27, consist of several small and scenic villages—East Boothbay, Boothbay Harbor, and Boothbay, among them—which are closer than Wiscasset to the open ocean. The former fishing port of Boothbay Harbor was discovered in the last century by wealthy rusticators who built imposing seaside homes and retreated here in summer to avoid the swelter of the cities along the Eastern Seaboard.

Having embraced the tourist dollar, the harborfront village never really looked back, and in more recent years it has emerged as one of the premier destinations of travelers in search of classic coastal Maine. This embrace has had an obvious impact. The village is often regarded as a mandatory stop on bus tours, which has, in turn, attracted kitschy shops and a slew of mediocre restaurants that seem to specialize in baked stuffed haddock.

If Boothbay Harbor is stuck in a time warp, then it's a Tourist Trap from 1974—bland and boxy motels hem in the harbor, and side-by-side boutiques hawk the same mass-market trinkets (Beanie Babies, T-shirts emblazoned with puffins). Despite it all, there's still an affable charm that manages to rise above the clutter and cheese, especially on foggy days when the horns bleat mournfully at the harbor's mouth. If you avoid the tourist clutter of the downtown harbor area itself, some of the outlying areas are uncommonly beautiful.

ESSENTIALS

GETTING THERE

Wiscasset is on Route 1 midway between Bath and Damariscotta. Boothbay Harbor is south of Route 1 on Route 27. Coming from the west, look for signs shortly after crossing the Sheepscot River at Wiscasset.

VISITOR INFORMATION

As befits a place where tourism is a major industry, the Boothbay region has three visitor information centers in and around town, reflecting the importance of the travel dollars to the region. At the intersection of Route 1 and Route 27 is a center that's open May to October and is a good place to stock up on brochures. A mile before you reach the village is the seasonal **Boothbay Information Center** on your right (open June–Oct). If you zoom past it or it's closed, don't fret. The year-round **Boothbay Harbor Region Chamber of Commerce,** P.O. Box 356, Boothbay Harbor, ME 04538 (© **800/266-8422** or 207/633-2353; www.boothbayharbor.com), is at the intersection of Rtes. 27 and 96.

EXPLORING WISCASSET

Aside from enjoying the town's handsome architecture and vaunted prettiness, there are several quirky, low-key attractions that will nicely break up a trip along the coast. You'll also find a handful of worthwhile antiques shops. Next to Red's Eats is the Wiscasset Hardware Co., a sublimely old-fashioned hardware store that has retained its roots while also stocking wares of interest to souvenir hunters.

Castle Tucker ⭐ This fascinating mansion at the edge of town overlooking the river was first built in 1807 and then radically added to and altered in a more ostentatious style in 1860. The home remains more or less in the same state it was in when reconfigured by cotton trader Capt. Richard Tucker; one of his descendants, Jane Tucker, still lives on the top floor. Tours of the lower floor are

---

⸢*Tips*⸥ **Get Your Kicks on Route 1? Umm . . . No.**

While there's a certain retro charm in the *idea* of traveling Maine on historic Route 1, the reality is quite different. It can be congested and unattractive, and you're not missing anything if you take alternative routes. For memorable explorations, be sure to leave enough time for forays both inland and down the lesser roads along the coast.

offered by the Society of New England Antiquities, which was given the house by Ms. Tucker in 1997. The detailing is exceptional and offers insight into the life of an affluent sea captain in the late 19th century. Be sure to note the extraordinary elliptical staircase and the painted plaster trim (it's not oak).

Lee and High sts. ℂ 207/882-7364. Admission $5. Tours leave on the hour 11am–4pm Fri–Sun. Open June to mid-Oct only.

Musical Wonder House   Talk about your obsession! Danilo Konvalinka has been collecting music boxes both grand and tiny for decades, and nothing seems to delight him more than to play them for awestruck visitors. The collection includes massive and ancient music boxes that sound as resounding as an orchestra (an 1870 Girard music box from Austria), to the tinnier, more ethereal sounds of the smaller contraptions. Music boxes are displayed (and played) in four rooms in a stately 1852 home; admission is charged by the room. It is quite pricey; if you're undecided whether it's worth the fee, try this: Visit the free gift shop and sample some of the coin-operated 19th-century music boxes in the adjoining hallway. Intrigued? Sign up for the next tour.

18 High St. ℂ 207/882-7163. www.musicalwonderhouse.com. $8 for half downstairs tour; $15–$30 for full house tour. Late May to Oct daily 10am–5pm. Closed Nov to late May.

EXPLORING THE BOOTHBAY REGION

Summer parking in Boothbay Harbor requires either great persistence or forking over a few dollars. A popular local attraction is the long, narrow **footbridge** across the harbor, built in 1901. It's more of a destination than a link—other than a couple of unnotable restaurants and motels, not much is on the other side. The winding streets that weave through town are filled with shops catering to tourists. Don't expect much merchandise beyond the usual trinkets and souvenirs.

If dense fog or rain socks in the harbor, bide your time at the vintage **Romar Bowling Lanes** ✦ (ℂ 207/633-5721). This log-and-shingle building near the footbridge has a harbor view and has been distracting travelers with traditional New England candlepin bowling since 1946.

In good weather, stop by a Boothbay region information center (see above) and request a free guide to the holdings of the **Boothbay Region Land Trust** ✦✦ (ℂ 207/633-4818). Eight pockets of publicly accessible lands dot the peninsula, most with quiet, lightly traveled trails good for a stroll or a picnic. Among the best: **Linekin Preserve,** a 95-acre parcel en route to Ocean Point (drive south from Rte. 1 in Boothbay Harbor on Rte. 96 for 3¾ miles; look for parking on the left) with 600 feet of riverfront. A hike around the loop trail (about 2 miles) will occupy a pleasant hour.

Coastal Maine Botanical Garden   This 128-acre waterside garden is relatively new and a work in progress, but it's already worth exploring. It's not a fancy, formal garden like you'll find elsewhere in Maine, but rather a natural habitat that's being gently coaxed into a more mannered state. Those overseeing this nonprofit organization have blazed several short trails through the mossy forest, good for a half-hour's worth of exploring, cutting through terrain that's delightfully quiet and lush. One trail follows along much of the 3,600 feet of tidal shoreline that's part of the property. Plans call for ornamental gardens featuring Maine's indigenous plants to be completed by 2005.

Barters Island Rd., Boothbay (near Hogdon Island). ℂ 207/633-4333. www.mainegardens.org. Free admission. Mon–Fri 8:30am–4:30pm. From Rte. 27 in Boothbay Center, bear right at the monument at the stop sign, and then make the first right on Barters Island Rd.; drive 1 mile and look for the stone gate on your left.

> ### *Tips* Escaping the Crowds
>
> Boothbay Harbor is overrun with summer visitors, but at nearby Ocean Point, leave most of the crowds behind as you follow a picturesque lane that twists along the rocky shore and past a colony of vintage summer homes. Follow Route 96 southward east of Boothbay Harbor, and you'll pass through the sleepy village of East Boothbay before continuing on toward the point. The narrow road runs through piney forests before arriving at the rocky finger; it's one of a handful of Maine peninsulas with a road edging its perimeter, which allows for fine ocean views. The colorful Victorian-era summer cottages bloom along the roadside like wildflowers. Ocean Point makes for a good bike loop. Mountain-bike rentals are available at Tidal Transit (see below).

Marine Resources Aquarium   Operated by the state's Department of Marine Resources, this compact aquarium offers context for life in the sea around Boothbay and beyond. You can view rare albino and blue lobsters and get your hands wet at a 20-foot touch tank—a sort of petting zoo of the slippery and slimy. Parking is tight at the aquarium, which is located on a point across the water from Boothbay Harbor, so visitors are urged to use the free shuttle bus (look for the Rocktide trolley) that connects downtown with the aquarium and runs frequently throughout the summer.

McKown Point Rd., West Boothbay Harbor. © 207/633-9542. Admission $5 adults, $3 children 5–18 and seniors. Daily 10am–5pm. Closed Oct to Memorial Day.

BOAT TOURS

The best way to see the timeless Maine coast around Boothbay is on a boat tour. Nearly two dozen tour boats berth at the harbor or nearby.

Balmy Days Cruises (© **800/298-2284** or 207/633-2284; www.balmydays cruises.com) runs several trips from the harbor, as many as five daily in summer. If you'd rather be sailing, ask about the 90-minute cruises on the *Bay Lady*, a 15-passenger Friendship sloop ($18). It's a good idea to call ahead for reservations.

The most personal way to see the harbor is via sea kayak. **Tidal Transit Kayak Co.** (© **207/633-7140**) offers morning, afternoon, and sunset tours of the harbor for $35 to $65 (sunset's the best bet). Kayaks can also be rented for $15 an hour or $50 per day. Tidal Transit is open daily in summer (except when it rains) on the waterfront at 47 Townshend Ave. (walk down the alley).

WHERE TO STAY

One of the coast's most memorable private campgrounds is located between Bath and Wiscasset. **Chewonki Campgrounds,** off Route 144 (© **800/465-7747** or 207/882-7426), occupies 50 acres overlooking a salt marsh and the confluence of lazy tidal streams. The 47 sites are sizable and private; there's a nicely maintained pool with a sweeping view; kayaks and canoes are available for rent. Campsites start at $23 per night, which is at the high end of the price scale but decidedly worth it. Drive 7 miles east of Bath on Route 1; turn right on Route 144 and then take the next right past the airport. Follow the signs for the campground.

Five Gables Inn ★   The handsome Five Gables Inn was painstakingly restored in the late 1980s and now sits proudly amid a small colony of summer homes on a quiet road above a peaceful cove. It's nicely isolated from the confusion and hubbub of Boothbay Harbor; the activity of choice here is to sit on the deck and enjoy the glimpses of the water through the trees. The rooms are pleasantly appointed, and five have fireplaces that burn manufactured logs; some also sport four-poster beds. Room 8 is a corner room with brilliant morning light; room 14 is the most requested, with a great view and a fireplace with a marble mantle. (Some of the first-floor rooms open onto a common deck and lack privacy.) The breakfast buffet is sumptuous, with offerings like tomato-basil frittata, cornbread with bacon and green onions, and blueberry-stuffed French toast.

Murray Hill Rd. (P.O. Box 335), East Boothbay, ME 04544. © **800/451-5048** or 207/633-4551. www.fivegables inn.com. 15 units. $130–$195 double. Rates include breakfast buffet. MC, V. Closed Nov to mid-May. Drive through East Boothbay on Rte. 96; turn right after crest of hill on Murray Hill Rd. Children 12 and older are welcome. *In room:* Fireplace (some).

The Inn at Lobsterman's Wharf ⟨*Value*⟩   This is our budget pick for the region. A clean, comfortable no-frills place located adjacent to a working boatyard, this nine-room inn was originally a coal depot and later a boarding house. It still has some of the boarding house informality to it (although all rooms now have small private bathrooms), but you get a lot for your money. Seven rooms face the water, and the innkeeper invited local people to decorate each of the rooms to reflect local history, giving them a unique, homespun flair. Hodgon Suites is the largest, located under the eaves with a view of the Hodgon Yacht boatyard. The Lobsterman's Wharf restaurant (see below) is just next door.

Rte. 96, East Boothbay. © **207/633-5481.** 9 units. $75–$95 double. Rates include continental breakfast. MC, V. Pets allowed in 2 rooms. *In room:* TV.

Lawnmeer Inn & Restaurant   The Lawnmeer, situated a short hop from Boothbay on the northern shore of Southport Island, offers easy access to town and a restful environment. This was originally built as a guest home in the late 19th century, and the main inn has been updated with some loss of charm. More than half of the guest rooms are located in a motel-like annex, which makes up for a lack of character with private balconies offering views of the placid waterway that separates Southport Island from the mainland.

Regional and global cuisine is served in a comfortable, homey dining room with windows overlooking the waterway. The inn serves some of the most consistently reliable food in a town that's come to expect high restaurant turnover. Look for contemporary fare, with entrees like grilled venison with a cranberry chutney, chicken satay, and poached salmon with dill hollandaise sauce. Reservations are recommended.

Rte. 27 (P.O. Box 29), Southport, ME 04576. © **800/633-7645** or 207/633-2544. www.lawnmeerinn.com. 32 units. Summer $100–$230 double; spring and fall $90–$210 double. 2-night minimum on holiday weekends. MC, V. Closed mid-Oct to mid-May. Pets accepted on limited basis; $10 extra per pet. **Amenities:** Dining room. *In room:* A/C (some).

Newagen Seaside Inn ★   This 1940s-era resort has seen more glamorous days, but it's still a superb small, low-key resort offering stunning ocean views and walks through a fragrant spruce forest. The inn is housed in a low, wide, white-shingled building that's furnished simply with country pine furniture. There's a classically austere dining room, narrow cruise ship–like hallways with pine wainscoting, and a lobby with a fireplace. Rooms have been recently renovated and feature polished wood floors and simple Amish-style quilts; country-themed decorations adorn the walls. Guests flock here for the 85-acre ocean-side grounds filled with decks, gazebos, and walkways that border on the magical. It's

hard to convey the magnificence of the ocean views, which could be the best of any inn in Maine.

The handsome, simple dining room with ocean views offers a menu with creative New England fare such as grilled salmon, pork tenderloin with tomato currant chutney, or broiled haddock with lemongrass and fruit salsa. It's closed Tuesday for dinner.

Rte. 27 (P.O. Box 29), Newagen, ME 04576. (©) **800/654-5242** or 207/633-5242. www.newagenseaside inn.com. 30 units, 3 cottages. $110–$250 double, including full breakfast; cottages $1,400 weekly. Ask about off-season discounts. AE, MC, V. Closed mid-Oct to mid-May. Located on south tip of Southport Island. Take Rte. 27 from Boothbay Harbor and continue on until the inn sign. **Amenities:** Dining room; freshwater and saltwater pools; tennis courts; badminton; horseshoes; free rowboats; bikes.

Spruce Point Inn ★★   The Spruce Point Inn was originally built as a hunting and fishing lodge in the 1890s, and it evolved into a summer resort in 1912. After some years of quiet neglect, it has benefited greatly from an overall spiffing up that's been ongoing since the late 1980s. A number of new units were built in the late 1990s; they match the older buildings architecturally and blend in nicely. Those looking for historic authenticity might be disappointed. Those seeking modern resort facilities (Jacuzzis, carpeting, updated furniture) along with accenting to provide a bit of historic flavor will be delighted. (Those who prefer their gentility a bit less polished should consider the Newagen Seaside Inn, see above.) Anyway, it's hard to imagine anyone being let down by the 15-acre grounds, situated on a rocky point facing west across the harbor. Guests typically fill their time idling in the Adirondack chairs or partaking of more strenuous activities that include croquet, shuffleboard, tennis on clay courts, or swimming. Although more of a couples' place, children's programs accommodate the growing number of families who vacation here. Also notable is the welcome recent addition of a spa facility.

Diners are seated in an elegant formal dining room (men are requested to wear jackets) and enjoy wonderful sunset views across the mouth of Boothbay Harbor as they peruse the evening menu. The menu features creative adaptations of traditional New England meals. Appetizers include lobster spring rolls with ginger sesame sauce and crab cakes with spicy peanut and Thai sauces, paired with marinated cucumber salad. Main courses offered include such things as rack of lamb with herb crust (served with a three-mustard glaze and a roasted shallot demiglace), pan-seared swordfish, or salmon Osaka—a Japanese take on the fish, employing pickled ginger and Asian noodles.

Atlantic Ave. (P.O. Box 237), Boothbay Harbor, ME 04538. (©) **800/553-0289** or 207/633-4152. www.spruce pointinn.com. 93 units. July–Aug $150–$270 double, $225–$350 suite; spring and fall $125–$210 double, $205–$250 suite; cottages and condos $295–$550. 2-night minimum weekends; 3 nights holidays. AE, DC, DISC, MC, V. Closed mid-Oct to Memorial Day. Turn seaward on Union St. in Boothbay Harbor; proceed 2 miles to the inn. Pets not allowed. **Amenities:** Dining room; 2 outdoor pools; 2 tennis courts; fitness center; spa; Jacuzzi; lawn games (shuffleboard, tetherball, etc); game room; concierge; conference rooms; massage; babysitting; laundry service; dry cleaning. *In room:* Kitchenette (some), fridge, coffeemaker, iron/ironing board, safe, Jacuzzi (some).

Topside   The old gray house on the hilltop looming over the dated motel buildings might bring to mind the Bates Motel, especially when a full moon is overhead. But get over that. Topside offers spectacular ocean views at a reasonable price from a quiet hilltop compound located right in downtown Boothbay. The inn itself—a former boarding house for shipyard workers—features several comfortable rooms, furnished with a somewhat discomfiting mix of antiques and contemporary furniture. At the edge of the inn's lawn are two outbuildings with basic motel units. These are on the small side, furnished simply with dated paneling and furniture. (You won't find this hotel profiled in *House Beautiful.*) Room nos. 9 and 14 have the best views, but most rooms offer a glimpse of the water and many have decks or patios. All guests have access to the wonderful lawn and the endless views, and the Reed family, which owns and operates the inn, is accommodating and friendly.

60 McKown Hill, Boothbay Harbor, ME 04538. ✆ **877/486-7466** or 207/633-5404. Fax 207/633-2206. http://home.gwi.net/topside. 21 units. June to early Oct $95–$150 double; mid-Apr to May and Oct to late Nov $75–$105 double. Rates include continental breakfast. AE, DISC, MC, V. Closed late Nov to Apr. *In room:* Patio (some).

WHERE TO DINE
IN WISCASSET

Red's Eats TAKEOUT   Red's is an innocuous roadside stand smack in downtown Wiscasset that's probably received more than its fair share of media ink about its famous lobster rolls. (They often crop up in "Best of Maine" surveys.) And they *are* good, consisting of moist and plentiful chunks of chilled lobster placed in a roll served with a little mayo on the side. But be aware that they're on the pricey end of the scale—you can find less expensive (although less meaty) versions elsewhere. The few tables behind the stand fill up quickly in summer, but you can walk a minute or two and be on a public riverfront deck, which has a better view anyway. One way to economize: Order one lobster roll and split it with a friend, and then fuel up on the budget fare (hot dogs, sandwiches) that dominates the rest of the menu.

Water St. (Rte. 1 just before the bridge). ✆ **207/882-6128**. Sandwiches $2–$5.25; lobster rolls typically $13–$14. No credit cards. Mon–Thurs 11am–11pm; Fri–Sat 11am–2am; Sun noon–6pm. Closed Oct–Apr.

Sarah's SANDWICHES/TRADITIONAL   Sarah's is a hometown favorite that opened quietly in Wiscasset in 1987 and then moved down the block to a place with a view of Sheepscot River a decade later. Expect personable service and filling and well-prepared (if unremarkable) food. It's usually crowded for lunch, with offerings including pita pockets (good choice: roasted turkey, tomato, red onion, and sprouts), croissant sandwiches, roll-ups on 12-inch tortillas, burritos, and a local favorite called a whaleboat, which is two-cheese turnovers (like a calzone) served with a broad choice of ingredients. The lobsters are fresh, hauled daily by Sarah's brother and father. This is our choice for an informal lunch break when motoring up Route 1—at least at those times we don't feel like splurging on a lobster roll at Red's.

Water St. and Rte. 1 (across from Red's). ✆ **207/882-7504**. Sandwiches $5–$6.25; pizzas $4.95–$17. AE, DISC, MC, V. Daily 11am–8pm (until 9pm Fri–Sat).

IN THE BOOTHBAYS

When wandering through Boothbay Harbor, watch for **"King" Brud and his famous hot-dog cart.** Brud started selling hot dogs in town in 1943, and he's still at it. He's usually at the corner of McKown and Commercial streets from 10am until 4pm from June to October.

More innovative dining can be found in the dining rooms at Spruce Point Inn and Lawnmeer Inn, listed in "Where to Stay," above.

Boothbay Region Lobstermen's Co-op SEAFOOD   WE ARE NOT RESPONSIBLE IF THE SEAGULLS STEAL YOUR FOOD reads the sign at the ordering window of this casual, harborside lobster joint. And that sets the tone pretty well. Situated across the harbor from downtown Boothbay, the lobstermen's co-op offers no-frills lobster and seafood. This is the best pick from among the cluster of usually dependable lobster-in-the-rough places that line the waterfront nearby. You order at a pair of windows and then pick up your meal and carry your tray either to the picnic tables on the dock or inside a garagelike two-story prefab building. Lobsters are priced to market (figure $8–$12), with extras like onion rings ($2.10) or coleslaw ($1). A bank of soda machines provides liquid refreshment. This is a fine place for a lobster on a sunny day, but it's uninteresting, at best, in rain or fog.

Atlantic Ave., Boothbay Harbor. (*C* 207/633-4900. Reservations not accepted. Fried and grilled foods $2–$10; dinners $7–$15. DISC, MC, V. Daily May to mid-Oct 11:30am–8:30pm. By foot: Cross footbridge and turn right; follow road for ⅓ mile to co-op.

Lobsterman's Wharf SEAFOOD   Located on the water in East Boothbay, the Lobsterman's Wharf has the comfortable, pubby feel of a popular neighborhood bar, complete with a pool table. And that's appropriate, since that's what it is. But it's that rarest of pubs—a place that's popular with the locals but that also serves up a decent meal and knows how to make travelers feel at home. If the weather's cooperative, sit at a picnic table on the dock and admire the views of a spruce-topped peninsula across the Damariscotta River; you can also grab a table inside amid the festive nautical decor. Entrees include a mixed-seafood grill, a barbecue shrimp and ribs platter, grilled swordfish with béarnaise, and succulent fresh lobster offered four different ways. At lunch, there's hamburger, baked haddock, lobster rolls, and steamed lobster.

Rte. 96, East Boothbay. (*C* 207/633-3443. Reservations accepted for parties of 6 or more only. Lunch $5–$14; dinner $14–$25 (mostly $14–$16). AE, MC, V. Daily 11:30am–10pm Apr–Oct. Closed Nov–Mar.

5 Pemaquid Peninsula ★★★

The Pemaquid Peninsula is an irregular, rocky wedge driven deep into the Gulf of Maine. It's much less commercial and trinkety than the Boothbay Peninsula just across the Damariscotta River, and more inviting for off-the-beaten-track exploration. (If you're given to such generalizations, the Boothbay peninsula is for tourists and the Pemaquid peninsula is for travelers.) The inland areas are leafy with hardwood trees and laced with narrow, twisting back roads that are perfect for bicycling. As you near the southern tip where small harbors and coves predominate, the region takes on a more remote maritime feel. When the surf pounds Pemaquid Point's rugged, rocky shore at the extreme southern tip of the peninsula, this can be one of the most dramatic destinations in Maine.

ESSENTIALS
GETTING THERE
The Pemaquid Peninsula is accessible from the west by turning southward on Route 129/130 in Damariscotta, just off Route 1. (Stay on Rte. 130 to Pemaquid Point.) From the east, head south on Route 32 just west of Waldoboro.

VISITOR INFORMATION
The **Damariscotta Region Chamber of Commerce,** P.O. Box 13, Main Street, Damariscotta, ME 04543 (*C* 207/563-8340), is a good source of local information and maintains a seasonal information booth on Route 1 during the summer months. To get there, follow Route 27 south, leaving Route 1 just east (across the bridge) after Wiscasset.

EXPLORING THE PEMAQUID PENINSULA
The Pemaquid Peninsula invites slow driving and frequent stops. Start out by heading south on Route 129 toward Walpole from the sleepy head-of-the-harbor village of Damariscotta. Keep an eye on your left for the austerely handsome

Walpole Meeting House, one of three meeting houses built on the peninsula in 1772. (Only two remain.) It's not regularly open to the public, but Sunday services are held here four times each summer (call for times), or try to sneak a look during the occasional wedding. (Dress well and don't eat too much of the wedding party's food.) History or architecture buffs bound and determined to see the interior when it's closed might also contact Charlene Hunter (© **207/563-5318**), who has the key.

Just north of the unassuming fishing town of South Bristol on Route 129, watch for the **Thompson Ice Harvesting Museum** ⭐ (© **207/644-8551**). During winter's deep freeze (usually in Feb), volunteers from around town carve out huge blocks of ice and relay them to the well-insulated icehouse (a 1990 replica of the original icehouse) to be packed in sawdust. Summer visitors can peer into the cool, damp depths and see the glistening blocks (the harvest is sold to fishermen throughout the summer to ice down their catch) and learn about the once-common practice of ice harvesting through photos and other exhibits in a tiny museum. The grounds are open during daylight hours year-round; the museum exhibits are open 1 to 4pm Wednesday, Friday, and Saturday only, and only in July and August. A $1 donation (50¢ for children) is requested.

Continue on Route 129 and arrive at picturesque **Christmas Cove,** so named because Capt. John Smith (of Pocahontas fame) anchored here on Christmas Day in 1614. While wandering about, look for the rustic **Coveside Bar and Restaurant** (© **207/644-8282**), a popular marina with a pennant-bedecked lounge and basic dining room. The food is okay, but the views are outstanding; you may catch a glimpse of the celebrity yachtsmen who tend to stop off here.

About 5 miles north of South Bristol, turn right on Pemaquid Road, which will take you to Route 130. Along the way, look for the **Harrington Meeting House** (the other 1772 structure), which is open to the public on occasional afternoons in July and August. It's an architectural gem inside, almost painfully austere, with a small museum of local artifacts on the second floor. Even if it's not open, stop to wander about the lovely cemetery out back, the final resting place of many sea captains.

Head south on Route 130 to the village of New Harbor and look for signs to **Colonial Pemaquid** (© **207/677-2423**). Open daily from Memorial Day to Labor Day 9am to 5pm, this state historic site features exhibits on the original 1625 settlement here; archaeological digs take place in the summer. The $1 admission charge (free for children under 12) includes a visit to stout **Fort William Henry,** a 1907 replica of a supposedly impregnable fortress that stood over the river's entrance. It was not impregnable, as it turned out, with tragic results for the settlement. Three French ships, under the command of Pierre Le Moyne and working in concert with a force of some 500 local native Americans, bombarded

---

⌒*Tips*　**Lobster Pricing**

Travelers may be in for a rude surprise when they get the bill for a meal at a casual wharfside lobster restaurant. Prices posted for lobsters are per *pound,* not per *lobster.* This can be inadvertently misleading, as a range of prices is often posted—for example, $6.99 for 1¼-pound lobsters, $7.99 for 1½-pound lobsters, and so on. That's the price per pound, not the total price, so you'll need do a little math to figure out the final price of your lobster.

and raided the fort, destroying it; little remains of the fort today. Nearby Pemaquid Beach allows for a bracing ocean dip and is a good spot for families.

Pemaquid Point ★★★, which is owned by the town of Bristol, is the place to while away an afternoon (© **207/677-2494**). Bring a picnic and a book, and find a spot on the dark, fractured rocks to settle in. The ocean views are superb, and the only distractions are the tenacious seagulls, which might take a profound interest in your lunch. While here, be sure to visit the **Fishermen's Museum** ★ (© **207/677-2494**) in the handsome lighthouse (open daily 9am–5pm). Informative exhibits depict the whys and wherefores of the local fishing trade and should answer those questions that invariably arise while watching lobstermen at work just offshore. There's a small fee to enter the park; admission to the museum is by donation.

From New Harbor, you can get a great view of the coast from the outside looking in with **Hardy Boat Cruises** (© **800/278-3346** or 207/677-2026; www.hardyboat.com). Tours are aboard the 60-foot *Hardy III*, and excursions include a 1-hour sunset and lighthouse cruise ($10 for adults, $7 for children 12 and under), 90-minute puffin tours out to Eastern Egg Rock ($18 for adults, $11 for children. Extra clothing for warmth is strongly recommended. Closed early September to mid-May.

Route 32 strikes northwest from New Harbor, and it's the most scenic way to leave the peninsula if you plan to continue eastward on Route 1. Along the way, look for the sign pointing to the **Rachel Carson Salt Pond Preserve** ★★, a Nature Conservancy property. The noted naturalist Rachel Carson studied these roadside tide pools extensively while researching her 1956 bestseller *The Edge of the Sea,* and today it's still an inviting spot for budding naturalists and experts alike. Pull off your shoes and socks, and wade through the cold waters at low tide looking for starfish, green crabs, periwinkles, and other creatures.

WHERE TO STAY

Bradley Inn ★   The Bradley Inn is located within easy walking or biking distance to the point, but there's plenty of reasons to lag behind at the inn. Start by wandering the nicely landscaped grounds or enjoying a game of croquet in the gardens. If the fog has moved in for a spell, settle in for a game of Scrabble at the pub, which is decorated with a lively nautical theme. The rooms are tastefully appointed; only the carriage house has a television. The third-floor rooms are the best, despite the hike, thanks to distant glimpses of John's Bay. The inn is popular with weddings on weekends in summer, so ask in advance if you're seeking solitude and quiet.

The fare served in the inn's handsome first-floor restaurant emphasizes local seafood, but the menu also features duck, steak, veal, and lamb.

Rte. 130, 3063 Bristol Rd, New Harbor, ME 04554. © **800/942-5560** or 207/677-2105. Fax 207/677-3367. www.bradleyinn.com. 15 units, 1 cottage. Late May to Oct $155–$225 double, $250–$275 suite; Apr to late May $125–$195 double, $195–$225 suite. Rates include full breakfast. AE, MC, V. Closed Nov–Mar. **Amenities:** Pub; access to nearby beach; free use of bikes; room service (7am–10pm).

Hotel Pemaquid *Kids*   This 1889 coastal classic isn't directly on the water— it's only a minute or two walk from Pemaquid Point—but the main inn has the flavor of an old-time seaside boarding house. The outbuildings are a bit more modern and have less character. The inn is aggressively old-fashioned (although most guest rooms now have private bathrooms), with narrow hallways and antiques, including a great collection of old radios and phonographs. The inn has a two- (or three-) bedroom suite, which is ideal for families.

Rte. 130, Pemaquid Point (mailing address: 3098 Bristol Rd., New Harbor, ME 04554). ℂ **207/677-2312.** www.hotelpemaquid.com. 23 units (4 share 2 bathrooms). Peak season $80–$100 double ($65–$70 for shared bathroom), $135–$190 suite; off-season $75–$80 double ($60 shared bathroom), $110–$150 suite. 2-night minimum stay on weekends. No credit cards. Closed mid-Oct to mid-May.

Newcastle Inn ★★   Located not far from Route 1 and just across the river from Damariscotta, the Newcastle Inn is the most luxurious (and most romantic) option in the Pemaquid region (Pemaquid Point is about 15 miles away). It's especially appealing to gourmands, who rave about the inn's restaurant ★. The inn has limited views of the tidal Damariscotta River, but the real charm lies within the well-appointed inn, which has an elegant, modern, country feel. Innkeepers Rebecca and Howard Levitan have aggressively expanded guest rooms by combining smaller rooms, and most are now spacious and bright. (Eight have air-conditioning, two have televisions, and nine have gas fireplaces.) Seguin Island is the smallest room; West Quoddy is the largest suite (they're named after lighthouses). The Pemaquid Point suite is very appealing, with gas fireplace, glimpses of the river, a small sitting room, and a large bathroom with a two-person Jacuzzi.

The inn's restaurant, **Lupines** ★★, is top rate—the Levitans report that Julia Child dined here on her birthday for 3 years running. Cocktails are served at 6pm in the inn's common room, followed by dinner at 7pm. The menu focuses on fresh Maine ingredients and changes nightly. Typical entrees might include a seared duck breast with calvados reduction sauce, beef tenderloin au poivre with oven-roasted cherry tomatoes, or pan-seared Chilean sea bass on jasmine rice with stir-fried vegetables and a Thai lobster curry sauce. The four-course meal offers good value at a fixed price of $46 (plus tax and gratuity).

River Rd., Newcastle, ME 04553. ℂ **800/832-8669** or 207/563-5685. www.newcastleinn.com. 15 units. Late May to Oct $155–$295 double; Nov to late May $125–$225 double. Rates include full breakfast. 2-night minimum stay some weekends. AE, MC, V. Children age 12 and up are welcome. **Amenities:** Restaurant. *In room:* A/C (some), TV (some), fireplace (some), Jacuzzi (some).

WHERE TO DINE

Shaw's Fish and Lobster Wharf ★ LOBSTER   Shaw's attracts hordes of tourists, but it's no trick to figure out why: It's one of the best-situated lobster pounds, with postcard-perfect views of the working harbor and the boats coming and going through the inlet that connects to the open sea. Customers stand in line to place their orders and then wait for their names to be called. While waiting, you can stake out a seat on either the open deck or the indoor dining room (go for the deck), or order up some appetizers from the raw bar. This is one of the few lobster joints in Maine with a full liquor license.

On the water, New Harbor. ℂ **207/677-2200.** Lobster priced to market (typically $7 per lb.). MC, V. Open mid-May to mid-Oct daily 11am–8pm (open until 9pm July–Aug). Closed mid-Oct to mid-May.

6 Monhegan Island ★★★

Brawny, wild, and remote, Monhegan Island is Maine's premier island destination. Visited by Europeans as early as 1497 (although some historians insist that earlier Norsemen carved primitive runes on neighboring Manana Island), the island was first settled by fishermen attracted to the sea's bounty in the offshore waters. Starting in the 1870s and continuing to the present day, noted artists discovered the island and came to stay for a spell. Their roster included Rockwell Kent (the artist most closely associated with the island), George Bellows, Edward Hopper, and Robert Henri. The artists gathered in the kitchen of the lighthouse to chat and drink coffee; it's said that the wife of the lighthouse keeper accumulated a tremendously valuable collection of paintings. Today Jamie Wyeth, scion of the Wyeth clan, claims the island as his part-time home.

It's not hard to figure why artists have been attracted to the place: There's a mystical quality to it, from the thin light to the startling contrasts of the dark cliffs and the foamy white surf. There's also a remarkable sense of tranquillity to this place, which can only help focus one's inner vision.

Be aware that this is not Martha's Vineyard—no ATMs, few pay phones, even electricity is in scarce supply. That's what visitors tend to like about it. If you have the time, I strongly recommend an overnight on the island at one of the several hostelries. Day trips are easily arranged, but the island's true character doesn't start to emerge until the last day boat sails away and the quiet, rustic appeal of the island starts to percolate back to the surface.

ESSENTIALS
GETTING THERE
Access to Monhegan Island is via boat from either New Harbor, Boothbay Harbor, or Port Clyde. The 70-minute trip from Port Clyde is the favored route among longtime island visitors. The trip from this rugged fishing village is picturesque as it passes the Marshall Point Lighthouse and a series of spruce-clad islands before setting out on the open sea.

Two boats make the run to Monhegan from Port Clyde. The *Laura B* is a doughty workboat (building supplies and boxes of food are loaded on first; passengers fill in the available niches on the deck and in the small cabin). A newer boat—the faster (50 min.), passenger-oriented *Elizabeth Ann*—also makes the run, offering a large heated cabin and more seating. You'll need to leave your car behind, so pack light and wear sturdy shoes. The fare is $27 round-trip for adults, $14 for children 2 to 12 years old, and $2 for pets. Reservations are advised: **Monhegan Boat Line,** P.O. Box 238, Port Clyde, ME 04855 (© **207/ 372-8848;** www.monheganboat.com). Parking is available near the dock for an additional $4 per day.

VISITOR INFORMATION
Monhegan Island has no formal visitor center, but it's small and friendly enough that you can make inquiries of just about anyone you meet on the island pathways. The clerks at the ferry dock in Port Clyde are also quite helpful. Be sure to pick up the inexpensive map of the island's hiking trail at the boat ticket office or at the various shops around the island. An informal website maintained by island resident Clare Durst offers helpful information for first-time visitors: **www. briegull.com/monhegan**.

Because wildfire could destroy this breezy island in short order, smoking is prohibited outside the village.

EXPLORING PORT CLYDE
Port Clyde's charm lies in the fact that it's still first and foremost a fishing village. While some small-scale tourist enterprises have made their mark on the village, located at the tip of a long finger about 15 miles south of Route 1, it still caters primarily to working fishermen and the ferry workers who keep Monhegan supplied.

Here's a favorite routine for spending a couple of hours in Port Clyde, either while waiting for the ferry or just snooping around. Head to the **Port Clyde General Store** ★★ (© **207/372-6543**) on the waterfront and soak up the cracker-barrel ambiance (there's actually a decent selection of wine here, attesting to encroaching upscalism). Order a sandwich to go, and then drive to the **Marshall Point Lighthouse Museum** (℗ **207/372-6450**); follow the road along the harbor eastward and bear right to the point.

This small lighthouse received a few moments of fame when Forrest Gump turned around here and headed back west during his cross-country walks in the movie, but it also happens to be one of the most peaceful and scenic lighthouses in the state. Carry your lunch around to the far side of the lightkeeper's house, and settle on one of the granite benches to watch the fishing boats come and go through the thoroughfare. Afterward, tour through the small but engaging museum (free, but donations encouraged) and learn a bit about the culture of lighthouses on the Maine Coast.

EXPLORING MONHEGAN

Walking is the chief activity on the island, and it's genuinely surprising how much distance you can cover on these 700 acres (about 1½ miles long and a ½ mile wide). The village clusters tightly around the harbor; the rest of the island is mostly wild land, laced with some 17 miles of trails. Much of the island is ringed with high, open bluffs atop fissured cliffs. Pack a picnic lunch and hike the **perimeter trail** 𝕬𝕬𝕬, spending much of the day just sitting, reading, or enjoying the surf rolling in against the cliffs. There are 18 numbered trails on the island, most on private property; tread lightly. The most difficult and all-encompassing of these is trail no. 1, known as the Cliff Trail, which takes you around the entire perimeter and up and down many cliffs and ravines; it requires at least a few hours (figure a half-day to be smart), and requires surprising exertion. There are some cutoffs that avoid the cliffs, marked as trail no. 1a at various points; be sure to consult the excellent map published by Monhegan Associates (available at the island store) before setting out.

The inland trails are appealing in a far different way. Deep, dark **Cathedral Woods** is mossy and fragrant; sunlight only dimly filters through the evergreens to the forest floor.

Bird-watching 𝕬 is a popular activity in the spring and fall. Monhegan Island is on the Atlantic flyway, and a wide variety of birds stop at the island along their migration routes. Swapping stories of the day's sightings is a popular activity at island inns and B&Bs.

The sole attraction on the island is the **Monhegan Historical and Cultural Museum,** located next to the 1824 lighthouse on a high point above the village. The museum, open from July through September, has a quirky collection of historic artifacts and provides context for this rugged island's history. Nearby is a small and select art museum that opened in 1998, featuring changing exhibits showcasing the works of illustrious island artists, including Rockwell Kent.

The spectacular view from the grassy slope in front of the **lighthouse** 𝕬𝕬 is the real prize. The vista sweeps across a marsh, past one of the island's most historic hotels, past melancholy Manana Island, and across the sea beyond. Get here early if you want a good seat for the sunset; it seems most visitors to the island congregate here after dinner. (Another popular place is the island's southern tip, where the wreckage of the *D.T. Sheridan,* a coal barge, washed up in 1948.)

If you time it right, you can also visit the **studios** of Monhegan artists, who still come here in great numbers. Artists often open their workspaces for limited hours and are happy to have visitors stop by and look at their work, chat, and perhaps buy a canvas or sculpture. Some of the artwork runs along the lines of predictable seascapes and sunsets, but much of it rises above the banal. Look for the bulletin board along the main pathway in the village for a listing of the days and hours the studios are open.

WHERE TO STAY & DINE ON MONHEGAN

Monhegan House   The handsome Monhegan House has been accommodating guests since 1870, and it has the comfortable, worn patina of a venerable lodging house. The accommodations at this four-floor walk-up are austere but comfortable, more so after recent renovations; there are no closets, and everyone uses clean dormitory-style bathrooms. The downstairs lobby with fireplace is a welcome spot to sit and take the fog-induced chill out of your bones (even in Aug, it can be cool here). The restaurant offers three meals a day, with a selection of filling but simple meat and (very fresh) fish dishes, along with vegetarian entrees.

Monhegan Island, ME 04852. (©) 207/594-7983. www.monheganhouse.com. 33 units (all with shared bathroom). Peak season $119–$225 double, off-season $99 double. MC, V. Closed Columbus Day to Memorial Day. **Amenities:** Dining room. *In room:* No phone.

Trailing Yew   At the end of long summer afternoons, guests congregate near the flagpole in front of the main building of this rustic hillside compound. They sit in Adirondack chairs or chat with newfound friends. But mostly they're waiting for the ringing of the bell, which signals them in for the included-with-the-price dinner, as if at summer camp. Inside, guests sit around long tables, introduce themselves to their neighbors, and then pour an iced tea and wait for the delicious family-style repast. (You're given a choice, including vegetarian options, but my advice is to opt for the fresh fish whenever it's available.)

Taking in guests since 1929, the Trailing Yew is a friendly, informal place that's popular with hikers and birders. Guest rooms are eclectic and simply furnished in a pleasantly dated summer-home style. Only one of the four guest buildings has electricity, however, and most, but not all, bathrooms have electricity—guests in rooms without electricity are provided a kerosene lamp and instruction in its use. (A small flashlight is helpful, just in case.) Rooms are unheated, so bring an extra layer if the weather's chilly.

Monhegan Island, ME 04852. (©) 800-592-2520 or 207/596-0440. 37 units in 4 buildings (all but 1 share bathrooms). $140 double, including breakfast, dinner, taxes, and tips. No credit cards. Closed mid-Oct to mid-May. Pets allowed. **Amenities:** Dining room. *In room:* No phone.

Midcoast

Traveling eastward along the Maine Coast, those who pay attention to such things will notice that they're suddenly heading almost due north around Rockland. The culprit behind this geographic quirk is Penobscot Bay, a sizable bite out of the Maine Coast that forces a lengthy northerly detour to cross the head of the bay where the Penobscot River flows in at Bucksport.

You'll find some of Maine's more pastoral coastal scenery in this area—spectacular offshore islands and high hills rising above the blue bay. Although the mouth of Penobscot Bay is occupied by two large islands, its waters can still churn with vigor when the tides and winds conspire.

Penobscot Bay's western shore gets a heavy stream of tourist traffic, especially along Route 1 through the scenic village of Camden. Nonetheless, this is a good destination to get a taste of the Maine coast. Services for travelers are abundant, although during the peak season a small miracle will be required to find a weekend guest room without a reservation.

Forming the eastern boundary of Penobscot Bay—though you must drive north and then *south* to get there —the lovely Blue Hill Peninsula is a back-roads paradise. If you're of a mind to get lost on country lanes that suddenly dead-end at the sea or inexplicably start to loop back on themselves, this is the place for you. In contrast to the western shores of Penobscot Bay, the peninsula attracts few tourists and has more of a lost-in-time character. The roads here are hilly, winding, and narrow, passing through leafy forests, venerable saltwater farms, and the edge of an azure inlet here or there.

By and large, it's overlooked by the majority of Maine's tourists, especially those who like their itineraries well structured and their destinations clear and simple.

1 Enjoying the Great Outdoors

BEACHGOING   The town-owned **Pemaquid Beach Park** (© 207/677-2754), near Damariscotta, and **Swan Lake State Park** (© 207/525-4404), 6 miles north of Belfast, are both worthy beaches, albeit small ones. Small admission fees are charged at both.

BICYLING   **Vinalhaven** and **North Haven** in Penobscot Bay and **Swan's Island** in Blue Hill Bay are popular with bikers.

GOLFING   With six of its holes bordering Penobscot Bay, the golf course at the **Samoset Resort** in Rockport (© 800/341-1650 or 207/594-2511) is easily the state's most dramatic. (It's also among the priciest, with greens fees running $95 during peak season—if you can even get a reservation.)

HIKING   A good destination for hilly coastal hiking is **Camden Hills State Park,** on the west shore of Penobscot Bay. *Fifty Hikes in Southern and Coastal Maine,* by John Gibson, is a reliable directory to trails in the Camden Hills area.

For a coastal walking vacation with all the details taken care of, contact **New England Hiking Holidays,** P.O. Box 1648, North Conway, NH 03860 (© **800/ 869-0949** or 603/356-9696; www.nehikingholidays.com), which offers excursions to the Maine coast each summer. Trips typically involve moderate day hiking coupled with nights at comfortable lodges.

SAILING   An ideal way to combine time in the outdoors with relative luxury and an easy-to-digest education in maritime history is aboard a windjammer cruise on the coast. Maine boasts a sizable fleet of sailing ships both vintage and modern that offer private cabins, meals, entertainment, and adventure. The ships range in size from 53 to 132 feet, and most are berthed in the region between Boothbay Harbor and Belfast. You choose your adventure: An array of excursions are available, from simple overnights to weeklong expeditions gunkholing among Maine's thousands of scenic islands and coves.

Several windjammer festivals and races are held along the Maine coast throughout the summer; these are perfect events to shop for a ship on which to spend a few days. Among the more notable events are **Windjammer Days** in Boothbay Harbor (late June) and the **Camden Windjammer Weekend** in early September. For information on windjamming vacations, contact **Maine Windjammer Association** at © **800/807-WIND,** or on the Web at www.sailmainecoast.com.

SKIING   The only downhill peak of any significance along the coast would be the **Camden Snow Bowl** (p. 164), and even it's not terribly lofty. If you'd like to detour inland a bit and ski while visiting the coast, get a pamphlet with basic information about Maine skiing from the **Ski Maine Association** (P.O. Box 7566, Portland, ME 04112; www.skimaine.com). The association's website also offers up-to-date reports on ski conditions during the winter.

2 Rockland & Environs ⭐

Rockland is 185 miles NE of Boston and 78 miles NE of Portland.

Located on the southwest edge of Penobscot Bay, Rockland has long been proud of its brick-and-blue-collar waterfront town reputation. Built around the fishing industry, Rockland historically dabbled in tourism on the side. But with the decline of the fisheries and the rise of the tourist economy in Maine, the balance has shifted—Rockland has recently been colonized by creative restaurateurs and innkeepers and other small-business folks who are painting it with an unaccustomed gloss. One of the most striking changes of the past 20 years has been the city's transformation from fish-processing center to arts-and-crafts center.

There's a small park on the waterfront from which the fleet of windjammers comes and goes, but more appealing than Rockland's waterfront is its commercial downtown—it's basically one long street lined with sophisticated historic brick architecture. If you're seeking picturesque harbor towns, head straight for Camden, Rockport, Port Clyde, or Stonington (take Rte. 90 to almost entirely skirt the city of Rockland). But Rockland does make a decent enough base for exploring this beautiful coastal region, especially if you have a low tolerance for trinkets and tourist hordes—and don't mind hanging out in what is still, despite the recent influx of artists and craftsmen hanging out their shingles, essentially a working-class town.

ESSENTIALS
GETTING THERE
Route 1 passes directly through Rockland. Rockland's tiny airport is served by **Colgan Air** (© **800/428-4322**) with daily flights from Boston and Bar Harbor.

Penobscot Bay

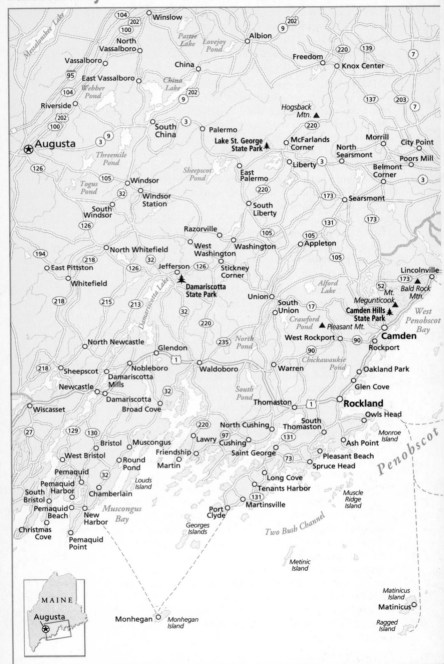

Winslow
104 202 100
North Vassalboro
Vassalboro
East Vassalboro
95
104
Riverside
202 100
Augusta
126
9
3
South China
China
9
202
Palermo
Lake St. George State Park
Albion
9 202
Freedom
220 139
Knox Center
7
137 203
7
Hogsback Mtn.
220
McFarlands Corner
North Searsmont
Morrill
City Point
Poors Hill
Belmont Corner
3
Liberty
3
East Palermo
220
South Liberty
173
Searsmont
173
Windsor
105
32
Windsor Station
South Windsor
126
Razorville
West Washington
Washington
105
131
105
Appleton
105
North Whitefield
32
Jefferson
126 126
Stickney Corner
Damariscotta State Park
Union
South Union
17
Alford Lake
52
Mt. Megunticook
Bald Rock Mtn.
173
Lincolnville
173
Camden Hills State Park
West Penobscot Bay
194
East Pittston
218
Whitefield
218
215
213
32
220
235
North Pond
Crawford Pond
Pleasant Mt.
West Rockport
90
90
Camden
Rockport
Oakland Park
Glen Cove
North Newcastle
Glendon
1
Waldoboro
Chickawaukie Pond
Warren
218
Sheepscot
Nobleboro
Damariscotta Mills
Newcastle
32
Damariscotta
Broad Cove
South Pond
Thomaston
1
Rockland
Owls Head
Wiscasset
27
129 130
Bristol
Muscongus
Lawry
97
Cushing
North Cushing
220
South Thomaston
131
Monroe Island
Ash Point
West Bristol
Round Pond
Friendship
Saint George
73
Pleasant Beach
Spruce Head
Pemaquid
32
Martin
Louds Island
Long Cove
Pemaquid Harbor
South Bristol
Chamberlain
Muscongus Bay
Tenants Harbor
Muscle Ridge Island
Pemaquid Beach
New Harbor
131
Martinsville
Christmas Cove
Pemaquid Point
Port Clyde
Georges Islands
Two Bush Channel
Metinic Island
Matinicus Island
Matinicus
Ragged Island
Penobscot

MAINE
Augusta

Monhegan
Monhegan Island

Concord Trailways (© **800/639-3317**) offers bus service from Rockland to Bangor and Portland.

VISITOR INFORMATION

The **Rockland/Thomaston Area Chamber of Commerce,** P.O. Box 508, Rockland, ME 04841 (© **800/562-2529** or 207/596-0376; www.therealmaine.com), staffs an information desk at Harbor Park. It's open daily 9am to 5pm Memorial Day to Labor Day, and weekdays only the rest of the year.

EVENTS

The **Maine Lobster Festival** (© **800/LOB-CLAW** or 207/596-0376) takes place at Harbor Park the first weekend in August (plus the preceding Thursday and Friday). Entertainers and vendors of all sorts of Maine products—especially the local crustacean—fill the waterfront parking lot and attract thousands of festival-goers who enjoy this pleasant event with a sort of buttery bonhomie. The event includes the Maine Sea Goddess Coronation Pageant. Admission costs $7 to $10 per day; food, of course, costs extra.

MUSEUMS

Farnsworth Museum ★★★   Rockland, for all its rough edges, has long and historic ties to the arts. Noted sculptor Louise Nevelson grew up in Rockland, and in 1935 philanthropist Lucy Farnsworth bequeathed a fortune large enough to establish the Farnsworth Museum, which has since become one of the most respected art museums in New England. Located in the middle of downtown, the Farnsworth has a superb collection of paintings and sculptures by renowned American artists with a connection to Maine. This includes not only Nevelson and three generations of Wyeths (N. C., Andrew, and Jamie), but also Rockwell Kent, Childe Hassam, and Maurice Prendergast. The exhibit halls are modern, spacious, and well designed, and the shows are professionally prepared. In 1998, the museum expanded with the opening of the **Farnsworth Center for the Wyeth Family,** housed in the former Pratt Memorial Methodist Church and containing Andrew and Betsy Wyeth's personal collection of Maine-related art.

The Farnsworth also owns two other buildings open to the public. The **Farnsworth Homestead,** located behind the museum, offers a glimpse into the life of prosperous coastal Victorians. And a 25-minute drive away, in the village of Cushing, is the **Olson House,** perhaps Maine's most famous home, immortalized in Andrew Wyeth's noted painting *Christina's World.* Ask at the museum for directions and information (closed in winter).

356 Main St., Rockland. © 207/596-6457. www.farnsworthmuseum.org. $9 adults, $8 seniors, $5 students 18 and older, free for 17 and under. MC, V. Summer Mon–Fri 10am–7pm, Sat–Sun 10am–5pm; spring and fall Tues–Sun 10am–5pm; winter Tues–Sat 10am–5pm, Sun 1–5pm.

Owls Head Transportation Museum ★ *Finds*   You don't have to be a car or plane buff to enjoy a day at this museum, located 3 miles south of Rockland on Route 73. Founded in 1974, the museum has an extraordinary collection of cars, motorcycles, bicycles, and planes, nicely displayed in a tidy, hangarlike building at the edge of the Knox County Airport. Look for the beautiful early Harley Davidson and the sleek Rolls-Royce Phantom dating from 1929. The museum is also a popular destination for hobbyists and tinkerers, who drive and fly their classic vehicles here for frequent weekend rallies in the summer. Call ahead or check the museum's website to ask about special events.

Rte. 73, Owls Head. © 207/594-4418. www.ohtm.org. $7 adults, $6 seniors, $5 children 5–17, $18 families. Apr–Oct daily 10am–5pm; Nov–Mar daily 10am–4pm.

WINDJAMMING

During the long transition from sail to steam, captains of fancy new steamships belittled old-fashioned sailing ships as "windjammers." The term stuck; through a curious metamorphosis, the name evolved into one of adventure and romance.

Today, windjammer vacations combine adventure with limited creature comforts—such as lodging at a backcountry cabin on the water. Guests typically bunk in small two-person cabins, which usually offer cold running water and a porthole to let in fresh air, but not much else. (You know it's not like a fancy inn when one ship's brochure boasts "standing headroom in all 15 passenger cabins" and another crows that all cabins "are at least 6 ft. by 8 ft.")

Maine is the windjammer cruising capital of the U.S., and the two most active Maine harbors are **Rockland** and **Camden** on Penobscot Bay. Cruises last from 3 days to a week, during which these handsome, creaky vessels poke around tidal inlets and small coves that ring the beautiful bay. It's a superb way to explore the coast the way it's historically been explored—from the water, looking inland. Rates run between about $110 and $150 per day per person, with modest discounts early and late in the season.

Cruises vary from ship to ship and from week to week, depending on the inclinations of captains and the vagaries of Maine weather. The "standard" cruise often features a stop at one or more of the myriad spruce-studded Maine islands (perhaps with a lobster bake onshore), hearty breakfasts enjoyed sitting at tables belowdecks (or perched cross-legged on the sunny deck), and a palpable sense of maritime history as these handsome ships scud through frothy waters. A windjammer vacation demands you use all your senses, to smell the tang of the salt air, to hear the rhythmic creaking of the masts in the evening, and to feel the frigid ocean waters as you leap in for a bracing dip.

More than a dozen windjammers offer cruises in the Penobscot Bay region during summer (some migrate south to the Caribbean for the winter). The ships vary widely in size and vintage, and accommodations range from cramped and rustic to reasonably spacious and well appointed. Ideally, you'll have a chance to look at a couple of ships to find one that suits you before signing up.

If that's not practical, call ahead to the **Maine Windjammer Association** (© **800/807-9463**) and request a packet of brochures, which enables you to comparison shop. The association's website is **www.sailmainecoast.com**.

Note: If you're hoping for a last-minute windjammer cruise, stop by the chamber of commerce office at the Rockland waterfront (see above) and inquire after any open berths.

WHERE TO STAY

Capt. Lindsey House Inn ⚔   The three-story, brick Capt. Lindsey House is located just a couple minutes' walk from the Farnsworth Museum. It was originally erected as a hotel in 1835, but it went through several subsequent incarnations, including headquarters of the Rockland Water Co. (The inn's front desk is where folks once paid their water bills.) Guests enter through a doorway a few steps off Rockland's Main Street into an opulent first-floor common area done up in rich tones, handsome dark-wood paneling, and a well-selected mix of antique and contemporary furniture. The upstairs rooms are also tastefully decorated in a contemporary country style, generally with bold modern colors and patterns mixed deftly with traditional design. Even the smaller rooms like room no. 4 are well done (this in a sort of steamship nouveau style); the rooms on the third floor all feature yellow pine floors and antique oriental carpets. All rooms but two have showers only, but all have pleasing extras, like handmade bedspreads, hair dryers, down comforters, and bathrobes. (Note that a few rooms have twin beds.) Reliable pub fare is available at the Waterworks next door (see below), which is owned by the same people who own the inn.

5 Lindsey St., Rockland, ME 04841. © 800/523-2145 or 207/596-7950. Fax 207/596-2758. www.lindseyhouse. com. 9 units. Peak season $140–$190 double; Columbus Day to Memorial Day $85–$125 double. Rates include continental breakfast. AE, DISC, MC, V. *In room:* A/C, hair dryer, robe.

East Wind Inn ⭐ The inn itself, formerly a sail loft, is perfectly situated next to the harbor with water views from all rooms and the long porch. It's a classic seaside hostelry with busy wallpaper, simple colonial reproduction furniture, and tidy rooms. (The 10 guest rooms across the way at a former sea captain's house have most of the private bathrooms.) The atmosphere is relaxed almost to the point of ennui, and the service is good.

Traditional New England fare is served in an Edwardian-era dining room (open Apr–Nov). The seafood is usually your best bet; the baked haddock is always popular. Sides include freshly cut french fries and "country mashed potatoes" ("made with milk, butter, and occasional lumps").

P.O. Box 149, Tenants Harbor, ME 04860. © 800/241-8439 or 207/372-6366. Fax 207/372-6320. www.eastwind inn.com. 26 units (7 with shared bathroom). Late June to early Sept $159 double ($129 with shared bathroom), $189–$299 suite and apt; mid-June to late June and mid-Sept to mid-Oct $109–$139 double, $169–$249 suite; mid-Oct to Nov rates lower, call ahead for specifics; Dec–May inn open only if prior arrangements have been made. Rates include full breakfast. 2-night minimum on suites and apts. AE, DISC, MC, V. Drive south on Rte. 131 from Thomaston to Tenants Harbor; turn left at post office. $15 extra for pets (by reservation). Children welcome. **Amenities:** Dining room.

LimeRock Inn ⭐⭐ This beautiful Queen Anne–style inn is located on a quiet side street just 2 blocks from Rockland's Main Street. Originally built for U.S. Rep. Charles Littlefield in 1890, it served as a doctor's residence from 1950 to 1994, after which it was renovated into a gracious inn. The innkeepers have done a commendable job converting what could be a gloomy manse into one of the region's better choices for overnight accommodation. Attention has been paid to detail throughout, from the choice of country Victorian furniture to the Egyptian cotton bed sheets. All the guest rooms are welcoming, but among the best choices is the Island Cottage Room, a bright and airy chamber wonderfully converted from an old shed and featuring a private deck and Jacuzzi; the wood floors are covered with throw rugs. The Turret Room has French doors into the bathroom, which features a claw-foot tub and a separate shower. If it's big elegance you're looking for, opt for the Grand Manan Room, which has a large four-poster bed, a fireplace, and a double Jacuzzi.

96 Limerock St. Rockland, ME 04841. © 800/546-3762 or 207/594-2257. www.limerockinn.com. 8 units. $120–$215 double. Rates include breakfast. DISC, MC, V. *In room:* Jacuzzi (some).

Samoset Resort ⭐⭐ The Samoset is a something of a Maine coast rarity—a modern, self-contained resort that offers contemporary styling, ocean views, and lots of golf. Both the hotel and town houses are surrounded by the handsome golf course, which opens up expansive views from almost every window on the property. The lobby is constructed of massive timbers (recovered from an old grain silo in Portland), and the guest rooms all have balconies or terraces. Bathrooms are extra-big, many with soaker tubs. Golfers like the place for its scenic 18-hole course with several waterside holes, and families will always find plenty of activities for kids (there's a summer camp during high season, and babysitting the rest of the year). The resort also has the best sunset stroll in the state—you

(Tips) Boat & Breakfast

A growing trend in Maine is the "boat-and-breakfast," a working fishing or tour boat that takes overnight lodgers and often serves a meal or does a cruise. You wake up in the morning and disembark. Many (though not all) of Maine's BO-&-B's are berthed in Penobscot. Try one if you're looking for a different way to experience the coast (and pack Dramamine if you tend to become nauseous at sea). A few of the best current options include:

Morning in Maine (© 207/691-SAIL; www.amorninginmaine.com), 58 E. Neck Rd., Nobleboro, ME 04555. Captain Bob Pratt runs a 55-foot ketch around Penobscot Bay, serving lobster dinners on board and making time for fishing or stargazing. Continental breakfast is also served in the morning. Cost is $350 for two, $150 for each addition person up to six.

Rachel B. Jackson (© 888/405-SAIL or 207/288-2216; www.downeast sail.com), P.O. Box 901, Bar Harbor ME 04609. A 67-foot topsail schooner based in Bar Harbor, the *Rachel B. Jackson* is a handsome reproduction ship of oak, pine, and brass (it was built in Maine). The overnight cruise begins at 6:30pm, discharges day travelers, then continues to anchorage somewhere in Acadia; cost, including breakfast but not dinner, is $175 per person.

Schooner Wendameen (© 207/594-1751; www.schooneryacht.com). This 67-foot schooner yacht cruises around Penobscot Bay, leaving at 2pm for an afternoon sail and anchoring for a night in a harbor specially chosen according to prevailing conditions. A buffet dinner is served (guests must bring aboard their own alcohol or drinks), as well as a light breakfast, and the ship returns to port by 9am next day. Cost is $180 per person, up to 14.

Symbion (© 207/725-0979). A 37-foot sloop captained by Ken Brigham, the *Symbion* ties up at pretty Cundy's Harbor and circumnavigates Casco Bay, allowing guests to take the wheel from time to time (with a bit of instruction). There's a private restroom for overnight guests, and the itinerary may take in local sights such as Eagle Island, Christmas Cove, a series of lighthouses, or Monhegan Island. Longer cruises, up to 5 days in length, are also possible; tour prices vary.

can ramble across the golf course to a breakwater that leads out to a picturesque lighthouse. The Flume Cottage is a recent luxury addition.

The Samoset offers four dining areas, including the Clubhouse Grill, the Breakwater Cafe, and the Poolhouse. The centerpiece restaurant is Marcel's, where specialty dinners are prepared tableside. These include lobster flambé, rack of lamb for two, and steak Diane.

Rockport, ME 04856. © **800/341-1650** (outside Maine) or 207/594-2511. www.samoset.com. 178 hotel units, plus 72 townhouse units. Early July to late Aug from $259–$289 double (from $369 suite); mid-Apr to early July and late Aug to early Oct from $179–$289 double (from $259–$289 suite); winter starting at $129 double (from $209 suite). Cottage $539–$769. Meals not included; ask about MAP packages. AE, DC, DISC, MC, V. Valet parking. **Amenities:** 4 restaurants; indoor and outdoor pools; 18-hole golf course ($95 for 18 holes); 4 tennis courts (night play); modern health club; Jacuzzi; sauna; jogging and walking trails; children's program; indoor video golf driving range; concierge; courtesy car; business center; gift shops; massage; babysitting; laundry service; dry cleaning; free newspaper. *In room:* A/C, safe.

WHERE TO DINE

Cafe Miranda ★ *Value* WORLD CUISINE Hidden away on a side street, this tiny contemporary restaurant features a huge menu with big flavors and a welcoming, hip attitude. ("We do not serve the food of cowards," says owner-chef Kerry Altiero). The fare draws liberally from cuisines from around the globe (Altiero again: "It's comfort food for whatever planet you're from"), and given its wide-ranging culinary inclinations, it comes as something of a surprise just how well prepared everything is. The chargrilled pork and shrimp cakes served with a ginger-lime-coconut sauce are superb. Other creative entrees include barbecue pork ribs with a smoked jalapeño sauce, and Indian almond chicken. (The menu changes often, so don't set your heart on these dishes in particular.) Or just go for some of the multitudes of changing small plates, dishes like gazpacho, roasted corn with pickled banana peppers, roasted shallots or apples with blue cheese, roasted fiddleheads, grilled rare beef with wasabi, tapenade, foie gras, gnocchi, seared shrimp, fried feta cheese, fried oysters with buttermilk-sherry vinegar, chicken livers with bacon—the list goes on almost forever. Go nuts. All things considered, I'd say that Cafe Miranda provides the best value—and opportunity for gustatory exploration—per your buck of any restaurant in Maine. Beer and wine are also available to wash it all down.

15 Oak St., Rockland. © 207/594-2034. Reservations strongly encouraged. Small plates $5–$11; main courses $12–$22. DISC, MC, V. Summer daily 5:30–9:30pm (until 8:30 in winter), off-season closed Mon.

Cod End Fish House LOBSTER POUND Part of the allure of Cod End is its hidden and scenic location—it seems as though you've stumbled upon a secret. Situated between the Town Landing and the East Wind Inn, Cod End is a classic lobster joint with fine views of tranquil Tenants Harbor. You walk through the fish market (where you can buy fish or lobster to go, along with various lobster-related souvenirs) and then place your order at the outdoor shack. While waiting to be called, you can check out the dock or just sit and relax in the sun. (If it's raining, there's limited seating in the market.) Lobsters are the draw here, naturally, but there's plenty else to choose from, including chowders, stews, linguini with seafood, rolls (like the clam or haddock rolls), and simple sandwiches for younger tastes (even peanut butter and jelly). As with most lobster pounds, the less complicated and sophisticated your meal is here, the better the odds are you'll be satisfied.

Next to the Town Dock, Tenants Harbor. © 207/372-6782. Lunch entrees $2.50–$8; dinner $7.95–$14. DISC, MC, V. July–Aug daily 11am–8:30pm; limited hours June, Sept–Oct; closed Nov–May.

Market on Main ★ *Kids* CONTEMPORARY DELI Run by the folks at Cafe Miranda, lively and hip Market on Main is a great choice for a midday break or easy dinner if you're driving up the coast or spending the day at the Farnsworth Art Museum down the block. Half deli, half restaurant, it's casual, with brick walls, exposed heating ducts, and galvanized steel tabletops. Selections range from sandwiches (including choices such as baked eggplant) to burgers to seafood, as well as salads and a children's menu (including peanut butter and honey).

315 Main St. © 207/594-0015. Main courses $5.50–$14. DISC, MC, V. Mon–Thurs 11am–7pm; Fri–Sat 11am–8pm; Sun 10am–3pm.

Primo ★★★ MEDITERRANEAN/NEW AMERICAN   Primo opened in April 2000 and quickly developed New York–size buzz, and with good reason. The restaurant, owned by executive chef Melissa Kelly and pastry chef Price Kushner, occupies two deftly decorated floors of a century-old home a short drive south of downtown Rockland (no views to speak of). Kelly graduated first in her class at the Culinary Institute of America and won the 1999 James Beard Foundation award for "best chef in the Northeast." The menu reflects the seasons and draws from local products wherever available: start with an appetizer such as foie gras, scallops, or wood oven-roasted Raspberry Point oysters with creamy leeks, tomato, bacon, and tarragon. For the main course, you might choose from one of the inventive daily pastas—ricotta Cavatelli with Italian sausage, kale, and eggplant in a tomato sauce, or spaghetti tossed with baby calamari, chiles, and roasted tomatoes in an almond pesto, for example. Or try the pepper-crusted venison with a rosemary spaetzle. Or just order one of the great wood-fired pizzas with matzoh-thin crusts. Finish with one of Kushner's desserts: an espresso float, a rhubarb-strawberry tartlet with vanilla gelato and strawberry sauce, homemade cannoli, or an apple crostata made from local apples and sided with pine nut-and-caramel ice cream. The wine list is also outstanding. It's hard to get a table during the peak summer season, but you can order off the menu from the cozy upstairs bar.

2 S. Main St. (Rte. 173), Rockland. ✆ 207/596-0770. www.primorestaurant.com. Reservations strongly suggested. Main courses $16–$30. AE, DC, DISC, MC, V. Summer daily 5:30–9pm; call for dates/hours in off-season.

The Waterworks PUB FARE   Set a half-block off Rockland's Main Street in the brick garage of the former waterworks (naturally), The Waterworks has the informal, comfortable feel of a brewpub without the brewery. The restaurant is divided into two spacious sections (where the sun streams through the room's tall windows during long, lazy afternoons). Turn left when you enter for the pub side, which is open and airy, with wooden floors and long oak tables where customers can be indelicate with their pints. To the right is the dining room, which is carpeted and quieter. Expect pub fare and "comfort food" (so billed) that includes roast turkey, pork loin, and meatloaf.

Lindsey St., Rockland. ✆ 207/596-7950. Reservations for parties of 6 or more only. Lunch $4–$8.95; dinner $8–$15. DISC, MC, V. Mon–Sat 11am–10pm. Closed Sun–Mon in winter.

3 Camden ★★

Camden is 8 miles N of Rockland.

Camden is the quintessential coastal Maine village. Set at the foot of the wooded Camden Hills on a picturesque harbor that no Hollywood movie set could improve, the affluent village of Camden has attracted the gentry of the Eastern Seaboard for more than a century. The elaborate mansions of the moneyed set still dominate the shady side streets (many have been converted into bed-and-breakfasts), and the continued presence of old-money New Englanders has given Camden a grace and sophistication (some say snootiness) that eludes most of Maine's other coastal towns.

The best way to enjoy Camden is to park your car as soon as you can—which could mean driving a block or two off Route 1. The village is of a perfect scale to reconnoiter on foot, which allows a leisurely browse of boutiques and galleries. Don't miss the hidden town park (look behind the library), which was designed by the landscape firm of Frederick Law Olmsted, the nation's most lauded landscape architect.

On the downside, all this attention and Camden's growing appeal to bus tours is having a deleterious impact, according to some longtime visitors. The merchandise at the shops seems to be trending downward to appeal to a lower common denominator, and the constant summer congestion distracts somewhat from the village's inherent charm. If you don't come expecting a pristine and undiscovered village, you're likely to enjoy the place all the more.

ESSENTIALS
GETTING THERE
Camden is on Route 1. Coming from the south, travelers can shave a few minutes off their trip by turning left on Route 90, 6 miles past Waldoboro, bypassing Rockland. The most traffic-free route from southern Maine is to Augusta via the Maine Turnpike, and then via Route 17 to Route 90 to Route 1. **Concord Trailways** (© **800/639-3317**) offers bus service to and from Bangor and Portland.

VISITOR INFORMATION
The **Camden-Rockport-Lincolnville Chamber of Commerce,** P.O. Box 919, Camden, ME 04843 (© **800/223-5459** or 207/236-4404; www.camdenme.org), dispenses helpful information from its center at the Public Landing in Camden, where there's also free parking (although spaces are scare in summer). The chamber is open year-round weekdays from 9am to 5pm, and Saturdays 10am to 5pm. In summer, it's also open Sundays 10am to 4pm.

EXPLORING CAMDEN
Camden Hills State Park ★★ (© **207/236-3109**) is located about a mile north of the village center on Route 1. This 6,500-acre park features an ocean-side picnic area, camping at 107 sites, a winding toll road up 800-foot Mount Battie with spectacular views from the summit, and a variety of well-marked hiking trails. The day-use fee is $3 for adults and $1 for children 5 to 11. It's open from mid-May to mid-October.

One hike I recommend is an ascent to the ledges of **Mount Megunticook** ★★, preferably early in the morning before the crowds have amassed and when the mist still lingers in the valleys. Leave from near the campground (the trail head is clearly marked) and follow the well-maintained trail to these open ledges. The hike requires only about a 30- to 45-minute exertion. Spectacular, almost improbable views of the harbor await, as do glimpses inland to the gentle vales. Depending on your stamina and desires, you can continue on the park's trail network to Mount Battie or into the less-trammeled woodlands on the east side of the Camden Hills.

The Camden area is also wonderful to explore by bike. A pleasant loop several miles long takes you from the town of Camden into the cute village of **Rockport** ★, which has an equally scenic harbor and lighter tourist traffic and makes for a scenic and worthwhile detour off Route 1. There's a boat landing, small park, one of the state's best art galleries (see below), and a highly regarded summer school of photography here in Rockport.

Try this bike route: Take Bayview Street from the center of town out along the bay, passing by opulent seaside estates. The road soon narrows and becomes quiet and pastoral, overarched with leafy trees. At the stop sign just past the cemetery, turn left and follow this route into Rockport. Along the way, you'll pass the local version of "landscape with cows": in this case, a small herd of belted Galloways. In Rockport, snoop around the historic harbor and then stop by the **Center for Maine Contemporary Art** ★★, 162 Russell Ave. (© **207/236-2875;** www.arts maine.org), a stately gallery that offers rotating exhibits of local painters, sculptors,

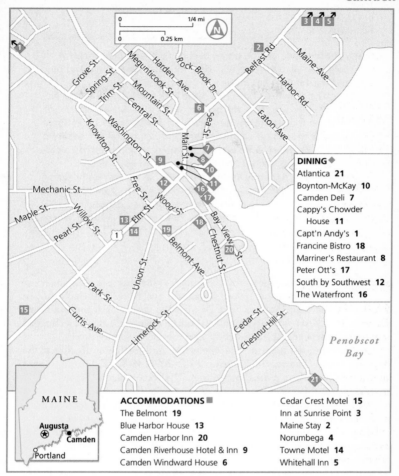

DINING ◆
Atlantica **21**
Boynton-McKay **10**
Camden Deli **7**
Cappy's Chowder
    House **11**
Capt'n Andy's **1**
Francine Bistro **18**
Marriner's Restaurant **8**
Peter Ott's **17**
South by Southwest **12**
The Waterfront **16**

ACCOMMODATIONS ■
The Belmont **19**
Blue Harbor House **13**
Camden Harbor Inn **20**
Camden Riverhouse Hotel & Inn **9**
Camden Windward House **6**
Cedar Crest Motel **15**
Inn at Sunrise Point **3**
Maine Stay **2**
Norumbega **4**
Towne Motel **14**
Whitehall Inn **5**

and crafts people. Admission is $3 per person; the gallery is open Tuesday to Saturday from 10am until 5pm and Sundays from 1 to 5pm.

There's also the **Prism Glass Studio & Gallery** (© **207/230-0061;** www.prism glassgallery.com) to visit while in Rockport. This combination glassblowing gallery and cafe cut its ribbon in 2004 at 297 Commercial St. in the heart of the village. Patti Kissinger and Lisa Sojka opened the 6,500-square-foot gallery to showcase blown glass by 85 of the top such artists in the country. There's also a stained glass studio where the partners fashion architectural commissions, Tiffany lamp reproductions, and the like. In addition to the work it shows, Kissinger produces her own paperweights, vessels, and fused glass jewelry designs.

The highlight, however, may be the gallery **cafe** ★★, which is garnering impressive raves for its upscale cuisine.

The Camden-Rockport Historical Society has prepared a 9-mile bike (or car) tour with brief descriptions of some of the historic properties along the way. The

Packing a Picnic

Grassy **Harbor Park**, on the upper part of Camden's main street is all you could want in a park: grassy, ideal for people-watching, and possessed of outstanding bay views.

Just north of town, **Camden Hills State Park** (p. 162) is ideal for a picnic, too, whether you're on the bottom section (sea views) or drive to the top of the toll road (great bay views). I'd pick up my picnic at **Boynton-McKay,** a superlative sandwich shop just across Main Street from Harbor Park, or **French & Brawn,** an upscale provisions shop on a corner just down the block; see "Where to Dine" for more details.

A little hard to find, tiny **Rockport** (p. 162) has its own scenic public park by the boat landing—small, with only a tiny sitting area, but there's a great view of the boats in the harbor. Snag it if you can. Failing that, **Walker Park** and **Mary Lea Park,** just uphill, offer grassy expanses and nice views.

brochure describing the tour is free; check for it at the chamber of commerce at Camden Public Landing (see above), or ask for one at the Whitehall Inn (see below). The brochure also includes a 2-mile walking tour of downtown Camden. Bike rentals, repairs, maps, and local riding advice are available at **Ragged Mountain Sports** (© 207/236-6664) at 46 Elm St. in Camden.

What to do in the evening? You might take in a foreign or art film at the **Bayview Street Cinema,** 10 Bayview St (© 207/236-8722), on the second floor just off Camden's central intersection. The theater boasts a superb sound system, and there's an excellent lineup of frequently changing films throughout the year. Screenings normally occur at 7 and 9pm nightly, with afternoon matinees on Sundays as well. Tickets generally cost $4.50 to $6.50 per show.

Come winter, there's skiing at the **Camden Snow Bowl** ☆ (© 207/236-3438), just outside of town on Hosmer's Pond Road. This small family-oriented ski area has a handful of trails and a modest vertical drop of 950 feet (lift tickets cost $12–$28 per day), but it also has good views of the open ocean and an exhilarating **toboggan run** ☆☆. Toboggans are available for rent for $1 per ride, or you can bring your own.

ON THE WATER

Several sailing ships make Camden their home base, and it's a rare treat to come and go from this harbor, which is considered by many to be the most beautiful in the state.

The 57-foot windjammer *Surprise* (© 207/236-4687) was launched in 1918 and today takes a maximum of 18 passengers on 2-hour nonsmoking cruises from the Camden Public Landing. Fruit juices and cookies are served on board; children 12 and older are permitted. Four excursions ($28 adults, $25 seniors) are offered daily July to mid-September; three are run daily in June, late September, and October. Reservations are helpful.

The *Schooner Lazy Jack* (© 207/230-0602) has been plying the waters since 1947 and is modeled after the Gloucester fishing schooners of the late 19th century. They run four cruises per day from mid-May through October. There's a maximum of 13 passengers; children must be 10 or older. The 2-hour tours are $25 per person; snacks are available on board, and you can BYOB.

For a more intimate view of the harbor, **Maine Sport Outfitters** (*℡* **800/722-0826** or 207/236-8797) offers sea-kayaking tours of Camden's scenic harbor. The standard tour lasts 2 hours, costs $45 for adults ($35 for children ages 10–15), and takes paddlers out to Curtis Island at the outer edge of the harbor. This beginner's tour is offered three times daily and is an easy, delightful way to get a taste of the area's maritime culture. Longer trips and instruction are also available. The outfitter's main shop, located on Route 1 in Rockport (a few minute's drive south of Camden), has a good selection of outdoor gear and is worth a stop for outdoor enthusiasts gearing up for local adventures or heading on to Acadia. Sign up for the tours either at the store or at the boathouse, which is located at the head of the harbor (near the town park).

EVENTS

Fall travelers will enjoy Camden's annual Fall Festival Arts & Crafts Show, a weekend of local art works displayed against the stunningly scenic backdrop of the Camden Hills' changing colors; call *℡* **207/236-4404** for more information. Rockport has its own October crafts show, the annual Work of the Hands show, featuring an opening bash and nine days of impressive contemporary crafts for sale. There's a small admission charge. Call *℡* **207/236-2875** for details.

And, of course, Rockland (not be left out) celebrates the changing of colors, too, during the last two weeks of the month—though with a unique twist: a scarecrow-making contest. It's part of the city's Festival of Scarecrows and Harvest Day celebration. Find the 'crows on the lawn of the Farnsworth Art Museum downtown.

Crafting a Vacation

The Maine coast has been a haven for visual artists, jewelers, sculptors, photographers, potters, and other creative types for as long as I can remember; studios, galleries, arts centers, and museums of surprising quality crop up nearly everywhere, even in the tiniest coastal villages.

While cruising the coast, you'd do well to drop into some of these craft studios—and the best way to find them quickly, is to contact the **Maine Crafts Association** (*℡* **207/780-1807**; www.mainecrafts.org), which publishes a comprehensive annual guidebook to its member artists, the *Maine Guide to Craft Artists and Culture* (the list is also available online). It contains everyone from the big Portland Museum of Art to tiny places like Handworks Gallery (in Blue Hill) or Isleford Pottery. The guide also includes small black-and-white photographs of member work, so you can get a handle on a particular style before you barrel 30 miles down a peninsula to find it.

Speaking of that, you may wish to call ahead to get studio hours before making the trek to an out-of-the-way craft studio or gallery. There *are* artists, after all—hours are likely to be a little whimsical. But who could blame them?

Later, in late November, Rockland's Festival of Lights kicks off with Santa arriving not by reindeer but by Coast Guard boat—make of that what you will—then moves on to a program of caroling, horse-drawn carriage rides, a parade, and interesting tours of some of the area's most historic inns. Call ℂ **207/596-0376** for more information.

WHERE TO STAY

Camden vies with Kennebunkport and Manchester, Vermont, for the title of bed-and-breakfast capital of New England. They're everywhere. Route 1 north of the village center—locally called High Street—is a virtual bed-and-breakfast alley, with many handsome homes converted to lodgings. Others are tucked on side streets.

Despite the preponderance of B&Bs, the total number of guest rooms (only about 300) is limited relative to the number of visitors, and during peak season lodging is tight. It's best to reserve well in advance. You might also try **Camden Accommodations and Reservations** (ℂ **800/344-4830** or 207/236-6090), which offers assistance with everything from booking rooms at local B&Bs to finding cottages for seasonal rental.

If the inns and B&Bs listed below are unavailable or out of your budget, a handful of area motels and hotels might be able to accommodate you. South of the village center are the **Cedar Crest Motel,** 115 Elm St. (ℂ **800/422-4964** or 207/236-4839), a handsome compound with a coffee shop and a shuttle-bus connection downtown (closed winter; peak season rates $119–$139); and long-time mainstay **Towne Motel,** 68 Elm St. (ℂ **207/236-3377**), which is within walking distance of the village (open year-round; $59–$125 double). Also right in town, just across the footbridge, is the modern, if generic, **Camden River-house Hotel and Inns,** 11 Tannery Lane (ℂ **800/755-7483** or 207/236-0500), which has an indoor pool, fitness center, and new Wi-Fi and high-speed Internet access (open year-round; peak season $179–$219).

One warning: High Street is a-rumble with cars and RVs during the summer months, and you might find that the steady hum of traffic diminishes the small-town charm of the establishments that flank this otherwise stately, shady road. Restless sleepers should request rooms at the rear of the property.

Finally, there's camping at **Camden Hills State Park** (see "Exploring Camden," above).

The Belmont ⭐   The Belmont is in a handsome, shingle-style 1890s home with a wraparound porch set in a quiet residential neighborhood of unpretentious homes away from Route 1. The Belmont has a sense of understated, light-Victorian style throughout—the decor is more targeted toward repose than ostentation. The inn features numerous floral prints by Maine artist Jo Spiller, and there's a large guest room with great morning light named after her. All the guest rooms have polished wood floors and are furnished simply with eclectic antiques. Downstairs, there's an elegant common room with a fireplace alcove and two built-in benches; adjacent is a cozy bar with a full liquor license.

6 Belmont Ave., Camden, ME 04843. ℂ **800/238-8053** or 207/236-8053. www.thebelmontinn.com. 6 units. Peak season $120–$175 double; off-season $90–$125 double. Rates include full breakfast. AE, MC, V. From south on Rte. 1: Turn right at first stop sign in Camden. Continue straight for 1 block; inn is on your left. From north: After passing through town on Rte. 1, turn left at blinking yellow light. Continue straight for 1 block; inn is on your left. Children 12 and older are welcome. *In room:* A/C.

Blue Harbor House ⭐   On busy Route 1 just south of town, this pale blue 1810 farmhouse has been an inn since 1978, decorated throughout with a sprightly country look. Guest rooms vary in size; some are rather small and noisy with traffic (earplugs and white-noise machines are in some rooms). Room 3 is especially nice, with wood floors, a handsome quilt, a bright alcove with plants, and a small TV. (Seven rooms have TVs, and two have Jacuzzis). The quietest and most spacious quarters are the two suites in the rear of the house, which offer the best value. Guests tend to return to this B&B not so much for the elegance of the accommodations, as for the congeniality of the hosts (they're especially good at helping plan day trips), and the familiar, familial feel of the place.

67 Elm St., Camden, ME 04843. © 800/248-3196 or 207/236-3196. Fax 207/236-6523. www.blueharbor house.com. 10 units. $115–$205 double. Rates include breakfast. AE, DISC, MC, V. Pets allowed in suite with prior permission. Closed mid-Oct to mid-May. **Amenities:** Dining room (by reservation only). *In room:* A/C, TV, hair dryer.

Camden Harbour Inn 🌟

The 1871 Camden Harbour Inn sits in a quiet neighborhood on a rise with a view of the sea and mountains beyond. It's one of the few old-fashioned Victorian-era hotels in town that hasn't been massively refurbished, and it still retains something of a creaky, seaside holiday feel with lots of floral wallpaper, a mix of simple antiques and ill-advised modern furnishings, and thin towels. (Happily, the place isn't threadbare.) All rooms have private bathrooms, most rooms have views, eight have balconies or terraces, and six have wood-burning fireplaces. It's within walking distance of downtown Camden and its restaurants.

83 Bayview St., Camden, ME 04843. © 800/236-4266 or 207/236-4200. Fax 207/236-7063. www.camden harbourinn.com. 22 units. Mid-June to mid-Oct $195–$275 double, including full breakfast; May to mid-June and mid-Oct to Nov $155–$195, including continental breakfast. 2-night minimum in peak season. AE, DISC, MC, V. Children 12 and older are welcome. Pets OK on ground floor only. *In room:* fireplace (some), balcony (some).

Camden Windward House 🌟

One of the frequent complaints about travelers staying in B&Bs on Camden's High Street is the noise from passing traffic. The Windward solved that problem by installing double windows in the front of this historic 1854 house to dampen the drone (all rooms are air-conditioned). As a result, when you walk in this historic house and close the door behind you, it feels as if you're miles away. The welcoming common rooms are decorated with a light Victorian touch and feature a great collection of cranberry glass; in the library, you'll find a guest refrigerator, icemaker, and afternoon refreshment. The guest rooms are varied in size, but all have televisions and phones with dataports. Four rooms have gas fireplaces; the Silver Birch Suite is a two-bedroom suite with a private balcony, a cathedral ceiling, a television with a VCR, and a Jacuzzi. Guests choose from seven or eight breakfast entrees, which are served in a pleasant dining room furnished with four maple tables.

6 High St., Camden, ME 04843. © 877/492-9656 or 207/236-9656. Fax 207/230-0433. bnb@windwardhouse. com. 8 units. Peak season $190–$280 double; off-season $120–$240 double. Rates include full breakfast. AE, MC, V. Children 12 and older are welcome. **Amenities:** Library. *In room:* A/C, VCR (1 room), Jacuzzi (1 room) fireplace (some).

Cedarholm Garden Bay 🌟🌟

Joyce and Barry Jobson—the daughter of the former owner and her husband—took over the inn in 1995, built a road down to the 460 feet of dramatic cobblestone shoreline, and constructed two modern, steeply gabled cedar cottages (named Loon and Puffin), each with two bedrooms. These are uniquely wonderful places, with great detailing like pocket doors, cobblestone fireplaces, wet bars, phones, handsome kitchenettes, and Jacuzzis. They're easily among the region's most quiet and peaceful retreats. There are also now two smaller, simpler waterfront cottages (Osprey and Tern) that are also quite suitable for couples; these lack the aforementioned kitchens, fireplaces, and Jacuzzis but have microwaves and great views. Guests staying up the hill in the two smallest, oldest cottages, dubbed Blueberry and Gooseberry respectively, can still wander down to the shore and lounge on the common deck overlooking the upper reaches of Penobscot Bay. It's somewhat noisier up above, where it's closer to Route 1, and the prices reflect that; as well, these latter units possess no phones.

Rte. 1, Lincolnville Beach, ME 04849. ⓒ 207/236-3886. www.cedarholm.com. 6 units. Cottage $159–$325 double. Rates include breakfast. 2-night minimum in some cottages. Closed late Nov to late Apr. MC, V. *In room:* Kitchenette (some), Jacuzzi (some), fireplaces (some), no phone.

Inn at Ocean's Edge ★★   This hidden waterside property crouches off the water side of Route 1, just a mile south of the Isleboro ferry; despite a recent change in ownership it remains a high-standard, well-kept secret retreat for honeymooners and vacationers alike. Units in the main inn and the newer hilltop annex are nearly identical: all possess Jacuzzi tubs, four-poster beds, ocean views, TVs with VCRs, and tasteful wallpaper prints and art. The hilltop units also add fridges and coffeemakers in the rooms, but sacrifice distance from the pleasant common room overlooking the bay and gardens; a full cooked breakfast, served in that room, is a highlight each morning—it might be eggs scrambled with boursin one day, an asparagus-egg dish the next. Delicious sweets and coffee are also dispensed for free from afternoon through evening in the same area, plus newspapers. Another highlight is the recent addition of Wi-Fi access in all rooms—if you've got a wireless card installed in your laptop, fine; if not, borrow a "bridge" at reception and you'll be hooked up in minutes. This is as friendly, personable, and well-kept a place as you'll find along this stretch of coast, and word is spreading. Future plans include the addition of a new outdoor pool with hot tub and an on-premises restaurant; for now, head either a mile up the road to Lincolnville Beach for lobster or 5 miles back to Camden for numerous fine dining options.

Rte. 1, Lincolnville Beach (P.O. Box 74, Camden, ME 04843). ⓒ 207/236-0945. Fax 207/236-0609. www. innatoceansedge.com. 33 units. $159–$295 double. AE, DISC, M, V. Rates include full breakfast. **Amenities:** Pub; fitness room. *In room:* AC, TV/VCR, coffeemaker (some), fridge (some), Jacuzzi, fireplace.

Inn at Sunrise Point ★★   This peaceful, private sanctuary 4 miles north of Camden Harbor seems a world apart from the bustling town. The service is crisp and helpful, and the setting can't be beat. Situated on the edge of Penobscot Bay down a long, tree-lined gravel road, the Inn at Sunrise Point consists of a cluster of contemporary yet classic shingled buildings set amid a nicely landscaped yard. The predominant sounds here are of birds and waves lapping at the cobblestone shore. A granite bench and Adirondack chairs on the front lawn allow guests to enjoy the bay view; breakfasts are served in a sunny conservatory. Guest rooms are spacious and comfortable and full of amenities, including fireplaces, VCRs, and individual heat controls. The cottages are at the deluxe end of the scale, and all feature double Jacuzzis, fireplaces, wet bars, and private decks. One new suite also has a queen bed, washer/dryer, and private deck.

Route 1 (P.O. Box 1344), Camden, ME 04843. ⓒ 207/236-7716. Fax 207/236-0820. www.sunrisepoint.com. 8 units (4 in cottages). $150–$250 double; $290–$440 suite; $205–$470 cottage. Rates include full breakfast. AE, MC, V. Closed Nov to late May. No children. *In room:* VCR, minibar, fridge (some), fireplace, Jacuzzi (some).

Maine Stay ★★   The Maine Stay is one of Camden's premier bed-and-breakfasts. Located in a home dating from 1802 but expanded in Greek Revival style in 1840, the Maine Stay is a classic slate-roofed New England homestead set in a shady yard within walking distance of both downtown and Camden Hills State Park. The eight guest rooms on three floors all have ceiling fans and are distinctively furnished with antiques and special decorative touches. Our favorite: the downstairs Carriage House Room, which is away from the buzz of traffic on Route 1 and boasts its own stone patio. The downstairs common rooms are perfect for unwinding, and the country kitchen is open to guests at all times. Hikers can set out on trails right from the yard into the Camden Hills. Of note to families is the Stichery Suite, which occupies the whole third floor.

22 High St., Camden, ME 04843. (C) 207/236-9636. www.mainestay.com. 8 units. Late May to Oct $125–$205 double, $150–$205 suite; off-season $100–$160 double, $150–$160 suite. Rates include breakfast. AE, MC, V. Children over 10 welcome. **Amenities:** Kitchen.

Norumbega ★★ You'll have no problem finding Norumbega. Just head north of the village and look for travelers pulled over taking photos of this Victorian-era stone castle overlooking the bay. The 1886 structure is both wonderfully eccentric and finely built, full of wondrous curves and angles throughout. There's extravagant carved-oak woodwork in the lobby and a stunning oak and mahogany inlaid floor. The downstairs billiards room is the place to pretend you're a 19th-century railroad baron. (Or an information-age baron—the home was owned for a time by Hodding Carter III.)

Guest rooms have been meticulously restored and furnished with antiques. Five of the rooms have fireplaces, and the three "garden-level rooms" (they're off the downstairs billiards room) have private decks. Most (not all) have televisions. Two rooms rank among the finest in New England—the Library Suite, housed in the original two-story library with an interior balcony, and the sprawling penthouse, with its superlative views, king-size bed, and oversize soaking tub. The inn is big enough to ensure privacy but also intimate enough for you to get to know the other guests—mingling often occurs at breakfast, at the optional evening social hour, and in the afternoon, when the inn puts out its famous fresh-baked cookies.

63 High St., Camden, ME 04843. (C) 207/236-4646. Fax 207/236-0824. www.norumbegainn.com. 12 units. July to mid-Oct $160–$365 double; mid-May to June $125–$290; mid-Oct to mid-May $95–$250. Suite $375–$475. All rates include full breakfast and evening refreshments. 2-night minimum in summer, weekends, and holidays. AE, DISC, MC, V. Children age 7 and older welcome. **Amenities:** Billiards room. *In room:* Fireplace (some).

Whitehall Inn ★ The Whitehall is a venerable Camden establishment, the sort of place you half expect to find the young Cary Grant in a blue blazer tickling the ivories on the 1904 Steinway in the lobby. Set at the edge of town on Route 1 in a structure that dates from 1834, this three-story inn has a striking architectural integrity with its columns, gables, and long roofline. The only downside is its location on Route 1—the traffic noise tends to persist through the evening and then start up early in the morning. (Ask for a room away from the road.) Inside, the antique furnishings—including the handsome Seth Thomas clock, Oriental carpets, and cane-seated rockers on the front porch—are impeccably well cared for. Guest rooms are simple but appealing; only some rooms have phones. The Whitehall also occupies a minor footnote in the annals of American literature—a young local poet named Edna St. Vincent Millay recited her poems here for guests in 1912, stunning the audience with her eloquence. Today the inn remains popular with a more mature, blueblood clientele, many of whom have been coming here each summer for generations

The dining room boasts a slightly faded glory and service that occasionally limps along, but it remains a good destination for reliable New England fare like scallops with basil and cherry tomatoes, and grilled lamb loin with rosemary and caramelized garlic. Of course, there's always boiled Maine lobster.

52 High St., Camden, ME 04843. ℂ **800/789-6565** or 207/236-3391. Fax 207/236-4427. www.whitehall-inn. com. 50 units (8 units share 4 bathrooms). July to late Oct $135–$170 double ($110–$120 shared bathroom); late May and June, $65–$125 double. Rates include full breakfast. AE, MC, V. Closed late Oct to late May. **Amenities:** Dining room, tennis court; nature trails; tour desk; conference rooms; babysitting. *In room:* Afternoon tea, safe.

WHERE TO DINE

In addition to its fine-dining options, downtown Camden offers a wealth of places to nosh, snack, lunch, and brunch. That's right: You can snack surprisingly well in this blueblood town.

Some of the best doughnuts in New England, for instance, are fried up at **Boynton-McKay** (ℂ **207/236-2465**) at 30 Main St.—also a superlative spot for lunch, coffee, or a sandwich. Just up the street, south of the main drag, pick up a bag of gourmet groceries at **French & Brawn** (ℂ **207/236-3361**) or lunch on Tex-Mex brunches and espresso at homey **South by Southwest** at 31 Elm St. Other local favorites include **Capt'n Andy's** (ℂ **207/236-2312**) at 156 Washington St., known for chowder and seafood; and the **Camden Deli** (ℂ **207/236-8343**) at 37 Main St., serving gourmet sandwiches, beer, and wine. All are located right in the heart of downtown.

Just up the road in Lincolnville Beach, the **Whale's Tooth Pub** (ℂ **207/789-5200**) is much more than a pub: the kitchen turns out shepherd's pie and burgers, but also steak au poivre, steamed lobsters, and salmon with pesto sauce—not to mention seafood crepes, Thai-style chicken, and even several eggplant dishes geared to vegetarians.

Atlantica ★★ SEAFOOD/ECLECTIC Atlantica gets high marks for its innovative seafood menu and its consistently well-prepared fare under the management of executive chef Ken Paquin, a graduate of the Culinary Institute of America (and former executive chef at a number of larger establishments, including the Equinox in Vermont). Located on the waterfront with a small indoor seating area and an equally small deck, Atlantica features subtly creative fare like morel mushroom- and scallion-encrusted tuna, or scallops glazed with ginger and brown sugar. You might start with a cup or bowl of the lobster corn chowder. The restaurant also now once again serves lunch, including upscale sandwiches such as fried calamari with an apricot, shallot, and chipotle dipping sauce; a rich lobster stew; and chicken pie.

1 Bayview Landing. ℂ **888/507-8514** or 207/236-6011. Reservations suggested. Lunch $5–$13; dinner main courses $17–$26. AE, MC, V. Wed–Mon 5:30–9pm (Sun also 12:30–2:30pm).

Cappy's Chowder House *Finds* SEAFOOD/AMERICAN "People always remember their meal here," say fans of Cappy's, a local institution smack in the middle of Camden. Travelers—especially families—tend to drift in here more to drink up the atmosphere than to sample rarified cuisine. Prime rib is served every day, there's a hearty seafood stew flavored with kielbasa, and there's also the famous chowder (it's been noted by *Gourmet* magazine). "Old-time sodas" are also a specialty and often a favorite with kids. The Crow's Nest upstairs is a bit quieter and offers glimpses of the harbor. Cappy's is well worth a stop if you're looking for a reasonably priced and filling meal, and if you don't expect to be treated like a member of the House of Windsor.

1 Main St. ℂ **207/236-2254**. Main courses, lunch and dinner $5.95–$14. MC, V. Daily 7:30am–11pm.

Chez Michel ⭐ *Value* FRENCH/SEAFOOD   This combination French-and-seafood restaurant, right across the road from the Isleboro ferry in Lincolnville Beach, offers good value amid a sea of higher-priced area options. And the menu successfully blends in elements of Maine and American cooking for those a bit too shy to go for, say, bouillabaisse. Begin with some mussels steamed in wine or a pâté of rabbit or locally smoked salmon, then move on to lamb kabobs, duck au poivre, steak, poached salmon, lamb shanks in a tomato-herb sauce, or haddock in a meunière sauce. If those sound too adventurous, choose a lobster dinner, pasta dish, or some fried oysters instead.

Rte. 1, Lincolnville Beach. *(C)* **207/789-6500**. Entrees $13–$18, lobster dishes market price. AE, DC, DISC, MC, V. Tues–Sat 4–9:30pm (sometimes later); Sun 11:30am–9pm.

Francine Bistro ⭐ FRENCH BISTRO   At this hot new local bistro, a meal might start with fish, onion, or lentil soup; a ceviche of halibut, serrano chiles, and red onions; mussels in Bordeaux and shallots; or skewers of grilled lamb served with white pesto, orange, and endive. The evening's entrees might run to roast chicken with a chèvre gratin or a cauliflower-cheese hash; duck a l'orange; crispy skate wing with Jerusalem artichokes; a roasted sea bass in caramelized garlic sauce; seared halibut with shrimp; a haddock stuffed with scallops; or steak frites (which are the only constant on the menu).

55 Chestnut St., Camden. *(C)* **207/230-0083**. Reservations recommended. Entrees $17–$25. MC, V. Tues–Sat 5:30–10pm. Closed mid-Mar to mid-Apr.

The Lobster Pound ⭐ LOBSTER POUND   Among the many lobster shacks up and down the midcoast, this one holds its own by offering a variety of surf-and-turf combos, shore dinners, and variations on, well, lobster. But they also serve noncrustacean meals, such as grilled steaks, roast turkey with all the trimmings, and your usual set of straightforward fish and shellfish dishes prepared in the standard ways: grilled swordfish, fried haddock, and combinations thereof. The baked scallops are excellent. There's a take-out shack adjacent for those who just don't have the time to stick around for a sit-down.

U.S. Rte. 1, Lincolnville Beach. *(C)* **207/789-5550**. Sandwiches $5.95–$7.20; lunch portions $9.95–$15; dinner entrees $12–$37. AE, DISC, MC, V. Daily 11:30am–8:30pm.

Marriner's Restaurant LUNCHEONETTE   "The last local luncheonette" is how Marriner's sums itself up, along with the legend "Down Home, Down East, No Ferns, No Quiche." As you might guess, this is a fairly small and simple affair, done up in a not-very-subtle nautical theme with pine booths and vinyl seats, some of which are held together with duct tape. (Another sign: COME ON IN, THE LOCALS WILL ENJOY YOUR ACCENT.) Marriner's has been dishing up filling breakfasts and lunch since 1942, and it's the place for early risers to get a quick start on the day—those getting here later in summer will likely find themselves facing a wait. Lunches are basic and good, and include burgers, franks, egg salad sandwiches, and homemade clam and fish chowders. The lobster and crab rolls are both superb, as are the homemade pies.

35 Main St., Camden. *(C)* **207/236-2647**. Breakfast $3.75–$5.95; lunch $4.25–$12 (mostly under $7). MC, V. Daily 6am–2pm.

Peter Ott's ⭐ AMERICAN   Peter Ott's has attracted a steady stream of satisfied local customers and repeat-visitor yachtsmen since it opened smack in the middle of Camden in 1974. While it poses as a steakhouse with its simple wooden tables and chairs and its manly meat dishes (like charbroiled Black

Angus with mushrooms and onions, and sirloin steak Dijonaise), it's grown beyond that to satisfy more diverse tastes. In fact, the restaurant offers some of the best prepared seafood in town, including a pan-blackened seafood sampler and grilled salmon served with a lemon caper sauce. Be sure to leave room for the specialty coffees and notable desserts, including a lemon-almond crumb tart.

16 Bayview St., Camden. © 207/236-4032. Main courses $17–$26. MC, V. Daily 5:30–9pm.

The Waterfront SEAFOOD   The Waterfront disproves the restaurant rule of thumb that "the better the view, the worse the food." Here you can watch multimillion-dollar yachts and handsome windjammers come and go (angle for a harborside seat on the deck), yet still be pleasantly surprised by the food. The house specialty is fresh seafood of all kinds. Lunch and dinner menus are an enterprising mix of old favorites and creative originals. On the old favorites side are fried clams, crab cakes, boiled lobster, and a fisherman's platter piled with fried seafood. On the more adventurous side are a warm duck breast salad sautéed with spinach, kalamata olives, roasted red peppers, balsamic vinaigrette, pine nuts, and feta cheese; and sautéed Gulf shrimp primavera with olive oil, Chablis-tossed linguini, vegetables, and Parmesan cheese. More earthbound fare for non-seafood eaters includes burgers, pitas, and strip steaks. A lighter pub menu is available between 2:30 and 5pm.

Bayview St. on Camden Harbor. © 207/236-3747. Main courses, lunch $6.95–$15; dinner $16–$18; lobsters market price. AE, MC, V. Daily 11:30am–2:30pm and 5–10pm. Closes earlier in off-season.

4 Belfast to Bucksport ★

Belfast is 18 miles N of Camden; Bucksport is 19 miles NE of Belfast.

The northerly stretch of Penobscot Bay is rich in history, especially maritime history. In the mid–19th century, Belfast and Searsport produced more than their share of ships, along with the captains to pilot them on trading ventures around the globe. In 1856 alone, 24 ships of more than 1,000 tons were launched from Belfast. The now-sleepy village of Searsport once had 17 active shipyards, which turned out some 200 ships over the years.

When shipbuilding died out, the Belfast area was sustained by a thriving poultry industry. Alas, that too declined as the industry moved south. In recent decades, the area has attracted artisans of various stripes who sell their wares at various shops. Tourists tend to pass through the region quickly, en route from the tourist enclave of Camden to the tourist enclave of Bar Harbor. It's worth slowing down for.

ESSENTIALS
GETTING THERE
Route 1 connects Belfast, Searsport, and Bucksport.

VISITOR INFORMATION
The **Belfast Area Chamber of Commerce,** P.O. Box 58, Belfast, ME 04915 (© **207/338-5900;** www.belfastmaine.org), staffs an information booth at 17 Main St. near the waterfront park that's open May to November daily, 10am to 6pm. Farther north, try the **Bucksport Bay Area Chamber of Commerce,** 252 Main St. (P.O. Box 1880), Bucksport, ME 04416 (© **207/469-6818;** www.bucksportchamber.org). Self-serve information is available 24 hours a day; the office is staffed 3 days weekly (days vary).

EXPLORING THE REGION

When approaching the area from the south, some splendid historic homes may be viewed by veering off Route 1 and entering downtown Belfast via High Street (look for the first DOWNTOWN BELFAST sign). The **Primrose Hill District** along High Street was the most fashionable place for prosperous merchants to settle during the early and mid–19th century, and their stately homes reflect an era when stature was equal to both the size of one's home and the care one took in designing and embellishing it. Downtown Belfast also has some superb examples of historic brick commercial architecture, including the elaborate High Victorian Gothic–style building on Main Street that formerly housed the Belfast National Bank.

Near Belfast's small waterfront park, you can take a diverting excursion on the scenic **Belfast and Moosehead Lake Railroad** (© 800/392-5500; www.belfast railroad.com). The railroad was chartered in 1867 and financed primarily by the town; in fact, until 1991 the B&ML railroad was the only railroad in the nation owned by a municipality. (It was also then locally called the "Broken and Mended.") The rail line was subsequently purchased by entrepreneurs, who have spruced it up considerably. The fleet features 11 vintage rail cars from Sweden, including a 1913 steam locomotive, and offers tours on the 33-mile rail line from both the village of Unity and downtown Belfast. (If you have your heart set on a steam locomotive, head to Unity; the Belfast train runs on diesel.)

The 1½-hour tour offers a wonderful glimpse of inland Maine and its thick forests and rich farmland. (The train also edges along Passagassawakeag River, a name that provokes considerable mirth in all but the most melancholy of children.) The Unity train features a dining car, where beer and wine can be purchased. Excursions run from mid-May to mid-October; call for hours and more information. The fare is $15 to $18 for adults, $10 for children 3 to 15, and free for children under 3.

If you'd like to explore the area by water, call Harvey Schiller at **Belfast Kayak Tours** (© 207/382-6204), or just show up at the Belfast City Pier boat ramp. With a great deal of charm and even more enthusiasm, Harvey will provide paddle instruction and take you out for a guided tour—the perfect way to get up close and personal with both the unspellable river and Penobscot Bay. (His handmade uniform is a kick, too.) Trips last 2 hours; the cost is $30 for adults and $15 for kids 12 and under; and are available from 9am to 6pm every day except Wednesday from July to Labor Day. Call for off-season hours, prices on longer tours, and group rates.

At the northern tip of the bay, the Penobscot River squeezes through a dramatic gorge near Verona Island, which Route 1 spans on an attractive suspension bridge. This easily defended pinch in the river was perceived to be of strategic importance in the 1840s, when solid and imposing **Fort Knox** was constructed. While it was never attacked, the fort was manned during the Civil War and Spanish-American War and today is run as a state park (© 207/469-7719). It's an impressive edifice to explore, with graceful granite staircases and subterranean chambers that produce wonderful echoes. Admission is $3 for adults and $1 for children under 12; the park opens from 9am until sunset daily, May through October.

Across the river from Fort Knox in the paper mill town of Bucksport is **Northeast Historic Film** (© 207/469-0924; www.oldfilm.org), an organization founded in 1986 and dedicated to preserving and showing early films

---

Moments **A Quirky Museum**

If you enjoy kitsch and uniquely American things, on a rainy day in Belfast you could do worse than make the 30-minute detour inland through the hills to little Thorndike and experience **Bryant's Stove Museum** (© **207/568-3665;** www.bryantstove.com), a nothing-if-not-entertaining experience. Joe and Bea Bryant exhibit, refurbish, and sell gorgeous cast-iron woodstoves. But looking these over is only part of the fun: The premises also house a huge selection of vintage dolls, toys, antique cars, player pianos, calliopes, concertinas, and oodles of other musical instruments and mechanical contraptions. Entering the rooms where the goodies are stored is like opening a door into an alternate universe—one presided over by suspender-wearing Joe, who sings lustily along with the pianos while puppets (rigged to the instruments) bob along in time. Get there by taking Waldo Avenue (Rte. 137) west out of Belfast for about 15 miles, then turning right onto Route 200 and continuing a bit farther. Admission is free.

---

related to New England. In 1992, the group bought Bucksport's Alamo Theatre, which was built in 1916 and closed (after a showing of *Godzilla*) in 1956. Films are shown weekends in the renovated theater; call or check the group's website to see what's coming up. Visitors can also stop by the store at the front of the theater (open Mon–Fri 9am–4pm) to browse videos and other items.

THE SEAFARING LIFE

Penobscot Marine Museum ★★★   The Penobscot Marine Museum is one of the best small museums in New England. Housed in a cluster of eight historic buildings atop a gentle rise in tiny downtown Searsport, the museum does a deft job of educating visitors about the vitality of the local shipbuilding industry, the essential role of international trade to daily life in the 19th century, and the hazards of life at sea. Exhibits (such as "The Art of Lobstering") are uncommonly well organized, and wandering from building to building induces a keen sense of wonderment at the vast enterprise that was Maine's maritime trade.

Among the most intriguing exhibits is a wide selection of dramatic marine paintings (including a stunning rendition of whaling in the Arctic), black-and-white photographs of many of the 286 weathered sea captains who once called Searsport home, exceptional photographs of a 1902 voyage to Argentina, and an early home decorated in the style of a sea captain, complete with lacquered furniture and accessories hauled back from trade missions to the Orient. Throughout, the curators do a fine job of both educating and entertaining visitors. It's well worth the price if you're the least interested in Maine's rich culture of the sea.

85 Main St. (corner Church St. and Rte. 1), Searsport. © 207/548-2529. Adults $8, seniors $6, children 7–15 $3. Memorial Day to mid-Oct Mon–Sat 10am–5pm; Sun noon–5pm. Last ticket sold at 4pm.

WHERE TO STAY

If you're stuck for a bed along this stretch of the coast and don't mind the chain-hotel ambience for a night, the **Comfort Inn,** 159 Searsport Ave. (Rte. 1) (© **207/338-2090**), is a good backup option. Some rooms have kitchenettes and/or whirlpools; there's a pool; a small breakfast is served; and some rooms come with sublime views of the bay (if there's no fog, that is). However, check early if possible—the place sometimes fills up early.

Homeport Inn ⭐ Sitting in this inn's front parlor a few miles north of Belfast, guests may be excused for feeling as if they were sitting inside a Persian carpet. The opulently furnished 1861 sea captain's house is filled with tchotchkes from Asia and elaborate decorative touches. Breakfast is served on an airy enclosed porch along the side (with glimpses of the bay beyond). Choose from one of four handsome period rooms in the old section of the house atop a grand staircase, or from one of six more modern rooms in the adjoining carriage house. The disadvantage of the older rooms is that they share a single bathroom; the disadvantage of the carriage house rooms is that they're somewhat lacking in historic charm. Note also that the inn faces a heavily traveled stretch of Route 1 east of Searsport village, which detracts somewhat from the historic charm.

Rte. 1 (P.O. Box 647), Searsport, ME 04974. ⓒ **800/742-5814** or 207/548-2259. 10 units (3 share 1 bathroom). $60–$120 double. Rates include breakfast. AE, DISC, MC, V. *In room:* No phone.

The White House ⭐⭐ This architecturally stunning Greek Revival home is just a 10-minute walk from downtown Belfast and offers more B&B than you might expect for the rates, which are somewhat low for this area of the coast. Originally built as a sea captain's home in the 1840s and topped with a striking eight-sided cupola, the James P. White House was exquisitely refurnished, painted, and wallpapered by the three innkeepers. Downstairs, guests have the run of a library, an elegant parlor area, and a dining room where the hearty breakfasts are served. All bedrooms (two with TVs) have private bathrooms with a hair dryer and gorgeously soft Egyptian cotton towels and robes. Owners even place fresh flowers in the guest rooms. One of the nicest (and also the priciest) is the Belfast Bay, an over-the-top Louis XVI–style room with a fireplace, a whirlpool, and water views. Less fancy but no less appealing is the Copperbeech Suite, located at the back of the house and featuring a sitting room and old pumpkin pine floors.

1 Church St., Belfast. ⓒ **888/290-1901** or 207/338-1901. Fax 207/338-5161. www.mainebb.com. 6 units (1 with private hall bathroom). $115–$175 double. Rates include full breakfast. DISC, MC, V. **Amenities:** Library; laundry service. *In room:* TV (some), hair dryer, Jacuzzi (1 room), fireplace (1 room), robe.

Wildflower Inn ⭐ Reopened after a hiatus, the former sail-maker's home in downtown Searsport is elegant yet extremely comfortable in its latest incarnation as a B&B. A bright and open sitting room and dining area are good for travelers looking for something more personal than a hotel, yet less fusty than your typical Inn with a capital "I." Translation? They don't put on airs here. Guest rooms have plenty of space and are spotless, and little extras—bottles of spring water, bowls of chocolates on the dresser—are quite welcome after long days of active sightseeing. The Delphinium Room is most luxurious, with its bay view, Jacuzzi and king bed; the Sage and Viola rooms feature antique sink fittings, while the Buttercup Room is furnished with a smaller double bed. The friendly

Packing a Picnic

Searsport has an outstanding little pocket park just off the hustle of busy Route 1; look for the post office, then walk downhill. It makes for a great quick picnic. Pick up rudimentary foods at **Tozier's Market** (on Rte. 1 just south of the Maritime Museum; you can't miss it).

innkeepers whip up breakfasts that might include blueberry pancakes, thick bacon, or Mexican quiche, and also put out homemade cookies and other sweets for daytime snacking. (Light sleepers, note that the inn sits right on Rte. 1; some guests may be sensitive to traffic noise in high summer.) The basement is a comfy television/game room where guests can escape to play backgammon, watch films, or snooze on the couch; and the gardens surrounding the home host an abundance of glorious, well-maintained (guess what?) wildflowers.

2 Black Rd. (Rte. 1), Searsport, ME 04974. ℂ 888/546-2112 or 207/548-2112. www.wildflowerinnme.com. 4 units. $85–$135 double. Rates include full breakfast. MC, V. *In room:* TV (some), coffeemaker, Jacuzzi (1 room).

WHERE TO DINE

While strolling around downtown Belfast, don't overlook the **Gothic** ★ (ℂ **207/ 338-4933**) at 108 Main St., a great little dessert and coffee shop. The ice cream, coffee drinks, milkshakes, and pastries here are all terrific (try an espresso milk-shake for a real kick), and there's usually a free *New York Times* kicking around the room for reading. It's part of a business that scrounges unique construction materials from area buildings; as a result, the adjacent room holds all sorts of interesting local signs, boards, clocks, and other decorative whatnot.

Just south of Belfast on Route 1, **Seng Thai** ★ (ℂ **207/338-0010**)—one of many Thai restaurants you'll be surprised to find as you cruise up and down the Maine coast—serves up well-spiced classic dishes such as pad Thai and various curries, but also a uniquely creative take on more upscale fare such as lobster and fish. Top off your meal with a potent Thai tea or coffee. (The two original Seng Thais in Portland are cheaper and more downscale, though equally authentic.) It's open daily from 11am until 10pm.

A surprisingly hip new spot in downtown Belfast is **three tides** (ℂ **207/ 338-1707**) at 3 Pinchy Lane (next to the waterfront); it's got a more contemporary, urban feel than Belfast's workaday bars and pubs. They serve raw fish, tapas, a selection of beers and a number of un-Maine drinks such as a chocolate martini—but they'll also do you a full-blown lobster bake, complete with sea-weed-baked clams. The outdoor deck is a good spot to relax while the sun goes down.

Finally, if you're packing a picnic, one of Maine's best natural-foods stores, **The Belfast Co-op** ★ (ℂ **207/338-2532**) is at 123 High St. Not everything here is for the virtuous: The selection of imported beers and the cuts of organic beef are surprisingly good. It's open 7:30am to 8pm daily.

Chase's Daily Restaurant ★ VEGETARIAN   A vegetarian restaurant that doesn't make a point of being too politically correct, Chase's maintains a good balance between simple, hearty food and more sophisticated menu items. Break-fast ranges from simple oatmeal to breakfast burritos and healthy fruit smooth-ies; lunch segues nicely into a menu of pizzas, sandwiches, soups, and salads with an emphasis on Asian, Latin American, and European themes. There's also a daily pasta dish. Coffee drinks here are high quality: The restaurant serves fair-trade beans roasted at New York's excellent Porto Rico coffeehouse. The whole room is inviting and light-filled; notice the wooden floorboards and pressed-tin ceiling.

96 Main St., Belfast. ℂ 207/338-0555. Main courses $3.50–$14. DISC, MC, V. Breakfast, lunch daily (din-ner Fri only). Mon–Thurs 7am–2pm; Fri 5:30am–8:30pm; Sat 7am–2pm; Sun 8am–1pm.

Darby's ★ AMERICAN/ECLECTIC   Located in a Civil War–era pub with attractive stamped tin ceilings and a beautiful back bar with Corinthian

columns, Darby's is a popular local hangout that boasts a comfortable, neigh-
borhoody feel. Order up a Maine microbrew or a single-malt whiskey while you
peruse the menu, which is more creative than you might expect for the pubby
surroundings. Darby's serves up not only basic bar favorites like burgers on a
bulky roll, but also inventive dishes like mahogany duck, pad Thai, and steak.
(The burgers and pad Thai are nothing special, but the convivial atmosphere at
the bar is.) Desserts here are all homemade and tend toward the basic, with
cheesecake, pies, and an interesting "Russian cream." If you like the artwork on
the wall, ask about it—it was probably painted by a local artist, and it's probably for sale.

155 High St., Belfast. ✆ 207/338-2339. Reservations suggested after 7pm. Main courses $7–$13 lunch;
$11–$19 dinner. AE, DC, DISC, MC. V. Mon–Sat 11:30am–3:30pm and 5–9pm; Sun noon–3:30pm and
5–8:30pm.

MacLeod's ECLECTIC HOME STYLE   MacLeod's is a comfortable, pubby
place in downtown Bucksport that teems on weekends with Bucksport residents—from workers at the pulp mill to local businessmen. With its simple
wood tables, Windsor chairs, and relentlessly upbeat background music,
MacLeod's won't be confused with a place for fancy dining, but it does offer
good meals, sizable portions, and consistent quality. For dinner, entrees include
grilled lamb shish kabob, raspberry chicken, baked sea scallops, and a unique
"lasagna al pescatore," made with shrimp, scallops, and crabmeat with a rich
lobster sauce.

Main St., Bucksport. ✆ 207/469-3963. Reservations recommended on weekends and in summer. Main
courses $4.95–$11 lunch, $8.95–$15 dinner. AE, DC, MC, V. Mon–Fri 11:30am–9pm; Sat–Sun 5–9pm (closed
Sun evenings in off-season).

The Rhumb Line NEW AMERICAN   The Rhumb Line features locally
grown ingredients—the tomatoes in a salad might have just been picked from the
garden in back of the inn, the tender horseradish-crusted salmon (served with a
rémoulade) farmed in nearby Ellsworth, the smoked salmon smoked in Belfast.
If you're not in the mood to start with one of the Rhumb Line's fresh salads, try
the escargot, shrimp wrapped in prosciutto, or the hot crab dip. As far as entrees
go, stick with favorites like grilled rack of lamb with mint-fig balsamic vinegar,
or the sautéed fillet of haddock with roasted garlic, basil oil, and olives.

200 East Main St. (Rte. 1), Searsport. ✆ 207/548-2600. Reservations suggested. Main courses $21–$28.
MC, V. Open year-round, daily in summer 5:30–9pm; call for off-season hours.

Twilight Cafe ★★ NEW AMERICAN   The food at the new downtown
home of this popular cafe sings, bringing a repeat clientele of knowledgeable
locals and the occasional tourist fortunate enough to locate it. Dinner offerings
are eclectic: lobster cakes might be served encrusted in pecans and served with a
gingery crème fraîche; Caribbean jerk shrimp might be paired with citrus linguine; lamb chops could come with shallots, mustard, and mint; and a chicken
breast may be stuffed with crabmeat. Salmon, tenderloin, and bouillabaisse are
often on the menu, and there's a small wine list. Desserts are great, as well. Artwork from the adjacent gallery, which promotes the work of artists with disabilities, hangs on the walls.

72 Main St., Belfast. ✆ 207/338-0937. Reservations recommended. Dinner entrees $16–$26. AE, DISC, MC,
V. Thurs–Sat 5:30–9:30pm.

Young's Lobster Pound ★ *Finds* LOBSTER   I love this place; it's one of my
favorite lobster shacks in Maine. Actually, even calling it a "shack" may be a

euphemism. When you first enter the dirt parking lot and spy the unlovely red corrugated industrial building, you may think, "This must be a mistake." But persevere; beyond the hangar-sized door, you'll find a counter where friendly folks take your order amid long, green lobster tanks loudly gurgling seawater, then shout it to the lobster guys in boots. Eat upstairs where picnic tables are arrayed in an open, barnlike area, or out on the deck, with views across the river to Belfast. This is a place to get good and messy; the lobsters, served on paper plates with butter and corn on the cob, are delicious and relatively inexpensive. Stick to the shore dinners and steer away from the stews. And *don't* wear your finest threads—unless you want them to smell like lobster. And get lots of napkins.

Mitchell Ave., E. Belfast. © 207/338-1160. Fax 207/338-3498. Reservations not accepted. Main courses $5.95–$17. MC, V. Daily 7am–8pm (until 7pm in spring and fall). Closed Dec–Mar. From Belfast, take Rtes. 1 and 3 eastward across the river; look for signs on right after bridge.

5 Castine & Environs ★★

Castine, off the beaten track, must be one of the most gracious villages in Maine. It's not so much the stunningly handsome, meticulously maintained mid-19th-century homes that fill the side streets. Nor is it the location on a quiet peninsula, 16 miles south of tourist-clotted Route 1. No, what lends Castine most of its charm are the splendid, towering elm trees that still overarch many of the village streets. Before Dutch elm disease ravaged the nation's tree-lined streets, much of America once looked like this, and it's easy to slip into a debilitating nostalgia for this most graceful tree, even if you're too young to remember the America of the elms. Through perseverance and a measure of luck, Castine has managed to keep several hundred elms alive, and it's worth the drive here for this alone.

For American history buffs, Castine offers more than trees. This outpost served as a strategic town in various battles among the British, Dutch, French, and feisty colonials in the centuries following its settlement in 1613. It was occupied by each of those groups at some point, and historical personages like Miles Standish and Paul Revere passed through during one epoch or another. The town has a dignified, aristocratic bearing, and it somehow seems appropriate that Tory-dominated Castine welcomed the British with open arms during the Revolution.

An excellent brief history of Castine by Elizabeth J. Duff is published in brochure form by the Castine Merchant's Association. The brochure, which also includes a walking tour of Castine, is entitled "Welcome to Castine" and is available at several shops in town, at the town hall, and at most state information centers.

Castine is most likely to appeal to those who can entertain themselves. It's a peaceful place to sit and read or take an afternoon walk. If it's outlet shopping or cute boutiques you're looking for, you're better off moving on.

ESSENTIALS
GETTING THERE
Castine is located 16 miles south of Route 1. Turn south on Route 175 in Orland (east of Bucksport) and follow this to Route 166, which winds its way to Castine. Route 166A offers an alternate route along Penobscot Bay.

VISITOR INFORMATION
Castine lacks a formal information center, but the clerk at the **Town Office** (© 207/326-4502) is often helpful with local questions. The office is open Monday to Friday, 11am to 3pm only. The **Blue Hill Peninsula Chamber of Commerce** (see later in this chapter) handles tourist inquiries.

EXPLORING CASTINE

One of the town's more intriguing attractions is the **Wilson Museum** ⛿ (© 207/ 326-1247; www.wilsonmuseum.org) on Perkins St., an appealing and quirky anthropological museum constructed in 1921. This small museum contains the collections of John Howard Wilson, an archaeologist and collector of prehistoric artifacts from around the globe. His gleanings are neatly arranged in a staid, classical arrangement of the sort that proliferated in the late 19th and early 20th centuries. The museum is open from the end of May to the end of September every day except Monday 2 to 5pm; admission is free.

Next door is the **John Perkins House** (© 207/326-9247), Castine's oldest home. It was occupied by the British during the Revolution and the War of 1812, and a tour features demonstrations of old-fashioned cooking techniques. The Perkins House is open July and August on Wednesday and Sunday only from 2 to 5pm. Admission is free.

Other attractions in this Wilson-Perkins complex (it's almost like a little historical campus, really) include a blacksmith shop and the Hearse House; both are free to tour.

Castine is also home to the **Maine Maritime Academy** (© 207/326-4311), which trains sailors for the rigors of life at sea with the merchant marine. The campus is on the western edge of the village, and the 498-foot vessel T.V. *State of Maine,* the hulking gray training ship, is often docked in Castine, all but overwhelming the village. Free half-hour tours of the ship are offered in summer whenever the ship is in port, on the hour from 10am to noon and from 1 to 4pm.

Also worth exploring is **Dice's Head Light,** at the extreme western end of Battle Avenue. While the 1828 light itself is no longer operating and is not open to the public, it's well worth scrambling down the trail to the rocky shoreline along the Penobscot River just beneath the lighthouse. A small sign indicates the start of the public trail.

ON THE WATER

This is a lovely open harbor, with open land and forest edging the watery expanse. A couple of options exist for cruising on the water.

Castine Kayak Adventures (© 207/866-3506; www.castinekayak.com) offers full- ($110) and half-day ($65) sea kayak tours departing from Dennett's Wharf restaurant. Both trips are appropriate for those without experience; a brief intro will get you started with this graceful and often meditative sport. You'll often spot wildlife, like bald eagles, harbor seals, and ospreys. The 6-hour tour includes a bag lunch. Ask also about the sunset tours, nighttime paddles, and overnight trips, which are also offered.

A TOUR OF CAPE ROSIER ⛿⛿

Across the Bagaduce River from Castine is Cape Rosier, one of Maine's best-kept secrets. The bad news is, to reach the cape you need to backtrack to Route 175, head south toward Deer Isle, and then follow Route 176 to the turnoff to Cape Rosier—about 18 miles of driving to cross 1 mile of water. As a dead-end peninsula, there's no through traffic and roads suddenly turn to dirt in sections. The cape still has a wild, unkempt flavor with salty views of Penobscot Bay; it's not hard to imagine that you're back in Maine of the 1940s.

A loop of 15 miles or so around the cape starting on Goose Falls Road—begin by following Route 176 to Brooksville, then taking Cape Rosier Rd.—is suitable for travel by mountain bike or as a leisurely car trip. The views are uncommonly beautiful, with a mix of blueberry barrens, boreal forest, farmsteads, summer estate houses, and coves dotted with yachts and lobster boats. There's virtually no commercial development of any sort. It's no accident that Helen and Scott Nearing, the late back-to-the-land gurus and authors of *Living the Good Life,* chose to settle here when Vermont became too developed for their tastes. A number of Nearing acolytes continue to live on Cape Rosier. Bike rentals are available at Eggemoggin Landing (p. 183).

If the weather's agreeable, stop for a walk on the state-owned **Holbrook Island Wildlife Sanctuary,** a 1,200-acre preserve laced with trails and abandoned roads. The sanctuary is located at the northern end of the cape (look for signs). Among the choices: The Backshore Trail passes along open meadows to the shoreline, and the Summit Trail is all mossy, mushroomy, and medieval, with teasing glimpses of the water from the top.

WHERE TO STAY

Castine Harbor Lodge ★ *(Kids* This is a great seasonal spot for families. Housed in a grand 1893 mansion (the only inn on the water in Castine), it's run with an informal good cheer that allows kids to feel at home amid the regal architecture. The main parlor is dominated by a pool table, and there's Scrabble and Nintendo for the asking. The spacious rooms are eclectically furnished, with some antiques and some modern. Two of the guest rooms share an adjoining bathroom—of note to traveling families. The family dog is welcome. And if you're not traveling with a family? It's still a great spot if you prefer well-worn comfort to high-end elegance. And the bathrooms might have the best views of any in the state.

Perkins St (P.O. Box 215), Castine, ME 04421. © 207/326-4335. www.castinemaine.com. 16 units (2 with shared bathrooms), 1 cottage. June to mid-Nov $85–$245 double; cottage $1,250 weekly. Mid-Nov to May $75–$195 double. Rates include continental breakfast. MC, V. Pets allowed ($10 per night). **Amenities:** Dining room; bar; pool table.

Castine Inn ★ The Castine Inn is a Maine Coast rarity: a hotel that was originally built as a hotel (not as a residence)—in this case, in 1898. This handsome cream-colored village inn, designed in an eclectic Georgian Federal–revival style, has a fine front porch and attractive gardens. Inside, the lobby takes its cue from the 1940s, with wingback chairs and loveseats and a fireplace in the parlor. There's also an intimate, dark lounge decked out in rich green hues, reminiscent of an Irish pub. The guest rooms on the two upper floors are attractively, if unevenly, furnished in early American style—the innkeepers are revamping the rooms one by one to an even gloss, adding luxe touches. Until they're all renovated, it might be wise to ask to view the available rooms before you sign in. The innkeepers have also recently added a sauna to the inn. The elegant dining room (see below) serves up Castine's best fare and some of the best food in the state.

Main St. (P.O. Box 41), Castine, ME 04421. © 207/326-4365. Fax 207/326-4570. www.castineinn.com. 19 units. Peak season $90–$225 double; off-season lower. Rates include full breakfast. Closed Nov–Apr. 2-night minimum July–Aug. MC, V. Children 8 and older are welcome. **Amenities:** Dining room; sauna.

Pentagöet Inn ★ Here's the big activity at the Pentagöet: Sit on the wrap-around front porch on cane-seated rockers and watch the slow-paced activity on Main Street. That's not likely to be overly appealing to those looking for a fast-paced vacation, but it's the perfect salve for someone seeking respite from urban life. This quirky yellow and green 1894 structure with its prominent turret is tastefully furnished downstairs with hardwood floors, oval braided rugs, and a woodstove. It's comfortable without being overly fussy, professional without being chilly, personal without being overly intimate. The rooms on the upper two floors of the main house are furnished eclectically, with a mix of antiques and collectibles. The five guest rooms in the adjacent Perkins Street building—a more austere Federal-era house—are furnished simply and feature painted floors. There's no air-conditioning, but all rooms have ceiling or window fans.

The inn's first floor features the cozy Passports Pub and a dining room with delightful outdoor seating in summer. Meals are a mix of the regional and global—chicken pot pie and Spanish seafood stew, for example. The restaurant is open daily in summer and limited days during the off-season.

Main St. (P.O. Box 4), Castine, ME 04421. © 800/845-1701 or 207/326-8616. Fax 207/326-9382. www. pentagoet.com. 16 units (2 with private hallway bathrooms). Peak season $85–$195 double; off-season lower. Rates include full breakfast. MC, V. Closed Nov–Apr. Pets by reservation. Suitable for older children only. **Amenities:** Dining room; pub; bikes. *In room:* Fireplace (some).

WHERE TO DINE

The best dinner in town is at the Castine Inn (see above). For lunch or more informal dinner fare, try the following.

Castine Inn ★★ NEW AMERICAN This handsome hotel dining room has Castine's best fare and some of the better food in the state. Chef/owner Tom Gutow served stints at Bouley and Verbena in New York, and isn't timid about experimenting with local meats and produce. Expect dishes such as lobster with vanilla butter, mango mayonnaise, and tropical-fruit salsa; or lamb loin with eggplant, green lentils, tomatoes, and rosemary *jus*. One night each week, the restaurant offers a buffet; that night, you're better off heading to Dennett's Wharf.

Main St. © 207/326-4365. Reservations recommended. Main courses $26–$33. MC, V. Daily 6–9pm. Closed mid-Dec to May.

Dennett's Wharf PUB FARE Located in a soaring waterfront sail loft with dollar bills tacked all over the high ceiling, Dennett's Wharf offers upscale bar food amid a lively setting leavened with a good selection of microbrews. If the weather's decent, there's outside dining under a bright yellow awning with superb harbor views. Look for grilled sandwiches, roll-ups, and salads at lunch; dinner includes lobster, stir-fry, and steak teriyaki. And how did all those bills get on the ceiling? Ask your server. It will cost you exactly $1 to find out.

15 Sea St. (next to the Town Dock). © 207/326-9045. Reservations recommended in summer and for parties of 6 or more. Lunch $4.75–$13; dinner $8.95–$27. AE, DISC, MC, V. Daily 11am–midnight. Closed mid-Oct to Apr 30.

6 Deer Isle ★★

Deer Isle is well off the beaten path but worth the long detour off Route 1 if your tastes run to pastoral countryside with a nautical edge. Loopy, winding roads cross through forest and farmland, and travelers are rewarded with sudden glimpses of the sun-dappled ocean and mint-green coves. An occasional settlement crops up now and again.

Deer Isle doesn't cater exclusively to tourists, as many coastal regions do. It's still occupied by fifth-generation fishermen, farmers, longtime rusticators, and artists who prize their seclusion. The village of Deer Isle has a handful of inns and galleries, but its primary focus is to serve locals and summer residents, not transients. The village of **Stonington,** on the southern tip, is a rough-hewn sea town. Despite serious incursions the past 5 years by galleries and enterprises dependent on seasonal tourism, it remains dominated in spirit by fishermen and the occasional quarry worker.

ESSENTIALS
GETTING THERE
Deer Isle is accessible via several winding country roads from Route 1. Coming from the west, head south on Route 175 off Route 1 in Orland, and then connect to Route 15 to Deer Isle. From the east, head south on Route 172 to Blue Hill, where you can pick up Route 15. Deer Isle is connected to the mainland via a high, narrow, and graceful suspension bridge built in 1938, which can be somewhat harrowing to cross in high winds.

VISITOR INFORMATION
The **Deer Isle–Stonington Chamber of Commerce** (© 207/348-6124; www. deerislemaine.com) staffs a seasonal information booth just beyond the bridge on Little Deer Isle. The booth is open daily in summer from 10am to 4pm, depending on volunteer availability.

EXPLORING DEER ISLE
Deer Isle, with its network of narrow roads to nowhere, is ideal for perfunctory rambling. It's a pleasure to explore by car and is also inviting to travel by bike, although hasty and careening fishermen in pickups can make this unnerving at times. Especially tranquil is the narrow road between Deer Isle and Sunshine to the east. Plan to stop and explore the rocky coves and inlets along the way. To get here, head toward Stonington on Route 15. Just south of the village of Deer Isle, turn east toward Stinson Neck and continue along this scenic byway for about 10 miles over bridges and causeways.

Stonington, at the very southern tip of Deer Isle, consists of one commercial street that wraps along the harbor's edge. The village took its name from the granite quarries that pockmark the area; local stone has been incorporated into some of America's most important buildings and bridges, and lately the quarrying industry has seen an upkick. Main Street, while small, does feature a gourmet foods shop (Penobscot Bay Provisions; © 207/367-5177), tackle shop, and bookshop. The town opera house is home to a summer-stock theater company; log onto www.operahousearts.org for a schedule and other details. Stonington is also another of Maine's fishing villages to feature some big-time **lobster boat racing;** this town's event occurs in late July. You'll be amazed at how quickly one of these workhorses can get going when the captain's going full throttle. While bed-and-breakfasts and boutiques have made some inroads here, it's still mostly a rough-and-tumble waterfront town with strong links to the sea, and you're likely to observe lots of activity in the harbor as lobster boats come and go.

If you hear industrial sounds emanating from just offshore, however, that might actually be the stone quarry on Crotch Island, which has been supplying architectural granite to builders nationwide for more than a century. You can learn more about the stone industry at the **Deer Isle Granite Museum,** on Main Street (© 207/367-6331). The museum features some historical artifacts from the quarry's golden years, but the real draw is a working diorama (8 by 15 ft.) of Crotch Island as it would have appeared around 1900. It features a little railroad, little boats, and little cranes moving little stones around. Kids under 10 years old find it endlessly fascinating. The museum is open from late May to August, Monday to Saturday from 9am to 5pm and Sunday from 1 to 4pm. Donations are requested.

Haystack Mountain School of Crafts ⭐ The 40-acre ocean-side campus of this respected summer crafts school is stunning. Designed in the 1960s, Edward Larrabee Barnes set the buildings on a hillside overlooking the waters of Jericho Bay. Barnes cleverly managed to play up the views while respecting the delicate landscape by constructing a series of small structures on pilings that seem to float above the earth. The classrooms and studios are linked by board-walks, many connected to a wide central staircase ending at the "Flag Deck," a sort of open-air commons just above the shoreline. These buildings and class-rooms are closed to the public, but summer visitors are welcome to walk to the Flag Deck and stroll the nature trail adjacent to campus. The drive to the cam-pus is outstanding, as well, and there's one public tour weekly June to August Wednesdays at 1pm, during which you can catch glimpses of the studios.

Sunshine Rd. ⓒ 207/348-2306. www.haystack-mtn.org. Donations appreciated. Summer daily 9am–5pm; tours Wed 1pm. Head south of the village of Deer Isle on Rte. 15; turn left on Greenlaw District Rd. and fol-low signs to the school, approximately 7 miles.

WHERE TO STAY

Located on the island side of the bridge from the mainland is **Eggemoggin Landing** (ⓒ **207/348-6115**), a recommended lodging option on the island for those looking to spend less than charged at the inns below. It's a standard motel with basic rooms, but it features a great location on the shores of Eggemoggin Reach with good views of the bridge. It's open from May to October, with rates of $67 to $85. Pets are allowed spring and fall only ($10 extra charge). A restau-rant serves three meals on the premises; the motel also offers kayaks, bike rentals (nonguests may also rent), and sailboat cruises.

Goose Cove Lodge ⭐⭐ _Kids_ A rustic compound adjacent to a nature preserve on a remote coastal point, Goose Cove Lodge is a superb destination for families and lovers of the outdoors. Exploring the grounds offers an adventure every day. You can hike out at low tide to salty Barred Island or take a guided nature hike on any of five trails. You can mess around in boats in the cove (the inn has kayaks and canoes) or borrow one of the inn's bikes for an excursion. Twenty of the rooms offer fireplaces or Franklin stoves; two newer, modern cottages sleep six and are available through the winter. Our favorites? The Elm and the Linnea, cozy cabins tucked privately in the woods on a rise overlooking the beach.

Each evening begins with a cocktail hour at 5:30 in the lodge, followed by dinner. Guests sit family style and dine while enjoying views of the cove and dis-tant islands. There's always a vegetarian option at dinner, along with other cre-ative entrees such as smoked salmon with chèvre served on potato pancakes with apple sour cream sauce, or lobster shepherd's pie with corn-cheddar mash, roasted tomato, and a smoked gouda fondue. The dining room is open to the public (reservations mandatory); come for lunch on the deck or for dinner as space permits.

Goose Cove Rd. (P.O. Box 40), Sunset, ME 04683. ⓒ **800/728-1963** or 207/348-2508. Fax 207/348-2624. www.goosecovelodge.com. 22 cottages. Mid-June to Aug $155–$575 double; mid-May to mid-June and Sept to mid-Oct $145–$295. Rates include full breakfast. Ask about low-season packages. Some units have 3-per-son minimum during high season. July-Aug 2-night minimum (1-week min. in cottages). MC, V. **Amenities:** Dining room. _In room:_ Woodstove (some).

Inn on the Harbor ⭐ This appealingly quirky waterfront inn has the best location in town—perched over the harbor and right on the main street. After a major makeover a few years ago, the guest rooms (10 of which overlook the har-bor) are now nicely appointed with antiques and sisal carpets. Swap notes about your room with other guests over complimentary sherry and wine served in the reception room or on the expansive deck in late afternoon. This is a great location for resting up before or after a kayak expedition, or a good base for a day trip out to Isle au Haut. All rooms except the suite, located across town in the innkeeper's home, feature in-room phones (but the suite does have a woodstove and private kitchen). Breakfast includes home-baked muffins and breads. Parking is on the street or at nearby lots and can be inconvenient during busy times.

Main St. (P.O. Box 69), Stonington, ME 04681. (C) **800/942-2420** or 207/367-2420. Fax 207/367-5165. www. innontheharbor.com. 13 units. Mid-May to mid-Oct $115–$195 double; mid-Oct to mid-May $60–$130 double. Rates include continental breakfast mid-May to mid-Oct only. AE, DISC, MC, V. Children 12 and older welcome. **Amenities:** Spa services. *In room:* Dataport.

Oakland House Seaside Resort/Shore Oaks ★ *Kids*

It doesn't get much more Maine than out-of-the-way Oakland House: Innkeeper Jim Littlefield is the great-grandson of the original owner, a retired sea captain who opened the inn back on July 4, 1889, on land acquired from King George. (The original inn sign remains.) Located on the mainland just north of the bridge to Deer Isle, it's a classic summer resort. The main house, known as Shore Oaks, was built in 1907 and consists of 10 Arts and Crafts-style rooms, seven with private bathrooms (and two with wood-burning fireplaces); as none have televisions or phones, guests tend to congregate in a living room of wicker, bay windows, and rocking chairs or the wraparound porch with its expansive views of the reach and the Pumpkin Island Lighthouse. An adjoining library of maps and books includes an archive of the hotel. In addition to the main inn, 15 cottages dot the property, offering a variety of amenities from kitchenettes to claw-foot tubs.

The main draw, however, is a cluster of shore-side cottages. These cottages—tucked among 50 acres and a half-mile of shore front with extraordinary views of Eggemoggin Reach, containing one to five bedrooms each—have televisions or phones, usually not both. These are mostly set aside for week-long stays (Sat–Sat) and are of varying vintages, but most have fireplaces with wood delivered daily. Lone Pine is the most modern, with an up-to-date kitchen with oven and refrigerator/freezer, two bedrooms, and a satellite TV with VCR; Boathouse is right at water's edge, with a wood-burning fireplace, dining table, and full kitchen. Scenic hiking trails also lace the grounds, sea breezes are omnipresent, and kayaks can be rented for offshore exploration. In peak season, the hotel dining room serves mussels, scallops, steaks, seafood, and the like on china and tablecloths (and Thurs nights bring lobster picnics on the beach). Further activities on the grounds include hiking trails (be sure to hike the Blue Dot Trail to Lookout Rock), dubbing around in rowboats, swimming in the frigid saltwater, hiking to a (warmer) lake for swimming (shared with a kids' summer camp), and watching videos in the barn after dinner. Boat charters and a lobster bake are options in the summer. In short, whatever this property may lack in luxury, it more than makes up for with hospitality and seaside relaxation. You might never leave.

435 Herrick Rd., Brooksville, ME 04617. (C) **800/359-RELAX** or 207/359-8521. www.oaklandhouse.com. 10 units (7 with private bathroom), 15 cottages. $226–$470 double; $475–$5,400 weekly cottage. Rates include five-course dinner and breakfast in high season. 2-night minimum for inn on weekends. MC, V. Closed mid-Oct to early May. Children age 14 and up welcome in inn; children welcome in all cottages. **Amenities:** Dining room; watersports equipment rental; fax service. *In room:* TV (some), fireplace (some), no phone (some).

Pilgrim's Inn ★

Set just off a town road and between an open bay and a mill pond, this is a historic, handsomely renovated inn. The inn was built in 1793 by Ignatius Haskell, a prosperous sawmill owner. His granddaughter opened the home to boarders, and it's been housing summer guests ever since. The interior is tastefully decorated in a style that's informed by early Americana but not beholden to historic authenticity. The guest rooms are well appointed with antiques and painted in muted colonial colors; especially intriguing are the rooms on the top floor with impressive diagonal beams. Two nearby cottages are also available. Activities include strolling around the village, using the inn's bikes, and taking scenic drives.

Dinners start with cocktails and hors d'oeuvres in the common room at 6pm, followed by one seating at 7pm in the adjacent barn dining room. Several entrees are offered, and the creative American cuisine is not likely to disappoint. You might feast on tenderloin of pork in phyllo with local shiitake mushrooms, or roasted ratatouille napoleon with a lemon balsamic vinaigrette and grilled spring onions. Dinner is also open to the public by reservation at a fixed price of about $32.

P.O. Box 69, Deer Isle, ME 04627. © **888/778-7505.** Fax 207/348-7769. www.pilgrimsinn.com. 12 units, 3 cottages. Summer $129–$209 double; fall $99–$189 double. Cottage $169–$239. Rates include breakfast. MC, V. Closed mid-Oct to mid-May (cottages open year-round). Pets allowed in cottages only. Children 10 and older are welcome. **Amenities:** Dining room; bikes.

WHERE TO DINE

For fine dining, check out the dining rooms at Goose Cove Lodge or the Pilgrim's Inn (see "Where to Stay," above); be aware, however, that both require dinner reservations.

Fisherman's Friend (Value) SEAFOOD   This is a local-eats place. Lively and boisterous, it's usually as crowded as it is unpretentious. The menu features basic home-cooked meals and typically includes a wide range of fresh fish prepared in a variety of styles, including charbroiled. If you find yourself beset with a fierce craving for lobster, do yourself a favor and bypass the usual; instead, order up a bowl of the lobster stew, which is brimming with meaty lobster chunks. It's not a light meal, but travelers often find themselves making excuses to linger in Stonington another day to indulge in a second bowl of stew. Dessert selections, including berry pies and shortcake, are extensive and traditional New England; $2 will buy a hearty serving of Grape-Nuts pudding with real whipped cream. BYOB.

School St., Stonington. © **207/367-2442.** Reservations recommended peak season and weekends. Sandwiches $2.50–$6.50; dinner entrees $6.95–$16. DISC, MC, V. July–Aug daily 11am–9pm; June and Sept–Oct daily 11am–8pm; Apr–May Tues–Sun 11am–8pm. Closed Nov–Mar. Located up the hill from the harbor past the Opera House.

A DAY TRIP TO ISLE AU HAUT ✦✦

Rocky and remote Isle au Haut offers the most unusual hiking and camping experience in northern New England. This 6-by-3-mile island, located 6 miles south of Stonington, was originally named Isle Haut (or High Island) in 1604 by French explorer Samuel de Champlain. The name and its pronunciation evolved—today it's generally pronounced "aisle-a-*ho*"—but the island itself has remained steadfastly unchanged over the centuries.

About half of the island is owned by the National Park Service and maintained as an outpost of Acadia National Park (see chapter 8). A 60-passenger "mailboat" makes a stop in the morning and late afternoon at Duck Harbor, allowing for a solid day of hiking while still returning to Stonington by nightfall. At Duck Harbor, the NPS also maintains a cluster of five Adirondack-style lean-tos, which are available for overnight camping. Advance reservations are essential: Contact **Acadia National Park,** Eagle Lake Rd. (P.O. Box 177), Bar Harbor, ME 04609, or call © **207-288-3338.** The park doesn't charge a fee to explore its island holdings.

Isle au Haut

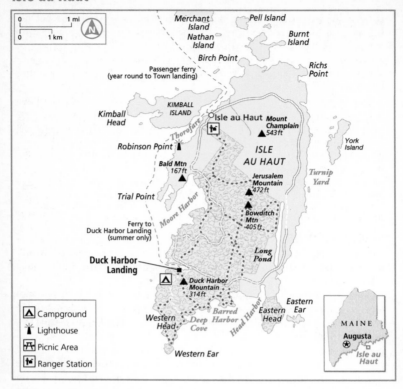

One-half of the island is privately owned, partly by fishermen who can trace their island ancestry back 3 centuries, and partly by summer visitors whose forebears discovered the bucolic splendor of Isle au Haut in the 1880s. The summer population of the island is about 300, with about 50 diehards remaining year-round. The mail boat also stops at the small harborside village, which has a few old homes, a handsome church, and a tiny schoolhouse, post office, and store. Day-trippers will be better served ferrying straight to Duck Harbor.

The **Isle au Haut Boat Company** operates a ferry (© **207/367-5193;** www. isleauhaut.com) to the island, which leaves from the pier at the end of Sea Breeze Avenue in Stonington. In summer (mid-June to mid-Sept), the *Miss Lizzie* departs for the village of Isle au Haut daily at 7am, 11:30am, and 4:30pm; the *Mink* departs for Duck Harbor daily at 10am and 4:30pm. (Limited trips go to Isle au Haut the remainder of the year, and Sunday schedules are different from the regular schedules—check the website for all the details.) The round-trip boat fare to either village or Duck Harbor is $32 for adults and $16 for children under 12. The crossing takes about 45 minutes to the village and 1 hour to Duck Harbor. Reservations are not accepted; it's best to arrive at least a half-hour before departure. The ferry has been working to set up online reservations; check the company's website for the status.

Note that bikes are *not* allowed on any of Isle au Haut's hiking trails.

SEA KAYAKING

Peer southward from Stonington, and you'll see dozens of spruce-studded islands between the mainland and the dark, distant ridges of Isle au Haut. These islands, ringed with salmon-pink granite, are collectively called Merchant's Row, and they're invariably ranked by experienced coastal boaters as among the most beautiful in the state. Thanks to these exceptional islands, Stonington is among Maine's most popular destinations for sea kayaking. Many of the islands are open to day visitors and overnight camping, and one of the Nature Conservancy islands even hosts a flock of sheep. Experienced kayakers should contact the **Maine Island Trail Association** (© **207/596-6456** or 207/761-8225; www.mita.org) for more information about paddling here; several of the islands are open only to association members.

    Old Quarry Charters (© **207/367-8977**; www.oldquarry.com), just outside the village of Stonington, offers guided kayak tours as well as kayaks for rent. (Old Quarry will rent only to those with prior experience, so it's best to call ahead to discuss your needs.) Tours range from 2 hours ($45) to a full-day, 7-hour tour that weaves out through the islands and includes a stop for a swim or a picnic at an abandoned quarry ($105). Overnight camping trips are also offered. Other services: parking and a launch site for those who've brought their own boats, sailboat tours and lessons, charter tours aboard a 38-foot lobster boat, and camping ($16–$26 per couple). For more information, visit the website.

    Outfitters based outside the region that offer guided overnight kayak trips around Merchant's Row include **Maine Island Kayak Co.** (© **800/796-2373** or 207/766-2373; www.maineislandkayak.com) or **Maine Sport Outfitters** (© **800/722-0826** or 207/236-8797; www.mainesport.com).

7 Blue Hill ★★

Blue Hill, population 1,900, is fairly easy to find—just look for gently domed Blue Hill Mountain, which lords over the northern end of Blue Hill Bay. Set between the mountain and the bay is the quiet and historic town of Blue Hill, clustering along the bay shore and a burbling stream. There's never much going on, and that seems to be exactly what attracts summer visitors back time and again—and it might explain why two excellent bookstores are located here. Many old-money families maintain retreats set along the water or in the rolling inland hills, but Blue Hill offers several excellent choices for lodging if you're not well endowed with local relatives. It's a good destination for an escape and will especially appeal to those deft at crafting their own entertainment.

ESSENTIALS
GETTING THERE
Blue Hill is southeast of Ellsworth on Route 172. Coming from the west, head south on Route 15 five miles east of Bucksport (it's well marked with road signs).

VISITOR INFORMATION
Blue Hill does not maintain a visitor information booth. Look for the "Blue Hill, Maine" brochure and map at state information centers, or write the **Blue Hill Peninsula Chamber of Commerce** (© **207/374-3242**), P.O. Box 520, Blue Hill, ME 04614. The staffs at area inns and restaurants are usually able to answer any questions you might have.

SPECIAL EVENTS
The **Blue Hill Fair** ★★ (© **207/374-3701** for information) is a traditional country fair with livestock competitions, displays of vegetables, and carnival

---

Tips   **Community Radio**

When in the Blue Hill area, tune to the local community radio station, WERU at 89.9 FM. Started by Noel Paul Stookey (the Paul in Peter, Paul, and Mary) in a former chicken coop, its idea was to spread good music and provocative ideas. It's become slicker and more professional in recent years, but still retains a pleasantly homespun flavor at times, with an eclectic range of music and commentary.

---

rides. The fair takes place at the fairgrounds northwest of the village on Route 172 on Labor Day weekend.

EXPLORING BLUE HILL

A good way to start your exploration is to ascend the open summit of **Blue Hill Mountain** ★★, from which you'll have superb views of the azure bay and the rocky bald mountaintops on nearby Mount Desert Island. To reach the trailhead from the village, drive north on Route 172, then turn west (left) on Mountain Road at the Blue Hill Fairgrounds. Drive 8 miles and look for the well-marked trail. An ascent of the "mountain" (elevation 940 ft.) is about a mile and requires about 45 minutes. Bring a picnic lunch and enjoy the vistas.

Blue Hill has traditionally attracted more than its fair share of artists, especially, it seems, potters. On Union Street, stop by **Rowantrees Pottery** (© 207/374-5535), which has been a Blue Hill institution for more than half a century. The shop was founded by Adelaide Pearson, who was inspired to pursue pottery as a career after a conversation with Mahatma Gandhi in India. Rowantrees' pottery is richly hued, and the potters who've succeeded Pearson continue to use glazes made from local resources.

Another inventive shop, the family-run **Rackliffe Pottery** on Ellsworth Road (© 888/631-3321 or 207/374-2297), uses native clay and lead-free glazes, and the bowls, vases, and plates produced here have a lustrous, silky feel. Visitors are welcome to watch the potters at work. Both shops are open year-round.

Even if you're not given to swooning over historic homes, you owe yourself a visit to the intriguing **Parson Fisher House** ★ (© 207/374-2459 for information), located on Routes 176 and 15, a half-mile west of the village. Fisher, Blue Hill's first permanent minister, was a countrified version of a Renaissance man when he settled here in 1796. Educated at Harvard, Fisher not only delivered sermons in six different languages, including Aramaic, but was also a writer, painter, and minor inventor whose energy was evidently boundless. On a tour of his home, which he built in 1814, you can see a clock with wooden works he made and samples of the books he not only wrote but also published and bound himself.

Parson Fisher House is open from July to mid-September every day except Sunday from 1 to 4pm. Admission is by donation, and $5 per person is suggested.

If you're an ardent antique hunter or bibliophile, it's worth your while to detour to the **Big Chicken Barn** (© 207/667-7308), on Route 1 between Ellsworth and Bucksport (it's 9 miles west of Ellsworth and 11 miles east of Bucksport). This sprawling antiques mall and bookstore is of nearly shopping mall proportions—more than 21,000 square feet of stuff in an old poultry barn. It's open daily from 9am to 6pm during summer, shorter hours in the off-season.

WHERE TO STAY

Blue Hill Farm Country Inn   Comfortably situated on 48 acres 2 miles north of the village of Blue Hill, the Blue Hill Country Farm Inn offers some of the most relaxing and comfortable common areas you'll find anywhere. The first floor of a vast barn has been converted to a spacious living room for guests, with a handful of sitting areas arrayed so that you can opt for privacy or the company of others. Or, in an adjoining old farmhouse, you can curl up in the cozy, intimate common room, which is amply stocked with a good selection of books. There's also the old kitchen, no longer used for cooking but now a fine place to linger or just store your cold drinks in the fridge.

It's fortunate that the common areas are so exceptionally well done because you're not likely to spend much time in the guest rooms, which tend to be small and lightly furnished. The more modern rooms are upstairs in the barn loft and are nicely decorated in a country farmhouse style, but these are a bit motel-like, with rooms set off a central hallway. The seven older rooms in the farmhouse have more character and share a single bathroom with a small tub and hand-held shower.

Rte. 15 (P.O. Box 437), Blue Hill, ME 04614. ℂ 207/374-5126. 14 units (7 with shared bathroom). June–Oct $85–$99 double; Nov–May $75–$85 double (no shared bathroom in off-season). Rates include continental breakfast. AE, MC, V.

Blue Hill Inn ★★   The Blue Hill Inn has been hosting travelers since 1840. Situated on one of Blue Hill's main thoroughfares and within walking distance of most everything, this Federal-style inn features a convincing colonial American motif throughout, with the authenticity enhanced by creaky floors and door jambs slightly out of true. The friendly innkeepers have furnished all the rooms pleasantly with antiques and down comforters; the four rooms in the main house feature wood-burning fireplaces, although these rooms are open only mid-May through the end of October. A large contemporary suite located in an adjacent, free-standing building features a cathedral ceiling, fireplace, full kitchen, living room, and deck with a tree growing out of it; this Cape House Suite is available to guests year-round. Ask about packages that include kayaking, hiking, or sailing. The inn also formerly operated a good restaurant, but now offers periodic wine dinners each summer; these cost about $75 per person and are excellent if you can get in, so call in advance if you're interested.

Union St. (P.O. Box 403), Blue Hill, ME 04614. ℂ 207/374-2844. Fax 207/374-2829. www.bluehillinn.com. 11 units, 1 cottage. Mid-May to Nov $138–$195 double, $235–$285 suite; Dec–mid-May $165–$200 suite. Rates include breakfast. 2-night minimum in summer. DISC, MC, V. Main inn closed Dec to mid-May. Children 13 and older are welcome. **Amenities:** Free hors d'oeuvres; wine dinners. *In room:* A/C, kitchen (1), fireplace.

WHERE TO DINE

Arborvine Restaurant ★★ FINE DINING   Blue Hill recently saw the closing of two of its longtime favorite dining spots (Firepond and the Left Bank Cafe); fortunately, the Arborvine has stepped in to fill the gap, once again giving this sleepy town a top-flight eatery. Ensconced in a beautifully renovated Cape Cod–style house, the restaurant's interior is warm and inviting—think rough-hewn timbers, polished wooden floors, and a cozy bar area. Diners are seated at simply dressed tables embellished with fresh flowers grown on the grounds. The husband-and-wife team that owns the place is careful to use locally grown and procured ingredients for appetizers such as Damariscotta River oysters on the half shell. Among the entrees are crispy roast duckling with a blood orange glaze, candied orange zest, and orange cranberry chutney; or vegetarian-friendly portobello mushroom and leek risotto cakes served on a bed of rocket with polenta and roasted red pepper cream. There's also a gourmet deli on the premises, an obvious choice for a picnic lunch. Reservations are highly recommended, as the place is already popular with locals and tourists alike.

Main St., Blue Hill, ME 04614. ✆ 207/374-2119. www.arborvine.com. Dinner $18–$22. MC, V. Summer daily 5:30–8:30pm; off-season Fri–Sun 5:30–8:30pm.

8 Bangor, Orono & Old Town

The towns of Bangor, Orono, and Old Town lie along the western banks of the Penobscot River—not far inland from Ellsworth and Belfast on the coast—and serve as gateways to the North Woods. They may be worth a day or a half-day if you're interested in sampling an inland slice of the real Maine.

Bangor is Maine's third largest city (after Portland and Lewiston), the last major urban outpost ith a full-fledged mall. It's a good destination for history buffs curious about the early North Woods economy. Bangor was once a thriving lumber port, shipping millions of board feet cut from the woods to the north and floated down the Penobscot River. While much of the town burned in 1911 and has since suffered from ill-considered urban renewal schemes, visitors can still discern a robust history just below the surface. Orono and Old Town, two smaller towns to the north, offer an afternoon's diversion on rainy days.

This is a major transportation hub and the commercial center for much of eastern and northern Maine. But, quite frankly, it's not much of a tourist destination. The downtown has a handful of buildings of interest to those intrigued by late Victorian architecture, and a new and fun children's museum, but overall the city has little of the charm or urbanity of Portland. Travelers may not wish to budget a significant amount of time for exploring Bangor.

ESSENTIALS

GETTING THERE   Bangor is located just off the Maine Turnpike. Take I-395 east, exit at Main Street (Rte. 1A), and follow signs for downtown.

As with many smaller regional airports, **Bangor International Airport** (✆ 207/947-0384) has had a tough time persuading airlines to keep a schedule of full-service flights; thus, many flights begin or end via commuter planes to or from Boston. Due in part to recent airline turnovers, many travelers have reported problems with delays and lost luggage at Bangor. Airlines currently serving Bangor include **Delta Connection** (✆ 800/221-1212; www.delta.com) and **US Airways Express** (✆ 800/428-4322; www.usair.com).

One exception to the downward trend is the arrival of a relatively new discount carrier. **Pan Am** (✆ 800/359-7262; www.flypanam.com) came back to life under new ownership and with a limited flight schedule serving Bangor, currently two flights daily from Bangor to Baltimore and onward to two Florida airports.

⟨Fun Fact⟩   I Left My Heart in Bangor, Maine

One of Bangor's claims to tourist fame is that in 1977 an addled German tourist, Erwin Kreuz, accidentally disembarked here during a transatlantic refueling stop. He spent a few days wandering the city, believing the whole time he was in San Francisco. This would be an urban legend except for the fact that it's true. It's a wonder that a statue hasn't been erected of this man.

Concord Trailways (© 800/639-3317; www.concordtrailways.com) and **Vermont Transit** (© 800/451-3292 or 800/642-3133; www.vermonttransit.com) offer bus service to Bangor from Portland; there's also connecting service to Bar Harbor, Houston, and the Downeast coast, including Machias and Calais.

VISITOR INFORMATION   The **Bangor Visitors Information Office** is staffed in summer near the big, scary statue of Paul Bunyan at the convention center on Main Street near I-395. Contact the **Bangor Region Chamber of Commerce,** 519 Main St., Bangor, ME 04401 (© 207/947-0307), open year-round from 8am to 5pm Monday through Friday, with extended hours in summer depending on volunteer availability.

EXPLORING BANGOR, ORONO & OLD TOWN

IN BANGOR   The **Bangor Historical Society** (© 207/942-5766) offers a glimpse of life in Bangor during the golden days of the late 19th century. The society is in a handsome brick home built in 1836 for a prominent businessman and now features displays of furniture and historical artifacts. The society's collections are at 159 Union St. (just off High St.) and are seen during 1-hour guided tours ($4 for adults, free for 12 and under). The museum is open April through December, Tuesday through Friday from noon to 4pm (last tour at 3pm); June through September, it's also open Saturdays from noon to 4pm (last tour at 3pm).

Vintage-car and early transportation buffs will enjoy a detour to the **Cole Land Transportation Museum** (© 207/990-3600; www.colemuseum.org), 405 Perry Rd. off Exit 45B of I-95 near the intersection with I-395 (left at the first light, then left onto Perry Rd.). The museum features old automobiles lined up in a warehouse-size display space, along with quirkier machinery such as snow rollers, cement mixers, power shovels, and tractors. Especially well represented are early trucks, appropriate given its connection with Cole Express, a Maine trucking company founded in 1917. The museum is open daily from May to mid-November from 9am to 5pm; admission is $5 for adults, $3 for seniors, and free for those under 18.

Despite the city's rich history and the distinguished architecture of the commercial district, Bangor is probably best known as home to horror novelist and one-man Maine industry **Stephen King.** King's sprawling Victorian home seems a fitting place for the Maine native author; it's got an Addams Family–like creepiness, which is only enhanced by the wrought-iron fence with bats on it. His home isn't open to the public, but it's worth a drive by. To find the house, take the Union Street exit off I-95, head toward town for 6 blocks, then turn right on West Broadway. I trust you'll figure out which one it is.

IN ORONO & OLD TOWN   Orono is home to the University of Maine, which was founded in 1868. The campus is spread out on a plain and features a pleasing mix of historic and contemporary buildings. (The campus was originally designed by noted landscape architect Frederick Law Olmsted, but its early look has been obscured by later additions.) On campus, the modern and spacious **Hudson Museum** (© 207/581-1901) features exhibits on anthropology and native culture. The museum displays crafts and artwork from native cultures around the world and is especially well represented with North American displays. Closed Mondays and holidays; admission is free.

A few minutes north on Route 178 is the riverside Old Town, famous for the canoes made here since the last turn of the century. **The Old Town Canoe Company** (© 207/827-5514) sits in its original brick factory in the middle of town and sells new and factory-second canoes from its showroom at 58 Middle St. (Open in summer Mon–Sat 9am–6pm; Sun 10am–3pm.) Old Town no longer offers tours of the creaky old factory, but a continuously running video in the showroom shows techniques used in contemporary canoe-making.

WHERE TO STAY

Bangor has plenty of guest rooms, many along charmless strips near the airport and the mall. If you're not choosy or if you're arriving late at night, these are fine. Be aware that even these can fill up during the peak summer season, so reservations are advised. Try the **Comfort Inn,** 750 Hogan Rd. (© **800/228-5150** or 207/942-7899), **Howard Johnson's Motor Lodge,** 336 Odlin Rd. (© **800/ 654-2000** or 207/942-5251), or the **Fairfield Inn,** 300 Odlin Rd. (© **800/228- 2800** or 207/990-0001).

Other options: Connected to Bangor's airport is **Four Points by Sheraton,** 308 Godfrey Blvd. (© **800/228-4609** or 207/947-6721; www.sheraton.com); near the Bangor Mall and other chain stores is **Country Inn at the Mall,** 936 Stillwater Ave. (© **207/941-0200;** www.maineguide.com/bangor/countryinn); and downtown is the **Holiday Inn,** 500 Main St. (© **800/799-8651** or 207/947- 8651; www.holiday-inn.com).

Mount Desert Island & Acadia National Park

Mount Desert Island is home to spectacular Acadia National Park, and for many visitors the two places are one and the same. Yes, tourism drives the island economy, and the presence of tourists defines the summer spirit of Maine's largest island. And the park does contain the most dramatic coastal real estate on the Eastern Seaboard.

Yet the park holdings are only part of the appeal of this immensely popular island, which is connected to the mainland via a short, two-lane causeway. Beyond the parklands are scenic harborside villages and remote backcountry roads, quaint B&Bs and fine restaurants, oversize 19th-century summer "cottages," and the unrepentant tourist trap of Bar Harbor. Those who arrive on the island expecting untamed wilderness invariably leave disappointed. Those who understand that Acadia National Park is but one chapter (albeit a very large one) in the intriguing story of Mount Desert Island will enjoy their visit thoroughly.

Mount Desert (pronounced "de-sert," like what you have after dinner) is divided into two lobes separated by Somes Sound, the only legitimate fjord in the continental U.S. (A fjord is a valley carved by a glacier that subsequently filled with rising ocean water.) Those with a poetic imagination see Mount Desert shaped as a lobster, with one large claw and one small one. Most of the parkland is on the meatier east claw, although large swaths of park exist on the leaner west claw as well. The eastern side is more developed, with Bar Harbor the center of commerce and entertainment. The western side has a more quiet, settled air and teems more with wildlife than tourists. The island isn't huge—it's only about 15 miles from the causeway to the southernmost tip at Bass Harbor Head—yet visitors can do a lot of adventuring in such a compact space. The best plan is to take it slowly, exploring whenever possible by foot, bicycle, canoe, or kayak, and giving yourself up to a week to do it. You'll be glad you did.

1 Enjoying the Great Outdoors

Acadia is a fine, even world-class destination for those who like their coastal vacations seasoned with adventure. While southern Maine has classic beach towns where the smell of salt air mixes with coconut oil and taffy, much of the rest of the Maine coast is unruly and wild. In parts, it seems to share more in common with Alaska—you can see bald eagles soaring above and whales breaching below. In between these two archetypes, you'll find remote coves perfect for a rowboat jaunt and isolated offshore islands accessible only by sea kayak.

The best places for coastal adventure are often not the most obvious places—those tend to be crowded and more developed. You'll need to do a bit of homework to find the real treasures. A growing number of specialized guidebooks and outfitters can help point visitors in the right direction; some of the best are mentioned below.

Keep in mind that no other New England state offers as much outdoor recreational diversity as Maine. Bring your mountain bike, hiking boots, sea kayak, canoe, fishing rod, and/or snowmobile—there'll be plenty for you to do here.

If your outdoor skills are rusty or nonexistent, you can brush up at **L.L. Bean Outdoor Discovery Schools** (© 888/552-3261; www.llbean.com/odp), which offers a series of lectures and workshops that run anywhere from 2 hours to 3 days. Classes are offered at various locations around the state, covering a whole range of subjects, including use of a map and compass, fly tying, bike maintenance, canoeing, kayaking, and cross-country and telemark skiing. L.L. Bean also hosts popular canoeing, sea kayaking, and cross-country skiing festivals that bring together instructors, lecturers, and equipment vendors for 2 or 3 days of learning and outdoor diversion. Call for a brochure or check the website for a schedule.

BEACHGOING   The average ocean temperature at Bar Harbor in summer is 54°F (12°C); farther east in Passamaquoddy Bay it's 51°F (11°C). Cold. But small, crescent-shaped **Sand Beach** in Acadia National Park makes for a wonderfully scenic day outing—and the water's wadable (if not exactly swimmable).

BICYCLING   **Mount Desert Island** and **Acadia National Park** are the premier coastal destinations for bikers, especially mountain bikers who prefer easy-riding terrain—the cycling here may be some of the most pleasant in America. Its 57 miles of well-maintained national-park carriage roads offer superb cruising through thick forests and to ocean views atop rocky knolls. No cars are permitted on these grass and gravel lanes; bikers and walkers have them all to themselves. You can rent mountain bikes in Bar Harbor, which has several bike shops from which to choose. The Park Loop Road, while often crowded with slow-moving cars, offers one of the more memorable road-biking experiences in the state. The rest of Mount Desert Island is also good for highway biking, especially on the quieter western half of the island, where traffic is almost never a problem.

CAMPING   Car campers traveling the Maine coast have plenty of choices, from well-developed private campgrounds to more basic state parks. **Acadia National Park** tends to be the biggest draw, but there's no shortage of other options on and near the coast.

Among the coastal state parks worthy of an overnight are **Lamoine State Park** (© 207/667-4778), which is convenient to Acadia National Park yet away from the thickest of the crowds, and remote **Cobscook Bay State Park** (© 207/726-4412), where most campsites are on the water, offering a great view of the massive 28-foot tides that slosh in and out. See chapter 9 for more details on Cobscook Bay State Park.

CANOEING   For many outdoor enthusiasts in the Northeast, Maine is very alluring to serious paddlers. In fact, you can't travel very far in Maine without stumbling upon a great canoe trip. The state's best canoeing tends to be far inland and deep in the woods, true, but day paddlers can still find good trips at several lakes along the coast or in some of the protected bays.

Mount Desert's ponds offer scenic if limited canoeing; most have public boat access. Canoe rentals are available at the north end of **Long Pond** (the largest pond on the island, at 3 miles long) in Somesville from **National Park Canoe**

Rentals (© 207/244-5854). The cost is $22 for 4 hours. Much of the west shore and southern tip are within park boundaries. Jet skis are banned in the park, and swimming is prohibited in ponds that serve as public water reservoirs (including Bubble, Jordan, Eagle, and the south end of Long Pond).

Two excellent sources of detailed canoeing information are the *AMC River Guide: Maine* and *Quiet Water Canoe Guide: Maine,* both published by the Appalachian Mountain Club, 5 Joy St., Boston, MA 02108.

CARRIAGE RIDES ★★   Carriage rides are offered by **Wildwood Stables** (© 207/276-3622; www.acadia.net/wildwood), about a half-mile south of Jordan Pond House. The 1-hour trip departs three times daily and takes in sweeping ocean views; it costs $14 for adults, $7 for children 6 to 12, and $4 for children 2 to 5. Longer tours are available, as is a special carriage designed to accommodate passengers with disabilities. Reservations are recommended.

FISHING   For freshwater fishing not too far from the Downeast coast, **Grand Lake Stream** is a popular and historic destination. Located deep in the woods of Washington County, close to the border with Canada, the area has a rich heritage as a fisherman's settlement, and a number of camps and outfitters cater to the serious angler, especially those in search of landlocked salmon, smallmouth bass, and brook trout. Among the classic fishing lodges in this area are **Weatherby's** (© 207/796-5558) and **Indian Rock Camps** (© 800/498-2821 or 207/ 796-2822).

GOLF   The historic **Kebo Valley Golf Club** (© **207/288-3000**) in the rolling hills outside of Bar Harbor is the state's oldest course, and it's a beauty. Greens fees are $50 per person for 18 holes, and it's very busy in summertime—try to reserve ahead if you're wanting a tee time.

HIKING   Maine is home to 10 peaks over 4,000 feet and hundreds of miles of maintained trails, but serious hiking—as opposed to strolling—is limited along the Maine coast. The most challenging and most rewarding trails are found at **Acadia National Park.** Although the peaks top out at 1,530 feet, the terrain might be more rugged than you expect and often leads to blustery hill-tops of granite and blueberry, offering exceptional vistas of islands and sea. The park also has numerous wonderful day hiking opportunities, though its trails can get crowded during the peak summer season. I have detailed some prime hikes below (see "Hiking in the Park"). Ask at the ranger station about hikes to such places as **The Bubbles, Parkman Mountain, St. Sauveur Mountain,** and many more.

Hikes at Great Wass Island, near **Cutler,** and at **West Quoddy Head** (and just over the border on Canada's Campobello Island) also provide a measure of remoteness and solitude that has been lost along much of the rest of the Maine coast. More inveterate explorers still should continue eastward along the coast to Washington County.

If you don't mind heading inland a bit, the **Appalachian Trail** traverses the range on its way from Grafton Notch (on the New Hampshire border) to the trail's terminus at **Mount Katahdin;** see chapter 10 for more information. A good source of trail info is the official Appalachian Trail *Data Book,* obtainable from bookstores or online for $5.95 at the trail's administrative website, www. atctrailstore.org.

Two guides to the state's trails are also highly recommended. *Fifty Hikes in Southern and Coastal Maine,* by John Gibson, is a reliable directory to trails at Acadia. *Fifty Hikes in the Maine Mountains,* by Chloe Chunn, is the best guide for the Bigelow Range and Baxter State Park. Both are published by Back-country Publications and are available at local bookstores or online.

MOUNTAIN BIKING   The 57 miles of **carriage roads** ★★★ built by John D. Rockefeller, Jr., are among the park's most extraordinary hidden treasures. These were maintained by Rockefeller until his death in 1960, after which they became shaggy and overgrown. A major restoration effort was launched in 1990, and today the roads are superbly restored and maintained. With their wide hard-packed surfaces, gentle grades, and extensive directional signs, they make for very smooth biking. Note that bikes are also allowed on the island's free shuttle buses (see "Getting Around," below). I give more information about biking the roads later in this chapter (see "Biking the Carriage Roads").

SKIING   Cross-country skiers have a glorious mix of terrain to choose from, especially within **Acadia National Park,** where skiing is allowed for free on park grounds throughout the winter. For more about cross-country ski areas in Maine, contact the **Maine Nordic Council** (© **800/754-9263;** www.mnsc.com).

2 Acadia National Park ★★★

It's not hard to fathom why Acadia is consistently one of the biggest draws in the U.S. national park system. The park's landscape is a rich tapestry of rugged cliffs, restless ocean, and deep, silent woods. Acadia's landscape, like so much of the rest of northern New England, was carved by glaciers some 18,000 years ago. A mile-high ice sheet shaped the land by scouring valleys into their distinctive U shapes, rounding many of the once-jagged peaks, and depositing huge boulders about the landscape, such as the famous 10-foot-high Bubble Rock, which appears to be perched precariously on the side of South Bubble Mountain.

The park's more recent roots can be traced back to the 1840s, when noted Hudson River School painter Thomas Cole packed his sketchbooks and easels for a trip to this remote island and then home to a small number of fishermen and boat-builders. His stunning renditions of the surging surf pounding against coastal granite were later displayed in New York and triggered an early tourism boom as urbanites flocked to the island to rusticate. By 1872, national magazines were touting Eden (Bar Harbor's name until 1919) as a desirable summer resort. It attracted the attention of wealthy industrialists and soon became the summer home to Carnegies, Rockefellers, Astors, and Vanderbilts, who built massive summer cottages with literally dozens of rooms. (One "cottage" even boasted 28 bathrooms.) More recently, lifestyle doyenne Martha Stewart occupied a multimillion-dollar hilltop compound in Seal Harbor originally built for Edsel Ford.

By the early 1900s, the huge popularity and growing development of the island began to concern its most ardent supporters. Boston textile heir and conservationist George Dorr and Harvard president Charles Eliot, aided by the largesse of John D. Rockefeller, Jr., started acquiring large tracts for the public's enjoyment. These parcels were eventually donated to the federal government, and in 1919 the public land was designated Lafayette National Park, the first national park east of the Mississippi. Renamed Acadia in 1929, the park has grown to encompass nearly half the island, with holdings scattered about piecemeal here and there.

Rockefeller purchased and donated about 11,000 acres—about one-third of the park. He's also responsible for one of the park's most extraordinary features. Around 1905, a dispute erupted over whether to allow noisy new motorcars onto the island. Resident islanders wanted these new conveniences to boost their mobility; John D. Rockefeller, Jr., whose fortune was from the oil industry (students of irony, take note), strenuously objected, preferring the tranquillity of the car-free island. Rockefeller went down to defeat on this issue, and the island was opened to cars in 1913. In response, the multimillionaire set about building an elaborate 57-mile system of private carriage roads, featuring a dozen gracefully handcrafted stone bridges. These roads, open today only to pedestrians, bicyclists, and equestrians, are concentrated most densely around Jordan Pond, but also ascend to some of the most scenic open peaks and wind through sylvan valleys.

Try to allow 3 or 4 days, at a minimum, for visiting the park. If you're passing through just briefly, try to work in at least two of the big three activities (hiking, biking, driving) I've described below.

And when you set out to explore the park, pack a picnic lunch and keep it handy. Once you're in the park, there are few places to stop for lunch or snacks. Having drinks and a bite to eat at hand will prevent breaking up your day with time-wasting backtracking into Bar Harbor or elsewhere in a desperate effort to fend off starvation. The more food you bring with you, the more your options for the day will expand.

ESSENTIALS
GETTING THERE
Acadia National Park is reached from the town of Ellsworth via Route 3. If you're coming from southern Maine, you can avoid the coastal congestion along Route 1 by taking the Maine Turnpike to Bangor, picking up I-395 to Route

Tips   **Avoiding Crowds in the Park**

Early fall is the best time to miss the mobs yet still enjoy the weather. If you do come midsummer, try to venture out in early morning or early evening to see the most popular spots, such as Thunder Hole or the summit of Cadillac Mountain. Setting off into the woods at every opportunity is also a good strategy. About four out of five visitors restrict their tours to the loop road and a handful of other major attractions, leaving the Acadia backcountry open for more adventurous spirits.

The best guarantee of solitude is to head to the more remote outposts managed by Acadia, such as Isle au Haut and Schoodic Peninsula, across the bay to the east. Ask for more information at the visitor centers.

1A, then continuing south on Route 1A to Ellsworth. While this looks longer on the map, it's by far the quickest route in summer.

Daily flights from Boston to the airport in Trenton, just across the causeway from Mount Desert Island, are offered year-round by U.S. Airways affiliate **Colgan Air** (© **800/428-4322**). From here, call a taxi or ride the free shuttle bus (late June to mid-October only) to downtown Bar Harbor.

Two major bus lines serve the island. **Vermont Transit Lines** (© **800/552-8737** or 207/288-3211; www.vermonttransit.com) is affiliated with **Greyhound** and serves Bangor from Boston's South Station, continuing onward (in summer only) once daily to Ellsworth and Bar Harbor.

Concord Trailways (© **800/639-3317** or 207/945-5000; www.concord trailways.com) serves Bangor from Boston, but does not continue to the smaller towns onward; you'll need to transfer at Bangor via taxi (a long ride) or Vermont Transit.

GETTING AROUND

A free **summer shuttle bus service** ★★ known as the *Island Explorer* was inaugurated in 1999 as part of an effort to reduce the number of cars on the island's roads. It's working. The propane-powered buses, which are equipped with racks for bikes, serve six routes that cover nearly the entire island and will stop anywhere you request outside the village centers, including trailheads, ferries, small villages, and campgrounds. Just be prepared to share the ride with garrulous fellow passengers—and/or bring a book; there are lots of stops. All routes begin or end at the Village Green in Bar Harbor, but you're encouraged to pick up the bus wherever you're staying, whether motel or campground, to avoid parking hassles in town. Route no. 3 goes from Bar Harbor along much of the Park Loop, offering easy access to some of the park's best hiking trails. The buses operate from late June to mid-October (there are fewer, but still enough, buses Sept to mid-Oct); ask for a schedule at any of the island information centers.

GUIDED TOURS

Acadia National Park Tours (© **207/288-3327** or 207/288-0300; www.acadia tours.com) offers 2½-hour park tours departing twice daily (10am and 2pm) from downtown Bar Harbor. The bus tour includes three stops (Sieur De Monts Springs, Thunder Hole, and Cadillac Mountain) and plenty of park trivia courtesy of the driver. This is an easy way for first-time visitors to get a quick introduction to the park before setting out on their own. Tickets are available at Testa's Restaurant, 53 Main St., Bar Harbor; $20 adults, $10 children under 14.

ENTRY POINTS & FEES

A 1-week park pass, which includes unlimited trips on Park Loop Road, now costs $20 per car; there's no additional charge per passenger. (No daily pass is available, but if you'll be here more than 2 weeks, purchase the $40 annual pass instead.) The main point of entry to Park Loop Road, the park's most scenic byway, is at the visitor center at **Hulls Cove.** Mount Desert Island consists of an interwoven network of park and town roads, allowing visitors to enter the park at numerous points. A glance at a park map (available free at the visitor center) will make these access points self-evident. The entry fee is collected at a toll-booth on Park Loop Road a half-mile north of Sand Beach.

VISITOR CENTERS & INFORMATION

Acadia staffs two visitor centers. The **Thompson Island Information Center** (✆ 207/288-3411) on Route 3 is the first you'll pass as you enter Mount Desert Island. This center is maintained by the local chambers of commerce, but park personnel are often on hand to answer inquiries. It's open daily May to mid-October from 6am until 10pm, and is a good stop for general lodging and restaurant information.

If you're interested primarily in information about the park itself, continue on Route 3 to the National Park Service's **Hulls Cove Visitor Center,** about 7½ miles beyond Thompson Island. This attractive stone-walled center includes profes-sionally prepared park service displays, such as a large relief map of the island, natural history exhibits, and a short introductory film. You can also request free brochures about hiking trails and the carriage roads, or purchase postcards and more detailed guidebooks. The center is open daily mid-May to October, 8:30am to 4:30pm (later in midsummer). Information is also available year-round, by phone or in person, from the park's **headquarters** (✆ 207/288-3338) on Route 233 between Bar Harbor and Somesville. Your questions might also be answered in advance on the park's Web page at **www.nps.gov/acad.**

SEASONS   Visit Acadia in September if you can. Between Labor Day and the foliage season of early October, the days are often warm and clear, the nights have a crisp northerly tang, and you can avoid the hassles of congestion, crowds, and pesky insects. It's not that the park is empty in September. Bus tours seem to proliferate this month, which can mean periodic crowds at the most popular sites such as Thunder Hole. Not to worry: If you walk just a minute or two off the road, you can find solitude and an agreeable peacefulness. Hikers and bikers have the trails and carriage roads to themselves.

Summer, of course, is peak season. The weather in July and August is perfect for about any outdoor activity. Most days are warm (in the 70s or 80s/low to

---

Regulations

The usual national park rules apply. Guns may not be used in the park; if you have a gun, it must be "cased, broken down, or otherwise packaged against use." Fires and camping are allowed only at designated areas. Pets must be on leashes at all times. Seat belts must be worn in the national park (this is a federal law). Don't remove anything from the park, either manmade or natural; this includes cobblestones from the shore.

mid-20s Celsius), with afternoons frequently cooler than mornings owing to ocean breezes. While sun seems to be the norm, come prepared for rain and fog, both frequent visitors to the Maine coast. Once or twice each summer, a heat wave settles into the area, producing temperatures in the 90s (30s Celsius), dense haze, and stifling humidity, but this rarely lasts more than a few days. Enjoy summer: Soon enough (sometimes even during the last 2 weeks of Aug), a brisk north wind will blow in from the Canadian Arctic, churning up the waters and forcing visitors into sweaters at night. You'll smell the approach of autumn, with winter not far behind.

Winter is an increasingly popular time to travel here, especially among those who enjoy cross-country skiing on the carriage roads. Be aware, though, that snow along the coast is inconsistent, and services—including most restaurants and many inns—are often closed in winter.

RANGER PROGRAMS   Frequent ranger programs are offered throughout the year. These include talks at campground amphitheaters and tours of various island locales and attractions. Examples include the Otter Point nature hike, walks across Mr. Rockefeller's stone bridges, Frenchman Bay cruises (rangers provide commentary on commercial trips), and a discussion of changes in Acadia's landscape. Ask for a schedule of events or more information at a visitor center or campground.

DRIVING TOUR   DRIVING THE PARK LOOP ROAD

The 20-mile **Park Loop Road** ★★★ is to Acadia what Half Dome is to Yosemite—the park's premier attraction, and magnet for the largest crowds. This remarkable roadway starts near the Hulls Cove Visitor Center and follows the high ridges above Bar Harbor before dropping down along the rocky coast. Here, earthy tones and spires of spruce and fir cap dark granite contrast sharply with frothy white surf and steely blue sea. After following the picturesque coast and touching on several coves, the road loops back inland along Jordan Pond and Eagle Lake, with a detour to the summit of the island's highest peak.

Ideally, visitors make two circuits on the loop road. The first is for the sheer exhilaration of it and to discern the lay of the land. On the second trip, plan to stop frequently and poke around on foot by setting off on trails or scrambling along the coastline. Scenic pull-offs are staggered at frequent intervals. The two-lane road is one-way along some coastal sections; the right-hand lane is set aside for parking, so you can stop wherever you'd like to admire the vistas.

From about 10am to 4pm in July and August, anticipate large crowds along the loop road, at least on those days when the sun is shining. Parking lots may fill at some of the more popular destinations, including Sand Beach, Thunder Hole, and the Cadillac Mountain summit. Travel early or late. Alternatively, make the best of wet days by donning rain gear and letting the weather work to your advantage. You'll discover that you have the place to yourself. Allow a few hours, or even a half-day for this drive.

From the Hulls Cove Visitor Center, the Park Loop initially runs atop

❶ Paradise Hill

The tour starts with sweeping views eastward over Frenchman Bay. You'll see the town of Bar Harbor far below, and just beyond it the Porcupines, a cluster of islands that look like, well, porcupines.

Following the Park Loop Road clockwise, you'll dip into a wooded valley and come to

❷ Sieur de Monts Spring

Here you'll find a rather uninteresting natural spring, artificially encased, along with a botanical garden with some 300 species showcased in 12 habitats. The original **Abbe Museum** (✆ **207/288-3519**) is here, featuring a small but select collection of Native American artifacts. Open daily from mid-May to mid-October; admission is $2 for adults, $1 for children. A larger, more modern branch is open in Bar Harbor itself, featuring more and better-curated displays (see below).

The Tarn is the chief reason to stop here; a few hundred yards south of the springs via footpath, it's slightly mystical-looking and forsaken pond sandwiched between steep hills. Departing from the south end of the Tarn is the fine **Dorr Mountain Ladder Trail** (see "Hiking in the Park," below).

Continue the clockwise trip on the loop road; views eastward over the bay soon resume, almost uninterruptedly, to

❸ The Precipice Trail

The park's most dramatic trail ✿, this ascends sheer rock faces on the east side of Champlain Mountain. Only about .75 miles to the summit, it's rigorous, and involves scrambling up iron rungs and ladders in exposed places (those with a fear of heights or under 5 ft. tall should avoid this trail). The trail is often closed midsummer to protect nesting peregrine falcons. Rangers are often on hand in the trailhead parking lot to point out the birds and suggest alternative hikes.

Between the Precipice Trail and Sand Beach is a tollbooth where visitors pay the park fee of $20 per car, good for 1 week.

Picturesquely set between the arms of a rocky cove is

❹ Sand Beach

Sand Beach ✿ is the only sand beach on the island, although swimming these cold waters (about 50°F/10°C) is best enjoyed on extremely hot days or by those with a freakishly robust metabolism. When it's sunny out, the sandy strand is crowded midday, often with picnickers and pale waders. (*Tip:* The water at the far end of the beach—where a gentle stream enters the cove—is often a few degrees warmer than the end closer to the access stairs.)

Two worthwhile hikes start near the beach. **The Beehive Trail** overlooks Sand Beach (see "Hiking in the Park," below); it starts from a trailhead across the loop road. From the east end of Sand Beach, look for the start of the **Great Head Trail,** a loop of about 2 miles that follows on the bluff overlooking the beach, then circles back along the shimmering bay before cutting through the woods back to Sand Beach.

About a mile south of Sand Beach is

❺ Thunder Hole

Thunder Hole ✿ is a shallow oceanside cavern into which surf surges, compresses, and bursts out (a walking trail on the road lets you leave your car parked at the beach). When the bay is as quiet as a millpond (it often is during the lulling days of summer), it's a drive-by. Spend your time elsewhere.

But on days when the seas are rough and large swells roll in off the Bay of Fundy, it's a must-see, three-star attraction; you can feel the ocean's power and force resonating under your sternum. *Tip:* The best viewing time is 3 hours before high tide. (Ask for a tidal guide at gift shops or at your hotel.)

Parents with overly inquisitive toddlers (or teenagers) needn't fear: Visitors walk to the cusp of Thunder Hole on a path girded with stout steel railings; on the most turbulent days, rangers gate off parts of the walk to keep visitors away from rogue waves.

Just before the road curves around Otter Point, you'll be driving atop

⑥ Otter Cliffs

This set of 100-foot-high precipices is capped with dense spruce that plummet down into roiling seas. Look for whales spouting in summer; in early fall, thousands of eider ducks can sometimes be seen floating in flocks just offshore. A footpath follows the brink of the crags.

At Seal Harbor, the loop road veers north and inland back toward Bar Harbor. On the route is

⑦ Jordan Pond

Jordan Pond ★★ is a small but uncommonly beautiful body of water encased by gentle, forested hills. A 3-mile hiking loop follows the pond's shoreline (see "Hiking in the Park," below), and a network of splendid carriage roads converge at the pond. After a hike or mountain-bike excursion, spend some time at a table on the lawn

of the Jordan Pond House restaurant (see "Where to Dine," below).

Shortly before the loop road ends, you'll pass the entrance to

⑧ Cadillac Mountain

Reach this mountain ★ by car, ascending an early carriage road. At 1,528 feet, it's the highest peak on the Eastern Seaboard between Canada and Brazil. During much of the year, it's also the first place in the U.S. touched by the sun. But because Cadillac Mountain is the only mountaintop in the park accessible by car, and because it's also the island's highest point, the parking lot at the summit can be jammed, and drivers testy. Views are undeniably great, but the shopping-mall-at-the-holidays atmosphere can put a serious crimp in your enjoyment of the place. Some lower peaks accessible only by foot—such as Acadia or Champlain mountains—offer equally excellent views and fewer crowds.

BIKING THE CARRIAGE ROADS ★★

The park's miles of carriage roads, though built for horse and carriage, are ideal for cruising by mountain bike and offer some of the most scenic, relaxing biking found anywhere in the United States. Park near Jordan Pond and plumb the tree-shrouded lanes that lace the area, taking time to admire the stonework on the uncommonly fine bridges. Afterward, stop for tea and popovers at the **Jordan Pond House** (see "Dining," below) which has been a popular island destination for over a century, although it's unlikely as much Lycra was in evidence 100 years ago.

A decent map of the carriage roads is available free at the park's visitor center. (Where the carriage roads cross private land—generally between Seal Harbor and Northeast Harbor—the roads are closed to mountain bikes.) More detailed guidebooks are sold at area bookstores.

Mountain bikes can be rented along Cottage Street in Bar Harbor, with rates around $17 to $18 for a full day, $12 to $13 for a half-day (which is actually only 4 hr. in the bike-rental universe). Most bike shops include locks and helmets as basic equipment, but ask what's included before you rent. Also ask about closing times, since you'll be able to get a couple extra hours in with a later-closing shop. **Bar Harbor Bicycle Shop** (© **207/288-3886**), at 141 Cottage St., gets our vote for the most convenient and friendliest; you might also try **Acadia Outfitters** (© **207/288-8118**), at 106 Cottage St., or **Acadia Bike & Canoe** (© **800/526-8615** or 207/288-9605), at 48 Cottage St.

HIKING IN THE PARK

This quintessential Acadia experience shouldn't be missed. The park is studded with low "mountains" (they'd be called hills elsewhere) that offer superb views over the island and the open ocean. The trails weren't simply hacked out of the hillside; many were crafted by experienced stonemasons and others with high aesthetic intent. The routes aren't the most direct, nor were they the easiest to build. But they're often the most scenic, taking advantage of fractures in the rocks, picturesque ledges, and sudden vistas.

Acadia National Park has 120 miles of hiking trails in addition to the carriage roads. The Hulls Cove Visitor Center offers a one-page chart of area hikes; combined with the park map, this is all you'll need since the trails are well maintained and well marked. It's not hard to cobble together loop hikes to make your trips more varied. Coordinate your hiking with the weather; if it's damp or foggy, you'll stay drier and warmer strolling the carriage roads. If it's clear and dry, head for the highest peaks with the best views.

One of the best trails is the **Dorr Ladder Trail** , which departs from Route 3 near The Tarn just south of the Sieur de Monts entrance to the Loop Road. This trail begins with a series of massive stone steps ascending along the base of a vast slab of granite and then passes through crevasses (not for the wide of girth) and up ladders affixed to the granite. The views east and south are superb.

An easy lowland hike is around **Jordan Pond,** with the northward leg along the pond's east shore on a hiking trail and the return via carriage road. It's mostly level, with the total loop measuring just over 3 miles. At the north end of Jordan Pond, consider heading up the prominent, oddly symmetrical mounds called **The Bubbles** . These detours shouldn't take much more than 20 minutes each; look for signs off the Jordan Pond Shore Trail.

On the western side of the island, an ascent of **Acadia Mountain** and return takes about an hour and a half, but hikers should schedule in some time for lingering while they enjoy the view of Somes Sound and the smaller islands off Mount Desert's southern shores. This 2½-mile loop hike begins off Route 102 at a trailhead 3 miles south of Somesville. Head eastward through rolling mixed forest, then begin an ascent over ledgy terrain. Be sure to visit both the east and west peaks (the east peak has the better views), and look for hidden balds in the summit forest that open up to unexpected vistas.

Many of the ocean-side rock faces attract experienced rock climbers, as much for the beauty of the climbing areas as the challenge of the climbs and the high-grade quality of the rock. For novices or experienced climbers, **Acadia Mountain Guides** (© **888/232-9559;** www.acadiamountainguides.com) offers rock-climbing lessons and guide services, ranging from a half-day introduction to rock climbing, to intensive workshops on self-rescue and instruction on how to lead climbs. The Bar Harbor shop, open during summer only, is located at 198 Main St., at the corner of Mount Desert Street.

CAMPING IN & NEAR THE PARK

The National Park Service maintains two campgrounds within Acadia National Park. Both are extremely popular; during July and August, expect both to fill by early to midmorning.

The more popular of the two is **Blackwoods** (© **207/288-3274**), located on the island's eastern side. Access is from Route 3, 5 miles south of Bar Harbor. Bikers and pedestrians have easy access to the loop road from the campground via a short trail. The campground has no public showers, but an enterprising business just outside the campground entrance offers clean showers for a modest fee. Camping fees are $20 per night and reservations are accepted; **reservations** can be made up to 5 months in advance by calling © **800/365-2267.** (This is to a national reservation service whose contract is revisited from time to

Packing a Picnic

Before you set out to explore, pack a lunch and keep it handy. Once in, the park has few places (other than Jordan Pond House) to stop for lunch or snacks. Having drinks and snacks at hand will prevent breaking up your day backtracking into Bar Harbor or elsewhere to fend off starvation. The more food you bring, the more your options for the day will expand, so hit one of the charming general stores in any of the island's villages for a wedge of cheese, fresh sandwich, chips, and bottled water.

Acadia National Park is full of picnic opportunities at every turn. **Sand Beach** is gloriously scenic (bring a blanket, plus a sweater for sea winds). A hike up any of the smaller mountains such as **Day Mountain** or **Flying Mountain** is rewarded with ocean views and cooling winds (or, in fall, a blaze of colors). If you're too tired to hike, truck over to **Jordan Pond** or to **The Bubbles** for good views.

time by the park service; if it's nonworking, call the campground directly to ask for the current toll-free reservation number.) Reservations can also be made on the Web between 10am and 10pm only at http://reservations.nps.gov. A park pass is also required for park entry; see above for details.

Seawall (© 207/244-3600) is on the quieter western half of the island near the fishing village of Bass Harbor. This is a good base for road biking, and several short coastal hikes are within easy striking distance. Many of the sites are walk-ins, which require carrying your gear a hundred yards or so to the site. The campground is open late May to September on a first-come, first-served basis. In general, if you get here by 9 or 10am, you'll be pretty much assured of a campsite, especially if you're a tent camper. There are no showers, but there's an unnamed supply store offering low-cost showers a half-mile from the campground. Note that the Parks Services is currently discussing the addition of showers to Seawall; stay tuned. Camping fees are $14 to $20 per night, depending on whether you want to drive directly to your site or pack a tent in for a distance of up to 450 feet. As with Blackwoods, possession of a park pass (minimum cost: $20) is also required to stay at the campground.

Private campgrounds handle the overflow. The region from Ellsworth south boasts 14 private campgrounds, which offer varying amenities. The **Thompson Island Information Center** (© 207/288-3411), open 6am to 10pm daily from May through mid-October, posts up-to-the-minute information on which campgrounds still have vacancies; it's a good first stop for those arriving without camping reservations.

Two private campgrounds stand above the rest. **Bar Harbor Campground,** Route 3, Salisbury Cove (© 207/288-5185; www.barharborcamping.com), on the main route between the causeway and Bar Harbor, doesn't take reservations, and you can often find a good selection of sites if you arrive before noon, even during the peak season. Some of its 300 sites are set in piney woods; others are on an open hillside edged with blueberry barrens. The wooded sites are quite private. There's a pool for campers, uncommonly clean bathhouses, and campers always get to pick their own sites rather than be arbitrarily assigned one. Rates range from $24 for a basic, no-services site to $28 for all hookups.

At the head of Somes Sound is **Mount Desert Campground,** Route 198 (*(C)* **207/244-3710**), which is especially well suited for campers (RVs to a maximum of 20 ft. only). This heavily wooded campground has very few undesirable sites and a great many desirable ones, including some walk-in sites right at the water's edge. The rate ranges from $28 to $39 per night in high season, $25 to $32 per site in the off-season. It's open from mid-June to about mid-September. (*Note:* This campground should not be confused with the Mount Desert Narrows Campground, which is more RV-oriented and located closer to the causeway.)

Another option is **Lamoine State Park** (*(C)* **207/667-4778**), which faces Mount Desert from the mainland across the cold waters of northernmost Frenchman Bay. This is an exceptionally pleasant, quiet park with private sites, a shower house, and a small beach about a half-hour's drive from the action at Bar Harbor. The campground has been belatedly discovered by travelers in the last half-dozen years, but still rarely fills to capacity. It's open from mid-May to early September, and sites cost $20 per night for non-residents of Maine.

Should all these options be full, don't despair: You can find a room, especially in Bar Harbor, which is teeming with motels and inns. The rest of the island also has a good, if scattered, selection of places to spend the night. See the "Where to Stay" sections for Bar Harbor and the rest of Mount Desert Island below. Still desperate? Head off-island to Trenton (a clutch of motels along Rte. 3) and then Ellsworth.

WHERE TO DINE

Just across the bridge connecting Mount Desert Island to the mainland, the very good **Trenton Bridge Lobster Pound** ⚓ (*(C)* **207/667-2977**) on Route 3 in Trenton (on the mainland side) is well worth a stop. It's a personal favorite of mine, salty and unpretentious as all get-out. Often overlooked due to its position—right on a fast, traffic-clogged straightaway, with the elusive island finally in sight—this place serves delicious lobsters and lobster stew. Finish with simple sweet treats such as ice cream and slices of blueberry pie. Containers of the stew also make ideal takeout fare.

Jordan Pond House ⚓⚓ *Finds* AMERICAN   The secret to the Jordan Pond House? Location, location, location. The restaurant traces its roots from 1847, when a farm was established on this picturesque property at the southern tip of Jordan Pond looking north toward The Bubbles, a picturesque pair of glacially sculpted mounds. It was popular during the mania for teahouses in the late 19th century. But tragedy struck in 1979 when the original structure and its birchbark dining room were destroyed by fire. A more modern two-level dining room was built in its place—it has less charm, but it still has the island's best dining location, on a nice lawn. If the weather's agreeable, ask for a seat on the lawn with its unrivaled views. Afternoon tea with popovers is a hallowed Jordan Pond House tradition. Ladies Who Lunch sit next to Mountain Bikers Who Wear Lycra, and everyone feasts on the huge, tasty popovers and strawberry jam served with a choice of teas or fresh lemonade before an expansive view of the Bubbles. The lobster and crab rolls are abundant and filling; the lobster stew is expensive but very, very good. Dinners include classic resort entrees like prime rib, steamed lobster, and baked scallops with a crumb topping.

Park Loop Rd. (near Seal Harbor), Acadia National Park. *(C)* 207/276-3316. www.jordanpond.com. Advance reservations not accepted; call before arriving to hold a table. Main courses: lunch $7.50–$15; afternoon tea $7.25–$8.50; dinner $14–$20. AE, DISC, MC, V. Mid-May to late Oct daily 11:30am–8pm (until 9pm July–Aug).

3 A Nature Guide to Acadia National Park

The human history of Acadia National Park is usually thought of as beginning in the early 20th century, when preservationists banded together with wealthy philanthropists to set aside and create the park we know today. In fact, of course, its clock winds much farther back than that—beginning thousands of years ago, when local native American tribes fished its shores and hunted its hills. But even *that* is just a flake off the deep, deep time that has been required to create Acadia. The rocks upon which you climb, sun yourself, and picnic are old—staggeringly old.

Before arriving, then, one would do well to acquaint oneself with the natural history of the place. Armed with a respect and appreciation for the landscape before you, you just might treat it a bit more reverently while you're here and help ensure it remains for future generations to behold for many years.

THE LANDSCAPE

The beginnings of Acadia National Park as we see it today are perhaps a half *billion* years old. At that time, deep wells of liquid rock known as magma were moving upward, exploding in underground volcanoes, then hardening—still underground, mind you—into granite-like rocks. Later, as natural forces such as wind and water wore away the upper layers of rock above these rocks, the rocks began to be exposed. Their journey was only beginning, however; soon enough (geologically speaking, that is), what is now eastern North America and most of Europe began to shove up against each other, slowly but inexorably. This "collision" (which was more like an extremely slow-motion car wreck), heated, squeezed, transformed, and thrust up the rocks that now form the backbone of Mount Desert Island. Now in place, the rocks were once again changed by everything around them. Ice ages came and went, but the rocks remained; the successive waves of great glaciation and retreat scratched up the rocks like old vinyl records, and the thick tongues of pressing ice cut deep notches out of the rock. Near Somesville, it nearly divided the island in two, creating the only natural fjord in the United States; farther "inland," the slowly flowing ice pushed forward and scooped out several more narrow, parallel valleys that would later be filled by rainwater to form Jordan Pond and Eagle Lake. Huge boulders were swept up and deposited by the ice in odd places, such as the tops of mountains (Bubble Rock is one).

When the glaciers finally retreated for the last time, tens of thousands of years ago, the water melting from the huge ice sheet covering North America swelled the level of the Atlantic high enough to submerge formerly free-flowing river valleys, and give Mount Desert Island the distinctive, knuckled-fist shape we know it for today.

Onto the bones of this landscape came plants and then animals. After each ice age, conifers such as spruce and fir trees—alongside countless grasses and weeds—began to reform, decompose, and form soils. It was tough work: Acadia is a rocky, acidic place. Yet they persevered, and soon the spruces, firs, and hemlocks formed an impenetrable thicket covering the bedrock. Land animals came here, too, some of them now extinct—the caribou, elk, eastern timber wolf, and sea mink among those extirpated by human presence. Many others survived, however, and there's plenty of wildlife here today; while the lynx and eastern cougar may no longer roam the woods, hills, and fields of Acadia, plenty of other creatures do.

The park, though it appears to be fixed in time now, is actually in constant flux. Islanders got a lesson in nature's restorative powers in 1947, when a huge forest fire swept across the park and island, devastating most of it; in the ashes soon grew not more spruces and firs, but rather an entire new set of flowers, weeds, and trees better adapted to grow in bright, sunny, nutrient-poor meadows. Fireweeds, wildflowers, aspens, birch, oak, pine and maple trees began to slowly fill in the denuded landscape and today help create the mixture of plants (and the fall foliage, and the deer, mice and other animals that favor this mixture) in the park today. The spruces and firs may, eventually, take over again—but it will take generations to happen.

Acadia's unique position—it is very near the warm Gulf Stream, yet possesses very cold waters; it is not far from the high, shallow undersea plateau known as Georges Bank—has also brought an astonishing variety of marine life to its doorstep. Migrating whales make for a wonderful spectacle twice each year (and whale-watch tours out of Bar Harbor bring the lives of whales closer to the visitor). Seabirds make similar passages, lighting upon the rocks and lakes of the park coming and going. And the waters teem—though not as they once did—with fish large and small, lobsters, crabs, dolphins, and a great deal more, each with their particular habits, habitats, diets, life cycles, and seasonal migration patterns.

This is to say almost nothing of Acadia's tide pools, in that precarious zone where land and rock meet crashing ocean; a closer look at these pools reveals an ever-changing world of seaweed, snails, barnacles, darting water bugs, clams, shellfish, mud-burrowing worms, and other creatures. Interestingly, the type of life you'll find changes in well-marked "bands" as you get closer to water; rocks that are always submerged contain one mixture of seaweeds and marine organism, rocks that are exposed and then resubmerged each day by the tides contain another. Mostly dry surfaces of the shore rocks contain yet another mixture of living things. It's fascinating to note how each particular organism has found its niche, maintained it, and continues to live hardily and well—within its particular band. Move it up or down a foot, and it would perish.

What follows is only the barest sketch of the natural world in Acadia. For a real look at it, go and see it yourself—preferably by as many means as possible. Whether you choose to explore Acadia on foot, bicycle, horse-drawn carriage, kayak, charter boat, or some other way, you're almost certain to see something here you've never seen before. If you're attentive, you'll come away with a deeper respect for things natural—here, and everywhere.

THE FLORA

Balsam fir   The best-smelling tree in the park must be the mighty balsam fir, whose tips are harvested elsewhere to fabricate aromatic Christmas-tree wreaths. It's sometimes hard to tell a fir from a spruce or hemlock, though the balsam's flat, paddle-like needles (white underneath) are nearly unique—only a hemlock's are similar. Pull one off the twig to be sure; a fir's needle comes off clean, a hemlock's ragged. Still not sure you've got a fir tree on your hands? The long, glossy, almost purplish cones are absolutely distinctive.

Balsam Fir

Red, white, and pitch pine The pines grow in Acadia's sandy soils, and normally like some sunlight. **White pine** is the familiar "King's pine" prevalent throughout Maine; its trunk was prized for the masts of British ships of war, and countless huge pines were floated down Maine rivers by loggermen. Sadly, very few virgin pine trees in Maine remain today. The white pine's extremely long, strong needles come five to a bunch. The **red pine,** not so common, can be distinguished by its pairs of needles and pitchy trunk. The presence of a **pitch pine** indicates poor, acidic soils, and this is one of the first trees to successfully rush in and take root in the wake of a fire. It can grow in the oddest places—along a cliff, on a lip of crumbling stone, in waste soil. The shorter, scrubby clumps of needles (arranged three to a group) don't look attractive but belie the tree's toughness.

Red Pine

White Pine

Red and sugar maple These two maple trees look vaguely alike when turning color in fall, but they're actually quite different—from the shapes of their leaves to the habitats they prefer. **Red maples** have skinny, gray trunks and like a swampy or wet area; often, several of the slim trunks grow together into a clump, and in fall the red maples' pointy leaves turn a brilliant scarlet color almost at once. **Sugar maples,** on the other hand, are stout-trunked trees with lovely, substantial leaves (marked with distinctive U-shaped notches), which autumn slowly changes to red and flame-orange. Sugar maples grow in or at the edges of mixed forests, often in combination with birch trees, oak trees, beech trees, hemlocks, and the like. Their sap, of course, can be collected and boiled down to make delicious maple syrup.

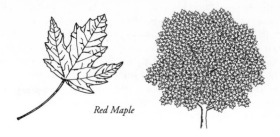

Red Maple

Lowbush blueberry   The lowbush blueberry, with its shrubby, tealike leaves and hardy, thick twigging, lies low to exposed rocks on sunny hillsides or sometimes crops up in shady woods; most of the year, it's inconspicuous as anything, trailing harmlessly underfoot. Come late summer, however, and it's suddenly the island's most popular plant—among bears as well as humans. The wild blueberries ripen slowly in the sun (look behind and beneath the leaves for the best bunches), and make for fine eating, pancake baking, and jam.

THE FAUNA
MAMMALS
Land mammals

Beaver   Reintroduced to Acadia in the 1920s (it had earlier nearly gone extinct from brisk world trade in beaver pelts), the beaver's lodge-building, stick-chewing, and hibernating habits are well known. You'll find it in streams, lakes, and ponds around Mount Desert Island.

Beaver

Black bear   Black bears do occur in Acadia, though in small numbers (still, you may want to keep a cover on that campfire food). The bears are mostly—emphasis on mostly—plant-eaters and docile. Though they'll eat just about anything, black bears prefer easily reached foods on the woodland floor such as berries, mushrooms, and nuts. They need them for a long winter hibernation that averages 6 months.

Black Bear

Moose Nothing says Maine like a moose, and the huge, skinny-legged, vegetarian moose is occasionally seen in Acadia National Park; not very often, however. It far prefers the deep woods, lakes, ponds, and uninhabited areas of Maine's Great North Woods. You can't miss it if you see it, though—the rack of antlers (on the male), the broad, lineman shoulder, the spindly (but quick) legs, and the sheer bulk of the thing—big as a truck—ensure you won't mistake it for anything else on the planet. Hope you don't run into one late at night, on a highway: each year, cars and moose meet up in Maine. Everybody loses, but the car gets a lot more banged up than the moose.

Moose

Shellfish
American lobster Everyone knows the lobster by sight and taste; what few know is that not so long ago it was once considered ugly, tasteless, and unfit to eat. In fact, there was a time when mainly prisoners in Maine were served lobster and lobster stew—three meals a day! Today, of course, the situation is very different. Lobsters, which are related to crabs and shrimp (and more generally to spiders and insects), slowly scour the ocean bottom in shallow, dark waters, locating food by smell. They actually see very poorly. The hard shell, which they periodically shed in order to grow, is the lobster's skeleton: a greenish-black color in life, bright red only after having been cooked.

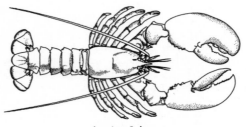

American Lobster

Whales, Dolphins, Porpoises & Seals

Finback whale   A seasonal visitor to Maine's waters twice a year when migrating between polar and equatorial waters, the finback is one of the biggest whales, and also one of the most collegial. It often travels in pairs or groups of a half dozen or more (most whales are relatively solitary), though it does not travel close to shore or in shallow waters; you'll need a whale-watch boat to spot it. Find it by its rather triangular head and a fin which sweeps backward (like a dolphin's) rather than standing straight up like many whales'.

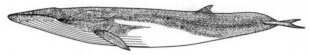

Finback Whale

Humpback whale   Though this whale's Latin name roughly translates as "large-winged New England resident," the gentle, gigantic humpback actually isn't so often seen off the coast of Acadia. (That's mostly because they were easy targets in the heyday of whaling.) But if you do see it, you'll know it: It's huge, dark black, blows tremendous amounts of water when surfacing, and does some amazingly playful acrobatics above water. The males also sing haunting songs, sometimes for as long as two days. The world population has shrunk to perhaps 20,000 individuals.

Minke whale   The smallest (and most human-friendly) of the whales, the minke swims off Acadia's coast, usually moving in groups of two or three whales—but much larger groups collect in feeding areas and seasons. It has a unique habit of approaching and congregating around boats and ships, making this a whale you're quite likely to see while on a whale-watch tour. The minke is dark gray on top; the throat has grooves; and each black flipper fin is marked with a conspicuous white band.

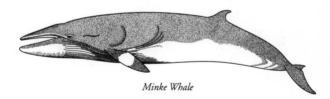

Minke Whale

Northern right whale   If you see a right whale, you've really seen something; it's the most endangered of all the living whales—there are probably fewer than a thousand left in all the oceans of the world, and the northern right is even scarcer—yet one has occasionally been seen off the coast of Acadia. Experts predict it will become extinct within a few more human generations, if not sooner. Huge and active as the humpback, the right is known for doing headstands (so to speak) underwater, poking its tail fins above. It can be spotted by its light color—often blue, brown, or even off-white—and the whitish calcium growths that often appear on its head.

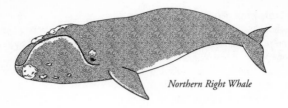

Northern Right Whale

Pilot whale   A smallish whale, the pilot is very rarely seen off Acadia, and very poorly understood. Its habits, world population, and diet are nearly unknown. It is known to congregate in large groups, sometimes up to several hundred, and even to swim with other species of whale at sea. Nearly unique among the whales that pass Maine, it has teeth, and the roundish fin is swept back like a dolphin's or shark's. Sightings are possible, and to be cherished.

Pilot Whale

Dolphins   Two very similar-looking species of dolphin—the **Atlantic white-sided dolphin** and the **white-beaked dolphin**—come rarely to the coast of Maine. Cute and athletic, these dolphins sometimes also occasionally turn up on southern New England's beaches, for a more tragic reason: large groups are occasionally stranded by the tide, then perish when they cannot get back to sea in time.

Atlantic White-Sided Dolphin

White-Beaked Dolphin

Harbor porpoise   Quiet in behavior and habit, the porpoise is not the same thing as a dolphin; in fact, it's darker, much less athletic, and with a blunter, triangular fin. (The dolphin jumps out of the water, and has a pointier fin that sweeps backward.)

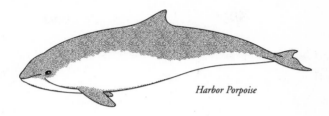

Harbor Porpoise

Seals
Harbor seal   Related to sea lions, the whiskered harbor seal is best seen using one of the charter boat services that leaves from Bar Harbor and other local harbors. You can also sometimes see it basking in the sun or on the rocks of an offshore island. You'll easily recognize it: the seal's flippers have five claws, almost like a human hand; its neck is stocky and strong (as are its teeth); and then there are those whiskers and that fur.

BIRDS
Waterfowl
Ducks   Between one and two dozen species of ducks and ducklike geese, brant, and teal seasonally visit the lakes, ponds, and tidal coves of Acadia every year, including—though hardly limited to—the **red-breasted merganser, common eider,** and the **bufflehead.** Mergansers, characterized by very white sides and very red bills (males) or reddish crests (females), occur year-round in the park but are more common in winter months. So is the eider, which inhabits offshore islands and coastal waters rather than Mount Desert Island's freshwater lakes; Maine is actually the southernmost tip of its breeding range—in winter, it forms huge rafts of birds. Males are marked with a sharp black-and-white pattern. The chubby, squat bufflehead is also distinctively black and white, with a glossy green and purple head; it is entirely absent from the park in summer, but passes through in spring and fall, sometimes lingering for the winter. It flies much more quickly than one might imagine from its appearance.

Red-Breasted Merganser

Common Eider

Great blue heron   Everyone knows a great blue at once, by its prehistoric flapping wings, comb of feathers, and spindly legs. These magnificent hunters wade tidal rivers, fishing with lightning strikes beneath the surface, from May through around October. The smaller, stealthier green heron occurs less commonly, and occasional sightings of black-crowned and yellow-crowned night herons have also been recorded within the park's boundaries.

Great Blue Heron

Loons   Two species of loon visit the island's lakes and tidal inlets, fishing for dinner. The **red-throated loon,** grayish with the red neck, is mostly a spring visitor and barely present at all in the heat of summer. The **common loon** is, indeed, more common—it can be distinguished by its black band around the neck, as well as black-and-white stripes and dots—and can be found in Acadia year-round, though it's most easily spotted in late spring and late fall. It gives the distinctive mournful, almost laughing cry for which the birds are famous. Both have been decimated by human environmental changes such as oil spills, acid rain, and airborne mercury.

Red-Throated Loon

Common Loon

Plovers   Plovers inhabit and breed in Acadia's muddy tidal flats, and their habitat is understandably precarious; a single human step could crush an entire generation of eggs. Only two species of plover visit the park, and they're here in significant numbers for only a relatively short time. The **black-bellied plover**—marked with a snowy black-and-white pattern—arrives in May, breeds in August and September, and is gone by Thanksgiving. The **semipalmated plover,** with its quite different brownish body and white breast, has a similar life cycle.

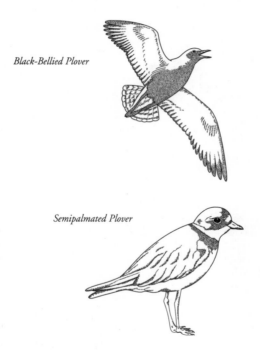

Black-Bellied Plover

Semipalmated Plover

Seagulls   No bird is so closely associated with Maine as the seagull. But, in fact, there's more than one kind of gull here; three or four distinct gulls are commonly found here year-round, a few more visit seasonally, and a few more pop up occasionally. Most common is the grayish **herring gull,** which is also the gull least afraid of humans. It's found in prevalence every month of the year. The aggressive great **black-backed gull** is similarly common, and is nearly all-white (except for that black back and wings); it will even eat the eggs of another gull, but in general avoids humans. Less common are the glaucous, **ring-billed gull,** and even the **laughing and Bonaparte's gulls** (in summer only), not to mention the related **black-legged kittiwake.** Each has a distinctive look; consult a bird guide if you're interested to tell them apart.

Herring Gull

Black-Backed Gull

Bonaparte's Gull

Storm-petrels   The tiny storm-petrel is a fascinating creature; these plucky little birds fly astonishing distances in winter, eating insects on the wing, only to return to Acadia each spring like clockwork, usually in May. They spend an amazing four months in the nest incubating, hatching, and tending to their single, white eggs. **Wilson's storm-petrel** is here for a shorter time than the **Leach's storm-petrel,** which restricts its visits and nests solely to offshore rocks and islands. Both breed in the height of summer, then pack up and head south again by fall.

Wilson's Storm-Petrel

Land Birds

Bald eagle Yes, they're here—year-round—and even breed in Acadia, though they're difficult to find and hardly conspicuous. (Their endangered status means you shouldn't really try to seek them out.) The bald eagle's black body, white head, and yellow bill make it almost impossible to confuse with any other bird. It was nearly wiped out by the 1970s, mainly due to environmental poisons such as DDT-based pesticides, which caused female eagles to lay eggs which were too weak to sustain growing baby chicks. However, the bird has begun to come back.

Bald Eagle

Common raven The park holds jays and crows aplenty, but the raven is a breed apart—tougher, more reclusive, more ragged, more interesting. Look (or listen) for it on cliff tops, mountains, and in deep woods.

Common Raven

Songbirds   There are literally dozens of species of songbirds coming to roost in
Acadia's open fields, forests, and dead snags—even in the rafters and bird boxes
of houses. They are not so common on this rocky, shady island as in Maine's sub-
urbia (Greater Portland, for instance) or in the farmlands of central and western
Maine, but they are here. One thing is for certain: Songbirds love human company, thus look for them near the settled areas. The park hosts perhaps 15 or
more distinct types of chirpy little **warblers,** each with unique and often liquid
songs; a half-dozen **thrushes** occurring in significant numbers; winter **wrens,
swallows, sparrows, vireos, finches, creepers,** and **thrashers;** the whimsical
black-capped **chickadee;** and occasional (and lovely) sightings of **bluebirds, car-
dinals,** and **tanagers,** among many other species.

Black-Capped Chickadee

Eastern Bluebird

Summer Tanager

4 Bar Harbor (★

Bar Harbor has historical roots in the grand resort era of the late 19th century. The region was discovered by wealthy rusticators, drawn by the mid-19th-century landscape paintings that were exhibited in Boston and New York. Later, sprawling hotels and boarding houses cluttered the shores and hillsides as the newly affluent middle class flocked here in summer by steamboat and rail from Eastern Seaboard cities. When the resort was at its zenith near the turn of the last century, Bar Harbor had rooms enough to accommodate some 5,000 visitors. Along with the hotels and guest houses, hundreds of cottages were built by those who came here season after season.

The tourist business continued to grow through the early part of the 1900s, then all but collapsed as the Great Depression and the growing popularity of automobile travel doomed the era of the extended vacation. Bar Harbor was dealt a further blow in 1947 when a fire fueled by an unusually dry summer and fierce northwest winds leveled many of the most opulent cottages and much of the rest of the town. (To this day, no one knows with any certainty how the fire started.) The fire destroyed 5 hotels, 67 grand cottages, and 170 homes. In all, some 17,000 acres of the island were burned. Downtown Bar Harbor was spared, and many of the in-town mansions along the oceanfront were missed by the conflagration.

After a period of quiet slumber (some storefronts were still boarded up as late as the 1970s), Bar Harbor has been rejuvenated and rediscovered in recent years as tourists have poured in, followed by entrepreneurs who have opened dozens of restaurants, shops, and boutiques. The less charitable regard Bar Harbor as just another tacky tourist mecca—the downtown hosts a proliferation of T-shirt vendors, ice-cream cone shops, and souvenir palaces. Crowds spill off the sidewalk and into the street in midsummer, and the traffic and congestion can be truly appalling.

Yet Bar Harbor's vibrant history, distinguished architecture, and beautiful location along Frenchman Bay allow it to rise above its station as mild diversion for tourists. Most of the island's inns, motels, and B&Bs are located here, as are dozens of fine restaurants, making it a desirable base of operations. Bar Harbor is also the best destination for supplies and services; there's a decent grocery story and coin-operated laundry, and you can stock up on other necessities of life.

As for the congestion, it's fortunate that Bar Harbor is compact enough that once you find a parking space or a room for the night, the whole town can be navigated on foot. Arriving here early in the morning also considerably improves your odds of securing parking within easy striking distance of the town center. My suggestion: Explore Bar Harbor before and after breakfast, then set off for the hills, woods, and coast the rest of the day.

ESSENTIALS
GETTING THERE
Bar Harbor is located on Route 3 about 10 miles southeast of the causeway onto Mount Desert Island. Daily flights from Boston to the airport in Trenton, just across the island causeway, are offered year-round by U.S. Airways affiliate **Colgan Air** (© 800/428-4322). From here, call a taxi or ride the free shuttle bus (late June to mid-October only) to downtown Bar Harbor.

Two major bus lines serve the island. **Vermont Transit Lines** (© 800/552-8737 or 207/288-3211; www.vermonttransit.com) is affiliated with **Greyhound** and serves Bangor from Boston's South Station, continuing onward (in summer only) once daily to Ellsworth and Bar Harbor.

Concord Trailways (© 800/639-3317 or 207/945-5000; www.concord trailways.com) serves Bangor from Boston, but does not continue to the smaller towns onward; you'll need to transfer at Bangor via taxi (a long ride) or Vermont Transit.

VISITOR INFORMATION

The **Bar Harbor Chamber of Commerce,** P.O. Box 158, Bar Harbor, ME 04609 (© 207/288-5103; www.barharborinfo.com), stockpiles a huge arsenal of information about local attractions at its offices at 93 Cottage St. Write, call, or e-mail in advance for a directory of area lodging and attractions. The chamber's website is chock-full of information and helpful links.

EXPLORING BAR HARBOR

Wandering the compact downtown on foot is a good way to get a taste of the town. Among the best views in town are those from the foot of Main Street at grassy **Agamont Park,** which overlooks the town pier and Frenchman Bay. From here, set off past the Bar Harbor Inn on the **Shore Path** ⋆, a winding, wide trail that follows the shoreline for a short distance along a public right of way. The pathway passes in front of many of the elegant summer homes (some converted to inns), offering a superb vantage point to view the area's architecture.

From the path, you'll also have an open view of **The Porcupines,** a cluster of spruce-studded islands just offshore. This is a good spot to witness the powerful force of glacial action. The south-moving glacier ground away at the islands, creating a gentle slope facing north. On the south shore, away from the glacial push (glaciers simply melted when they retreated north), is a more abrupt, clifflike shore. The resulting islands look like a small group of porcupines migrating southward—or so early visitors imagined.

A short stroll from the Village Green is the **Bar Harbor Historical Society,** 33 Ledgelawn Ave. (© 207/288-0000 or 207/288-3807). The society moved into this handsome 1918 former convent in 1997, where they've showcased artifacts of life in the old days—dishware and photos from the grand old hotels, and exhibits on noted landscape architect Beatrix Farrand. Leave enough time to spend a few minutes thumbing through the scrapbooks about the devastating 1947 fire. The museum is open June to October Monday to Saturday from 1 to 4pm; admission is free.

Located on the grounds of one of Bar Harbor's more magnificent summer estates is the **College of the Atlantic** (© 207/288-5015), a school founded in 1969 with a strong emphasis on environmental education. The campus, with its old and new buildings, is uncommonly picturesque (great views of Frenchman Bay!). The school's **Museum of Natural History** ⋆, 105 Eden St. (© 207/288-5395), features exhibits prepared by current and former students that focus on the interaction between island residents, including the two-legged, the four-legged, the finned, and the furred. The building housing the museum was originally the Acadia National Park headquarters and was moved and expanded prior to its opening in June 2000.

The museum is open Monday through Saturday mid-June to Labor Day 10am to 5pm; the rest of the year, it's open Thursday to Saturday from 1 to 4pm and Sunday 10am to 4pm. Admission is $3.50 for adults, $2.50 for seniors, $1.50 for teens, and $1 for children ages 3 to 12.

One of downtown's less obvious attractions is the **Criterion Theater** (© 207/288-3441), a movie house built in 1932 in a classic Art Deco style and that so far has avoided the degradation of multiplexification. The 900-seat theater,

Bar Harbor

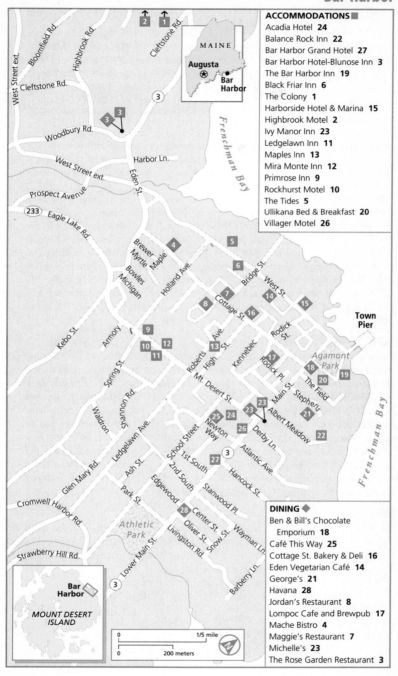

ACCOMMODATIONS

Acadia Hotel **24**
Balance Rock Inn **22**
Bar Harbor Grand Hotel **27**
Bar Harbor Hotel-Blunose Inn **3**
The Bar Harbor Inn **19**
Black Friar Inn **6**
The Colony **1**
Harborside Hotel & Marina **15**
Highbrook Motel **2**
Ivy Manor Inn **23**
Ledgelawn Inn **11**
Maples Inn **13**
Mira Monte Inn **12**
Primrose Inn **9**
Rockhurst Motel **10**
The Tides **5**
Ullikana Bed & Breakfast **20**
Villager Motel **26**

DINING

Ben & Bill's Chocolate
   Emporium **18**
Café This Way **25**
Cottage St. Bakery & Deli **16**
Eden Vegetarian Café **14**
George's **21**
Havana **28**
Jordan's Restaurant **8**
Lompoc Cafe and Brewpub **17**
Mache Bistro **4**
Maggie's Restaurant **7**
Michelle's **23**
The Rose Garden Restaurant **3**

> ⟨ *Tips* **Parking in Bar Harbor**
>
> If parking spaces are scarce downtown, head to the end of Albert Meadow (a side street across from the Village Green). At the end of the road is a small waterfront park with free parking, great views of the bay, and foot access to Shore Path. It's not well marked or publicized, so you can often find a place to park when much of the rest of town is filled up.

located on Cottage Street, shows first-run movies in summer and is worth the price of admission for the fantastic, if somewhat faded, interiors; the movie is secondary. As once was the case at most movie palaces, it still costs extra to sit in the more exclusive loges upstairs.

For an eye-opening adventure, consider watching the sunrise from atop Cadillac Mountain, followed by a bike descent back to Bar Harbor. **Acadia Bike & Canoe** (48 Cottage St.; © 207/288-9605) hauls you and a rental bike to the top of the island's highest peak, serves you coffee and a light breakfast while the sun edges over the horizon, then leads you on a delightfully brisk coasting and pedaling trip 6 miles down the mountain into Bar Harbor. Be aware that this is a *really* early-morning adventure: Tours meet at about 4:15am in early July (about 5am by late Aug) and last about 3 hours. Trips are Monday through Friday during peak season, and reservations are recommended. The price is $34 per person.

WHALE-WATCHING

Bar Harbor is a base for several ocean endeavors, including whale-watching tours. Operators offer excursions in search of humpbacks, finbacks, minkes, and the infrequently seen endangered right whale. The sleekest is the *Friendship V* (© 800/942-5374 or 207/288-2386; www.whalesrus.com), which operates from the municipal pier in downtown Bar Harbor. Tours are on a fast, twin-hulled three-level excursion boat that can hold 200 passengers in two heated cabins. The tours run three hours plus; the cost is $45 per adult, $42 per senior citizen. A puffin- and whale-watch tour is also offered for $43 per adult, $25 per child 5 to 14, and $8 per child under age 5. There's free on-site parking and a money-back guarantee that you'll see whales. Tours begin in May and run throughout the summer. Call ahead for exact dates.

WHERE TO STAY

Bar Harbor is the bedroom community for Mount Desert Island, with hundreds of hotel, motel, and inn rooms. They're invariably filled during the busy days of summer, and even the most basic of rooms can be quite expensive in July and August. It's essential to reserve as early as possible.

Reputable motels in or near town that offer at least some rooms under $100 in peak season include the conveniently located **Villager Motel,** 207 Main St. (© 207/288-3211), with 63 rooms; the in-town, pet-friendly **Rockhurst Motel,** 68 Mount Desert St. (© 207/288-3140); and the smoke-free **Highbrook Motel,** 94 Eden St. (© 800/338-9688 or 207/288-3591). About 4 miles west of Bar Harbor on Route 3 is **Hanscom's Motel and Cottages** (© 207/288-3744; www.hanscomsmotel.com), an old-fashioned motor court with 12 units (some two-bedroom) that have been well maintained. Its rates range from $88 to $120 in summer; from $68 off-season.

VERY EXPENSIVE

Balance Rock Inn ★★★   Tucked down a quiet side alley just off Bar Harbor's main drag, the Balance Rock (built in 1903 for a Scottish railroad magnate) reaches for and achieves a gracefully upscale Long Island beach house feel. The entrance alone is nearly worth the steep rack rates: You enter a sitting room, which looks out onto the sort of azure outdoor swimming pool you'd expect to find in a Tuscan villa, and just beyond looms the Atlantic. Rooms are as elegant as any on the island, with a variety of layouts, some with sea views; some also have whirlpools and saunas, while the penthouse suite adds a full kitchen as well. The comfortable king beds are adjustable using controls and have been fitted with both feather beds and quality linens. The poolside bar, piano room, gracious staff, and fragrant flowers lining the driveway complete the romance of the experience.

21 Albert Meadow, Bar Harbor, ME 04609. © **800/753-0494** or 207/288-2610. www.barharborvacations.com. 17 units. Peak season $255–$525 double, $455–$625 suite; spring and late fall $115–$295 double, $195–$595 suite. Rates include full breakfast. AE, DISC, MC, V. Closed late Oct to early May. **Amenities:** Poolside bar; outdoor pool; fitness room; piano. *In room:* A/C, kitchen (1), hair dryer, iron and ironing board, robes, whirlpool (some), sauna (some).

EXPENSIVE

Bar Harbor Hotel–Bluenose Inn ★★   Owned by the same folks who operate the waterside Bar Harbor Inn (see below), this resort-style complex—situated in two buildings topping a small rise—offers even better views of the surrounding terrain than its companion property. Facilities here are more modern, too: Expect spacious carpeted rooms with huge bathrooms, small refrigerators, and balconies, a good fitness center, indoor and outdoor pools, and one of the island's best dining rooms (see "Where to Dine," later in this chapter). Upper-floor rooms with sea views are definitely worth the extra cost, particularly if the weather is good, and the staff here is professional and friendly.

90 Eden St., Bar Harbor, ME 04609. © **800/445-4077** or 207/288-3348. www.bluenoseinn.com. 97 units. Mid-June to mid-Oct $145–$405 double; spring and late fall $79–$299 double. AE, DC, DISC, MC, V. Closed Nov–Apr. **Amenities:** Restaurant; 2 pools; fitness center; Jacuzzi. *In room:* A/C, fridge, coffeemaker, hair dryer, iron and ironing board, robe, balcony.

Packing a Picnic

Even in downtown Bar Harbor, you can have a nice picnic experience simply by settling onto a bench on the **Village Green**—that's the green, rectangular space tucked behind and between Mount Desert and Kennebec streets (beside from which island buses depart; it's a block off Cottage St.). People-watching abounds, and art shows and festivals sometimes come to the green.

Closer to the water, at the tip of the land (at the end of West and Main sts.), the pocket **Agamont Park** is superlative for its picnic spot and a view of boats and islands. There's also the quiet campus of earthy **College of the Atlantic,** back on Route 3; they surely won't mind if you plunk down a basket and graze—in the interests of researching the college for future enrollment, of course. You're surrounded by food in downtown Bar Harbor; the natural foods store **Alternative Market** (© **207/288-8227**) is probably your best choice for prepared foods, drinks, and natural snacks.

Bar Harbor Grand Hotel ⭐   Bar Harbor's newest hotel (it opened in the summer of 2003) nicely fills a lodging gap between quaint, expensive inns and B&Bs and the family-owned motels, hotels, and cottages scattered about the island. It's owned by the Witham family, the same folks behind the Bar Harbor and Bluenose hotels (see elsewhere in these listings). The hotel's blocky, two-towered design faithfully copies the style of the Rodick House, a now-defunct 19th-century lodging in Bar Harbor that could once boast of being Maine's largest hotel; the Grand, however, does the former one better with spacious rooms and bathrooms and, of course, all-modern fixtures. Rooms are decked out in the same floral bedspreads and curtains you'd expect in any upscale business hotel, but the access to downtown Bar Harbor and the nearby ocean are big pluses. Concessions to business and tourist travelers include a guest laundry facility, gift shop, and high-speed Internet access. Not surprisingly, they're getting a lot of tour groups. Expect comfort, not island character.

269 Main St. ℂ **888/766-2529** or 207/288-5226. www.barharborgrand.com. 70 units. Early Apr to late June and late Oct to mid-Nov $75–$139 double; late June to early Sept $175–$195 double; early Sept to late Oct $135–$159 double. Suites $20–$70 extra. Rates include continental breakfast. Closed mid-Nov to early Apr. **Amenities:** Outdoor pool. *In room:* A/C, fridge, coffeemaker, DVD player.

The Bar Harbor Inn ⭐⭐   The Bar Harbor Inn, located just off Agamont Park, nicely mixes traditional and contemporary. Situated on shady waterfront grounds just a minute's stroll from downtown boutiques (it's also at the start of the Shore Path), the inn offers convenience and gracious charm. The main shingled inn, which dates from the turn of the 19th century, has a settled, old-money feel, with its semicircular dining room with ocean views and the button-down elegance of the lobby. The guest rooms, located in the main inn and two additional structures, are decidedly more contemporary. Guest rooms in the Oceanfront Lodge and Main Inn both offer spectacular views of the bay, and many have private balconies; the less expensive Newport Building lacks views but is comfortable and up-to-date. The inn's semiformal dining room serves up resort fare along with the best ocean view in town. Entrees include grilled vegetable ravioli, filet mignon, and grilled strip steak. The Terrace Grille, serving simpler fare like chowders, salads, and boiled lobster, is downstairs; it also overlooks the bay, features outdoor seating in good weather, and is open daily for lunch and dinner.

Newport Dr. (P.O. Box 7), Bar Harbor, ME 04609. ℂ **800/248-3351** or 207/288-3351. www.barharborinn.com. 153 units. Mid-June to late Oct $129–$319 double; spring and late fall $79–$255 double. Rates include continental breakfast. AE, DISC, MC, V. Closed Dec to late Mar. **Amenities:** Dining room; heated outdoor pool; Jacuzzi; conference space; limited room service; afternoon coffee and cookies; free newspaper. *In room:* A/C, balcony (some).

Harborside Hotel & Marina ⭐⭐   Once a family-style motel known as the Golden Anchor, the Harborside is the town's newest luxury property—and it's got great water views to boot. When completed, the renovation will have transformed the formerly midlevel lodging into something else again: a wide variety of studios, and two- and three-bedroom suites sporting fancy bathrooms, business-hotel amenities, and large televisions. The priciest suites are more like condominium units, with various combinations of Jacuzzis, fireplaces, balconies, water views, and even—in a few cases—full kitchens and dining rooms. The large swimming pool and hot tub will be big drawing cards, and a new marina was also in the works at press time. There's a family-style restaurant, **The Pier,** as well.

55 West St., Bar Harbor, ME 04609. ℂ **800/328-5033** or 207/288-5033. www.theharborsidehotel.com. 160 units. $139–$259 double; $225–$850 suite. Off-season rates sometimes lower. DISC, MC, V. Closed Nov–Apr. **Amenities:** Outdoor pool. *In room:* A/C, TV, dataport.

Ivy Manor Inn The Ivy Manor quickly proved a welcome addition to Bar Harbor's upscale lodging pool when it opened in 1997. Located in a 1940s-era Tudor-style house that was once the home and office of a doctor, the Ivy Manor was thoroughly done over in an understated French Victorian style, mostly in lush, rich colors such as burgundy. The rooms are larger than average; most are carpeted and furnished with attractive, tasteful antiques from the innkeeper's collection. Some rooms have antique claw-foot tubs; others have small outdoor sitting decks (none with views to speak of). Among my favorite rooms: no. 6, a small suite with a private sitting room and small fireplace; and no. 1, the honeymoon room, with an imposing walnut headboard and matching armoire. All rooms have small TVs. Leave time for a cocktail in the cozy first-floor lounge after you return from your day's outing. The inn restaurant, Michelle's, is described below under "Where to Dine."

194 Main St., Bar Harbor, ME 04609. © **888/670-1997** or 207/288-2138. www.ivymanor.com. 7 units. Mid-June to Oct $200–$325; Apr to mid-June $185–$275 double. Rates include full breakfast. Closed Nov–Mar. 2-night minimum on holiday weekends. AE, DISC, MC, V. Children over 12 welcome. **Amenities:** Restaurant; lounge. *In room:* A/C.

The Tides ✶ The Tides features just four guest rooms (three of which are suites) in a sprawling yellow mansion dating from 1887. It's located at the head of a long, lush lawn that descends to the water's edge, all on 1½ acres in a neighborhood of imposing homes within easy strolling distance of the village center. Guests can unwind in one of the two spacious living rooms (one upstairs and one down) or, more likely, on the veranda, which has a unique outdoor fireplace. Breakfast is served on the porch in good weather; otherwise, it's enjoyed in the regal dining room, with polished wood floors and views out to Bar Island.

119 West St., Bar Harbor, ME 04609. © **207/288-4968.** www.barharbortides.com. 4 units. $225 double; $375–$395 suite. Rates include full breakfast. DISC, MC, V. Closed Nov to mid-June. *In room:* VCR, dataport, fireplace (some).

MODERATE

Acadia Hotel ✶ The Acadia Hotel is nicely situated overlooking the Village Green, easily accessible to in-town activities and free shuttles to elsewhere on the island. This handsome, simple home dating from the late 19th century has a wraparound porch and guest rooms decorated with busy floral motifs. Rooms vary widely in size and amenities; two have whirlpools, two have phones, one has a kitchenette. Ask for the specifics when you book. The smaller rooms offer good value for those who don't plan to spend much time inside.

20 Mt. Desert St., Bar Harbor, ME 04609. © **207/288-5721.** www.acadiahotel.com. 10 units. Summer $100–$160 double; fall $80–$130 double; winter and spring $55–$100 double. MC, V. *In room:* A/C, TV, no phone.

Black Friar Inn The Black Friar Inn, tucked on a side street overlooking the municipal building parking lot, is easily overlooked. But this yellow-shingled structure with quirky pediments and a somewhat eccentric air offers good value for Bar Harbor. A former owner "collected" interiors and installed them throughout the house. Among them is a replica of the namesake Black Friar Pub in London, complete with elaborate carved-wood paneling (it's now a common room), stamped tin walls in the breakfast room, and a doctor's office (now a guest room). The Black Friar's rooms are carpeted and furnished with a mix of antiques, and most are rather small. The least expensive are the two garret rooms on the third floor, each of which has a detached private bathroom down the hall. Staff can also arrange for kayak and fly-fishing tours.

10 Summer St., Bar Harbor, ME 04609. (C) **207/288-5091.** Fax 207/288-4197. www.blackfriar.com. 7 units. Peak season $110–$160 double; off-season lower. Rates include full breakfast. 2-night minimum mid-June to mid-Oct. DISC, MC, V. Closed Dec–Apr. Children 12 and older welcome. *In room:* A/C.

Ledgelawn Inn ⭐ If you want great location with considerably more flair than a motel, this is a good bet. This hulking cream and maroon 1904 "cottage" sits on a village lot amid towering oaks and maples and has an early-20th-century elegance, updated with modern amenities (some rooms are air-conditioned); on the property, you'll also find a small, no-frills pool. The Ledgelawn first gets your attention with a handsome sun porch lounge with full bar, and when you set foot here, you half expect to find Bogart flirting with Bacall in a corner. Guest rooms vary somewhat in size and mood, but all are comfortably if not stylishly furnished with antiques and reproductions. Room 221 has a working fireplace, a shared balcony, and a pair of oak double beds; room 122 has an appealing sitting area with fireplace. Some rooms have bathrooms shoehorned into small spaces.

66 Mt. Desert St., Bar Harbor, ME 04609. (C) **800/274-5334** or 207/288-4596. Fax 207/288-9968. www. ledgelawninn.com. 33 units. July–Aug $125–$275 double; off-season lower. Rates include breakfast. AE, DISC, MC, V. Closed late Oct to early May. Pets allowed ($15 per day).

Maples Inn The Maples is a popular destination among those attracted to outdoor activities. You'll often find guests swapping stories of the day's adventure on the handsome front porch or lingering over breakfast to compare notes about the best hiking trails. The rather modest (by Bar Harbor standards) yellow farmhouse-style home is tucked away on a leafy side street among other B&Bs; it's an easy walk downtown to a movie or dinner. The innkeepers have a good way of making guests comfortable, with board games and paperbacks scattered about, and down comforters in all rooms. Rooms are small to medium-size, but you're not likely to feel cramped—and all do now have private bathrooms. The two-room White Birch has a fireplace and is the largest; Red Oak has a private deck with plastic patio furniture. Breakfasts—including dishes like Bananas Holland America—are appropriately filling for a full day outdoors.

16 Roberts Ave., Bar Harbor, ME 04609. (C) **207/288-3443.** www.maplesinn.com. 6 units. Mid-June to mid-Oct $110–$160 double; off-season $70–$110. Memorial Day weekend $20 higher. Rates include full breakfast. 2-night minimum on holiday weekends. DISC, MC, V. Closed Nov–Apr. No children under 12. **Amenities:** Board games.

Mira Monte Inn A stay at this grayish-green Italianate mansion, built in 1864, feels a bit like a trip to Grandmother's house—a grandmother who inherited most of her furniture from *her* grandmother. The antiques are more intriguing than elegant, and the common rooms are furnished in a pleasant country Victorian style. The 2-acre grounds, located within a few minutes' walk of Bar Harbor's restaurants and attractions, are attractively landscaped and include a cutting garden to keep the house in flowers. There's a nice brick terrace away from the street, which makes a fine place to enjoy breakfast on warm summer mornings. Most guest rooms are blessed with either a balcony, a fireplace, or both. The room styles vary widely; some are heavy on the Victorian, others have the feel of a country farmhouse. If you're a light sleeper, avoid the rooms facing Mount Desert Street; those facing the gardens in the rear are far more peaceful. Families should inquire about the suites in the adjacent outbuilding.

69 Mount Desert St., Bar Harbor, ME 04609. (C) **800/553-5109** or 207/288-4263. Fax 207/288-3115. www.miramonte.com. 12 units. Late June to late Oct $165–$230 double, $144–$285 suite; spring and fall $95–$166 double. Rates include breakfast. 2-night minimum stay in midsummer. AE, DC, DISC, MC, V. Closed Nov to early May. **Amenities:** Garden; Internet access. *In room:* A/C, fireplace (some), balcony (some).

Primrose Inn ⚡ *Kids*   This handsome pale-green-and-maroon Victorian stick-style inn, originally built in 1878, is one of the more notable properties on mansion row along Mount Desert Street. Its distinctive architecture has been not only preserved, but even improved upon with an addition in 1987 that added 10 rooms with private bathrooms and a number of balconies. The inn is comfortable and furnished with "functional antiques" and more modern reproductions, and many rooms have a floral theme and thick carpets. It's not a stuffy place—it has a distinctly informal air that encourages guests to mingle and relax in the common room, decorated in a light country Victorian style complete with piano. Two guest rooms feature whirlpools or fireplaces. The suites in the rear are spacious and comfortable, and the efficiencies make sense for families that could benefit from a kitchen (for rent by the week only).

73 Mount Desert St., Bar Harbor, ME 04609. © **877/846-3424** or 207/288-4031. www.primroseinn.com. 10 units plus 5 efficiencies. Peak season $110–$210 double; spring and fall $85–$165 double; efficiencies $600–$1,150 per week. Daily rates include breakfast. 2-night minimum summer weekends. DISC, MC, V. Closed late Oct to Apr. Pets allowed ($75 fee; call first). **Amenities:** Piano. *In room:* A/C, kitchenette (some), iron and ironing board, hair dryer, Jacuzzi (some), fireplace (some).

Ullikana Bed & Breakfast   This Tudor cottage dates from 1885 and is tucked on a quiet side street near Agamont Park and the Bar Harbor Inn (the owners report that its name has long been shrouded in mystery). The 10-bedroom "cottage" is solidly built, and the downstairs, with its oak trim and wainscoting, is heavy and dark in an English gentleman's club kind of way. The guest rooms are varied in size, but all are spacious and nicely decorated in a country Victorian mode, some with iron or brass cottage beds. Audrey's Room has a pleasant, storybook feel to it, with pastel colors, high ceilings, and a cozy bathroom with a claw-foot tub. Summery room no. 6 has a deck with glimpses of the bay, along with a sofa and a claw-foot tub for relaxing. Across the lane is the attractive Yellow House, which has six additional rooms. The house and rooms are both simpler in style than the main cottage, but they boast a large common area on the first floor and a nice porch that's great for late afternoon relaxing. Especially appealing here are the porch rockers, with views of the whimsical sculpture on the grounds.

16 The Field, Bar Harbor, ME 04609. © **207/288-9552**. Fax 207/288-3682. www.ullikana.com. 10 units (2 with detached bathroom), plus 6 across street in Yellow House. $160–$295 double ($240 in Yellow House). Rates include full breakfast. MC, V. Closed Nov to early May. Children age 8 and up are welcome. *In room:* No phone.

INEXPENSIVE

The Colony *Value*   The Colony is a vintage motor court consisting of a handful of motel rooms (starting at $105) and a battery of cottages arrayed around a long green. It will be most appreciated by those with a taste for the authentically retro; others might decide to look for accommodation more lavishly appointed. The rooms are furnished in a simple '70s style that won't win any awards for decor, but all are comfortable; many have kitchenettes. It's situated just across Route 3 from a cobblestone beach, and it's a 10-minute drive from Bar Harbor. The Colony offers one of the better values on the island.

Route 3 (P.O. Box 56), Hulls Cove, ME 04644. © **800/524-1159** or 207/288-3383. www.acadia.net/thecolony. 55 units. $65–$125 double (discounts in Oct). Closed mid-Oct to early June. AE, DC, DISC, MC, V. *In room:* A/C, kitchenette (some), fridge (some), no phone (some).

WHERE TO DINE

If you're wanting a light bite or breakfast, my local favorite is **Cottage Street Bakery and Deli** ⚡ (© **207/388-1010**) at 59 Cottage St. Egg dishes, omelets, blueberry pancakes, and baked goods are all well done, and there are plenty of coffee drinks; I also like the outdoor patio. The kid's menu is fun and welcome.

If you're craving something sweet, head over to **Ben & Bill's Chocolate Emporium** (66 Main St.; ✆ **800/806-3281** or 207/288-3281), for a big ice-cream cone. In the evenings, you may have to join the line spilling out the door. Visitors are often tempted to try the house novelty, lobster ice cream. Resist.

VERY EXPENSIVE

The Rose Garden Restaurant ★★★ NEW AMERICAN   One of only a handful of fine-dining establishments in Bar Harbor that actually delivers a big-league dining experience, this unassuming room—located within the Bluenose Inn resort complex (see "Where to Stay," earlier in this chapter)—turns out wonderful meals. The prix-fixe isn't cheap ($63 per person, at last check), but the chef's seared tenderloin is perfectly done and paired with tender pot-roast vegetables; a tasty hunk of grilled salmon comes with mustard sauce, caramelized onions, and a potato cake. Other choices could include lobster served with pasta, a roasted rack of lamb with pesto potatoes, or a peppercorn-seared venison with wild rice, squash puree and cranberry sauce. Inventive appetizers include a Scandinavian-style plate of smoked salmon, caviar, and pumpernickel slices; foie gras; crunchy crab cakes; strudel filled with asparagus, toasted walnuts, and Gruyère; Maine lobster bisque with tarragon reduction and sweet brandy cream; and chilled mango soup with jumbo shrimp and fresh mint. And dessert doesn't let up, either—the chocolate mousse cake and the unusual sweet potato crème brûlée with shortbread are out of sight, as are a warm Granny Smith apple tart, the mango mascarpone cheesecake, an espresso panna cotta, and almost everything else. There's a new pair of new three- and five-course tasting menus now available; ask your server about them.

90 Eden St. ✆ **800/445-4077** or 207/288-3348. Reservations recommended. Breakfast $10–$17; prix-fixe dinner $56. MC, V. Breakfast 7–10:30am; dinner 5:30–9:30pm. Closed Nov–Apr.

Moments **Eating Lobster by the Pound**

The ingredients for a proper feed at a local lobster pound are a pot of boiling water, a tank of lobsters, some well-worn picnic tables, a good view, and a six-pack of Maine beer—no pretensions, no frills. The best lobster restaurants are those right on the water.

Among the best on Mount Desert Island is the famous **Beal's Lobster Pier** (✆ **207/244-7178**) in Southwest Harbor, one of the oldest pounds in the area. **Thurston's Lobster Pound** (✆ **207/244-7600**) in tiny Bernard (across the water from Bass Harbor) is atmospheric enough to have been used as a backdrop for the Stephen King miniseries *Storm of the Century;* it's a fine place to linger toward dusk, with great views of fishing and lobster boats. See "Elsewhere on Mount Desert Island," later in this chapter, for a full review. **Abel's Lobster Pound** (✆ **207/276-5827**) on Route 198, 5 miles north of Northeast Harbor, overlooks the deep blue waters of Somes Sound; eat at picnic tables under the pines or indoors at the restaurant. It's quite a bit pricier than other lobster restaurants at first glance, but they don't charge for the extras that many other lobster joint do—and some visitors claim that lobsters here are more succulent.

EXPENSIVE

George's ★★ CONTEMPORARY MEDITERRANEAN   George's takes some sleuthing to find, but it's worth the effort. This is a Bar Harbor classic, offering fine dining in classy but informal surroundings for more than 2 decades. (It's located in the small clapboard cottage behind Main St.'s First National Bank.) George's captures the joyous feel of summer nicely with four smallish dining rooms (and plenty of open windows) and additional seating on the terrace outside, which is the best place to watch the gentle dusk settle over town. The service is upbeat and the meals are wonderfully prepared. All entrees sell for one price ($25) and include salad, vegetable, and potato or rice. Offerings change with the season and availability. You won't go wrong with basic choices, like steamed lobster, roast chicken, or grilled beef with ancho chile sauce and masa cakes, but you're better off opting for the more adventurous fare, like lobster strudel or the "To Die For" mustard shrimp (also offered as an appetizer). The house specialty is lamb in its many incarnations, including chargrilled lamb tenderloin with a rosemary-infused three-bean ragout. Finish with a delectable dessert such as coconut panna cotta, speckled chocolate cake with orange Bavarian cream, a pear and almond tart, maple sugar crème brûlèe, or just some black currant sorbet. The restaurant consistently receives the annual *Wine Spectator* award of excellence. Note that the original owner (George) has sold the place, but the new owners have kept up the traditions, with help from George himself.

7 Stephens Lane. ✆ 207/288-4505. www.georgesbarharbor.com. Reservations recommended. Entrees $25; appetizer, entree, and dessert packages $37–$40. AE, DISC, MC, V. Daily 5:30–10pm; shorter hours after Labor Day. Closed Nov to early May.

Havana ★★ LATINO/FUSION   Havana established a new creative standard for restaurants when it opened in 1999 in this town of fried fish and baked stuffed haddock. The spare but sparkling decor in the old storefront is as classy as you'll find in Boston or Washington, D.C., and the menu could compete in any urban area as well. Owner Michael Boland says his menu is inspired by Latino fare, which he melds nicely with New American ideas. While the offerings change weekly, expect items like appetizers of monkfish ceviche, Thai tofu with a plantain crust, shrimp stuffed with jicama and coconut, served with a sweet potato puree and peanut dipping sauce, and tenderloin brochettes. Recent entrees included choices as adventurous as Chilean black bean stew; grilled pork chops rubbed with maple sugar and chiles; filet mignon rubbed with Cuban coffee and black pepper; and tuna grilled and spiced with *guajillo* chiles. Finish with an equally dazzling dessert such as coconut ice cream, a pecan tart, a Nicaraguan *tres leches* cake, pistachio-mousse popovers with chocolate Cointreau sauce, or guava mousse in a chocolate waffle cone. The wine list here is small and basic but won't offend anyone.

318 Main St. ✆ 207/288-2822. www.havanamaine.com. Reservations recommended. Main courses $16–$33. AE, DC, DISC, MC, V. Daily 5:30–10pm. Closed Jan–Mar.

Mache Bistro ★ BISTRO   Relative newcomer Mache has developed a devoted following among those who know quality food and preparation. The small restaurant (nine tables) with soothing but plain decor hides a sophisticated kitchen. (For instance, one wouldn't expect an imported cheese course offered in a place with plywood floors. Yet there you have it.) The menu changes monthly; appetizers could include a salad with bleu cheese, apples, and truffle oil; or a smoked-lobster bisque. Main courses recently featured a seared steak with black trumpet infused jus, and a Brittany fisherman's soup made with local seafood. Duck is often on the menu, and it's often a good choice.

135 Cottage St. ℂ **207/288-0447.** Reservations recommended. Main courses $16–$22. AE, MC, V. May–Dec daily 6–10pm; Jan–Apr closed Mon–Tues.

Michelle's ⭑ FRENCH   Michelle's is located in the graceful Ivy Manor Inn (see review earlier in the chapter), and it caught the attention of the state's epicures when it opened in 1997. The three dining rooms are elegant and set out with fresh roses and candles (there's outside seating when the weather's good). The extensive menu elaborates on traditional French cuisine with subtle New England twists. The appetizers include smoked salmon layered with a chervil mousse, and foie gras with black truffle. Main courses are elaborate affairs, with dishes like chateaubriand for two carved at the table, roasted lobster in basil cream sauce, rack of lamb, and Michelle's bouillabaisse for two, which includes lobster, mussels, clams, scallops and the fresh catch of the day. (Appropriately for Bar Harbor, the seafood selection is extensive.) Finish with the unique "bag of chocolate," which comes served in an edible chocolate bag, or one of several outstanding soufflés.

194 Main St. ℂ **207/288-0038.** Reservations required during peak season. Main courses $26–$34. AE, DISC, MC, V. Daily 6–9pm. Closed late Oct to early May.

MODERATE

Café This Way ⭑ NEW AMERICAN   This is the kind of place where they know how to do wonderful things with relatively simple ingredients. Café This Way has the feel of a casually hip coffee house and is much more airy than one might guess upon first looking at this cozy cottage tucked on a side street down from the village green. Bookshelves line one wall, and there's a small bar tucked in a nook. Unusually, they serve breakfast and dinner but no lunch. The breakfasts are excellent and mildly sinful—it's more like an everyday brunch—with offerings such as eggs Benedict with spinach, artichoke, and tomato, big breakfast burritos, and a range of omelets. The red-skinned potatoes are crispy and delicious; the robust coffee requires two creamers to lighten it. Dinners are equally appetizing, with tasty starters that might run to a spicy Portuguese stew of mussels and sausages or a small flat-bread pizza of pears and blue cheese, followed by main courses such as lemon-vodka lobster cooked in Absolut citron, a Thai seafood pot, grilled tuna served with apples and smoked shrimp, corn-crusted fish, "east-west" duck, maple salmon, or grilled and peppered lamb chops.

14½ Mount Desert St. ℂ **207/288-4483.** www.cafethisway.com. Reservations recommended for dinner. Main courses breakfast $4.95–$7.50; dinner $13–$23. MC, V. Mid-Apr to Oct Mon–Sat 7–11am; Sun 8am–1pm; dinner daily 6–9pm.

Eden Vegetarian Café ⭑ *Finds* VEGETARIAN   Have you ever seen a vegetarian restaurant where people dress up for dinner? Right across the street from the bay, chef Mark Rampacek operates Bar Harbor's only vegetarian eatery, bringing high culinary flair and atmosphere to the cause; most dishes here use organic and/or locally grown ingredients, and you'll even possibly want to dress up a bit if you dine here. The changing daily menu could include lunches of faux tuna salad, a Thai salad of tofu, coconut, and vegetables, vegan mac-and-"cheese," grapefruit gazpacho, or chickpea burritos. Dinners are more elaborate, beginning with starters such as roasted fig bruschetta, seared crablike vegetable cakes, ratatouille-stuffed mushroom caps, fresh local salads, or a beet tartare with capers and a delicate arrangement of 'stained glass' potato. The main course might be a bento box of tofu, edamame, seaweed salad, and the like; grilled vegetables, tempeh, or seitan; roasted portobello mushroom with polenta cake; or bright red lentil dal paired with eggplant. For dessert, try chocolate fondue for two, dairy-free ice cream with caramel and coconut, or sponge cake with lemon curd and blueberries. There's a full range of coffees and teas, and a full bar.

78 West St. ✆ **207/288-4422**. www.barharborvegetarian.com. Reservations strongly recommended. Main courses $9–$17. MC, V. Apr–Sept Mon–Sat 11am–9:30pm; Oct–Nov Mon–Sat 5–9pm. Closed Dec–Mar.

Maggie's Restaurant ⋆ SEAFOOD   The slogan for Maggie's is "Notably fresh seafood," and the place invariably delivers on that understated promise. (Only locally caught fish is used.) It's a casually elegant spot tucked off Cottage Street, good for a romantic evening with soothing music and attentive service. Appetizers include smoked salmon, lobster spring rolls, and steamed oysters with a saffron hollandaise. Main courses range from basic boiled lobster and simple grilled salmon to more innovative offerings like Maine seafood Provençal, and sautéed halibut with lime butter and heirloom beans. The place now also offers steak, but finned creatures remain the prime attraction here. Desserts, which include apple crepes with cinnamon ice cream, Maine blueberry pie, and the island's best array of sundaes—including everything from peach with praline sauce and pecans to white chocolate ice cream with almond crumbles, are home-made and worth leaving room for.

6 Summer St. ✆ **207/288-9007**. Reservations recommended July–Aug. Main courses $16–$24. DISC, MC, V. Mon–Sat 5–9:30pm; closed mid-Oct to mid-June.

INEXPENSIVE

Jordan's Restaurant (Value) DINER   This unpretentious breakfast and lunch joint has been dishing up filling fare since 1976, and it offers a glimpse of old Bar Harbor before the local economy was dominated by T-shirt shops. It's a popular haunt of working folks in town on one errand or another, but the staff is also genuinely friendly to tourists. (Still, with its atmosphere of senior citizens at coffee klatch and rock-bottom prices, this is not a gourmet experience.) Diners can settle into one of the pine booths or at a laminated table and order off the placemat menu, choosing from basic fare like grilled cheese with tomato or a slight but serviceable hamburger. The soups and chowders are all homemade. Breakfast is the specialty here, with a broad selection of three-egg omelets, along with muffins and pancakes made with wild Maine blueberries.

80 Cottage St. ✆ **207/288-3586**. Breakfast $2.95–$6.75; lunch $2.25–$8.25. MC, V. Daily 4:30am–2pm. Closed Feb–Mar.

Lompoc Cafe and Brewpub AMERICAN/ECLECTIC   The Lompoc Cafe has a well-worn, neighborhood bar feel to it—little wonder, since waiters and other workers from around Bar Harbor congregate here after hours. The cafe consists of three sections—there's the original bar, a tidy beer garden just outside (try your hand at bocce), and a small and open barnlike structure at the garden's edge to handle the overflow. The brewery next door produces several unique beers, including a blueberry ale (intriguing concept, but ask for a sample before ordering a full glass) and the smooth Coal Porter, available in sizes up to the 20-ounce "fatty." Bar menus are usually yawn-inducing, but this one has some pleasant surprises, like the Persian plate (hummus and grape leaves), Szechuan eggplant wrap, and crab and shrimp cakes. Vegetarians will also find a decent selection. Alas, the kitchen's executions don't always live up to its aspirations. Live music is offered some evenings, when there's a small cover charge.

36 Rodick St. ✆ **207/288-9392**. www.lompoccafe.com. Reservations not accepted. Sandwiches $4.25–$14; dinner items $8.50–$19. MC, V. May–Nov daily 11:30am–1am. Closed Dec–Apr.

SHOPPING

Bar Harbor is full of boutiques and souvenir shops along two intersecting commercial streets, Main Street and Cottage Street. Many proffer the expected T-shirt and coffee-mug offerings—the stuff that crops up wherever tourists congregate—but look a little harder and you'll find some original items for sale.

Business hours are generally 10am to 6pm for most retail stores, but individual store hours may vary. Many stores stay open later in summer. Always call ahead before heading out.

Bar Harbor Hemporium   The Hemporium is dedicated to promoting products made from hemp, an environmentally friendly (and nonpsychoactive) fibrous plant that can be used in making paper, clothing, and more. There's some interesting stuff. 116 Main St. ℂ 207/288-3014. www.barharborhemp.com.

Cadillac Mountain Sports   Sleeping bags, backpacks, outdoor clothing, and hiking boots are found at this shop, which caters to the ragged wool and fleece set. There's a good selection of hiking and travel guides to the island. 26 Cottage St. ℂ 207/288-4532. www.cadillacmountain.com.

In the Woods   Wood products from Maine are the focus here, with items including—in addition to bowls and cutting boards—children's games and puzzles, peg coat racks, and spice racks. 160 Main St. ℂ 207/288-4519.

Island Artisans   This is the place to browse for products of local and Maine craftspeople. Products are mostly of the size you can bring home in a knapsack, and include tiles, sweetgrass baskets, pottery, jewelry, and soaps. There's a second location in Northeast Harbor. 99 Main St. ℂ 207/288-4214. www.islandartisans.com.

RainWise   Bar Harbor–based RainWise manufactures reliable weather stations for the serious hobbyist. Its factory store, located off Cottage Street, sells the firm's products, plus a variety of third-party thermometers and barometers. 25 Federal St. ℂ 800/762-5723 or 207/288-5169. www.rainwise.com.

5 Elsewhere on Mount Desert Island ★★

There's plenty to explore outside of Acadia National Park and Bar Harbor. Quiet fishing villages, deep woodlands, and unexpected ocean views are among the jewels that turn up when one peers beyond the usual places.

ESSENTIALS
GETTING AROUND

The east half of the island is best navigated on Route 3, which forms the better part of a loop from Bar Harbor through Seal Harbor and past Northeast Harbor before returning up the eastern shore of Somes Sound. Route 102 and Route 102A provide access to the island's western half. See information on the free island-wide shuttle service in "Getting Around" in the section on Acadia National Park, earlier in this chapter.

VISITOR INFORMATION

The best source of information on the island is at the **Thompson Island Information Center** (ℂ 207/288-3411), on Route 3 just south of the causeway connecting Mount Desert Island with the mainland (see above). Another source of local information is the **Mount Desert Chamber of Commerce,** P.O. Box 675, Northeast Harbor, ME 04662 (ℂ 207/276-5040).

EXPLORING THE REST OF THE ISLAND

On the tip of the eastern lobe of Mount Desert Island is the staid, prosperous community of **Northeast Harbor** ☆, long one of the favored retreats among the Eastern Seaboard's upper crust. Those without personal invitations to come as house guests will need to be satisfied with glimpses of the shingled palaces set in the fragrant spruce forests and along the rocky shore. But the village itself is worth investigating. Situated on a scenic, narrow harbor, with the once-grand Asticou Inn at its head, Northeast Harbor is possessed of a refined sense of elegance that's best appreciated by finding a vantage point and then sitting and admiring.

One of the best, least publicized places for enjoying views of the harbor is from the understatedly spectacular **Asticou Terraces** ☆. Finding the parking lot can be tricky: Head a half-mile east (toward Seal Harbor) on Route 3 from the junction with Route 198, and look for the small gravel lot on the water side of the road with a sign reading ASTICOU TERRACES. Park here, cross the road on foot, and set off up a magnificent path made of local rock that ascends the sheer hillside, with expanding views of the harbor and the town. This pathway, with its precise stonework and the occasional bench and gazebo, is one of the nation's hidden marvels of landscape architecture. Created by Boston landscape architect Joseph Curtis, who summered here for many years prior to his death in 1928, the pathway seems to blend in almost preternaturally with its spruce-and-fir surroundings, as if it were created by an act of God rather than of man. Curtis donated the property to the public for quiet enjoyment.

Continue on the trail at the top of the hillside, and you'll soon arrive at Curtis's cabin (open to the public daily in summer), behind which lies the formal **Thuya Gardens,** which are as manicured as the terraces are natural. These wonderfully maintained gardens, designed by noted landscape architect Charles K. Savage, attract flower enthusiasts, students of landscape architecture, and local folks looking for a quiet place to rest. It's well worth the trip. A small donation of a few dollars is requested of visitors to the garden; admission to the terraces is free.

From the harbor, visitors can depart on a seaward trip to the beguilingly remote **Cranberry Islands** ☆. You have a couple of options: Either travel with a national park guide to Baker Island, the most distant of this small cluster of low islands, and explore the natural terrain; or hop one of the ferries to either Great or Little Cranberry Island and explore on your own. On Little Cranberry, there's a small historical museum run by the National Park Service that's worth a few minutes. Both islands feature a sense of being well away from it all, but neither offers much in the way of shelter or tourist amenities, so travelers should head out prepared for the possibility of shifting weather. For ferry information, contact **Beal & Bunker** (© **207/244-3575**), which runs about a half-dozen boats out to the islands each day in peak summer season from Northeast Harbor. The cost is $14 round-trip for adults, $7 for children ages 3 to 12, $5 per bike; if you're going, be sure to check the schedule and ensure that you don't miss the last ferry back to Mount Desert.

When leaving Northeast Harbor, plan to drive out via **Sargent Drive** ☆☆. This one-way route runs through Acadia National Park along the shore of Somes Sound, affording superb views of this glacially carved inlet.

On the far side of Somes Sound, there's good hiking (see above) and the towns of Southwest Harbor and Bass Harbor. These are both home to fishermen and boatbuilders and are rather more humble than the settlements of the landed gentry at Northeast and Seal harbors across the way.

In Southwest Harbor, look for the intriguing **Wendell Gilley Museum of Bird Carving** (© 207/244-7555), on Route 102 just north of town. Housed in a new building constructed specifically to display the woodcarvings, the museum contains the masterwork of Wendell Gilley, a plumber who took up carving birds as a hobby in 1930. His creations, ranging from regal bald eagles to delicate chickadees, are startlingly lifelike and beautiful. The museum offers woodcarving classes for those inspired by the displays, and a gift shop sells fine woodcarving. It's open Tuesday to Sunday 10am to 4pm June to October, Friday to Sunday in May, November, and December. The museum is closed January to April. Admission is $5 adults, $2 children 5 to 12.

WHERE TO STAY

Asticou Inn ⋆   The once-grand Asticou Inn, which dates from 1883, occupies a prime location at the head of Northeast Harbor. Its weathered gray shingles and profusion of overhanging eaves give it a stern demeanor, but it also has elements of eccentricity. The Asticou is more elegant on the exterior and in its location than in the interior, although renovations in 1999 spruced things up a bit. Despite some incipient shabbiness, a wonderful old-world gentility seems to arise from the creaking floorboards and through the thin guest room walls. The rooms are furnished in a simple summer-home style, as if a more opulent decor was somehow too ostentatious. Recent wholesale changes have improved the dining room, where longtime guests had noted a decline in quality. The dinner dance and elaborate "grand buffet" on Thursday nights in summer remain hallowed island traditions and worth checking out. (Expect smoked seafood, lobster Newburg, salads and relishes, a dessert tray, and more.) Seatings are on the hour; jackets are requested for men in the evening.

Rte. 3, Northeast Harbor, ME 04662. © 800/258-3373 or 207/276-3344. www.asticou.com. 41 units, 2 cottages. Late May to June $130–$180 double, $160–$200 suite; July–Aug $225–$285 double, $220–$325 suite; Sept to mid-Oct $155–$215 double, $175–$230 suite. Rates include breakfast; MAP plans available July–Aug only. MC, V. Valet parking. Closed mid-Oct to late-May. Children 6 and older welcome. **Amenities:** Outdoor pool; tennis court; concierge; business center; limited room service; babysitting; laundry; Thurs dances.

Claremont ⋆   Early prints of the 1884 Claremont show an austere four-story wooden building with a single gable overlooking Somes Sound from a grassy rise. And the place hasn't changed all that much since. The Claremont offers nothing fancy or elaborate—just simple, classic New England grace. It's wildly appropriate that the state's most high-profile and combative croquet tournament takes place here annually in early August; all those folks in their whites seem right at home. The common areas and dining rooms are pleasantly appointed in an affable country style. There's a library with rockers, a fireplace, and jigsaw puzzles waiting to be assembled. Two other fireplaces in the lobby take the chill out of the morning air. Most of the guest rooms are bright and airy, furnished with antiques and some old furniture that doesn't quite qualify as "antique." The bathrooms are modern. Guests opting for the full meal plan at the inn are given preference in reserving rooms overlooking the water; it's almost worth it, although dinners are lackluster. There's also a series of cottages, available for a 3-day minimum—some are set rustically in the piney woods, while others offer pleasing views of the sound. The Claremont's dining room is open nightly, and meals are mainly reprises of American classics like salmon, grilled lamb, and steamed lobster; guests sometimes report being underwhelmed by the fare. The dining room is open to the public; jackets and ties are requested on men.

P.O. Box 137, Southwest Harbor, ME 04679. ℭ **800/244-5036** or 207/244-5036. www.theclaremonthotel.com. 30 inn rooms, 14 cottages. Inn rooms: summer $200–$325 double; spring and fall $125–$250 double. Cottages: mid-June to mid-Sept $180–$250 double; late May to mid-June and mid-Sept to mid-Oct $135–$185 double. Closed mid-Oct to late May. **Amenities:** Dining room; tennis court; bicycles (free to guests); babysitting; croquet; rowboats; library.

Inn at Southwest   There's a decidedly late-19th-century air to this mansard-roofed Victorian home, but it's restrained on the frills. The guest rooms are named after Maine lighthouses and are furnished with both contemporary and antique furniture. All rooms have ceiling fans and down comforters. Among the most pleasant rooms is Blue Hill Bay on the third floor, with its large bathroom, sturdy oak bed and bureau, and glimpses of the scenic harbor. Breakfasts offer ample reason to rise and shine, featuring specialties like vanilla Belgian waffles with raspberry sauce, and crab potato bake.

371 Main St. (P.O. Box 593), Southwest Harbor, ME 04679. ℭ 207/244-3835. www.innatsouthwest.com. 7 units. Late June to mid-Oct $110–$165 double; off-season $75–$135 double. All rates include full breakfast. DISC, MC, V. Closed Nov–Apr. *In room:* No phone.

Lindenwood Inn ★★   The Lindenwood offers a refreshing change from the fusty, overly draperied inns that tend to proliferate along Maine's coast; affable innkeeper Jim King gave up cabinetmaking to open a string of successful B&Bs in Southwest Harbor, and his latest is his best—one of my favorites in Maine. The place feels like you've rented an island home for the summer with a bunch of your friends. Housed in a handsome 1902 Queen Anne–style home at the harbor's edge, the inn has modern and uncluttered rooms, with colors that are simple and bold. Most have balconies, some have fireplaces, and all possess won-derfully comfy mattresses. The adornments are few (those that do exist are mostly from King's wonderful collection of African and Pacific art and artifacts), but clean lines and bright natural light more than create a relaxing mood—you'll even begin to view the cobblestone doorstops as works of art. The spacious suite with its great harbor views is especially appealing, featuring a deck, a cathedral ceiling, and a Jacuzzi. Breakfasts of French toast or blueberry pancakes are very good, and there's a small bar for a late-night drink. As if you needed it, there's one further reason to stay: This is the closest lodging to Beal's lobster take-out pier (see below).

118 Clark Point Rd. (P.O. Box 1328), Southwest Harbor, ME 04679. ℭ **800/307-5335** or 207/244-5335. www.lindenwoodinn.com. 8 units, 1 bungalow. Mid-June to mid-Oct $105–$275 double; mid-Oct to mid-June $95–$225 double. Rates include full breakfast. AE, MC, V. **Amenities:** Bar; outdoor pool; Jacuzzi. *In room:* Kitchenette (some), fireplace (some), Jacuzzi (1).

WHERE TO DINE

Ten years ago, there were virtually no serious dining options anywhere on the quiet side of Mount Desert Island. All that has changed. From fits and starts in the mid-'90s, Southwest Harbor has gradually become the sort of place where one can eat a bistro meal, buy a bottle of quality wine for a picnic, or go whole-hog and have an (almost) Manhattanesque meal.

The current big three include Red Sky, Fiddlers' Green, and Seaweed Café (see below for details on all of them). There's also the **Café Drydock** at 357 Main St. (ℭ **207/244-5842**), with an extensive seafood menu, landlubber-friendly lunch and dinner options such as pasta, burgers, and salads, and a Sun-day brunch.

Should you tire of eating both gourmet fare and seafood, fear not. Instead, head for one of several cafés lining the town's main street. The **Quietside Café** (360 Main St.; ℭ **207/244-9444**) serves inexpensive club sandwiches and ice cream cones. The **Little Notch Café** (340 Main St.; ⓒ **207/244-3357**), an offshoot of a nearby bakery, makes gourmet sandwiches on its own bread in the vein of grilled chicken in focaccia with onions and aioli, prosciutto with Asiago and roasted peppers on an onion roll, and grilled flank steak on a baguette. The pizzas are also quite good. **Eat-A-Pita** (326 Main St.; ⓒ **207/244-4344**) serves pitas, salads, and egg dishes.

In Bass Harbor and Bernard, a few miles south of Southwest Harbor, head for outstanding lobsters at Thurston's (see below) or fill up on seafood from **Freya's** (ⓒ **207/244-9404**) or the **Seafood Ketch** (ⓒ **207/244-7463**). Both do standard surfs and turfs.

For a quick bite or a picnic lunch to go in Northeast Harbor, don't overlook the informal **Docksider Restaurant,** hidden a block off the main commercial drag at 14 Sea St. (ⓒ **207/276-3965**). The crab rolls and lobster rolls are outstanding, made simply and perfectly. The small restaurant also features a host of other fare, including lobster dinners, sandwiches, chowder, fried seafood, and grilled salmon.

Beal's Lobster Pound *(Finds)* LOBSTER POUND   Purists claim this is among the best lobster shacks in Maine. It's certainly got the atmo down: Creaky picnic tables on a plain deck, overlooking a working-class harbor and right next to the Coast Guard base. Don't wear a tie. You go inside to pick out and order your lobster from tanks (pay by the pound), then choose sides (corn on the cob, slaw, steamed clams—the usuals—are good), then wait eagerly for your number to be called. There are absolutely no pretensions here; your meal will arrive on Styrofoam or paper plates, but you won't care a bit. There's also a takeout window across the deck serving fried fare such as fries, clams, and fish boats, as well as chowder (it's only so-so) and ice cream.

182 Clark Point Rd., Southwest Harbor. ⓒ 207/244-7178 or 207/244-3202. www.bealslobster.com. Lobsters market price. AE, DISC, MC, V. Summer daily 9am–8pm; after Labor Day 9am–5pm. Closed Columbus Day to Memorial Day.

The Burning Tree ★★ *(Finds)* REGIONAL/ORGANIC   Located on busy Route 3 between Bar Harbor and Northeast Harbor, The Burning Tree is an easy restaurant to speed right by. But that's a mistake. This low-key restaurant, with its bright, open, and sometimes noisy dining room, serves up the freshest food in the area. Much of the produce and herbs comes from its own gardens, with the rest of the ingredients supplied locally whenever possible. Seafood is the specialty here, and it's consistently prepared with imagination and skill. The menu changes often to reflect local availability.

Rte. 3, Otter Creek. ⓒ 207/288-9331. Reservations recommended. Main courses $18–$23. DISC, MC, V. Mid-June to Columbus Day Wed–Mon 5–9pm. Closed Columbus Day to mid-June.

Fiddlers' Green ★ CREATIVE AMERICAN/SEAFOOD   Derek Wilbur's bistro is certainly something different in these parts, and very welcome indeed. Begin with something from the cold seafood bar: smoked salmon wrapped in gravlax and horseradished chèvre, oysters on the half shell, or Wilbur's unique "sashimi martini," a cup of smoked mussels, scallop ceviche, and raw tuna in a pear-tahini marinade. Alternately, you could begin with mussels steamed in Guinness beer, crab cakes with a honey mango sauce, or skewers of beef with Chinese herbs and sided with a Thai-style relish. There are always a few good pasta dishes on the menu, such as penne with merguez and mushrooms or farfalle with lemon and artichokes. Meatier main dishes offered nightly could include scallops, spicy salmon served with crab, lightly seared yellowfin tuna, steamed lobster, steak frites, a bacon-wrapped saddle of rabbit, and venison chops. Martini drinkers should take special note: Wilbur's bar serves a dozen classic versions and nine rather more obscure versions of the drink, such as one created for Miles Davis in 1949 and another featuring Absolut Currant vodka. Careful if you order the Ancient Martini (vodka, Gran Marnier, and a twist of orange): "After a couple," the menu reads, "you're history."

411 Main St., Southwest Harbor. ⓒ 207/244-9416. Reservations recommended. Main courses $18–$25. AE, DISC, MC, V. Tues–Sun 5:30–9pm. Closed Columbus Day to Memorial Day.

Red Sky ★★ CREATIVE AMERICAN   Terry Preble closed his former Preble Grill but, after a spell, reopened right off Southwest Harbor's main drag; like the other two gourmet restaurants in the area, it brings a big-city sensibility to the island last seen in Midtown Manhattan. Meals begin with intriguing starters such as carrot-red curry soup, "lollipop" lamb chops dusted with bitter chocolate and minty vinaigrette, shrimp dumplings, scallion crepes, or house-fashioned duck-and-pork sausages served with dipping sauces. Main courses run to lobster risotto with asparagus and porcini mushrooms, strip steak served with blue cheese, panko-crusted sea scallops in tamari sauce, or a simple pan-roasted breast of duck served with a plum wine demiglace. There's also a cheese course and a full dessert selection.

14 Clark Point Rd., Southwest Harbor. ⓒ 207/244-0476. Entrees $16–$25. AE, DISC, MC, V. Thurs–Mon 5:30–9pm.

Seaweed Café ★★ CREATIVE AMERICAN/SEAFOOD   Chef Bill Morrison, formerly a personal chef to Don Johnson and Melanie Griffith, opened this Asian-inflected seafood eatery just outside "downtown" Manset. Though it's an unlikely location for gourmet fare, so far the reviews are nearly all raves. Many diners begin with sushi: a lobster inside-out roll, smoked trout, Maine crab and avocado, and the like. Others begin with lamb skewers, scallop ceviche, or Thai mussels soaked in sake. Then follow with lobster-meat maki rolls, lightly seared yellowfin tuna, pan-fried noodles, a Szechuan-style stir-fry, or an entree of gingered lobster, Georgian-style chicken tabaka, or monkfish medallions braised in a spicy Burmese both.

146 Seawall Rd., Manset. ⓒ 207/244-0572. Entrees $13–$21; lobster dishes market price. MC, V. Daily 5:30–9pm. Closed Jan–Apr. From Southwest Harbor, follow Rte. 102 south 1 mile and turn left onto Rte. 102A at sign for Manset. Restaurant is on right.

Thurston's Lobster Pound ★ Finds LOBSTER POUND   Right off the end of a dock (the same place they load the lobsters up), Thurston's possesses all three key requirements of a great Maine lobster shack: one, a great view of Bass Harbor and its fishing boats, two, great lobster and side dishes at reasonable prices, and three, an unpretentious vibe blended with a dash of friendly sass. It's like a place out of the movies. The lobsters come quickly, their claws precracked for easier access; the corn on the cob is perfectly cooked; scallop chowder, crunchy crab cakes, and bags of steamed mussels and clams all provide toothsome sides; and the "plain dinner" option (five bucks extra) finishes with a wonderfully eggy cinnamon-blueberry cake. There are two decks, upstairs and down—and a convivial atmosphere pervades at both, as perfect strangers break the ice over crustaceans. This place is a true Maine classic.

Steamboat Wharf Rd. (at the docks), Bernard. ⓒ 207/244-7600. Lobsters market price. MC, V. Memorial Day to Labor Day daily 11am–8:30pm.

9

The Downeast Coast

The term *Downeast* comes from the old sailing ship days. Ships heading east had the prevailing winds at their backs, making it an easy "downhill" run to the eastern ports. Heading the other way took more skill and determination.

Today it's a rare traveler who gets far Downeast to explore the rugged coastline of Washington County. Few tourists venture beyond Acadia National Park, discouraged perhaps by the lack of services for visitors and the low number of high-marquee attractions. They might also be creeped out by the sometimes spooky remoteness of the region. But Downeast Maine has substantial appeal. There's an authenticity that's been lost in much of coastal Maine and is only a distant memory in the rest of New England. Many long-time visitors to the state say that this is how all of Maine used to be back in the 1940s and 1950s, when writer E. B. White first arrived. *Pad Thai,* the *New York Times,* and designer coffee have not yet crossed the border into Washington County. Those seeking a glimpse of a rugged, hardscrabble way of life where independence is revered above all else aren't likely to go away disappointed.

Many residents still get by as their forebears did—by scratching a living from the land. Scalloping, lobstering, and fishing remain major sources of income, as do logging and other forest work. Grubbing for bloodworms in spring, picking wild blueberries in the barrens in late summer, and tipping fir trees for wreath making in late fall round out the income. In recent years, aquaculture has become an important part of the economy around Passamaquoddy and Cobscook bays; travelers will see vast floating pens, especially around Eastport and Lubec, where salmon are raised for markets worldwide.

As I said, the geographical isolation of this region means that not many tourists make it this far north—most have long since been waylaid by the charms of Kennebunkport, Portland, Camden, Acadia National Park, and the like. But if you're hoping to get a peek at the *real* Maine, the Maine beyond the tourist chintz, you'd be wise to make a trip here for at least a day or two. You might never view Maine the same way again.

1 Essentials

GETTING THERE
Downeast Maine is most commonly reached via Route 1 from Ellsworth. Those heading directly to Washington County in summer can take a more direct, less congested route via Route 9 from Brewer (across the river from Bangor), connecting south to Route 1 via Routes 193 or 192.

VISITOR INFORMATION
For information on the Machias area or other parts of Downeast Maine, visitors should check in with the **Machias Bay Area Chamber of Commerce,** 12 E. Main

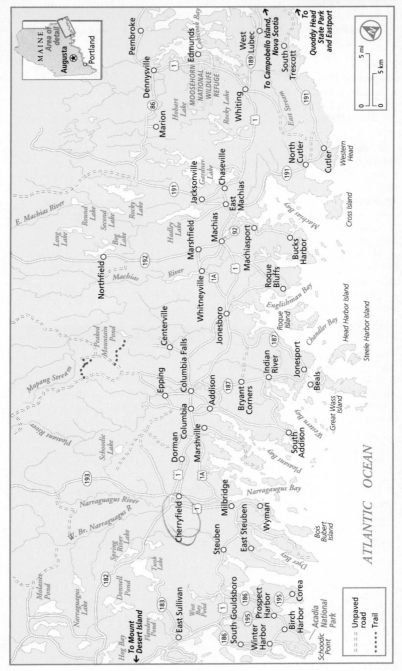

St. (P.O. Box 606), Machias, ME 04654 (© **800/377-9748** or 207/255-4402; www.machiaschamber.org). They provide tourist information from their offices at 23 E. Main St. (Rte. 1), and are open weekdays from 10am to 3pm.

EVENTS

Eastport celebrates the **Fourth of July** in extravagant hometown style each year, a tradition that began in 1820 after the British gave up possession of the city (they captured it during the War of 1812). Some 15,000 people come to this city of 1,900 during the 4-day event, which includes vendors, games, and contests, and culminates with a grand parade on the afternoon of the Fourth.

The popular **Machias Wild Blueberry Festival** ⍟, operated by the local Congregation Church, celebrates the local cash crop each summer. Washington County claims to produce an astonishing 85% of the world's blueberry crop, so there's bound to be some for the tasting when you show up. The festivities begin Friday with a children's parade and fish fry, continue with a Saturday blueberry pancake breakfast (of course!) and road race, then motor along through lobster feeds, the raffling of a blueberry quilt, a book sale, and—the highlight, perhaps—a blueberry pie-eating contest. There are also performances and the sales of blueberry-theme gift items. Stamp collectors should plan to drop by the Machias Post office for special-issue cancellation stamps, uniquely themed to blueberries each year.

Contact the local chamber of commerce (© **207/255-4402**) for the exact dates of the festival; usually it takes place in late August.

2 Enjoying the Great Outdoors

There are several good tour outfitters and boat tour operators in these parts, offering everything from kayak day trips to whale watches.

Bold Coast Charter Co. ⍟ (© **207/259-4484;** www.boldcoast.com) captain Andrew Patterson operates cruises out of little Cutler harbor to Machias Seal Island, May through August, and Cross Island from May through October. Patterson's 40-foot *Barbara Frost* tour boat sometimes lights ashore, sometimes doesn't, but in either case close-up viewing of puffins and razorbills on Machias Seal Island (which is claimed by both Canada and the U.S. as territory, no resolution in sight) is all but guaranteed. You might see Arctic terns, petrels, seals, eagles, or porpoises en route to or in the vicinity of Cross Island, as well, which is also a noted bird and wildlife refuge; Patterson even makes occasional trips past Libby Island and its lighthouse. The 5-hour bird-watching tours leave around 7 or 8am and cost $60 per person; remember that many birds will have headed south by Labor Day. Board at Cutler's little boat ramp on the harbor.

Machias Bay Boat Tours and Sea Kayaking (© **207/259-3338;** www. machiasbay.com) on Cutler Road in Machiasport, offers both kayaking tours of the coastline and boat cruises around Machias Bay aboard a 34-foot working lobster boat, the *Martha Ann.* You may spot seals or whales, and you'll definitely spy seabirds and lobsters as the traps are pulled up by hand from the deep. Ask the captain about making a cruise past the old Libby Island Lighthouse, the local islands—some of which hold nesting populations of bald eagles and osprey, others home to pastures of grazing sheep—and the famed Machias Bay petroglyphs, several-thousand-year-old stone carvings scattered in several locations around the bay.

Mooselook Guide Service (© **207/963-7720;** www.mooselookguideservice. com) at 761 South Gouldsboro Rd. (Rte. 186) in South Gouldsboro also operates kayak, canoe, cycling, and other tours of the Downeast region. Contact the service for further details of tour itineraries and rates.

3 Exploring Downeast Maine

Ellsworth is 27 miles SE of Bangor.

The best way to see this area—the only way, really—is to simply drive Route 1 and a few associated back roads and shortcuts north from Ellsworth all the way to the Canadian border and then beyond, if you fancy it.

ELLSWORTH TO MACHIAS

Ellsworth doesn't get much due from travelers hell-bent on making it to Mount Desert Island by dinnertime, but those in the know are increasingly stopping to partake of a town that has significantly expanded its cultural offerings. In fact, though it seems pedestrian and overcommercialized—the town's Main Street was long ago usurped by Route 1, lending it a chaotic air out of step with Ellsworth's actual character—the community gives Bar Harbor a serious run for the title of Downeast arts capital.

The town was first settled by Passamaquoddy and Penobscot tribes; later, French woodsmen explored the area, and the British inevitably followed with bridges, sawmills, and ships on the Union River. By the late 19th century, Ellsworth had become both a significant port of departure for lumber cut from the big Maine woods and an important shipbuilding center. Those industries soon faded away, but Ellsworth swiftly reinvented itself as tourist's jumping-off point—playing off its proximity of Mount Desert Island—and arts center, capitalizing on the concentration of artists and musicians attracted to its concentration of services and closeness to genuine wilderness.

Traveling north from Ellsworth, it's about 13 miles to prettily situated **Sullivan** on a rise overlooking Frenchman's Bay. The town was briefly home to a mini gold rush, but today is little more than a quiet fishing village consisting mostly of a general store. Sullivan is also home to an intriguing combination smokehouse/rental cottage operation where you can buy smoked fish for picnics (see "Where to Stay & Dine," later in this chapter).

It's 8 miles farther on Route 1 to **Gouldsboro,** which is actually a series of five villages. The area contains a handful of accommodations. For a look at genuine fishing villages, strike south off Route 1 down Rte. 186 to Winter Harbor, Prospect Harbor, and Corea. And absolutely do not miss Schoodic Point, at the end of the road (see below); it's a disconnected sliver of Acadia National Park, and a fine spot for dramatic photographs of surf crashing over big rocks.

Continue north 10 more miles to **Milbridge,** a former shipbuilding town, the little **Milbridge Historical Museum** (see later in this chapter) captures some of the local history; as recently as 1983 a boat was built and launched here.

From here, it's shorter to cut north along Route 1A, but if you do so you'll miss quaint Cherryfield. The **Cherryfield-Narraguargus Historical Society** (© **207/546-7979**), housed right on Main Street in Cherryfield, maintains its own small museum of tools, 19th-century home items, photographs, and genealogical collections. It's open in July and August only, Wednesdays and Fridays from 1 to 4pm.

Five more miles to the north, the center of tiny **Columbia Falls** (pop. 560) retains its longtime charm thanks to the good fortune of having been bypassed by Route 1; if you're stopping here to visit the historic **Ruggles House** (see later in this chapter), also check out April Adams' excellent **Columbia Falls Pottery** shop (© **800/235-2512** or 207/483-2905) in the restored schoolhouse next door, looking over nature-inspired designs such as Lupine, Blueberry, Flag Iris, and Lady's-Slipper.

Just north of Columbia Falls, detour south along Route 187 (it makes a complete loop of the peninsula) to the end of the point, where you come to **Jonesport,** a photogenic, lost-in-time fishing village dominated by the lobster trade and boat work. Beyond the pretty village and the dramatic local tides, you'll also find—should you venture offshore—some of the largest puffin colonies in the world. July 4th is a surprisingly big deal here, featuring an impressive little parade, games, food, fireworks, and lobster boats racing in the harbor.

Jonesport is the jumping-off point for the nature preserve on Great Wass Island (see later in this chapter), too, as well as some puffin tour operators. **Barna and John Norton** run boat tours to Machias Seal Island (and its colony of 3,000-plus puffins) out of Jonseport aboard the *Chief;* call © **207/497-5933** for details of the tours, which cost $50 per person.

Rejoin Route 1 at **Jonesboro,** from which you can sally eastward once again —down unnumbered highways—to find remote and scenic Roque Bluffs State Park (see later in this chapter), a good place to go swimming in both saltwater and freshwater pools.

MACHIAS
Machias is about 90 miles E of Bangor and 64 miles E of Ellsworth.

Back on Route 1, continue 10 or so more miles north to the trim market town of **Machias** (mah-*chy*-us)—the county seat and only town of size in Washington County. Its year-round population of 2,400 seems positively Manhattanesque around here, and a University of Maine satellite campus has attracted the requisite (and welcome) clutch of coffee shops, galleries, and other trappings of outside culture that a college town brings. Its name is a native word translating approximately to "Bad Little Falls," in tribute to the rough meeting place of river and coast originally settled by Native Americans as a fishing camp.

Early explorers used the same river mouth as a trade port, though true colonial settlement of the town waited until 1763. The river became the site of the Revolutionary War's first naval battle on June 12, 1775, when locals here turned back the British gunboat the *Margaretta,* a story told today at the Burnham Tavern (see below).

Downtown Machias possesses a surprising number of historic structures. The **George Foster House** and Andrew Gilson House on North Street both display distinctive mansards, while Court Street is also packed with historic structures: Machias' town offices are housed inside an Italianate former schoolhouse, the **Clark Perry House** has peaked lintels, and the granite **Porter Memorial Library** incorporates ballast and andirons from the *Margaretta.* The **Carrie Albee House** is a Victorian dating from 1900 at the corner of West and Court streets. If you're a church buff, check out the stained glass and organ inside the **Center Street Congregational Church** at Center and Court streets. The gorgeous stained glass windows date from 1899, using state-of-the-art (at the time) opalescent and drapery glass. The organ was installed in 1867 by noted Boston organ builder George Stevens. It's open daily except Saturdays, 2 to 5pm though no formal tours are given.

Just outside town, on Route 92 in **Machiasport,** the **Gates House Museum** (© **207/255-8461**)—riverside home to the Machiasport Historical Society— also functions as a small local museum. It's open June to August, Tuesday to Sunday 12:30 to 4:30pm.

MACHIAS TO EASTPORT

Just north of Machias, be sure to detour south and east on Route 191 to find **Cutler** (pop. 400), an attractive small harbor village once actively devoted to shipbuilding but now a sleepy place of lobster boats and enormous salmon farms. The coastal scenery north of the village, known as the **Bold Coast**—and it is—makes for an impressive drive or hike (see below).

In addition to being the home of a former navy base (see box), Cutler is a good place to shove off for **whale-watching cruises,** some of which also take in rare seabirds and basking seals.

Back on Route 1, you pass through nondescript **Whiting,** one entry point to the easternmost national wildlife refuge on the Atlantic migration corridor. **Moosehorn National Wildlife Refuge** was created back in 1937 with proceeds from President Teddy Roosevelt's Duck Stamp program; it is one of America's oldest such refuges, and home to eagles, osprey, and the unusual woodcock and its remarkable courtship flights. Cycling, skiing, hiking, and leashed pets are allowed on the refuge roads, though not in the wildlife areas; there are more than 50 miles of trails, plus observation decks for watching some of the many birds here. Tours are often given in summer. Note that the refuge consists of *two* disjoined chunks of land—one here along Cobscook Bay on Route 1 between Dennysville and Whiting, the other to the southwest of Calais.

If you continue north along Route 1, north of Dennysville you cross Cobscook Bay at **Pembroke** (once the site of an ironworks) and an unusual reversing falls; the direction of the river—actually a tidal inlet—and the falls reverses direction twice each day, depending on the prevailing tides. From here to French-inflected **Calais,** there are only tiny towns along Cobscook Bay and the St. Croix River. Calais is connected by bridge to St. Stephen, New Brunswick (with a chocolate factory and museum worth checking out); proceed here if you're planning to visit lovely St. Andrews or seafaring Grand Manan island, both described in chapter 10.

If you plan to confine your explorations to American soil, however, split off Route 1 at Routes 189 or 190, where you'll discover charming **Lubec** and **Eastport,** as well as the gateway to Campobello Island and Deer Isle, two lovely slices of New Brunswick also described in the next section.

Lubec is at the end of the line, literally, the northeasternmost community in the United States and one connected by a bridge to Canada. (Locals joke that although this isn't the end of the Earth, you can see it—the end—from here.) The tidal mixing of two bays here proved an ideal environment for fish, and canning and packing plants once filled the town with work and wealth. Today the town is notable chiefly for its vistas of the ocean and offshore lighthouses; set a

Moments Radar Love

Cutler is more than a fishing village; it was once an important Navy communications outpost, its proximity to Europe and northerly location making it ideal for communicating with submarines plying European waters.

Those two dozen or so big antennas poking up above the coast? They're said to make up the most powerful VLF transmitter in the world, and this quiet headland was for years considered a very high-risk target in the event of war. If you're an aficionado of things military, be sure to have a look. However, you should also know that the base's usefulness has greatly diminished in modern times, and the equipment is now operated by civilian personnel; most of the Navy property, located on a scenic peninsula, is now in the process of being redeveloped.

course for Quoddy Head (see later in this chapter) if you crave high tides, early sunrises, and a view that would stretch all the way to Europe and Africa if not for the curve of the Earth.

If Lubec doesn't grab you, get back onto Route 1 and continue north to Perry, a turn down Route 190 takes you to Eastport. First, however, you must traverse the **Pleasant Point Passamaquoddy Indian Reservation,** one of a handful of Maine's native American reservations (**Note to self:** Don't speed as you pass through). The Passamaquoddy tribe, long based here, won a landmark lawsuit in 1981 and received a huge land-and-cash settlement as an award; in exchange, the tribe agreed to drop a series of contentious land claims. There are few tourist facilities here, save a tribal museum (open sporadic hours) and a few souvenir shops.

EASTPORT

Eastport, on a small island across a causeway at the tip of America, was once among the busiest ports on the entire east coast; later, it became a major center for sardine tinning. Today it's a sleepy fishing village rather than a shipping destination, but the historic downtown has lately begun to make itself over as an artsy place of writers, musicians, and other creative types attracted to the slow pace of life and closeness to the sea. (The fishing industry has also reinvented itself: salmon farm pens now fill the near-shore waters.)

The most interesting things here are the growing arts scene, the local historic district (see below), and an honest-to-goodness mustard mill (see below).

Eastport is also very well-known along this part of the coast for its **Fourth of July** celebrations, which run several days and include pie-eating competitions, a flotilla of boats and ships in the harbor, a huge torch-lit parade (Maine's largest), parachutes, pipe bands, and the like. You get the idea: They go over the top here, culminating in impressive (for the town's size) fireworks. The **Eastport Salmon Festival** (© 207/853-4644) takes over town during the third weekend in September.

Though Eastport's rather quiet, the 90-acre peninsula of **Shackford Head State Park** is even quieter; get there by following Route 190 almost into town, then turning right at the gas station and continue almost 1 mile along Deep Cove Road.

Finally, if you're into whirlpools, you've come to the right place. Just north of Eastport is the **Old Sow,** said to be the largest whirlpool in the Western Hemisphere. It's a bit finicky and is impressive only during the highest tides; the best way to see it is to take a seasonal ferry to Deer Island in New Brunswick, Canada (see chapter 10), and back. There's a nominal fee for passengers, and you don't have to go through the Canadian Customs check if you don't want to disembark. The ferry departs from behind the Eastport Fish and Lobster House at 167 Water St.

4 What to See & Do

Below are some of the highlights of the region. The driving time direct from Ellsworth to Lubec via Routes 1 and 189 is about two hours with no stops. Allow considerably more time for visiting the sites mentioned below and just plain snooping around.

Burnham Tavern   In June 1775, a month after the Battle of Lexington in Massachusetts, a group of patriots hatched a plan at the gambrel-roofed Burnham Tavern that led to the first naval battle of the Revolutionary War. The armed schooner *Margaretta* was in Machias harbor to obtain wood for British barracks. The patriots didn't think much of this idea and attacked the ship using much smaller boats they had commandeered, along with muskets, swords, axes, and pitchforks. The patriots prevailed, killing the captain of the *Margaretta* in the process. Visitors can learn all about this episode during a tour of the tavern, which was built on a rise overlooking the river in 1770—it's the oldest existing building in eastern Maine. On display is booty taken from the British ship, along with the original tap table and other historic furniture and ephemera. The tours last around 1 hour.

Main St. (Rte. 192), Machias. © 207/255-4432. Admission $2 adult, 25¢ children. Mid-June to early Sept Mon–Fri 9am–5pm.

Cobscook Bay State Park ★★★   One of Maine's hidden jewels, this state park is an outstanding camping or day-trip destination for the family. Tides flow back and forth across cribworked rocks, exposing deep tidal pools, rocks, and clam-rich mudflats; bird life is also prodigious. There are some 900 acres of trails (cross-country skiable in winter) and tidal exposure in all, and the hundred-plus campsites here include a number of waterside sites.

U.S. Rte. 1 (RR#1, Box 127, Dennysville ME 04628), 4 miles south of Dennysville. © 207/726-4412. Open mid-May to mid-Oct. Admission $3 adults; $1 children 5–11.

Cutler Coastal Trail ★   Marked by a sign at a small parking lot, this dramatic loop trail passes through diverse ecosystems, including bogs, barrens, and dark and tangled spruce forests. But the highlight of this trail, which traverses state-owned land, is the mile-long segment along the rocky headlands high above the restless ocean. Some of the most dramatic coastal views in the state are located along this isolated stretch, which overlooks dark-gray-to-black rocks and an often tumultuous sea. Visible on the horizon across the Bay of Fundy are the west-facing cliffs of the Canadian island of Grand Manan. Plan on at least 2 or 3 hours for the whole loop, although more time spent whiling away the afternoon hours on the rocks is well worth the while. If it's damp or foggy, rain pants are advised to fend off the moisture from the low brush along the trail.

Rte. 191, Cutler. Contact Maine Bureau of Park and Recreation © 207/827-1818. Free admission. Always open. Directions: From the village of Cutler, head NE on Rte. 191; approx. 4½ miles outside of town, look for parking lot and signs on right.

Eastport Historic District In the 1880s, the city of Eastport—3 miles from Lubec by water, but 50 minutes by car—had a population of nearly 5,000 and 18 bustling sardine plants. The population is now less than 2,000, and all the sardine plants are gone. But much of the handsome commercial brick architecture remains on downtown's Water Street, a compact thoroughfare that also affords lovely views of Campobello Island and Passamaquoddy Bay. The majority of the buildings between the post office and the library are on the National Register of Historic Places. Here you'll find the nation's oldest operating ship chandlery (S.L. Wadsworth & Son, 42 Water St.; ⓒ **207/853-4343**).

Water St., Eastport. From Rte. 1 in Perry, take Rte. 190 south for 7 miles.

Great Wass Island Preserve ⭐ This exceptional 1,524-acre parcel, acquired by the Nature Conservancy in 1978, contains an excellent 5-mile loop hike covering a wide cross-section of native terrain, including bogs, heath, rocky coastline, and forests of twisted jack pines. Maps and a birding checklist are found in a stand at the parking lot. Follow one fork of the trail to the shoreline; work your way along the storm-tossed boulders to the other fork, then make your way back to your car. If a heavy fog has settled into the area, as often happens, don't let that deter your hike. The dense mist creates a medieval tableau that makes for magical hiking.

Black Duck Cove Rd., Great Wass Island, Jonesport. Contact Nature Conservancy ⓒ 207/729-5181. Free admission. Open daylight hours. From Jonesport, cross bridge to Beals Island (signs); continue across causeway to Great Wass Island. Bear right at next fork; pavement ends. Continue past lobster pound to a small parking lot on the left marked by Nature Conservancy logo (oak leaf).

Milbridge Historical Museum This low-key museum focuses mostly on shipbuilding and fishing as a local way of life, with exhibits such as "Getting Through the Long Winter," "Old Ways of Fishing," and "Rusticators" (about summer tourists seeking to escape to a more basic way of life here). The displays include vintage photos, shipbuilding tools, and a time capsule filled with items from Downeast Maine.

Main St. (Rte. 1), Milbridge. ⓒ 207/546-4471. Admission free. July–Aug Tues, Sat–Sun 1–4pm; June, Sept Sat–Sun 1–4pm. Oct–Feb by appointment. Closed Mar–May.

New England Museum Of Telephony It's not exactly comprehensive, but the tiny telephone museum here in a barn about 10 miles outside Ellsworth nevertheless makes for a rainy-day diversion as you explore the ins and outs of the hand-crank system that first made it possible to reach out and touch someone in America. Talk to a switchboard operator—the early heroines of the system

---

⌒ *Moments* **Touring Eastport Via the "Woody"**

One of the most distinctive ways to see the town is to take Jim Blankman's "woody" (wood-paneled station bus) tour. Blankman, who works as a coffin maker/woodworker/luthier/salmon smoker when he's not giving tours—people tend to double up around here—bought and restored a 1947 Dodge 1-ton bus from a local family and now runs it around town; the tour includes a picnic lunch of salmon and chicken, and seats a maximum of 11. Contact Blankman's **Moose Island Tour Bus** outfit at ⓒ **207/853-4831** for schedule and fee details.

(my mom was one)—and learn about telephone poles, line, linesmen, switching stations, and how they kept it all running smoothly back in a day where cell phones were just science fiction.

166 Winkumpaugh Rd. (P.O. Box 1377), Ellsworth. © 207/667-9491. http://ellsworthme.org/ringring. Admission $4 adults, $2 children. July–Sept Thurs–Sun 1–4pm. From Rte. 1 in Ellsworth, go 7 miles south on Rte. 1 to Happytown Rd., turn right and continue 6 miles to crossroads. Turn right onto Winkumpaugh Rd. Museum is on left.

Petit Manan National Wildlife Refuge ★★   A series of islands and parcels of land protected as habitat for nesting seabirds and birds of prey. The refuge now includes some 42 islands and three on-shore areas, more than 7,300 acres in all. Here you'll find terns, plovers, bald eagles, puffins, razorbills, storm-petrels, and eiders, among other birds; hiking trails run through forest, marsh, and mudflat habitats; there's even a loop along stony beaches (the Hollingsworth Trail, 6 miles off Rte. 1 in Steuben) and another passing through a blueberry field (the Birch Point Trail). Note that some parts of the refuge are open to the public (Cross, Scotch, Halifax, and Bois Bubert islands), some are always closed (Seal Island), and the rest are only open in the off-season (Sept–Mar), closed April to August. You'll need to arrange a personalized tour from a charter boat operator such as **Maine Expressions** (© 207/622-0884; www.maineexpressions.com) or **Sea Venture** (© 207/288-3355) if you want to view these islands from afar when they are closed, and if you set foot on those which are open, respect the rules: no open fires or unleashed dogs.

P.O. Box 279, Milbridge. © 207/546-2124. http://petitmanan.fws.gov.

Raye's Mustard *Finds*   Foodies may feel they've gone to heaven after stumbling across Raye's artisanal mustard factory here in downtown Eastport, powered by one of the last true stone mills in America. The family has been cold-grinding mustard seeds and bottled various mustard concoctions since 1903, when J. W. "Wes" Raye built the place to create mustards for a booming local sardine tinning trade. Now he supplies sardine plants as far away as Norway too. Free hourly tours of the factory are given, where new flavors are sometimes in the offing; in the gift shop, pick up gifts for the mustard-crazed back home.

P.O. Box 2, Eastport, ME 04631. © 800/853-1903 or 207/853-4451. www.rayesmustard.com. Tours given Mon–Fri 10am–3pm on the hour; also sometimes Sat. Gift shop open 1 hr. later.

Roque Bluffs State Park *Kids*   A day-use only park, Roque Bluffs features impressive coastal scenery plus the added attraction of both freshwater and saltwater swimming areas. Jasper Beach is particularly noteworthy for the uniformly smoother jasper stones which make it up. There are family-friendly amenities here such as grills, changing areas, a playground, and a lifeguard.

145 Schoppee Point Rd. (6 miles off U.S. Rte. 1), Roque Bluffs ME 04654. © 207/255-3475. $2 adults; $1 children age 5–11, children under 5 free. Open mid-May to Sept.

Ruggles House   This fine Federal home dates from 1818 and was built for Thomas Ruggles, an early timber merchant and civic leader. The home is very grand and opulent, but in a curiously miniature sort of way. There's a flying staircase in the central hallway, pine doors hand-painted to resemble mahogany, and detailed wood carvings in the main parlor, done over the course of 3 years by an English craftsman equipped, legend says, with only a penknife. Locals once said his hand was guided by an angel. Tours last 20 minutes to a half-hour

Main St., Columbia Falls. © 207/483-4637. Suggested donation $3 adults; $1.50 children. June to mid-Oct Mon–Sat 9:30am–4:30pm, Sun 11am–4:30pm.

Schoodic Point ★★ This remote unit of Acadia National Park is just 7 miles from Mount Desert Island across Frenchman Bay, but it's a long 50-mile drive to get here via Ellsworth. A pleasing loop drive hooks around the tip of Schoodic Point. The one-way road (no park pass required) winds along the water and through forests of spruce and fir. Good views of the mountains of Acadia open up across Frenchman Bay; you'll also see buildings of a historic naval station housed on the point. Park near the tip of this isolated promontory and explore the salmon-colored rocks that plunge into the ocean. It's especially dramatic when the seas are agitated and the surf crashes loudly.

Acadia National Park, Winter Harbor. ✆ 207/288-3338. Free admission. Drive east from Ellsworth on Rte. 1 for 17 miles to W. Gouldsboro; then turn south on Rte. 186 to Winter Harbor. Outside Winter Harbor, look for the brown-and-white national park signs.

West Quoddy Head Light & Quoddy Head State Park ★★ This famed red-and-white light (it's been likened to a barbershop pole and a candy cane) marks the easternmost point of the United States and ushers boats into the Lubec Channel between the U.S. and Canada. (Interestingly, this is also the nearest geographical point in the U.S. to Africa!) The light, operated by the Coast Guard, isn't open to the public, but visitors can walk the grounds near the light and along headlands at the adjacent state park. The West Quoddy Head Light Keepers Association opened a new visitors center in spring 2002 inside the lightkeeper's house. The park overlooks rocky shoals that are ceaselessly battered by high winds, pounding waves, and some of the most powerful tides in the world. Watch for fishing boats straining against the currents, or seals playing in the waves and sunning on the offshore rocks. The park also consists of 480 acres of coastline and bog, and several trails wind through the dark conifer forest and crest the tops of rocky cliffs. Some of the most dramatic views are just a short walk down the path at the far end of the parking lot.

W. Quoddy Head Rd., Lubec. ✆ 207/733-0911. www.westquoddy.com. Lighthouse grounds: free admission. Park: $2 adults; $1 children 5–11. Grounds open 9am–sunset daily mid-May to mid-Oct.; visitors center open late May to mid-Oct daily 10am–4pm. Closed mid-Oct to mid-May.

5 Passamaquoddy Bay

Once in Lubec or Eastport, it's only a short drive to Canada, where you'll find Campobello Island, a quiet jewel once favored by former U.S. President Franklin D. Roosevelt.

From Campobello, you can catch a ferry to quiet Deer Island, then onward to the New Brunswick's Passamaquoddy Bay region, which adjoins the Maine coast and is easily reached via a boat ride from Campobello. Or, take a 1-minute drive across a bridge in Calais, Maine (assuming the border checks go smoothly) to St. Stephen, New Brunswick, for a look at a French town with a yummy chocolate museum.

You might also push a bit farther into New Brunswick and check out the lovely seaside town of St. Andrews. For more information about this scenic town, see chapter 10. It's a worthwhile day trip or overnight trip.

CAMPOBELLO ISLAND ★

Campobello is a compact island (about 10 miles long and 3 miles wide) at the mouth of Passamaquoddy Bay. Among its other distinctions, it's connected by a graceful modern bridge to Lubec, Maine, and is thus easier to get to from the United States than from Canada. To get here from the Canadian mainland without

---

Tips   **Like Bikes? You'll Love Campobello.**

If you like bikes, the islands and peninsulas of Passamaquoddy Bay lend themselves nicely to cruising in the slow lane—especially pretty Campobello, which has plenty of good dirt roads perfect for mountain biking. But you'll need a guide to show you the way. Fortunately, Kent Thompson has written a handy one, called *Biking to Blissville*. It covers 35 lovely rides in the Maritimes, including some on the island, and costs C$14.95 (about US$11). Unfortunately, it was published in 1993. Try to order it through the publisher, Goose Lane Editions, 469 King St., Fredericton, NB E3B 1E5 (© **888/926-8377** or 506/450-4251).

---

driving through the United States requires two ferries, one of which operates only during the summer.

Campobello has been home to both humble fishermen and wealthy families over the years, and both have coexisted quite nicely. (Locals approved when summer folks built golf courses earlier this century, since it gave them a place to graze their sheep.) Today, the island is a mix of elegant summer homes and less interesting tract homes of a more recent vintage.

The island offers excellent shoreline **walks** at both Roosevelt Campobello International Park (see below) and **Herring Cove Provincial Park** (© **506/752-7010**), which opens from mid-May to mid-October. The landscapes are extraordinarily diverse. On some trails you'll enjoy a Currier and Ives tableau of white houses and church spires across the channel in Lubec and Eastport; 10 minutes later you'll be walking along a wild, rocky coast pummeled by surging waves. Herring Cove has a mile-long beach that's perfect for a slow stroll in the fog. Camping and very scenic golf are also offered at the provincial park.

Nature lovers should note that Campobello's mixed terrain also attracts a good mix of birds, including sharp-shinned hawk, common eider, and black guillemot. Ask for a checklist and map at the visitor center.

ESSENTIALS
GETTING THERE   Campobello Island is accessible year-round from the United States. From Route 1 in Whiting, Maine, take Route 189 to Lubec, where a bridge links Lubec with Campobello. In the summer, there's another option. From the Canadian mainland, take the free ferry to **Deer Island**, drive the length of the island, and then board the small seasonal ferry to Campobello. The ferry is operated by **East Coast Ferries** (© **506/747-2159**) and runs from late June to early September. The fare is C$13 (US$9) for car and driver, C$2 (US$1.40) for each additional passenger, with a maximum of C$17 (US$12) per car.

VISITOR INFORMATION   The **Campobello Welcome Center,** 44 Route 774, Welshpool, NB E5E 1A3 (© **506/752-7043**), is on the right side just after you cross the bridge from Lubec. It's open mid-May to early September 9am to 7pm, then 10am to 6pm until mid-October.

Roosevelt Campobello International Park ★★   Take a brief excursion out of the country and across the time zone. The U.S. and Canada maintain a joint national park here, celebrating the life of Franklin D. Roosevelt, who summered here with his family in the early 1900s. Like other affluent Americans, the

Roosevelt family made an annual trek to the prosperous colony at Campobello Island. The island lured folks from the sultry cities with a promise of cool air and a salubrious effect on the circulatory system. ("The extensive forests of balsamic firs seem to affect the atmosphere of this region, causing a quiet of the nervous system and inviting sleep," read an 1890 real estate brochure.) The future U.S. president came to this island every summer between 1883—the year after he was born—and 1921, when he was suddenly stricken with polio. Franklin and his siblings spent those summers exploring the coves and sailing around the bay, and he always recalled his time here fondly. (It was his "beloved island," he said, coining a phrase that gets no rest in local promotional brochures.)

You'll learn much about Roosevelt and his early life at the visitor center, where you can view a brief film, and during a self-guided tour of the elaborate mansion, covered in cranberry-colored shingles. For a "cottage" this huge, it is surprisingly comfortable and intimate. The park is truly an international park, run by a commission with representatives from both the U.S. and Canada, making it like none other in the world. Because of new Homeland Security measures in place I suggest you bring with you either a passport or birth certificate, although checks are rarely enforced.

Leave some time to explore farther afield in the 2,800-acre park, which offers scenic coastline and 8½ miles of walking trails. Maps and walk suggestions are available at the visitor center.

Rte. 774, Campobello Island, New Brunswick. © **506/752-2922**. www.fdr.net. Free admission. Daily 10am–6pm. Closed mid-Oct to late May.

ST. STEPHEN

St. Stephen is the gateway to Canada for many travelers arriving from the United States. It's directly across the tidal St. Croix River from Calais, Maine, and the two towns share a symbiotic relationship—it's a local call across the international border from one town to the other, fire engines from one country will often respond to fires in the other, and during the annual summer parade the bands and floats have traditionally marched right through customs without stopping. (There was no word, at press time, about whether this practice would be discontinued in the wake of new, tighter border controls.)

ESSENTIALS

VISITOR INFORMATION   The **Provincial Visitor Information Centre** (© **506/466-7390**) is open daily 10am to 6pm mid-May to mid-October. It's in the old train station on Milltown Boulevard, about a mile from Canadian customs; turn right after crossing the border (following signs for St. Andrews and Saint John), and watch for the information center at the light where the road turns left.

EXPLORING ST. STEPHEN

St. Stephen is a town in transition. The lumber industry and wood trade that were responsible for the handsome brick and stone buildings that line the main street have by and large dried up. The town now depends on a paper mill and the large Ganong chocolate factory as its economic mainstays. (For the truly cocoa bean–obsessed, there's also a small Chocolate Festival in mid-Aug.) As a regional commercial center, it has a gritty, lived-in feel to it, and not much in the way of stylish boutiques or upscale restaurants.

You can learn about the region's history with a brief stop at the **Charlotte County Museum,** 443 Milltown Blvd. (© **506/466-3295**).

The Chocolate Museum *Kids*   St. Stephen's claim to fame is that it's the home of the chocolate bar—the first place (1910) where somebody thought to wrap chocolate pieces in foil and sell them individually. At least that's according to local lore. Chocolate is still big around here—not quite like Hershey, Pennsylvania, but still a part of the local psyche and economy. The Ganong brothers started selling chocolate from their general store here in 1873, and from this an empire was built, employing some 700 people by the 1930s. Ganong was also the first to package chocolates in heart-shaped boxes for Valentine's Day, and still holds 30% of the Canadian market for heart-box chocolates.

Ganong's modern new plant is on the outskirts of town and isn't open for tours, but in 1999 the nonprofit Chocolate Museum was opened in one of Ganong's early factories, a large brick structure on the town's main street. Here you'll view an 11-minute video about the history of local chocolates, then see the displays and exhibits, including 19th-century chocolate boxes, interactive multimedia displays about the making of candy on iMacs, and games for young children (my favorite: "Guess the Centers"). A highlight of a visit is watching one of the expert hand-dippers make chocolates the old fashioned way; samples are available afterward.

Want more? Ganong's Chocolatier, an old-fashioned candy shop, is located in the storefront adjacent to the museum. Don't miss the budget bags of factory seconds.

73 Milltown Blvd. (C) 506/466-7848. chocolate.museum@nb.aibn.com. Admission C$5 (US$3.50) adults, C$4 (US$2.75) students, C$3 (US$2) children under 6, C$15 (US$11) family. Mid-June to Aug Mon–Sat 9am–6:30pm, Sun 1–5pm; Mar to mid-June and Sept–Nov weekdays 9am–5pm. Closed Dec–Feb.

6 Where to Stay & Dine

IN MAINE

Small motels, inns, and B&B's abound along this part of the Maine coast; resorts, on the other hand, are almost nonexistent. The message: Prepare to rusticate.

The upside of this situation is that budget travelers seeking to minimize costs can do well here. Low-end offerings include the Machias Motor Inn, with 35 riverside rooms at 26 East Main St (Rte. 1) in Machias (C) **207/255-4861**); the Margaretta Motel (C) **207/255-6500**), with swimming pool and air-conditioning, and the Bluebird Motel (C) **207/255-3332**) with 40 units, both also on U.S. 1 in Machias; the Blueberry Patch Motel & Cabins (C) **207/434-5411**), on Route 1 in Jonesboro; the Eastland Motel, on Route 189 in Lubec (C) **207/733-5501**), or the Motel East, at 23A Water St. in downtown Eastport (C) **207/853-4747**).

Those with RVs can camp out at Pleasant River RV Park, 8 West Side Rd., Addison (C) **207/483-4083**).

In addition to gleaning the listings below, you might also think about renting a cottage or farmhouse by the week or month; there are plenty to choose from along this stretch of coast in summer, though digging them up can take some doing. Among the many offerings, check out **Yellow Birch Farm Guest Cottage** (C) **207/726-5807**), 272 Young's Cove Rd. in Pembroke, a farmstead on Cobscook Bay halfway between Lubec and Eastport with an outdoor shower and outhouse; **Tide Mill Farm** (C) **207/733-2110**), Tide Mill Road, Dennysville, a five-bedroom farmhouse anchoring a 1,600-acre farm (also right on Cobscook Bay); or the unique **Quoddy Head Station** (C) **207/733-4452**), West Quoddy Head Rd. in Lubec, a former Coast Guard lifesaving station built in 1918. You can rent the five-bedroom station house or five other units, all with terrific coastal views.

Eats are likewise thin on the ground up here. If you're simply looking to fuel up on fast food or family-style fare, Ellsworth is your main (and, actually, only) supply depot; expect the usual franchise chains along Route 1, especially near the point where Routes 1 and 3 diverge.

On the town's main drag, you can also fuel up with standard Mexican fare at **The Mex,** 191 Main St. (© **207/667-4494;** www.themex.com), which serves a variety of Mexican dishes plus some seafood surprises (crab enchiladas, ceviche, haddock Veracruz) as a tip of the sombrero to Maine. Large entrees run about $7 to $16, though you can spend less. More usual coastal dining is found in Ellsworth at **Union River Lobster Pot,** 8 South St. (© **207/ 667-5077**).

To stock up for a picnic at Quoddy Head, make a beeline for **Bold Coast Smokehouse** (© **888/733-0807** or 207/733-8912; www.boldcoastsmokehouse. com) on Route 189 in Lubec; it's got to be the nation's easternmost smokehouse. Vinny and Holly Gartmayer smoke up hot salmon, gravlax, kabobs, and trout pâté, among other products. Another smokehouse, **Sullivan Farm,** is covered below.

Black Duck Inn
There isn't much to the pretty village of Corea, mostly just a clutch of fishing boats and some island views, but there is a bed-and-breakfast if you care to stay the night. The Black Duck consists of four rooms (two share a bathroom, the others have private facilities), a suite, and a waterfront cottage. It's a simple place set among beautiful scenery. Rooms here are uncluttered and dotted with antiques; three, including the cottage (which has a kitchenette), possess excellent vistas of the picturesque harbor and the lupine-strewn headland.

36 Crowley Island Rd. (P.O. Box 39), Corea ME 04624. © 207/963-2689. Fax 207/963-7495. www.blackduck. com. 5 units (2 with shared bathroom), 1 cottage. $105-$165 double. Full breakfast included with rate. V, MC, DISC. Open Apr–Nov. Children 8 and older welcome. *In room:* No phone.

Captain Cates Bed & Breakfast
This trim blue house on a point of water, built by a sailor in the 1850s and now operated by the Duckworth family, is a simple yet accommodating place; five of the six units have ocean views. The J. W. Room, with an extra long mahogany bed from 1865 and matching commode and dresser, sports water views, while the Olevia Room is furnished with a queen bed and late 19th-century French provincial bedroom set. Up on the third floor, the Starboard Room is done in cream and blue-green tones. There are three more units as well, containing double beds or, in the case of the Puffin Room, a single bed; all bathrooms are shared, however. The lack of televisions and phones is made up for by a communal game room with a single TV and puzzles.

Route 92 at Phinney Lane (P.O. Box 314), Machiasport ME 04655. © 207/255-8812. Fax 207/255-6705. captcates@ptc-me.net. 6 units. $75–$95 double. Pets not allowed. No smoking. **Amenities:** 2 dining rooms; game room. *In room:* No phone.

Crocker House Country Inn ✦
Built in 1884, this handsome, shingled inn is off the beaten track on picturesque Hancock Point, across Frenchmen Bay from Mount Desert Island. It's a cozy retreat, perfect for rest, relaxation, and quiet walks (it's about a 4-min. walk from the water's edge). The rooms are tastefully decorated with comfortable country decor. Two rooms are located in the adjacent carriage house. The common areas are more relaxed than fussy, like the living room of a friend who's always happy to see you. The inn has a few bikes for guests to explore the point; nearby are four clay tennis courts. Dinner here is a highlight, with tremendous care taken with the meals and a fun, convivial atmosphere, featuring live piano on weekends. The menu focuses on traditional favorites, including French onion soup, artichoke hearts with crabmeat, and oysters Rockefeller

for starters. Entrees include a good selection of fresh seafood, such as scallops, salmon, and shrimp, all creatively prepared; nonseafood items include filet mignon and rack of lamb. The desserts and breads are homemade.

HC 77 (Box 171), Hancock Point, ME 04640. © 207/422-6806. Fax 207/422-3105. www.crockerhouse.com. 11 units. Mid-June to mid-Oct $105–$150 double; off-season $85–$110 double. Rates include full breakfast. AE, MC, V. Closed Jan–Feb; open weekends only in Mar. Pets allowed with prior permission. **Amenities:** Dining room; bikes.

Harbor House on Sawyer Cove B&B ⭑

Once the local telegraph office and an outpost for ship's equipment, early-19th-century Harbor House may now be Jonesport's most luxurious lodging choice—which is not to say it is superluxurious; there are only two suites. But both feature truly impressive coastal scenery from their third-floor windows. The Beachrose Room is a funkily-shaped space (narrow with low ceilings) with outstanding ocean views, while the Lupine Room features a king featherbed and private breakfast nook; both have private entrances. Breakfast is served on a wonderful inn porch, and a backyard picnic table is yet another perfect spot from which to take in the changing light over the reach and islands.

27 Sawyer Sq. (P.O. Box 468), Jonesport ME 04649. © 207/497-5417. Fax 207/497-3211. www.harborhs.com. 2 units. Summer $110 double; June and Sept $95 double; winter $85 double. Rates include full breakfast. DISC, MC, V. *In room:* No phone.

Helen's Restaurant *Finds*

This is the original Helen's, a cut-above-the-rest diner and one of the premier places in all of Maine to eat pie. (And, yes, there was a Helen.) You can get pork chops, fried fish, burgers, meatloaf, and other American-style square meals. But absolutely save room for the amazingly creamy and fruity pies; strawberry rhubarb or blueberry, when in season, are out of this world, but chocolate cream, banana cream, or just about anything else will satisfy the sweet tooth equally well in a pinch. Check for daily specials. There's another Helen's on the strip just north of Ellsworth.

28 E. Main St., Machias. © 207/255-8423. Entrees $3–$16. DISC, MC, V. Daily 6am–8:30pm.

Home Port Inn ⭑

The 1880 Home Port was built as a family home and converted into lodgings in 1982. Right on a quiet street in downtown Lubec, its rooms mostly possess tremendous views of both Cobscook Bay and the Bay of Fundy. The central living room and fireplace are the focal points; guests can sleep in a queen-bedded library; a "dining room"; a queen-bedded room with hand-painted tiles; a master bedroom with four-poster queen bed; a king room (with bathroom down the hall); or a double-bedded room. The inn's dining room is surprisingly skillful, too, and serves passable seafood dinners nightly, starting with smoked fish and continuing on to lobsters, scallops, salmon, crab, and other dishes cooked with local catches. (It also serves chicken and steak.) Finish with cheesecake, shortcake, and ice cream sundaes.

45 Main St. (P.O. Box 50), Lubec ME 04652. © 207/733-2077. www.homeportinn.com. 7 units. $85–$99 double. Rates include continental breakfast. AE, DISC, MC, V. Closed Nov–Apr. *In room:* No phone.

Le Domaine ⭑⭑

An epicure's delight, Le Domaine long ago established its reputation as one of the most elegant and delightful destinations in Maine. Set on Route 1 about 10 minutes east of Ellsworth, this inn has the Continental flair of an impeccable French *auberge*. While the highway in front can be a bit noisy, the garden and woodland walks out back offer plenty of compensating serenity. The rooms are comfortable and tastefully appointed without being pretentious; a couple of years ago, the innkeeper combined four rooms to create two suites and added air-conditioning and phones to all of the rooms. The guest rooms are on the second floor in the rear of the property; private terraces face the gardens and the 90 acres of forest owned by the inn. Rooms (which are named after small towns from the region of France where the owner's mother grew up) are loaded with extras such as Bose radios, bathrobes, fresh fruit and flowers, lighted makeup mirrors, wineglasses, and corkscrews. Each room also has its own library.

The real draw here is the exquisite dining room ★★, which is famed for its understated elegance. Chef Nicole Purslow carries on the tradition established when her French-immigrant mother opened the inn in 1946, offering superb country cooking in the handsome candle-lit dining room with pine-wood floors and sizable fireplace. The ever-changing meals still sing. Best-named appetizer? It's called "My mother's pâté recipe that I cannot improve upon," and is fashioned from organic chicken livers. Entrees, which run from about $11 to $29 apiece, might include baby grilled lamb chops in a house marinade, or lightly crusted sweetbreads with capers and lemon juice; don't forget to choose something from the extensive wine cellar, which holds some 5,000 bottles of French vintage. Plan to check in by 5:30pm, as dinner is served Tuesday to Sunday between 6 and 9pm. Dinner is also available to nonguests and is highly recommended if you're passing through this otherwise unremarkable stretch of Route 1. The wine cellar here, it almost goes without saying, is outstanding considering the out-of-the-way location.

Rte. 1 (P.O. Box 496), Hancock, ME 04640. ✆ **800/554-8498** or 207/422-3395. www.ledomaine.com. Fax 207/422-3252. 5 units. $200 double; $285 suite. Rates include full breakfast. AE, DISC, MC, V. Closed mid-Oct to mid-June. **Amenities:** Dining room. *In room:* A/C, radio, robes.

Little River Lodge   Overlooking Cutler's tiny but impressively situated harbor, this Victorian inn—once known as the Cutler Hotel— was built in the late 19th century to lodge steamship passengers bound from Boston to Canada. The inn has just five rooms, three of them facing the water; all have been decorated in nautical themes and simple, pleasing colors, such as forest green and eggshell blue, then stocked with old books and antiques. Note that most rooms are still furnished with twin or double beds, although the Roosevelt Room (where T. R. himself is said to have once slept) does contain a bigger queen bed. Also take note that the five rooms share three bathrooms. But if you're wanting to stay in Cutler, it's your only option.

Rte. 191 (P.O. Box 251), Cutler ME 04626. ✆ **207/259-4437.** www.cutlerlodge.com. 5 units, 2 with private bathroom. $70–$90 double. Rates include breakfast. No credit cards. Some rooms 2-night minimum stay weekends. From Rte. 1 in E. Machias, turn onto Rte. 191 South and continue 13 miles to hotel on left. **Amenities:** Dining room. *In room:* No phone.

Micmac Farm ★   Based in a 1763 home with intriguing history (the founder's family is buried in a cemetery on the premises), Micmac Farm consists of three units: two rustic, wood-paneled "guesthouses" in the woods, furnished with two double beds apiece plus kitchenettes, as well as a more luxurious guest room located inside the main house, with a big deck, queen bed, TV, and Jacuzzi tub. This room also adjoins the house library. An outdoor deck at the inn overlooks the Machias River, a good spot for watching the water and contemplating nothing.

47 Micmac Lane (Rte. 92), Machiasport ME 04655. ✆ **207/255-3008.** 1 unit, 2 guesthouses. $70–$85 double, $425–$525 guesthouses weekly. MC, V.

The Milliken House ★   Guests of this friendly B&B are greeted with glasses of port or sherry in a big living room sporting two fireplaces. It's a nice welcome, and the five rooms are equally fine, done up with marble-top furnishings and the original home builder's collection of books. (Benjamin Milliken made his small fortune by building a dock and outfitting the big ships passing in and out of the busy port in Eastport's 19th-century heyday.) Expect small touches such as pillow-side chocolates and fresh flowers. The house is located only 2 blocks from Eastport's historic district (see earlier in this chapter) as well, making it ideal for local explorations; breakfast might run to buttermilk pancakes served with a berry sauce, crepes, or a quiche Lorraine, sided with homemade bread.

29 Washington St., Eastport, ME 04631. (C) **888/507-9370** or 207/853-2955. www.eastport-inn.com. 5 units. $65–$75 double. Rates include full breakfast. MC, V. Call about off-season availability. "Well-trained pets" welcome. *In room:* Fireplace, no phone.

Peacock House Bed & Breakfast ★   The Peacock House was built in end-of-the-line Lubec in 1860 by an English sea captain; it has since hosted prominent Mainers, including U.S. Senators Margaret Chase Smith and Edmund Muskie, among others. Three second-floor rooms are queen-bedded and simple. The Margaret Chase Smith Suite has a queen-size bed, while the king-bedded Meadow Suite has the inn's largest bathroom and a sitting area. (It's also handicapped-accessible.) The Wedgwood Suite's queen bed is augmented by a day bed with trundle and is best for small families. The Peacock Suite is the most romantic of the rooms, with a gas fireplace, four-poster queen bed, sitting area, wet bar, refrigerator, and DVD player. Tinkle the keys of the living room's baby grand piano if you so fancy; it's allowed, and even encouraged.

27 Summer St., Lubec ME 04652. (C) **888/305-0036** or 207/733-2403. 7 units. $85–$125 double. Rates include full breakfast. MC, V. Children age 7 and older welcome. *In room:* VCR (some).

Redclyffe Shore Motor Inn ★   I don't often recommend motor inns or motels in this guidebook, but here's one that packs a great deal more historic and scenic punch than most. The complex, consisting of a Gothic Revival main house dating from the 1860s (note the steep gables) and a cluster of motel units, perches on an ocean-side cliff with genuinely expansive views of Passamaquoddy Bay and the St. Croix River. Simply gazing at the water makes for a wonderful few hours, particularly if you've booked one of the so-called "patio rooms" with private balcony. Whether in the main house or the motel section, the 16 double-bedded and king-bedded rooms and suites sport all the necessary basics: phones, televisions with HBO, and coffeemakers. Those balcony rooms are a steal considering the vistas, and the glassed-in dining room—it's open nightly from 5 to 9pm, serving standard American meals—features yet another knock-out ocean view.

Rte. 1, Robbinston ME 04671. (C) **207/454-3270**. Fax 207/454-8723. www.redclyffeshoremotorinn.com. 16 units. $62–$73 double. MC, V. **Amenities:** Dining room. *In room:* AC (some), TV, coffeemaker.

Riverside Inn   When you're up Downeast, it isn't easy to find a frilly place, but this small three-room inn just outside Machias proper does sport some of the requisite chintz, antiques, and library/reading room one might seek out in an old-fashioned lodging house. The second-floor Mrs. Chase Room, named for the former captain's wife, comes with a claw-foot tub and skylight. The two-bedroom Lower Coach Suite features a wraparound deck overlooking the East Machias River and the small inn garden, while the Upper Coach Suite possesses even better views—from a private balcony. (It also sports a kitchenette with fridge, microwave, stovetop, and true oven). If the rooms are just a bit fusty, they're also uniformly attractive and clean. The dining room, a rarity as well up here, serves breakfasts of quiche, eggs, and the like, plus a range of pork, shrimp, beef, salmon, and pasta dishes for dinner.

Rte. 1 (P.O. Box 373), E. Machias ME 04630. (*) 207/255-4134. Fax 207/255-0577. www.riversideinn-maine. com. 3 units. May–Oct $95–$130 double; Nov–Apr $80–$115 double. AE, MC, V. **Amenities:** Dining room. *In room:* Kitchenette (some), fridge (some).

Sullivan Harbor Farm Smokehouse *Finds*   One of the last independently owned smokehouses in New England, this award-winning operation, run out of a farmhouse right on Route 1, specializes in delicious cuts of salmon, cured, hand-rubbed with salt and brown sugar, and cold-smoked over hickory smudge fires. They also produce gravlax, hot-roasted salmon, smoked scallops, smoked char, and pâté. If you're stumped for a place to stay near Mount Desert Island, consider renting one of three cottages on the smokehouse property; each is differently equipped—one has a full modern kitchen, another a washer/dryer, phone, and cable TV, and a third, simpler cottage comes with few extras. The cottages rent by the week in high summer season (shorter rentals possible in fall), for from $875 to $1,450 weekly.

Rte. 1 (P.O. Box 96), Sullivan, ME 04664. (*) **800/422-4014** or 207/422-3735. www.sullivanharborfarm.com. 3 cottages, $875-$1,450 weekly. MC, V. *In room:* Kitchenette (1 unit), washer/dryer (some), no phone.

Todd House Bed & Breakfast   A bright yellow house out on Todd's Head overlooking Cobscook and Passamaquoddy bays, this 1775 Cape features classic New England architectural touches such as a huge center chimney and a fireplace with bake oven. It has served as a former Mason's Hall and temporary military barracks; today the six inn rooms come in various configurations, including three suites, two rooms with private bathrooms, and two with kitchenettes. The yard features cookout equipment, but the ocean views are the real draw. It's also only about a ¾-mile walk from the central downtown district.

1 Capen Ave., Eastport ME 04631. (*) 207/853-2328. Fax 207/853-2328. 6 units, 2 with private bathroom. $50–$95 double. Rates include breakfast. MC, V. *In room:* TV/VCR (some), kitchenette (some), fridge (some), fireplace (some), no phone.

Weston House   A whitewashed, hillside 1810 Federal looking out onto the bay and Campobello, the Weston House features rooms with antiques and Asian furnishings, with classical music playing in the background. John James Audubon lodged here once upon a time, and today the four units (sharing two bathrooms) are brightly furnished with prints and poster beds. Breakfasts are better than you might expect; brunches are served on the weekend along with glasses of sherry, while picnic lunches and dinners can be ordered by special arrangement. For relaxation, there's an attractive patio with wicker furniture. Two Scottish terriers are in residence.

26 Boynton St., Eastport ME 04631. (*) **800/853-2907** or 207-853-2907. Fax 207/853-0981. www.weston house-maine.com. 4 units, all with shared bathroom. $70–$85 double. Rates include full breakfast. No credit cards. *In room:* TV (some), fireplace (some).

IN NEW BRUNSWICK

Lupine Lodge *Value*   In 1915, cousins of the Roosevelts built this handsome compound of log buildings not far from the Roosevelt cottage. A busy road runs between the lodge and the water, but the buildings are located on a slight rise and have the feel of being removed from the traffic. Guest rooms are in two long lodges adjacent to the main building and restaurant. The rooms with bay views cost a bit more but are worth it—they're slightly bigger and better furnished in a log-rustic style. All guests have access to a deck that overlooks the bay. The lodge's attractive restaurant exudes rustic summer ease with log walls, a double stone fireplace, bay views, and mounted moose head and swordfish. Three meals are served daily. Dinner entrees include favorites such as salmon, T-bone, turkey, and steamed lobster.

610 Rte. 774, Welshpool, Campobello Island, NB E5E 1A5. (✆ **888/912-8880** or 506/752-2555. www. lupinelodge.com. 11 units. C$50–C$125 (US$36–US$89) double. MC, V. Closed mid-Oct to mid-June. Pets accepted for additional C$15 (US$11). **Amenities:** Restaurant.

Owen House, A Country Inn & Gallery   This three-story clapboard captain's house dates from 1835 and sits on 10 tree-filled acres at the edge of the bay. The first-floor common rooms are nicely decorated in a busy Victorian manner with Persian and braided carpets and mahogany furniture. The guest rooms are a mixed lot, furnished with an eclectic mélange of antique and modern furniture that sometimes blends nicely. Likewise, some rooms are bright and airy and filled with the smell of salty air (room 1 is the largest, with waterfront views on two sides); others, like room 5, are tucked under stairs and rather dark, but the Owens are slowly renovating the old house with bigger bathrooms and new showers. The third-floor rooms share a single bathroom but also have excellent views. A filling breakfast served family style is included in the room rates.

11 Welshpool St., Welshpool, Campobello, NB E5E 1G3. (✆ **506/752-2977.** www.owenhouse.ca. 9 units, 7 with private bathroom. C$112–C$213 (US$80–US$151) double. Rates include breakfast. MC, V. Closed mid-Oct to late May. No children under 6 in Aug.

10

Side Trips from the Maine Coast

Once ensconced on the coast of Maine, you'd be easily forgiven if you didn't wish to do anything more strenuous than turn the pages of a book while lying in a hammock. But if you're a back-roads adventurer, an outdoors enthusiast, or a connoisseur of gourmet meals, there are some rather interesting places to be found if you're willing to journey a bit farther afield.

Portsmouth, New Hampshire, for instance, is well worth a quick detour across the bridge from Kittery for its coffee shops, inns, shops, and pleasing snugness. Coastal New Brunswick is worth a visit for its pretty seaside villages, islands, and high tides. And, just inland from the midcoast, huge Baxter State Park—featuring the lofty and impressive peak of Mount Katahdin—is one of Maine's finest moments.

I have described each of these three side trips below, going in order—as does this book—from south to north.

1 Portsmouth, New Hampshire ⋆⋆

Portsmouth is a civilized little seaside city of bridges, brick, and seagulls, and quite a little gem. Filled with elegant architecture that's more intimate than intimidating, this bonsai-size city projects a strong, proud sense of its heritage without being overly precious. Part of the city's appeal is its variety: Upscale coffee shops and art galleries stand alongside old-fashioned barbershops and tattoo parlors. Despite a steady influx of money in recent years, the town still retains an earthiness that serves as a tangy vinegar for more saccharine coastal spots. Portsmouth's humble waterfront must actually be sought out; when found, it's rather understated.

The city's history runs deep, a fact that is evident on a walk through town. For the past 3 centuries, the city has been the hub for the region's maritime trade. In the 1600s, Strawbery Banke (it wasn't renamed Portsmouth until 1653) was a major center for the export of wood and dried fish to Europe. In the 19th century, it prospered as a center of regional trade. Across the Piscataqua River in Maine, the Portsmouth Naval Shipyard, founded in 1800, evolved into a prominent base for the building, outfitting, and repair of U.S. Navy submarines. Today, Portsmouth's maritime tradition continues with a lively trade in bulk goods (look for scrap metal and minerals stockpiled along the shores of the Piscataqua River on Market St.). The city's de facto symbol is the tugboat, one or two of which are almost always tied up near the waterfront's picturesque "tugboat alley."

Visitors to Portsmouth will find a lot to see in such a small space, including good shopping in the boutiques that now occupy much of the historic district, good eating at many small restaurants and bakeries, and plenty of history to explore among the historic homes and museums set on almost every block.

ESSENTIALS

GETTING THERE Portsmouth is served by Exits 3 through 7 on I-95. The most direct access to downtown is via Market Street (Exit 7), which is the last New Hampshire exit before crossing the river to Maine.

Portsmouth, New Hampshire

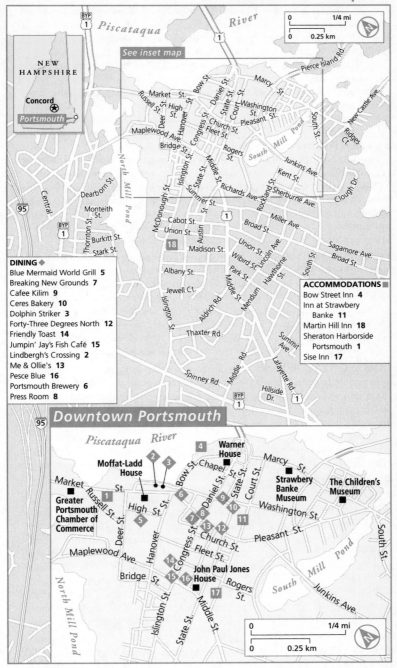

NEW HAMPSHIRE

Concord ☆

Portsmouth ○

Piscataqua River

See inset map

DINING ◆
Blue Mermaid World Grill **5**
Breaking New Grounds **7**
Cafee Kilim **9**
Ceres Bakery **10**
Dolphin Striker **3**
Forty-Three Degrees North **12**
Friendly Toast **14**
Jumpin' Jay's Fish Café **15**
Lindbergh's Crossing **2**
Me & Ollie's **13**
Pesce Blue **16**
Portsmouth Brewery **6**
Press Room **8**

ACCOMMODATIONS ■
Bow Street Inn **4**
Inn at Strawbery
  Banke **11**
Martin Hill Inn **18**
Sheraton Harborside
  Portsmouth **1**
Sise Inn **17**

Downtown Portsmouth

Piscataqua River

Warner House
Moffat-Ladd House
Greater Portsmouth Chamber of Commerce
Strawbery Banke Museum
The Children's Museum
John Paul Jones House

In 2000, discount airline **Pan Am** (© **800/359-7262;** www.flypanam.com) launched operations out of a former military base on Portsmouth's outskirts. The only airline that serves Portsmouth (don't expect onward connections), it has flights to a limited but growing roster of second-tier airports, including Gary, Indiana; Sanford, Florida; and Baltimore. Call or check the carrier's website for an updated list of airports currently served.

Amtrak (© **800/872-7245;** www.amtrak.com) operates four trains daily from Boston's North Station to downtown Dover, New Hampshire; a one-way ticket is about $15 per person, and the trip takes about 1¼ hours. You then take the #2 **COAST** bus (© **603/743-5777;** www.coastbus.org) to the center of downtown Portsmouth, a 40-minute trip that costs just $1.

Greyhound (© **800/229-9424;** www.greyhound.com), **C&J Trailways** (© **800/258-7111;** www.cjtrailways.com), and **Vermont Transit** (© **800/ 552-8737;** www.vermonttransit.com) all run about five buses daily from Boston's South Station to downtown Portsmouth, plus one to three daily trips from Boston's Logan Airport. The one-way cost for each service is about $15. A one-way Greyhound trip from New York City's Port Authority bus station to downtown Portsmouth is about $44 and takes about 6½ hours.

VISITOR INFORMATION The **Greater Portsmouth Chamber of Commerce,** 500 Market St. (© **603/436-1118;** www.portcity.org), has an information center between Exit 7 and downtown. From Memorial Day to Columbus Day, it's open Monday through Wednesday, 8:30am to 5pm; Thursday and Friday, 8:30am to 7pm; and Saturday and Sunday, 10am to 5pm. The rest of the year, hours are Monday through Friday, 8:30am to 5pm. In summer, a second booth is at Market Square in the middle of the historic district. A good website with extensive information on the region may be found at **www.seacoastnh.com.**

PARKING Most of Portsmouth can be easily reconnoitered on foot, so you need park only once. Parking can be tight in and around the historic district in summer. The municipal parking garage nearly always has space and costs just 50¢ per hour; it's located on Hanover Street between Market and Fleet streets. Strawbery Banke museum (see below) also offers limited parking for visitors.

There's also now a free "**trolley**" (© **603/743-5777**) circulating central Portsmouth in a one-way loop from July to early September. It hits all the key historical points. Catch it at Market Square, Prescott Park, or Strawbery Banke.

A MAGICAL HISTORY TOUR

Portsmouth's 18th-century prosperity is evident in the Georgian-style homes that dot the city. Strawbery Banke occupies the core of the historic area and is well worth visiting. If you don't have the budget, time, or inclination to spend half a day at Strawbery Banke, a walking tour takes you past many other significant homes, some of which are maintained by various historical or colonial societies and are open to the public. A helpful map and brochure, *The Portsmouth Trail: An Historic Walking Tour,* is available free at information centers.

Tired? Take a break at **Prescott Park** ★★, between Strawbery Banke and the water. It's one of my favorite municipal parks in New England. Water views, lemonade vendors, benches, grass, and occasional festivals make it worth a visit.

Strawbery Banke ★★★   In 1958, the city planned to raze this neighborhood, first settled in 1653, to make way for urban renewal. A group of local citizens resisted and won, establishing an outdoor history museum that's become one of the largest in New England. Today it consists of 10 downtown acres and 46 historic buildings. Ten buildings have been restored with period furnishings;

eight others feature exhibits. (The remainder may be seen from the exterior only.) While Strawbery Banke employs staffers to assume the character of historic residents, the emphasis is more on the buildings, architecture, and history than the costumed reenactors.

The neighborhood surrounds an open lawn (formerly an inlet) and has a settled, picturesque quality. At three working crafts shops, watch coopers, boat builders, and potters are at work. The most intriguing home is the split-personality Drisco House, half of which depicts life in the 1790s and half of which shows life in the 1950s, nicely demonstrating how houses grow and adapt to each era.

Hancock St. ℂ 603/433-1100. www.strawberybanke.org. Admission $12 adults, $11 seniors, $8 children 7–17, free for children under 6; $28 per family. May–Oct Mon–Sat 10am–5pm, Sun noon–5pm; winter (except Jan) Mon–Sat 10am–2pm, Sun noon–2pm. Closed Jan. Look for directional signs posted around town.

John Paul Jones House ★★   Revolutionary War hero John Paul ("I have not yet begun to fight") Jones lived in this 1758 home during the war. He was here to oversee the construction of his sloop, *Ranger,* believed to be the first ship to sail under the U.S. flag (a model is on display). Immaculately restored and maintained by the Portsmouth Historical Society, costumed guides offer tours.

43 Middle St. ℂ 603/436-8420. Admission $5 adults, $4.50 seniors, $2.50 children 6–14, free for children under 6. Thurs–Tues 11am–5pm. Closed mid-Oct to mid-May.

Moffat-Ladd House ★★   Built for a family of prosperous merchants and traders, the elegant garden is as notable as the 1763 home, with its great hall and elaborate carvings. The home belonged to one family between 1763 and 1913, when it became a museum; many furnishings have never left the premises. The house will appeal to aficionados of early American furniture and painting.

154 Market St. ℂ 603/436-8221. Admission $5 adults, $2.50 children under 12. Mon–Sat 11am–5pm; Sun 1–5pm. Closed Nov–May.

Warner House ★   This house, built in 1716, was the governor's mansion in the mid–18th century when Portsmouth was the state capital. After a time as a private home, it has been open to the public since the 1930s. This stately brick structure with graceful Georgian architectural elements is a favorite among architectural historians for its wall murals (said to be the oldest murals still in place in the U.S.), early wall marbleizing, and original white pine paneling.

150 Daniel St. ℂ 603/436-5909. www.warnerhouse.org. Admission $5 adults, $2.50 children 7–12, free for children 6 and under. Mon–Sat 11am–4pm; Sun noon–4pm. Closed Nov to early June.

Wentworth-Gardner House ★★★   Arguably the most handsome mansion in the Seacoast region, this is considered one of the nation's best examples of Georgian architecture. The 1760 home features many period elements, including some very notable *quoins* (blocks on the building's corners), pedimented window caps, plank sheathing (to make the home appear as if made of masonry), an elaborate

---

⸦Finds **Around the Wentworth-Gardner House**

Most travelers tend to visit just Strawbery Banke, then perhaps do a little shopping at the downtown boutiques. To get a fuller sense of historic Portsmouth, walk a bit off the beaten track. The neighborhood around the Wentworth-Gardner House is a great area to snoop around—with lanes too narrow for SUVs, twisting roads, and wooden houses, both restored and unrestored. Get a real taste of the early 19th century here.

doorway with Corinthian pilasters, a broken scroll, and a paneled door topped with a pineapple, the symbol of hospitality. Perhaps most memorable is its scale—though a grand home of the colonial era, it's modest in scope; some circles today may not consider it much more than a pool house.

50 Mechanic St. (℃ **603/436-4406**. Admission $4 adults, $2 children 6–14, free for children 5 and under. Tues–Sun 1–4pm. Closed mid-Oct to May. From rose gardens on Marcy St. across from Strawbery Banke, walk south 1 block, turn left toward bridge, make a right before crossing bridge; house is down the block on your right.

BOAT TOURS

Portsmouth is especially attractive seen from the water. A small fleet of tour boats ties up at Portsmouth, offering scenic tours of the Piscataqua River and the historic Isle of Shoals throughout the summer and fall.

The **Isle of Shoals Steamship Co.** ★★ (℃ **800/441-4620** or 603/431-5500) sails from Barker Wharf on Market Street and is the most established of the tour companies. The firm offers a variety of tours on the 90-foot, three-deck *Thomas Laighton* (a modern replica of a late-19th-century steamship) and the 70-foot *Oceanic,* especially designed for whale-watching. One popular excursion is to the Isle of Shoals, at which passengers can disembark and wander about Star Island, a dramatic, rocky island that's part of an island cluster far out in the offshore swells. Reservations are strongly encouraged. Other popular trips include 6-hour whale-watching voyages and a sunset lighthouse cruise. Fares range from $10 to $22 to $35 for adults, $12 to $19 for children. Parking costs an additional charge.

Portsmouth Harbor Cruises ★ (℃ **800/776-0915** or 603/436-8084; www. portsmouthharbor.com) specializes in tours of the historic Piscataqua River aboard the *Heritage,* a 49-passenger cruise ship with plenty of open deck space. Cruise by five old forts or enjoy the picturesque tidal estuary of inland Great Bay, a scenic trip upriver from Portsmouth. Trips run daily; reservations are suggested. Fares are $11 to $18 for adults, $9.50 to $17 for seniors, and $7 to $10 for children.

ESPECIALLY FOR KIDS

The Children's Museum of Portsmouth ★★ *Kids* The Children's Museum is a bright, lively arts and science museum that offers a morning's worth of hands-on exhibits of interest to younger artisans and scientists (it's designed to appeal to children between 1 and 11). Popular displays include exhibits on earthquakes, dinosaur digs, and lobstering, along with the miniature yellow submarine and space shuttle cockpit, both of which invite clambering.

280 Marcy St., 2 blocks south of Strawbery Banke. (℃ **603/436-3853**. www.childrens-museum.org. Admission $5 adults and children; $4 seniors; free for ages 1 and under. Tues–Sat 10am–5pm; Sun 1–5pm. Also open Mon during summer and school vacations.

WHERE TO STAY

Downtown accommodations are preferred, as everything is within walking distance, but prices tend to be higher. For budget accommodations, less-stylish chain hotels are located at the edge of town along I-95. Among them are the **Anchorage Inn & Suites,** 417 Woodbury Ave. (℃ **603/431-8111**); the **Fairfield Inn,** 650 Borthwick Ave. (℃ **603/436-6363**); and the **Holiday Inn of Portsmouth,** 300 Woodbury Ave. (℃ **603/431-8000**).

In addition to the options listed below, see the Portsmouth Harbor Inn and Spa in chapter 4.

Bow Street Inn This is an adequate destination for travelers willing to give up charm for convenience. The former brewery was made over in the 1980s in

Packing a Picnic

Portsmouth's **Prescott Park** is about as pretty a spot as you could expect to find for an al fresco bite, with views of the harbor, a well-kept green, free gardens, the occasional music festival, and vendors dispensing slushies and other fun treats in the summer. And it's free. There are a few benches, but tote a blanket just in case—the lawn makes a great spot for splaying out and catching some rays.

Get provisions right nearby at **Richardson's Market** (© 603/436-5104) just 2 blocks away on State Street. There's a good selection of beers, an outstanding sandwich counter (a lot of locals eat lunch on the fly here), and plenty of snacks and ice cream products. Or just hit the vendors.

a bit of inspired recycling: condos occupy the top floor, while the **Seacoast Repertory Theatre** (© 603/433-4472) occupies the first. The second floor is the Bow Street Inn, a ten-room hotel that offers good access to historic Portsmouth. Guest rooms, set off a rather sterile hallway, are clean, comfortable, small, and, for the most part, unexceptional. Only rooms 6 and 7 feature good views of the harbor, and a premium is charged for these. Parking is on the street or at a nearby paid garage; a parking pass is included with harbor-view rooms.

121 Bow St., Portsmouth, NH 03801. © 603/431-7760. Fax 603/433-1680. 10 units. Peak season (summer and holidays) $119–$175 double; off-season $99–$155 double. Rates include continental breakfast. 2-night minimum stay on some holidays. AE, DISC, MC, V. *In room:* A/C, TV, dataport, hair dryer.

Inn at Strawbery Banke ⚹ This historic inn, located in an 1814 home tucked away on Court Street, is ideally located for exploring Portsmouth: Strawbery Banke is a block away, and Market Square (the center of the action) is 2 blocks away. The friendly innkeepers have done a nice job of taking a cozy antique home and making it comfortable for guests. Rooms are tiny but bright and feature stenciling, wooden shutters, and beautiful pine floors; one has a bathroom down the hall. Common areas include two sitting rooms with TVs, lots of books, and a dining room where a full breakfast is served each morning.

314 Court St., Portsmouth, NH 03801. © 800/428-3933 or 603/436-7242. www.innatstrawberybanke.com. 7 units. Spring, summer, and early fall $145–$150 double; off-season $100–$115 double. Rates include breakfast. 2-night minimum stay Aug and Oct weekends. AE, DISC, MC, V. Children 10 and older welcome. *In room:* A/C, no phone.

Martin Hill Inn Bed & Breakfast ⚹⚹ Innkeepers Paul and Jane Harnden keep things running smoothly and happily at this friendly B&B in a residential neighborhood a short walk from downtown, and that's why I like it so much. The inn consists of two period buildings: a main house (built around 1815) and a second guesthouse built 35 years later. All rooms have queen-size beds, writing tables, and sofas or sitting areas, and are variously appointed with distinguished wallpapers, porcelains, antiques, love seats, four-poster or brass bedding, and the like. Each has its own character, from the master bedroom, with pine floors, to the Victorian Rose Room to the mahogany-lined Library Room (the only room with two beds). There's also a relaxing greenhouse—a suite, really, with sitting room, solarium, and access to the outdoors. A stone path leads to a small, beautiful garden, and the gourmet breakfast is a highlight: It usually consists of blueberry-pecan pancakes, served with Canadian bacon and real maple syrup, or delicious apple Belgian waffles topped with a nutmeg-ginger sauce. The Harndens gladly share their encyclopedic knowledge of local sights and restaurants.

404 Islington St., Portsmouth, NH 03801. ⓒ 603/436-2287. 8 units. Summer $125–$145 double; off-season $98–$125 double. Holiday rates higher. Rates include full breakfast. MC, V. Children 16 and over are welcome. *In room:* A/C.

Sheraton Harborside Portsmouth 🏨🏨 This five-story, in-town brick hotel is nicely located—the attractions of downtown Portsmouth are virtually at your doorstep (Strawbery Banke is about a 10-min. walk), and with parking underground and across the street, a stay here can make for a relatively stress-free visit. It's a modern building inspired by the low brick buildings of the city, and wraps around a circular courtyard. This is a well-maintained, well-managed, uniformly bland property popular with business travelers, as well as leisure travelers looking for the amenities of a larger hotel. Some rooms have views of the working harbor.

250 Market St., Portsmouth, NH 03801. ⓒ 877/248-3794 or 603/431-2300. Fax 603/431-7805. 200 units. Summer $200–$255 double; ask about off-season discounts. Suites higher. AE, DISC, MC, V. **Amenities:** Restaurant (American); fitness center; business center; limited room service; executive rooms. *In room:* A/C, TV w/pay movies, dataport, minibar, coffeemaker, hair dryer, iron.

Sise Inn 🏨🏨 A modern, elegant hotel in the guise of a country inn, this solid Queen Anne–style home was built for a prominent merchant in 1881; the hotel addition was constructed in the 1980s, amid other renovations. The effect is happily harmonious, with antique stained glass and copious oak trim meshing well with the more contemporary elements. An elevator serves the three floors; modern carpeting is throughout, but many rooms feature antique armoires, updated Victorian styling, and whirlpool or soaking tubs. I like room 302, a bi-level, two-bedroom suite with a claw-foot tub; 406, a suite with soaking tub and private sitting room; 120, with its private patio; and 216 (in the carriage house), which has an actual working sauna, a two-person whirlpool, and lovely natural light. A continental breakfast is served in the huge old kitchen and adjoining sunroom. This is a popular hotel for business travelers, but if you're on holiday you won't feel out of place. As an added bonus, new ownership recently added free Wi-Fi access throughout the property, allowing guests to cruise the Internet wirelessly.

40 Court St. (at Middle St.), Portsmouth, NH 03801. ⓒ 877/747-3466 or 603/433-0200. Fax 603/433-1200. www.siseinn.com. 34 units. June–Oct $189–$269 double; Nov–May $119–$189 double. Rates include breakfast. AE, DC, DISC, MC, V. **Amenities:** Laundry service. *In room:* A/C, TV/VCR, hair dryer, iron and ironing board, Jacuzzi (some), DVD (some).

Three Chimneys Inn 🏨🏨 About 20 minutes northwest of Portsmouth at the edge of the pleasant university town of Durham, the Three Chimneys Inn is a wonderful retreat. The main part of the inn dates from 1649, but later additions and a full-scale renovation in 1997 have given it more of a regal Georgian feel. All units are above average in size and lushly decorated with four-poster or canopied beds, mahogany armoires, and Belgian carpets. Seventeen rooms have either gas or Duraflame log fireplaces. One favorite is the William Randolph Hearst Room, with photos of starlets on the walls and a massive bed that's a replica of one at San Simeon. Five rooms are on the ground-floor level beneath the restored barn and have outside entrances, Jacuzzis, and gas fireplaces; these tend to be a bit more cavelike than the others, but also more luxurious. Note that the inn is a popular spot for weddings on summer weekends, and University of New Hampshire events such as graduation and homecoming weekend book it full.

17 Newmarket Rd., Durham, NH 03824. ℂ 888/399-9777 or 603/868-7800. Fax 603/868-2964. www.three chimneysinn.com. 23 units. May to mid-Nov $169–$249 double ($30 less midweek); off-season $169–$219 double. Rates include breakfast. 2-night minimum stay on weekends. AE, DISC, MC, V. Children 6 and older welcome. **Amenities:** 2 restaurants (upscale regional, tavern fare). *In room:* A/C, TV, coffeemaker.

Wentworth by the Sea ★★★   The reopening of this historic resort in 2003 was a major event in seacoast hospitality; this is now, in my view, one of the top resort properties in New England. The photogenic grand hotel, which opened on New Castle Island in 1874 but later shut down due to neglect, was refurbished by the Ocean Properties group (owners of the Samoset in Rockland, Maine) and is operated jointly with Marriott in professional, luxurious fashion. As befits an old hotel, room sizes vary, but most rooms are spacious, with good views of the ocean or harbor. Particularly interesting are the suites occupying the three turrets, such as no. 601, in the middle turret: it's two stories tall, with the grandest view in the house. Eighteen rooms contain gas-powered fireplaces, while 15 include private balconies; all feature luxury bath amenities, new bathroom fixtures, and beautiful detailing and furnishings. Free high-speed Internet access is a welcome addition, with wireless access said to be on the way very soon. Families should note that many units here contain two queen beds. Just downhill, beside the marina, a set of new bi-level luxury suites opened in 2004 in a new facility (with private pool) and are truly outstanding: each possesses a water view, full modern kitchen stocked with pots and utensils, and a marble bathroom with Jacuzzi. The full-service spa features a full range of treatments such as facials and body wraps, while the adjacent privately operated country club is reserved for hotel guests. The **dining room** ★ fare here is also top-rate, served beneath the remarkable (and original) frescoed dome; entrees might include grilled swordfish, lobster with filet mignon, seared yellowfin tuna, a clambake, a lobster pie, or something more Continental. There is a moderate dress code (men are asked to wear a collared shirt).

Wentworth Rd. (P.O. Box 860), New Castle NH 03854. ℂ 866/240-6313 or 603/422-7322. Fax 603/422-7329. www.wentworth.com. 164 units. Peak season midweek from $259 double, from $479 suite; weekend from $359 double, $489–$659 suite. Off-season midweek double from $159, suite from $199; weekend double from $169. AE, DISC, MC, V. Ask about packages. **Amenities:** 2 restaurants (creative American), indoor pool; outdoor pool; spa. *In room:* AC, TV, kitchen (some), coffeemaker, hair dryer.

WHERE TO DINE

Portsmouth has perhaps the best cafe scene in New England; in at least 10 places downtown you can get a good cup of coffee and decent baked goods and while away the time. There's a Starbucks, of course, but my favorites are the relocated **Breaking New Grounds** (ℂ **603/436-9555**), 14 Market Sq., with outstanding espresso shakes, good tables for chatting, and late hours; **Caffe Kilim** (ℂ **603/436-7330**) at 79 Daniel St., across from the post office, a bohemian choice; and **Me and Ollie's** (ℂ **603/436-7777**) at 10 Pleasant St., well known locally for its bread, sandwiches, and homemade granola.

If you want a bit more of a bite with your coffee, three outstanding places leap to mind. The tie-dyed **Friendly Toast** (ℂ **603/430-2154**), at 121 Congress St., serves a variety of eggs and other breakfast dishes all day long, plus heartier items such as burgers. Funky **Ceres Bakery,** 51 Penhallow St. (ℂ **603/436-6518**), on a side street, has a handful of tiny tables; you may want to get a cookie or slice of cake to go and walk to the waterfront rose gardens.

Blue Mermaid World Grill ★★ GLOBAL/ECLECTIC   The Blue Mermaid is a Portsmouth favorite for its good food, good value, and refusal to take itself too seriously. A short stroll from Market Square, in a historic area called the Hill, it's not pretentious—locals congregate here, Tom Waits drones on in the background, and the service is casual but professional. The menu is adventurous in a low-key global way—you might try lobster and shrimp pad Thai, Bimini chicken with walnuts and a bourbon-coconut sauce, or crispy duck with guava and andouille stuffing. Other items include seafood, burgers, pasta, and pizza from the wood grill, plus a fun cocktail menu (mojitos, Goombay smash, and a dozen different margaritas) and homemade fire-roasted salsa.

The Hill (at Hanover and High sts., facing the municipal parking garage). $\mathcal{C}$ 603/427-2583. www.bluemermaid. com. Reservations recommended for parties of 6 or more. Lunch main courses $5.95–$14; dinner main courses $13–$21 (most around $15–$17). AE, DISC, MC, V. Sun–Thurs 11:30am–9pm; Fri–Sat 11:30am–10pm.

Dolphin Striker *✿* NEW ENGLAND   In a historic brick warehouse in Portsmouth's most charming area, the Dolphin Striker offers reliable if unexciting traditional New England seafood dishes, such as haddock filet piccata and lobster with ravioli. Seafood loathers can find refuge in one of the grilled meat dishes, such as grilled beef tenderloin, rack of lamb, and duck breast. The main dining room features a rustic, public house atmosphere with wide pine-board floors and wooden furniture; or order meals downstairs in a comfortable pub.

15 Bow St. $\mathcal{C}$ 603/431-5222. www.dolphinstriker.com. Reservations recommended. Lunch main courses $6.95–$11; dinner main courses $17–$28. AE, DC, DISC, MC, V. Tues–Sun 11:30am–2pm and 5–10pm.

43 Degrees North *✿✿✿* ECLECTIC   Right off the city's main square, Portsmouth's newest fancy eatery of note pulls off the neat trick of managing to be both a classy restaurant and a capable wine bar. Chef Evan Hennessey works magic with local seafood, Continental sauces, and game meats. You can fill up on a selection of his small plates such as cumin-fried oysters, seared Maine crabs, or blackberry-juniper braised short ribs, or go straight to a main course such as chile-spiced tuna steak, grilled tenderloin of pork, rabbit, boar, or even ostrich, or a grilled five-spice duck in a blood orange reduction with a duck confit crepe. Beguiling side dishes could be anything from applewood bread pudding to andouille-scallion potato cake. And of course, you can get plenty of wines by the glass or half-bottle. Note that in December lunch is served just 3 days a week.

75 Pleasant St. $\mathcal{C}$ 603/430-0225. Reservations recommended. Small plates $7–$10; entrees $18–$28. AE, MC, V. Mon–Sat 5–9pm.

Jumpin' Jay's Fish Café *✿✿* SEAFOOD   One of Portsmouth's more urbane eateries, Jay's is a welcome destination for those who like their seafood more sophisticated than simply deep-fried. A sleek and spare spot dotted with splashes of color, it also features an open kitchen and a polished steel bar. Jay's attracts a younger, culinary-attuned clientele. The day's fresh catch is posted on blackboards; you pick the fish, and pair it up with sauces, such as salsa verde, ginger-orange, or roasted red pepper. Pasta dishes are also an option—add scallops, mussels, or chicken as you like. The food's great, and the attention to detail by the kitchen and waitstaff is admirable.

150 Congress St. $\mathcal{C}$ 603/766-3474. Reservations recommended (call by Wed for weekends). Dinner $14–$23. AE, DISC, MC, V. Mon–Thurs 5:30–9:30pm (closes at 9pm in winter); Fri–Sat 5–10pm; Sun 5–9pm.

Lindbergh's Crossing *✿* BISTRO   For exotic comfort food, head to this restaurant, which serves what it calls hearty French country fare. Located in an old waterfront warehouse, this intimate, two-story restaurant has a bistro menu that's subtly creative without calling too much attention to itself. You can partake of starters such as seared rare tuna with white beans, then move on to main courses like pan-roasted cod with beet polenta, a Moroccan bouillabaisse, or braised beef short ribs with a Guinness and molasses sauce over baked polenta. They also offer steaks and $14 burgers of mixed lamb and tenderloin. If you don't have reservations, ask about sitting in the bar; they may have room.

29 Ceres St. © **603/431-0887**. Reservations recommended. Main courses $16–$27. AE, DC, MC, V. Sun–Thurs 5:30–9:30pm; Fri–Sat 5:30–10pm. Bar opens 4pm daily, with a limited menu.

Pesce Blue ★★ SEAFOOD/ITALIAN   Yet another upscale seafood eatery invades downtown Portsmouth, and yet again it's a smashing success so far. Chef Mark Segal serves seafood (but also other meals) with an Italian accent. Lunch might be a piece of grilled flat bread topped with maple smoked salmon and white bean puree, a tuna burger, a smoked trout salad, a salad Niçoise, or a crispy cut of Icelandic char with roasted fingerling potatoes and lemon caper sauce. Dinner might be a grilled tuna or some prawns, or a small plate of seafood-inflected pasta such as linguine with Maine peekytoe crab or spaghetti served with mahogany clams, white wine sauce, and peporoncino. There's also an outdoor terrace open from May through October.

106 Congress St. © **603/430-7766**. www.pesceblue.com. Small plates and entrees $9.50–$27. Lobsters market price. AE, DISC, MC, V. Sun–Thurs 5–9:30pm; Fri–Sat 5–10pm; also Mon–Fri 11:45am–2pm.

Portsmouth Brewery PUB FARE   In the heart of the historic district (look for the tipping tankard suspended over the sidewalk), New Hampshire's first brewpub opened in 1991 and draws a clientele loyal to the superb beers. The tin-ceiling, brick-wall dining room is open, airy, echoey, and redolent of hops. Brews are made in 200-gallon batches and include specialties such as Old Brown Ale and a delightfully creamy Black Cat Stout. An eclectic menu complements the robust beverages, with selections including burgers, veggie jambalaya, hickory-smoked steak, grilled pizza, and bratwurst. Recently the kitchen has become more adventurous with offerings such as cioppino and London broil with white-bean cassoulet. The food's okay, the beer excellent.

56 Market St. © **603/431-1115**. www.portsmouthbrewery.com. Reservations accepted for parties of 10 or more. Lunch main courses $5.25–$8.95; dinner main courses $11–$22. AE, DC, DISC, MC, V. Daily 11:30am–12:30am.

Press Room TAVERN FARE   Locals flock here more for the convivial atmosphere and the easy-on-the-budget prices than for creative cuisine. An in-town favorite since 1976, the Press Room likes to boast that it was the first in the area to serve Guinness stout, so it's appropriate that the atmosphere is rustic Gaelic charm. On cool days, a fire burns in the woodstove, and quaffers flex their elbows at darts amid brick walls, pine floors, and heavy wooden beams overhead. Choose your meal from a basic bar menu of inexpensive selections, including a variety of burgers, fish and chips, stir-fries, and salads.

77 Daniel St. © **603/431-5186**. Reservations not accepted. Sandwiches $3.50–$6.50; main courses $7.50–$13. AE, DISC, MC, V. Sun–Thurs 5–11pm; Fri–Sat 11:30am–11pm.

SHOPPING

Portsmouth's historic district is home to dozens of boutiques offering unique items. The fine contemporary **N.W. Barrett Gallery,** 53 Market St. (© **603/431-4262**), features the work of area craftspeople, offering a classy selection of ceramic sculptures, glassware, lustrous woodworking, and handmade jewelry. The **Robert Lincoln Levy Gallery,** operated by the New Hampshire Art Association, 136 State St. (© **603/431-4230**), frequently changes exhibits and shows and is a good destination for fine art produced by New Hampshire artists.

Bibliophiles and collectors of cartography should plan a detour to the **Portsmouth Bookshop,** #1-7 Islington St. (℅ **603/433-4406**), which specializes in old and rare books and maps; it's open daily. The **Book Guild** (℅ **603/436-1758**) at 58 State St. holds a more general, but very good, selection of used travel guides, geographies, sports books, poetry, novels, and more. **Chaise Lounge,** 104 Congress St. (℅ **603/430-7872**), offers a wonderfully eclectic range of home furnishings—sort of Empire meets modern—including wonderful photo lamps made in Brooklyn. **Nahcotta,** 110 Congress St. (℅ **603/433-1705**), is a gallery that boasts of "cool goods" including high-end paintings and sculptures, many of which are quietly edgy and entertaining.

Bailey Works, 146 Congress St. (℅ **603/430-9577**), makes rugged, waterproof bike messenger bags in several styles and colors. The attention to detail is superb; the popular "253" is billed as "great for students and briefcase haters."

Paradiza, 63 Penhallow St. (℅ **603/431-0180**), has an array of clever greeting cards, along with exotica such as soaps and bath products from Israel and Africa. **Macro Polo,** 89 Market St. (℅ **603/436-8338**), specializes in retro-chic gifts, toys, magnets, and gadgets.

PORTSMOUTH AFTER DARK
Performing Arts
The Music Hall This historic theater dates from 1878 and was thankfully restored to its former glory by a local nonprofit arts group. A variety of shows are staged here, from magic festivals to comedy revues to concerts by visiting symphonies and pop artists. Call for the current line-up. 28 Chestnut St. ℅ **603/436-2400.** Tickets $12–$50 (average price about $25).

Bars & Clubs
Dolphin Striker Live jazz, classical guitar, and low-key rock is offered most evenings Tuesday through Sunday. 15 Bow St. ℅ **603/431-5222.**

Muddy River Smokehouse Blues are the thing at Muddy River's downstairs lounge, which is open evenings Wednesday through Saturday. Weekends offer blues with well-known performers from Boston, Maine, and beyond. Cover charges vary, but admission is free for some shows if you arrive before 7:30pm. 21 Congress St. ℅ **603/430-9582.** www.muddyriver.com.

The Press Room A popular local bar and restaurant (see "Where to Dine," above), the Press Room offers casual entertainment almost every night, either upstairs or down. Tuesday nights are the popular Hoot nights, with an open mike hosted by local musicians. Friday nights are for contemporary folk, starring name performers from around the region; but the Press Room may be best known for its live jazz on Sunday, when the club brings in quality performers from Boston and beyond. 77 Daniel St. ℅ **603/431-5186.** No cover charge Mon–Thurs; around $5 Fri–Sun (2nd floor only).

2 Baxter State Park & Mount Katahdin

There are two versions of the Maine Woods. There's the grand and unbroken forest threaded with tumbling rivers that unspools endlessly in the popular perception, and then there's the reality.

The perception is that this region is the last outpost of big wilderness in the East, with thousands of acres of unbroken forest, miles of free-running streams, and more azure lakes than you can shake a canoe paddle at. A look at a road map

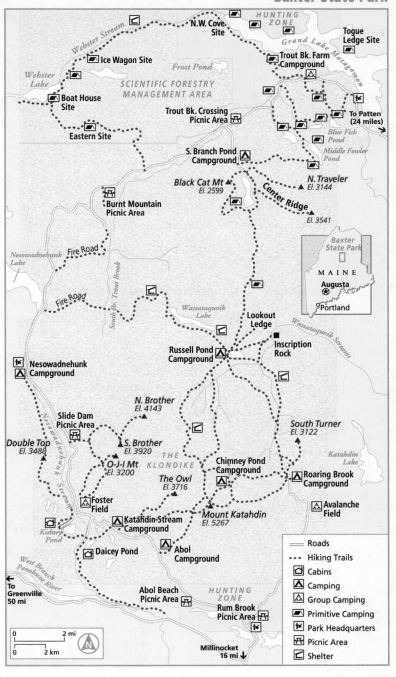

Webster Stream

N.W. Cove Site

HUNTING ZONE

Grand Lake Matagamon

Togue Ledge Site

Ice Wagon Site

Frost Pond

Webster Lake

Trout Bk. Farm Campground

Boat House Site

SCIENTIFIC FORESTRY MANAGEMENT AREA

To Patten (24 miles)

Eastern Site

Trout Bk. Crossing Picnic Area

Blue Fish Pond

Middle Fowler Pond

S. Branch Pond Campground

Black Cat Mt
El. 2599

N. Traveler
El. 3144

Burnt Mountain Picnic Area

Center Ridge

El. 3541

Nesowadnehunk Lake

Fire Road

South Br. Trout Brook

Baxter State Park

MAINE

Augusta

Portland

Fire Road

Wassataquoik Lake

Lookout Ledge

Wassataquoik Stream

Russell Pond Campground

Inscription Rock

Nesowadnehunk Campground

N. Brother
El. 4143

South Turner
El. 3122

Slide Dam Picnic Area

Double Top
El. 3488

S. Brother
El. 3920

THE KLONDIKE

Chimney Pond Campground

Katahdin Lake

O-J-I Mt
El. 3200

Roaring Brook Campground

The Owl
El. 3716

Avalanche Field

Foster Field

Katahdin Stream Campground

Mount Katahdin
El. 5267

Kidney Pond

Daicey Pond

Abol Campground

West Branch Penobscot River

To Greenville 50 mi

Abol Beach Picnic Area

HUNTING ZONE

Rum Brook Picnic Area

	Roads
	Hiking Trails
	Cabins
	Camping
	Group Camping
	Primitive Camping
	Park Headquarters
	Picnic Area
	Shelter

0   2 mi

0   2 km

Millinocket 16 mi

seems to confirm this, with only a few roads shown here and there amid terrain pocked with lakes; but undeveloped does not mean untouched.

The reality is that this forestland is a massive plantation, largely owned and managed by a handful of international paper and timber companies. An extensive network of small timber roads feeds off major arteries and opens the region to extensive clear-cutting. This is most visible from the air. In the early 1980s, *New Yorker* writer John McPhee noted that much of northern Maine "looks like an old and badly tanned pelt. The hair is coming out in tufts." That's even more the case today following the acceleration of timber harvesting thanks to technological advances in logging and demands for faster cutting to pay down large debts incurred during the large-scale buying and selling over the past decade and a half.

The Debate over Maine's North Woods

Much of Maine's outdoor recreation takes place on private lands—especially in the North Woods, 9 million acres of which are owned by fewer than two dozen timber companies. This sprawling, uninhabited land is increasingly at the heart of a simmering debate over land-use policies.

Hunters, fishermen, canoeists, rafters, bird-watchers, and hikers have been accustomed to having the run of much of the forest, with the tacit permission of local timber companies, many of which had long and historic ties to woodland communities. But a lot has changed in recent years.

Among the biggest changes is the value of lakefront property, which has become far more valuable as second-home properties than as standing timber. A number of parcels have been sold off, and some formerly open land was closed to visitors.

At the same time, corporate turnovers in the paper industry led to increased debt loads, followed by greater pressure from shareholders to produce more from their woodlands, which led to accelerated timber harvesting and quickened land sales. Environmentalists maintain that the situation in Maine is a disaster in the making. They insist that the forest won't provide jobs in the timber industry or remain a recreational destination if the state continues on its present course. Timber companies deny this, and insist that they're practicing responsible forestry.

A number of proposals to restore and conserve the forest have circulated in recent years, ranging from sweeping steps such as establishing a new 2⅔-million-acre national park, to more modest notions such as encouraging timber companies to practice sustainable forestry and keep access open for recreation through tax incentives.

In the 1990s, statewide referendums calling for a clear-cutting ban and sweeping new timber harvesting regulations were twice defeated, but the land-use issue has a ways to go in sorting itself out. The debate over the future of the forest isn't as volatile here as in the Pacific Northwest, where public lands are involved, but few residents lack strong opinions.

While the North Woods are not a vast, howling wilderness, the region still has fabulously remote enclaves where moose and loon predominate, and where the turf hasn't changed all that much since Thoreau paddled through in the mid–19th century and found it all "moosey and mossy." If you don't arrive expecting utter wilderness, you're less likely to be disappointed.

Baxter State Park is one of Maine's crown jewels, even more spectacular in some ways than Acadia National Park. This 204,000-acre state park in the remote north-central part of the state is unlike more elaborate state parks you may be accustomed to elsewhere—don't look for fancy bathhouses or groomed picnic areas. When you enter Baxter State Park, you enter near-wilderness.

Former Maine governor and philanthropist Percival Baxter single-handedly created the park, using his inheritance and investment profits to buy the property and donate it to the state in 1930. Baxter stipulated that it remain "forever wild." Caretakers have done a good job fulfilling his wishes.

You won't find paved roads, RVs, or hookups at the eight drive-in campgrounds. (Size restrictions keep RVs out.) Even cellphones are banned. You will find rugged backcountry and remote lakes. You'll also find Mount Katahdin, a lone and melancholy granite monolith that rises above the sparkling lakes and severe boreal forest of northern Maine.

To the north and west of Baxter State Park are several million acres of forestland owned by timber companies and managed for timber production. Twenty-one of the largest timber companies own much of the land and manage recreational access through a consortium called North Maine Woods, Inc. If you drive on a logging road far enough, expect to run into a North Maine Woods checkpoint, where you'll be asked to pay a fee for day use or overnight camping on their lands.

Note: Don't attempt to tour the timberlands by car. Industrial forestland is boring at best, downright depressing at its overcut worst. A better strategy is to select a pond or river for camping or fishing and spend a couple of days getting to know a small area. Buffer strips have been left around all ponds, streams, and rivers, and it can often feel like you're getting away from it all as you paddle along, even if the forest sometimes has a Hollywood facade feel to it. Be aware that, outside of Baxter State Park, no matter how deep you get into these woods, you may well hear machinery and chain saws in the distance.

ESSENTIALS

GETTING THERE   Baxter State Park is 86 miles north of Bangor. Take I-95 to Medway (Exit 56) and head west 11 miles on Route 11/157 to the mill town of Millinocket, the last major stop for supplies. Head northwest through town and follow signs to Baxter State Park. The less-used entrance is near the park's northeast corner. Take I-95 to the exit for Route 11, drive north through Patten and then head west on Route 159 to the park. The speed limit in the park is 20 mph; motorcycles and ATVs are not allowed.

VISITOR INFORMATION   Baxter State Park offers maps and information from its **headquarters,** 64 Balsam Dr., Millinocket, ME 04462 (© **207/ 723-5140;** www.baxterstateparkauthority.com). Note that no pets are allowed in Baxter State Park, and all trash you generate must be brought out.

For information on canoeing and camping outside of Baxter State Park, contact **North Maine Woods, Inc.,** P.O. Box 421, Ashland, ME 04732 (© **207/ 435-6213;** www.northmainewoods.org). Help finding cottages and outfitters is available through the **Katahdin Area Chamber of Commerce,** 1029 Central St., Millinocket, ME 04462 (© **207/723-4443**).

FEES   Baxter State Park visitors with out-of-state license plates are charged a per-day fee of $12 per car. (It's free to Maine residents.) The day-use fee is charged only once per stay for those camping overnight. Camping reservations are by mail or in person only (see below). Private timberlands managed by North Maine Woods levy a per-day fee of $4 per person for Maine residents, $7 per person for nonresidents. Camping fees are additional (see below).

GETTING OUTDOORS

BACKPACKING   Baxter State Park maintains about 180 miles of backcountry hiking trails and more than 25 backcountry sites, some accessible only by canoe. Most hikers coming to the park are intent on ascending 5,267-foot Mount Katahdin; but dozens of other peaks are well worth scaling, and just traveling through the deep woods is a sublime experience. Reservations are required for backcountry camping; many of the best spots fill up shortly after the first of the year. Reservations can be made by mail or in person, but not by phone.

En route to Mount Katahdin, the Appalachian Trail winds through the "100-Mile Wilderness," a remote and bosky stretch where the trail crosses few roads and passes no settlements. It's the quiet habitat of loons and moose. Trail descriptions are available from the **Appalachian Trail Conference,** P.O. Box 807, Harpers Ferry, WV 25425 (© **304/535-6331;** www.appalachiantrail.org).

CAMPING   Baxter State Park has eight campgrounds accessible by car and two backcountry camping areas, but don't count on finding anything available if you show up without reservations. The park starts taking reservations in January, and dozens of die-hard campers traditionally spend a cold night outside headquarters the night before the first business day in January to secure the best spots. Many of the most desirable sites sell out well before the snow melts from Mount Katahdin. The park is stubbornly old-fashioned about its reservations, which must be made either in person or by mail, with full payment in advance. No phone reservations are accepted. Don't even mention e-mail. The park starts processing summer camping mail requests on a first-come, first-served basis the first week in January; call well in advance for reservations forms. Camping at Baxter State Park costs $6 per person ($12 minimum per tent site), with cabins and bunkhouses available for $7 to $17 per person per night.

North Maine Woods, Inc. (see above), maintains dozens of primitive campsites on private forestland throughout its 2 million-acre holdings. While you may have to drive through massive clear-cuts to reach the campsites, many are located on secluded coves or picturesque points. A map showing logging road access and campsite locations is $3 plus $1 postage from the North Maine Woods headquarters (see "Visitor Information," above). Camping fees are $5 per person in addition to the day-use fee outlined above.

CANOEING   The state's premier canoe trip is the Allagash River, starting west of Baxter State Park and running northward for nearly 100 miles, finishing at the village of Allagash. The **Allagash Wilderness Waterway** (© **207/941-4014**) was the first state-designated wild and scenic river in the country, protected from development in 1970. The river runs through heavily harvested timberlands, but a buffer strip of at least 500 feet of trees preserves forest views along the entire route. The trip begins along a chain of lakes involving light portaging. At Churchill Dam, a stretch of Class I–II white water runs for about 9 miles, then it's back to lakes and a mix of flat-water and mild rapids. Toward the end is a longish portage (about 450 ft.) around picturesque Allagash Falls before finishing up above the village of Allagash. (Leave enough time for a swim at the base of the falls.) Most paddlers spend between 7 and 10 days making the trip from Chamberlain Lake to Allagash. Eighty campsites are maintained along the route; most have outhouses, fire rings, and picnic tables. The camping fee is $4 per night per person for Maine residents, $5 for nonresidents.

Several outfitters offer Allagash River packages, including canoes, camping equipment, and transportation. **Allagash Wilderness Outfitters,** Box 620, Star Route 76, Greenville, ME 04441 (they don't have a direct phone line in summer; call Folsom's Air Service at *✆* **207/695-2821** and an operator will relay messages/requests via shortwave radio), rents a complete outfit (including canoe, life vests, sleeping bags, tent, saw, axe, shovel, cooking gear, first-aid kit, and so on) for $23 per person per day. **Allagash Canoe Trips** (*✆* **207/695-3668;** www.allagash canoetrips.com) in Greenville offers 7-day guided descents of the river, including all equipment and meals, for $650 adults, $500 children under 18.

More experienced canoeists looking for a longer expedition should head to the **St. Croix River** on the U.S. border, where you can embark on a multiday paddle trip and get lost in the woods, spiritually if not in fact. Martin Brown's tour outfitter **Sunrise International** (*✆* **800/RIVER-30;** www.sunrise-exp.com), headquartered in Bangor with a base camp in Cathance Grove (about 20 miles inland from Machias), runs highly regarded canoe trips along the St. Croix (and also along the Machias River); call for current prices and tour schedules.

HIKING   With 180 miles of maintained backcountry trails and 46 peaks (including 18 over 3,000 ft.), Baxter State Park is the destination of choice in Maine for serious hikers.

The most imposing peak is 5,267-foot **Mount Katahdin** ★★★—the northern terminus of the Appalachian Trail. An ascent up this rugged, glacially scoured mountain is a trip you'll not soon forget. Never mind that it's not even a mile high (though a tall cairn on the summit claims to make it so). The raw drama and grandeur of the rocky, windswept summit is equal to anything you'll find in the White Mountains of New Hampshire.

Allow at least 8 hours for the round-trip, and be prepared to abandon your plans for another day if the weather takes a turn for the worse while you're en route. The most popular route leaves and returns from Roaring Brook Campground. (To get there, follow signs from the park's southern entrance.) In fact, it's popular enough that it's often closed to day hikers—when the parking lot fills, hikers are shunted to other trails. You ascend first to dramatic Chimney Pond, which is set like a jewel in a glacial cirque, then continue to Katahdin's summit via one of two trails. (The Saddle Trail is the most forgiving, the Cathedral Trail the most dramatic.) From here, the descent begins along the aptly named "Knife's Edge," a narrow, rocky spine between Baxter Peak and Pamola Peak. This is not for acrophobes or the squeamish: In places, the trail narrows to 2 or 3 feet with a drop of hundreds of feet on either side. It's also not a place to be if high winds or thunderstorms threaten. From here, the trail follows a long and gentle ridge back down to Roaring Brook.

Katahdin draws the largest crowds, but the park maintains numerous other trails where you'll find more solitude and wildlife. A pleasant day hike is to the summit of **South Turner Mountain,** which offers wonderful views of Mount Katahdin and blueberries for the picking in late summer. The trail also departs from Roaring Brook Campground and requires about 3 to 4 hours for a round-trip. To the north, there are several decent hikes out of the South Branch Pond Campground. You can solicit advice from the rangers and purchase a trail map at park headquarters, or consult *Fifty Hikes in Northern Maine* by Cloe Caputo.

WHITE-WATER RAFTING   A unique way to view Mount Katahdin is by rafting the west branch of the Penobscot River. Flowing along the park's southern border, this wild river offers some of the most technically challenging white water in the East. Along the upper stretches, it passes through a harrowing gorge that appears to be designed by cubists dabbling in massive blocks of granite. The river widens after this, interspersing sleepy flat water (with views of Katahdin) with several challenging falls and runs through turbulent rapids. At least a dozen rafting companies offer trips on the Penobscot, with prices around $90 to $115 per person, including a lunch along the way.

Among the better-run outfitters in the area is **New England Outdoor Center** (© 800/766-7238; www.neoc.com), on the river southeast of Millinocket. **The River Driver Restaurant** ⚓ is among the best in Millinocket; the owners also run nearby **Twin Pine Camps,** a rustic lodge on the shores of Millinocket Lake with stellar views of Mount Katahdin (cabins for two start at $120).

For other rafting options, **Raft Maine** (© 800/723-8633 or 207/824-3694; www.raftmaine.com) will connect you to one of their member outfitters.

3 St. Andrews & Grand Manan Island, New Brunswick

Once you've reached the northernmost limits of coastal Maine, it's just a skip (well, boat ride) onward to the pleasures of maritime Canada. For a sampling of one pocket of briny goodness, head for the **Bay of Fundy.** Its top attractions close to Maine include Campobello, Deer Isle, Grand Manan, and St. Andrews.

Note that the bay is rich with plankton, and therefore rich with whales. Some 15 types of whales can be spotted in the bay, including finback, minke, humpback, the infrequent orca, and the endangered right whale. Whale-watching expeditions sail throughout the summer from Campobello Island, Deer Island, Grand Manan, St. Andrews, and St. George. Any visitor information center can point you in the right direction; the province's travel guide also lists many of the tours, which typically cost around C$40 (US$28) to C$50 (US$36) for 2 to 4 hours of whale-watching.

The province has also put together a well-conceived campaign—called **"The New Tide of Adventure"**—to encourage visitors of all budgets to explore its outdoor attractions. The province has funded Day Adventure Centers (well marked from most major roads), where you can stop in, peruse the local adventure options, and then sign up on the spot. The Travel Planner also outlines dozens of day and multi-day adventures ranging from a C$10 (US$7) guided hike at Fundy National Park to C$389 (US$276) biking packages that include inn accommodations and gourmet dinners. For more information on the program, call © 800/561-0123.

I further detail coastal New Brunswick in *Frommer's Nova Scotia, New Brunswick & Prince Edward Island* (Wiley Publishing, Inc., 2004).

ST. ANDREWS ✮✮

The lovely village of St. Andrews—or St. Andrews By-The-Sea, as the chamber of commerce likes to call it—traces its roots from the days of the Loyalists. After the American Revolution, New Englanders who supported the British in the struggle were made to feel unwelcome. They decamped first to Castine, Maine, which they presumed was safely on British soil. It wasn't; the St. Croix River was later determined to be the border between Canada and the United States. Uprooted again, the Loyalists dismantled their houses, loaded the pieces aboard ships, and rebuilt them on the welcoming peninsula of St. Andrews. Some of these saltbox houses still stand today.

This historic community later emerged as a fashionable summer resort in the late 19th century, when many of Canada's affluent and well-connected nabobs built homes and gathered annually here for an active social season. Around this time, the Tudor-style Algonquin Hotel was built on a low rise overlooking the town in 1889, and it quickly became the town's social hub and defining landmark.

St. Andrews is beautifully sited at the tip of a long, wedge-shaped peninsula. Thanks to its location off the beaten track, the village hasn't been spoiled much by modern development, and walking the wide, shady streets—especially those around the Algonquin—invokes a more genteel era. Some 250 homes around the village are more than a century old. A number of appealing boutiques and shops are spread along Water Street, which stretches for some distance along the town's shoreline. Also don't miss the weekly farmer's market, held Thursdays in summer from 9am to about 1pm on the waterfront.

ESSENTIALS

GETTING THERE   St. Andrews is located at the apex of Route 127, which dips southward from Route 1 between St. Stephen and St. George. The turnoff is well marked from either direction. **SMT bus lines** (© 800/567-5151 or 506/859-5060), runs one bus daily between St. Andrews and Saint John; the one-way fare is C$17 (US$12).

VISITOR INFORMATION   St. Andrews has two information centers. At the western intersection of Route 1 and Route 127 is the seasonal **St. Andrews Tourist Bureau** (© 506/466-4858), which is staffed by local volunteers from May to the end of September. A second facility, the **Welcome Centre** (© 506/529-3556), is located at 46 Reed Ave., on your left as you enter the village. It's in a handsome 1914 home overarched by broad-crowned trees. It's open in May and September daily from 9am to 6pm, and in July and August to 8pm. The rest of the year, contact the **chamber of commerce** in the same building (© 800/563-7397 or 506/529-3555) by writing P.O. Box 89, St. Andrews, NB E0G 2X0.

EXPLORING ST. ANDREWS

The chamber of commerce produces two brochures, the *Town Map and Directory* and the *St. Andrews by-the-Sea Historic Guide,* both of which are free and can be found at the two visitor information centers. Also look for *A Guide to Historic St. Andrews,* produced by the St. Andrews Civic Trust. With these in hand you'll be able to launch an informed exploration. To make it even easier, many of the private dwellings in St. Andrews feature plaques with information on their origins. Look in particular for the saltbox-style homes, some of which are thought to be the original Loyalist structures that traveled here by barge.

For a guided tour, contact **Heritage Discovery Tours,** 205 Water St. at Market Wharf (© 506/529-4011). Elaine Bruff's "Magical History Tour" is recommended; prices start at C$15 (US$11) per person. She gives one tour daily from May 15 to October 15, starting at 10am. If she's booked full (it happens), another outfit in town, **HMS Transportation** (© 506/529-3371), offers a similar tour at the same price and even the same time.

The village's compact and handsome downtown flanks Water Street, a lengthy commercial street that parallels the bay. You'll find low, understated commercial architecture, much of it from the turn of the 20th century, that encompasses a gamut of styles. Allow an hour or so for browsing at boutiques and art galleries. There's also a mix of restaurants and inns.

Two blocks inland on King Street, you'll get a dose of local history at the **Ross Memorial Museum,** 188 Montague St. (© 506/529-5124). The historic home was built in 1824; in 1945 the home was left to the town by Rev. Henry Phipps Ross and Sarah Juliette Ross, complete with their eclectic and intriguing collection of period furniture, carpets, and paintings. Open late June to mid-October, Monday through Saturday 10am to 4:30pm. Admission is by donation.

Walk up the hill to the head of King Street, and you'll eventually come to the **Kingsbrae Garden** (see below).

On the west end of Water Street, you'll come to Joe's Point Road at the foot of Harriet Street. The stout wooden **blockhouse** that sits just off the water behind low grass-covered earthworks was built by townspeople during the War of 1812, when the British colonials anticipated a U.S. attack that never came. This structure is all that remains of the scattered fortifications created around town during that war.

Across the street from the blockhouse is the peaceful Centennial Gardens, established in 1967 to mark the centenary of Canadian confederation. The compact, tidy park has views of the bay and makes a pleasant spot for a picnic.

To the east of the blockhouse is the **Niger Reef Tea House,** 1 Joe's Point Rd. (© **506/529-8007**), built in 1926 as the chapter house of the Imperial Order of the Daughters of the Empire. Tea was served summer afternoons, with the proceeds going to support the group's charitable endeavors. In 1999, the building was restored by the St. Andrews Civic Trust, with profits going to support the Trust's preservation efforts. Notable are the dreamy, evocative landscape murals on the walls, painted in 1926 by American artist Lucille Douglass. A very limited selection of light meals is served here, along with excellent tea and coffee drinks (including espresso and cappuccino). Afternoon tea is served 3 to 5pm (about C$8/US$5.75), and includes tea with cakes, sweets, and finger sandwiches. If the weather's right, it's hard to top afternoon tea on the outside deck.

At the other end of Water Street, headed east from downtown, is the open space of Indian Point and the Passamaquoddy Ocean Park Campground. The views of the bay are panoramic; somehow it's even dramatic on foggy days, and swimming in these icy waters will earn you bragging rights.

Look for history at your feet when exploring the park's rocky beaches. You'll sometimes turn up worn and rounded flint and coral that washed ashore. It's not native, but imported. Early traders sailing here loaded their holds with flint from Dover, England, and coral from the Caribbean to serve as ballast on the crossing. When they arrived, the ballast was dumped offshore, and today it still churns up from the depths.

For a more protected swimming spot, wander down **Acadia Drive,** which runs downhill behind the Algonquin Hotel. You'll come to popular Katy's Cove, where floating docks form a sort of natural swimming saltwater pool along a lovely inlet. You'll find a snack bar, a playground, and an affable sense of gracious ease here, and it's a fine place for families to while away an afternoon. There's a small fee.

BOAT TOURS
St. Andrews is an excellent spot to launch an exploration of the bay, which is very much alive, biologically speaking. On the water you'll look for whales, porpoises, seals, and bald eagles, no matter which trip you select.

Quoddy Link Marine (© **877/688-2600** or 506/529-2600) offers whale-watch tours on a 50-foot power catamaran, and the tour includes use of binoculars and seafood snacks. Whale-watch and sunset tours are offered aboard the *Seafox* (© **506/636-0130**), a 40-foot Cape Islander boat with viewing from two decks. Two-hour tours in search of wildlife aboard 24-foot rigid-hull Zodiacs are offered by **Fundy Tide Runners** (© **506/529-4481**); passengers wear flotation suits as they zip around the bay. For a more traditional experience, sign up for a trip aboard the *Tallship Cory* (© **506/529-8116**), which offers 3-hour tours under sail, with music and storytelling on board.

Seascape Kayak Tours (© **866/747-1884** or 506/747-1884), in nearby Deer Island offers an up-close and personal view of the bay on full- and half-day tours, with lunch provided on full-day trips, and snacks on the half-day (2½-hr.) tour. No kayaking experience is needed. The daylong trip costs C$105 (US$75); the half-day trip runs C$59 (US$42).

GOLF

In St. Andrews, the **Algonquin hotel**'s newly expanded golf course is a beauty—easily among eastern Canada's top 10, right behind the bigger-name stars on Cape Breton Island and Prince Edward Island. It features nine newer inland holes (the front nine), and then nine older seaside holes that become increasingly spectacular as you approach the point of land separating New Brunswick from Maine. (All 18 of them are challenging, so bring your "A" game.) Service and upkeep are impeccable here, and there's both a snack bar on premises and a roving club car with sandwiches and drinks. Greens fees are C$125 (US$89) for 18 holes, lessons are offered, and there's a short-game practice area in addition to a driving range; call © **888/460-8999** or 506/529-8165 for tee times.

WHAT TO SEE & DO

Atlantic Salmon Interpretive Centre   The splashy new visitor center of the Atlantic Salmon Federation, sometimes called Salar's World after the main exhibit, opened in 1999 for its first full season and is dedicated to educating the public about the increasingly rare and surprisingly intriguing Atlantic salmon. Located in a bright and airy post and beam facility, the center allows visitors to get oriented through exhibits and presentations and viewing salmon through underwater windows or strolling the outdoor walkways along Chamcook Stream.

24 Chamcook Rd. (4 miles from St. Andrews via Rte. 127). © **506/529-1384**. Admission C$4 (US$2.75) adults, C$3.50 (US$2.50) seniors and college students, C$2 (US$1.40) children, C$10 (US$7) families. Daily 9am–5pm. Closed mid-Oct to mid-May.

Kingsbrae Garden *Kids*   This 27-acre public garden opened in 1998, using the former grounds of a long-gone estate. The designers incorporated the existing high hedges and trees, and have ambitiously planted open space around the mature plants. The entire project is very promising, and as the plantings take root and mature it's certain to become a noted stop for garden lovers. The grounds include almost 2,000 varieties of trees (including old-growth forest), shrubs, and plants. Among the notable features: a day lily collection, an extensive rose garden, a small maze, a fully functional Dutch windmill that circulates water through the two duck ponds, and a children's garden with an elaborate Victorian-mansion playhouse.

With views over the lush lawns to the bay below, the on-site Garden Cafe is a pleasant place to stop for lunch. Try the thick, creamy seafood chowder and one of the focaccia bread sandwiches.

220 King St. © **866/566-8687** or 506/529-3335. Admission C$8 (US$6) adults, C$6.50 (US$4.50) students and seniors, free for children under 6. Daily 9am–6pm. Closed early Oct to mid-May.

Ministers Island Historic Site/Covenhoven ★★   This rugged, 500-plus-acre island is linked to the mainland by a sandbar at low tide, and the 2-hour tours are scheduled around the tides. (Call for upcoming times.) You'll meet your tour guide on the mainland side, then drive your car out convoy-style across the ocean floor to the magical island estate created in 1890 by Sir William Van Horne.

Van Horne was president of the Canadian Pacific Railway, and the person behind the extension of the rail line to St. Andrews. He then built a sandstone mansion (Covenhoven) with some 50 rooms (including 17 bedrooms), a circular bathhouse (where he indulged his passion for landscape painting), and one of Canada's largest and most impressive barns. The estate also features heated greenhouses, which produced grapes and mushrooms, along with peaches that weighed up to 2 pounds each. When Van Horne was home in Montréal, he had fresh dairy products and vegetables shipped daily (by rail, of course) so that he could enjoy fresh produce year-round.

Rte. 127 (northeast of St. Andrews), Chamcook. ℭ **506/529-5081** for recorded tour schedule. Admission C$5 (US$3.50) adults, C$2.50 (US$1.75) children 13–18, free for children under 12. Closed late Oct to May 31.

WHERE TO STAY

St. Andrews offers an abundance of fine B&Bs and inns. Those traveling on a budget should head for the **Picket Fence Motel,** 102 Reed Ave. (ℭ **506/529-8985**). This trim and tidy motel is near the handsome, newly expanded Algonquin golf course (see "Golf," above) and within walking distance of the village center. Rooms are C$55 to C$75 (US$39–US$53) in peak season.

The Fairmont Algonquin 🔅🔅   The Algonquin's distinguished pedigree dates from 1889, when it first opened its doors to wealthy vacationers seeking respite from city heat. The original structure was destroyed by fire in 1914, but the surviving annexes were rebuilt in sumptuous Tudor style; in 1993 an architecturally sympathetic addition was built across the road, linked by a gatehouse-inspired bridge.

The red-tile-roofed resort commands one's attention through its sheer size and aristocratic bearing (not to mention through its kilt-wearing, bagpipe-playing staff). The inn is several long blocks from the water's edge, but it perches on the brow of a hill and affords panoramic bay views from the second-floor roof garden and many guest rooms. The rooms were recently redecorated and are comfortable and tasteful; all have coffeemakers and hair dryers. One caveat: The hotel happily markets itself to bus tours and conferences, and if your timing is unfortunate you might feel a bit overwhelmed and small. The resort's main dining room is one of the more enjoyable spots in town—it's often bustling (great people-watching) and the kitchen produces some surprisingly creative meals. Informal dining options include The Library (just off the main lobby) and the downstairs lounge. Further afield, the Italian bistro food at the Algonquin Clubhouse on the resort's golf course is well worth the drive—try the seared salmon with cilantro corn salsa served over pasta.

184 Adolphus St., St. Andrews, NB E5B 1T7. ℭ **800/441-1414** or 506/529-8823. Fax 506/529-7162. www. fairmont.com. 234 units. C$130–C$350 (US$92–US$249) double. Rates include continental breakfast year-round. Meal package C$45 (US$32) per person. Other packages available. AE, DC, DISC, MC, V. Valet parking. Pets accepted on 1st floor only. **Amenities:** 2 restaurants; outdoor pool; golf course; 2 tennis courts; health club; Jacuzzi; sauna; bike rentals; children's programs; game room; salon; massage; babysitting; laundry service; dry cleaning. *In room:* Minibar, coffeemaker, hair dryer.

Inn on the Hiram Walker Estate 🔅🔅   Innkeeper Elizabeth Cooney has put her indelible stamp on this exceptionally romantic getaway, a former home to the scion of the Walker distilling empire (which still makes Canadian Club whiskey). Rooms are filled with period antiques and furnished with four-poster beds and fireplaces; room 1 comes with a double Jacuzzi and views of lawn and sea, room 2 has a claw-foot tub and also looks out on the ocean—for half the price. Cooney also cooks sumptuous prix-fixe dinners, for guests only, for about C$60 (US$40) per person; an excellent hot breakfast is also available for an extra charge. Both are served in the cozy dining room, where an attached golf-themed bar completes the experience—this is St. Andrews, after all, where the town's excellent Algonquin golf course (see above) runs just alongside.

109 Reed Ave., St. Andrews, NB E5B 2J6. (© 800/470-4088 or 506/529-4210. Fax 506/529-4311. www.walker estate.com. 13 units. High season C$250–C$450 (US$178–US$320) double. Off-season rates lower. AE, MC, V. **Amenities:** Restaurant; bar; outdoor pool; Jacuzzi. In room: Jacuzzi (some), fireplace (some).

Kingsbrae Arms Relais & Châteaux ★★★   Kingsbrae Arms, part of the
upscale Relais & Châteaux network, is a five-star inn informed by an upscale European polish/sophistication. Kingsbrae brings to mind a rustic elegance—a bit of Tuscany, perhaps, melded with a genteel London town house. Located atop King Street, this intimate inn occupies an 1897 manor house, where the furnishings—from the gracefully worn leather chesterfield to the Delft-tiled fire-place—all seem to have a story to tell. The grand, shingled home, built by prosperous jade merchants, occupies 1 acre, all of which has been well employed. A heated pool sits amid rose gardens at the foot of a lawn, and immediately next door is the 27-acre Kingsbrae Horticultural Gardens (some guest rooms have wonderful views of the gardens, others a panoramic sweep of the bay; one has both). Guests will feel pampered here, with 325-thread-count sheets, plush robes, VCRs, and hair dryers in all rooms, and a complete guest-services suite stocked with complimentary snacks and refreshments. Five rooms have Jacuzzis; all have gas fireplaces. Guests can also enjoy a four-course meal around a stately table in the dining room during peak season. (This dining room is not open to the public.) One meal is offered nightly, and the new Canadian-style cuisine is ever-changing and scrumptious. Entrees might include Fundy salmon, Prince Edward Island (PEI) mussels, New Zealand rack of lamb, or Alberta steaks; high-quality wines are carefully paired with these meals.

219 King St., St. Andrews, NB E5B 1Y1. (© 506/529-1897. Fax 506/529-1197. www.kingsbrae.com. 8 units. C$250–C$1,000 (US$167–US$400) double. 2-night minimum; 3-night minimum July–Aug weekends. 5% room service charge additional. Meal packages available. AE, MC, V. Pets allowed with advance permission. **Amenities:** Babysitting; dry cleaning; laundry service. In room: A/C, TV/VCR, hair dryer, robes, Jacuzzi (some).

Salty Towers   Behind this somewhat staid Queen Anne home on Water
Street lurks the soul of a wild eccentric. Salty Towers is equal parts turn-of-the-20th-century home, 1940s boarding house, and 1960s commune. Overseen with great affability by artist-naturalist Jamie Steel, this is a world of wondrous clutter—from the early European landscapes with overly wrought gilt frames to exuberant modern pieces. Think *Addams Family* meets Timothy Leary.

The guest rooms lack the visual chaos of the public spaces and are nicely done up, furnished with eclectic antiques and old magazines. (Especially nice is room 2, with hand-sponged walls and a private sitting area surrounded by windows.) The top floor is largely given over to single rooms; these are a bargain at C$30 (US$20) with shared bathroom. Guests have full run of the large if sometimes confused kitchen. Don't be surprised to find musicians strumming on the porch, artists lounging in the living room, and others of uncertain provenance swapping jokes around the stove. If that sounds pretty good to you, this is your place.

340 Water St., St. Andrews, NB E5B 2R3. (© 506/529-4585. steeljm@nbnet.nb.ca. 15 units. C$40–C$65 (US$28–US$46) double. V. **Amenities:** Babysitting.

The Windsor House ⭐ Located in the middle of the village on busy Water Street, the lovely Windsor House offers guests a quiet retreat amid lustrous antiques in a top-rate restoration. The three-story home was originally built in 1798 by a ship captain. It's served almost every purpose since then, including stagecoach stop, oil company office, and family home, before reopening its doors as a luxury inn in 1999. The new owners—Jay Remer and Greg Cohane—spent more than 2 years and C$2 million renovating the home, and their attention to detail shows. The rooms are furnished with antiques (no reproductions) far above what one normally expects at an inn; Remer spent 5 years at Sotheby's in New York and knows what he's looking for. All of the rooms are superbly appointed, most with detailed etchings of animals adorning the walls; four have working fireplaces. The best two are the suites on the third floor, with peaceful sitting areas, exposed beams, Oriental carpets, handsome armoires, and limited views of the bay. (Both also have claw-foot tubs and glass shower stalls.) The basement features an appealing terra-cotta-floored billiard room. The hotel's restaurant (see below) can be found on the first floor, and the adjacent pub is the perfect spot for an early evening libation or after-dinner drink.

132 Water St., St. Andrews, NB E5B 1A8. ℂ 506/529-3330. Fax 506/529-4063. 6 units. C$125–C$300 (US$89–US$213) double. AE, DC, MC, V. Restaurant closed Jan–Apr. **Amenities:** Restaurant; bar. *In room:* Fireplace (some).

WHERE TO DINE

The Gables SEAFOOD/PUB FARE   This informal eatery is located in a trim home with prominent gables fronting Water Street, but you enter down a narrow alley where sky and water views suddenly blossom through a soaring window from a spacious outside deck. Inside, expect a bright and lively spot with a casual maritime decor; outside there's a plastic-porch-furniture informality. Breakfast is served during peak season, with homemade baked goods and rosemary potatoes. Lunch and dinner options include burgers, steaks, and such seafood entrees as breaded haddock, daily specials, and a lobster clubhouse—a chopped lobster salad served with cheese, cucumber, lettuce, and tomato; there's a kids' menu, as well. Margaritas and sangria are available by the pitcher. The view here tends to outclass the menu, but those ordering simpler fare will be satisfied.

143 Water St. ℂ 506/529-3440. Main courses C$3.95–C$6.95 (US$2.75–US$5) at breakfast, C$7.50–C$25 (US$5.25–US$17) at lunch and dinner. MC, V. July–Aug daily 8am–11pm; Sept–June daily 11am–9pm.

L'Europe ⭐⭐ CONTINENTAL   In an intriguing yellow building that once housed a movie theater and dance hall, Bavarian husband-and-wife transplants Markus and Simone Ritter whip up fine French-, Swiss-, and German-accented Continental cuisine for a 35-seat room. Starters include smoked salmon with rosti and capers; scallops in Mornay sauce, baked with cheese; French onion soup; and escargot. Main courses run to haddock in Champagne sauce, scallops fried Provençal-style, Zurich-style chicken in cream sauce, loin of lamb, pork cordon bleu, tenderloin steak with béarnaise sauce, and (as a nod to Canada) venison in a red-currant sauce, though it's sided with spaetzle. All are prepared with skill and restraint. Finish with chocolate mousse or homemade almond parfait. The wine list, as one might expect, is also surprisingly strong given that this is such a small, out-of-the-way place in a small, out-of-the-way town.

48 King St. ℂ 506/529-3818. Main courses C$19–C$28 (US$14–US$20). MC, V. June–Oct daily 5–9pm; Nov–May weekends (by reservation only).

Lighthouse Restaurant SEAFOOD   Located on the water at the eastern edge of the village, this spot rewards diners with a great view while they enjoy fresh-from-the-boat seafood. It's a bustling, popular place that seems to attract families and those who crave lobster. Look for a good selection of fish and lobster served with little fanfare or pomp. The menu includes sautéed scallops, seafood pasta, and lobster prepared any number of ways. The surf-and-turf specials (including filet mignon and lobster tail for C$34/US$23) are especially popular, and children's meals are offered at both lunch and dinner. The owners also rent out three suites on nearby Queen Street under the name Harry's Hatch B&B for C$95 (US$63). If you're in a pinch for a room, inquire about them.

Patrick St. (drive eastward on Water St. toward Indian Point; look for signs). ⓒ 506/529-3082. Reservations recommended. Lunch C$5.50–C$11 (US$4–US$8); dinner main courses C$15–C$36 (US$10 –US$26); most C$18–C$24 (US$13–US$17). AE, DC, MC, V. Mid-May to Labor Day daily 11:30am–2pm and 5–9pm. Closed Labor Day to mid-May.

The Windsor House ★★ FRENCH/CONTINENTAL   Guests are seated in one of two intimate dining rooms on the first floor of this historic home (see "Where to Stay," above), which serves only dinner on weekdays. The setting is formal, the guests are dressed with a bit more starch than you'll find elsewhere in town, and the service is excellent. The weekend brunches are somewhat less formal and very delectable, including such treats as Windsor gravlax, omelets, crepes, and Neptune's bounty (a kind of seafood chowder), while dinner offerings might include beef Oscar, cedar-planked salmon, or a host of other entrees.

132 Water St., ⓒ 506/529-3330. Reservations recommended. Brunch Sat–Sun C$4–C$12 (US$2.75–US$8.50); dinner C$26–C$35 (US$19–US$25). AE, DC, MC, V. Mon–Sat 5:30–9:30pm; Sun 11am–2pm and 5:30–9:30pm. Spring and fall closed Mon–Tues; closed Jan–Apr.

GRAND MANAN ISLAND ✸

Geologically rugged, profoundly peaceable, and indisputably remote, this handsome island of 2,800 year-round residents is a 90-minute ferry ride from Blacks Harbour, southeast of St. George. For adventurous travelers Grand Manan is a much-prized destination and a highlight of their vacation. Yet the island remains a mystifying puzzle for others who fail to be smitten by its rough-edged charm. "Either this is your kind of place, or it isn't," said one island resident. "There's no in between." The only way to find out is to visit.

Grand Manan is a good destination for independent-minded hikers who enjoy the challenge of finding the trail as much as the hike itself. An excellent resource is *A Hiking Guide to New Brunswick,* published by Goose Lane Editions. It's C$14.95 (US$11) and available in bookstores around the province, or directly from the publisher (469 King St., Fredericton, NB E3B 1E5; ⓒ **888/ 926-8377** or 506/450-4251). The island also holds considerable appeal for cyclists, although the main road (Rte. 776) has narrow shoulders and fast cars.

Hiking some of Grand Manan's trails, don't be surprised to come across knots of very quiet people peering intently through binoculars. These are the birders; the island is located smack on the Atlantic flyway, and Ur-birder John James Audubon lodged here when studying local bird life more than 150 years ago. Nearly 300 different species of birds either nest here or stop by the island during their long migrations, and it's a good place to add to one's life list, with birds ranging from bald eagles to puffins (you'll need to sign up for a boat tour for the latter). September is typically the best month for sightings, and it's not hard to swap information with other birders: On the ferry, look for excitable folks with binoculars and Tilley hats dashing from port to starboard and back. Talk to them. Boat tours from Grand Manan will bring you to Machias Seal Island, with its colonies of puffins, Arctic terns, and razorbills.

The island is also a special favorite among enthusiasts of the novelist Willa Cather. Cather kept a cottage here and wrote many of her most beloved books while living on the island. Her fans are as easy to spot as the birders, say locals. In fact, islanders are still talking about a Willa Cather conference some summers ago, when 40 participants wrapped themselves in sheets and danced around a bonfire during the summer solstice. "Cather people, they're a wild breed," one innkeeper intoned gravely to me.

ESSENTIALS

GETTING THERE   Grand Manan is connected to Blacks Harbour on the mainland via frequent ferry service in summer. **Coastal Transport ferries** (© **506/662-3724;** www.coastaltransport.ca), each capable of hauling 60 cars, depart from the mainland and the island every 2 hours between 7:30am and 5:30pm during July and August; a ferry makes three to four trips the rest of the year. The round-trip fare is C$9.60 (US$6.75) per passenger (C$4.80/US$3.35 ages 5–12), C$30 (US$21) per car. Boarding the ferry on the mainland is free; tickets are purchased when you leave the island.

Reserve your return trip at least a day ahead to avoid getting stranded on the island, and get in line early to secure a spot. A good strategy for departing from Blacks Harbour is to bring a picnic lunch, arrive an hour or two early, put your car in line, and head to the grassy waterfront park adjacent to the wharf. It's an attractive spot; there's even an island to explore at low tide.

VISITOR INFORMATION   The island's **Visitor Information Centre,** P.O. Box 193, Grand Manan, NB E0G 2M0 (© **888/525-1655** or 506/662-3442), is open daily in summer (10am–4pm except Sun, when it's open 1–5pm) in the town of Grand Harbour. It's beneath the museum, across from the elementary school. If the center is closed, ask around at island stores or inns for one of the free island maps published by the Grand Manan Tourism Association, which includes a listing of key island phone numbers.

EXPLORING THE ISLAND

Start your explorations before you arrive. As you come abreast of the island aboard the ferry, head to the starboard side. You'll soon see **Seven Day's Work** in the rocky cliffs of Whale's Cove, where seven layers of hardened lava and sill (intrusive igneous rock) have come together in a sort of geological Dagwood sandwich.

You can begin to open the puzzle box that is local geology at the **Grand Manan Museum** (© **506/662-3524**) in Grand Harbour, one of three villages on the island's eastern shore. The museum's geology exhibit, located in the basement, offers pointers about what to look for as you roam the island. Birders will enjoy the Allan Moses collection upstairs, which features 230 stuffed and mounted birds in glass cases. The museum also has an impressive lighthouse lens from the Gannet Rock Lighthouse, and a collection of stuff that's washed ashore from the frequent shipwrecks. The museum is open mid-June to mid-September Monday through Saturday 10:30am to 4:30pm, Sunday 1 to 5pm. Admission is C$4 (US$2.75) adults, C$2 (US$1.40) seniors and students, and free for children under 12.

This relatively flat and compact island is perfect for exploring by bike; the only stretches to avoid are some of the faster, less scenic segments of Route 776. All the side roads offer **superb biking.** Especially nice is the **cross-island road** ★★ (paved) to **Dark Harbour,** where you'll find a few cabins, dories, and salmon pens.

The route is wild and hilly at times but offers a memorable descent to the ocean on the island's west side.

Bike rentals are available at **Adventure High** (✆ **800/732-5492** or 506/662-3563) in North Head, not far from the ferry. (Day-trippers might consider leaving their cars at **Blacks Harbour** and exploring by bike before returning on the last ferry.) **Adventure High** also offers sea kayak tours of the island's shores for those who prefer a cormorant's-eye view 𝕬 of the impressive cliffs. Bikes rent for C$22 (US$16) per day, C$16 (US$11) for a half-day. Kayak tours run from C$39 (US$27) for a 2-hour sunset tour to C$99 (US$70) for a full-day excursion.

If Grand Manan seems too crowded and hectic (unlikely, that), you can find more solitude at **White Head Island.** Drive to Ingalls Head (follow Ingalls Head Rd. from Grand Harbour) to catch the half-hour ferry to this rocky island, home to about 200 people. On the island, you can walk along the shore to the lighthouse between Battle Beach and Sandy Cove. The ferry holds 10 cars, is free of charge, and sails up to 10 times daily in summer.

HIKING

Numerous hiking trails lace the island, and they offer a popular diversion throughout the summer. Trails can be found just about everywhere, but most are a matter of local knowledge. Don't hesitate to ask at your inn or the tourist information center, or to ask anyone you might meet on the street. *A Hiking Guide to New Brunswick* (Goose Lane Editions; ✆ **506/450-4251**) lists 12 hikes with maps; this handy book is often sold on the ferry.

The most accessible clusters of trails are at the island's northern and southern tips. Head north up Whistle Road to Whistle Beach, and you'll find both the **Northwestern Coastal Trail** 𝕬 and the **Seven Day's Work Trail** 𝕬, both of which track along the rocky shoreline. Near the low lighthouse and towering radio antennae at Southwest Head (follow Rte. 776 to the end), trails radiate out along cliffs topped with scrappy forest; the views 𝕬 are remarkable when the fog's not in.

WHALE-WATCHING & BOAT TOURS

A fine way to experience island ecology is to mosey offshore. Several outfitters offer complete nature tours, providing a nice sampling of the world above and beneath the sea. **Island Coast Whale Tours** (✆ **877/662-9393** or 506/662-8181) sets out for 4- to 5-hour expeditions in search of whales and birds from July to mid-September. On an excursion you might see minke, finback, or humpback whales, along with exotic birds including puffins and phalaropes. The cost is C$48 (US$34) adults, C$24 (US$17) children. **Sea Watch Tours** (✆ **877/662-8552** or 506/662-8552) runs 5-hour excursions from July to late September, with whale sightings guaranteed, aboard a 42-foot vessel with canopy. The rate is C$48 (US$34) adults, and C$28 to C$38 (US$20–US$27) per child, depending on age.

WHERE TO STAY

Anchorage Provincial Park 𝕬 (✆ **506/662-7022**) has about 100 campsites scattered about forest and field. There's a small beach and a hiking trail on the property, and it's well situated for exploring the southern part of the island. It's very popular midsummer; call before you board the ferry to ask about campsite availability. Sites are C$24 (US$17) with hookups for RVs, C$22 (US$15) for a tent. From Blacks Harbour ferry landing, follow main island road (Rte. 776) south to turnoff; it's about 7 miles.

Inn at Whale Cove Cottages ✦   The Inn at Whale Cove is a delightful, family-run compound set in a grassy meadow overlooking a quiet and picturesque cove. The original building is a cozy farmhouse that dates from 1816. It's been restored rustically with a nice selection of simple country antiques. The guest rooms are comfortable (Sally's Attic has a small deck and a large view); the living room has a couple years' worth of good reading and a welcoming fireplace. The cottages are scattered about the property, and they vary in size from one to four bedrooms, renting at C$700–C$800 (US$497–US$568). The 10-acre grounds, especially the path down to the quiet cove-side beach, are wonderful to explore. Innkeeper Laura Buckley received her culinary training in Toronto, and she demonstrates a deft touch with local ingredients. The menu might include bouillabaisse, seafood risotto, salmon in phyllo, or pork tenderloin with a green peppercorn sauce. Dinner is served nightly from 6 to 8:30pm; on Saturday night a full dinner is served with one seating at 7pm. Dinner is open to the public. They have 30 seats available and take reservations.

Whistle Rd. (P.O. Box 233), North Head, Grand Manan, NB E0G 2M0. 🕐 506/662-3181. 7 units. C$105 (US$75) double. Rates include full breakfast. MC, V. Closed late Oct to Apr. Pets accepted. *In room:* Kitchenette.

Shorecrest Lodge ✦ *(Value* *(Kids*   This century-old inn is a fine place to put your feet up and unwind. Located just a few hundred yards from the ferry, the inn is nicely decorated with a mix of modern furniture and eclectic country antiques. Most of the guest rooms have private bathrooms (a rarity for Grand Manan). The best is room 8 with burgundy leather chairs and a great harbor view. Kids like the spacious TV room in the back, which also has games and a library that's strong in local natural history. The homey country-style dining room has a fireplace and hardwood floors, and a menu that includes local fresh seafood and filet mignon. It's open daily from 5 to 9pm during peak season; hours are limited during the shoulder season.

100 Rte. 776, North Head, Grand Manan, NB E5G 1A1. 🕐 506/662-3216. shorcres@nbnet.nb.ca. 10 units, 8 with private bathroom. C$65–C$109 (US$43–US$66) double. Rates include continental breakfast. MC, V. Closed Dec–Mar. **Amenities:** Fitness equipment; TV room.

WHERE TO DINE

Options for dining out aren't exactly extravagant on Grand Manan. The three inns listed above offer appetizing meals and decent value.

In the mood for a dare? Try walking into **North Head Bakery** ✦✦ (🕐 **506/ 662-8862**) and walking out without buying anything. It cannot be done. This superb bakery (open Tues–Sat 6am–6pm) has used traditional baking methods and whole grains since it opened in 1990. Breads made daily include a crusty, seven-grain Saint John Valley bread and a delightful egg-and-butter bread. Nor should the chocolate-chip cookies be overlooked. The bakery is on Route 776 on the left when you're heading south from the ferry.

For a ready-made picnic, detour to **Cove Cuisine** (open Mon–Sat 11am–5pm) at the Inn at Whale Cove (🕐 **506/662-3181**). Laura Buckley offers a limited but tasty selection of "new traditional" fixins, such as hummus, tabouli, and curried chicken salad to go. The inn is on Whistle Road, which forks off Route 776 near the bakery.

Appendix:
The Maine Coast in Depth

Boiled down to simplest terms, the Maine coast basically consists of two regions: southern Maine—"down there," also sometimes derisively referred to as "Vacationland" or "not Maine")—and Downeast—"up there" or "the real Maine" or, possibly "miles from nowhere" (just kidding). The two regions are as different as night and day; broadly speaking, the gourmet cuisine, fine cars, and luxury inns of the south coast gradually (and then quickly) give way to cottages, used cars tacked together with baling wire, and fried fish.

Maine's legendary aloofness is important to keep in mind when visiting the area, because getting to know the region requires equal amounts of patience and persistence. New England doesn't wear its attractions on its sleeve. It keeps its best destinations hidden in valleys and on the side streets of small villages. Your most memorable experience might come in cracking open a boiled lobster at a roadside lobster pound marked only with a scrawled paper sign, or exploring a cobblestone alley that's not on the maps. There's no Disneyland or Space Needle or Grand Canyon here. The coast is, instead, the sum of dozens of smaller attractions, and resists being defined by a few big ones.

Of course, the natural elements—wind, light, water—take the greatest hold on the traveler, and these elements are as rejuvenating as they are capricious; you're just as likely to get a shiny, gold-star, blue-sky day when islands sparkle like gems in the harbor as you are 3 days of fog and spitting rain or snow. Maybe both. Attempting to understand this weather—just like trying to explore the coast as a regular tourist, hitting attraction after attraction—is frustrating and pointless. Better you let the mood of a day catch you, cycling or driving a back road in search of something (a byway, an old house, a handmade sign advertising PIES) you've never seen before.

Some writers maintain that Maine's character is still informed by a Calvinist doctrine, which decrees nothing will change one's fate and that hard work is a virtue. The Mainer's longstanding deep belief that the Red Sox (and, by extension, the Mainer) will never again win another world series—a delusion happily and forever shattered late on the night of October 11, 2004, to the everlasting joy of countless New Englanders (not least of all yours truly)—is often trotted out as evidence of the region's enduring Calvinism, as is the inhabitants' perverse celebration of the often-brutish climate.

But that's not to say travelers should expect rock-hard mattresses and nutritional but tasteless meals. Luxurious country inns and restaurants serving food rivaling what you'll find in Manhattan have become part of the landscape in the past 2 decades. Be sure to visit these places. But also set aside enough time to spend an afternoon rocking and reading on a broad inn porch, or to wander an unknown rocky beach path with no particular destination in mind.

1 The Maine Coast Today

It's a common question, so don't be embarrassed about asking it. You might be on Monhegan Island, or traveling Downeast along Route 1. You'll see houses and people. And you'll wonder: "What do these people do to earn a living?"

As recently as a few decades ago, the answer was probably this: living off the land. They might have fished the seas, harvested woodlots, or managed gravel pits. Of course, many still do, but this hardscrabble work is no longer the sole economic backbone of Maine. Today, scratch a coastal Mainer and it's possible you might find an editor for a magazine that's published in Boston or New York, a farmer who grows specialized produce for gourmet restaurants, or a banking consultant who handles business by fax and e-mail. And you'll find *lots* of folks whose livelihood is dependent on tourism, whether it's the tour guide, the high-school kid working a local T-shirt shop—or even the tow-truck driver hauling fancy cars around Mount Desert Island when they break down. There's a lot of trickle-down going on here.

This slow change in the economy is but one of the tectonic shifts facing the region. The most visible and wracking change involves development and growth. For a region long familiar with economic poverty, a spell of recent prosperity and escalating property values has threatened to bring to Maine that curious homogenization already marking much of the rest of the nation. Once a region of distinctive villages, green commons, and courthouse squares, coastal Maine in a few places is beginning to resemble suburbs everywhere else—a pastiche of strip malls dotted with fast food chains, big-box discount and home-improvement stores, and the like.

This change pains longtime residents. Coastal towns have long maintained their identities in the face of considerable pressure. The region has always taken pride in its low-key, practical approach to life. In smaller communities, town meetings are still the preferred form of government. Residents gather in a public space to speak out about—sometimes rather forcefully—and vote on the issues of the day, such as funding for their schools, road improvements, fire trucks, or even symbolic gestures such as declaring their towns nuclear-free. "Use it up, wear it out, make do, or do without" is a well-worn phrase that aptly sums up the attitude of many long-standing Mainers—and it's the polar opposite of the designer-outlet ethos filtering in.

It's still unclear how town meetings and that sense of knowing where your town ends and the next one begins will survive the slow but inexorable encroachment of Wal-Marts and Banana Republics. Of course, suburban Connecticut communities in the orbit of New York City and Boston have long since capitulated to sprawl, as have pockets elsewhere in the region—including a mall-heavy area outside Portland, the shopping outlets of Kittery and Freeport, the conglomeration of Route 1 near Bucksport or Ellsworth. Here, little regional identity can still be found.

But the rest of coastal Maine is still figuring out how best to balance the principles of growth and conservation—how to allow the economy to edge into the modern age, without sacrificing those qualities that make Maine such a distinctive place. Development is a hot issue, to be sure; but it isn't white-hot—yet. Few locals feel that development should be allowed at all costs. And few locals tend to think that the land should be preserved at all costs. They're not all that happy about rising property taxes and land prices, either—unless they happen to own a chunk of the coast. Then, it's more complex.

Pinching off all development would mean the offspring of longtime Maine families will have no jobs, and Maine will be fated to spend its days as a sort of quaint theme park. But if development continues unabated, many of the characteristics that make this place unique—and attract tourist dollars—will vanish. Will the Maine coast be able to sustain its tourism industry if it's blanketed with strip malls and fast-food joints, making them look like every other place in the nation? Not likely. The question is how to respect the conservation ethic while leaving room for growth. And that question won't be resolved in the near future.

Maine's economy has been quixotic, with tourism on the uptick but in no way growing steadily. The mid-'90s saw a slump, and things have been flat of late; even when the economy has nosed back downward, however, resourceful locals somehow find a way to buy and fix up farmhouses and keep their pickup trucks and dogs happy. Turn over a few stones, and it's remarkable how many self-owned enterprises you'll find along the coast.

But one change is all but inevitable: Property values will continue to rise as city folks increasingly seek a piece of whatever makes rural Maine special. Commentators point out that this change, while welcome after decades of slow growth, will bring new conflicts. The continuing rise of an information culture will make it increasingly likely that telecommuters and info-entrepreneurs will move in and settle the coast's most pristine villages, running their businesses via modem or satellite. How will these affluent newcomers feel about increased coastal development or increasing numbers of tour buses cruising their harbor-side streets? How will locals respond to the new money—with envy? With open arms? And, how will the area's precious natural resources be stressed by increased tourism or development?

Change doesn't come rapidly to the Maine coast. But there's a lot to sort out, and friction will certainly continue to build, one waterfront condo at a time. One thing is for sure: It will be interesting to see how it plays out.

2 History 101

Viewed from a distance, Maine's history mirrors that of its progenitor, England. The coast rose from nowhere to gain tremendous historical prominence, captured a good deal of overseas trade, and became an industrial and marine powerhouse and center for creative thought. And then the party ended relatively abruptly, as commerce and culture sought more fertile grounds to the west and south.

To this day, Maine refuses to be divorced from its past. As you walk through Portland, layers of history are evident at every turn, from the church steeples of colonial times to ocean-view parklands and elaborate residences that bespeak the refined sensibility of the late Victorian era.

Dateline

- 1000–15 Viking explorers land in Canada, and may or may not sail southward to New England. (Evidence is spotty.)
- 1497 John Cabot, seeking to establish trade for England, reaches the island of Newfoundland in Canada and sails south as far as the Maine coast.
- 1604 The French explorer Samuel de Champlain spots Mount Desert Island but does not stop. French colonists settle, instead, on an island on the St. Croix River between present-day Maine and New Brunswick. They leave after a single miserable winter.

continues

History is even more inescapable in the off-the-beaten-track coast. Travelers in Downeast Maine, for instance, will find clues to what Henry Wadsworth Longfellow called "the irrevocable past" every way they turn, from stone walls running through woods to Federal-style homes.

Here's a brief overview of some historical episodes and trends that shaped New England:

INDIGENOUS CULTURE Native Americans have inhabited Maine since about 7000 B.C. The state was inhabited chiefly by Algonquins and Abenakis who lived a nomadic life of fishing, trapping, and hunting; they changed camp locations several times each year to take advantage of seasonal fish runs, wildlife movements, and the like.

After the arrival of the Europeans, French Catholic missionaries succeeded in converting many Native Americans, and most tribes sided with the French in the French and Indian Wars in the 18th century. Afterward, the Indians fared poorly at the hands of the British, and were quickly pushed to the margins. Today, they are found in greatest concentration at several reservations in Downeast Maine. Other than that, the few remnants left behind by Indian cultures have been more or less obliterated by later settlers.

THE COLONIES In 1604, some 80 French colonists spent a winter on a small island on what today is the Maine–New Brunswick border. They did not care for the harsh weather of their new home and left in spring to resettle in present-day Nova Scotia. In 1607, 3 months after the celebrated Jamestown, Virginia, colony was founded, a group of 100 English settlers established a community at Popham Beach, Maine. The Maine winter demoralized these would-be colonists, as well, and they returned to England the following year.

- 1614 Capt. John Smith maps the New England coast, and calls the area a paradise.
- 1616 Smallpox kills large numbers of Indians in Maine.
- 1620 The *Mayflower*, carrying 100 colonists (including many Pilgrims, fleeing religious persecution in England), arrives at Cape Cod. Colonists begin to filter north to Maine almost immediately.
- 1624 York Village is settled, the first community in what would later become Maine.
- 1675–76 Native Americans attack colonists in New England in what is known as "King Philip's War."
- 1765 Maine's European population reaches 23,000.
- 1812 War of 1812 with England batters Maine's economy.
- 1820 Maine, formerly a district of Massachusetts, becomes a state.
- 1844 Hudson River School painter Thomas Cole begins painting the Mount Desert Island area, beginning a long process of attracting summer visitors to the area.
- 1903 Maine legislature begins steps to preserve parts of Mount Desert Island.
- 1915–1933 Oilman/philanthropist John D. Rockefeller, Jr., finances the construction of 57 miles of (car-free) carriage roads throughout Mount Desert Island.
- 1919 Acadia National Park (then called Lafayette National Park, in honor of the French general) is established, due largely in part to Rockefeller, who donates 11,000 total acres of land to it.
- 1929 Acadia National Park is renamed and expanded with the inclusion of Schoodic Point on the mainland.
- 1930s The Great Depression devastates Maine's already reeling industrial base.
- 1938 A major hurricane sweeps into New England, killing hundreds and destroying countless buildings and trees.
- 1947 A fire, apparently set by a careless cigarette, ravages nearly the entirety of Acadia National Park, razing many of Mount Desert Island's trees and buildings.

The colonization of the region began in earnest with the arrival of the Pilgrims at Plymouth Rock in 1620. The Pilgrims—a religious group that had split from the Church of England—established the first permanent colony, although it came at a hefty price: Half the group perished during the first winter. But the colony began to thrive over the years, in part thanks to helpful Native Americans. The success of the Pilgrims lured other settlers from England, who established a constellation of small towns outside Boston that became the Massachusetts Bay Colony. Throughout the 17th century, colonists from Massachusetts pushed northward into what is now Maine (but was once actually part of Massachusetts). The first areas to be settled were lands near protected harbors along the coast and on navigable waterways.

- 1972 Maine's Native Americans head to court, claiming the state illegally seized their land in violation of a 1790 act. They settle 8 years later for $82 million.
- 1980s Land boom and economic bubble hits Portland area, resulting in job creation and significant waterfront development. Within a decade, the bubble bursts.
- 1997 Bangor native William Cohen is sworn in as U.S. Secretary of Defense under President Bill Clinton.
- 1998 High-speed ferry service from Bar Harbor to Yarmouth, Nova Scotia debuts.
- 2002 Camden resident Richard Russo wins Pulitzer Prize for his novel Empire Falls.
- 2004 Boston Red Sox win the World Series, ending 86 years of frustrations and triggering wild celebrations from Kittery to Eastport.

The more remote settlements came under attack in the 17th and early 18th centuries in a series of raids by Indians conducted both independently and in concert with the French. These proved temporary setbacks; colonization continued throughout New England into the 18th century.

THE AMERICAN REVOLUTION   Starting around 1765, Great Britain launched a series of ham-handed economic policies to reign in the increasingly feisty colonies. These included a direct tax—the Stamp Act—to pay for a standing army. The crackdown provoked strong resistance. Under the banner of "No taxation without representation," disgruntled colonists engaged in a series of riots, resulting in the Boston Massacre of 1770, when five protesting colonists were fired upon and killed by British soldiers.

In 1773, the most infamous protest took place in Boston. The British had imposed the Tea Act (the right to collect duties on tea imports), which prompted a group of colonists dressed as American Indians to board three British ships and dump 342 chests of tea into the harbor. This well-known incident was dubbed the Boston Tea Party. Hostilities reached a peak in 1775, when the British sought to quell unrest in Massachusetts. A contingent of British soldiers was sent to Lexington to seize military supplies and arrest two high-profile rebels—John Hancock and Samuel Adams. The militia formed by the colonists exchanged gunfire with the British, thereby igniting the revolution ("the shot heard round the world"). Hostilities formally ended in February 1783, and in September, Britain recognized the United States as a sovereign nation.

While no notable battles were fought in Maine, a number of forts were established along the coast of Maine—first for the purpose of defending the British from the French, and then for the purpose of defending the new America from, well, the British. Many of these forts remain well preserved today, as state parks.

A Literary Legacy

New Englanders have generated whole libraries, from the earliest days of hellfire-and-brimstone Puritan sermons to Stephen King's horror novels set in fictional Maine villages.

Henry Wadsworth Longfellow (1807–82), the Portland poet who later settled in Cambridge, was perhaps the most famous coastal Maine writer (until recently; see below). Longfellow caught the attention of the public with evocative narrative poems focusing on distinctly American subjects. His popular works included "The Courtship of Miles Standish," "Paul Revere's Ride," and "Hiawatha." Poetry in the mid–19th century was the equivalent of Hollywood movies today—Longfellow could be considered his generation's Steven Spielberg (apologies to literary scholars).

The zenith of New England literature occurred in the mid- and late 19th century with the Transcendentalist movement. These exalted writers and thinkers included **Ralph Waldo Emerson** (1803–82) and **Henry David Thoreau** (1817–62). They fashioned a way of viewing nature and society that was uniquely American. They rejected the rigid doctrines of the Puritans, and found sustenance in self-examination, the glories of

FARMING & TRADE   As the new republic matured, economic growth in New England followed two tracks. Residents of inland communities survived by farming, and trading in furs.

On the Maine coast, however, boatyards sprang up anywhere there was a good anchorage, and ship captains made tidy fortunes trading lumber for sugar and rum in the Caribbean. Trade was dealt a severe blow following the Embargo Act of 1807, but commerce eventually recovered, and Maine-ported ships could be encountered everywhere around the globe. Entire towns such as Searsport developed almost solely as exclusive (at the time) hometowns for the sea captains who stayed at sea for long months on these difficult journeys; many of their homes contained distinctive "widow's walks," from which their wives could watch for their returns.

The growth of the railroad in the mid–19th century was another boon. The train opened up much of the coast to trade by connecting Maine with Boston. The rail lines allowed local resources—such as timber from the Maine woods, floated downriver to the coast via log drives—to be much more easily shipped to markets to the south.

INDUSTRY   Maine's industrial revolution found seed around the time of the embargo of 1807. Barred from importing English fabrics, New Englanders simply pulled up their bootstraps and built their own textile mills. Other common household products were also manufactured domestically, especially shoes. Coastal towns like Biddeford, Saco, and Topsham became centers of textile and shoe production. Today, however, industry no longer plays the prominent role it once did—manufacturing first moved to the South, then overseas.

TOURISM   In the mid– and late 19th century, Mainers discovered a new cash crop: the tourist. All along the Eastern Seaboard, it became fashionable for the gentry and eventually the working class to set out for excursions to the nature, and a celebration of individualism. Thoreau's *The Maine Woods* explored Maine (although not the coast) in detail, at a time when few white men had yet penetrated the interior of the state—and there were still significant dangers involved in doing that. His canoe trip to Katahdin was a genuine adventure.

Among other regional writers who left a lasting mark on American literature was **Edna St. Vincent Millay** (1892–1950), the poet from Camden, and **Sarah Orne Jewett** (1849-1909) who wrote the indelible *The Country of the Pointed Firs*. The bestselling *Uncle Tom's Cabin,* the book Abraham Lincoln half-jokingly accused of starting the Civil War, was written by **Harriet Beecher Stowe** (1811–86) in Brunswick.

New England continues to attract writers drawn to the noted educational institutions and the privacy of rural life. Prominent contemporary writers and poets who live in the region at least part of the year include **John Updike, Nicholson Baker, Christopher Buckley, P. J. O'Rourke, Bill Bryson, John Irving,** and **Donald Hall.** Bangor, Maine, is also the home of **Stephen King,** who is considered not so much a novelist as Maine's leading industry; he does write about coastal subjects often, however.

mountains and the shore. Aided by the dramatic paintings of the Hudson River School painters, Acadia and the Downeast Coast were suddenly lifted by a tide of summer visitors; this tourism wave crested in the 1890s in Bar Harbor. Several grand resort hotels from tourism's golden era still host summer travelers in the area.

ECONOMIC DOWNTURN   While the railways helped Maine to thrive in the mid–19th century, the train played an equally central role in undermining its prosperity. The driving of the Golden Spike in 1869 in Utah, linking America's Atlantic and Pacific coasts by rail, was heard loud and clear in Maine, and it had a discordant ring. Transcontinental rail meant manufacturers could ship goods from the fertile Great Plains and California to faraway markets; the coastal shipping trade was dealt a fatal blow. And the tourists, too, began to set their sights on the suddenly accessible Rockies and other stirring sites in the West.

Beginning in the late 19th century, Maine lapsed into an extended economic slumber. Families commonly walked away from their farmhouses (there was no market for resale) and set off for regions with more promising opportunities. The abandoned, decaying farmhouse became almost an icon for the Maine coast, and vast tracts of farmland were reclaimed by forest. With the rise of the automobile, the grand resorts further succumbed, and many closed their doors as inexpensive motels siphoned off their business.

BOOM TIMES   During the last 2 decades of the 20th century, much of Maine rode an unexpected wave of prosperity. A massive real-estate boom shook the region in the 1980s, driving land prices sky-high as prosperous buyers from New York and Boston acquired vacation homes or retired to the most alluring areas. In the 1990s, the rise of the high-tech industry also sent ripples from Boston north into Maine. Tourism rebounded as harried urbanites of the Eastern Seaboard opted for shorter, more frequent vacations closer to home.

Travelers to more remote regions, however, will discover that some communities never benefited from this boom; they're still waiting to rebound from the economic malaise earlier in the century. Especially hard hit have been places like Downeast Maine, where many residents still depend on local resources—lobsters, fish, farmland, maybe a bed-and-breakfast or crafts business on the side— to eke out a living. And, remarkably, it still works.

3 Maine Architecture

You can often trace the evolution of a place by its architecture, as styles evolve from basic structures to elaborate mansions. The primer below should help you with basic identification.

- **Colonial** (1600–1700): The New England house of the 17th century was a simple, boxy affair, often covered in shingles or rough clapboards. Don't look for ornamentation; these homes were designed for basic shelter from the elements, and are often marked by prominent stone chimneys.
- **Georgian** (1700–1800): Ornamentation comes into play in the Georgian style, which draws heavily on classical symmetry. Georgian buildings were in vogue in England at the time, and were embraced by affluent colonists. Look for Palladian windows, formal pilasters, and elaborate projecting pediments. Portsmouth, New Hampshire, has abundant examples of later Georgian styles.
- **Federal** (1780–1820): Federal homes (sometimes called Adams homes) may best represent the New England ideal. Spacious yet austere, they are often rectangular or square, with low-pitched roofs and little ornament on the front, although carved swags or other embellishments are frequently seen near the roofline. Look for fan windows and chimneys bracketing the building. In Maine, excellent Federal-style homes are found throughout the region in towns such as Kennebunkport, Bath, and Brunswick.
- **Greek Revival** (1820–60): The most easy-to-identify Greek Revival homes feature a projecting portico with massive columns, like a part of the Parthenon grafted onto an existing home. The less dramatic homes may simply be oriented such that the gable faces the street, accenting the triangular pediment. Greek Revival didn't catch on in New England the way it did in the South, however.
- **Carpenter Gothic** and **Gothic Revival** (1840–80): The second half of the 19th century brought a wave of Gothic Revival homes, which borrowed their aesthetic from the English country home.
- **Victorian** (1860–1900): This is a catchall term for the jumble of mid- to late-19th-century styles that emphasized complexity and opulence. Perhaps the best-known Victorian style—almost a caricature—is the tall and narrow Addams-Family-style house, with mansard roof and prickly roof cresting. You'll find these scattered throughout the region.

  The Victorian style also includes squarish **Italianate** homes with wide eaves and unusual flourishes, such as the outstanding Victoria Mansion in Portland.

  Stretching the definition a bit, Victorian can also include the **Richardsonian Romanesque** style, which was popular for railroad stations and public buildings.
- **Shingle** (1880–1900): This uniquely New England style quickly became preferred for vacation homes on the Maine coast. They're marked by a

profusion of gables, roofs, and porches, and are typically covered with shingles from roofline to foundation.

- **Modern** (1900–present): Maine has produced little in the way of notable modern architecture; you won't find a Fallingwater (one of Frank Lloyd Wright's best-known works, near Pittsburgh), though you might spy a surprising modernist building somewhere on an enclave of wealth such as Mount Desert Island or Cape Elizabeth—if you can get past the security.

4 A Taste of Maine

All along the coast you'll be tempted by seafood in its various forms. You can get fried clams by the bucket at divey shacks along remote coves and busy highways. The more upscale restaurants offer fresh fish, grilled or gently sautéed.

Live lobster can be bought literally off the boat at lobster pounds, especially along the Maine coast. The setting is usually rustic—maybe a couple of picnic tables and a shed where huge vats of water are kept at a low boil.

In summer, small farmers set up stands at the end of their driveways offering fresh produce straight from the garden. You can usually find berries, fruits, and sometimes home-baked breads. These stands are rarely tended; just leave your money in the coffee can.

Restaurateurs haven't overlooked New England's bounty. Many chefs serve up delicious meals consisting of local ingredients—some places even tend their own gardens. Some of the fine dishes we've enjoyed while researching this guide include curried pumpkin soup, venison medallions with shiitake mushrooms, and wild boar with juniper berries.

But you don't have to have a hefty budget to enjoy the local foods. A number of regional classics fall under the "road food" category. Here's an abbreviated field guide:

- **Beans:** Boston is forever linked with baked beans (hence the nickname "Beantown"), which are popular throughout the region. A Saturday-night supper traditionally consists of baked beans and brown bread. Many small coastal towns host "bean hole" suppers featuring this food, and there's a famous B&M baked-bean plant still operating in Portland.

- **Lobster rolls:** Lobster rolls consist of lobster meat plucked from the shell, mixed with just enough mayonnaise to hold it all together, then served on a hot-dog roll. You'll find them almost everywhere on the coast; expect to pay between $9 and $15 per roll, and for that price you'd better get a lot of meat. (One of the meatiest is served at Red's Eats in Wiscasset.)

- **Moxie:** Early in the 20th century, Moxie outsold Coca-Cola. Part of its allure was the fanciful story behind its 1885 creation: A traveler named Moxie was said to have observed South American Indians consuming the sap of a native plant, which gave them extraordinary strength. The drink was "re-created" by Maine native Dr. Augustin Thompson. It's still quite popular in Maine, although some folks liken the taste to a combination of medicine and topsoil. I happen to like it a lot.

- **Blueberries:** One gets the feeling that Downeast Maine's economy would be in serious trouble without the humble blueberry; it's grown and harvested everywhere around here. To taste it, look for roadside stands and diners advertising pies made with fresh berry in mid- to late summer. Also note that the tiny wild blueberries (which grow on low shrubs, often on windswept rocks or hilltops) are tastier than the bigger, commercially grown highbush variety.

Finally, no survey of comestibles would be complete without mention of something to wash it all down: beer. Maine alone has more microbreweries than any other region outside of the Pacific Northwest. Popular brewpubs that rank high on the list include Federal Jack's Brewpub (Kennebunkport), the Sea Dog Brewing Co. (now located in Topsham, originally in Camden) and Portland, Maine's clutch of terrific minibreweries—at least a half-dozen, at last count, all making mighty good beer.

5 Lighthouses: A Tour Up the Coast

Unlike its neighbor of Nova Scotia, Canada, Maine doesn't maintain, advertise, or market a "Lighthouse Trail"—but it might be a good idea to cobble one together, because this state has quietly assembled some of the best lighthouses in the U.S. of A. Most were built of stone in the early– to mid–19th century, and nearly all were automated in the 1960s or 1970s with very few exceptions. (Today no keepers live full-time in any Maine lighthouses.) To see them all, you'd need to drive the coast bottom to top—in other words, follow the chapters of this book in geographical order—and also be in possession of a boat.

Let's forget about the boat for a minute, and concentrate on those most easily seen by car; I've sprinkled references to Maine's most visible lighthouses throughout this guidebook, but henceforth, a quick primer on connecting the dots and seeing them one-by-one, beginning with the southern coast. (*Note:* If you're taking on a side trip to Portsmouth, New Hampshire—described in greater detail in chapter 10—you've got a shot at even adding a few *more* lighthouses to your "seen-in-lifetime" list. See below for more on those.)

THE SOUTHERN COAST

Almost from the moment you cross the state line in Kittery, you're on the scent of our imagined Lighthouse Trail. Make a beeline for Fort McClary, on the back road from Portsmouth to York (Rte. 103); from Portsmouth, simply follow State Street across the bridge to Maine, then turn right at the sign for Route 103. Follow the winding road a few miles to a sharp right-hand bend, and the park's there on the right before you round the bend. From here, you can view squat, gray-granite **Whaleback Light.** It's not much to look at, though a private boat would help you get closer; public access to the lighthouse grounds is not permitted, however.

A few miles north of Kittery, detour off Route 1 to York Beach and head for Long Sands. Here, from the comfort of nothing more than a blanket or beach chair, you can—with good eyes—spy *two* lighthouses at once!

The first one, **Nubble Light** (p. 72), is obvious at the northern end of the beach. It sticks far out on a promontory and is the archetypal Maine light. For a closer look at it, drive to the northern end of the beach and hang a right, then drive the winding cape road to the turnoff for Sohier Park (parking is free). Here, from a rock or bench, you can get almost close enough to the fabled light to touch it—don't try however; a dangerous narrow passage of water separates the viewing area from the rock-bound lighthouse. Snap a photo, then head up the hill for an ice cream cone at Brown's, again keeping your gaze fixed on the lighthouse as you eat.

The other lighthouse visible from Long Sands, the tall, slim, ghostly **Boon Island light,** demands a perfectly clear day and binoculars or exceptional vision; gaze out to sea, roughly in the middle of the stretch between both ends of crescent-shaped Long Sands, and its hazy outline may appear to you. Though nearly

10 miles offshore, the granite tower stands more than 13 stories tall—New England's tallest—and that's why it can be seen.

Tiny, windswept Boon Island itself has an appropriately murky history: when a British ship ran aground here in 1710, survivors resorted to cannibalism for nearly 3 weeks to survive until a member of the party somehow sailed ashore and fetched help. Author Kenneth Roberts wrote a popular novel, *Boon Island,* fictionalizing parts of this incident. Incredibly, the barren rock and its lighthouse was still inhabited as recently as 1978, when one of the worst winter storms in New England history destroyed all the outbuildings and part of the tower, where the keeper's family cowered for several days, awaiting rescue. Soon afterward, it was automated.

It's a bit farther north to the next light. The small **Goat Island Light** lies just off the lovely little hamlet of Cape Porpoise, north of Kennebunkport. (From Dock Sq. in the center of Kennebunkport, follow coastal Rte. 9 about 2½ miles north and east to find the village.) The light has a storied history, including its use as a command post for U.S. Secret Service agents defending the family compound of President George H. W. Bush; a keeper who did a 34-year stint of duty on the rock; a caretaker who died in a boating accident in 2002; and Maine's last lighthouse-keeping family, the Culps, who departed the light in 1990 and turned it over to automation and the care of the Kennebunkport Conservation Trust, which maintains the 25-foot tower and keeper's house and plans to restore the property further in the future. Boat visits are welcome.

At the mouth of the Saco River, where the big river enters the Atlantic at the Biddeford-Saco line, the cute little **Wood Island Lighthouse** and its keeper's house still guards this passage—though you'd never know it, as the light's almost impossible to view, except by boat. The light actually has a rich history, however, including tales of ghosts, murder most foul, and a keeper's dog smart enough to ring bells by himself. The Friends of Wood Island Lighthouse (www.woodislandlighthouse.org) offer summertime boat tours to the island; otherwise, its premises can't be visited by the public.

GREATER PORTLAND

Greater Portland contains perhaps the finest—and most-visited and -photographed—lights on the whole of the Maine coast.

To view **Cape Elizabeth Light,** the southernmost light in the Portland area, head straight for Two Lights State Park (there were previously two working lights here; one was phased out). The lightkeeper's home is now privately owned, but this lighthouse has a rich lore, including daring rescues of shipwrecked sailors in the boiling, stormy sea and the work of painter Edward Hopper, who featured the light in several early 20th-century paintings. It is still an important signal on this rocky part of the coast. If you're hungry after viewing it, be sure to drop by the outstanding Two Lights Lobster Shack (see the sidebar "Lucky 77" in chapter 5) for a bite, and also visit the small souvenir shack on the rocks.

Just to the north, **Portland Head Light** (p. 114) possesses lovely proportions, an 80-foot beveled tower, a handsome keeper's home (now a small museum), and a scenic position on a cliff before the horizon and the Atlantic. This is one of the very best lighthouses in Maine to view with the family—and one of the most popular and often-photographed, as well. (Don't come here for solitude.) Hundreds of thousands of visitors come each year to the free park from which it can be viewed, just off Shore Road in Cape Elizabeth. There's also a gift shop.

From Portland Head Light, you can get a very good view of another light-house just offshore: the often-overlooked (probably due to its crude looks) **Ram Island Ledge Light,** built of Maine granite in 1905.

Next up, reachable by following South Portland's Broadway to its end, is the **Spring Point Light,** an amusingly-shaped light that somewhat resembles a fire hydrant. But take it seriously: it guards the heavily trafficked passage between Portland Harbor and the so-called Calendar Islands, a passage critical to oil and freight transport into and out of Maine. The light is set out at the end of the narrow stone breakwater, and can be walked up to and viewed but not entered except during special open houses held periodically, where you may view the keeper's room, which is slowly being outfitted with period furnishings. There's a museum, the Portland Harbor Museum (© **207/799-6337**), on the land side of the breakwater with plenty more information about the area. The light is also adjacent to both the pretty campus of Southern Maine Community College and the ruins of Fort Preble, good places for a picnic and a walk.

Nearby around the point, the Portland Breakwater Light—locally known as "**Bug Light**"—is a smaller, squatter version of the Spring Point light sitting on land that was once an important shipbuilding complex. A small, free city park surrounds the light.

FREEPORT TO MIDCOAST

From either Bath or South Freeport, you can take a boat tour to view the attractive, high rock housing **Seguin Island Light** a few miles off Popham Beach. Contact Atlantic Seal Cruises (© **207/865-6112**), which runs twice-weekly tours in summertime, or the Maine Maritime Museum (© **207/443-1316**), which offers periodic cruises past the light. Due to the heavy fogs that frequently move into this area, the house sports Maine's strongest (and most valuable) lens; it's 12 feet high, and has been operating since 1857, the same year the keeper's home and stone light tower were also constructed.

Smaller, weaker **Pond Island Light, Cuckolds Light**, the **Perkins Island Light, Ram Island Light,** and the mainland-based **Squirrel Point Light** are all located in the same general vicinity as Seguin, and the quartet can also be viewed during the Maine Maritime Museum's cruises or during other charter runs from the Boothbay Harbor waterfront. Squirrel Point's light can also be hiked to via a rough trail that begins off Bald Head Road in Arrowsic.

Also in Arrowsic, some of **Doubling Point Light's** grounds are free to roam—reach it by crossing the huge bridge from Bath, making an immediate right onto Route 127 south, and following signs to the Doubling Point Road turnoff on the right. The light is connected to the keeper's quarters by a long causeway which is closed to the public. Two small related lights, known as the **Range Lights,** are housed in octagonal wooden towers near the Doubling Point grounds; these lighthouse grounds are also free to visit, and the towers are architecturally singular on the coast, though unsigned and a bit difficult to find. Once again, the Maine Maritime Museum's special lighthouse cruises often pass by this set of lights.

From the Boothbay Harbor pier, it's easy to visit the handsome **Burnt Island Light** and its attractive complex of outbuildings: catch a ferry (© **207/633-2284**) from the pier, then settle in for one of the twice-daily summertime tours. Plan ahead, however; the tours take 2 to 3 hours apiece. Now owned by the state of Maine, the complex, still active as a navigational aid, is now also home to a program of nature, arts, and even music courses—a real success story.

Before leaving Boothbay Harbor, you may wish to detour down the long peninsula to West Southport (take Rte. 27 to the turnoff for the village) to get a view of offshore **Hendricks Head Light,** now privately owned and beautifully restored.

Finally, there's the **Pemaquid Point Light** (in Bristol) and its museum and the **Marshall Point Light** (in Port Clyde) and its museum, both of which I describe in greater detail in chapter 6; and, offshore, there's the **Monhegan Island Light** and *its* museum (open July–Sept; ℂ **207/596-7003**), which I haven't mentioned. But it's well worth a look if you're out on the island, and makes a fine, fitting end to this section of our ad hoc Lighthouse Trail.

PENOBSCOT BAY

The midcoast region harbors plenty of lights, though many are small and posted on offshore rocks, thus inaccessible (and unviewable) by car. However, the squat **Owls Head Light,** now owned by the Coast Guard, sits on a promontory in Owls Head State Park (ℂ **207/941-4014**); it can be viewed by anyone who can wrangle a parking spot in the lot. (The light itself, of course, is off-limits.) Interestingly, there's a long walkway and set of stairs connecting the keeper's house to the actual light, making this one of the most visually pleasing of all Maine's lighthouses.

The southernmost light of the two in the city of Rockland is known as **Rockland Harbor Southwest Light,** and this light is fascinating—it's the only one in Maine that was built by a private citizen! A local dentist constructed the light as both an aid to ships and a kind of homage to the other Rockland light (see below), and it began blinking on and off in 1987; today, it's an official navigational light, and still privately held. From downtown Rockland, head south about 2 miles on Route 73 and hang a left onto North Shore Road.

The **Rockland Breakwater Light** is at the northern edge of the harbor, sitting atop a handsome brick home about a mile out on a rugged stone breakwater; it's easily viewed from the Samoset resort complex (see "Where to Stay," in chapter 7, but the grounds are only open to the public during summer weekends.

Rockport's Marine Park is a good spot to look out at the attractive keeper's house and its **Indian Island Light;** however, the light itself no longer functions. Just north in Camden, the **Curtis Island Light** is quite attractive—it sits on a private island, now owned by the city—but can only really be seen well from the deck of a sightseeing charter or windjammer cruise leaving from the harbor.

Again just north, in Lincolnville, stand on the ferry dock for a look at the **Grindle Point Light,** with its unusual squarish light tower—or, better yet, hop the ferry for an up-close look; it docks on Isleboro nearly beside the lighthouse. The light is part of a public park that includes a small museum built as a memorial to sailors.

Continuing north, pull off Route 1 at signs for Stockton Springs if you want a look at the tiny **Fort Point Light,** still active and now a state historic site. It's not the most impressive of the state's lights, however.

Castine is already attractive enough, but the presence of the **Dice Head Light** (p. 179) makes it even more so; the light, privately owned and resided in, features an unusual rough, conical stone tower (though the actual light is no longer atop this interesting structure). Simply follow Route 166 to its very end at the water for a look; do not approach the tower, however; it's private property.

There are three lighthouses on or just offshore Deer Isle, but one is no longer active and the other two can only be seen from a boat cruising off the island's back shore.

Finally, the **Robison Point Light** on Isle au Haut is accessible to the public—in fact, you can sleep in the keeper's house, the only lighthouse in Maine for which this is true. Contact The Keeper's House (© **207/460-0257;** www.keepers house.com) for current rates and availability; there's no phone and no electricity, but the owners will prepare a gourmet meal for you if you wish.

MOUNT DESERT ISLAND & DOWNEAST

Mount Desert Island and its surrounding islands are home to very few lights that can be visited or viewed by the public. One that can is the **Bass Harbor Head Light,** on Mount Desert's western lobe, down Route 102A past Southwest Harbor. The complex includes a cylindrical light tower, simple keeper's house, triangular fog signal, and even a barn.

From Bass Harbor, head for another light that can be visited by the public: the **Burnt Coat Harbor Light** (also known as Hockamock Head Light). To get here, however, you'll need to catch a ferry from Bass Harbor to Swan's Island. The squared brick tower and keeper's home were built in 1872.

The Downeast section of the Maine coast is rife with little ledges and lighthouses, often steeped in fog and usually off-limits to the public (and too far offshore or too indistinct to be seen anyway). The inactive **Winter Harbor Light** can be glimpsed from the Schoodic Peninsula loop road, although distantly; at press time (late 2004), this lighthouse was actually up for sale for more than $1 million—care to make a bid? According to the realtors, the keeper's home is well equipped with such amenities as a music room, woodstove, and a boat dock with moorings (plus boathouse, of course).

The slim stone tower of the **Petit Manan Light** near Milbridge pokes an impressive 120 feet above the surrounding sea. However, it's off-limits and difficult to see anyway. While taking a tour of the Petit Manan National Wildlife Refuge (see "What to See & Do" in chapter 9) you can get a better look at it.

Finally, the **West Quoddy Head Light** in Lubec is part of the state park of the same name I've described in chapter 9. This is America's easternmost point, and there's a museum on the lighthouse grounds, open daily from spring through Columbus Day. Check it out, then sit awhile to reflect on all you've seen on your lighthouse tour.

A LITTLE SOMETHING EXTRA

If you decide to begin your Maine coasting in Portsmouth, you can take a side trip to the coast and glimpse a few more lighthouses. The cast-iron **Fort Point Light,** part of the state's Fort Constitution Historic Site (© **603/436-1552**), is located on Route 1B near the Wentworth by the Sea resort described in "Where to Stay" in chapter 10. It can be viewed from the historic site—which is free to enter—from May through October, but can only be entered on one special open-house day each month during that season; check with the park each year for the open house dates.

There's also the brick **White Island Light,** offshore in the Isles of Shoals and too far to be seen except when taking a cruise of the islands. Contact the Isle of Shoals Steamship Co. (© **800/441-4620** or 603/431-5500) about periodic lighthouse cruises of the area.

For more on Maine's (and New Hampshire's) lighthouses and preservation efforts, contact the **American Lighthouse Foundation,** P.O. Box 889, Wells, ME 04090 (© **207/646-0245;** www.lighthousefoundation.org).

Index

See also Accommodations and Restaurant indexes, below.

GENERAL INDEX

A
AAA (American Automobile Association), 50, 61
AARP, 25
Abacus American Crafts, 118
Abbe Museum, 2, 201
Acadia Bike & Canoe, 202, 222
Acadia Drive, 276
Acadia Mountain, 203
Acadia Mountain Guides, 203
Acadia National Park, 2, 5–7, 193, 196–218
　avoiding crowds in, 198
　camping in and near, 203–205
　driving tour, 200–202
　entry points and fees, 199
　getting around, 198
　guided tours, 198–199
　history of, 196–197
　nature guide to, 206–218
　outdoor activities, 193–196, 202–203
　ranger programs, 200
　regulations, 199–200
　restaurants, 205
　seasons, 199
　traveling to, 197–198
　visitor centers and information, 199
Acadia Outfitters, 202
Accessible Journeys, 23
Accommodations. See also Camping; and Accommodations Index
　best, 9–10
　surfing for, 28–29
　tips on, 44–48
Active vacations, 36–41
　best, 7
　general advice, 39
　information and resources, 40–41
　special-interest, 41
Adventure High, 283
Agamont Park, 220, 223
Airfares, 27–28, 33–35
　for international visitors, 60

Airlines, 31–33, 44, 59–60
Airport security, 33
Allagash Canoe Trips, 273
Allagash Wilderness Outfitters, 273
Allagash Wilderness Waterway, 272–273
Alternative Market, 223
Amaryllis Clothing Co., 118–119
Amato's, 106
American Airlines, 32
American Automobile Association (AAA), 50, 61
American Express, 50
　traveler's checks, 15
American Foundation for the Blind, 24
American lobster, 210
American Revolution, 289
Anchorage Provincial Park, 283
Annual Fiddlers Contest, 18
Annual Windjammer Days, 18
Antiques, Portland, 118
Appalachian Mountain Club, 40
Appalachian Trail, 5–6, 196
Architecture, 292–293
Area code, 50
Arts and crafts, 165
Asticou Terraces, 233
Atlantic Salmon Interpretive Centre, 277
ATMs (automated teller machines), 14–15, 50, 58–59
Aucocisco Gallery, 1
Autumn, 16

B
Back Cove, 110
Back Cove Pathway, 115
Backpacking, Baxter State Park, 272
Bailey Works, 268
Bald eagles, 217
Balmy Days Cruises, 141
Balsam fir, 207
Bangor, 190–192

Bangor Historical Society, 191
Bar Harbor, 8, 26, 193, 194, 196–205, 219–232
　accommodations, 222
　exploring, 220
　history of, 219
　parking, 222
　restaurants, 227
　shopping, 232
　traveling to, 219–220
　visitor information, 220
Bar Harbor Bicycle Shop, 202
Bar Harbor Campground, 204–205
Bar Harbor Hemporium, 232
Bar Harbor Historical Society, 220
Baseball, Portland, 118
Bass Harbor, 233–234
Bass Harbor Head Light, 298
Bath, 131–136
Baxter State Park, 268–274
Bay Ferries, 118
Bay of Fundy, 274
Bayview Street Cinema, 164
Beaches, 37
　Acadia National Park, 201
　Biddeford, 98
　Cape Elizabeth, 111, 117
　Harpswell Peninsula, 137
　the Kennebunks, 89
　Midcoast Maine, 152
　Mount Desert Island, 194
　Ogunquit, 79–80
　Portland, 117
　southern Maine, 3
　the Yorks, 72–73
Beal & Bunker, 233
Beavers, 209
Bed & breakfasts (B&Bs). See also Accommodations Index
　best, 9
The Beehive Trail, 201
Belfast, 172–178
Belfast and Moosehead Lake Railroad, 173
The Belfast Co-op, 176
Belfast Kayak Tours, 173

Biddeford, 97–98
Biddeford Pool, 98
BiddingForTravel, 28
Big Chicken Barn, 188
Biking and mountain
  biking, 37
    Bar Harbor, 222
    Camden, 164
    Campobello, 249
    Grand Manan Island,
      282–283
    the Kennebunks, 89
    Midcoast Maine, 152
    Mount Desert Island and
      Acadia National Park, 7,
      194, 196, 202
    Route 1A, 7, 37
Birding, 37–38, 41
    Downeast Maine, 246, 247
    Monhegan Island, 150
Birds, 213–218
Black-backed gull, 216
Black bears, 209
Blacks Harbour, 283
Blackstones, 24
Blackwoods, 203–204
Blueberry, lowbush, 209
Blueberry barrens, 6, 180,
  204
Blue Hill, 6, 186–189
Blue Hill Fair, 19, 187–188
Blue Hill Mountain, 188
Boat-and-breakfast, 159
Boat trips and cruises. See
  also Ferries
    around Boothbay, 141
    Downeast Maine, 240
    Grand Manan Island, 283
    Kennebunkport, 88
    Monhegan Island, 149
    Ogunquit, 78–79
    Pemaquid Peninsula, 147
    Portsmouth (New
      Hampshire), 262
    St. Andrews, 276–277
    Sebago and Long lakes, 122
Boingo, 30
Bold Coast, 243
Bold Coast Charter Co, 240
The Book Guild, 268
Books, recommended, 50
Boon Island light, 294–295
Boothbay Harbor Fisherman's
  Festival, 18
Boothbay Region Land Trust,
  140
The Boothbays, 138–145
Booth Theatre, 79
Boucher Memorial Park, 98
Bowdoin College, 131
Bowdoin College Museum of
  Art, 133

Boynton-McKay, 164
Bradbury Brothers Market,
  95
Bradford Camps, 42
Brian Ború, 120
Brick Store Museum, 87
Brown's Ice Cream, 72
Brunswick, 131–136
Bryant's Stove Museum, 174
The Bubbles, 203, 204
Bucket shops, 34
Bucksport, 172–178
Burnham Tavern, 245
Burnt Coat Harbor Light, 298
Burnt Island Light, 296
Business hours, 61–62
Bus travel, 36, 43
    for international visitors,
      60–61

Cabot Mill Antiques, 133
Cadillac Mountain, 202
Cadillac Mountain Sports,
  232
Calais, 243
The Calendar Islands, 3–4,
  296
Calendar of events, 18–20
Camden, 6, 161–172
    accommodations, 166–170
    exploring, 162–164
    traveling to, 162
    visitor information, 162
Camden Deli, 170
Camden Hills, 4–6
Camden Hills State Park,
  152, 162, 164, 166
Camden Snow Bowl,
  153, 164
Camden Windjammer
  Weekend, 153
Camping, 14, 38, 42
    in and near Acadia
      National Park, 203
    Anchorage Provincial Park,
      283
    between Bath and
      Wiscasset, 141
    Baxter State Park, 272
    Maine Island Trail, 10
    Mount Desert Island, 194
Campobello Island, 248–250
Candlelight Stroll, 20
Canoeing, 7
    Baxter State Park, 272
    Mount Desert Island,
      194–195
Cape Able Bike Shop, 89
Cape Arundel Golf Club, 38
Cape Elizabeth beaches,
  111, 117

Cape Elizabeth Light, 295
Cape Neddick, 68
Cape Porpoise Kitchen, 95
Cape Rosier, 179–180
Car rentals, 29, 41, 61
Carriage rides, Mount Desert
  Island, 195
Carrie Albee House, 242
Car travel, 35, 41–42, 61, 62
Casco Bay Lines, 110, 116
Castine and environs, 6,
  178–181
Castle Tucker, 139–140
Cathedral Woods, 150
Cellphones, 30–31
Center for Cultural
  Exchange, 121
Center for Maine
  Contemporary Art,
  162–163
Center Street Congregational
  Church, 242
Chaise Lounge, 268
Charlotte County Museum,
  250
Chebeague Island, 37
Cherryfield-Narraguargus
  Historical Society, 241
Chewonki Campgrounds,
  141
Children, families with
    best destinations for, 8
    information and resources,
      25–26
Children's Museum of Maine,
  113–114
The Children's Museum of
  Portsmouth (New Hamp-
  shire), 262
Chiltern Mountain Club, 24
The Chocolate Museum, 251
Christmas Cove, 146
Christmas Prelude, 20
City Hall (Portland), 113
Clark Perry House, 242
Cliff Walk, 71
Coastal Maine Botanical
  Garden, 140
Cobscook Bay State Park,
  194, 245
Cobweb Bridge, 137
Cole Land Transportation
  Museum, 191
Colgan Air, 32
College of the Atlantic,
  220, 223
Colonial Pemaquid, 146
Columbia Falls, 241
Columbia Falls Pottery,
  241–242
Common Ground Country
  Fair, 19

Concord Trailways, 36, 43
Consolidators, 34
Continental Airlines, 32
Council Travel, 26
Country Walkers, 40
Cranberry Islands, 233
Credit cards, 15, 58
Crescent Beach State Park,
    111, 117
Criterion Theater, 220, 222
Cuckolds Light, 296
Cuddledown of Maine, 125
Cuisine, 293–294
Currency and currency
    exchange, 57–58
Curtis Island Light, 297
Customs regulations, 56–57
Cutler, 243
Cutler Coastal Trail, 245

Day Mountain, 204
D. Cole Jewelers, 119
Deer Isle, 181–186
Deer Isle Granite Museum,
    182
DeLorme Map Store, 124
Delta Airlines, 32
Dice Head Light, 179, 297
Diners, 84–85
Disabilities, travelers with,
    23–24
Dock Square, 88
Dolphins, 212
Dolphin Striker, 268
Dorr Mountain Ladder Trail,
    201, 203
Doubling Point Light, 296
Douglas Mountain, 122
Downeast Maine,
    12, 238–257
    accommodations and
        restaurants, 251–257
    exploring, 241–245
    outdoor activities,
        240–241
    sights and attractions,
        245–248
    special events, 240
    traveling to, 238
    visitor information,
        238, 240
Drinking laws, 62
Driver's licenses, foreign, 54
Ducks, 213

Eagle Island Tours, 116
East End Beach, 117
Eastern Promenade, 110, 113
Eastern Prom Pathway,
    115–116

East Point Sanctuary, 98
Eastport, 6, 243, 244
Eastport Historic District,
    246
Eastport Salmon Festival,
    244
Elderhostel, 25
ElderTreks, 25
Electricity, 62
Elizabeth Perkins House, 71
Ellsworth, 241
ELTExpress, 34
Embassies and consulates, 62
Emergencies, 51, 63
Emerging Horizons, 24
Emerson, Ralph Waldo, 290
Emerson-Wilcox House, 71
Entry requirements, 53–56
Exchange Street, 113
Expedia, 27, 28

Fall Festival Arts & Crafts
    Show, 19, 165
Fall foliage, 16–17
    best places to see, 6
Fall Foliage Fair, 19
Families with children
    best destinations for, 8
    information and resources,
        25–26
Farnsworth Center for the
    Wyeth Family, 156
Farnsworth Homestead, 156
Farnsworth Museum, 156
Fax machines, 65
Ferries
    Cranberry Islands, 233
    Isle au Haut, 186
    Portland, 116–118
Ferry Beach, 117
Festival of Lights
    Rockland, 20, 166
    York Village, 20
Festival of Scarecrows and
    Harvest Day, 19
Festivals and special events,
    18–20
Fiddlehead, Antique Car, &
    Antique Aeroplane
    Festival, 18
Film, flying with, 35
Finback whale, 211
First Parish Church, 113
Fisherman's Walk, 71
Fishermen's Museum, 147
Fishing, 38
    Mount Desert Island, 195
    Ogunquit, 79
    Portland, 116
FlyCheap, 34
Fly-fishing, 41

Flying Mountain, 204
Flying Wheels Travel, 23
Folia, 1, 119
Foliage hot line, 17
Footbridge Beach, 80
Foreign visitors, 53–66
    customs regulations, 56–57
    entry requirements, 53–56
    fingerprinting of, 54
    getting to and around
        coastal Maine, 59–61
    money matters, 57–59
Fort Knox, 173
Fort Point Light, 297, 298
Fortunes Rocks Beach,
    90, 98
Fort William Henry, 146–147
Fort Williams State Park,
    111, 117
Fourth of July (Eastport),
    240, 244
Freeport, 11, 123–131
Freeport Knife Co., 125–126
Freeport Trading & Shipping
    Co., 125
French & Brawn, 164, 170
Frommers.com, 28
Fundy Tide Runners, 277

Gasoline, 63
Gates House Museum, 242
Gay and lesbian travelers,
    information and resources,
    24–25
George Foster House, 242
Giardia, 21
Gilsland Farm Sanctuary,
    111
Goat Island Light, 295
Golden Age Passport, 25
Golf, 38
    Bar Harbor, 196
    Midcoast Maine, 152
    St. Andrews, 277
    South Berwick, 72
Gooch's Beach, 89
Goose Rocks Beach, 90
GoToMyPC, 29–30
Gouldsboro, 241
Grand Lake Outfitters, 42
Grand Lake Stream, 42, 195
Grand Manan Island,
    281–282
Grand Manan Museum,
    282
Great blue heron, 214
Great Head Trail, 201
Great Lost Bear, 120
Great North Woods, 7, 210,
    270, 271
Great Wass Island, 196

Great Wass Island Preserve, 246
Green Design Furniture, 119
Greyhound, 36
Grindle Point Light, 297
Gritty McDuff 's Brew Pub, 119–120
GSM (Global System for Mobiles) wireless network, 31
Guided tours, 40
Guides, 39–40

Hamilton House, 72
Hancock Wharf, 70–71
Harbor Fish Market, 119
Harbor Park, 164
Harbor porpoise, 213
Harbor seal, 213
Hardy Boat Cruises, 147
Harpswell Peninsula, 136–138
Harrington Meeting House, 146
Haystack Mountain School of Crafts, 183
H.B. Provisions, 90
Health concerns, 21–22
Health insurance, 22, 57
Hendricks Head Light, 297
Heritage Discovery Tours, 275
Herring Cove Provincial Park, 249
Herring gull, 216
Hiking and walking, 38
    Baxter State Park, 273
    Douglas Mountain, 122
    Downeast Maine, 245, 246, 249, 250
    Grand Manan Island, 283
    guided tours, 40
    Holbrook Island Wildlife Sanctuary, 180
    Midcoast Maine, 152–153
    Monhegan Island, 6, 150
    Mount Desert Island and Acadia National Park, 196, 201, 202–203, 233
    Mount Megunticook, 162
    Ogunquit, 78
    Portland, 115
    Vaughn Woods State Park, 72
    the Yorks, 72
History, 287–292
HMS Transportation, 275
Holbrook Island Wildlife Sanctuary, 180
Holidays, 63
Hospitals, 51

Hotwire, 28
Hudson Museum, 191
Hulls Cove Visitor Center, 199
Humpback whale, 211

I Can, 24
IGLTA (International Gay & Lesbian Travel Association), 24
Immigration and customs clearance, 60
Independence Day, 19
Indian Island Light, 297
Indian Rock Camps, 195
Insurance, 20–21
Intellicast, 31
The International Gay & Lesbian Travel Association (IGLTA), 24
International Student Identity Card (ISIC), 26
International visitors, 53–66
    customs regulations, 56–57
    entry requirements, 53–56
    fingerprinting of, 54
    getting to and around coastal Maine, 59–61
    money matters, 57–59
International Youth Travel Card (IYTC), 26
Internet access, 29–30, 51
In the Woods, 232
InTouch USA, 31
iPass, 30
ISIC (International Student Identity Card), 26
Island Artisans, 232
Island Coast Whale Tours, 283
Isle au Haut, 185–186
Isle au Haut Boat Company, 186
Isle of Shoals Steamship Co., 262
Itinerary, suggested, 48–50
I2roam, 30
IYTC (International Youth Travel Card), 26

Jefferds Tavern, 70
Jewett, Sarah Orne, 291
    House, 72
J.L. Coombs Footwear and Fine Casuals, 126–127
John Paul Jones House, 261
John Perkins House, 179
Jones, John Paul, House, 261
Jonesboro, 242
Jonesport, 242
Jordan Pond, 202–204
Jordan Pond House, 202

Katahdin, Mount, 5–6, 196, 273
Kayaking, 7, 38–39, 42
    around Boothbay, 141
    Belfast, 173
    Castine, 179
    Deer Isle, 186
    Downeast Maine, 240
    Merchant's Row, 7
    Ogunquit, 78
    St. Andrews, 277
Kebo Valley Golf Club, 196
Kennebunk Beach, 89, 90
The Kennebunks (Kennebunk and Kennebunkport), 86–97
    accommodations, 90–95
    beaches, 89–90
    exploring, 87–89
    traveling to, 87
    visitor information, 87
King, Stephen, 191
"King" Brud and his famous hot-dog cart, 144
Kingsbrae Garden, 277
Kittery, 11, 68–77, 126
KT Aviation, 42

Lady Pepperell House, 70
La Kermesse, 98
Lamoine State Park, 194, 205
Languages, 63
Laudholm Farm, 80
Legal aid, 63–64
LeRoux Kitchen, 119
Libby Island Light, 243
Lighthouses, 294–298
Linekin Preserve, 140
Liquor laws, 51
L.L. Bean, 41, 127–128
L.L. Bean Factory Store, 119, 126
L.L. Bean Outdoor Discovery Schools, 194
Lobster, American, 210
Lobster boat racing, 182
Lobster pricing, 146
Longfellow, Henry Wadsworth, 290
Long Pond, 194
Long Sands Beach, 37, 72–73, 76
Long Sands General Store, 76
Loons, 214
Lost and found, 51
Lost-luggage insurance, 21
Lowbush blueberry, 209
Lubec, 243–244
Luggage Express, 34
Lyme disease, 21–22

Machias, 242–243
Machias Bay Boat Tours and
    Sea Kayaking, 240
Machiasport, 242
Machias Wild Blueberry
    Festival, 240
Macro Polo, 268
Mail, 64
Mail2web, 29
Maine Atlas and Gazetteer,
    42–43
Maine Audubon Society, 41
Maine Boatbuilders'
    Show, 18
Maine Campground Owners
    Association, 38
Maine Crafts Association, 165
Maine History Gallery, 115
Maine Island Kayak Co.,
    39, 40, 186
Maine Island Trail, 10, 38–39
Maine Island Trail
    Association, 39
Maine Lobster Festival,
    19, 156
Maine Mall, 127
Maine Maple Sunday, 18
Maine Maritime Academy,
    179
Maine Maritime Museum &
    Shipyard, 133–134
Maine Medical Center, 51
Maine Narrow Gauge
    Railroad Co. & Museum,
    114
Maine Potters Market, 119
Maine Professional Guides
    Association, 40
Maine Sport Outfitters,
    39, 165, 186
Manana Island, 150
Mangy Moose, 128
Map Adventures, 40
MapQuest, 31
Maps, 52
Marathon, Mount Desert
    Island, 19
Marginal Way, 78
Marine Resources Aquarium,
    141
Market Square Day, 18
Marshall Point Light, 297
Marshall Point Lighthouse
    Museum, 150
Mary Lea Park, 164
MasterCard
    ATM Locator, 31
    traveler's checks, 15
Mast Landing Sanctuary, 124
MedicAlert identification
    tag, 22

Medical insurance, 22, 57
Medical requirements for
    entry, 54
Megunticook, Mount, 162
Merchant's Row, 7
Mercy Hospital, 51
Midcoast Maine,
    12, 152–192
Milbridge, 241
Milbridge Historical
    Museum, 241, 246
Ministers Island Historic
    Site/Covenhoven,
    277–278
Minke whale, 211
Moffat-Ladd House, 261
Money matters, 13–15
    for international visitors,
    57–59
Monhegan Boat Line, 149
Monhegan Historical and
    Cultural Museum, 150
Monhegan Island, 6, 8,
    148–151
Monhegan Island Light, 297
Moody Beach, 80
Moose, 44, 210
Moosehorn National
    Wildlife Refuge, 243
Moose Island Tour Bus,
    246
Mooselook Guide Service,
    240–241
Morning in Maine, 159
Moss-Rehab, 23
Mountain biking. See
    Biking and mountain
    biking
Mount Desert Campground,
    205
Mount Desert Island, 2, 8,
    193–237. See also
    Acadia National Park;
    Bar Harbor
Mount Desert Island
    Marathon, 19
The Movies, 120
Muddy River Smokehouse,
    268
Museum of Natural History,
    220
Musical Wonder House, 140
The Music Hall, 268

Nahcotta, 268
National Park Canoe
    Rentals, 194–195
Native Americans, 288
New Brunswick, 256–257
New England Hiking
    Holidays, 40

New England Museum Of
    Telephony, 246–247
New England Outdoor
    Center, 274
Newspapers and magazines,
    52, 64
New Year's Portland, 18, 101
Nickelodeon Cinemas, 120
Niger Reef Tea House, 276
Northeast Harbor, 6, 233
Northeast Historic Film,
    173–174
Northern right whale, 211
North Haven, 152
Northwest Airlines, 32
Northwestern Coastal Trail,
    283
The North Woods, 7, 210,
    270, 271
North Woods Ways, 39
Norton, Barna and John, 242
Nova Scotia, ferries to,
    116–118
Now, Voyager, 24–25
Nubble Light, 72, 76, 294
N.W. Barrett Gallery, 267

Off-season, 14
Ogunquit, 24, 37, 77–86
    accommodations, 80–83
    beaches, 79–80
    exploring, 78–79
    restaurants, 83–86
    transportation, 78
    traveling to, 77
    visitor information, 77–78
Ogunquit Fest, 19
Ogunquit Museum of
    American Art, 79
Ogunquit Playhouse, 79
Olde Port Mariner Fleet, 116
Old Gaol (York Village), 71
Old Orchard Beach, 8, 26,
    37, 121
Old Port, 112–113
Old Port Festival,
    18, 101–102
Old Quarry Charters, 186
Old Sow, 245
Old Town, 190–192
The Old Town Canoe
    Company, 191–192
Old York Historical Society, 70
Olson House, 156
Open World Magazine, 24
Orbitz, 27
Orono, 190–192
Otter Cliffs, 202
Outdoor activities. See
    Active vacations; and
    specific destinations

Outdoor Discovery Program, 41
Owls Head Light, 297
Owls Head Transportation Museum, 156

Palace Playland, 121
Pan Am, 33
Paradiza, 268
Park Loop Road, 7, 200
Parson Fisher House, 8, 188
Passamaquoddy Bay, 248–251
Passport information, 55–56
Peaks Island, 37
Peary, Robert E., home, 116
Peary-MacMillan Arctic Museum, 133
Pemaquid Beach Park, 152
Pemaquid Peninsula, 145–148
Pemaquid Point, 147
Pemaquid Point Light, 297
Pembroke, 243
Penobscot Marine Museum, 174
Perkins, John, House, 179
Perkins Cove, 78
Perkins Island Light, 296
Petit Manan Light, 298
Petit Manan National Wildlife Refuge, 247
Pets, traveling with, 27
Picnics
    Acadia National Park, 204
    Bar Harbor, 223
    Belfast, 176
    Brunswick, 133
    Camden, 164
    Cape Porpoise, 95
    Freeport, 130
    the Kennebunks, 90
    Portland, 110–111
    Portsmouth (New Hampshire), 263
    Searsport, 175
    York, 76
Pilot whale, 212
The Pink Pages, 24
Pitch pine, 208
Pleasant Point Passamaquoddy Indian Reservation, 244
Plovers, 215
Poison ivy, 21
Pond Island Light, 296
Popham Beach State Park, 37, 137
The Porcupines, 220
Porpoises, 213
Port Clyde, 149
Port Clyde General Store, 149–150

Porter Memorial Library, 242
Portland, 1, 99–122
    accommodations, 102–106
    average temperatures, 18
    baseball, 118
    beaches, 37, 117
    coffee shops, 106
    exploring, 112–119
    gay and lesbian travelers, 24
    layout of, 100–101
    nightlife, 119–121
    outdoor activities, 39
    parking, 101
    restaurants, 106–112
    shopping, 11, 118–119
    side trips, 121–122
    special events and festivals, 18–20, 101
    traveling to, 100
    visitor information, 100
Portland Breakwater Light, 296
Portland Head Light & Museum, 114, 295
Portland International Jetport, 32, 100
Portland Museum of Art, 114
Portland Observatory, 113
Portland Public Market, 106–107, 114–115
Portland Sea Dogs, 118
Portland Stage Company, 121
Portland Symphony Orchestra, 121
Portsmouth (New Hampshire), 8–9, 11, 258–268
    accommodations, 262–265
    nightlife, 268
    parking, 260
    restaurants, 265–267
    shopping, 267–268
    sights and attractions, 260–262
    traveling to, 258, 260
    visitor information, 260
Portsmouth Bookshop, 268
Portsmouth Harbor Cruises, 262
The Precipice Trail, 201
Prescott Park, 260, 263
Prescription medications, 22
The Press Room, 268
Priceline, 28
Primrose Hill District, 173
Prism Glass Studio & Gallery, 163

Quoddy Air, 44
Quoddy Head State Park, 248
Quoddy Link Marine, 276–277

Rabies, 22
Rachel B. Jackson, 159
Rachel Carson Salt Pond Preserve, 147
Rackliffe Pottery, 188
Raft Maine, 274
Ragged Mountain Sports, 164
RainWise, 232
Ram Island Ledge Light, 296
Ram Island Light, 296
Range Lights, 296
Ravens, 217
Raye's Mustard, 247
Red maples, 208
Red pine, 208
Regions of Maine, 12
Reid State Park, 37, 137
Resorts. *See also* Accommodations Index
    best, 9
Resourceful Home, 119
Restaurants. *See also* Restaurant Index
    best, 10–11
Restrooms, 66
Richard A. Nott House, 88
Richardson's Market, 263
RoadPost, 31
Robert Lincoln Levy Gallery, 267
Robison Point Light, 298
Rockefeller, John D., Jr., 196
Rockland and environs, 153–161
Rockland Breakwater Light, 297
Rockland Harbor Southwest Light, 297
Rockport, 162, 164, 165
Romar Bowling Lanes, 140
Roosevelt Campobello International Park, 249–250
Roque Bluffs State Park, 247
Ross Memorial Museum, 275–276
Rotary Park, 90, 98
Route 103, 37
Rowantrees Pottery, 188
Ruggles House, 241, 247

Sabbathday Lake Shaker Community, 8, 122
Saco, 97–98
Saco Museum, 98

Saco River, 98
Safety, 22–23, 59
Sailing, Midcoast Maine, 153
St. Andrews, 274–281
St. Croix River, 273
St. Stephen, 250–251
St. Vincent Millay, Edna, 291
Samoset Resort, golf course
    at, 152
Sand Beach, 194, 201, 204
Sarah Orne Jewett House, 72
Sargent Drive, 233
Satellite phones, 31
Sayward-Wheeler House, 71
Scarborough Beach Park,
    111, 117
Schoodic Point, 248
School House (York
    Village), 70
Schooner Lazy Jack,
    164–165
Schooner Wendameen, 159
Seagulls, 216
Sea kayaking, 7, 38–39, 42
    Belfast, 173
    around Boothbay, 141
    Castine, 179
    Deer Isle, 186
    Downeast Maine, 240
    Merchant's Row, 7
    Ogunquit, 78
    St. Andrews, 277
Seals, 213
Searsport, 172, 174–177
Seascape Kayak Tours, 277
The Seashore Trolley
    Museum, 88–89
Seasons, 16
Seawall, 204
Sea Watch Tours, 283
Sebago Lake, 122
Sebago Lake State Park,
    37, 122
Seguin Island Light, 296
Senior travelers, 25
Seven Day's Work, 282
Seven Day's Work Trail, 283
Shackford Head State Park,
    244
Shipping your luggage, 34
Shopping, best destinations
    for, 11
Shore Path, 220
Short Sands Beach,
    37, 72–73, 76
Sieur de Monts Spring, 201
Sisters, 24
Site59.com, 28
Skiing
    Acadia National Park, 196
    Camden Snow Bowl, 153

SkyCap International, 34
Smarter Living, 28
Smoking, 45
Society for Accessible Travel
    and Hospitality, 23
Songbirds, 218
South Berwick, 72
Southern Maine coast,
    12, 67–98
South Harpswell, 137
South Turner Mountain, 273
Southwest Airlines, 32
Southwest Harbor, 233–234
Special events and festivals,
    18–20
Spring, 17
Spring Point Light, 296
Squirrel Point Light, 296
Standard Baking Company,
    106, 111
STA Travel, 26, 34
Stonewall Kitchen, 119
Stonington, 181–186
Storm-petrels, 216
Stowe, Harriet Beecher, 291
Strawbery Banke, 260–261
Student travelers, 26–27
Styxx, 120
Sugar maples, 208
Sullivan, 241
Summer, 16
Summer Performance
    Series, 19
Sunrise International, 273
Supper at Six, 106, 111
Surprise, 164
Swan Lake State Park, 152
Swan's Island, 152
Symbion, 159

The Tarn, 201
Taxes, 52, 64
Telegraph and telex
    services, 65
Telephone, 64–65
Theater, Ogunquit, 79
Thomas Point Beach
    Bluegrass Festival, 19, 132
Thompson Ice Harvesting
    Museum, 146
Thompson Island Information
    Center, 199, 204
Thoreau, Henry David,
    290–291
Thos. Moser Cabinetmakers,
    128
Three-Dollar Dewey's, 119
Thunder Hole, 201
Thuya Gardens, 233
Tidal Transit Kayak Co., 141

Time zone, 52, 65
Tipping, 65–66
T-Mobile Hotspot, 30
Toboggan Championships,
    U.S. National, 18
Tobogganing, 18, 164
Toilets, 66
Tom's of Maine, 87
Tozier's Market, 175
Train travel, 36, 44
    for international visitors, 60
Transportation, 41–44
TravelAxe, 29
Travel CUTS, 26–27
Traveler's checks, 15, 58
Travel insurance, 20–21
Travelocity, 27, 29
Trip-cancellation
    insurance, 20
Twin Peaks Press, 24
Two Lights State Park,
    111, 117

United Express, 32
US Airways, 32
U.S. Custom House, 113
USIT Campus, 26
U.S. National Toboggan
    Championships, 18

Vaughn Woods State
    Park, 72
Vermont Bicycle Touring, 40
Vermont Transit Lines, 36, 43
Victoria Mansion, 8, 115
Victorian Holiday, 20
Video, flying with, 35
Village Green, 223
Vinalhaven, 152
Virtual Bellhop, 34
Visa
    ATM Locator, 31
    traveler's checks, 15
Visas, 53–54
Visitor information, 13

Wadsworth-Longfellow
    House & Center for Maine
    History, 115
Walker Park, 164
Walkers Point, 88
Walking tours, guided, 40
Walpole Meeting House, 146
Warner House, 261
Wayport, 30
Weatherby's, The Fisherman's
    Resort, 42, 195
Weather.com, 31

Websites
  traveler's toolbox, 31
  travel-planning and
    booking, 27–29
Wedding Cake House, 87–88
Wendell Gilley Museum of
  Bird Carving, 234
Wentworth-Gardner House,
  261–262
WERU, 188
Western Promenade,
  110, 113
Western Union, 51
West Quoddy Head, 196
West Quoddy Head Light,
  248, 298
Whaleback Light, 294
Whales, 211–212
Whale-watching
  Bar Harbor, 222
  Downeast Maine, 243
  Grand Manan Island, 283
  Ogunquit, 78
White Head Island, 283
White Island Light, 298
White pine, 208
White-water rafting, Baxter
  State Park, 274
Whiting, 243
Wi-Fi access, 30
Wiggly Bridge, 71
Wild Blueberry Festival, 19
Wildwood Stables, 195
Willard Beach, 117
Wilson Museum, 179
Windjammer cruises, 7
  Camden, 164–165
  Rockland and Camden, 157
Windjammer Days, 153
Windjammers, 10
  special events, 18, 19, 153
Winslow Park, 130
Winter, 17
Winter Harbor Light, 298
Wiscasset, 138–145
Wolfe Neck Woods State
  Park, 124
Wolfe's Neck Farm, 124
Wood Island Lighthouse, 295
Work of the Hands
  show, 165
Wyeth Family, Farnsworth
  Center for the, 156

Yahoo! Mail, 29
Yahoo! Maps, 31
York Beach, 8, 26
York Days, 19

The Yorks (York Village;
  York Harbor; York Beach),
  6, 68–77
York Village Festival of
  Lights, 20

ACCOMMODATIONS

Above Tide Inn, 80
Acadia Hotel, 225
Anchorage Inn (York
  Beach), 73
Anchorage Inn & Suites
  (Portsmouth, NH), 262
Asticou Inn, 234
Balance Rock Inn, 223
Bar Harbor Grand Hotel,
  2, 224
Bar Harbor Hotel–Bluenose
  Inn, 223
The Bar Harbor Inn, 224
Beach House Inn, 90
Beachmere Inn, 80, 82
The Belmont, 166
Black Duck Inn, 252
Black Friar Inn, 225–226
Black Point Inn, 9, 102
Blue Harbor House, 166–167
Blue Hill Farm Country Inn,
  189
Blue Hill Inn, 189
Bow Street Inn (Portsmouth,
  NH), 262–263
Bradley Inn, 147
Brunswick Bed & Breakfast,
  134
Camden Harbour Inn, 167
Camden Riverhouse Hotel
  and Inns, 166
Camden Windward House,
  167
Captain Cates Bed &
  Breakfast, 252
Captain Jefferds Inn, 93
The Captain Lord Mansion,
  9, 92
Capt. Lindsey House Inn,
  157–158
Castine Harbor Lodge, 180
Castine Inn, 180
Cedar Crest Motel, 166
Cedarholm Garden Bay,
  167–168
Claremont, 9, 234–235
Coastline Inn, 102
The Colony Hotel, 9, 93, 227
Comfort Inn (Bangor), 192
Comfort Inn (Searsport), 174
Comfort Suites, 128
Country Inn at the Mall, 192

Crocker House Country Inn,
  252–253
The Danforth, 104
Days Inn, 102
Dockside Guest Quarters, 73
Driftwood Inn & Cottages,
  10, 137–138
The Dunes, 82
The Eastland Park Hotel, 105
East Wind Inn, 158
Edwards' Harborside Inn, 74
Eggemoggin Landing, 183
Extended Stay America, 102
Fairfield Inn, 192, 262
The Fairmont Algonquin, 278
Five Gables Inn, 141–142
Four Points by Sheraton, 192
Franciscan Guest House,
  10, 90
Galen C. Moses House, 134
Goose Cove Lodge, 183
Grand Hotel, 82
Grey Havens, 9, 134–135
Hanscom's Motel and
  Cottages, 222
Harbor House on Sawyer
  Cove B&B, 253
Harborside Hotel & Marina,
  2, 224
Harraseeket Inn, 128–129
Highbrook Motel, 222
Hilton Garden Inn, 1, 102
Holiday Inn (Bangor), 192
Holiday Inn by the Bay, 102
Holiday Inn of Portsmouth
  (NH), 262
Home Port Inn (Lubec), 253
Homeport Inn (Searsport),
  175
Hotel Pemaquid, 147–148
Howard Johnson's Motor
  Lodge (Bangor), 192
The Inn at Lobsterman's
  Wharf, 142
Inn at Ocean's Edge, 168
Inn at Park Spring, 105
Inn at Southwest, 235
Inn at Strawbery Banke
  (Portsmouth, NH), 263
Inn at Sunrise Point, 168
Inn at Whale Cove
  Cottages, 284
Inn on the Harbor, 183–184
Inn on the Hiram Walker
  Estate, 278–279
Isaac Randall House, 129
Ivy Manor Inn, 225
Kendall Tavern Bed &
  Breakfast, 129
Kingsbrae Arms Relais &
  Châteaux, 279

Lawnmeer Inn & Restaurant, 142
Ledgelawn Inn, 226
Le Domaine, 253–254
LimeRock Inn, 158
Lindenwood Inn, 9, 235
Little River Lodge, 254
Lodge at Turbat's Creek, 94–95
Lupine Lodge, 256–257
Maine Idyll Motor Court, 10, 129
Maine Stay (Camden), 168–169
Maine Stay Inn and Cottages (Kennebunkport), 93–94
Maples Inn, 226
Marginal Way House and Motel, 82–83
Martin Hill Inn Bed & Breakfast (Portsmouth, NH), 263–264
Micmac Farm, 254
The Milliken House, 254–255
Mira Monte Inn, 226
Monhegan House, 151
Nellie Littlefield House, 83
Newagen Seaside Inn, 142–143
Newcastle Inn, 148
Nicholson Inn, 129–130
Norumbega, 169
Oakland House Seaside Resort/Shore Oaks, 184
Old Fort Inn, 94
Owen House, A Country Inn & Gallery, 257
Peacock House Bed & Breakfast, 255
Pentagöet Inn, 180–181
The Percy Inn, 105–106
Picket Fence Motel, 278
Pilgrim's Inn, 184–185
Pomegranate Inn, 9, 104–105
Portland Harbor Hotel, 1, 102–104
Portland Regency Hotel, 104
Portsmouth Harbor Inn and Spa, 1, 73
Primrose Inn, 227
Quoddy Head Station, 251
Redclyffe Shore Motor Inn, 255
Riverside Inn, 255–256
Rockhurst Motel, 222
Salty Towers, 279
Samoset Resort, 158–160
Sea Latch, 73
Sebasco Harbor Resort, 135
Sheraton Harborside Portsmouth (NH), 264
Shorecrest Lodge, 284

Sise Inn (Portsmouth, NH), 264
Spruce Point Inn, 143
Stage Neck Inn, 74
Studio East Motel, 80
Super 8, 128
Three Chimneys Inn (Portsmouth, NH), 264–265
Tide Mill Farm, 251
The Tides Inn, 94, 225
Todd House Bed & Breakfast, 256
Topside, 143–144
Towne Motel, 166
Trailing Yew, 151
Twin Pine Camps, 274
Ullikana Bed & Breakfast, 227
Union Bluff Hotel, 74–75
Villager Motel, 222
Wentworth by the Sea (Portsmouth, NH), 2, 265
Weston House, 256
White Barn Inn, 1, 9, 92
Whitehall Inn, 169–170
The White House, 175
Wildflower Inn, 175
The Windsor House, 280
The Yachtsman Lodge & Marina, 95
Yellow Birch Farm Guest Cottage, 251

RESTAURANTS

Abel's Lobster Pound, 228
Amore, 83
Angelone's, 106
Arabica, 106
Arborvine Restaurant, 189–190
Arrows, 10, 83
Atlantica, 170
Back Bay Grill, 107
Beale Street BBQ, 108
Beal's Lobster Pier, 228
Beal's Lobster Pound, 236
Becky's, 11, 111
Bella Cucina, 108
Ben & Bill's Chocolate Emporium, 228
Benkay, 108–109
Bintliff's Diner, 85
Blue Mermaid World Grill (Portsmouth, NH), 265–266
Bob's Clam Hut, 75
Bold Coast Smokehouse, 252
Boothbay Region Lobstermen's Co-op, 144–145
Borealis Breads, 86

Boynton-McKay, 170
Breaking New Grounds (Portsmouth, NH), 2, 265
The Burning Tree, 236
Café Drydock, 235
Cafe Miranda, 160
Café This Way, 230
Café Uffa!, 109
Caffe Kilim (Portsmouth, NH), 265
Cape Porpoise Lobster Co., 95
Cappy's Chowder House, 170
Capt'n Andy's, 170
Castine Inn, 181
Ceres Bakery (Portsmouth, NH), 265
Chase's Daily Restaurant, 176
Chauncey Creek Lobster Pier, 75
Chez Michel, 171
Chowder Express & Sandwich Shop, 130
Cod End Fish House, 160
Congdon's Doughnuts Family Restaurant & Bakery, 79
Cook's Lobster House, 138
Corsican Restaurant, 130
Cottage Street Bakery and Deli, 227–228
Cove Cuisine, 284
Coveside Bar and Restaurant, 146
Darby's, 176–177
Dennett's Wharf, 181
Docksider Restaurant, 236
Dolphin Marina, 11, 138
Dolphin Striker (Portsmouth, NH), 266
Eat-A-Pita, 236
Eden Vegetarian Café, 2, 230–231
Estes Lobster House, 138
Falcon Restaurant, 130
Federal Jack's Restaurant and Brew Pub, 95–96
Federal Spice, 112
Fiddlers' Green, 2, 236–237
Fisherman's Friend, 185
Five Islands Lobster Co., 135–136
Five-O, 83–84
Flatbread Company, 109
Flo's Steamed Hot Dogs, 84
Fore Street, 11, 107
43 Degrees North (Portsmouth, NH), 266
Francine Bistro, 1–2, 171
Freya's, 236
Friendly Toast (Portsmouth, NH), 265

The Gables, 280
George's, 229
Gilbert's Chowder House, 112
Goldenrod Restaurant, 75–76
Gothic, 176
Great Lost Bear, 120
Grissini, 96
Gritty McDuff's, 130
Harraseeket Lunch & Lobster, 130–131
Havana, 229
Helen's (Ellsworth), 85
Helen's Restaurant (Machias), 253
Hurricane (Kennebunkport), 96
Hurricane (Ogunquit), 10, 84–86
Jameson Tavern, 131
Jordan Pond House, 205
Jordan's Restaurant, 231
Jumpin' Jay's Fish Café (Portsmouth, NH), 266
Katahdin, 109
L'Europe, 280
Lighthouse Restaurant, 280–281
Lindbergh's Crossing (Portsmouth, NH), 266–267
Line House, 84
Little Notch Café, 236
Lobster Cooker, 130
Lobster Cove, 76
Lobsterman's Wharf, 145
The Lobster Pound, 171
Lompoc Cafe and Brewpub, 231

Lupines, 148
Mache Bistro, 229–230
MacLeod's, 177
Maggie's Restaurant, 231
Maine Diner, 84
Market on Main, 160
Marriner's Restaurant, 171
Me and Ollie's (Portsmouth, NH), 265
The Mex, 252
Michelle's, 230
Miss Brunswick Diner, 85
Miss Wiscasset Diner, 85
Moody's Diner, 85
Natasha's, 109–110
98 Provence, 86
North Head Bakery, 284
Nunan's Lobster Hut, 95
Palace Diner, 84
Pesce Blue (Portsmouth, NH), 2, 267
Peter Ott's, 171–172
Pier 77 Restaurant, 1, 96–97
Portland Coffee Roasting Co., 106
Portsmouth Brewery (NH), 267
Press Room (Portsmouth, NH), 267
Primo, 11, 161
Quietside Café, 235
Red's Eats, 144
Red Sky, 2, 237
The Rhumb Line, 177
Ricetta's, 106
RíRá, 110
The River Driver Restaurant, 274

Robinhood Free Meetinghouse, 136
The Rose Garden Restaurant, 228
Sarah's, 144
Sea Dog Brewing Co., 1, 136
Seafood Ketch, 236
Seaweed Café, 2, 237
Seng Thai, 176
Shaw's Fish and Lobster Wharf, 148
Siam City Cafe, 110
Silly's, 11, 112
South by Southwest, 170
Star Fish Grill, 136
Stonewall Kitchen Café, 76–77
Street & Co., 107–108
Sullivan Harbor Farm Smokehouse, 256
three tides, 176
Thurston's Lobster Pound, 11, 228, 237
Trenton Bridge Lobster Pound, 205
Twilight Cafe, 177
Two Lights Lobster Shack, 117
Union River Lobster Pot, 252
The Waterfront, 172
The Waterworks, 161
Whale's Tooth Pub, 170
White Barn Inn, 97
Wild Oats Bakery and Café, 133
The Windsor House, 281
Young's Lobster Pound, 177–178

FROMMER'S® NATIONAL PARK GUIDES

Algonquin Provincial Park
Banff & Jasper
Family Vacations in the National
  Parks

Grand Canyon
National Parks of the American
  West
Rocky Mountain

Yellowstone & Grand Teton
Yosemite & Sequoia/Kings
  Canyon
Zion & Bryce Canyon

FROMMER'S® MEMORABLE WALKS

Chicago
London

New York
Paris

San Francisco

FROMMER'S® WITH KIDS GUIDES

Chicago
Las Vegas
New York City

Ottawa
San Francisco
Toronto

Vancouver
Walt Disney World® & Orlando
Washington, D.C.

SUZY GERSHMAN'S BORN TO SHOP GUIDES

Born to Shop: France
Born to Shop: Hong Kong,
  Shanghai & Beijing

Born to Shop: Italy
Born to Shop: London

Born to Shop: New York
Born to Shop: Paris

FROMMER'S® IRREVERENT GUIDES

Amsterdam
Boston
Chicago
Las Vegas
London

Los Angeles
Manhattan
New Orleans
Paris
Rome

San Francisco
Seattle & Portland
Vancouver
Walt Disney World®
Washington, D.C.

FROMMER'S® BEST-LOVED DRIVING TOURS

Austria
Britain
California
France

Germany
Ireland
Italy
New England

Northern Italy
Scotland
Spain
Tuscany & Umbria

THE UNOFFICIAL GUIDES®

Beyond Disney
California with Kids
Central Italy
Chicago
Cruises
Disneyland®
England
Florida
Florida with Kids
Inside Disney

Hawaii
Las Vegas
London
Maui
Mexico's Best Beach Resorts
Mini Las Vegas
Mini Mickey
New Orleans
New York City
Paris

San Francisco
Skiing & Snowboarding in the
  West
South Florida including Miami &
  the Keys
Walt Disney World®
Walt Disney World® for
  Grown-ups
Walt Disney World® with Kids
Washington, D.C.

SPECIAL-INTEREST TITLES

Athens Past & Present
Cities Ranked & Rated
Frommer's Best Day Trips from London
Frommer's Best RV & Tent Campgrounds
  in the U.S.A.
Frommer's Caribbean Hideaways
Frommer's China: The 50 Most Memorable Trips
Frommer's Exploring America by RV
Frommer's Gay & Lesbian Europe
Frommer's NYC Free & Dirt Cheap

Frommer's Road Atlas Europe
Frommer's Road Atlas France
Frommer's Road Atlas Ireland
Frommer's Wonderful Weekends from
  New York City
The New York Times' Guide to Unforgettable
  Weekends
Retirement Places Rated
Rome Past & Present

Travel Tip: He who finds the best hotel deal has more to spend on facials involving knobbly vegetables.

Hello, the Roaming Gnome here. I've been nabbed from the garden and taken round the world. The people who took me are so terribly clever. They find the best offerings on Travelocity. For very little cha-ching. And that means I get to be pampered and exfoliated till I'm pink as a bunny's doodah.

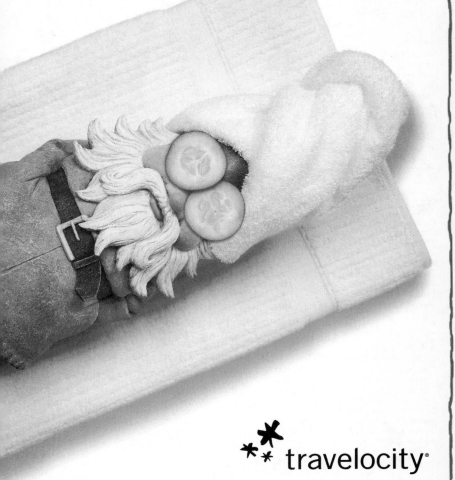

*** travelocity®

Travel Tip: Make sure there's customer service for any change of plans — involving friendly natives, for example.

One can plan and plan, but if you don't book with the right people you can't seize le moment and canoodle with the poodle named Pansy. I, for one, am all for fraternizing with the locals. Better yet, if I need to extend my stay and my gnome nappers are willing, it can all be arranged through the 800 number at, oh look, how convenient, the lovely company coat of arms.

travelocity®

1-888-TRAVELOCITY / travelocity.com / America Online Keyword: Travel